Business in Action

THIRD EDITION

Courtland L. Bovée

Professor of Business Administration

C. Allen Paul Distinguished Chair

Grossmont College

John V. Thill

Chief Executive Officer

Communication Specialists of America

PEARSON

Prentice Hall

Upper Saddle River, New Jersey 07458

Library of Congress Cataloging-in-Publication Data

Bovée, Courtland L.
    Business in action / Courtland L. Bovée, John V. Thill.—3rd ed.
      p. cm.
Includes bibliographical references and index.
ISBN 0-13-149266-7
    1. Business. 2. Commerce. 3. Industrial management. I. Thill, John V. II. Title.
HF1008.B685 2005
650—dc22   2004052224

Acquisitions Editor: David Parker
Editor-in-Chief: Jeff Shelstad
Editorial Assistant: Denise Vaughn
Marketing Manager: Shannon Moore
Senior Managing Editor (Production): Judy Leale
Production Editor: Marcela Boos
Permissions Coordinator: Charles Morris
Associate Director, Manufacturing: Vincent Scelta
Production Manager: Arnold Vila
Manufacturing Buyer: Michelle Klein
Design Manager: Maria Lange
Art Director: Janet Slowik
Interior Design: Liz Harasymczuk
Cover Design: Liz Harasymczuk
Cover Photo: EStock Photo, LLC
Art Studio: Accurate Art, Inc.
Manager, Print Production: Christy Mahon
Composition: UltraGraphics
Full-Service Project Management: Heidi Allgair, UltraGraphics
Printer/Binder: Courier-Kendallville

Credits and acknowledgments borrowed from other sources and reproduced, with permission, in this textbook appear on appropriate page within text.

Microsoft® and Windows® are registered trademarks of the Microsoft Corporation in the U.S.A. and other countries. Screen shots and icons reprinted with permission from the Microsoft Corporation. This book is not sponsored or endorsed by or affiliated with the Microsoft Corporation.

Pearson Prentice Hall™ is a trademark of Pearson Education, Inc.
Pearson® is a registered trademark of Pearson plc
Prentice Hall® is a registered trademark of Pearson Education, Inc.
Pearson Education LTD.
Pearson Education Singapore, Pte. Ltd
Pearson Education, Canada, Ltd
Pearson Education–Japan
Pearson Education Australia PTY, Limited
Pearson Education North Asia Ltd
Pearson Educación de Mexico, S.A. de C.V.
Pearson Education Malaysia, Pte. Ltd
Pearson Education Upper Saddle River, New Jersey

ISBN 0-13-149266-7
10 9 8 7 6 5 4 3

Contents in Brief

Contents

Preface

Tour the Text That Lets Students Experience Business in Action!

From the productivity gains of online meetings to the public controversy erupting over offshoring, business continues to change at speeds unimagined just a few years ago. *Business in Action* leads students on an intriguing journey through the new world of business with more coverage of leading-edge topics than any comparable text.

Students will explore the technologies that are revolutionizing business, from wireless networks to nanotechnology, and get practical advice on financing and organizing a business, hiring employees, delivering vital services, and succeeding at other important tasks. Throughout, *Business in Action* ensures student learning by carefully presenting complex issues such as free-market systems and motivational theories, which can be among the more challenging to learn—and to teach.

Business in Action lets students experience business firsthand through a variety of highly involving activities and real-life examples that no other textbook can match. Students will appreciate the broad selection of featured companies and the text's user-friendly layout, manageable length, eye-catching graphics, conversational tone, and tie-in with Business PlanPro software. From the global economy to the world of small business, *Business in Action* takes students on an engaging journey of the fundamentals, strategies, and dynamics of successful business management.

Business in Action is a compelling model of today's most effective instructional techniques. The text uses an extraordinary number of devices that simplify teaching, promote active learning, stimulate critical thinking, and develop career skills. In short, this text is the most effective teaching and learning tool you'll find for an introductory business course. As you'll see on the pages that follow, *Business in Action* will make your classes livelier, more relevant, and more enjoyable.

EXCITING NEW FEATURES

Learning from Business Blunders. These miniboxes throughout the book highlight a recent business mistake and help students relate the story to chapter content. These examples are both entertaining and relevant, such as Mitsubishi's recent effort to market the Eclipse to college-aged buyers with cut-rate financing—the company lost a half billion dollars because many of these young buyers defaulted on their loans.

Technologies That Are Revolutionizing Business. A series of miniboxes feature cutting-edge developments such as nanotechnology, wireless networking, virtual meetings, RFID, and XML; the boxes introduce the technology, explain its potential impact, and point students to appropriate websites for more information.

Learning from Business Blunders

Oops: Filling out a loan application is always an unpleasant task; it's hard to avoid the feeling that you're being forced to divulge your most private personal secrets. Imagine how it must feel to see all those secrets on display on the World Wide Web. Dealerskins, a company that hosts websites for car dealers, failed to take even the most basic steps to protect the private financial information of a thousand car-loan applicants. Anyone could view the applications simply by clicking on "View Source" in Internet Explorer.

Technologies That Are Revolutionizing Business

Instant messaging
If you're a serious user of instant messaging (IM), do you remember what it was like those first few times you communicated? Chances are it changed the way you interacted with friends and family.

How it's changing business
IM may have started as a way for individual computer users to stay in touch, but it is quickly becoming a major communication tool for businesses worldwide. Businesses use IM to replace in-person meetings and phone calls, to supplement online meetings, and to interact with customers. Key benefits include rapid response to urgent messages and lower cost than both phone calls and e-mail. Business-class IM systems offer a range of advanced capabilities in addition to basic chat, including *presence awareness* (the ability to quickly see who's at their desks and available to IM), remote display of documents, remote control of other computers, video, and even automated *bot* capabilities that mimic simple conversations with human beings.

Where you can learn more
To learn more about how IM works, check out computer.howstuffworks.com/instant-messaging.htm. For the latest on the business applications of IM, log on to www.instantmessagingplanet.com.

Business Buzz. A special margin note called "Business Buzz" features some of the latest buzzwords in the business world, such as "e-mail hygiene: technologies and practices that reduce spam and protect a computer from viruses and other threats embedded in or attached to e-mail messages."

Personal Finance: Getting Set for Life. This major new appendix gives students practical advice for every stage in their financial lives, from getting through college to preparing for retirement. Unlike personal finance sections in many other texts, which are often little more than descriptive catalogs of financial topics, this appendix makes financial planning much more relevant by introducing students to the financial decisions they'll need to make as they transition from each life stage to the next. And in response to the debt crisis that affects so many college students today, this appendix highlights the serious problem of credit card debt and offers strategies for extricating oneself from a financial black hole.

> ## Business Buzz
>
> *Experience economy:*
> Goods and services designed to give consumers unique, memorable experiences, such as adventure travel in exotic locations or fantasy sports camps

TRADEMARK FEATURES—ALL UPDATED FOR THIS EDITION

Behind the Scenes

Chapter-Opening Vignette

Each chapter begins with a slice-of-life vignette that attracts student interest by vividly portraying a challenge faced by a real businessperson. Each vignette ends with thought-provoking questions that draw students into the chapter.

Chapter-Ending Case

Each chapter ends with a case that expands on the chapter-opening vignette. The case includes three critical-thinking questions that require students to apply the concepts covered in the text. Plus, students can find out more about the company featured in the case by completing the "Learn More Online" exercise.

Special-Feature Boxes

Two special-feature boxes in each chapter make the world of business come alive with current examples to further enhance student learning. Each box includes two critical-thinking questions that are ideal for developing team or individual problem-solving skills.

Video Cases

Professionally produced videos take students behind the scenes at some of the world's most fascinating organizations. Each case includes a synopsis, five discussion questions, and an online exploration exercise.

End-of-Chapter Material

Test Your Knowledge

Questions for Review
Five questions reinforce learning and help students review the chapter material.

Questions for Analysis
Five questions help students analyze chapter material. One of these questions is ethics based and labeled "Ethical Considerations."

Questions for Application
Five questions give students the opportunity to apply principles presented in the chapter material. Selected questions labeled "Integrated" ask students to tie material learned in previous chapters to the topics in the chapter they're currently studying.

Practice Your Knowledge

Sharpening Your Communication Skills

These exercises call on students to practice a wide range of communication activities, including one-on-one and group discussions, personal interviews, panel sessions, oral and written papers, and letter- and memo-writing assignments.

Building Your Team Skills

These exercises teach students important team skills, such as brainstorming, collaborative decision making, developing a consensus, debating, role playing, and resolving conflict.

Expand Your Knowledge

Exploring Career Opportunities

Students are given the opportunity to explore career resources on campus, observe businesspeople on their jobs, interview businesspeople, and perform self-evaluations to assess their own career skills and interests.

Developing Your Research Skills

These exercises familiarize students with the wide variety of business reference material that's available, and they give students practice in developing research skills.

See It on the Web

"See It on the Web" exercises acquaint students with the wealth of information on the web that relates to the content of each chapter. Students explore three websites and answer questions that reinforce and extend chapter learning.

Learning Interactively

Students are directed to the text's website so they can take advantage of the interactive study guide to test their knowledge of the chapter and get instant feedback on whether additional studying is necessary.

E-Business in Action

THE BIGGEST AUDIENCE IN THE WHOLE WIDE WORLD WIDE WEB

As signs of progress go, it's not one that will make anybody happy, but it's a sign of progress nonetheless: The Peoples' Republic of China is now the world's number two receiver of junk e-mail, second only to the United States. The dubious distinction goes hand in hand with China's rapid rise as an online market. More than 80 million Chinese residents were online in 2004, and that number is expected to reach 150 or 200 million by 2006. At that point, China will have more Internet users than the United States (and, presumably, more spam).

The game company Kingsoft is a good example of how rapidly Chinese consumers are embracing new online offerings. After attempting to sell software to consumers for years, the company gave up and shifted to the Internet, starting with an action game called Sword Online. Within six months, Kingsoft had signed up 1.7 million customers and has plans to keep growing into a technology leader. Forecasters expect the online game market in China to surpass $800 million by 2007.

Internet + Mobile Phones = Profits

The marriage of the Internet and wireless technology promises to be another hot business across China. The country already has twice as many mobile phone subscribers as the United States, and online portals now deliver a variety of information and entertainment services to phone users—news, games, dating services, even voice greeting cards featuring NBA star Yao Ming. The wireless multimedia market alone jumped from $200 million in 2001 to $3 billion in 2004. Kingsoft is among the companies developing phone games that combine movies, voice, and data.

Multimedia phone services proved to be an enormous blessing for China's leading web portals, which include Sina, Sohu, and NetEase. (A web portal is a multifaceted website such as www.yahoo.com, which provides a variety of information and entertainment offerings, along with site directories, search engines, and other services.) Because advertising opportunities in China were so minuscule to begin with, Sina and the other Chinese portals avoided a misstep that hobbled many U.S. e-commerce companies during the early days of the Internet boom—trying to support themselves by selling online advertising. That business model never really took off in the United States and, in fact, proved to be the financial undoing of many promising young companies that invested millions of dollars in the untested

hope that ad dollars would show up sooner or later. In contrast, the Chinese portals are already profitable, thanks to wireless content services.

Rapid Evolution

This sizzling growth is a far cry from just a few years ago, when the Chinese government generally viewed e-commerce as a threat to its tight control over the economy and consumer behavior. Now, the country's leadership is intent on making China a global technology leader, showing strengths in both networking and wireless technologies. In rapid succession, the country is evolving from a low-cost manufacturer to a high-quality manufacturer and is on its way to being a technical innovator as well. As Robert Mao, CEO of greater China operations for networking giant Nortel, put it, China is now "part of the leading edge."

This isn't to say that growth is easy, by any means. Peggy Lu, head of DangDang.com, which roughly models itself after Amazon.com, faced the challenge of selling products online without a financial feature that marketers in many countries take for granted—credit cards (most Chinese citizens don't have them yet). To get around this hurdle, Lu's company accepts money orders and lets customers pay in cash when products are delivered.

Internet entrepreneurs such as Lu are becoming role models for a new generation who see that they can get ahead on their own initiative, without relying on official connections. In an economy under tight state control, "people used to think you could only get rich with stocks or smuggling," says one Chinese CEO. "Now, with the Internet, they know they can get rich using their intelligence."

Freedom to Profit, Not Freedom of the Press

Does all this free-market fervor mean that China's communist government is relaxing its control over the country's citizens? Hardly. Site operators are forbidden to publish information about Falun Gong, an outlawed religious group, or to raise the call for political reform, for instance. Moreover, the government has been known to demand free advertising space on portal sites.

Web logs, or blogs, the newest online rage in the United States, also come under close scrutiny in China. In 2004, for instance, the government shut down two blogs for carrying content it deemed objectionable—rumored to be discussions relating to the 1989 crackdown on a student protest in Beijing's Tiananmen Square. A year earlier, officials blocked

88

E-BUSINESS IN ACTION

From small dot-coms to lumbering global giants, e-business is influencing the way all companies do business today. Smart companies have learned the lessons of the dot-com bubble and are now using Internet technology and e-commerce techniques to boost productivity, hone marketing efforts, and improve virtually every aspect of business operations. "E-Business in Action" is a dedicated section that appears at the end of each text part and will expand student learning by explaining in depth the important challenges companies are facing in the world of e-business.

BUSINESS PLANPRO EXERCISES

The end-of-part "Business PlanPro Exercises" enable students to use the knowledge they've gained from reading chapters within that part. Each exercise has two tasks: "Think Like a Pro" tasks require students to navigate the software, find and review information in sample business plans, and evaluate and critique some of the thinking that went behind these plans. "Create Your Own Business Plan" tasks provide students with an opportunity to apply their skills to creating their own winning business plan.

YOUR BUSINESS PLAN (APPENDIX D)

Instructors who want a more complete business-planning experience for their students will want to take advantage of this text's new appendix. Using Business PlanPro software as a foundation, this appendix carefully takes students through each step toward creating a winning business plan. In addition, by completing the chapters in the text, and after studying numerous business plan examples, students will be able to build their own complete business plan by the end of the term.

ADDITIONAL TEACHING AND LEARNING SUPPORT

OneKey Online Courses

OneKey offers the best teaching and learning online resources all in one place. OneKey is all instructors need in order to plan and administer their course. OneKey is all students need for anytime, anywhere access to online course material. Conveniently organized by textbook chapter, these compiled resources help save time and help students reinforce and apply what they have learned. OneKey for convenience, simplicity, and success. OneKey is available in three course-management platforms: Blackboard, CourseCompass, and WebCT.

For the student:

- **Learning Modules**, which include section reviews, learning activities, and pretests and posttests
- **Student PowerPoints**—easy-to-print black-and-white PowerPoints
- **Research Navigator**—four exclusive databases of reliable source content to help students understand the research process and complete assignments

Instructor's Resource Center Available Online, in OneKey, or on CD-ROM

The Instructor's Resource Center, available on CD, at www.prenhall.com, or in your OneKey online course, provides presentation and other classroom resources. Instructors can collect the materials, edit them to create powerful class lectures, and upload them to an online course-management system.

Using the Instructor's Resource Center on CD-ROM, instructors can easily create custom presentations. Desired files can be exported to the instructor's hard drive for use in classroom presentations and online courses.

With the Instructor's Resource Center, you will find the following faculty resources:

- **PowerPoints**
  There are two versions of Instructor's PowerPoints available with this text. The first is a fully developed set of PowerPoints. The second is an essential grab-and-go version of the first set of PowerPoints.

- **TestGen Test-Generating Software**
  The test bank contains approximately 150 questions per chapter, including multiple-choice, true/false, fill-in, and essay questions. (*Print version also available.*)

- **Annotated Instructor's Media Edition (AIME)**
  Ready . . . AIME . . . Teach!

  Have you ever wanted to incorporate instructor media tools offered with a textbook but didn't know where to start or were simply too busy to spend hours planning your lectures? Here's your solution: **A**nnotated **I**nstructor's **M**edia **E**dition.

  Integrated . . . Accessible . . . A Turnkey Solution

  Integrated
  Recognizing that your students have a variety of learning styles, we've selected highlights from our instructor's supplements to complement your lectures. You'll find lecture notes, PowerPoints, selected classroom activities, and videos—all in one place.

Accessible

Thumbnail tabs found at the beginning of each chapter put selected teaching supplements at your fingertips.

A Turnkey Solution

1. Open to the chapter insert that you will be teaching.
2. Plan your lecture using the detailed chapter outline provided.
3. Select the appropriate PowerPoint slides, consider using the suggested classroom activities, plan your video presentation, and you are ready!

■ **Instructor's Manual**
  Designed to assist instructors in quickly finding and assembling the resources available for each chapter of the text, it includes the following: Learning Objectives, Summary of Learning Objectives, Chapter Outline, Lecture Notes and Chapter Outline, Potential Difficulties and Suggested Solutions, Real-World Cases, Behind the Scenes, Answers to End-of-Chapter Questions, Answers to Boxed Features, and Chapter Pop Quiz. (*Print version also available.*)

■ **Test Item File**
  Printed version of the test bank. (*Word file*)

Companion Website

The text website www.prenhall.com/bovee features chapter quizzes and student PowerPoints, which are available for review or can be conveniently printed three to a page for in-class note taking.

PERSONAL ACKNOWLEDGMENTS

A very special acknowledgment goes to George Dovel, whose superb editorial skills, distinguished background, and wealth of business experience assured this project of clarity and completeness.

Also, recognition and thanks to Jackie Estrada for her outstanding skills and excellent attention to details.

The supplements package for *Business in Action* has benefited from the able contributions of numerous individuals. We would like to express our thanks to them for creating the finest set of instructional supplements in the field.

We want to extend our warmest appreciation to the devoted professionals at Prentice Hall. They include Jerome Grant, president; Jeff Shelstad, vice president and editor-in-chief; David Parker, editor; Denise Vaughn, editorial assistant; Anke Braun, marketing manager; all of Prentice Hall Business Publishing; and the outstanding Prentice Hall sales representatives. Finally, we thank Judy Leale, senior managing editor of production; Janet Slowik, art director; and Marcy Boos, production editor, for their dedication, and we are grateful to Heidi Allgair, assistant manager of production services at GGS Book Services; Patricia Leal Welch, copy editor; Charles Morris, permissions coordinator; Melinda Alexander, photo researcher; and Liz Harasymczuk, designer, for their superb work.

Courtland L. Bovée

John V. Thill

Part 1

Conducting Business in the Global Economy

Chapter 1

Understanding the Fundamentals of Business and Economics

LEARNING OBJECTIVES
After studying this chapter, you will be able to

1 Define what a business is and identify four key social and economic roles that businesses serve

2 Differentiate between goods-producing and service businesses and list five factors that are contributing to the increase in the number of service businesses

3 Differentiate between a free-market system and a planned system

4 Explain how supply and demand interact to affect price

5 Discuss the four major economic roles of the U.S. government

6 Explain how a free-market system monitors its economic performance

7 Identify five challenges that businesses are facing in the global economy

Behind **the Scenes**

Making Dollars and Sense of Online Music at Apple iTunes

www.apple.com/itunes

Success in business is often a matter of connecting the dots: looking at your own strengths and weaknesses, exploring customer needs, and analyzing the various legal, technical, and social forces at work in the marketplace. You consider what you're capable of doing, what your competitors might do, what customers would like you to do—and what forces are reshaping the business landscape. Then you look for connections and opportunities. How can you capitalize on changing markets? What can you do to meet customer needs better than anyone else?

Apple CEO Steve Jobs spotted an opportunity in linking online music with his company's popular iPod digital music players.

Apple Computer CEO Steve Jobs has spent his career connecting those dots, leading the development of innovative products that have changed the way people work and play, including the way people listen to music. Although Apple didn't start out in the music business, by 2003 the company was a significant force in music, at least indirectly. Many musicians and creative professionals favored Apple computers, and the company's sleek new iPod portable music players were a must-have item for trendsetting music fans everywhere.

Outside the company, though, the music industry was in a state of turmoil. Music fans, tired of buying entire CDs for just one or two favorite songs, were downloading millions of songs for free from the Internet. However, many people consider this practice unethical and the recording industry considers it illegal. Performers, songwriters, and music companies were all looking for better ways to address customer complaints about the music industry while protecting their legal rights and financial assets. As is often the case, technology seemed to be one step ahead of business strategy. Everybody agreed that online distribution was central to the future of the music business, but nobody had quite figured out how to make it work.

Jobs wasn't the only person pondering this situation, of course. A diverse group of companies, from Wal-Mart and Sony to RealNetworks and a reborn Napster, wanted a piece of the new online music market. Amazon.com, eBay, and other companies had proven the potential for selling over the Internet, but was it possible to make money selling something as inexpensive as an individual song? If you were Steve Jobs, how would you approach the challenges and opportunities of online music? How would you connect the dots between Apple's strengths and the complex dynamics of the marketplace?[1] ∎

WHY STUDY BUSINESS?

No matter where your career plans take you, the dynamics of business will affect your work and life in innumerable ways. If you aspire to be a manager or an entrepreneur, knowing how to run a business is vital, of course. If you plan a career in a professional specialty such as law, engineering, or finance, knowing how businesses operate will help you interact with clients and colleagues more effectively and thereby contribute to your career success. Even if you plan to work in government, education, or some other non-commercial setting, business awareness can help you as well; many of these organizations look to business for new ideas and leadership techniques. And in your role as a consumer and taxpayer, knowing more about business will help you make better financial decisions.

In fact, your experiences as a consumer have already taught you a great deal about the business world. As you progress through this course, though, you'll begin to look at things from the eyes of an employee or a manager instead of a consumer. You'll develop a fundamental business vocabulary that will help you keep up with the latest news and make more-informed decisions. By participating in classroom discussions and completing the chapter exercises, you'll gain some valuable critical-thinking, problem-solving, team-building, and communication skills that you can use on the job and throughout your life.

This course will also introduce you to a variety of jobs in business fields such as accounting, economics, human resources, management, finance, marketing, and so on. You'll see how people who work in these fields contribute to the success of a company as a whole. You'll gain insight into the types of skills and knowledge these jobs require—and you'll discover that a career in business today is fascinating, challenging, and often quite rewarding.

In addition, a study of business management will help you appreciate the larger context in which businesses operate and the many legal and ethical questions managers must consider as they make business decisions. Both government regulators and society as a whole have numerous expectations regarding the ways businesses treat employees, shareholders, the environment, other businesses, and the communities in which they operate.

Learning from Business Blunders

Oops: Filling out a loan application is always an unpleasant task; it's hard to avoid the feeling that you're being forced to divulge your most private personal secrets. Imagine how it must feel to see all those secrets on display on the World Wide Web. Dealerskins, a company that hosts websites for car dealers, failed to take even the most basic steps to protect the private financial information of a thousand car-loan applicants. Anyone could view the applications simply by clicking on "View Source" in Internet Explorer.

What You Can Learn: In today's electronic economy, all businesses have an obligation to protect any confidential data they collect from customers. No system is absolutely foolproof, but readily available e-commerce systems provide secure, reliable ways to protect data.

WHAT IS A BUSINESS?

A **business** is any profit-seeking activity that provides goods and services designed to satisfy customers' needs. Apple's iTunes, for example, satisfies an important aspect of consumers' entertainment needs. In addition to providing a society with necessities such as housing, clothing, food, transportation, communication, health care, and much more, businesses provide people with jobs and a means to prosper; they pay taxes that are used to build highways, fund education, and provide grants for scientific research; and they reinvest their profits in the economy, thereby creating a higher standard of living and quality of life for society as a whole.

The driving force behind most businesses is the prospect of earning a **profit**—money that remains after all expenses have been deducted from the sales revenue the business has brought in. Such a prospect is commonly referred to as a *profit motive*. Businesses may keep and use their profits as they wish, within legal limits. Still, not every organization exists to earn a profit. **Nonprofit organizations** such as museums, public schools and universities, symphonies, libraries, government agencies, and charities exist to provide society with a social, educational, or other service. The American Red Cross, for example, provides relief to victims of disasters and helps people prevent, prepare for, and respond to emergencies. Although nonprofit organizations do not have a profit motive, they must operate efficiently and effectively to achieve their goals. All nonprofit organizations, from a student club with only a few dozen members to a multi-billion-dollar operation such as the Red Cross, can learn from business opportunities, challenges, and activities discussed throughout this course.

business
A profit-seeking activity that provides goods and services that a society wants or needs

profit
Money left over after expenses and taxes have been deducted from revenue generated by selling goods and services

nonprofit organizations
Firms whose primary objective is something other than returning a profit to their owners

Goods-Producing Businesses Versus Service Businesses

Most businesses can be classified into two broad categories: goods-producing businesses and service businesses. **Goods-producing businesses** produce tangible goods by engaging in activities such as manufacturing, construction, mining, and agriculture. Boeing, the world's largest manufacturer of commercial jetliners, military aircraft, and satellites, is a goods-producing business. The company's Everett, Washington, factory is the largest building, by volume, in the world. Spanning 98 acres under one roof, the facility is big enough to handle construction of 20 wide-body jets at once.[2] Of course, most manufacturing operations do not require a facility as big as Boeing's. Nonetheless, it's difficult to start a goods-producing business without substantial investments in buildings, machinery, and equipment. For this reason, most goods-producing businesses are **capital-intensive businesses**: they generally require large amounts of money or equipment to get started and to operate.

Service businesses, by contrast, produce intangible products (ones that cannot be held in your hand) and include those whose principal product is finance, insurance, transportation, utilities, wholesale and retail trade, banking, entertainment, health care, repairs, or information. America Online, Nordstrom, Jiffy Lube, and eBay are examples of service businesses. Most service businesses are **labor-intensive businesses**. That is, they rely more on human resources than buildings, machinery, and equipment to prosper. A consulting firm is an example of a labor-intensive service business because its existence is heavily dependent on the knowledge and skills of its consultants. A group of consultants can go into business with little more than a few computers and some telephones—although the consultants must possess considerable knowledge and experience.

Goods and services are useful categories, but the line between the two is often blurry. For example, IBM is well known as a manufacturer of computers and other technological goods, but roughly half the company's sales now come from computer-related services such as systems design, consulting, and product support.[3] Similarly, Boeing provides flight training, fleet and logistics support, and a number of aviation services to support sales of its commercial aircraft. As more and more manufacturers such as Boeing and IBM focus on servicing and supporting their products, it becomes increasingly difficult to classify many companies as either goods-producing businesses or service businesses. In addition, economists don't always agree on what constitutes production of goods versus delivery of services. Does McDonald's "manufacture" hamburgers or simply provide the service of assembling and selling materials created elsewhere? Such questions might seem a bit silly at times, but they can have important implications for taxation and other economic decisions.[4]

goods-producing businesses
Businesses that produce tangible products

capital-intensive businesses
Businesses that require large investments in capital assets

service businesses
Businesses that provide intangible products or perform useful labor on behalf of another

labor-intensive businesses
Businesses in which labor costs are more significant than capital costs

To meet the needs of its customers, Boeing offers both tangible products and a variety of services, from flight training to professional engineering services.

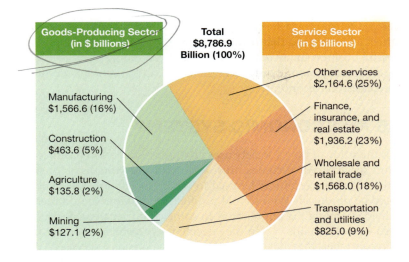

Goods-Producing Sector (in $ billions)
Total $8,786.9 Billion (100%)
Service Sector (in $ billions)

Manufacturing $1,566.6 (16%)
Construction $463.6 (5%)
Agriculture $135.8 (2%)
Mining $127.1 (2%)

Other services $2,164.6 (25%)
Finance, insurance, and real estate $1,936.2 (23%)
Wholesale and retail trade $1,568.0 (18%)
Transportation and utilities $825.0 (9%)

Exhibit 1.1

Sectors of the U.S. Economy

The service sector accounts for 74 percent of U.S. economic output, and the goods-producing sector accounts for the remaining 26 percent.

Growth of the Service Sector

Over the past two decades, service businesses have grown from providing about half of the nation's business output to providing roughly three-quarters of the output today (see Exhibit 1.1). This trend will likely continue into the foreseeable future as well, with service businesses creating the vast majority of new jobs.[5] Although the United States remains one of the world's manufacturing powerhouses, about half of the 1,000 largest U.S. companies are now service based.[6] The service sector is growing for a number of reasons:

- *Consumers have more disposable income.* The 76 million baby boomers in the United States (people born between 1946 and 1964) are in their peak earning years. These consumers find themselves with more disposable income and look for services to help them invest, travel, relax, and stay fit.

- *Services target changing demographic patterns and lifestyle trends.* The United States has more elderly people, more single people living alone, more two-career households, and more single parents than ever before. These trends create opportunities for service companies that can help people with all the tasks they no longer have time for, including home maintenance, food service, and child care.[7]

- *Services are needed to support complex goods and new technology.* Computers, home entertainment centers, recreational vehicles, security systems, and automated production equipment are examples of products that require specialized installation, repair, user training, or extensive support services. As new technology is incorporated into more and more products, companies will need to provide more of these product-support services to remain competitive.

- *Companies are increasingly seeking professional advice.* To compete in the global economy, many firms turn to consultants and professional advisers for help as they seek ways to cut costs, refine their business processes, expand overseas, and engage in **electronic commerce (e-commerce)**—buying and selling over the Internet.

- *Barriers to entry are lower for service businesses.* Capital-intensive manufacturing businesses generally have high **barriers to entry**, which are the requirements a company must meet before it can start competing in a given market. Conditions vary widely by industry, but manufacturers sometimes need to invest many millions of dollars in facilities and equipment before they can produce a single product. Other barriers to entry can include government testing and approval, tightly controlled markets, strict licensing procedures, supplies of raw materials, and the need for highly skilled employees. Of course, many of these barriers apply to various service businesses as well, but in general, service businesses are easier to start than manufacturing businesses of comparable size.

Business Buzz

Experience economy:
Goods and services designed to give consumers unique, memorable experiences, such as adventure travel in exotic locations or fantasy sports camps

electronic commerce (e-commerce)
The general term for the buying and selling of goods and services on the Internet

barriers to entry
Factors that make it difficult to launch a business in a particular industry

Whether you're running a service or a goods-producing business, world economic situations affect all businesses that compete in the global economy. Consequently, running a successful business today requires a firm understanding of basic economic principles, of the different economic systems in the world, and of how businesses compete in the global and electronic economy.

WHAT IS AN ECONOMIC SYSTEM?

Economics is the study of how a society uses its scarce resources to produce and distribute goods and services. All societies must deal with the same basic questions: How should limited economic resources be used to satisfy society's needs? What goods and services should be produced? Who should produce them? How should these goods and services be divided among the population? In some countries these decisions are made by individuals (or households) when they decide how to spend or invest their income and by businesses when they decide what kinds of goods and services to produce; in other countries these decisions are made by governments.

Economists call the resources that societies use to produce goods and services *factors of production*. To maximize a company's profit, businesses use five **factors of production** in the most efficient way possible:

- **Natural resources**—things that are useful in their natural state, such as land, forests, minerals, and water
- **Human resources**—anyone (from company presidents to grocery clerks) who works to produce goods and services
- **Capital**—resources (such as money, computers, machines, tools, and buildings) that a business needs to produce goods and services
- **Entrepreneurs**—innovative businesspeople who are willing to take the risks involved in creating and operating new businesss (see Exhibit 1.2)
- **Knowledge**—the collective intelligence of an organization

Traditionally, a business was considered to have an advantage if it was located in a country with a plentiful supply of natural resources, human resources, capital, and entrepreneurs. But in the global marketplace, intellectual assets are the key. Today companies can obtain capital from one part of the world, purchase supplies from another, and locate production facilities in still another. They can relocate their operations to wherever they find a steady supply of affordable workers. Thus, countries with the greatest supply of knowledge workers and ones with economic systems that give workers the freedom to pursue their own economic interests will have an advantage in the new economic landscape (see Exhibit 1.3 on page 8).

Types of Economic Systems

The role that individuals and government play in allocating a society's resources depends on the society's **economic system**, the basic set of rules for allocating resources to satisfy its citizens' needs. Economic systems are generally categorized as either *free-market systems* or *planned systems*, although these are really theoretical extremes; virtually every system in use today exhibits aspects of both approaches.

Free-Market System

In a **free-market system**, individuals are free to decide what products to produce, how to produce them, whom to sell them to, and at what price to sell them. Thus, they have the chance to succeed—or to fail—by their own efforts. **Capitalism** and *private enterprise* are the terms most often used to describe the free-market system—one in which individuals own and operate the majority of businesses and where competition, supply, and demand determine which goods and services are produced. Capitalism owes its philosophical origins to 18th-century philosophers such as Adam Smith. According to Smith,

economics
The study of how society uses scarce resources to produce and distribute goods and services

factors of production
Basic inputs that a society uses to produce goods and services, including natural resources, labor, capital, entrepreneurship, and knowledge

natural resources
Land, forests, minerals, water, and other tangible assets usable in their natural state

human resources
All the people who work for an organization

capital
The physical, human-made elements used to produce goods and services, such as factories and computers; can also refer to the funds that finance the operations of a business

entrepreneurs
Businesspeople who create and run new businesses and accept the risks involved in the private enterprise system

knowledge
Expertise gained through experience or association

economic system
Means by which a society distributes its resources to satisfy its people's needs

free-market system
Economic system in which decisions about what to produce and in what quantities are decided by the market's buyers and sellers

capitalism
Economic system based on economic freedom and competition

Exhibit 1.2	Rags to Riches

Few start-up companies are resource rich. Still, they become successful because an entrepreneur substitutes ingenuity for capital resources.

THE COMPANY	ITS START
Clorox	In May 1913, five men pooled $100 each and started Clorox. The group had no experience in bleach-making chemistry but suspected that the brine found in salt ponds in San Francisco Bay could be converted into bleach.
The Limited	In 1963, 26-year-old Leslie Wexner left his family's retail store after having an argument with his father. He opened one small store in a strip mall in Columbus, Ohio. Today the company operates thousands of stores across the United States.
Gateway 2000	Using $10,000 he borrowed from his grandmother, Ted Waitt started the company in his father's South Dakota barn in 1985. Because a typical computer-industry campaign would have been too costly, Waitt invented Gateway's now-famous cowhide-print boxes. Today Gateway's revenues exceed $3 billion.
Coca-Cola	Pharmacist John Pemberton invented a soft drink in his backyard in 1886. Asa Chandler bought the company for $2,300 in 1891. Current sales now exceed $20 billion every year.
Marriott	Willard Marriott and his fiancée-partner started a nine-seat A & W soda fountain with $3,000 in 1927. They demonstrated a knack for hospitality and clever marketing from the beginning.
Nike	In the early 1960s, Philip Knight and his college track coach sold imported Japanese sneakers from the trunk of a station wagon. Start-up costs totaled $1,000.
United Parcel Service	In 1907 two Seattle teenagers pooled their cash, came up with $100, and began a message and parcel delivery service for local merchants.
Wrigley's Gum	In 1891 young William Wrigley Jr. started selling baking soda in Chicago. To entice new customers, he threw in two packages of chewing gum with every sale. Guess what the customers were more excited about?
Amazon.com	In 1994 Jeff Bezos came across a report projecting annual web growth at 2,300 percent. So Bezos left his Wall Street job, headed to Seattle in an aging Chevy Blazer, and drafted his business plan en route. His e-business, Amazon.com, initially focused on selling books over the Internet, but Bezos later expanded his product offerings to include toys, consumer electronics, software, home improvement products, and more. Today Amazon.com generates over $5 billion in annual sales.

in the ideal capitalist economy (pure capitalism), the *market* (an arrangement between buyer and seller to trade goods and services) serves as a self-correcting mechanism—an "invisible hand" to ensure the production of the goods that society wants in the quantities that society wants, without regulation of any kind.[8]

Because the market is its own regulator, Smith was opposed to government intervention. He held that if anyone's prices or wages strayed from acceptable levels that were set for everyone, the force of competition would drive them back. In modern practice, however, the government sometimes intervenes in free-market systems to accomplish goals that leaders deem socially or economically desirable. This practice of limited intervention is characteristic of a *mixed economy* or *mixed capitalism*, which is the economic system of the United States and most other countries. For example, federal, state, and local governments intervene in the U.S. economy in a variety of ways, such as influencing particular allocations of resources through tax incentives, prohibiting or restricting the sale of certain goods and services, or setting *price controls*. Price controls can involve

The new economy is different from the old economy in a number of key ways. Besides being faster and more volatile, it's highly dependent on the use of information technology to gain a competitive advantage.

	OLD ECONOMY	NEW ECONOMY
General Characteristics	• Competitive advantage based on physical assets	• Competitive advantage based on intellectual assets
	• Profits maximized by controlling costs	• Profits maximized by adding value to products and services
Technology	• Mechanical technology is main influence on economic growth	• Information technology is main influence on economic growth
Workforce	• Job-specific skills	• Transferable skills and lifelong learning
Geography	• Firms locate near resource to reduce costs	• Firms locate near collaborators and competitors to boost innovation
Capital	• Debt financing	• Venture capital

both maximum allowable prices (such as limiting rent increases or capping the price on gasoline or other products during emergencies and shortages) and minimum allowable prices (such as supplementing the prices of agricultural goods to ensure producers a minimum level of income or establishing minimum wage levels).[9]

Mixed economies, particularly those with a strong capitalist emphasis, offer opportunities for wealth creation but usually attach an element of risk to the potential reward. For instance, it's relatively easy to start a company in a mixed economic system such as the United States, but you could lose all of your start-up money if the company isn't successful. Entrepreneurs and investors willing to face these risks are a vital force in capitalist economies, and they can be rewarded handsomely when they are successful.

Planned System

planned system
Economic system in which the government controls most of the factors of production and regulates their allocation

communism
Economic system in which the government owns and operates all productive resources and determines all significant economic choices

socialism
Economic system characterized by public ownership and operation of key industries combined with private ownership and operation of less-vital industries

In a **planned system** governments control all or part of the allocation of resources and limit the freedom of choice in order to accomplish government goals. Because social equality is a major goal of planned systems, private enterprise and the pursuit of private gain are generally regarded as wasteful and exploitive.

The planned system that allows individuals the least degree of economic freedom is **communism**, which still exists in such countries as North Korea and Cuba. (Keep in mind that even though communism and socialism are discussed here as economic systems, they can be political and social systems as well.) The degree to which communism is actually practiced varies. In its purest form, almost all resources are under government control. Private ownership is restricted to personal and household items. Resource allocation is handled through rigid centralized planning by a handful of government officials who decide what goods to produce, how to produce them, and to whom they should be distributed.[10] Although pure communism still has its supporters, the future of communism is dismal. As economists Lester Thurow and Robert Heilbroner put it, "It's a great deal easier to design and assemble the skeleton of a mighty economy than to run it."[11]

Socialism lies somewhere between capitalism and communism in the degree of economic freedom that it permits. Like communism, socialism involves a relatively high degree of government planning and some government ownership of land and capital resources (such as buildings and equipment). However, government involvement is limited to industries considered vital to the common welfare, such as transportation, utilities, medicine, steel, and communications. In these industries, the government owns or controls all the facilities and determines what will be produced and how the output will be distributed. Private ownership is permitted in industries that are not considered vital, and in these areas both businesses and individuals are allowed to benefit from their own efforts. Taxes are high in socialist states because the government must cover the costs of medical care, education, subsidized housing, and other social services.

The Trend Toward Privatization

Although varying degrees of socialism and communism are practiced around the world today, several socialist and communist economies are moving toward free-market systems. Anxious to unload unprofitable businesses for badly needed cash and to experiment with free-market capitalism, countries such as Great Britain, Mexico, Argentina, Israel, France, Sweden, and China are **privatizing** some of their government-owned enterprises by selling them to privately held firms. Great Britain, for example, has sold the national phone company, the national steel company, the national sugar company, Heathrow Airport, water suppliers, and the company that makes Rover automobiles. Like Great Britain, China is also privatizing its major industries and plans to convert the majority of its state-owned industries.[12]

privatizing
The conversion of public ownership to private ownership

HOW DOES A FREE-MARKET ECONOMIC SYSTEM WORK?

This section takes a closer look at three factors that differentiate a free-market system from other economic systems: supply and demand, competition, and limited government intervention.

The Theory of Supply and Demand in a Free-Market System

The theory of supply and demand is the immediate driving force of the free-market system. It is the basic tool that economists use to describe how the market works in determining prices and the quantity of goods produced. **Demand** refers to the amount of a good or service that customers will buy at a given time at various prices. **Supply** refers to the quantities of a good or service that producers will provide on a particular date at various prices. Simply put, *demand* refers to the behavior of buyers, whereas *supply* refers to the behavior of sellers. Both work together to impose a kind of order on the free-market system.

demand
Buyers' willingness and ability to purchase products

supply
Specific quantity of a product that the seller is able and willing to provide

On the surface, the theory of supply and demand seems little more than common sense. Customers should buy more when the price is low and buy less when the price is high. Producers would offer more when the price is high and offer less when the price is low. In other words, the quantity supplied and the quantity demanded continuously interact, and the balance between them at any given moment should be reflected by the current price on the open market. However, a quick look at any real-life market situation shows that balancing supply with demand by adjusting price isn't quite that simple, nor does it automatically guarantee profitability.

Consider the airline industry. Airline travel is a cyclical business; its revenues rise and fall with the economy. When the economy is robust, consumers and businesses are willing to spend more on discretionary travel. When the economy falters, they cut back on such spending (see Exhibit 1.4). Airlines can respond by reducing ticket

By adjusting prices, airlines can influence demand for their services to a degree, but such factors as security threats and the general health of the economy often have more influence on customer behavior.

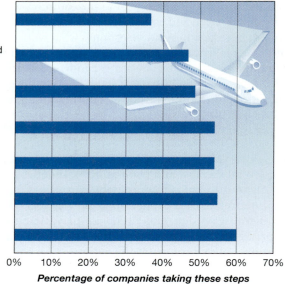

Increase use of corporate or chartered aircraft

Reduce number of conventions and conferences employees attend

Use alternative airports, even if less convenient

Reduce number of employees traveling

Reduce number of domestic trips

Increase use of Saturday-night stayovers

Increase use of videoconferencing and teleconferencing

0%   10%   20%   30%   40%   50%   60%   70%

Percentage of companies taking these steps

prices, by offering promotions, and by scaling back the number of flights. But airlines must plan their businesses years in advance, which means they must always be able to provide a base level of service regardless of how many people want to use it. Maintaining a fixed network of scheduled flights as traveler demand fluctuates is expensive: Major airlines own or lease hundreds of aircraft, each of which can cost several hundred million dollars and must be ordered years before it is needed. Add the costs of airport leases, landing fees, jet fuel, and employees such as pilots, flight attendants, and maintenance crews, and you can begin to see why airlines simply can't shrink their way back to profitability when demand falls.

Nevertheless, in broad terms, the interaction of supply and demand regulates a free-market system by determining what is produced and in what amounts. For example, a movie studio might produce more comedies if ticket sales for similar films are brisk. On the other hand, it might decide to produce fewer comedies and more action-adventure movies if attendance at comedies lags. The result of such decisions—in theory, at least—is that consumers will get what they want and producers will earn a profit by keeping up with public demand.

Buyer's Perspective

The forces of supply and demand determine the market price for products and services. Say you're shopping for blue jeans, and the pair you want is priced at $35. This is more than you can afford, so you don't make the purchase. When the store puts them on sale the following week for $18, however, you run right in and buy a pair.

But what if the store had to buy the jeans from the manufacturer for $20? It would have made a profit selling them to you for $35, but it loses money selling them for $18. Is there a price that will make both the supplier and the customer happy? The answer is yes—the price at which the quantity of jeans demanded equals the quantity supplied.

This relationship is shown in Exhibit 1.5. A range of possible prices is listed vertically at the left of the graph, with the lowest at the bottom and the highest at the top. Quantity of blue jeans is represented along the horizontal axis. The points plotted on the curve labeled *D* indicate that on a given day the store would sell 10 pairs of jeans if they were priced at $35, 15 pairs if they were priced at $27, and so on. The curve that describes this relationship between price and quantity demanded is a *demand curve*. (Demand curves are not necessarily curved; they may be straight lines.)

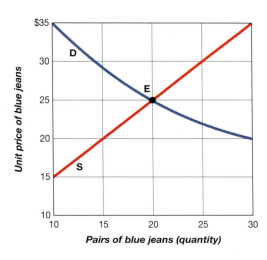

Exhibit 1.5

The Relationship Between Supply and Demand

In a free-market system, prices aren't set by the government; nor do producers alone have the final say. Instead, prices reflect the interaction of supply (*S*) and demand (*D*). The equilibrium price (*E*) is established when the amount of a product that producers are willing to sell at a given price equals the amount that consumers are willing to buy at that price.

Seller's Perspective

Now think about the situation from the seller's point of view. In general, the more profit the store can make on a particular item, the more of that item it will want to sell. This relationship can also be depicted graphically. Again, look at Exhibit 1.5. The line labeled *S* shows that the store would be willing to offer 30 pairs of jeans at $35, 25 pairs at $30, and so on. The store's willingness to carry the item increases as the price it can charge and its profit potential per item increase. In other words, as the price goes up, the quantity supplied goes up. The line tracing the relationship between price and quantity supplied is called a *supply curve*.

As much as the store would like to sell 30 pairs of jeans at $35, you and your fellow consumers are likely to want only 10 pairs at that price. If the store offered 30 pairs, therefore, it would probably be stuck with some that it would have to mark down. How does the store avoid this problem? It looks for the point at which the demand curve and the supply curve intersect, the point at which the intentions of buyers and sellers coincide. The point marked *E* in Exhibit 1.5 shows that when jeans are priced at $25, consumers are willing to buy 20 pairs of them and the store is willing to sell 20 pairs. In other words, at the price of $25, the quantity supplied and the quantity demanded are in balance. The price at this point is known as the **equilibrium price**.

Note that this intersection represents both a specific price—$25 in our example—and a specific quantity of goods—here, 20 pairs of jeans. It is also tied to a specific point in time. Note also that it is the mutual interaction between quantity demanded and quantity supplied that determines the equilibrium price.

equilibrium price
Point at which quantity supplied equals quantity demanded

Competition in a Free-Market System

In a free-market system, customers are free to buy whatever and wherever they please. Therefore, companies must compete with rivals for potential customers. Apple's iTunes service, for example, competes with other online music stores as well as CDs and even live music. **Competition** is the situation in which two or more suppliers of a product are rivals in the pursuit of the same customers.

The nature of competition varies widely by industry. In theory, the ideal type of competition is **pure competition**, which is characterized by three conditions: a marketplace of multiple buyers and sellers, a product or service with nearly identical features such as wheat or cotton, and low barriers of entry (that is, the ability to easily enter and exit the marketplace). When these three conditions exist, no single firm or group of firms in an industry becomes large enough to influence prices and thereby distort the workings of the free-market system. At the other extreme, in a **monopoly** there is only one supplier of a product in a given market, and thus the supplier is able to determine

competition
Rivalry among businesses for the same customer

pure competition
Situation in which so many buyers and sellers exist that no single buyer or seller can individually influence market prices

monopoly
Market in which there are no direct competitors so that one company dominates

LivePerson Puts a Pulse on the Web

You're shopping online, but you'd like some more information. Does that sweater come in red? Will those tires fit your motocross bike? Before you click and buy, sometimes you need the help of a real, live person. That's why Robert LoCascio developed LivePerson.com, a New York software company that puts the human touch in online shopping.

LoCascio knows that many retail websites are ineffective. They confuse and frustrate shoppers and force them to sift through page after page of detail to find the information they need. As a result, many consumers give up and abandon their electronic shopping carts. But Lo Cascio's LivePerson helps companies doing business on the Internet maximize their online shopping experience. Websites with LivePerson services invite online shoppers to chat with a real, live person. Shoppers simply click on the LivePerson icon, and a pop-up window appears on the screen. Type in your name, and you're instantly greeted by a customer service rep who asks, "What can I do for you?" Because pre-scripted responses to common questions are prepared in advance, customer service reps can chat with four or five customers at the same time.

The reps can also help customers with their unique product questions and selections. For instance, LivePerson reps can suggest alternatives to customers by clicking on different webpages to show similar products. They can also supply customers with valuable information about their past purchases and previous visits to the website. As LoCascio explains, the reps "embrace the customer and help them through the process of shopping."

All in all, LoCascio's LivePerson helps e-commerce companies compete by providing a high level of customer service. "If you walk into a store, and there's no person there to help you, the experience is pretty bad," says LoCascio. "The same thing is true online."

Questions for Critical Thinking

1. How can a service such as LivePerson help Internet retailers gain a competitive advantage?
2. A business is a profit-seeking activity that provides goods and services that satisfy customers' needs. What customer needs does LivePerson try to satisfy?

---

the price (within regulatory limits). For instance, the only gas station within a hundred-mile radius has an effective monopoly in that particular local market. In another example of government intervention in a mixed economy, the U.S. Postal Service has a legal monopoly on first-class mail service in this country, although Congress must approve its prices.

Most industries exist somewhere in between the extremes of pure competition and pure monopoly. For instance, commercial aircraft manufacturing is dominated by only a few suppliers (primarily Boeing and Airbus Industries), a situation known as an **oligopoly**. Like monopoly suppliers, oligopoly suppliers can sometimes exercise a degree of power over customers, based simply on the customer's lack of alternatives. Toy maker Mattel discovered this when it threatened to stop buying advertising time on Nickelodeon because the cable TV channel wouldn't air a Mattel-produced Barbie movie in prime time. Nickelodeon's corporate parent Viacom responded by threatening not to sell Mattel advertising on *any* Viacom-owned media outlet, which includes MTV, VH-1, the CBS television network, billboards, and radio stations across the country. To avoid being cut off from so many advertising venues, Mattel relented.[13]

In contrast, most of the competition in advanced free-market economic systems is **monopolistic competition** in which a large number of sellers (none of which dominates the market) offer products that can be distinguished from competing products in at least some small way. Toothpaste, cosmetics, soft drinks, Internet search engines, and restaurants are examples of products that can vary in the features each offers.

When markets become filled with competitors and products start to look alike, companies use price, speed, quality, service, or innovation to gain a **competitive advantage**—something that sets one company apart from its rivals and makes its products more appealing to consumers. For example, Southwest Airlines tries to compete on price by offering lower fares than its competitors. Jiffy Lube competes on speed: Mechanics change a car's oil and oil filter in 15 minutes or less while customers wait. Starbucks competes on quality by delivering a premium product that has changed the definition of

oligopoly
Market dominated by a few producers

monopolistic competition
Situation in which many sellers differentiate their products from those of competitors in at least some small way

competitive advantage
Ability to perform in one or more ways that competitors cannot match

"a good cup of coffee." The risk/reward nature of capitalism promotes constant innovation in pursuit of competitive advantage, rewarding companies that do the best job of creating appealing goods and services.

Government's Role in a Free-Market System

Although the free-market system generally works well, it's far from perfect. If left unchecked, the economic forces that make capitalism succeed may also create severe problems for some groups or individuals. To correct these types of problems, the government serves four major economic roles: It enacts laws and creates regulations to foster competition; it regulates and deregulates certain industries; it protects stakeholders' rights; and it intervenes to contribute to economic stability.

Fostering Competition

Because competition generally benefits the U.S. economy, the U.S. federal government and state and local governments create thousands of new laws and regulations every year to preserve competition and ensure that no single enterprise becomes too powerful. For instance, if a company has a monopoly, it can harm consumers by raising prices, cutting output, or stifling innovation. Furthermore, because most monopolies have total control over certain products and prices and the market share for those products, it's extremely difficult for competitors to enter markets where monopolies exist. For these reasons, over the last century or so, a number of laws and regulations have been established to help prevent individual companies or groups of companies from gaining control of markets in ways that restrain competition or harm consumers.

The potential rewards available in a free-market economy encourage innovators to create new and exciting products; a single innovative product can often revolutionize an entire industry.

Antitrust Legislation   Antitrust laws limit what businesses can and cannot do to ensure that all competitors have an equal chance of producing a product, reaching the market, and making a profit. Some of the earliest government moves in this arena produced such landmark pieces of legislation as the Sherman Antitrust Act, the Clayton Antitrust Act, and the Federal Trade Commission Act, which generally sought to rein in the power of a few huge companies that had financial and management control of a significant number of other companies in the same industry. Usually referred to as *trusts* (hence the label *antitrust legislation*), these huge companies controlled enough of the supply and distribution in their respective industries to muscle smaller competitors out of the way.

More recently, government regulators have focused their attention on companies such as Microsoft, which has been accused by some competitors of using its dominance in the operating systems market (through Microsoft Windows) to unfairly influence competition and customer choice in the application software market (where it offers such products as Word and Excel). In 2000, a U.S. federal judge even ordered that Microsoft be split into two independent companies so that other application software companies could compete against it more effectively. This decision was overturned the following year, but the issue didn't fade away. In 2004, antitrust regulators in the European Union hit the company with a fine of more than $600 million. The company appealed immediately, and the case is expected to be tied up in the courts for several years to come.[14]

Mergers and Acquisitions   To preserve competition and customer choice, governments may occasionally prohibit two companies in the same industry from combining through a merger or acquisition. Over the years, regulators in the United States and other countries have halted some blockbuster deals, such as the proposed mergers between United Airlines and U.S. Airways and between book retailer Barnes & Noble and book wholesaler Ingram Book Group.[15] In other cases, regulators will allow the merger or acquisition, but only after the companies meet certain conditions. For instance, when AOL wanted to merge with media giant Time Warner, the government stipulated that the companies make their powerful cable television and Internet networks available to competitors.

Government regulators in both the United States and Europe have kept a close eye on industry giant Microsoft over the years, periodically responding to complaints that the company's dominance give it unfair competitive advantages. CEO Steve Ballmer argues that the company should be free to innovate as long as it follows appropriate regulations.

stakeholders
Individuals or groups to whom business has a responsibility

Without such requirements, regulators were concerned that the combined AOL Time Warner (now known simply as Time Warner), by virtue of its enormous size, would have too much power and influence over access to the Internet.[16]

Regulating and Deregulating Industries

Sometimes the government imposes regulations on specific industries to ensure fair competition, ethical business practices, safe working conditions, or general public safety. The establishment of the Transportation Security Administration and the federalization of U.S. airport security following the September 11, 2001, terrorist attacks is an example of one such case where the U.S. government has assumed control of a private industry for the safety of its citizens.

In a *regulated industry*, close government control is substituted for free competition, and competition is either limited or eliminated. In extreme cases, regulators may even decide who can enter an industry, what customers they must serve, and how much they can charge. For years, the telecommunications, airline, banking, and electric utility industries fell under strict government control. However, the trend over the past few decades has been to open up competition in regulated industries by removing or relaxing existing regulations. Hopes are that such *deregulation* will allow new industry competitors to enter the market, create more choices for customers, and keep prices in check. But the debate is ongoing about whether deregulation achieves these goals. In some instances, deregulation has produced disastrous results. When the state of California deregulated some aspects of retail electricity in 2000, the result was a year's worth of skyrocketing prices and unreliable supply. The fiasco contributed heavily to a financial crisis that the state has yet to recover from.[17] If nothing else, the California experiment shows that deregulation needs to be approached with great care and a full understanding of the economic forces at work in any given industry.

Protecting Stakeholders

In addition to fostering competition, another important role the government plays is to protect the stakeholders of a business. Businesses have many **stakeholders**—groups that are affected by (or that affect) a business's operations, including colleagues, employees, supervisors, investors, customers, suppliers, and society at large. In the course of serving one or more of these stakeholders, a business may sometimes neglect the interests of other stakeholders in the process. For example, managers who are too narrowly focused on generating wealth for shareholders might not spend the funds necessary to create a safe work environment for employees or to reduce waste. Similarly, a public company that withholds information about its true financial performance may hamper the ability of investors to make solid decisions and may even harm the wealth of stakeholders, as has happened in several high-profile instances in recent years, notably Enron and WorldCom.

To protect consumers, employees, shareholders, and the environment from the potentially harmful actions of business, the government has established several regulatory agencies (see Exhibit 1.6). Many of these agencies have the power to pass and enforce rules and regulations within their specific area of authority. Such regulations are intended to encourage businesses to behave ethically and in a socially responsible way. Chapter 2 takes a closer look at society's concerns for ethical and socially responsible behavior, specific government agencies that regulate such behavior, and the efforts by businesses to become better corporate citizens.

Contributing to Economic Stability

A nation's economy never stays exactly the same size. Instead, it grows and contracts in response to the combined effects of such factors as technological breakthroughs, changes in investment patterns, shifts in consumer attitudes, world events, and basic economic forces. *Economic expansion* occurs when the economy is growing and people are spending more money. Consumer purchases stimulate businesses to produce more

Exhibit 1.6   Major Government Agencies and What They Do

Government agencies protect stakeholders by developing and promoting standards, regulating and overseeing industries, and enforcing laws and regulations.

GOVERNMENT AGENCY OR COMMISSION	MAJOR AREAS OF RESPONSIBILITY
Consumer Product Safety Commission (CPSC)	Regulates and protects public from unreasonable risks of injury from consumer products
Environmental Protection Agency (EPA)	Develops and enforces standards to protect the environment
Equal Employment Opportunity Commission (EEOC)	Protects and resolves discriminatory employment practices
Federal Aviation Administration (FAA)	Sets rules for the commercial airline industry
Federal Communications Commission (FCC)	Oversees communication by telephone, telegraph, radio, and television
Federal Energy Regulatory Commission (FERC)	Regulates rates and sales of electric power and natural gas
Federal Highway Administration (FHA)	Regulates vehicle safety requirements
Federal Trade Commission (FTC)	Enforces laws and guidelines regarding unfair business practices and acts to stop false and deceptive advertising and labeling
Food and Drug Administration (FDA)	Enforces laws and regulations to prevent distribution of harmful foods, drugs, medical devices, and cosmetics
Interstate Commerce Commission (ICC)	Regulates and oversees carriers engaged in transportation between states: railroads, bus lines, trucking companies, oil pipelines, and waterways
Occupational Safety and Health Administration (OSHA)	Promotes worker safety and health
Securities and Exchange Commission (SEC)	Protects investors and maintains the integrity of the securities markets

goods and services, which in turn stimulates employment. *Economic contraction* occurs when such spending declines. Businesses cut back on production, employees are laid off, and the economy as a whole slows down.

If the period of downward swing is severe, the nation may enter into a **recession**, traditionally defined as two consecutive quarters of decline in real gross domestic product. When a downward swing or recession is over, the economy enters into a period of *recovery*: Companies buy more, factories produce more, employment is high, and workers spend their earnings.

These recurrent up-and-down swings are known as the **business cycle**. Although such swings are natural and to some degree predictable, they cause hardship. In an attempt to avoid such hardship and to foster economic stability, the government can levy new taxes or adjust the current tax rates, raise or lower interest rates, and regulate the total amount of money circulating in our economy. These government actions have two facets: monetary policy and fiscal policy.

Monetary Policy   Every economy has a certain amount of "spendable" money in it at any given time, a quantity known as the *money supply*. (Some types of money are more spendable than others; cash in your pocket is easier to spend than money tied up in a certificate of deposit, for instance; the U.S. government has several different measures of the money supply, which go by such names as M1, M2, and M3.) The money supply sounds like an arcane topic, but government efforts to manage the money supply affect every consumer and business manager in the country. **Monetary policy** involves adjusting the nation's money supply by increasing or decreasing interest rates. In the United

recession
Period during which national income, employment, and production all fall

business cycle
Fluctuations in the rate of growth that an economy experiences over a period of several years

monetary policy
Government policy and actions taken by the Federal Reserve Board to regulate the nation's money supply

Exhibit 1.7

Influencing the Money Supply

The Federal Reserve uses four tools to influence the money supply as it attempts to stimulate economic growth while keeping inflation and interest rates at acceptable levels.

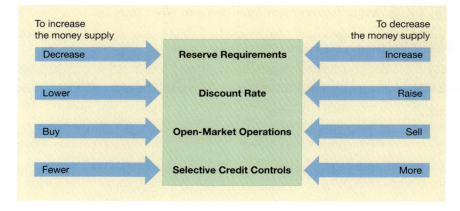

States, monetary policy is controlled primarily by the Federal Reserve Board (the Fed), a group of appointed government officials who oversee the country's central banking system.

The Fed influences the money supply to make certain that enough money and credit are available to fuel a healthy economy. However, it must act carefully because altering the money supply affects interest rates, inflation, and the economy. When the money supply is increased, more money is available for loans, so banks can charge lower interest rates to borrowers. On the other hand, an increased money supply can lead to more consumer spending and can result in the demand for goods exceeding supply. When demand exceeds supply, sellers may raise their prices, leading to inflation. In turn, inflation can slow economic growth—a situation the Fed wants to avoid. And because so many companies now buy and sell across national borders, the Fed's changes may affect the interlinked economies of many countries, not just the United States.[18] For both domestic and international reasons, the Fed keeps a close eye on the size of the money supply and moves cautiously when it's time to make adjustments.

The Fed can use four basic tools to influence the money supply (see Exhibit 1.7):

- *Changing the reserve requirement.* All financial institutions must set aside *reserves,* sums of money equal to a certain percentage of their deposits. The Fed can change the *reserve requirement,* the percentage of deposits that banks must set aside, to influence the money supply. However, the Fed rarely uses this technique because a small change can have a drastic effect. Increasing the reserve requirement slows down the economy: Banks have less money to lend, so businesses can't borrow to expand and consumers can't borrow to buy goods and services. Conversely, reducing this requirement boosts the economy, because banks have more money to lend to businesses and consumers.

discount rate
Interest rate the Federal Reserve charges on loans to commercial banks

prime interest rate (prime)
Lowest interest rate banks offer on short-term loans to preferred borrowers

- *Changing the discount rate.* The Fed can also change the **discount rate**, the interest rate it charges on loans to commercial banks and other depository institutions. When the Fed raises the discount rate, member banks generally raise the **prime interest rate**, the lowest interest rate on short-term loans to preferred borrowers. This increase discourages loans and in so doing tightens the money supply, which can slow down economic growth. By contrast, lowering the discount rate results in lower lending rates, which can encourage more borrowing and stimulate economic growth.

- *Conducting open-market operations.* The tool the Fed uses most often to influence the money supply is the power to buy and sell U.S. government bonds (a *bond* is a mechanism for borrowing money). Because anyone can buy these bonds on the open market, this tool is known as *open-market operations.* If the Fed is concerned about inflation, it can reduce the money supply by selling U.S. government bonds, which takes cash out of circulation. And when the Fed wants to boost the economy, it can buy back government bonds, putting cash into circulation and increasing the money supply.

- *Establishing selective credit controls.* The Fed can also use *selective credit controls* to set the terms of credit for various kinds of loans. This tool includes the power to set *margin requirements*, the percentage of the purchase price that an investor must pay in cash when purchasing a stock or a bond on credit. By altering the margin requirements, the Fed is able to influence how much cash is tied up in stock market transactions.

In addition to the initial impact that an increase in the money supply can have, money injected into the economy also has a *multiplier effect* as it makes its way through the system. For example, if a company spends money to build a large office complex, thousands of construction workers will be gainfully employed and earn wages. If some of these workers decide to spend their extra income to buy new cars, car dealers will have more income. The car dealers, in turn, might spend their income on new clothes, and the salesclerks (who earn commissions) might buy compact discs, and so on. This *circular flow* of money through the economic system links all elements of the U.S. economy by exchanging goods and services for money, which is then used to buy more goods and services and so on.

Fiscal Policy   **Fiscal policy** involves changes in the government's revenues and expenditures to stimulate a slow economy or dampen a growing economy that is in danger of overheating. On the revenue side, governments can adjust the revenue they bring in by changing tax rates and various fees collected from individuals and businesses (see Exhibit 1.8). When the federal government lowers the income tax rate, for instance, it does so with the hope that consumers and businesses will spend and invest the additional money in their pockets.

On the expenditure side, local, state, and federal government bodies constitute a huge market for goods and services, with billions of dollars of collective buying power. Governments can stimulate the economy by increasing their purchases, sometimes even to the point of creating new programs or projects with the specific purpose of expanding employment opportunities and increasing demand for goods and services.

Fiscal policy decisions nearly always involve discussions of budget deficits, both annual deficits (when the government spends more than it takes in during any given year) and the accumulating national debt (the result of the many years in which the government spends more than it receives). In 2004, the federal budget rang up a record annual deficit of more than $500 billion, and the national debt is now over $7 trillion. These numbers are almost incomprehensible, but they affect every business and every consumer in the country. The interest payment alone on the national debt costs U.S. taxpayers several

fiscal policy
Use of government revenue collection and spending to influence the business cycle

TYPE OF TAX	LEVIED ON
Income taxes	Income earned by individuals and businesses. Income taxes are the government's largest single source of revenue.
Real property taxes	Assessed value of the land and structures owned by businesses and individuals.
Sales taxes	Retail purchases made by customers. Sales taxes are collected by retail businesses at the time of the sale and then forwarded to the government.
Excise taxes	Selected items such as gasoline, tobacco, and liquor. Often referred to as "sin" taxes, excise taxes are implemented to help control potentially harmful practices.
Payroll taxes	Earnings of individuals to help fund Social Security, Medicare, and unemployment compensation. Corporations match employee contributions.

Exhibit 1.8

Types of Taxes

From road repair to regulation, running a government is an expensive affair. To fund government operations and projects, national governments, states, counties, and cities levy and collect a variety of revenue-raising taxes.

hundred billion dollars a year. And that's not all; the federal government currently has a $44 trillion hole in its financial planning—that's the difference between the amount of money committed to future Medicare and Social Security benefits and the government's projected ability to meet those commitments. Closing this gap is going to require dramatic changes in fiscal policy.[19] In other words, fiscal policy decisions may be able to solve or minimize short-term problems, but they often have considerable long-term effects.

How a Free-Market System Monitors Its Economic Performance

economic indicators
Statistics that measure variables in the economy

Each day we are deluged with complex statistical data that depict the current status and past performance of the economy. Sorting, understanding, and interpreting these data are difficult tasks even for professional economists. **Economic indicators** include statistics such as interest rates, unemployment rates, and housing data that are used to monitor and measure economic performance. Statistics that point to what may happen to the economy in the future are called *leading indicators*; statistics that signal a swing in the economy after the movement has begun are called *lagging indicators*.

Watching Economic Indicators

Economists monitor the performance of the economy by watching a variety of indicators. Unemployment statistics, for example, signal future changes in consumer spending. When unemployment rises, people have less money to spend, and the economy suffers. Housing starts, another leading indicator, show where several industries are headed. Housing is very sensitive to interest rate changes. If mortgage rates are high, fewer people can afford to build new homes. When housing starts drop, builders stop hiring and may even lay off workers. Meanwhile, orders fall for plumbing fixtures, carpets, and appliances, so manufacturers decrease production and workers' hours. These cutbacks ripple through the economy and lead to slower income and job growth and weaker consumer spending.[20] Another leading indicator is durable-goods orders, or orders for goods that typically last more than three years (which can mean everything from desk chairs to airplanes). A rise in durable-goods orders is a positive indicator that business spending is turning around. Informal indicators can also provide insights into economic health, such as the nature of buying and selling on Internet auction giant eBay. When buyers seem to be in a hopeful mood with cash to spend, luxury items are more popular. When times are tougher, people tend to shop for more run-of-the-mill, practical items.[21] In addition to all these indicators, economists closely monitor price changes and national output to get a sense of how well the economy is working.

Measuring Price Changes

Price changes, especially price increases, are another important economic indicator. In a period of rising prices, the purchasing power of a dollar erodes, which means that you can purchase fewer things with today's dollar than you could in a prior period. Over time, price increases tend to lead to wage increases, which in turn add pressures for higher prices, setting a vicious cycle in motion.

inflation
Economic condition in which prices rise steadily throughout the economy

deflation
Economic condition in which prices fall steadily throughout the economy

Inflation and Deflation   **Inflation** is a steady rise in the prices of goods and services throughout the economy. When the inflation rate begins to decline, economists use the term *disinflation*. **Deflation** on the other hand, is the sustained fall in the general price level for goods and services. It is the opposite of inflation; that is, purchasing power increases because a dollar held today will buy more tomorrow. In a deflationary period, investors postpone major purchases in anticipation of lower prices in the future. Keep in mind that although prices in the overall economy tend to increase year after year, not all industries and product categories necessarily follow this trend. The average price of a new car and a new computer might drop while the prices of the gasoline and electricity needed to power them increase.[22]

Consumer Price Index   The **consumer price index (CPI)** measures the rate of inflation by comparing the change in prices of a representative basket of goods and services, such as clothing, food, housing, and utilities, over time. A numerical weight is assigned to each item in the representative basket to adjust for each item's relative importance in the marketplace. The CPI has always been a hot topic because it is used by the government to index Social Security payments, and it is widely used by businesses in private contracts to calculate cost-of-living increases. But, like most economic indicators, the CPI is not perfect. The representative basket of goods and services may not reflect the prices and consumption patterns of the area in which you live or of your specific household. The U.S. Bureau of Labor Statistics periodically adjusts the mix of products used in the CPI, but the CPI should always be viewed as a general indicator of price trends, not as a specific measurement.[23]

consumer price index (CPI)
Monthly statistic that measures changes in the prices of about 400 goods and services that consumers buy

Measuring a Nation's Output

The broadest measure of an economy's health is the **gross domestic product (GDP)**. The GDP measures a country's output—its production, distribution, and use of goods and services—by computing the sum of all goods and services produced for *final* use in a market during a specified period (usually a year). The goods may be produced by either domestic or foreign companies—as long as these companies are located within a nation's boundaries. Sales from a Honda assembly plant in California, for instance, would be included in the GDP. Although far from perfect, the GDP enables a nation to evaluate its economic policies and to compare its current performance with prior periods or with the performance of other nations.

GDP has largely replaced an earlier measure called the **gross national product (GNP)** which excludes the value of production from foreign-owned businesses within a nation's boundaries and includes receipts from the overseas operations of domestic companies. GNP considers *who* is responsible for the production; GDP considers *where* the production occurs.

gross domestic product (GDP)
Value of all the final goods and services produced by businesses located within a nation's borders; excludes receipts from overseas operations of domestic companies

gross national product (GNP)
Value of all the final goods and services produced by domestic businesses that includes receipts from overseas operations and excludes receipts from foreign-owned businesses within a nation's borders

CHALLENGES OF A GLOBAL ECONOMY

Whether economic indicators suggest that the economy is in a period of contraction or expansion, businesses must be prepared to meet the many challenges of a global economy. **Globalization**—the increasing tendency of the world to act as one market instead of a series of national ones—opens new markets for a company's goods and services and new sources of natural resources, labor, and skills. But at the same time it creates tougher competition and a raft of new challenges for businesses:

globalization
Tendency of the world's economies to act as a single interdependent economy

- *Producing quality products and services that satisfy customers' changing needs.* Today's customer has access to considerable amounts of information about product choices and often has a wide range of goods and services from which to choose. For many businesses, competing in the global economy means competing on the basis of *speed* (getting products to market sooner), *quality* (doing a better job of meeting customer expectations), and *customer satisfaction* (making sure buyers are happy with every aspect of the purchase, from the shopping experience until they're through using the product).
- *Starting and managing a small business in today's competitive environment.* Starting a new business or successfully managing a small company in today's global economy requires creativity and a willingness to exploit new opportunities. Small companies often lack the resources to buffer themselves from competition. Furthermore, once

The Electronic Economy: Redefining Reality

Jumping on the Internet to check your test scores, reserve a plane ticket, or find an apartment might feel like business as usual to you these days, but the business and technology revolution that enabled these online conveniences has been anything but usual. And it's not over yet. No matter where your career takes you, inside the business arena or not, the electronic economy will affect you personally and professionally.

Throughout this course, you'll get insights into the interplay of technology and business. As you explore the ins and outs of business management, pay attention to the Internet's impact in areas such as these:

- **Competitive opportunities and threats.** The Internet creates new business opportunities for some companies and creates new competitive threats for others. Small companies can now reach customers halfway around the world—but the customers they used to have across the street can now shop just about anywhere as well.
- **The speed of business.** The good news is that technology can accelerate virtually every aspect of business. That's also the bad news. The faster things go, the faster everybody expects them to go. The pace can lead to rushed decision making and wear out both employees and managers.
- **Consumer power.** Researching and shopping for many products used to be a laborious, time-consuming chore in many cases, leaving buyers wondering if they had really explored all their options and gathered enough

information to make smart decisions. Not anymore. The Internet shifts power from sellers to buyers, who can usually gather mountains of information within minutes and jump from one seller to the next with the click of a mouse.

- **Security and privacy.** People who can't think of living without the Internet—a population that surely includes most college students—may find it hard to believe that more than 40 percent of the U.S. population manages to get by without it quite nicely, thank you. Among their top reasons for staying away: fear of being barraged by online pornography and scammed by credit card thieves. Until these and other problems (including spam) are fixed, electronic business will never reach its full potential.

With the dot-com boom and collapse in the rearview mirror, technology is getting down to business, with an emphasis on sensible solutions to real-world problems. As you move into your career, you'll no doubt encounter all these issues—and perhaps make your mark somewhere in the ever-changing world of electronic business.

Questions for Critical Thinking

1. Select a business that you purchase from regularly; how could the Internet help or threaten this company?
2. How has the Internet helped (or perhaps hurt) your college experience?

---

a new product or process is brought to the market, competitors need only a short time to be up and running with something similar. Thus, the biggest challenge for small businesses today is to make a product or provide a service that is hard to imitate.

Thinking globally and embracing a culturally diverse workforce. Globalization opens new markets for a company's goods, increases competition, and changes the composition of the workforce into one that is more diverse in race, gender, age, physical and mental abilities, lifestyle, culture, education, ideas, and background. As population patterns evolve and businesses continue to reach across national and cultural borders, businesses must also embrace the increasingly diverse workforce—both to support the needs of everyone in the workforce and to realize the benefits of having workers who represent a wider range of cultural backgrounds.

Behaving in an ethically and socially responsible manner. As businesses become more complex through global expansion and technological change, they must deal with an increasing number of ethical and social issues. These include the marketing of unhealthful products, the use of questionable accounting practices to compute financial results, and the pollution of the environment (as Chapter 2 discusses). In the future, businesses can expect continued pressure from environmental groups, consumers, employees, and government regulators to act ethically and responsibly.

Keeping pace with technology and electronic commerce. Everywhere we look, technology is reshaping the world. The Internet and innovations in computerization, miniaturization, and telecommunication have made it possible for people anywhere in the world to exchange information and goods. Such technologies are collapsing boundaries and changing the way customers, suppliers, and companies interact. Technology is also changing the way people shop for books, cars, vacations, advice—even the way they wash clothes. At the same time, technology can introduce unwanted complexities (no one ever had a typewriter crash in the middle of a term paper), security problems, and unwelcome elements such as spam (junk e-mail), spim (junk instant messages), and computer viruses.[24] In short, the Internet has touched every business and industry and is changing all facets of business life. (Consult Appendix A for a review of Internet and e-commerce fundamentals; the following chapters will assume that you know this material.)

As these challenges suggest, doing business in the 21st century means working in a world of increasing uncertainty where change is the norm, not the exception. In the coming chapters, we explore specific challenges that businesses are facing in the global economy and we provide real-world examples of how companies are tackling and meeting these challenges.

Summary of Learning Objectives

1 Define what a business is and identify four key social and economic roles that businesses serve.

A business is a profit-seeking activity that provides goods and services to satisfy consumers' needs. The driving force behind most businesses is the chance to earn a profit; however, nonprofit organizations exist to provide society with a social or educational service. Businesses serve four key functions: They provide society with necessities; they provide people with jobs and a means to prosper; they pay taxes that are used by the government to provide services for its citizens; and they reinvest their profits in the economy, thereby increasing a nation's wealth.

2 Differentiate between goods-producing and service businesses, and list five factors that are contributing to the increase in the number of service businesses.

Goods-producing businesses produce tangible goods and tend to be capital-intensive, whereas service businesses produce intangible goods and tend to be labor-intensive. The number of service businesses is increasing because (1) consumers have more disposable income to spend on taking care of themselves; (2) many services target consumers' needs brought about by changing demographic patterns and lifestyle trends; (3) consumers need assistance with using and integrating new technology into their business operations and lifestyles; (4) companies are turning to consultants and other professionals for advice to remain competitive; and (5) in general, barriers to entry are lower for service companies than they are for goods-producing businesses.

3 Differentiate between a free-market system and a planned system.

In a free-market system, individuals have a high degree of freedom to decide what is produced, by whom, and for whom. Moreover, the pursuit of private gain is regarded as a worthwhile goal. In a planned system, governments limit the individual's freedom of choice in order to accomplish government goals, control the allocation of resources, and restrict private ownership to personal and household items. The pursuit of private gain is nonexistent under a planned system.

4 Explain how supply and demand interact to affect price.

In the simplest sense, supply and demand affect price in the following manner: When the price goes up, the quantity demanded goes down but the supplier's incentive to produce more goes up. When the price goes down, the quantity demanded increases, whereas the quantity supplied may (or may not) decline. When the interests of buyers and sellers are in balance, an equilibrium price is established. However, adjusting price or supply to meet or spur demand does not guarantee profitability; business may not be able to adjust costs and price far enough and quickly enough. The important thing to remember is that in a free-market system, the interaction of supply and demand determines what is produced and in what amounts.

5 Discuss the four major economic roles of the U.S. government.

The U.S. government fosters competition by enacting laws and regulations, by enforcing antitrust legislation, and by approving mergers and acquisitions, with the power to block those that might restrain competition. It regulates certain industries where competition would be wasteful or excessive. It protects stakeholders from potentially harmful actions of businesses. And it contributes to economic stability by regulating the money supply and by spending for the public good.

6 Explain how a free-market system monitors its economic performance.

Economists evaluate economic performance by monitoring a variety of economic indicators, such as unemployment statistics, housing starts, durable-goods orders, and inflation. They compute the consumer price index (CPI) to keep an eye on price changes—especially inflation. In addition, economists measure the productivity of a nation by comput-

ing the country's gross domestic product (GDP)—the sum of all goods and services produced by both domestic and foreign companies as long as they are located within a nation's boundaries.

7 Identify five challenges that businesses are facing in the global economy.

The five challenges identified in the chapter are (1) producing quality products and services that satisfy customers' changing needs, (2) starting and managing a small business in today's competitive environment, (3) thinking globally and committing to a culturally diverse workforce, (4) behaving in an ethically and socially responsible manner, and (5) keeping pace with technology and electronic commerce.

Behind **the Scenes**

Moving the Music at Apple iTunes

When Steve Jobs surveyed the marketplace for online music, he no doubt liked some of the things he saw more than others. On the plus side, Apple was a well-known and highly regarded presence in both the computer and music industries, so almost anything the company chose to do would have the support and respect of many consumers and potential business partners. Plus, 2 million people were already walking around with Apple iPods, an enormously popular portable music player. Moreover, Apple's design team had a proven knack for making technology easier to use, a critical issue in the technically complicated arena of digital music.

On the minus side, Jobs knew there would be serious challenges in any effort to turn online music into a successful business venture. The technology would be complex, starting from the need to collect and store hundreds of thousands of songs and to make them easily available to thousands or even millions of online customers at once. The technology might've been the easiest part of the whole problem, however. The music business is a complex stew of strong personalities, strong traditions, tangled legal contracts, and lots of people who want a piece of the financial action, including performers, songwriters, music publishers, and record companies. Some artists refuse to sell songs individually out of fear it will hurt CD album sales (and some refuse to sell their music online at all). As a result, Apple and other companies often need to negotiate deals one song at a time—all of which takes time and costs money. To complicate matters even further, contractual terms differ from country to country, requiring a new round of negotiations each time. Then there are the millions of music listeners who were already in the habit of simply making copies of pirated songs. How

could they be convinced to pay for a product that they'd already been taking for free?

After 20 years of doing commercial battle with the likes of IBM and Microsoft, though, Steve Jobs has never been one to back down from a challenge. He added up those pluses and minuses, then decided to lead Apple into the fray. In 2003, the company launched iTunes.com, a web-based music store that offers more than a half million legally downloadable songs, all for 99 cents each. iTunes enjoyed widespread media coverage when it was first launched and even more when it was expanded to support Windows-based personal computers. Industry experts applaud its simplicity and breadth of musical offerings. Apple's efforts were no doubt also helped by some high-profile lawsuits that the recording industry launched against hundreds of people who had been downloading pirated tunes. By early 2004, iTunes had sold only 75 million or so of the 100 million songs it had hoped to sell by then, but Jobs claimed to be thrilled with the new business's performance nonetheless.

Jobs and his team have probably done about as good a job as anyone could in this wild new world of online music, but nobody knows yet if that is good enough. Recorded music is a multi-billion-dollar industry, but success or failure in online music will literally come down to pennies. When Apple collects those 99 cents for each song it sells, it first hands over 70 cents to whichever company controls the rights to the song (typically a record company in the United States). This company then has to divide those 70 cents among music publishers, performers, and songwriters. From the 29 cents Apple keeps, it needs to cover its costs for advertising, staffing, computer systems, and other business expenses. A single nationwide advertising campaign can cost millions of dollars, so you can get an idea of how hard it is to stretch those 29 cents to cover costs and turn a profit.

In fact, some experts don't think online music will ever be profitable and that the only reason companies will continue to offer it is to help sell related goods and services. In Apple's case, iTune's best success might mean selling even more of those popular iPods. Either way, if online music does turn out to be a viable business long-term, you can expect to see Steve Jobs and iTunes leading the way.[25]

Critical Thinking Questions

1. If Steve Jobs decides to let iTunes operate at a loss in order to generate more sales of iPods, does iTunes still qualify as a profit-seeking business? Explain your answer.
2. Is iTunes a goods-producing business or a service business? Why?
3. What barriers to entry did iTunes have to overcome in order to enter the online music business?

LEARN MORE ONLINE

Visit the iTunes website by going to Chapter 1 of this text's website at www.prenhall.com/bovee and clicking on the Apple iTunes hotlink. How does the website appeal to customers? What other products and services are offered? In what ways does the website encourage visitors to make purchases? ∎

Key Terms

barriers to entry (5)
business (3)
business cycle (15)
capital (6)
capital-intensive businesses (4)
capitalism (6)
communism (8)
competition (11)
competitive advantage (12)
consumer price index (CPI) (19)
deflation (18)
demand (9)
discount rate (16)
economic indicators (18)
economic system (6)
economics (6)

electronic commerce (e-commerce) (5)
entrepreneurs (6)
equilibrium price (11)
factors of production (6)
fiscal policy (17)
free-market system (6)
globalization (19)
goods-producing businesses (4)
gross domestic product (GDP) (19)
gross national product (GNP) (19)
human resources (6)
inflation (18)
knowledge (6)
labor-intensive businesses (4)
monetary policy (15)

monopolistic competition (12)
monopoly (11)
natural resources (6)
nonprofit organizations (3)
oligopoly (12)
planned system (8)
prime interest rate (prime) (16)
privatizing (9)
profit (3)
pure competition (11)
recession (15)
service businesses (4)
socialism (8)
stakeholders (14)
supply (9)

Test Your Knowledge

Questions for Review

1. Why do businesspeople study economics?
2. Why are knowledge workers a key economic resource?
3. How is capitalism different from communism and socialism in the way it achieves economic goals?
4. Why is government spending an important factor in economic stability?
5. Why might a government agency seek to block a merger or acquisition?

Questions for Analysis

6. Why is it often easier to start a service business than a goods-producing business?
7. Why is competition an important element of the free-market system?

8. Why do governments intervene in a free-market system?
9. How do countries know if their economic system is working?
10. **Ethical Considerations.** Because knowledge workers are in such high demand, you decide to enroll in an evening MBA program. Your company has agreed to reimburse you for 80 percent of your tuition. You haven't revealed, however, that once you earn your degree, you plan to apply for a management position at a different company. Is it ethical for you to accept your company's tuition reimbursement, given your intentions?

Questions for Application

11. Company sales are skyrocketing, and projections show that your computer consulting business will outgrow its

current location by next year. What factors should you consider when selecting a new site for your business?

12. How would a decrease in Social Security benefits to the elderly affect the economy?

13. Graph a supply and demand chart for iTunes pricing structure. Make up any data you need, but show the equilibrium price for an individual song to be 99 cents.

14. Think about the many ways that technology has changed your life as a consumer. Record your thoughts on a sheet of paper. On that same sheet of paper, make a second list of how you envision technology will change your life in the near future. Compare your thoughts to those of your classmates.

Practice Your Knowledge

Sharpening Your Communication Skills

Select a local service business you are familiar with. How does that business try to gain a competitive advantage in the marketplace? Write a brief summary, as directed by your instructor, describing whether the company competes on speed, quality, price, innovation, service, or a combination of those attributes. Be prepared to present your analysis to your classmates.

Building Your Team Skills

Economic indicators help businesses and governments determine where the economy is headed. You may have noticed news headlines such as the following, each of which offers clues to the direction of the U.S. economy:

1. Housing Starts Lowest in Months
2. Fed Lowers Discount Rate and Interest Rates Tumble

3. Retail Sales Up 4 Percent Over Last Month
4. Business Debt Down from Last Year
5. Businesses Are Buying More Electronic Equipment
6. Industry Jobs Go Unfilled as Area Unemployment Rate Sinks to 3 Percent
7. Telephone Company Reports 30-Day Backlog in Installing Business Systems

Discuss each of those headlines with the other students on your team. Is each item good news or bad news for the economy? Why? What does each news item mean for large and small businesses? Report your team's findings to the class as a whole. Did all the teams come to the same conclusions about each headline? Why or why not? With your team, discuss how these different perspectives might influence the way you interpret economic news in the future.

Expand Your Knowledge

Discovering Career Opportunities

Thinking about a career in economics? Find out what economists do by reviewing the *Occupational Outlook Handbook* in your library or online at www.bls.gov/oco. This is an authoritative resource for information about all kinds of occupations. Search for "economists," then answer these questions:

1. Briefly describe what economists do and their typical working conditions.
2. What is the job outlook for economists? What is the average salary for starting economists?
3. What training and qualifications are required for a career as an economist? Are the qualifications different for jobs in the private sector as opposed to those in the government?

Developing Your Research Skills

Gaining a competitive advantage in today's marketplace is critical to a company's success. Look through recent copies of business journals and newspapers (online or in print) to find an article about a company whose practices have set that company apart from its competitors. Use your favorite online search engine or metacrawler (see Appendix A for a list if you don't already have a favorite) to find more information about that company online.

1. What products or services does the company manufacture or sell?
2. How does the company set its goods or services apart from those of its competitors? Does the company compete on price, quality, service, or innovation?
3. Does the company have a website, and if so, how does the company use it? What kinds of information does the company include on its website?

SEE IT ON THE WEB

For live links to the websites that follow, go to this text's website at www.prenhall.com/bovee. When you log on, select Chapter 1, then select "Featured Websites," click on the URL of the website you wish to visit, review the website, and complete these exercises.

Explore these chapter-related websites, review their content, and answer the following questions for each website you visit:

1. What is the purpose of this website?
2. What kinds of information does this website contain? Please be specific.
3. How is the information provided at this website useful for businesspeople? Consumers?
4. How did you expand your knowledge of economics by reviewing the material at this website? What new things did you learn about this topic?

Find the Right Stuff

Learn about thousands of businesses around the world by visiting Corporate Information, a website with links to over 350,000 company profiles, data on 30 industries in 65 countries, and current economic information for over 100 countries. You'll also find research reports analyzing sales, dividends, earnings, and profit ratios on some thousands of companies, current foreign exchange rates, and the definitions of commonly used global company extensions such as GmBH, SA, de CV, and more. www.corporateinformation.com

Step Inside the Economic Statistics Briefing Room

Want to know where the economy is headed? Visit the Economic Statistics Briefing Room to get the latest economic indicators compiled by a number of U.S. agencies. Click on Federal Statistics by category to enter the room, and check out the stats and graphs for new housing starts; manufacturers' shipments, inventories, and orders; unemployment; average hourly earnings; and more. Are monthly housing starts, unemployment, and annual median household income increasing or decreasing? Make your own projections about which direction the economy is heading. www.whitehouse.gov/fsbr/esbr.html

Discover What's in the CPI

The CPI is an important tool that allows analysts to track the change in prices over time. But the CPI doesn't always match a given individual's inflation experience. Find out why by visiting the website maintained by the U.S. Bureau of Labor Statistics (look for Consumer Price Index). Be sure to check out how the CPI measures homeowners' costs, how the CPI is used, what goods and services it covers, and whose buying habits it reflects. stats.bls.gov

Companion Website

Learning Interactively

Go to the Companion Website at www.prenhall.com/bovee. For Chapter 1, take advantage of the interactive "Study Guide" to test your knowledge of the chapter. Get instant feedback on whether you need additional studying.

Also, visit this site's "Study Hall," where you'll find an abundance of valuable resources that will help you succeed in this course.

Video Case

Helping Businesses Do Business: U.S. Department of Commerce

LEARNING OBJECTIVES

The purpose of this video is to help you:

1. Understand world economic systems and their effect on competition.
2. Identify the factors of production.
3. Discuss how supply and demand affect a product's price.

SYNOPSIS

The U.S. Department of Commerce seeks to support U.S. economic stability and help U.S.-based companies do business in other countries. In contrast to the planned economy of the People's Republic of China, the United States is a market economy where firms are free to set their own missions and buy from and sell to any other business or individual. In the United States, companies must comply with government regulations that set standards such as minimum safety requirements. When doing business in other countries, they must consider tariffs and other restrictions that govern imports to those markets. In addition, supply and demand affect a company's ability to set prices and generate profits.

Discussion Questions

1. *For analysis:* If a U.S. company must pay more for factors of production such as human resources, what is the likely effect on its competitiveness in world markets?
2. *For analysis:* Is the equilibrium price for a company's product likely to be the same in every country? Explain your answer.
3. *For application:* To which factors of production might a small U.S. company have the easiest access? How would this affect the company's competitive position?
4. *For application:* Is a company likely to see more competitors enter a market when supply exceeds demand or when demand exceeds supply?
5. *For debate:* Should the U.S. Department of Commerce, funded by citizens' tax payments, be providing advice and guidance to U.S. companies that want to profit by doing business in other countries? Support your chosen position.

ONLINE EXPLORATION

Visit the U.S. Department of Commerce website at www.commerce.gov and follow some of the links from the homepage to see some of this government agency's resources for businesses. Also follow the link to read about the DOC's history. What assistance can a U.S. business expect from this agency? How have the agency's offerings evolved over the years as the needs and demands of business have changed?

Reviewing Internet and E-Commerce Fundamentals

As Chapter 1 demonstrates, it's virtually impossible to study business today without understanding the Internet and electronic commerce. Chances are you already have a fair amount of experience with e-mail, web surfing, and possibly instant messaging, but this appendix reviews these and many other topics from a business perspective. And if you haven't had the opportunity to spend much time online, this appendix will help you understand what it's all about. In either case, this textbook assumes that you're familiar with these fundamentals.

Understanding the Internet

The **Internet** is the world's largest computer network. Started in 1969 by the U.S. Department of Defense, the Internet is a voluntary, cooperative undertaking; no one individual, organization, or government owns it. The Internet is accessible to individuals, companies, colleges, government agencies, and other institutions in countries all over the world. It links thousands of smaller computer networks and millions of individual computer users in homes, businesses, government offices, and schools worldwide. You can learn more about the Internet by taking the tour at www.lib.berkeley.edu/TeachingLib/Guides/Internet/FindInfo. html or www.learnthenet.com.

You can access the Internet in a variety of ways. As a student, you might have access to your school's local network, which is in turn connected to the global Internet. If you don't have such network access, you can connect via a phone line, cable TV, a satellite link, or a wireless hot spot, depending on what's available in your area and how much you want to spend. Dial-up access, in which you connect your computer to a phone line via a modem to reach an **Internet service provider (ISP)**—a company that provides access to the Internet—is usually the slowest means of access. However, it's also the cheapest in most cases and available wherever you can find a phone. Both cable TV systems that offer Internet service and **digital subscriber line (DSL)** service offer faster access but aren't available in all areas. Both offer what is commonly known as **broadband** access, a somewhat vague term that usually means anything faster than dial-up. Satellite access offers a broadband alter-

native for people who can't get cable or DSL service, although it tends to be more expensive. Wireless access, often called "WiFi" for short, is available in an increasing number of public places and private networks. For instance, many Starbucks and McDonald's locations now offer wireless access for a modest fee. You need a wireless card in your laptop PC or handheld computer to use these wireless "hot spots." In addition to these options, a number of mobile phones, watches, and other devices are now equipped with some form of Internet access as well.

The most widely used part of the Internet is the **World Wide Web (WWW)**, more commonly known as simply the *web*. Developed in 1990, the web enables users to search for, display, and save a wide range of resources, from simple text pages to advanced **multimedia** pages that combine graphics, text, audio, and video files. This information is typically stored on a series of **webpages**, which are related files containing multimedia data that are made available on a **website**. You need a web **browser**—software such as Microsoft's Internet Explorer or Netscape Navigator—to read webpages.

The **homepage** of a website is the primary screen that users first access when visiting a site. Furthermore, each page in a website is identified by a unique address known as a **uniform resource locator (URL)**. Take www.yahoo.com, for example. The address begins with *http*, which is the abbreviation for **hypertext transfer protocol (HTTP)**, the communications protocol that allows you to navigate the web. The address continues with *www*, indicating that the site is located on the World Wide Web. The next part of the address is the registered **domain name** (in this case *yahoo.com*), a name unique to that site. The abbreviation following the period (com in Yahoo's case) is the top-level domain (TLD). The original seven TLDs identified commercial enterprises (com), educational institutions (edu), government agencies (gov), international sources (int), the military (mil), network resources (net), and nonprofit organizations (org). To keep up with demand, additional TLDs (such as pro, biz, info, coop, museum, and name) have been introduced. Websites based in other countries often include a two-letter country designator, such as .uk (United Kingdom) or .jp (Japan), along with .co for commercial enterprises or .ac for academic institutions. For instance, the URL of Amazon.com's United

Kingdom web presence is www.amazon.co.uk, and the website for University College London is www.ucl.ac.uk.

The basic language of the web is **hypertext markup language (HTML)**, which defines how text and graphics are displayed on your screen. (You don't need to worry about learning HTML unless you want to build your own websites, and even then you can build simple sites without knowing any HTML.) The most powerful element of HTML is the **hyperlink** or *hotlink*, which lets you click on specified text or graphic elements to jump to another webpage (or to download a file, launch another program, and so on). Once you get to your new destination, you can **bookmark** the site by using a browser feature that places the site's URL in a file on your computer for future use. Then, whenever you are online and you click on a bookmark, you automatically go to that site's address. Another handy browser feature is the ability to navigate your trail backward or forward at any time by using the *back* and *forward* buttons on your browser software. See the glossary at the end of this appendix for more definitions of Internet-related terms.

Finding Information on the Internet

Experienced business researchers know that the Internet can be a tremendous source of both **data** (recorded facts and statistics) and **information** (meaningful insights, knowledge, reports, and other higher-level results), much of it free and all of it available more or less instantly. They also know that the Internet can waste hours and hours of precious time and deliver inaccurate or biased information, exaggerated claims, and unsubstantiated rumors. You must remember that anyone (including you) can post virtually anything on a website, and much of that information will be unverified by the editorial boards and fact checkers commonly used in traditional publishing. If possible, try to learn something about an unfamiliar topic from a trusted source (such as an industry journal or an experienced colleague) before you start searching online. You'll be better able to detect skewed or erroneous information, and you can be more selective about which websites and documents to use.

One good place to start on the web is the Internet Public Library at www.ipl.org. Modeled after a real library, this site provides you with a carefully selected collection of links to high-quality business resources that offer such information as company profiles, trade data, business news, corporate tax and legal advice, small-business information, prepared forms and documents, biographies of executives, financial reports, job postings, online publications, and so on.

If you're looking for specific company information, your best source may be the company's website (if it maintains one, which virtually all large and medium-size companies do, as well as many smaller companies). These websites generally include detailed information about a firm's products, services, history, mission, strategy, financial performance, and employment needs. Many sites provide links to related company information, such as SEC filings, news releases, and more. Reputable companies are careful about the information they put online, but beware of the possibility of biases and mistakes.

Understanding Search Engines, Web Directories, and Databases

You've probably used one or more search engines, web directories, or databases for school and personal projects already. All three provide online access to secondary source material (and in some cases via CD-ROM), but each operates in a unique way and therefore offers distinct advantages and disadvantages for business researchers.

Search engines identify individual webpages that contain a specific word or phrase you've asked for. Search engines have the advantage of scanning millions or billions of individual webpages, and the best engines use powerful ranking algorithms to present the pages that are probably the most relevant to your search request. Note that search engines don't actually search the web when you submit a query; doing so would be painfully slow. Instead, they search through an index of pages that the search engine updates periodically. This is why you occasionally see webpages listed in the search results that you can't access; they've been moved or deleted since the last index update.

For all the ease and power they offer, search engines have three disadvantages that could affect the quality of your research. First, the process that search engines use to find and present lists of webpages is computerized, with no human editors involved to evaluate the quality of the content you find on these pages. Second, search engines can't reach the content held in limited-access collections, such as the back issues of many newspapers, magazines, professional journals, and subpages that search indexes don't index (although you can access many of these via www.invisible-web.net). Third, various search engines use different techniques to find, classify, and present pages, so you might be able to find certain pages through one engine but not through another.

The good news is that you can get around all three shortcomings when conducting research—although doing so is sometimes expensive. **Web directories** address the first major shortcoming of search engines by using human editors to categorize and evaluate websites. Directories such as those offered by Yahoo! About, and the Open Directory at http://dmoz.org present lists of websites chosen by a team of editors. For instance, the Open Directory lists more than 200,000 business-related websites by category, from individual companies to industry associations, all of which have been evaluated and selected by a team of volunteer editors.[1]

Online databases address the second shortcoming of search engines by offering access to the newspapers, magazines, and journals that you're likely to need for many research projects. You can access such sources as *BusinessWeek* and the

Amazon.com's "Search inside the book" feature adds a powerful new dimension to online research by letting you look for specific words within the content of published books (the words highlighted in this example were the keywords in the search). This feature can help you quickly identify books that will make good business research sources.

Wall Street Journal either through the individual publishers' own sites or through a commercial database that offers access to multiple sources. Individual publisher sites usually require a subscription to that publication for anything beyond the current issue, and commercial databases require subscriptions to access all content. Some commercial databases, such as HighBeam (www.highbeam.com) (formerly elibrary), are priced to attract individual users, whereas others, such as LexisNexis and ProQuest, are intended for use by libraries and other institutions. In addition to databases that primarily feature content from newspapers and periodicals, specialized databases such as Hoover's (www.hoovers.com) and OneSource's CorpTech (www.corptech.com) offer detailed information on thousands of individual companies. You can obtain company news releases from the free databases maintained by PRNewswire (www.prnewswire.com) and Business Wire (www.businesswire.com). News releases are good places to look for announcements of new products, management changes, earnings, dividends, mergers, acquisitions, and other company information.

Metacrawlers or *metasearch engines* address the third shortcoming of search engines by formatting your search request for the specific requirements of multiple search engines and then telling you how many hits each engine was able to find for you. The more popular **metacrawlers** include Dogpile.com and Mamma.com. Exhibit A.1 lists some of the more popular search engines, web directories, metacrawlers, and other tools available today.

As often happens in technology and business, the lines between these three types of tools are beginning to blur. For instance, Dogpile.com provides both metacrawler and directory functions, and LookSmart.com provides features of all three: a search engine, a directory, and a database of articles (although the database is limited to publications that provide free access to articles, which does not include major business publications such as *BusinessWeek* or *Fortune*).[2]

Using Search Tools Effectively

Search engines, metacrawlers, and databases offer a variety of ways to find information. That's the good news. The bad news is that no two of them work in exactly the same way, and many continue to refine and simplify their approaches, so you might have to modify your search techniques as you move from one tool to the next. The most basic form of searching is a *keyword search*, in which the engine or database attempts to find items that include all of the words you enter. A *Boolean search* expands on this capability by using search operators that let you define a query with greater precision. Common **Boolean operators** include AND (the search must include both words before and after the AND), OR (it can include either or both words), or NOT (the search ignores items with whatever word comes after NOT). For example:

- *corporate AND profits* finds webpages or database entries that contain both *corporate* and *profits*.
- *corporate OR profits* finds items that contain either *corporate* or *profit* but not necessarily both.
- *corporate NOT profit* finds items that contain *corporate* but excludes all those that contain the word *profit*.

Boolean searches can also include operators that let you find a particular word in close proximity to other words or use *wildcards* to find similar spellings (such as *profit, profits,* and *profitability*).

To overcome the perceived complexity of Boolean searches, some search engines and databases offer *natural language searches*, which let you ask questions in normal, everyday English ("Which videogame companies are the most profitable?"). For instance, HighBeam lets you select either Boolean or natural language searches. However, if a site or database doesn't specifically say that it offers natural language searching, the results might be unpredictable.

Recently, search engines such as Google, Yahoo!, and AllTheWeb have implemented *forms-based searches* that help you create powerful queries without the need to learn any special techniques.[3] As the name implies, you simply fill out an online form that typically lets you specify such parameters as date ranges, word to include or exclude, language, Internet domain name, and even file and media types. To access these forms, look for "advanced search" or a similar option. (Note that these forms use Boolean and other techniques in the background, but you don't have to learn any special commands.)

Exhibit A.1

Best of Internet Searching

Search engines, metacrawlers, directories, and other online research tools provide multiple ways to find vital business information.

MAJOR SEARCH ENGINES

AllTheWeb	www.alltheweb.com
Alta Vista	www.altavista.com
Ask Jeeves	www.askjeeves.com
Google	www.google.com
Lycos	www.lycos.com
MSN	http://search.msn.com
Teoma	www.teoma.com

METACRAWLERS AND HYBRID SITES

Dogpile	www.dogpile.com
Fazzle	www.fazzle.com
Infonetware RealTerm Search	www.infonetware.com
IXQuick	www.ixquick.com
Kartoo	www.kartoo.com
LookSmart	www.looksmart.com
Mamma	www.mamma.com
MetaCrawler	www.metacrawler.com
ProFusion	www.profusion.com
Query Server	www.queryserver.com
Search.com	www.search.com
Surfwax	www.surfwax.com
Vivisimo	www.vivisimo.com
Web Brain	www.webbrain.com
WebCrawler	www.webcrawler.com
Yahoo!	www.yahoo.com
Zapmeta	www.zapmeta.com
Zworks	www.zworks.com

WEB DIRECTORIES

About	www.about.com
Beaucoup	www.beaucoup.com
Internet Public Library	www.ipl.org
Open Directory	http://dmoz.org

NEWS SEARCH ENGINES

AllTheWeb News	www.alltheweb.com/?cat=news
AltaVista News	http://news.altavista.com
Daypop	www.daypop.com
Google News	http://news.google.com

NewsTrove.com	www.newstrove.com
World News Network	www.wn.com
Yahoo News	http://news.yahoo.com
MAGAZINE AND PERIODICAL SEARCH ENGINES	
FindArticles.com	www.findarticles.com
MagPortal	www.magportal.com

To make the best use of any search engine or **database**, keep the following points in mind:

- *Read the instructions.* Unfortunately, there is no universal set of instructions that apply to every search tool. You can usually find a "Help" page that explains both basic and advanced functions, with advice on how to use a particular tool most effectively.

- *Pay attention to the details.* Details can make all the difference in a search. For instance, most search engines treat *AND* (upper case) as a Boolean search operator and look only for pages or entries that contain both words. In contrast, *and* (lower case) and similar basic words (called *stopwords*) are excluded from many searches because they are so common they'll show up in every webpage or database entry. Similarly, some engines and databases interpret the question mark as a wildcard to let you search for variations of a given word, but Google does not (Google searches for word variations automatically). Again, you need to know how to operate each search engine or database, and don't assume they all work in the same way.

- *Review the search and display options carefully.* Some sites and databases provide few options to control your queries, but others, such as AllTheWeb.com, let you make a variety of choices to include or exclude specific types of files and pages from specific sites. When the results are displayed, verify the presentation order. On HighBeam, for instance, you can choose to sort the results by either date or relevancy. If you're looking for an article that you know was recently published, it might not show up near the top of the list if the list is sorted by relevancy instead of date. Also, pay attention to whether you are searching in the title, subject, or document field of the database. Each will return different results.

- *Try variations of your terms.* If you can't find what you're looking for, try abbreviations (*CEO, CPA*), synonyms (*man, male*), related terms (*child, adolescent, youth*), different spellings (*dialog, dialogue*), singular and plural forms (*woman, women*), nouns and adjectives (*manager, management, managerial*), and open and compound forms (*online, on line, on-line*).

- *Adjust the scope of your search if needed.* If a search yields little or no information, broaden your search by specifying fewer terms. For example, "Sony" yields many more hits than "Sony PlayStation." Conversely, if you're inundated with too many hits, use more terms to narrow your search.

Using Agents

For years, Internet users have been dreaming of intelligent software agents that automatically prowl the online world and bring back high-quality information. Nothing like this is available quite yet, but a capability called RSS (which stands for Rich Site Summary or Really Simple Syndication) can automate the delivery of new content from your favorite websites. RSS news aggregators such as NewsGator (www.newsgator. com) and NewzCrawler (www.newzcrawler.com) let you subscribe to channels at thousands of websites, newsgroups, and **blogs**—informal, web-based journals. New information is automatically delivered to your computer, saving you the trouble of searching multiple sites over and over again.[4]

How the Internet Is Changing the Way Companies Do Business

The Internet is revolutionizing all facets of business life. In the space of just a few years, the Internet has penetrated virtually every aspect of the economy. It's changing the way customers, suppliers, and companies interact, creating huge opportunities as well as unforeseen competitive threats. It's changing the way companies work internally—collapsing boundaries and redefining relationships among various functions, departments, and divisions. It's the fastest-growing marketplace in the world economy, spawning new businesses, transforming existing ones, and creating enormous wealth, opportunities, and risk. And it's changing the way companies communicate.[5]

The Internet offers businesses a wide variety of choices for online communication, including

- *E-mail.* Electronic mail, generally called **e-mail**, enables users to create, send, and read written messages entirely on the computer. An e-mail document can be a simple text message or can be formatted in HTML. Many types of files can be attached to e-mail messages as well.

■ *Discussion mailing lists.* **Discussion mailing lists**, also known as *listservs*, are discussion groups to which you subscribe by sending a message to the list's e-mail address. From then on, copies of all messages posted by any other subscriber are sent to you via e-mail. It's like subscribing to an electronic newsletter to which everyone can contribute.

■ *Newsgroups.* **Usenet newsgroups** consist of posted messages on a particular subject and responses to them. They differ from discussion mailing lists in two key ways. First, messages are posted at the newsgroup site, which you must access by using a news reader program. Second, messages posted to a newsgroup can be viewed by anyone. You can think of a newsgroup as a *place* you visit to read posted messages, whereas a discussion mailing list *delivers* posted messages to you.

■ *Instant messaging and chat.* Many companies encourage the use of **instant messaging (IM)** and **chat** to collaborate. Both allow online conversations in which any number of computer users can type in messages to each other and receive responses in real time. IM has become particularly popular in customer service applications.

■ *Telnet.* **Telnet** is a class of Internet application programs that allow you to communicate with other computers on a remote network even if your computer is not a permanent part of that network. For instance, you could use Telnet to access your county library's electronic card catalog from your home computer (although many libraries now provide access directly through your web browser so you don't always have to use Telnet).

■ *Internet telephony.* Internet users can converse vocally over the Internet using **Internet telephony**, also known as *VoIP* (short for Voice over Internet Protocol). Internet telephony promises lower costs and expanded service options, but technical and regulatory hurdles have slowed its advance. However, many experts predict that Internet telephony will become widely adopted once these issues are ironed out.[6]

■ *File transfers.* **File transfer protocol** (**FTP**) is an Internet service that enables you to **download** files or transfer data from a server to your computer and **upload** files or transfer data from your computer to another system.[7] FTP also allows you to attach formatted documents to your e-mail messages and download formatted files.[8] Sometimes users compress or *zip* large files—such as graphics files—to make them easier and faster to transfer. If you receive a zipped file, you must use special software to decompress it before you can read it. The Internet also makes *peer-to-peer file sharing* possible. Using the Internet and software, people can exchange files directly (from user to user) without going through a central server.

In addition to these communication choices, companies can use intranets and extranets—two types of websites specifically designed for internal and external communication.

Intranets

Companies that want to set up special employee-only websites can use an **intranet**, a private, internal corporate network. Intranets use the same technologies as the Internet and the World Wide Web, but the information provided and the access allowed are restricted to members of the organization (regardless of their actual location). Whereas employees can use a password to log onto the corporate intranet and then move to public areas of the Internet, unauthorized people cruising the Internet can't get into the internal site.

The majority of companies with 500 employees or more have corporate intranets, and smaller companies are also boosting productivity through intranet technology. Three factors are fueling this intranet boom: (1) the desire to share global knowledge, (2) the need for greater access to company information, and (3) the web's ease of use and flexibility.[9] For example, Ford Motor Company uses its intranet to enable engineers and designers worldwide to collaborate in real time on the design of new car models. Every model has its own internal website to track design, production, quality control, and delivery processes. And at IBM, employees can log onto the corporate intranet to more conveniently check their health benefits.[10]

As these examples show, intranets can be used for numerous communication functions. In addition to sending e-mail, other uses are filing electronic forms and reports, gaining access to the company information from remote locations, and publishing electronic phone directories, company newsletters, and other company material such as:[11]

■ *Policy manuals.* The most current version is always available to all employees without the need to reprint manuals when policies change.

An intranet set up by his law firm enables attorney David Beckman to view documents and other legal resources whether he's in the office or in the courtroom.

- *Employee benefits information.* Employees can find out about benefits, reallocate the funds in their retirement and benefit plans, fill out electronic W-4 forms, view an electronic pay stub, and sign up for training programs.

- *Presentation materials used by marketing and sales departments.* Sales representatives can download marketing materials at customer sites all over the world. In addition, changes made by marketing representatives at company headquarters are immediately available to field salespeople.

- *Company records and information.* Company directories, customer information, employee skills inventories, project status reports, company calendars and events, and many other records can be stored on an intranet so that they're accessible from anywhere in the world by using an Internet connection and a password.

Putting this material on an intranet allows employees to find information quickly and more easily than they would by digging through multiple filing cabinets or contacting different offices to find what they need.

Extranets

Once a company has an intranet in place, the cost of adding external capabilities is minimal, but the benefits can be substantial. An **extranet** is an external intranet that allows people to communicate and exchange data within a secured network.[12] Unlike intranets, which limit access to employees, extranets allow qualified people from the outside—such as suppliers and customers—to enter the network using a password. Extranets can enhance communication with clients, suppliers, and colleagues, and they can save companies time and money.

Consider Boeing. Every year the Chicago-based aerospace giant would ship a mountain of technical manuals, parts lists, and other maintenance documents to its 600 airline customers—enough papers to make a stack 130,000 feet tall—at an annual cost of millions of dollars. But now Boeing places all this information on an extranet so customers can review the data, obtain product updates, and discuss maintenance issues in chat areas.[13]

Extranets have many other uses. Some executive search firms and employment agencies are allowing clients to tap into their extranets to search for job prospects. More companies are inviting customers to use their extranets to check on the status of orders and shipping details. Doctors and hospitals are also using extranets to share best practices among their individual organizations. In the past they faxed this information to each other, but there was no guarantee that the right person would get a fax or even know it existed before the information became obsolete.

The latest twist on intranets and extranets is *darknets*, small, invitation-only networks that are typically more secure than other networks. Although they are popular with people sharing pirated music files, darknets have legitimate

business uses as well, primarily to exchange highly confidential information.[14]

By carefully combining Internet technologies on both the public network and private intranets, extranets, or even darknets, companies now use technology in multiple ways to become more efficient and more competitive:

- Locating information from external sources
- Collaborating with local, national, and international business partners
- Finding new business partners and attracting new customers
- Communicating with customers about orders, questions, and problems
- Promoting and selling goods and services to customers at any location
- Providing customers with service, technical support, and product information
- Searching out and buying parts and materials from domestic and international suppliers
- Permitting employees to **telecommute**, or work away from a conventional office, whether at home, on the road, or across the country
- Cost-effectively recruiting and training employees
- Sharing text, photos, presentation slides, videos, and other data within the organization
- Informing investors, industry analysts, government regulators, customers, and other stakeholders about business developments
- Conducting online meetings as an alternative to face-to-face meetings

You've probably noticed that all of these applications involve communication—one of the Internet's greatest contributions to business management.

Understanding Electronic Commerce

In addition to using the Internet for communication, businesses are using it to conduct electronic commerce. Chapter 1 defined electronic commerce (e-commerce) as the buying and selling of goods and services over an electronic network. Specifically, e-commerce is classified into four broad categories:

- **Business-to-consumer e-commerce.** Referred to as B2C, e-tailing, or electronic retailing, this form of e-commerce involves interactions and transactions between a company and consumers, with a strong focus on selling goods and services and marketing to consumers. Typical business-to-consumer transactions include such functions as sales, marketing (promotions, advertising, coupons, catalogs), order processing and tracking, credit authorization, customer service, and electronic payments.

- **Business-to-business e-commerce.** Known as B2B, this form of e-commerce uses the Internet to conduct transactions between businesses. Business-to-business e-commerce typically involves a company and its suppliers, distributors, manufacturers, and retailers but not consumers. Virtually every kind of business product imaginable is sold online today, from high-technology parts to advertising services.

- **Consumer-to-consumer e-commerce.** This category of e-commerce involves consumers who sell products directly to each other using the Internet as the intermediary. Auction sites such as eBay are consumer-to-consumer electronic channels. Sellers list their products with the auction site and buyers bid on listed sellers' products. Once a bid is accepted, the seller ships the product directly to the buyer.

- **Mobile commerce (m-commerce).** This category of e-commerce uses wireless Internet access and wireless handheld devices, such as cell phones, palm pilots, and pagers, to transact business. M-commerce is becoming increasingly popular in Europe and will become more popular in the United States once the required technology is in place.

Companies engage in e-commerce for a wide variety of reasons: to improve their image, improve customer service, simplify processes, compress time, increase productivity, eliminate paper transactions, expedite access to information, reduce transportation costs, find new benefits, increase flexibility, locate new customers, and reduce operating costs.[15] For instance, companies can reduce the costs of publishing, processing, distributing, storing, and retrieving information by engaging in electronic commerce. Moreover, processing customer orders electronically can be done at a fraction of the cost of using traditional paper-based and labor-intensive processes. Dell Computer reports that prior to launching its website, customers called an average of once or twice per purchase to check on the status of their orders. Now with online order tracking, customers check their order status electronically instead of calling a customer service rep. This process reduces Dell's costs significantly.[16]

Many companies also engage in e-commerce to generate new revenue streams by (1) creating new online markets for existing products, (2) creating new products specifically designed for online markets, and (3) expanding existing or new products into international markets.[17]

Customers stand to gain as much if not more from e-commerce than companies do. Electronic commerce[18]

- Enables customers to shop or conduct other transactions 24 hours a day, every day, from almost any location

- Provides customers with more choices; they can select from many vendors and from more products and price levels

- Allows for quick delivery of digitized products and information

- Allows customers to interact with other customers and exchange ideas as well as compare experiences

- Facilitates competition—which can keep prices in line

With a few clicks of the mouse, for example, travelers can plan and price trips, purchase tickets, receive travel confirmations, review current reservations, and review the status of their mileage rewards accounts. In short, today's customers can make buying decisions as if they had an army of intelligent helpers running to all the stores around the world to find the best products and prices. This ability is putting customers in a position of unprecedented control.

What Is the Difference Between E-Commerce and E-Business?

As discussed earlier, e-commerce involves buying and selling over electronic networks. By contrast, an **electronic business (e-business)** uses Internet technology to do much more than set up a website to sell or deliver goods. E-commerce is indeed an important part of becoming an e-business, but it is only one step in the evolutionary process. To become an e-business, a company must develop systems and structures that facilitate its ability to innovate constantly, react rapidly, and handle dynamic change. An e-business also integrates technology and the Internet into every phase of the business process—production, marketing, sales, customer support, advertising, public relations, and more—with one goal in mind: to meet customers' changing needs and priorities.[19]

Hot Topics and Issues in E-Commerce and E-Business

Electronic commerce may be a merchant's and consumer's dream, but once the website is up and running, companies must confront a variety of hot topics and issues as they begin to transact business. Among them are channel management, privacy, employee productivity, data security, and sabotage and theft.

Channel Management

As discussed in Chapter 12, the Internet has dramatically reshaped distribution channels in many industries. It created some entirely new companies, such as Amazon.com, and allowed others, such as REI, to integrate online and offline distribution. Some producers are using the Internet to eliminate intermediaries such as retailers, others are using it to restructure their distribution channels to make them more cost-effective, and still others are using the Internet to expand their reach. You'll also see that the Internet has created new risks of *channel conflict*, such as when manufacturers try to sell directly to consumers and compete with the retailers who also sell their products.

Information Privacy

Information privacy in today's workplace is another hot issue. Employers must find the right balance between protecting valuable company information and respecting employees' privacy rights. For instance, many employees erroneously believe that their e-mail and voice mail messages are private, and they're surprised when e-mail ends up in places they did not intend it to go. But employers have the legal right to monitor everything from employees' web access to the content of their company e-mail or voice mail messages. Moreover, both e-mail and voice mail can be used as evidence in court cases. Therefore, a good rule of thumb is not to say anything in e-mail or voice mail that you would not want to see published in a newspaper.

According to an American Management Association survey, 74 percent of major U.S. companies keep tabs on workers by recording phone calls or voice mail and by checking employees' computer files and e-mail.[20] Such surveillance is helping companies crack down on abuse: Just months after Xerox began monitoring web usage, it fired 40 employees for viewing inappropriate websites—primarily pornographic sites.[21]

Employee Productivity

Maintaining a high level of employee productivity is another challenge companies are facing. Whereas employees once had to deal only with incoming phone calls and the occasional fax, many now have to manage regular phone service, a mobile phone, e-mail, and IM—and still get their work done throughout the day. In addition to these interruptions, the Internet and other office technologies provide plenty of opportunities for employees to engage in personal business while on the job. To help prevent abuses of company resources and ensure that employees spend their work time doing company business, many employers either have policies regarding e-mail and Internet use or actually monitor e-mail and web surfing.[22]

Data Security

Before computers, companies typically conducted business mainly on paper, locking up sensitive documents and using security precautions when transporting important files. Furthermore, only a limited number of people had access to vital company data. But today's move from paper-based systems to electronic data management poses a real threat to corporate data security.[23]

Global networks increase the possibility that crucial information on an intranet or sent over the Internet will be altered or destroyed. Criminals and assorted mischief makers attempt to penetrate corporate networks thousands of times every year.[24] These infiltration attempts include **hacking**, or breaking into a computer network such as an intranet to steal, delete, or change data, and **cracking**, or entering a computer network for nondestructive reasons, such as to play a prank or show off, under the misguided impression that their activities don't cause any harm.

Unfortunately, hacking and cracking are on the rise. For these reasons, most companies go beyond simple identification and password protection to prevent unauthorized computer access by installing security software called a **firewall**, a special type of gateway that controls access to the company's local network. The firewall allows access only to users who present the proper password and system identification. In addition to firewalls, companies protect their data by (1) determining which employees should receive passwords to vital networks; (2) providing ongoing security enforcement and education; (3) conducting background checks on all new employees; (4) adopting a security policy that requires employees to use passwords, turn computers off when not in use, encrypt sensitive e-mail, and apply stronger security measures to safeguard trade secrets; and (5) developing a plan for data recovery if disaster strikes.[25]

Taking these measures will, of course, deter potential offenders, but doing so will not guarantee the security of information or completely protect data from sabotage or cyberterrorism.

Sabotage and Cyberterrorism

Today, criminals are using technology to disrupt website and computer operations and cause other problems for companies, governments, and individuals. Among the most common forms of sabotage are viruses and worms:

- **Viruses** are programs that can change or delete files or programs. Embedded in legitimate software (without the manufacturer's knowledge) or in files passed from one computer to another, vicious viruses can quickly do tremendous damage.

- **Worms** are programs specifically designed to replicate over and over again. Spread by e-mail, these send more worms to everyone in the recipient's e-mail address book—taking up precious network space and snarling connections.

Viruses and worms create immense financial damage, upwards of $10 billion a year according to some estimates, through lost productivity, lost sales, lost information, and the cost of protective software and hardware.[26] One way or another, these costs get passed on to consumers and investors in the form of higher prices or lower profits. Even if nothing is stolen, hacking and cracking present an enormous cost to society.

Cyberterrorism—orchestrated attacks on a company's information systems for political or economic purposes—is another form of sabotage that is being taken even more seriously since the terrorist attacks on buildings in New York City and Washington, D.C., in September 2001. Computer security experts say that the country's computer networks and the Internet are vulnerable to coordinated attacks that could interrupt power supplies to millions of homes, disrupt air traffic control systems, shut down water supplies, cut off emergency 911 services, and cripple corporate America, causing billions of dollars in business losses.[27]

To better police data security threats from domestic and international sources, the U.S. Justice Department has set up the National Infrastructure Protection Center (NIPC) at the FBI. The FBI has also begun using a software program called Carnivore to screen e-mail messages for clues to crippling electronic and physical terrorist attacks. Although privacy advocates fear that Carnivore and other security measures are too intrusive and could lead to false accusations, government officials—and many citizens—are willing to trade off some privacy for a higher degree of security against all types of terrorism.[28]

Regardless of the type of sabotage, the FBI estimates that reported computer losses as a result of sabotage total $10 billion annually—and the biggest threat comes from within. Up to 60 percent of computer break-ins are caused by employees. Other violators include laid-off workers, contractors, and consultants who destroy, alter, or expose critical data.[29] And the situation could get worse. With the use of web-browsing cell phones, wireless communication devices, and other computerized and networked products and services, companies may find their systems even more vulnerable to sabotage and theft in the coming years.

Glossary

blogs Web-based journals, usually presented by a single writer and updated frequently

bookmark A browser feature that places selected URLs in a file for quick access, allowing you to automatically return to the website by clicking on the site's name

Boolean operators The term *Boolean* refers to a system of logical thought developed by the English mathematician George Boole; it uses the operators AND, OR, and NOT

broadband Exact definitions vary, but generally, broadband refers to any method of Internet access that offers higher speeds than dial-up

browser Software, such as Microsoft's Internet Explorer or Netscape Navigator, that enables a computer to search for, display, and download the multimedia information that appears on the World Wide Web

business-to-business e-commerce Electronic commerce that involves transactions between companies and their suppliers, manufacturers, or other companies

business-to-consumer e-commerce Electronic commerce that involves transactions between businesses and the end user or consumer

chat A form of interactive communication that enables computer users in separate locations to have real-time conversations. Usually takes place at websites called chat rooms

consumer-to-consumer e-commerce Electronic commerce that involves transactions between consumers

cracking Entering a computer network for nondestructive reasons, such as to play a prank

cyberterrorism Orchestrated attacks on a company's information systems for political or economic purposes

data Recorded facts and statistics; data need to be converted to information before they can help people solve business problems

digital subscriber line (DSL) High-speed phone line that carries both voice and data

discussion mailing lists E-mail lists that allow people to discuss a common interest by posting messages, which are received by everyone in the group

domain name The portion of an Internet address that identifies the host and indicates the type of organization it is

download Transmitting a file from one computer system to another; on the Internet, bringing data from the Internet into your computer

electronic business (e-business) A company that has transformed its key business processes to incorporate Internet technology into every phase of the operation

e-mail Communication system that enables computers to transmit and receive written messages over electronic networks

extranet Similar to an intranet but extending the network to select people outside the organization

file transfer protocol (FTP) A software protocol that lets you copy or move files from a remote computer—called an FTP site—to your computer over the Internet; it is the Internet facility for downloading and uploading files

firewall Computer hardware and software that protects part or all of a private computer network attached to the Internet by preventing public Internet users from accessing it

hacking Breaking into a computer network to steal, delete, or change data

homepage The primary website for an organization or individual; the first hypertext document displayed on a website

hyperlink A highlighted word or image on a webpage or document that automatically allows people to move to another webpage or document when clicked on with a mouse

hypertext markup language (HTML) The software language used to create, present, and link pages on the World Wide Web

hypertext transfer protocol (HTTP) A communications protocol that allows people to navigate among documents or pages linked by hypertext and to download pages from the World Wide Web

information   Insights, summaries, analyses, comparisons, and other meaningful elements of knowledge

instant messaging (IM)   Online conversations in which any number of computer users can type in messages to each other and receive responses in real time

Internet   A worldwide collection of interconnected networks that enables users to share information electronically and provides digital access to a wide variety of services

Internet service provider (ISP)   A company that provides access to the Internet, usually for a monthly fee, via telephone lines, cable, or satellite; ISPs can be local companies or specialists such as America Online

Internet telephony   Telephone service that uses the Internet instead of traditional phone lines; also called VoIP

intranet   A private network, set up within a corporation or organization, that operates over the Internet and may be used to link geographically remote sites

metacrawlers   Special engines that search several search engines at once

mobile commerce (m-commerce)   Transaction of electronic commerce using wireless devices and wireless Internet access instead of PC-based technology

multimedia   Typically used to mean the combination of more than one presentation medium—such as text, sound, graphics, and video

online database   A collection of data arranged for ease and speed in searching and retrieving online

search engines   Internet tools for finding websites on the topics of your choice

telecommute   To work from home and communicate with the company's main office via computer and communication devices

Telnet   A way to access a remote computer via the Internet

uniform resource locator (URL)   Web address that gives the exact location of an Internet resource

upload   Sending a file from your computer to a server or host system

Usenet newsgroups   One or more discussion groups on the Internet where people with similar interests can post articles and reply to messages

viruses   Form of computer sabotage embedded in software or passed from one computer to the next that changes or deletes computer files or programs

web directory   A search tool that searches for information by subject categories, created by real people rather than by automation

webpages   Related files containing multimedia data that are made available on a website

website   A related collection of files on the World Wide Web

World Wide Web (WWW)   A hypertext-based system for finding and accessing Internet resources such as text, graphics, sound, and other multimedia resources

worms   Form of computer sabotage sent by e-mail that reproduces—taking up network space and snarling connections

Chapter 2

Practicing Ethical Behavior and Social Responsibility

LEARNING OBJECTIVES

After studying this chapter, you will be able to

1 Discuss what it means to practice good business ethics and highlight three factors that influence ethical behavior

2 Identify three steps that businesses are taking to encourage ethical behavior and explain the advantages and disadvantages of whistle-blowing

3 List four questions you might ask yourself when trying to make an ethical decision

4 Explain the difference between an ethical dilemma and an ethical lapse

5 Discuss the relationship between corporate social responsibility and profits

6 Discuss how businesses can become more socially responsible

7 Outline activities the government and businesses are undertaking to improve the environment

Behind the Scenes

Beyond the Pursuit of Profits: Patagonia Gears Up to Protect the Environment

www.patagonia.com

Yvon Chouinard admits that he likes the rush of adrenaline that comes from scaling frozen waterfalls and steep mountains. Never one to refuse a challenge, the daredevil sportsman became an icon in the world of ice and rock climbing during the 1970s. But Chouinard faced another test of endurance in the 1990s when he encountered a business problem as challenging as the mountains he loved to climb.

As the founder and owner of Patagonia, a lead-ing designer and distributor of outdoor gear, Chouinard worked hard to build a successful company that catered to extreme sports enthusiasts like himself. Along the way, he incorporated his personal passion for environmental protection into Patagonia's operating principles. As Chouinard explains, "We want it all. We want the best quality and the lowest environmental impact."

Under Chouinard's leadership, the company rigor-ously pursued its environmental values. For instance, Chouinard created a self-imposed "earth tax," amount-ing to the greater of 1 percent of sales or 10 percent of pretax profits, and donates the tax (about $1 million each year) to a variety of environmental causes.

By the end of the 1980s, Patagonia had carved its own niche among sports enthusiasts by producing the best outdoor products in the marketplace at the lowest possi-

Environmentally friendly products such as those sold by Patagonia give consumers a chance to make a difference while meeting their needs.

ble cost to the environment. With an annual growth rate of 30 percent, the company expanded its offerings to 375 products, including a line of casual apparel that appealed to the masses. But adhering to rigid environmental stan-dards in the production of its high-priced goods cre-ated enormous operating expenses. So when sales leveled off in the 1990s, Patagonia was forced to scale back its operations and lay off one-fifth of its workforce.

Consultants advised Chouinard to sell the com-pany and create a charitable foundation for environmen-tal causes instead of donating a million or so from com-pany profits each year. But Chouinard hadn't established Patagonia for the sole purpose of giving money away to environmental groups. He wanted to "use the company as a tool for social change," believing that Patagonia could lead the way in developing new, environmentally sensi-tive methods of producing high-quality goods.

Moreover, Chouinard knew that no one would ben-efit from the environmental agenda of a business in bankruptcy, so he faced a challenging dilemma: How could Patagonia continue to grow, expand, and make a profit without compromising its commitment to the environment? If you were Yvon Chouinard, how would you balance Patagonia's economic needs with its envi-ronmental principles?[1] ■

ETHICS AND SOCIAL RESPONSIBILITY IN CONTEMPORARY BUSINESS

Yvon Chouinard works hard to make sure that Patagonia does the right thing. But as Chouinard knows, a business can't take action or make decisions; only the individuals within a business can do that. From the CEO to the newest entry-level clerk, every individual in an organization makes choices and decisions that have moral implications. These choices and decisions affect the company and its stakeholders. Moreover, they ultimately determine whether the company is recognized as a responsible corporate citizen.

This chapter explains what it means to conduct business in an ethically and socially responsible manner and discusses the importance of doing so. Some people use the terms *social responsibility* and *ethics* interchangeably, but the two are not the same. **Social responsibility** is the idea that business has certain obligations to society beyond the pursuit of profits. **Ethics**, by contrast, is defined as the principles and standards of moral behavior that are accepted by society as right versus wrong. To make the right choice, or at least the best choice from among competing alternatives, individuals must think through the consequences of their actions. *Business ethics* is the application of moral standards to business situations.

Thanks to a number of high-profile scandals involving finances and product safety, corporate social responsibility and managerial ethics have been pushed to center stage in recent years. Several of these in particular have clearly and often painfully demonstrated that corporate responsibility and ethics are not just intriguing philosophical questions but real-life issues, where mistakes by just a handful of people can erase billions of dollars of shareholder value (including the life savings of many employees), destroy tens of thousands of jobs, and affect families and communities for years. Throughout your business studies and into your career, you'll continue to hear references to the following half-dozen cases (note that civil and criminal lawsuits are still active in several of these, so the final outcomes have yet to be determined):

social responsibility
The concern of businesses for the welfare of society as a whole

ethics
The rules or standards governing the conduct of a person or group

Business BUZZ

Enronomics: Suspect business practices that rely on impossibly optimistic forecasts, dubious accounting, or unsustainable spending

- **Enron.** Once the nation's seventh-largest company and a poster child for "new economy" companies, Houston-based energy conglomerate Enron all but collapsed in 2001 thanks to a complex stew of hidden partnerships (designed to overstate profits and hide losses from investors), management mistakes, and insider trading. Thousands of employees lost their jobs, and many lost their life savings when Enron stock became almost worthless. More than 20 executives have been investigated by the Justice Department; at least a dozen have been indicted, and several pled guilty before they could be indicted. Lawsuits and trials will continue for years. Charges were also brought against several of Enron's banks for their role in hiding financial information from investors.[2]

- **Arthur Andersen.** One of the world's oldest and most distinguished public accounting firms, Arthur Andersen served as both Enron's independent financial auditor and management adviser (Chapter 13 discusses this conflict of interest in more detail). The company was indicted for shredding Enron accounting documents and later convicted of obstruction of justice for hiding information about Enron finances, making it the first major accounting firm ever convicted of a felony. As a consequence, Arthur Andersen was required to stop performing public audits—the core of its business—and shed two-thirds of its employees.[3]

- **Tyco.** Former CEO Dennis Kozlowski and several top executives were charged with taking $600 million from Tyco, a diversified manufacturing company; his trial ended in a mistrial in 2004 for reasons unrelated to the case, but prosecutors plan to put him on trial again.[4]

- **Adelphia.** Once the nation's sixth-largest cable television company, Adelphia is now in bankruptcy, and founder John Rigas and two of his sons were arrested for defrauding investors out of billions of dollars.[5]

- **WorldCom.** Telecommunications giant WorldCom (which now goes by the name MCI), filed for bankruptcy and cut more than 22,000 jobs after revealing accounting frauds totaling $11 billion.[6]

- **Ford and Firestone.** Faulty Firestone tires on Ford Explorers are blamed for 271 deaths and more than 800 injuries worldwide—numbers that investigators said could've been much lower if both companies had reacted sooner to evidence of product failure. Firestone blamed the problem on Ford (and on Explorer drivers);

Ford blamed the problem on Firestone. Firestone refused to recall the tires, then Ford stepped in and replaced the tires on nearly 50,000 vehicles in 16 countries outside the United States—but neither company bothered to inform U.S. authorities or customers until similar failures started to show up in this country.[7]

Although these cases involve only a few companies, the fallout from their actions continues to affect managers in thousands of companies. As you'll see in Chapter 13, for instance, publicly traded companies (those that sell stock to investors) must now comply with new federal regulations, the Sarbanes-Oxley Act of 2002, that require much more stringent financial reporting. This new level of information may be a good thing for investors, but it comes at a cost. Estimates vary, but U.S. businesses will probably spend several billion dollars and countless hours of employee and executive time to ensure compliance with the new regulations—time and money that could've been invested in creating better products, improving customer service, and other productive activities.[8] And consumers ultimately pay the price when these added costs are passed along. Even though those new costs are a small fraction of the amount investors lost in these scandals, the unethical behavior of a small group of executives raised costs for everyone else.

The news is not all bad, of course. As you read about illegal (or legal but unethical) behavior on the part of a few managers, bear in mind that the vast majority of businesses are run by ethical managers and staffed by ethical employees whose positive contributions to their communities are unfortunately overshadowed at times by headline-grabbing scandals. When Cummins Engine discovered that poor children without a school were sneaking into their Brazilian factory to steal metal to sell, the company funded the construction of a school that now serves 800 kids—and their parents in the evenings.[9] When John Wheeler, CEO of Rockford Construction, found out how poorly inner-city students in Grand Rapids, Michigan, were being treated, he mobilized his entire company to help. The 60 or 70 projects the company has initiated range from building a playground to buying two dilapidated schools and spending $18 million to resurrect them to simply handing one principal an envelope with $5,000 in it, to be used whenever a low-income student's family can't afford to pay a gas or electricity bill.[10]

Like all managers, these people face issues that aren't always clear-cut either, so identifying the "right" choice is not always easy. You can start to appreciate the dilemmas these managers face by first understanding what constitutes ethical behavior.

What Is Ethical Behavior?

As Patagonia's Yvon Chouinard knows, wanting to be an ethical corporate citizen isn't enough; people in business must actively practice ethical behavior. In business, besides obeying all laws and regulations, practicing good ethics means competing fairly and honestly, communicating truthfully, and not causing harm to others.

Competing Fairly and Honestly

Businesses are expected to compete fairly and honestly and not knowingly deceive, intimidate, or misrepresent customers, competitors, clients, or employees. While most companies compete within the boundaries of the law, some do knowingly break laws or take questionable steps in their zeal to maximize profits and gain a competitive advantage. For example, to get ahead of the competition, some companies have engaged in corporate spying, stealing patents, hiring employees from competitors to gain trade secrets, and electronically eavesdropping. Although businesses need to gather as much strategic information as they can, ethical companies steer clear of such practices.

In some cases, the line between legal and ethical behavior is blurred. For instance, breaking into an office to gather sensitive information or crucial documents from the trash is illegal, but once the refuse makes its way to a Dumpster on public property, it's fair game. Still, rifling through a competitor's trash bins—a practice commonly referred to as *Dumpster diving*—is widely considered to be unethical. Procter & Gamble (P&G) recently admitted that several of its employees had hired corporate detectives to retrieve

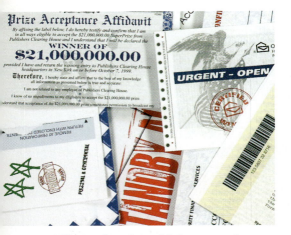

Mailings such as these misled consumers into believing that they were winners of the Publishers Clearing House sweepstakes. In particular, notice the prominent use of the words "priority," "personal and confidential," "urgent," and "prize acceptance affidavit."

documents related to Unilever's hair care operations from a Dumpster outside Unilever's Chicago offices. While P&G denied doing anything illegal, the company voluntarily told Unilever that it had obtained information "in a way that was clearly outside our company's policies in the area of business information gathering." Executives at P&G voluntarily returned the documents to Unilever, agreed to pay their rival $10 million, and promised not to use any of the information it had obtained.[11]

Communicating Truthfully

Companies that practice good ethical behavior refrain from issuing false or misleading communications. Publishers Clearing House learned this ethical lesson when it had to pay $34 million to settle lawsuits by 26 states claiming that it deceived consumers by mailing "you are winner" notices that looked like checks for large amounts. The company was also charged with accompanying such notices with deceptive communications that led consumers to believe they could increase their chances of winning a grand prize by purchasing magazine subscriptions. As part of the settlement agreement, Publishers Clearing House promised it would stop mailing simulated checks and stop sending consumers misleading information. It also promised that future mailings would disclose the odds of winning and inform the public that buying subscriptions would not increase the chances of winning.[12]

Not Causing Harm to Others

According to a recent *BusinessWeek*/Harris poll, some 79 percent of Americans believe corporate executives put their own personal interests ahead of workers' and shareholders'.[13] Placing one's personal welfare above the welfare of the organization can cause harm to others. For instance, every year tens of thousands of people are the victims of investment scams. Lured by promises of high returns, people sink more than a billion dollars annually into nonexistent oil wells, gold mines, and other fraudulent operations touted by complete strangers over the telephone and the Internet.[14]

Even legitimate companies can mislead investors by withholding vital information. For example, Enron and WorldCom both showed that with a little "creative accounting," a business that is in financial trouble can be made to look attractive, even to government regulators and astute investors.

Some business executives take advantage of the investor by using the company's earnings or resources for personal gain. Perhaps the most common approach is to cheat on expense accounts. Padding invoices and then splitting the overcharge with the supplier is another common ploy. Other tactics include selling company secrets to competitors and using confidential, nonpublic information gained from one's position in a company to benefit from the purchase and sale of stocks. Such **insider trading** is illegal and is closely checked by the Securities and Exchange Commission (SEC).

Another way that businesspeople can harm others is by getting involved in a **conflict of interest** situation. A conflict of interest exists when choosing a course of action will benefit one person's interests at the expense of another or when an individual chooses a course of action that advances his or her personal interests over those of the employer. For example, a lawyer would find himself in a conflict of interest situation if he represented both the plaintiff and the defendant in a lawsuit. Similarly, independent auditors could be in a conflict of interest situation if their firm also served as the client's consultants, as Arthur Andersen did with Enron.

insider trading
The use of unpublicized information that an individual gains from the course of his or her job to benefit from fluctuations in the stock market

conflict of interest
Situation in which a business decision may be influenced by the potential for personal gain

Factors Influencing Ethical Behavior

Although a number of factors influence the ethical behavior of businesspeople, three in particular appear to have the most impact: cultural differences, knowledge, and organizational behavior.

Cultural Differences

Globalization exposes businesspeople to a variety of different cultures and business practices. What does it mean for a business to do the right thing in Thailand? In Nigeria? In Norway? What may be considered unethical in the United States may be an accepted practice in another culture. Managers may need to consider a wide range of issues, including acceptable working conditions, minimum wage levels, product safety issues, and environmental protection. Chapter 3 explores these issues in more detail.

Learning from Business Blunders

Oops: When KFC launched a new ad campaign that presented fried chicken as an acceptable part of a "healthy, balanced diet" (or at least healthier than other fast-food alternatives), consumer advocates were quick to point out that the bucket of chicken being advertised contained more than 3,000 calories. *Advertising Age* magazine attacked the campaign, calling it "laughable." KFC quickly pulled the ads.

What You Can Learn: Whether people can occasionally enjoy fried chicken as part of a generally healthy diet is probably an issue for dieticians to resolve, but one thing is clear: Showing a 3,000-calorie, deep-fat fried product while talking about healthy diets is only asking for criticism. Many businesses now operate under constant scrutiny, so any suspect product claims are likely to come under close, critical examination from any number of regulators and advocacy groups.

Knowledge

Generally speaking, greater knowledge increases the chance of making the right decision. Making decisions without all the facts or a clear understanding of the consequences could harm employees, customers, the company, and other stakeholders. As an employee or manager, you are held accountable for your decisions and actions. So be sure to ask questions and gather enough information before making a decision or choosing a course of action. For instance, if a business superior tells you to shred a file drawer full of documents, you might want to ask why and inquire whether doing so would be in violation of the law.

Organizational Behavior

The foundation of an ethical business climate is ethical awareness and clear standards of behavior. Organizations that strongly enforce company codes of conduct and provide ethics training help employees recognize and reason through ethical problems. Similarly, companies with strong ethical practices set a good example for employees to follow. On the other hand, companies that commit unethical acts in the course of doing business open the door for employees to follow suit.

To avoid such ethical breaches, many companies proactively develop programs designed to improve their ethical conduct. Boeing, for example, requires all employees to undergo at least one hour of ethical training a year; the company's senior managers must undergo five hours. Lockheed Martin has created a newspaper called *Ethics Daily* that runs articles based on ethical problems employees have faced and how they resolved them.[15]

Additionally, more than 80 percent of large companies have adopted a written **code of ethics**, which defines the values and principles that should be used to guide decisions (see Exhibit 2.1 for an example). By itself, however, a code of ethics can't accomplish much. "You can have grand motives, but if your employees don't see them, they aren't going to mean anything," says one ethics manager.[16] To be effective, a code must be supported by employee communications efforts, a formal training program, employee commitment to follow it, and a system through which employees can get help with ethically difficult situations.[17]

In addition to setting a good example, top executives must also be sensitive to ethical pressures they may be placing on their employees. For instance, a number of U.S. employers, including Wal-Mart, Pep Boys, Family Dollar, Taco Bell, and Toys "R" Us, have recently been accused of "time shaving," a practice in which supervisors alter employees' work records in order to cut costs (typically to avoid paying overtime when employees log more than 40 hours a week). All of these companies have formal policies prohibiting time shaving, but some supervisors say they are under such intense pressure to control costs that they fear they'll lose their own jobs if they don't shave time off their employees' time cards. Compensation experts say the practice is far more common than most people believe.[18]

code of ethics
Written statement setting forth the principles that guide an organization's decisions

Exhibit 2.1

IEEE Code of Ethics

The Institute of Electrical and Electronics Engineers promotes the public policy interests of its U.S. members. The organization's code of ethics serves as a model for members to adopt.

THE INSTITUTE OF ELECTRICAL AND ELECTRONICS ENGINEERS, INC. CODE OF ETHICS

We, the members of the IEEE, in recognition of the importance of our technologies affecting the quality of life throughout the world, and in accepting a personal obligation to our profession, its members and the communities we serve, do hereby commit ourselves to the highest ethical and professional conduct and agree:

1. to accept responsibility in making engineering decisions consistent with the safety, health and welfare of the public, and to disclose promptly factors that might endanger the public or the environment;

2. to avoid real or perceived conflicts of interest whenever possible, and to disclose them to affected parties when they do exist;

3. to be honest and realistic in stating claims or estimates based on available data;

4. to reject bribery in all its forms;

5. to improve the understanding of technology, its appropriate application, and potential consequences;

6. to maintain and improve our technical competence and to undertake technological tasks for others only if qualified by training or experience, or after full disclosure of pertinent limitations;

7. to seek, accept, and offer honest criticism of technical work, to acknowledge and correct errors, and to credit properly the contributions of others;

8. to treat fairly all persons regardless of such factors as race, religion, gender, disability, age, or national origin;

9. to avoid injuring others, their property, reputation, or employment by false or malicious action;

10. to assist colleagues and co-workers in their professional development and to support them in following this code of ethics.

Codes of ethics are so important that according to the Federal Sentencing Guidelines (1991), a company found to be violating federal law might not be prosecuted if it has the proper ethics policies and procedures in place. As one ethics expert explains, "If you have an active ethics program in place ahead of time, then bad things shouldn't happen; but if they do happen, it won't hurt you as badly."[19] Perhaps inspired by these guidelines, some companies have created an official position—the ethics officer—to guard morality. Originally hired to oversee corporate conduct—from pilfering company pens to endangering the environment to selling company secrets—many ethics officers today function as corporate coaches for ethical decision making. Keep in mind, however, that ethical behavior starts at the top. The CEO and other senior managers must set the tone for people throughout the company. At Aveda, a cosmetics company, the corporate mission is to bring about positive effects through responsible business methods. "We do this, quite frankly, out of self-preservation," says founder and chairman Horst Rechebecher.[20]

Another way companies support ethical behavior is by establishing a system for reporting unethical or illegal actions at work, such as an ethics hot line. Companies that value ethics will try to correct reported problems. If a serious problem persists, or in cases where management may be involved in the act, an employee may choose to blow the whistle. *Whistle-blowing* is an employee's disclosure to the media or government authorities of illegal, unethical, or harmful practices by the company. Both the Enron and WorldCom fraud cases came to light through the efforts of whistle-blowers: Sherron Watkins at Enron and Cynthia Cooper at WorldCom (both women strongly dislike the term whistle-blower, by the way; they don't see themselves as tattletales but as good employees doing their jobs).[21]

Actions Speak Louder Than Codes

Once you write a code of ethics and establish an ethics hot line, what more does your business need? A lot more, according to experts. When Walker Information surveyed 2,000 U.S. employees, it found that many people still didn't trust their employers' ethics. Nearly 30 percent of respondents said that employers sometimes ignored ethics and even deliberately broke the law. Fewer than half trusted employers: Only 46 percent believed leaders take responsibility for their actions, just 45 percent believed leaders act with fairness, and only 40 percent believed employers keep promises.

Some companies developed detailed codes of behavior and established ethics hot lines only to pay them lip service. Perhaps that's why 81 percent of top managers believe they use ethics in day-to-day decision making, whereas 43 percent of employees believe managers routinely overlook ethics. When leaders make decisions that clearly show profits winning out over ethics, employees become skeptical and mistrustful, attitudes that lead to unethical behavior.

To avoid the lip-service trap, support your ethics programs with a dose of reality:

- *Inspire concretely.* Tell employees how they will personally benefit from participating in ethics initiatives. People respond better to personal benefits than to company benefits.

- *Acknowledge reality.* Admit errors. Discuss what went right and what went wrong. Solicit employee opinion: What do you think? What's your view? And act on those opinions.

- *Incorporate reality into your solutions.* Use practical strategies that can be accomplished in the time available. Obtain real feedback by asking employees to name three realities the company isn't facing, three reasons the company won't meet its goals, and three competitive weaknesses the company exhibits in the marketplace.

- *Be honest.* Tell employees what you know as well as what you don't know. Talk openly about real results, not about what you'd like them to be. Accept criticism—and listen to it.

Make personal benefits, company errors, and tactical solutions more concrete by being straightforward and specific. By acknowledging the realities in every situation, you turn your words into action and build trust with your employees.

Questions for Critical Thinking

1. How does building trust encourage employees to be more ethical?
2. Some companies ask job candidates to take preemployment tests such as drug tests or lie detector tests. Does such testing build trust with potential employees? Explain.

Whistle-blowing can bring with it high costs: Public accusation of wrongdoing hurts the business's reputation, requires attention from managers who must investigate the accusations, and damages employee morale. Moreover, whistle-blowers risk being fired or demoted, and they often suffer career setbacks, financial strain, and emotional stress. The fear of such negative repercussions may allow unethical or illegal practices to go unreported. Still, all things considered, many employees do the right thing, as Exhibit 2.2 suggests.

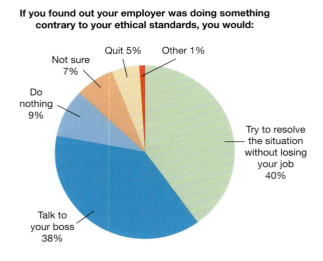

If you found out your employer was doing something contrary to your ethical standards, you would:

Not sure 7%
Quit 5%
Other 1%
Do nothing 9%
Try to resolve the situation without losing your job 40%
Talk to your boss 38%

Exhibit 2.2

Doing the Right Thing

According to a recent survey of 1,002 randomly selected adults, when it comes to ethics in the workplace, most employees try to do the right thing.

How Do You Make Ethical Decisions?

Determining what's ethically right in any given situation can be difficult. One approach is to measure each act against certain absolute standards. In the United States, these standards are often grounded in teachings such as "Do not lie" and "Do not steal." Another place to look for ethical guidance is the law. If saying, writing, or doing something is clearly illegal, you have no decision to make; you obey the law.

Even though legal considerations will resolve some ethical questions, you'll often have to rely on your own judgment and principles. When trying to decide the most ethical course of action, you might apply the Golden Rule: Do unto others as you would have them do unto you. Or you might examine your motives: If your intent is honest, the decision is ethical; however, if your intent is to mislead or manipulate, your decision is unethical. Don't automatically assume you're viewing a situation fairly and objectively, either. Psychological research suggests that many people are influenced by unconscious biases that may even run counter to their stated beliefs.[22] You might also consider asking yourself a series of questions:

1. Is the decision legal? (Does it break any laws?)

2. Is it balanced? (Is it fair to all concerned?)

3. Can you live with it? (Does it make you feel good about yourself?)

4. Is it feasible? (Will it actually work in the real world?)

When you need to determine the ethics of any situation, these questions will get you started. You may also want to consider the needs of stakeholders, and you may want to investigate one or more philosophical approaches such as those mentioned in the right-hand column of Exhibit 2.3. These approaches are not mutually exclusive alternatives. On the contrary, most businesspeople combine them to reach decisions that will satisfy as many stakeholders as possible without violating anyone's rights or treating anyone unjustly.

ethical dilemma
Situation in which both sides of an issue can be supported with valid arguments

ethical lapse
Situation in which an individual makes a decision that is morally wrong, illegal, or unethical

When making ethical decisions, keep in mind that most ethical situations can be classified into two general types: ethical dilemmas and ethical lapses. An **ethical dilemma** is a situation in which one must choose between two conflicting but arguably valid sides. All ethical dilemmas have a common theme: the conflict between the rights of two or more important groups of people. The second type of situation is an **ethical lapse**, in which an individual makes a decision that is clearly wrong, such as divulging trade secrets to a competitor. Be careful not to confuse ethical dilemmas with ethical lapses. A company faces an ethical dilemma when it must decide whether to continue operating a production facility that is suspected, but not proven, to be unsafe. A company makes an ethical lapse when it continues to operate the facility even after the site has been proven unsafe. Other examples of ethical lapses would include inflating prices for certain customers, hiring employees from competitors to gain trade secrets, selling technological secrets to unfriendly foreign governments, switching someone's long-distance service without their consent (a practice known as slamming), slipping unauthorized charges into phone bills (a practice known as cramming), and using insider information to profit on the sale of company securities—something Enron executives were accused of doing.

Perspectives on Corporate Social Responsibility

Conflicts over ethics and social responsibility are often fueled by differing perspectives on the issues at hand. People with equally good intentions can arrive at different conclusions based on different assumptions about business's role in society. These perspectives can be grouped into three general categories: (1) the only responsibility of business is to make money, (2) business has a larger responsibility to society—and ethical behavior leads to financial success, and (3) businesses must balance social responsibility and financial objectives.

Exhibit 2.3	Itemized List for Making Ethical Decisions

Companies with the most success in establishing an ethical structure are those that balance their approach to making decisions.

IS THE DECISION ETHICAL?	DOES IT RESPECT STAKEHOLDERS?	DOES IT FOLLOW A PHILOSOPHICAL APPROACH?
IS IT LEGAL?	WILL OUTSIDERS APPROVE?	IS IT A UTILITARIAN DECISION?
Does it violate civil law?	Does it benefit customers, suppliers, investors, public officials, media representatives, and community members?	Does it produce the greatest good for the greatest number of people?
Does it violate company policy?		DOES IT UPHOLD INDIVIDUAL, LEGAL, AND HUMAN RIGHTS?
IS IT BALANCED?	WILL SUPERVISORS APPROVE?	Does it protect people's own interests?
Is it fair to all concerned, in both the short and the long term?	Did you provide management with information that is honest and accurate?	Does it respect the privacy of others and their right to express their opinion?
CAN YOU LIVE WITH IT?	WILL EMPLOYEES APPROVE?	Does it allow people to act in a way that conforms to their religious or moral beliefs?
Does it make you feel good about yourself?	Will it affect employees in a positive way?	DOES IT UPHOLD THE PRINCIPLES OF JUSTICE?
Would you feel good reading about it in a newspaper?	Does it handle personal information about employees discreetly?	Does it treat people fairly and impartially?
IS IT FEASIBLE?	Did you give proper credit for work performed by others?	Does it apply rules consistently?
Does it work in the real world?		Does it ensure that people who harm others are held responsible and make restitution?
Will it improve your competitive position?		
Is it affordable?		
Can it be accomplished in the time available?		

The Traditional Perspective: The Business of Business Is Making Money

The classic perspective on this issue states that the sole responsibility of business is to make money for the investors who put their money at risk to fund companies. This stance seems blunt, but it can be more subtle than you might think at first glance. In the 19th and early 20th centuries, the prevailing view among U.S. industrialists was that business had only one responsibility: to make a profit. "The public be damned," said railroad tycoon William Vanderbilt, "I'm working for the shareholders."[23] *Caveat emptor*— "Let the buyer beware"—was the rule of the day. If you bought a product, you paid the price and took the consequences.

In 1970, influential economist Milton Friedman updated this view by saying "There is only one social responsibility of business: to use its resources and engage in activities designed to increase its profits so long as it stays within the rules of the game, which is to say, engages in open and free competition without deception or fraud." Friedman argued that only real people, not corporations, could have responsibilities and that dividends and profit maximization would allow the shareholders to contribute to the charities and causes of their choice.[24] As he saw it, the only social responsibility of business was to provide jobs and pay taxes.

The subtlety that is sometimes overlooked by critics of business is that companies cannot fund the many good things businesses today are expected to provide—decent wages, health care, child care, community assistance, philanthropy, and so on—if they don't make enough money to do so. The benefits of a healthy economy are numerous, from lower crime rates to better education, but socially healthy economies cannot exist without financially healthy companies because business is the primary generator of wealth in the economy.

The Contemporary Perspective: Ethics Pays

Most people in the United States, as much as 95 percent of the population according to one survey, now reject the notion that a corporation's only role is to make money.[25] In the last couple of decades, a new view of corporate social responsibility has replaced the classic view in the minds of many people both inside and outside business. This perspective states that not only do businesses have a broader responsibility to society, but doing good for society helps companies do well for themselves. In other words, ethics pays.

Many investors and managers now support a broader view of social responsibility. They argue that a company has an obligation to society beyond the pursuit of profits and that becoming more socially responsible can actually improve a company's profits. This line of thinking is best captured by a *New York Times* headline: "Do Good? Do Business? No, Do Both!" "You can't put one in front of the other. You can't be successful if you can't do both," says Seth Goldman, cofounder of Honest Tea, a company that manufactures barely sweetened ice tea and totally biodegradable tea bags. In other words, companies must be profitable businesses to advance their social mission, and their socially responsible activities should enhance the business.

Companies that support this line of thinking link the pursuit of socially responsible goals with their overall strategic planning. Such socially responsible companies are just as dedicated to building a viable, profitable business as they are to hewing to a mission—and they think strategically to make both happen. Increasingly, companies and employees are caring about their communities and want to be a part of the greater cause (see Exhibit 2.4). They want to be good corporate citizens and satisfy shareholders' needs for a return on their investment. Still, finding the right balance can be challenging.

Exactly how much can businesses contribute to social concerns? This is a difficult decision for most companies because they have limited resources. They must allocate

Exhibit 2.4

Civic Responsibilities

Executives generally support the notion that companies should serve their communities and be socially responsible citizens in a number of ways.

PERCENTAGE OF EXECUTIVES WHO "STRONGLY AGREE" OR "AGREE" THAT COMPANIES SHOULD	
Be environmentally responsible	100
Be ethical in operations	100
Earn profits	96
Employ local residents	94
Pay taxes	94
Encourage and support employee volunteering	89
Contribute money and leadership to charities	85
Be involved in economic development	75
Be involved in public education	73
Involve community representatives in business decisions that impact community	62
Target a proportion of purchasing toward local vendors	61
Help improve quality of life for low-income populations	54

their resources to a number of goals, such as upgrading facilities and equipment, developing new products, marketing existing products, and rewarding employee efforts, in addition to contributing to social causes. This juggling act is a challenge that every business faces. For example, if a company consistently ignores its stakeholders, its business will suffer and eventually fold. If the company disregards society's needs (such as environmental concerns), voters will clamor for laws to limit the offensive business activities, consumers who feel their needs and values are being ignored will spend their money on a competitor's products, investors who are unhappy with the company's performance will invest elsewhere, and employees whose needs are not met will become unproductive or will quit and find other jobs. As Exhibit 2.5 shows, stakeholders' needs sometimes conflict. In such cases, which stakeholders should be served first—society, consumers, investors, or employees?

An Emerging Perspective: Dynamically Balancing Ethics and Profits

Some business theorists now promote a third view, that ethics needs to be one of the cornerstones of business but that in the real world, profits and ethics are often at odds. Managers need to evaluate every situation within the context of the organization's "moral personality." In some cases, the ethical approach will pay off financially as well, but in others it won't.[26] The decision by 3M to discontinue Scotchgard Fabric Protector is a noteworthy example of this perspective. The government did not order 3M to stop manufacturing products with perfluorooctane sulfonate (PFOs), and there was no evidence as yet that PFOs harmed humans. But when traces of the chemical showed up in humans, 3M decided to pull the plug on the product and not wait until scientific evidence might someday link PFOs to a disease. This decision cost 3M $500 million in annual sales because the company did not have a substitute product to fill Scotchgard's void.[27] Even though the decision had painful financial implications, it fit the moral personality that 3M's leaders want to maintain for the organization.

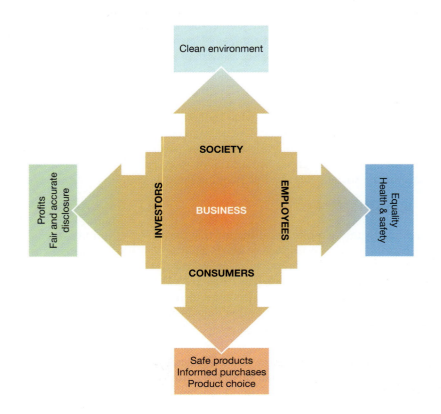

Exhibit 2.5

Balancing Business and Stakeholders' Rights

Balancing the individual needs and interests of a company's stakeholders is one of management's most difficult tasks.

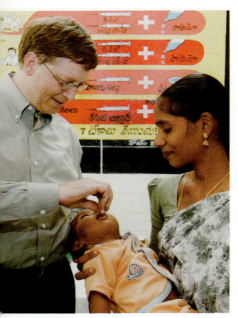

Bill Gates originally made his name as the co-founder and guiding force behind Microsoft, but in recent years he and his wife Melinda (not pictured) have become increasingly well known for their generous contributions to worldwide healthcare and education.

social audit
Assessment of a company's performance in the area of social responsibility

philanthropic
Descriptive term for altruistic actions such as donating money, time, goods, or services to charitable, humanitarian, or educational institutions

pollution
Damage to or destruction of the natural environment caused by the discharge of harmful substances

BUSINESS'S EFFORTS TO INCREASE SOCIAL RESPONSIBILITY

Particularly in times of highly publicized corporate scandals, it's important to remember that thousands of socially responsible businesses remain committed to having a positive impact on their local communities, the nation, and the world as a whole. *IndustryWeek*'s 100 Best Managed Companies all actively engage in socially responsible activities. Some work to curb child abuse or domestic violence. Others provide generous benefits packages for employees. Still others have strong recycling programs to keep the environment clean. Microsoft's Bill Gates is admired by many and criticized by some for his aggressive competitive approach to business, but through the Bill and Melinda Gates Foundation, he has become one of the world's most generous executives. The foundation supports health and education efforts in poorer countries with billions of dollars' worth of grants. In fact, one expert in international health issues predicts that Gates will ultimately be known more for what he's doing to improve world health than for what he does in the computer industry.[28]

In addition to doing good, those who give back to society are finding that their efforts can lead to a more favorable public image and stronger employee morale. Thus, more and more organizations are attempting to be socially responsible citizens by conducting a *social audit*, by engaging in *cause-related marketing*, or by being *philanthropic*.

A **social audit** is a systematic evaluation and reporting of the company's social performance. The report typically includes objective information about how the company's activities affect its various stakeholders. Companies can also engage in *cause-related marketing*, in which a portion of product sales helps support worthy causes. For example, Johnson & Johnson gives the World Wildlife Fund a cut from sales of a special line of children's toiletries. Similarly, PeaceWorks encourages joint business ventures among people of different backgrounds who live in volatile regions of the world. One of the company's product lines is *sprate* (a combination of *spread* and *paté*), uniquely flavored spreads produced in Israel by a Jewish-owned company that buys all its ingredients from Israeli Arabs and Palestinians. When consumers buy a jar of sprate, they not only get a tasty spread but they also support the peace process in the Middle East.[29]

Some companies choose to be socially responsible corporate citizens by being **philanthropic**; that is, they donate money, time, goods, or services to charitable, humanitarian, or educational institutions. Food company Newman's Own, established by actor Paul Newman and writer A. E. Hotchner, gives away all of its profits. The company has donated well over $100 million so far for hunger relief, for medical research, and to fund camps for seriously ill children.[30] Similarly, corporations such as Microsoft, General Electric, Dell, and Wal-Mart donate billions of dollars in cash and products to charity each year.

No matter what size they are or what industry they're in, businesses have endless opportunities to give back to society—donating computers, taking kids on field trips, supporting basketball teams, building houses for people, or helping people find jobs. "We try to function as though we live next door to everybody in our community," says the director of the Socially Responsible Banking Fund at Vermont National Bank.[31]

Responsibility Toward Society and the Environment

Environmental issues exemplify the difficulty that businesses encounter when they try to reconcile conflicting interests: Society needs as little pollution as possible from businesses. But producing quality products to satisfy customers' needs can cause pollution to some degree. Business executives such as Patagonia's Yvon Chouinard try to strike a balance by making environmental management a formal part of their business strategy—along with quality, profits, safety, and other daily business operations.[32]

The Pervasiveness of Pollution

For decades, environmentalists have warned businesses and the general public about the dangers of **pollution** (the contamination of the natural environment by the discharge of harmful substances). Our air, water, and land can easily be tainted by industrial dis-

Ben & Jerry's: A Double Scoop of Irony?

Few companies have a better reputation for environmental and social responsibility than Ben & Jerry's Homemade, the folksy, irreverent ice cream company. Since its inception in 1978, the company has donated 7.5 percent of pretax profits to various causes, including saving the family farm, promoting world peace, saving the world's rain forests, and keeping French nuclear testing out of the South Pacific. Even as the company grew, it managed to stay focused on Ben Cohen and Jerry Greenfield's mission and their intent to be a different kind of company. Cohen and Greenfield brought in professional management to balance the desire to do good with the need to maintain financial viability. To the surprise of many, the vision even survived a corporate buyout in 1999, when the company was purchased by Unilever, a $45 billion global food colossus. Today, Ben & Jerry's continues to put its money where its mouth is, promoting a variety of admirable causes.

Here's the catch. Well, three of them, actually. First, even with the company's high standards of environmental responsibility—and you'd have to look far and wide to find a company with higher standards—it can be hard to make a case that the production of ice cream is an environmentally friendly endeavor. For instance, ice cream requires refrigeration at every step of the manufacturing and distribution process, refrigeration requires prodigious amounts of electricity, and nearly all the electricity in this country is generated by coal-fired, natural gas, nuclear, or hydroelectric power plants. And while the company has done a great job of removing chlorine and other nasty elements from the production of its ice cream cartons, those cartons are delivered to your local grocery store by fume-spewing diesel trucks. Second, obesity is now generally considered the nation's number one health problem, and most of Ben & Jerry's products are high-fat, high-calorie concoctions. Third, all of this discussion concerns products that no one really needs. After all, this is ice cream, not medical supplies or drinking water.

Ben & Jerry's may well be the most environmentally and socially responsible ice cream company in history, but that still leaves the question: Should *anybody* be in the ice cream business?

Questions for Critical Thinking

1. Could Ben & Jerry's environmental stance be considered hypocritical, given the electricity demands of the ice cream industry? Why or why not?
2. How might Ben & Jerry's respond to the three issues discussed above while still remaining true to its philosophical roots?

---

charges, aircraft and motor vehicle emissions, and a number of chemicals that spill out into the environment as industrial waste products. Moreover, the pollution in any one element can easily taint the others. For instance, when emissions from coal-burning factories and electric utility plants react with air, they can cause acid rain, which damages lakes and forests. No business is immune from pollution issues, either. Internet-based companies such as Yahoo! or Google strike some people as "clean" because there seems to be no visible pollution, but the Internet has a voracious appetite for electricity, and the generation of electricity nearly always affects the environment—two-thirds of the electricity used in the United States is generated by burning coal, oil, or natural gas.[33]

The Government Effort to Reduce Pollution

Widespread concern for the environment has been growing since the 1960s with the popularization of **ecology**, or the study of the relationship between organisms and the natural environment. In 1963, federal, state, and local governments began enacting laws and regulations to reduce pollution. In 1970, the federal government established the Environmental Protection Agency (EPA) to regulate air and water pollution by manufacturers and utilities, supervise the control of automobile pollution, license pesticides, control toxic substances, and safeguard the purity of drinking water. A landmark piece of legislation, the Clean Air Act, was also passed that year. Many individual states and cities have also passed their own tough clean-air laws.

Cleaning up major industrial pollution sources is a complex technical and financial task, however, and the clean-air effort has been bogged down in lawsuits and political wrangling for years. In 2003, EPA officials appointed by President George W. Bush attempted to relax pollution standards for coal-burning power plants, one of the most

ecology
Study of the relationships among living things in the water, air, and soil, their environments, and the nutrients that support them

A modern economy needs metals, minerals, and fuels, but the effort to extract these materials can create unsafe conditions for nearby populations.

significant sources of air pollution in the country, but a federal appeals court blocked the change. The situation is not likely to be resolved for years.[34]

In addition, the country's love affair with the automobile has slowed progress toward cleaner air. Three of the most popular types of vehicles—pickups, minivans, and sport utility vehicles—are considered light trucks by government regulators and therefore aren't required to meet the more stringent pollution standards set for passenger cars. The situation is not helped by the runaway success of gas guzzlers such as the Hummer H2 (8 to 10 miles per gallon, according to dealers) and the Cadillac Escalade or moves such as the one Subaru recently made to get its popular Outback sedan reclassified as a small truck in order to skirt passenger car fuel-efficiency requirements.[35] The EPA blames the popularity of these vehicles and a dramatic increase in the miles driven on U.S. streets and highways for the lack of progress in reducing smog in the past 10 or 15 years.[36]

Progress has been made in reducing water pollution, thanks in large part to the Clean Water Act passed in 1972. As with the Clean Air Act, though, the conflict between environmental and commercial forces rages on in such areas as the dumping of mining wastes into rivers and streams and the annual discharge of millions of gallons of animal waste from large "factory" farms.[37] Drinking water quality has improved somewhat in the past couple of decades but still varies considerably across the country.[38] The complex war on toxic waste has marked a number of successes over the years, although as with air and water pollution, overall results are mixed. The EPA's Superfund program, designed to clean up the worst toxic waste dumps in the country, is now cleaning up only 40 or 50 sites a year, with more than a thousand left to go.[39] Some of these sites date from decades ago, when environmental awareness and corporate accountability were far below today's presumed standards. Some of the companies that created the worst messes no longer exist, and cleanup at many sites has been mired in lawsuits.

The Business Effort to Reduce Pollution

As you might expect, business's own efforts to reduce pollution range from corporations that must be dragged kicking and screaming to do the right thing to those that take the initiative on their own, such as 3M, Patagonia, and Ben & Jerry's. Du Pont, once labeled the country's biggest polluter, has shifted its corporate strategy to focus on *sustainable growth*, developing businesses that can operate forever without depleting natural resources. Among its current efforts: creating clothing fabrics with corn instead of petroleum as a key ingredient.[40] These and many other companies are addressing environmental concerns by taking a variety of positive actions:[41]

Electronics recycling centers like this one near the Lianjiang River in China are releasing toxic pollutants, environmental groups say.

- Considering environmental issues a part of everyday business and operating decisions
- Accepting environmental staff members as full-fledged partners in improving the company's competitiveness
- Measuring environmental performance
- Tying compensation to environmental performance
- Determining the long-term environmental costs *before* such costs occur
- Considering environmental impact in the product-development process
- Challenging suppliers to improve environmental performance
- Conducting environmental training and awareness programs

In addition to these actions, companies are reducing the amount of solid waste they send to landfills by implementing companywide recycling programs, a key effort in grappling with the hundreds of millions of pounds of solid waste this country generates every year—much of which is electronic waste (computer monitors, circuit boards, and so on).[42] McDonald's has reduced the amount of solid waste it generates by 300 million pounds a year, for instance. Hundreds of thousands of tons of waste have also been eliminated through conservation and more efficient production.[43] Some companies are using high-temperature incineration to destroy hazardous wastes or are giving their wastes to other companies that can use them in their manufacturing processes. Some even neutralize wastes biologically or have redesigned their manufacturing processes so that they don't produce the wastes in the first place.

Businesses that recognize the link between environmental performance and sustained financial well-being are discovering that spending now to prevent pollution can end up saving more money down the road (by reducing cleanup costs, litigation expense, and production costs). From building eco-industrial parks to improving production efficiency, these activities are a part of the *green marketing* movement, in which companies distinguish themselves by using less packaging materials, recycling more waste, and developing new products that are easier on the environment. In addition to ethical and financial concerns, green marketing efforts can also help companies build goodwill with customers, communities, and other stakeholders.

Responsibility Toward Consumers

The 1960s activism that awakened business to its environmental responsibilities also gave rise to **consumerism**, a movement that put pressure on businesses to consider consumer needs and interests. Consumerism prompted many businesses to create consumer-affairs departments to handle customer complaints. It also prompted state and local agencies to set up bureaus to offer consumer information and assistance. At the federal level, President John F. Kennedy announced a "bill of rights" for consumers, laying the foundation for a wave of consumer-oriented legislation. These rights include the right to safe products, the right to be informed, the right to choose, and the right to be heard.

consumerism
Movement that pressures businesses to consider consumer needs and interests

The Right to Safe Products

The U.S. government imposes many safety standards that are enforced by the Consumer Product Safety Commission (CPSC), as well as by other federal and state agencies. Theoretically, companies that don't comply with these rules are forced to take corrective action. Moreover, the threat of product-liability suits and declining sales motivates many companies to meet safety standards. After all, a poor safety record can damage a company's reputation. But with or without government action, many consumer advocates complain that some unsafe products still slip through the cracks, such as the faulty Firestone tires on Ford Explorers.

The Right to Be Informed

Consumers have a right to know what is in a product and how to use it. They also have a right to know the sales price of goods or services and the details of any purchase contracts. The Food and Drug Administration, the Federal Trade Commission, and the Agriculture Department are the federal agencies responsible for regulating product labels to make sure no false claims are made. These agencies are concerned not only with safety but also with accurate information. Research shows that nearly three-quarters of shoppers read labels when deciding whether to buy a food product the first time, so labels are an important element in informing consumers.[44]

If a product is sufficiently dangerous, a warning label is required by law, as in the case of cigarettes. However, warning labels can be a mixed blessing for consumers. To some extent, the presence of a warning protects the manufacturer from product-liability suits, but the label may not deter people from using the product or from using it incorrectly. The billions of dollars a year still spent on cigarettes in the United States illustrate this point.

By the time Firestone finally admitted that it made "bad tires," the company had been aware of peeling tire tread problems for at least three years. Most of the recalled tires were sold with Ford Explorer vehicles.

Technologies That Are Revolutionizing Business

Location and tracking technologies

Science fiction movies sometimes feature amazing technologies that can track people anywhere in the universe. They might still be amazing, but they're no longer science fiction; a variety of tracking devices can now keep tabs on both people and products.

How they're changing business

Location and tracking technologies cover a wide range of capabilities, some already in use and some just now hitting the market. Here are some of the more common uses and a few examples:

- **Personal security.** Parents and caregivers can use tracking technologies to check on children, elderly relatives, and medical patients.
- **Inventory management.** Radio frequency identification (RFID) tags combine tiny computer chips with small antennas. Retail giant Wal-Mart is moving to require its suppliers to attach RFID tags to incoming merchandise in order to enhance inventory management.
- **Location-based services and marketing campaigns.** Customers who are on the move can benefit from instant information that reflects their immediate shopping needs—and marketers would love to offer the right information at the right time, including notifications of nearby sales.

These new capabilities present considerable technological, social, and ethical issues, however, so expect to hear plenty of discussion about them in the coming years. For instance, privacy advocates launched a boycott campaign (www.boycottbenetton.org) when a supplier to the Italian apparel retailer Benetton announced that the company planned to embed RFID tags in its clothing items. (The premature announcement was denied by the company.)

Where you can learn more

This is a broad and dynamic field, with new information available nearly every day. Here are a few of the many sources online: MIT's Auto-ID Lab, autoidlabs.mit.edu, *RFID Journal*, www.rfidjournal.com, and the Federal Communications Commission, www.fcc.gov/911/enhanced.

The Right to Choose Which Products to Buy

Especially in the United States, the number of products available to consumers is truly amazing. But how far should the right to choose extend? Are we entitled to choose products that are potentially harmful, such as cigarettes, liquor, or guns? To what extent are we entitled to learn about these products? Consumer groups and businesses are concerned about these questions, but no clear answers have emerged. Moreover, some consumer groups say that government does not do enough. For example, when a product has been proven to be dangerous, does the fact that it is legal justify its sale? Should the government take measures to make the product illegal, or should consumers be allowed to decide for themselves what they buy?

Consider cigarettes, for example. Scientists determined long ago that the tar and nicotine in tobacco are both harmful and addictive. In 1965, the Federal Cigarette Labeling and Advertising Act was passed, requiring all cigarette packs to carry the now-famous Surgeon General's warnings. Over the years, tobacco companies have spent billions of dollars to defend themselves in lawsuits brought by smokers suffering from cancer and respiratory diseases. As recently as 1996, the Liggett Group (a major U.S. tobacco company) admitted publicly that cigarettes cause cancer, are addictive, and have been promoted to encourage smoking among minors. And in 1997 the tobacco industry agreed to pay $368.5 billion over 25 years and an additional $15 billion per year after that to settle lawsuits brought by smoking victims and 40 state governments. Even so, consumers can still purchase cigarettes in the marketplace. RJR Nabisco chairman Steve Goldstone reminds us that "behind all the allegations . . . is the simple truth that we sell a legal product."[45]

The Right to Be Heard

Many companies have established toll-free numbers for consumer information and feedback and print these numbers on product packages. In addition, more and more companies are establishing websites to provide product information and a vehicle for customer feedback. Companies use such feedback to improve their products and services and to make informed decisions about offering new ones. Technology has been a boon to consumers in this respect, with the opportunity to share information and voice their complaints via websites and online newsgroups.

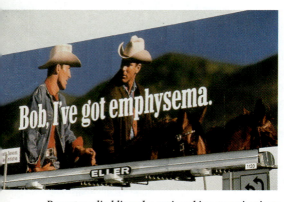

Recent media blitzes by antismoking organizations have appeared in magazines, on billboards, and in television commercials. The hope is that ads such as this one will elevate consumer awareness about the health problems cigarette smoking causes.

Responsibility Toward Investors

A growing number of investors are concerned about the ethics and social responsibility of the companies in which they invest. Allegations range from executives dumping stock ahead of bad news to companies using dirty accounting tricks to misrepresenting the investment.

The job of looking out for a company's investors falls to its board of directors. Lately, more investors are turning up the heat on the individuals who sit on those boards (as you'll explore in Chapter 4). Concerned investors are targeting board members who fail to attend meetings, who sit on the boards of too many companies, who are underinvested (own very little stock in the companies they direct), and who sit on boards of companies with which their own firms do business. Aggrieved investors are also filing lawsuits not just against the management of companies that admit to "accounting irregularities" but against their boards of directors and their audit committees.

The audit committee signs off on all financial statements and is supposed to protect shareholders, acting as a check on management's corporate reporting methods and asking tough questions about accounting practices. Looking out for investors is no easy task, but investors are finding that holding individual directors more accountable improves overall performance.[46] Of course, any action that cheats the investors out of their rightful profits is unethical.

Responsibility Toward Employees

Patagonia's Yvon Chouinard has always emphasized employee relationships that are ethical and supportive. For some companies, the past 30 years have brought dramatic changes in the attitudes and composition of the workforce. These changes have forced businesses to modify their recruiting, training, and promotion practices, as well as their overall corporate values and behaviors. (Consult Chapter 10 for an in-depth discussion of the staffing and demographic challenges employers are facing in today's workplace.)

The Push for Equality in Employment

The United States has always stood for economic freedom and the individual's right to pursue opportunity. Unfortunately, until the past few decades many people were targets of economic **discrimination**; relegated to low-paying, menial jobs; and prevented from taking advantage of many opportunities solely on the basis of their race, gender, disability, or religion.

The Civil Rights Act of 1964 established the Equal Employment Opportunity Commission (EEOC), the regulatory agency that battles job discrimination. The EEOC is responsible for monitoring the hiring practices of companies and for investigating complaints of job-related discrimination. It has the power to file legal charges against companies that discriminate and to force them to compensate individuals or groups who have been victimized by unfair practices. The Civil Rights Act of 1991 extended the original act by allowing workers to sue companies for discrimination and by granting women powerful legal tools against job bias.

Affirmative Action   In the 1960s, **affirmative action** programs were developed to encourage organizations to recruit and promote members of minority groups. Proponents of the programs believe that minorities deserve and require preferential treatment to boost opportunities and to make up for years of discrimination. Opponents of affirmative action believe that creating special opportunities for women and minorities creates a double standard that infringes on the rights of other workers and forces companies to hire, promote, and retain people who are not necessarily the best choice from a business standpoint. Moreover, studies show that affirmative action has not been entirely successful because efforts to hire more minorities do not neces-

discrimination
In a social and economic sense, denial of opportunities to individuals on the basis of some characteristic that has no bearing on their ability to perform in a job

affirmative action
Activities undertaken by businesses to recruit and promote women and minorities, based on an analysis of the workforce and the available labor pool

sarily change negative attitudes about differences among individuals. Regardless, any company that does business with the federal government must have an affirmative action program.

In addition to affirmative action programs, the majority of U.S. companies have established **diversity initiatives**. These initiatives include increasing minority employment and promotion, contracting with more minority vendors, adding more minorities to boards of directors, and targeting a more diverse customer base. Many companies also offer employees diversity training to promote understanding of the unique cultures, customs, and talents of all employees.

diversity initiatives
Company policies designed to enhance opportunities for minorities and to promote understanding of diverse cultures, customs, and talents

People with Disabilities   In 1990 people with a wide range of physical and mental difficulties got a boost from the passage of the federal Americans with Disabilities Act (ADA), which guarantees equal opportunities for an estimated 50 million to 75 million people who have or have had a condition that might handicap them. As defined by the 1990 law, *disability* is a broad term that protects not only those with obvious physical handicaps but also those with less-visible conditions, such as cancer, heart disease, diabetes, epilepsy, AIDS, drug addiction, alcoholism, and emotional illness. In most situations, employers cannot legally require job applicants to pass a physical examination as a condition of employment. The law also forbids firing people who have serious drinking or drug problems unless their chemical dependency prevents them from performing their essential job functions.

Occupational Safety and Health

Each day more than a dozen U.S. workers lose their lives on the job and thousands more are injured (see Exhibit 2.6).[47] During the 1960s, mounting concern about workplace hazards resulted in passage of the Occupational Safety and Health Act of 1970, which set mandatory standards for safety and health and which established the Occupational Safety and Health Administration (OSHA) to enforce them.

Today, OSHA's ergonomic safety regulations protect millions of workers from repetitive stress injuries such as carpal tunnel syndrome (from repetitive tasks such as keyboarding) and back injuries (from repetitive lifting). The rules grant workers up to 90 days of employer-paid sick leave for people injured on the job as a result of repetitive actions. Studies show that about 1.8 million U.S. workers each year suffer musculoskeletal injuries at work from performing repetitive actions and that about one-third of the cases are serious enough to require time off.[48]

Concerns for employee safety have also been raised by the international expansion of businesses. Many U.S. companies subcontract production to companies in foreign coun-

---

Exhibit 2.6

Workplace Killers

Transportation accidents are the leading workplace killer.

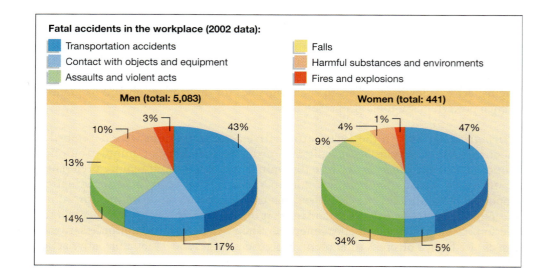

tries, making it more difficult to maintain proper standards of safety and compensation for workers. For example, when a local labor advocacy group inspected a Nike factory in Vietnam, members discovered violations of minimum wage and overtime laws, as well as physical abuse of workers. Nike has been criticized in recent years for similar conditions in its other Southeast Asian and Chinese factories. Many other companies, including The Gap, Guess, and the Body Shop, have come under similar criticism. In 1997 a presidential task force composed of apparel industry representatives, labor unions, and human rights groups drafted a code of conduct to uphold the rights of foreign workers of U.S. manufacturing companies. Among the provisions of the code are minimum wage requirements and limits on the number of hours employees work in a week.[49]

As with many ethical matters, raising the visibility of the issue can make the difference in how effectively a company responds. At computer chip maker Intel, for instance, CEO Craig Barrett demands a report within 24 hours whenever an Intel employee suffers an injury that results in even a single day of lost time. Thanks to the executive-level attention that workplace safety gets at Intel, the injury rate among the company's 80,000 employees is 25 times lower than the industry average.[50]

ETHICS AND SOCIAL RESPONSIBILITY AROUND THE WORLD

As complicated as ethics and social responsibility can be for U.S. businesses, these issues grow even more complex when cultural influences are applied in the global business environment. Corporate executives may face simple questions regarding the appropriate amount of money to spend on a business gift or the legitimacy of a payment to "expedite" business. Or they may encounter out-and-out bribery, environmental abuse, and unscrupulous business practices. As you read about global business in Chapter 3, you'll have the opportunity to see how a country's ethical codes of conduct, laws, and cultural differences are indeed put to the test as more and more companies transact business around the globe.

Summary of Learning Objectives

1 **Discuss what it means to practice good business ethics, and highlight three factors that influence ethical behavior.**

Businesspeople who practice good business ethics obey all laws and regulations, compete fairly and honestly, communicate truthfully, and avoid causing harm to others. Of the many factors that influence your ethical behavior, the three most common are cultural differences, knowledge of the facts and consequences involving a decision or action, and the ethical practices and commitment to ethical behavior at your place of work.

2 **Identify three steps that businesses are taking to encourage ethical behavior, and explain the advantages and disadvantages of whistle-blowing.**

Businesses are adopting codes of ethics, appointing ethics officers, and establishing ethics hot lines. In spite of these efforts, if illegal, unethical, or harmful practices persist, an employee may need to blow the whistle or disclose such problems to outsiders. Doing so may force the company to stop the problematic practices. But bringing these issues into the public eye has consequences. It can hurt the company's reputation, take managers' time, damage employee morale, and impact the informant's job with the company.

3 **List four questions you might ask yourself when trying to make an ethical decision.**

When making ethical decisions ask yourself: (1) Is the decision legal? (Does it break any law?) (2) Is it balanced? (Is it fair to all concerned?) (3) Can you live with it? (Does it make you feel good about yourself?) (4) Is it feasible? (Will it work in the real world?)

4 **Explain the difference between an ethical dilemma and an ethical lapse.**

An ethical dilemma is an issue with two conflicting but arguably valid sides, whereas an ethical lapse occurs when an individual makes a decision that is illegal, immoral, or unethical.

5 Discuss the relationship between corporate social responsibility and profits.

For years, many companies believed that the only role of a company was to make money and that social problems were the concern of the state. It was believed that socially responsible companies could not be profitable. But supporters of social responsibility now argue that a company has an obligation to society beyond the pursuit of profits and that companies can be both socially responsible and profitable. In fact, being a socially responsible company can help improve profits and being profitable can help companies stick to their social mission.

6 Discuss how businesses can become more socially responsible.

Companies can conduct social audits to assess whether their performance is socially responsible; they can engage in cause-related marketing by using a portion of product sales to help support worthy causes; and they can become philanthropic by donating their money, time, goods, or services to charitable, humanitarian, or educational institutions. Companies can also protect and improve the environment by taking a variety of actions to reduce pollution. They can become good citizens by considering consumers' needs and respecting their four basic rights: the right to safe products; the right to be informed—which includes the right to know a product's contents, use, price, and dangers; the right to choose which products to buy; and the right to be heard, such as the right to voice a complaint or concern. They can look out for a company's investors and protect the value of their interests. And they can foster good employee relationships by treating employees fairly and equally and by providing a safe working environment.

7 Outline activities the government and businesses are undertaking to improve the environment.

In 1970 the government set up the Environmental Protection Agency to regulate the disposal of hazardous wastes and to clean up polluted areas. Many individual states have also passed their own tough clean-air laws. Companies are taking these steps to improve the environment: (1) considering them a part of everyday business and operating decisions, (2) making environmental staff members full-fledged partners in improving competitiveness, (3) measuring environmental performance, (4) tying compensation to environmental performance, (5) determining environmental costs *before* they occur, (6) considering the environmental impact of the product-development process, (7) helping suppliers improve their environmental performance, and (8) conducting training and awareness programs.

Behind **the Scenes**

Patagonia: Reaching the Top by Doing the Right Thing

Convinced that Patagonia could serve as an example for others to follow, owner Yvon Chouinard wanted to prove that a "green" company could help the environment. But a mountain of obstacles blocked Patagonia's path to success during the 1990s. Faced with sagging sales and a severe cash crunch, Chouinard was determined to put Patagonia back on solid ground without compromising environmental values. To solve immediate problems, Chouinard focused his attention on the company's founding philosophy: Produce the best outdoor gear in the market at the lowest possible cost to the environment.

First he got the company "back to the basics" by eliminating one-third of its 375 products and by reducing the workforce by 20 percent. Then he took his case to the public. He informed customers about plans to limit Patagonia's growth by designing and developing products that emphasized function rather than fashionable styles, and he educated consumers on environmental issues. Lengthy catalog essays by Chouinard explained the company's philosophies about saving the Earth's resources and Patagonia's rationale for developing environmentally sensitive techniques in the production of merchandise. The ultimate aim behind the messages, of course, was to generate product demand as consumers recognized the added environmental value of Patagonia's merchandise.

To reinforce the sincerity of Patagonia's commitment to the environment, Chouinard established numerous internal procedures to validate its public image of a "green business." For instance, he created an internal assessment group to study the environmental impact of everything the company does—from production methods to office procedures—and then offer suggestions for improvement. He also constructed a new distribution center with recycled materials and an energy-saving heating system.

Next Chouinard focused on his suppliers. He challenged them to improve their performance and helped them develop techniques for meeting Patagonia's environmental standards. Working with outside contractors, Patagonia developed Synchilla fleece (a fabric made from recycled plastic soda bottles), which now accounts for the recycling of some 8 million plastic bottles each year. Patagonia also worked with farmers to produce 100 percent organic cotton—grown without artificial pesticides or fertilizers. To offset higher production costs for the cotton, the company split the increased costs with consumers, hoping that they would find value in an environmentally sensitive product. They did. Once the catalogs reached consumers, Patagonia immediately sold out of the new line of all-organic cotton sweaters.

Today, Patagonia is a leader and pioneer of "green" profits. But while other outdoor clothing companies have gone public, Chouinard has resisted the temptation. "As a climber, I'm pretty aware of what I am capable of," says Chouinard. "The same goes for the company." As Chouinard sees it, Patagonia will always be more about life than clothing, gear, and profits. "For me, profit is what happens when you do everything else right."

This philosophy not only permeates the company's six core catalogs but is the foundation of the company's existence. For instance, Chouinard clearly understands that workers need to balance their professional and personal work lives. At Patagonia, long-term employees can take a fully paid two-month internship to work at environmental nonprofit organizations. Moreover, he gives workers lots of time to pursue their outdoor and environmental passions, knowing that

employees who feed their passion will bring that passion back to the company—a philosophy that has indeed paid off. Named one of *Fortune* magazine's "100 Best Companies to Work For," Patagonia has proven that companies can achieve success while supporting their environmental values.[51]

Critical Thinking Questions

1. Which of the company's stakeholders are most affected by Patagonia's environmentalism?
2. How does Patagonia's environmentalism exemplify the consumer's right to safety?
3. Why does Patagonia allow workers to take time off to feed their passion?

LEARN MORE ONLINE

Patagonia's environmentalism is communicated through the company's catalog, product labels, and website. Go to Chapter 2 of this text's website at www.prenhall.com/bovee, and click on Patagonia to read about the company. Click on Enviro Action to read current and older reports on environmental issues. What types of environmental concerns are being addressed? How are proceeds from the Earth Tax (environmental grants) being distributed? Do you agree with the causes Patagonia supports? Explain your answer. ■

Key Terms

affirmative action (55)
code of ethics (43)
conflict of interest (42)
consumerism (53)
discrimination (55)

diversity initiatives (56)
ecology (51)
ethical dilemma (46)
ethical lapse (46)
ethics (40)

insider trading (42)
philanthropic (50)
pollution (50)
social audit (50)
social responsibility (40)

Test Your Knowledge

Questions for Review

1. Who shapes a company's ethics?
2. What is a conflict of interest situation?
3. How do companies support ethical behavior?
4. How are businesses responding to the environmental issues facing society?
5. What can a company do to assure customers that its products are safe?

Questions for Analysis

6. Why can't legal considerations resolve every ethical question?
7. How do individuals employ philosophical principles in making ethical business decisions?

8. Why does a company need more than a code of ethics to be ethical?
9. Why is it important for a company to balance its social responsibility efforts with its need to generate profits?
10. **Ethical Considerations.** How do business scandals such as the Enron, Ford/Firestone, and WorldCom cases impact all businesses?

Questions for Application

11. You sell musical gifts on the web and in quarterly catalogs. Your 2-person partnership has quickly grown into a 27-person company, and you spend all your time on quality matters. You're losing control of important environmental choices about materials suppliers, product

packaging, and even the paper used in your catalogs. What steps can you take to be sure your employees continue making choices that protect the environment?

12. At quitting time, you see your new colleague filling a briefcase with expensive software programs that aren't supposed to leave the premises. What do you do? Explain your answer.

13. **Integrated.** Chapter 1 identified knowledge workers as the key economic resource of the 21st century. If an employee leaves a company to work for a competitor, what types of knowledge would be ethical for the employee to share with the new employer and what types of knowledge would be unethical to share?

14. **Integrated.** Is it ethical for state and city governments to entice businesses to relocate their operations to that state or city by offering them special tax breaks that are not extended to other businesses operating in that area?

Practice Your Knowledge

Sharpening Your Communication Skills

All organizations, not just corporations, can benefit from having a code of ethics to guide decision making. But whom should a code of ethics protect, and what should it cover? In this exercise, you and your team are going to draft a code of ethics for your school.

Start by thinking about who will be protected by this code of ethics. What stakeholders should the school consider when making decisions? What negative effects might decisions have on these stakeholders? Then think about the kinds of situations you want your school's code of ethics to cover. One example might be employment decisions; another might be disclosure of confidential student information.

Next, using Exhibit 2.1 as a model, draft your school's code of ethics. Write a general introduction explaining the purpose of the code and who is being protected. Next, write a positive statement to guide ethical decisions in each situation you identified earlier in this exercise. Your statement about promotion decisions, for example, might read: "School officials will encourage equal access to job promotions for all qualified candidates, with every applicant receiving fair consideration."

Compare your code of ethics with the codes drafted by your classmates. Did all the codes seek to protect the same stakeholders? What differences and similarities do you see in the statements guiding ethical decisions?

Building Your Team Skills

Choosing to blow the whistle on your employees or co-workers can create all kinds of legal, ethical, and career complications. Here are five common workplace scenarios that might cause you to search your soul about whether or not to go public with potentially damaging charges. Read them carefully and discuss them with your teammates. Then decide what your team would do in each situation.[52]

1. You believe your company is overcharging or otherwise defrauding a customer or client.

2. With all of the headlines generated by sexual harassment cases lately, you'd think employees wouldn't dare break the law, but it's happening right under your company's nose.

3. You discover that your company, or one of its divisions, products, or processes, presents a physical danger to workers or to the public.

4. An employee is padding overtime statements, taking home some of the company's inventory, or stealing equipment.

5. You smell alcohol on a co-worker's breath and notice that individual's work hasn't been up to standard lately.

Expand Your Knowledge

Discovering Career Opportunities

Businesses, government agencies, and not-for-profit organizations offer numerous career opportunities related to ethics and social responsibility. How can you learn more about these careers?

1. Search through Appendix E to identify jobs related to ethics and social responsibility. One example is occupational health and safety manager, a job concerned with a company's responsibility toward its employees. What are the duties and qualifications of the jobs you have identi-

fied? Are the salaries and future outlooks attractive for all of these jobs?

2. Select one job for further consideration. Following the suggestions in Appendix E, what sources of employment information might provide more details about this job? Which of these sources are available in your school or public library? What additional sources can you consult for more information about the daily activities of this job and for ideas about locating potential employers?

3. What skills, educational background, and work experience do you think employers are seeking in applicants for the specific job you are researching? What keywords do you think employers would search for when scanning electronic résumés submitted for this position?

Developing Your Research Skills

Articles on corporate ethics and social responsibility regularly appear in business journals and newspapers. Look in recent issues (print or online editions) to find one or more articles discussing one of the following ethics or social responsibility challenges faced by a business:

- Environmental issues, such as pollution, acid rain, and hazardous-waste disposal
- Employee or consumer safety measures
- Consumer information or education
- Employment discrimination or diversity initiatives

- Investment ethics
- Industrial spying and theft of trade secrets
- Fraud, bribery, and overcharging
- Company codes of ethics

1. What was the nature of the ethical challenge or social responsibility issue presented in the article? Does the article report any wrongdoing by a company or agency official? Was the action illegal, unethical, or questionable? What course of action would you recommend the company or agency take to correct or improve matters now?

2. What stakeholder group(s) is affected? What lasting effects will be felt by (a) the company and (b) this stakeholder group(s)?

3. Writing a letter to the editor is one way consumers can speak their mind. Review some of the letters to the editor in newspapers or journals. Why are letters to the editor an important feature for that publication?

SEE IT ON THE WEB

For live links to the websites that follow, go to this text's website at www.prenhall.com/bovee. When you log on, select Chapter 2, then select "Featured Websites," click on the URL of the website you wish to visit, review the website, and answer the following questions:

1. What is the purpose of this website?
2. What kinds of information does this website contain? Please be specific.
3. How is the information provided at this website useful for businesspeople? Consumers?
4. How did you expand your knowledge of ethics and social responsibility in business by reviewing the material at this website? What new things did you learn about this topic?

Build a Better Business

One way to distinguish your business as an ethical organization is to join the Better Business Bureau (BBB). Members of this private, not-for-profit business group agree to maintain specific standards for operating ethically and addressing customer complaints. The BBB website is packed with information about the organization, member businesses, and programs that benefit businesses and consumers alike. You can find reports on companies, register complaints, get help with consumer problems, and access publications on all kinds of consumer issues, such as avoiding business scams and investigating charitable organizations. www.bbb.org

Surf Safely

Although the majority of telemarketing and online businesses are legitimate, unethical businesses bilk consumers out of billions of dollars every year. Fortunately, the National Fraud Information Center (NFIC) can help consumers fight back. The center was established by the National Consumers League (NCL) to safeguard consumers against telemarketing and Internet fraud. Resources on the center's website include reports about current online and telephone scams, tips for online safety, advice on how to file a fraud report, statistics about telemarketing fraud, and special advice for seniors, who are targeted by con artists. Even if you consider yourself a savvy consumer, the site contains a lot of valuable information to help you avoid being ripped off. www.fraud.org

Protect the Environment

For 30 years, the United States Environmental Protection Agency (EPA) has been working for a cleaner, healthier environment for the American people. Visit the agency's website to get the latest information on today's environmental issues. Become familiar with the major environmental laws and proposed regulations and learn how to report violations. Expand your knowledge about air pollution, ecosystems, environmental management, and hazardous waste. Visit the EPA newsroom to get regional news. Read the current articles and follow the links to hot lines, publications, and more. This site is a must for all businesses. www.epa.gov

Companion Website

Learning Interactively

Go to the Companion Website at www.prenhall.com/bovee. For Chapter 2, take advantage of the interactive "Study Guide" to test your knowledge of the chapter. Get instant feedback on whether you need additional studying.

Also, visit this site's "Study Hall," where you'll find an abundance of valuable resources that will help you succeed in this course.

Video Case

Doing the Right Thing: American Red Cross

LEARNING OBJECTIVES

The purpose of this video is to help you:

1. Identify some of the social responsibility and ethics challenges faced by a nonprofit organization.
2. Discuss the purpose of an organizational code of ethics.
3. Understand the potential conflicts that can emerge between an organization and its stakeholders.

SYNOPSIS

Founded in 1881 by Clara Barton, the American Red Cross is a nonprofit organization dedicated to helping victims of war, natural disasters, and other catastrophes. The organization's 1,000 chapters are governed by volunteer boards of directors who oversee local activities and enforce ethical standards in line with the Red Cross's code of ethics and community norms. Over the years, the Red Cross has been guided in its use of donations by honoring donor intent. This helped the organization deal with a major ethical challenge after the terrorist attacks of September 11, 2001. The Red Cross received more than $1 billion in donations and initially diverted some money to ancillary operations such as creating a strategic blood reserve. After donors objected, however, the organization reversed its decision and—honoring donor intent—used the contributions to directly benefit people who were affected by the tragedy.

Discussion Questions

1. *For analysis:* What are the social responsibility implications of the American Red Cross's decision to avoid accepting donations of goods for many local relief efforts?

2. *For analysis:* What kinds of ethical conflicts might arise because the American Red Cross relies so heavily on volunteers?
3. *For application:* What can the American Red Cross do to ensure that local chapters are properly applying the nonprofit's code of ethics?
4. *For application:* How might a nonprofit such as the American Red Cross gain a better understanding of its stakeholders' needs and preferences?
5. *For debate:* Should the American Red Cross have reversed its initial decision to divert some of the money donated for September 11th relief efforts to pressing but ancillary operations? Support your chosen position.

ONLINE EXPLORATION

Visit the American Red Cross site at www.redcross.org and scan the headlines to read about the organization's response to recent disasters. Also look at the educational information available through links to news stories, feature articles, and other material. Next, carefully examine the variety of links addressing the needs and involvement of different stakeholder groups. What kinds of stakeholders does the American Red Cross expect to visit its website? Why are these stakeholders important to the organization? Do you think the organization should post its code of ethics prominently on this site? Explain your answer.

Chapter 3
Competing in the Global Economy

Behind the Scenes

Whirlpool: Caught in the Wringer of Global Business

www.whirlpool.com

Everybody is talking about going global these days, but most people don't understand what that means. David Whitwam, chairman and CEO of Whirlpool, does. When he first began eyeing the global marketplace, this Michigan-based appliance maker was concentrating only on the U.S. market, producing and marketing washers, refrigerators, and other household appliances under the Whirlpool, KitchenAid, Consul, and other brand names.

Determined to convert Whirlpool from a U.S. company to a major global player, Whitwam purchased N. V. Philips's European appliance business. The CEO's first challenge was to integrate and coordinate the many European operations with the U.S. operation. Some companies accomplish this task by imposing the parent's systems on the acquired companies, but Whitwam started down a more ambitious path. He created cross-cultural teams with members from the European and North American operations, and together they designed a program to ensure quality and productivity throughout Whirlpool's worldwide operation. In the eyes of other corporate leaders, Whirlpool was doing everything right. The company was even featured in a *Harvard Business Review* article titled "The Right Way to Go Global."

Whirlpool, the world's leading manufacturer and marketer of major home appliances, sells products in more than 170 countries worldwide.

Whitwam soon discovered, however, that developing global strategies was easier than executing them. Whirlpool had not counted on the difficulty in marketing appliances—a process that is consistent in local markets all across the United States—to the fragmented cultures of Europe, Asia, and Latin America. For instance, clothes washers sold in northern European countries such as Denmark must spin-dry clothes much better than washers in southern Italy, where consumers often line-dry clothes in warmer weather. And consumers in India and southern China prefer small refrigerators because they must fit in tight kitchens. Whitwam was also caught off guard by poor economic conditions in Europe, Asia, and Brazil. There, because of economic downturns, consumers were postponing appliance purchases or buying lower-priced models—translating into low sales for Whirlpool.

Despite these challenges, Whitwam was convinced that he could remake Whirlpool into a truly global company. But how? If you were David Whitwam, what would you do to help Whirlpool navigate the rough waters of the global marketplace? How would you learn more about consumer needs to develop suitable appliances for each market? What steps would you take to boost sales of the Whirlpool brand around the world?[1] ■

FUNDAMENTALS OF INTERNATIONAL TRADE

The success of U.S. businesses such as Whirlpool, Wal-Mart, UPS, and others that operate in the global marketplace depends, in part, on the international economic relationships the United States maintains with other countries. Basically, the U.S. objective is to devise policies that balance the interests of U.S. companies, U.S. workers, and U.S. consumers. Other countries are trying to do the same thing. As you might expect, the many players in world trade sometimes have conflicting goals.

Why Nations Trade

No single country has the resources to produce everything its citizens want or need. Businesses and countries specialize in the production of certain goods and engage in international trade to obtain raw materials and goods that are unavailable to them or too costly for them to produce. International trade has many benefits: It increases a country's total output, it offers lower prices and greater variety to consumers, it subjects domestic oligopolies and monopolies to competition, and it allows companies to expand their markets and achieve cost, production, and distribution efficiencies, known as **economies of scale**.[2]

How does a country know what to produce and what to trade for? In some cases, the answer is easy: A nation may have an **absolute advantage**, which means it can produce a particular item more efficiently than *all* other nations, or it is virtually the only country producing that product. Absolute advantages rarely last, however, unless they are based on the availability of natural resources. Saudi Arabia, for example, has an absolute advantage in crude oil production because of its huge, developed reserves. Thus, it makes sense for Saudi Arabia to specialize in providing the world with oil and to trade for other items it needs.

In most cases, a country can produce many of the same items that other countries can produce. The **comparative advantage theory** explains how a country chooses which items to produce and which items to trade for. The theory states that a country should produce and sell to other countries those items it produces more efficiently or at a lower cost, and it should trade for those it can't produce as economically. To see how the theory works, consider the United States and Brazil. Each can produce both steel and coffee, but the United States is more efficient at producing steel than coffee, while Brazil is more efficient at producing coffee than steel. According to the comparative advantage theory, the two countries will be better off if each specializes in the industry in which it is more efficient and if the two trade with each other, with the United States selling steel to Brazil and Brazil selling coffee to the United States.[3] The basic argument behind the comparative advantage theory is that such specialization and exchange will increase a country's total output and allow both trading partners to enjoy a higher standard of living.

How International Trade Is Measured

In Chapter 1 we discussed how economists monitor certain key economic indicators to evaluate how well their country's economic system is performing. One trend that economists watch carefully is the level of a nation's imports and exports. For instance, at any given time, a country may be importing more than it is exporting. As Exhibit 3.1 illustrates, the United States imports more consumer goods than it exports, but it exports more services than it imports. Two key measurements of a nation's level of international trade are the *balance of trade* and the *balance of payments*.

The total value of a country's exports *minus* the total value of its imports, over some period of time, determines its **balance of trade**. In years when the value of goods and services exported by the United States exceeds the value of goods and services it imports, the U.S. balance of trade is said to be positive: People in other countries buy more goods and services from the United States than the United States buys from them, creating a **trade surplus**. Conversely, when the people of the United States buy more from foreign countries than the foreign countries buy from the United States, the U.S. balance of trade is said to be negative. That is, imports exceed exports, creating a **trade deficit**. As Exhibit 3.2 shows, in 2003 the U.S. trade deficit soared to nearly $500 billion.[4]

The **balance of payments** is the broadest indicator of international trade. It is the total flow of money into the country *minus* the total flow of money out of the country over some period of time. The balance of payments includes the balance of trade plus the net dollars received and spent on foreign investment, military expenditures, tourism,

economies of scale
Savings from manufacturing, marketing, or buying in large quantities

absolute advantage
A nation's ability to produce a particular product with fewer resources per unit of output than any other nation

comparative advantage theory
Theory that states that a country should produce and sell to other countries those items it produces most efficiently

balance of trade
Total value of the products a nation exports minus the total value of the products it imports, over some period of time

trade surplus
Favorable trade balance created when a country exports more than it imports

trade deficit
Unfavorable trade balance created when a country imports more than it exports

balance of payments
Sum of all payments one nation receives from other nations minus the sum of all payments it makes to other nations, over some specified period of time

Exhibit 3.1

U.S. Exports and Imports

The United States actively participates in global trade by exporting and importing goods and services.

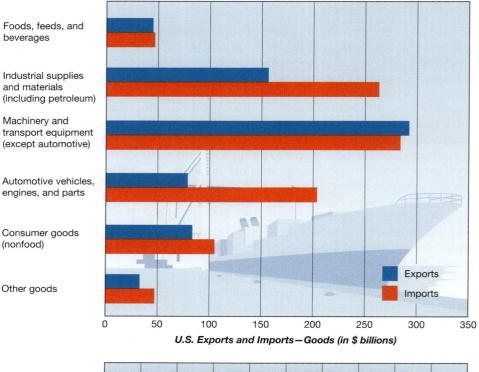

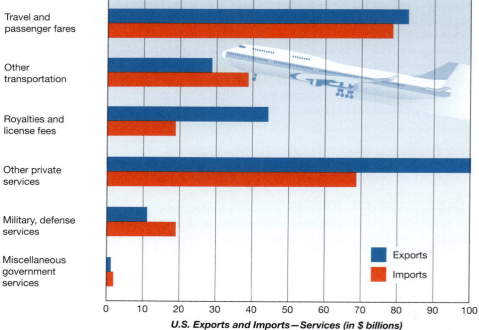

foreign aid, and other international transactions. For example, when a U.S. company such as Whirlpool buys all or part of a company based in another country, that investment is counted in the balance of payments but not in the balance of trade. Similarly, when a foreign company such as Daimler-Benz buys a U.S. company such as Chrysler or purchases U.S. stocks, bonds, or real estate, those transactions are part of the balance of payments. The U.S. government, like all governments, desires a favorable balance of payments. That means more money is coming into the country than is flowing out.

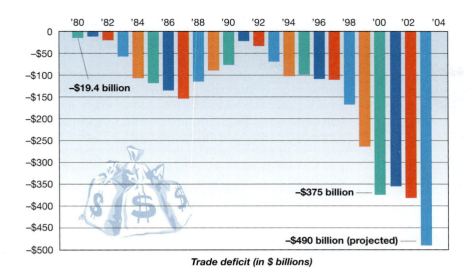

Exhibit 3.2

Trade Deficit on the Rise

U.S. officials say the exploding trade deficit is evidence that the United States maintains the world's most open markets.

Trade deficit (in $ billions)

Trade Restrictions

Even though international trade has many economic advantages, sometimes countries practice **protectionism**; that is, they restrict international trade for one reason or another. Sometimes they restrict trade to shield specific industries from foreign competition and the possible loss of jobs in these industries. Sometimes they try to protect certain industries that are key to their national defense and the health and safety of their citizens. And sometimes they engage in protectionist measures to give new or weak industries an opportunity to grow and strengthen.[5]

    Are trade restrictions a good idea or a bad idea? Study after study has shown that in the long run, they hurt a country because they remove competition, stifle innovation, and allow domestic producers to charge more for their goods. However, short-term pressures on politicians, from both business owners and labor groups, can override long-term thinking on occasion. The most commonly used forms of trade restrictions include:

- *Tariffs.* **Tariffs** are taxes, surcharges, or duties levied against imported goods. Sometimes tariffs are levied to generate revenue for the government, but more often they are imposed to restrict trade or to punish other countries for disobeying international trade laws.

- *Quotas.* **Quotas** limit the amount of a particular good that countries can import during a year. The United States puts ceilings on foreign sugar, peanuts, and dairy products. Limits may be set in quantities, such as pounds of sugar, or in values, such as total dollars' worth of peanuts. In some cases, a product faces stiff tariffs once it reaches its quota. After foreign tobacco products hit their quotas, for example, additional shipments face 350 percent tariffs.[6]

- *Embargoes.* In its most extreme form, a quota becomes an **embargo**, a complete ban on the import or export of certain products. For example, Canada forbids the importation of oleomargarine in order to protect its dairy industry, and the United States bans the importation of toys with lead paint because of health concerns.

- *Sanctions.* Sanctions are politically motivated embargoes that revoke a country's normal trade relations status; they are often used as forceful alternatives short of war. Sanctions can include arms embargoes, foreign-assistance reductions and cut-offs, trade limitations, tariff increases, import-quota decreases, visa denials, air-link cancellations, and more. Most governments (including the United States) use sanctions sparingly, because studies show that sanctions are ineffective at getting countries to change.[7]

protectionism
Government policies aimed at shielding a country's industries from foreign competition

tariffs
Taxes levied on imports

quotas
Fixed limits on the quantity of imports a nation will allow for a specific product

embargo
Total ban on trade with a particular nation (a sanction) or of a particular product

Automobiles are just one of the many products that have been subject to trade restrictions by various governments over the years.

In addition to restricting foreign trade, governments sometimes give their domestic producers a competitive edge by using these protectionist tactics:

- *Restrictive import standards.* Countries can assist their domestic producers by establishing restrictive import standards, such as requiring special licenses for doing certain kinds of business and then making it difficult for foreign companies to obtain such a license. For example, Saudi Arabia restricts import licenses for a variety of products, including chemicals, pasteurized milk, and information technology products.[8] Other countries restrict imports by requiring goods to pass special tests.

- *Subsidies.* Rather than restrict imports, some countries subsidize domestic producers so that their prices can compete favorably in the global marketplace. Airbus, originally an alliance of state companies from Germany, France, England, and Spain, was subsidized for years to help the company compete against rival Boeing. Now that Airbus is a strong competitor, the complex alliance has been sold to a joint venture composed of two private companies—the French-German-Spanish European Aeronautic Defense and Space Company and Britain's BAE Systems PLC.[9]

- *Dumping.* The practice of selling large quantities of a product at a price lower than the cost of production or below what the company would charge in its home market is called **dumping**. This tactic is often used to try to win foreign customers or to reduce product surpluses. Most industrialized countries have antidumping regulations. Section 301 of the U.S. Trade Act of 1988, for instance, obligates the U.S. president to retaliate against foreign producers that dump products on the U.S. market. So when reports showed that Japan was dumping coated steel, which is used primarily in metal containers, cans, bake ware, and home builders' hardware, on the U.S. market, the United States imposed a 95 percent antidumping penalty on the coated steel to prevent Japan from materially injuring the U.S. steel industry.[10]

dumping
Charging less than the actual cost or less than the home-country price for goods sold in other countries

Agreements and Organizations Promoting International Trade

To prevent trade disputes from escalating into full-blown trade wars, and to ensure that international business is conducted in a fair and orderly fashion, countries worldwide have created trade agreements and organizations. Philosophically, most of these agreements and organizations support the basic principles of **free trade**. The assumption is that each nation will ultimately benefit by freely exchanging the goods and services it produces most efficiently for the goods and services it produces less efficiently. The major trade agreements and organizations include the GATT, the WTO, the APEC, the IMF, and the World Bank.

free trade
International trade unencumbered by restrictive measures

The General Agreement on Tariffs and Trade (GATT)

The General Agreement on Tariffs and Trade (GATT) is a worldwide pact that was first established in the aftermath of World War II. The pact's guiding principle—most favored nation (MFN) status—is one of nondiscrimination: Any trade advantage a GATT member gives to one country must be given to all GATT members, and no GATT nation can be singled out for punishment. In 1995 GATT established the World Trade Organization (WTO), which has replaced GATT as the world forum for trade negotiations.

The World Trade Organization (WTO)

The World Trade Organization (WTO) is a permanent forum for negotiating, implementing, and monitoring international trade procedures and for mediating trade disputes among its 144 member countries. The organization's goals include facilitating free trade, lowering the costs of doing business, enhancing the international investment environment, simplifying customs, and promoting technical and economic cooperation. Experts believe that the WTO should ultimately prove to be more effective than the GATT because the WTO has a formal legal structure for settling disputes.

Admission to the organization is by application process and requires approval by two-thirds of the members. All WTO members enjoy "favored" access to foreign markets in exchange for adhering to a long list of fair-trading rules and laws governing patents, copyrights, and trademarks. After 15 years of negotiations, China was finally admitted to the WTO in November 2001. As a condition to its membership, China made extraordinary concessions. Over a 5-year period, China must eliminate many tariffs and quotas on a wide range of products and open its market of 1.4 billion people to foreign goods. One group that spoke out strongly against China's admission to the WTO was U.S. textile workers, who feared that the lifting of U.S. quotas on foreign textiles will increase imports of foreign textiles and severely affect the U.S. textile industry.[11]

Technologies That Are Revolutionizing Business

Telepresence

Telepresence systems start with the basic idea of videoconferencing but go far beyond with imagery so real that colleagues thousands of miles apart appear to be in the same room together. Business executives dissatisfied with the delays and image quality of conventional videoconferencing are turning to telepresence systems to stay connected with colleagues and customers—while avoiding the disruptions, costs, or perceived risks of international travel.

How it's changing business

Telepresence enhances communication for teams spread around the country or around the world. For example, Duke University's Fuqua School of Business installed a telepresence system to link its campuses in Durham, North Carolina, and Frankfurt, Germany. When meeting participants sit down at a table in one city, virtual participants from the other city appear to be sitting on the other side of the table. The effect is so real that some people think it's downright eerie. Not only can participants make eye contact across the Atlantic, but "you can stick your head in the room in Durham and hear the traffic of downtown Frankfurt," says associate dean Nevin Fouts.

Developers are even working on robotic telepresence, in which you'll be able to control a robot surrogate hundreds or thousands of miles away. Before long, you'll be able to run your global empire from the conference room down the hall.

Where you can learn more

Teliris is one of the early innovators in telepresence technology; check out the company's website at www.teliris.com.

The Asia Pacific Economic Cooperation Council (APEC)

The Asia Pacific Economic Cooperation Council (APEC) is an organization of 18 countries that is making efforts to liberalize trade in the Pacific Rim (the land areas that surround the Pacific Ocean). Among the member nations are the United States, Japan, China, Mexico, Australia, South Korea, and Canada. In 1994 the members agreed to eliminate all tariffs and trade barriers among industrialized countries of the Pacific Rim by 2010 and among developing countries by 2020.[12]

The International Monetary Fund (IMF)

The International Monetary Fund (IMF) was founded in 1945 and is now affiliated with the United Nations. Its primary function is to provide short-term loans to countries that are unable to meet their budgetary expenses. As such, the IMF is often looked upon as a lender of last resort. For example, the IMF provided a combined total of over $150 billion in loans to South Korea, Indonesia, Brazil, Thailand, and other countries to help rescue them from a global financial crisis at the end of the 20th century.[13]

The World Bank

Officially known as the International Bank for Reconstruction and Development, the World Bank was founded to finance reconstruction after World War II. It now provides low-interest loans to developing nations for improvement of transportation, telecommunications, health, and education. Currently the World Bank is focused on bringing the Internet to the less-developed regions of the world, such as Africa. World Bank officials and telecommunication executives hope that Internet connections will attract more companies to the region and lead to more rapid economic development.[14] Both the IMF and the World Bank are funded by deposits from its 182 member nations. The bulk of the funds come from the United States, western Europe, and Japan.

Trading Blocs

Trading blocs are another type of organization that promotes international trade. Generally comprising neighboring countries, trading blocs promote free trade among regional members. Although specific rules vary from group to group, their primary objective is to ensure the economic growth and benefit of members. As such, trading blocs generally promote trade inside the region while creating uniform barriers against goods and services entering the region from nonmember countries. Trading blocs are becoming a significant force in the global marketplace.[15]

Trading blocs can be advantageous or disadvantageous in promoting world trade, depending on one's perspective. Some economists are apprehensive about the growing importance of regional trading blocs. They fear that the world is splitting into three camps, revolving around the Americas, Europe, and Asia. Any nation that does not fall into one of these economic regions could suffer, they say, because members of the trading blocs could place severe restrictions on trade with nonmember countries. The critics fear that overall world trade could decline as members become more protective of their own regions. As a result, consumers could find themselves with fewer choices, and many producers could lose sales in lucrative foreign markets.

Others claim that trading blocs could improve world trade. The growth of commerce and the availability of customers and suppliers within a trading bloc could be a boon to smaller or younger nations that are trying to build strong economies. The lack of trade barriers within the bloc could help member industries compete with producers in more-developed nations, and, in some cases, member countries could reach a wider market than before.[16] Furthermore, close ties to more stable economies could help shield emerging nations from fluctuations in the global economy and could promote a greater sharing of knowledge and technology; both outcomes could aid future economic development. If nothing else, the ongoing disagreement is evidence of just how complicated global trade really is. No one can truly predict how trade agreements will affect each country involved because so many variables and competing forces are at work.

The four most powerful trading blocs today are the Association of Southeast Asian Nations (ASEAN), South America's Mercosur, the North American Free Trade Agreement (NAFTA), and the European Union (EU), with the latter two being the largest and most powerful (see Exhibit 3.3). Because many trading nations see Latin America as an area for large-scale economic growth in the future, they are eager to establish ties with Mercosur, which links Argentina, Brazil, Paraguay, and Uruguay and encompasses a population of 210 million people who produce more than $1 trillion in goods and services.[17] Like other trading blocks, Mercosur's objectives include the free movement of goods and services across the borders of its members. Furthermore, the group seeks an economic integration that it hopes will make the four countries more competitive in the global marketplace.[18] Some U.S. officials hope that Mercosur will eventually join NAFTA to form a Free Trade Area of the Americas (FTAA).[19]

NAFTA

In 1994 the United States, Canada, and Mexico formed a powerful trading bloc, the North American Free Trade Agreement (NAFTA). The agreement paved the way for the free flow of goods, services, and capital within the bloc by eliminating all tariffs and quotas on trades among the three nations.[20]

Now, after more than a decade in action, has NAFTA lived up to its promises, particularly regarding trade between the United States and Mexico? That depends on where you look. Mexico has tripled its exports, and U.S. and other foreign companies have invested billions of dollars in the country. Some companies are thriving, thanks to those export opportunities, while others, particularly in agriculture, have been hurt severely

European Union (EU)	North American Free Trade Agreement (NAFTA)	Association of Southeast Asian Nations (ASEAN)	Mercosur
Austria	Canada	Brunei	Argentina
Belgium	Mexico	Cambodia	Brazil
Cyprus	United States	Indonesia	Paraguay
Czech Republic		Laos	Uruguay
Denmark		Malaysia	
Estonia		Myanmar	
Finland		Philippines	
France		Singapore	
Germany		Thailand	
Great Britain		Vietnam	
Greece			
Hungary			
Ireland			
Italy			
Latvia			
Lithuania			
Luxembourg			
Malta			
Netherlands			
Poland			
Portugal			
Slovakia			
Slovenia			
Spain			
Sweden			

Exhibit 3.3

Members of Major Trading Blocs

As the economies of the world become increasingly linked, many countries have formed powerful regional trading blocs that trade freely with one another and limit foreign competition.

by low-cost imports from the United States. NAFTA didn't drain U.S. jobs away, as some early critics feared, although job growth within Mexico has not lived up to expectations, either. Many of the manufacturing jobs Mexico hoped to attract wound up in China instead. And outside the business sphere, hoped-for improvements in education and health care haven't materialized to the extent NAFTA backers expected, either, although they place the blame on government inaction, not on the free-trade agreement.[21]

Ultimately, NAFTA's supporters would like to see the agreement expanded to include all of Central and South America—making it the largest free-trade zone on the planet. However, Mexico's experience has soured many workers throughout Latin America on the prospects of free trade.[22]

The European Union

One of the largest trading blocs is the European Union (EU), which now combines 25 countries and nearly a half billion people. Talks are under way to admit several more countries in 2007.[23] EU nations are working to eliminate hundreds of local regulations, variations in product standards, and protectionist measures that limit trade among member countries. Eliminating barriers enables the nations of the EU to function as a single market, with trade flowing among member countries as it does among states in the United States.

The European Union's Impact on the Rules of Global Trade   Increasingly, the rules governing the food we eat, the software we use, and the cars we drive are set in Brussels, Belgium, the administrative home of the European Union. The EU, which tends to regulate more frequently and more rigorously than the United States—especially when it comes to consumer protection—significantly impacts global product standards. Twenty years ago if manufacturers designed something to U.S. standards, they could pretty much

The euro eases price comparisons for products sold in the member countries of the European Union.

euro
A unified currency used by most nations in the European Union

exchange rate
Rate at which the money of one country is traded for the money of another

sell it all over the world. Now items destined for export must conform to EU standards.

When it comes to consumer or environmental protections, EU regulators believe it's better to be safe than sorry. That approach evolved partly from a series of food scares in Europe over the past decade or two, such as mad cow disease. It also reflects the fact that Europeans are more inclined than Americans to expect government to protect them. Because of stricter EU rules, McDonald's has stopped serving soft-plastic toys with its Happy Meals and United Technologies has redesigned its Carrier air conditioners to comply with European recycling rules, which are tougher than U.S. standards.[24]

U.S. farmers also tend to cater to European tastes—especially when it comes to genetically modified food. The U.S. Food and Drug Administration has approved the use of most genetically modified crops in human food, but the EU has placed strict limits on which genetically modified seeds can be planted and how they can be used in Europe. Thus, many U.S. food processors won't buy genetically modified corn or soybeans so that they can sell their products internationally.[25]

The Euro   In 1999, 12 of the 15 countries that were EU members at that time formed the economic and monetary union (EMU) and turned over control of their individual monetary policies to the newly created European Central Bank. With a combined population of about 376 million people, these 12 countries account for about 20 percent of the world's gross domestic product (GDP), making them the world's second-largest economy.[26] These countries also adopted a unified currency called the **euro**.

Officially launched in 1999 (with notes and coins available in 2002), the euro got off to a rocky start. But European leaders believe it will build a bond among Europe's cities and improve trade. Moreover, the euro could wipe out some $65 billion annually in currency exchange costs among participants and cut the intermediary out of trillions of dollars' worth of foreign exchange transactions. U.S. businesses and travelers alone could save as much as 50 percent of the costs they now pay to convert dollars into multiple European currencies. And, with prices in these nations now visible in one currency, consumers can compare prices on similar items whether they are sold in Lisbon or Vienna.[27]

Foreign Exchange Rates and Currency Valuations

When companies buy and sell goods and services in the global marketplace, they complete the transaction by exchanging currencies. For instance, if a Japanese company borrows money from a U.S. bank to build a manufacturing plant in Japan, it must repay the loan in U.S. dollars. Or if a South Korean car manufacturer imports engine parts from Japan, it must pay for them in yen (Japan's currency). To do so, companies exchange their currency at any international bank that handles *foreign exchange*, the conversion of one currency into an equivalent amount of another currency. The number of yen, francs, or pounds that must be exchanged for every dollar, mark, or won is known as the **exchange rate** between currencies.

Most international currencies operate under a *floating exchange rate system*; thus, a currency's value or price fluctuates in response to the forces of global supply and demand. The supply and demand of a country's currency are determined in part by what is happening in the country's own economy. Moreover, because supply and demand for a currency are always changing, the rate at which it is exchanged for other currencies may change a little each day. Japanese currency might be trading at 107.6 yen to the dollar on one day and 106.8 on the next.

Even though most governments let the value of their currency respond to the forces of supply and demand, sometimes a government will intervene and adjust the exchange rate of its country's currency. Why would a government do this? One reason is to keep the price of a nation's goods and services more affordable in the global marketplace and to protect the nation's economy against trade imbalances. Another is to boost or slow down the country's economy.

Devaluation, or the drop in the value of a nation's currency relative to the value of other currencies, can at times boost a country's economy because it makes the country's products and services more affordable in foreign markets while it increases the price of imports. Because fewer units of foreign currency are required to purchase the devalued currency, such situations tend to raise a country's exports and lower its imports. Conversely, a strong currency boosts imports and dampens exports.

Some countries fix, or peg, the value of their currencies to the value of more stable currencies, such as the dollar or the yen, instead of letting it float freely. Hong Kong, for example, pegs its currency to the U.S. dollar. If a currency is pegged, its value fluctuates proportionately with the value of the foreign currency to which it is linked. So if the U.S. dollar declines, so will the Japanese yen and other currencies that are pegged to it. This system works well as long as the proportionate relationship between the two currencies remains valid. But if one partner suffers economic hardship, demand for its currency will decline significantly and the exchange rate at which the two are pegged will become unrealistic. Such was the case with Thailand's currency (the baht), Indonesia's currency (the rupiah), and Argentina's currency (the peso). When these countries unpegged their currencies from the U.S. dollar to let them gradually seek their true value, the currencies went into a free fall.

Argentines gathered in front of a Buenos Aires currency exchange as the government lifted restrictions against citizens' trading pesos at a free-floating rate against the dollar.
Source: Horacio Paone/The New York Times.

THE GLOBAL BUSINESS ENVIRONMENT

Like Whirlpool, more and more enterprises are experiencing the challenge and excitement of conducting business in the global marketplace. Even firms that once thought they were too tiny to expand into a neighboring city have discovered that they can tap the sales potential of overseas markets with the help of fax machines, overnight delivery services, e-mail, and the Internet. The small farming town of Waterloo, Wisconsin, might seem an unlikely place for the headquarters of an international bicycle business, but it's where five workers began assembling bike frames by hand in 1976. Today, Trek Bicycle sells more than half a million bikes annually in more than 70 countries. Over 40 percent of the company's sales come from international business.[28]

Companies such as Trek Bicycle and Whirlpool know that selling goods and services in foreign markets can generate increased sales, produce operational efficiencies, expose companies to new technologies, and provide greater consumer choices. But venturing abroad also exposes companies to many new challenges, as Whirlpool's David Whitwam discovered. For instance, each country has unique ways of doing business, which must be learned: laws, customs, consumer preferences, ethical standards, labor skills, and political and economic stability (see Exhibit 3.4). All these factors can affect a firm's international

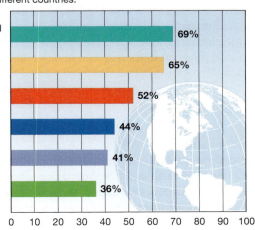

Challenges U.S. and European senior executives say they face when managing across different countries:

Changing individual behavior	69%
Cultural differences	65%
Business practice differences	52%
Headquarters too remote	44%
Labor law differences	41%
Accounting and tax differences	36%

0 10 20 30 40 50 60 70 80 90 100

Exhibit 3.4

Going Global Has Its Barriers

Learning a country's business customs and cultural differences is the first step in going global.

How to Avoid Business Mistakes Abroad

Doing business in another country can be extremely tricky. Here are some issues to consider when you conduct business abroad.

THE IMPORTANCE OF PACKAGING

Numerous problems result from the failure to adapt packaging for other cultures. Sometimes only the color of the package needs to be altered to enhance a product's sales. For instance, white symbolizes death in Japan and much of Asia; green represents danger or disease in Malaysia. Using the wrong color in these countries might produce negative reactions.

THE LANGUAGE BARRIER

Some product names travel poorly. For instance, the gasoline company Esso found out that its name means "stalled car" in Japan. However, some company names have traveled well. Kodak may be the most famous example. A research team deliberately developed this name after searching for a word that was pronounceable everywhere but had no specific meaning anywhere.

PROBLEMS WITH PROMOTIONS

In its U.S. promotion, one company had effectively used this sentence: "You can use no finer napkin at your dinner table." The U.S. company decided to use the same commercials in England because, after all, the British do speak English. To the British, however, the word *napkin* or *nappy* actually means "diaper." The ad could hardly be expected to boost sales of dinner napkins in England.

LOCAL CUSTOMS

Social norms vary greatly from country to country, and it is difficult for any outsider to be knowledgeable about all of them, so local input is vital. For example, one firm pro-moted eyeglasses in Thailand with commercials featuring animals wearing glasses. However, in Thailand animals are considered a low form of life; humans would never wear anything worn by an animal.

TRANSLATION PROBLEMS

The best translations of an advertising message convey the concept of the original but do not precisely duplicate the original. PepsiCo learned this lesson when it reportedly discovered that its slogan "Come alive with Pepsi" was translated into German as "Come alive out of the grave with Pepsi." In Asia, the slogan was once translated as "Bring your ancestors back from the dead."

THE NEED FOR RESEARCH

Proper market research may reduce or eliminate most international business blunders. Market researchers can uncover needs for product adaptations, potential name problems, promotional requirements, and useful market strategies. Good research may even uncover potential translation problems.

As you can see, doing business in other cultures can be risky if you're unprepared. However, awareness of differences, consultations with local people, and concern for host-country feelings can reduce problems and save money.

Questions for Critical Thinking

1. If you were thinking of selling a breakfast cereal in Japan, what issues might you want to consider?
2. What steps can companies take to avoid business blunders abroad?

---

prospects. Furthermore, volatile currencies, international trade relationships, and the threat of terrorism can make global expansion a risky proposition. Still, in most cases the opportunities of the global marketplace greatly outweigh the risks. When UPS began its rapid global expansion program in the 1980s, it had to attain air rights into each country, unravel a patchwork of customs laws, learn how to deal with varying work ethics and employment policies, and so on. But the company's efforts paid off. Today UPS delivers over 13 million documents and packages daily in more than 200 countries. [29]

Cultural Differences in the Global Business Environment

Cultural differences present a number of challenges in the global marketplace, as David Whitwam's experience shows. For one thing, companies must recognize and respect differences in language, social values, ideas of status, decision-making habits, attitudes toward time, use of space, body language, manners, and ethical standards. Otherwise, such differences can lead to misunderstandings in international business relationships, particularly if differences in business practices also exist. Furthermore, companies that sell their products overseas must often adapt the products to meet the unique needs of international customers, as Whirlpool discovered.

The best way to prepare yourself for doing business with people from another culture is to study that culture in advance. Learn everything you can about the culture's history, religion, politics, and customs—especially its business customs. Who makes decisions? How are negotiations usually conducted? Is gift giving expected? What is the proper attire for a business meeting? In addition to the suggestion that you learn about the culture, seasoned international businesspeople offer the following tips for improving intercultural communication:

Learning From Business Blunders

Oops: Toyota thought it had a clever ad slogan that played off the Chinese proverb, "When you get to the foot of the mountain, a road will appear." The Japanese automaker launched an advertising campaign with the slogan, "Wherever there is a road, there is a Toyota." Not precisely true, to be sure, but it's the sort of advertising-speak that consumers are used to just about everywhere in the world. Not in China, however. Government authorities accused Toyota of false advertising.

What You Can Learn: Most advertisers wouldn't think twice about saying things like "Wherever there is a road, there is a Toyota," but the Chinese government has strict rules about truth in advertising and, after all, there really isn't a Toyota on every road—in China or anywhere else. The message: Don't assume anything when you're doing business in another country; research is vital.

- *Be alert to the other person's customs.* Expect the other person to have values, beliefs, expectations, and mannerisms different from yours. For instance, don't be surprised when businesspeople in Pakistan excuse themselves in the middle of a meeting to conduct prayers. Moslems pray five times a day.

- *Deal with the individual.* Don't stereotype the other person or react with preconceived ideas. Regard the person as an individual first, not as a representative of another culture.

- *Clarify your intent and meaning.* The other person's body language may not mean what you think, and the person may read unintentional meanings into your message. Clarify your true intent by repetition and examples. Ask questions and listen carefully. The Japanese are generally appreciative when foreigners ask what is proper behavior, because it shows respect for the Japanese way of doing things.[30]

- *Adapt your style to the other person's.* If the other person appears to be direct and straightforward, follow suit. If not, adjust your behavior to match. In many African countries, people are suspicious of others who seem to be in a hurry. Therefore, you should allow plenty of time to get to know the people you are dealing with.

- *Show respect.* Learn how respect is communicated in various cultures—through gestures, eye contact, and so on. For example, in Spain let a handshake last five to seven strokes; pulling away too soon may be interpreted as a rejection. In France, however, the preferred handshake is a single stroke.

These are just a few tips for doing business in the global marketplace. Successful international businesses learn as much as they can about political issues, cultural factors, and the economic environment before investing time and money in new markets. Exhibit 3.5 can guide you in your efforts to learn more about a country's culture before doing business abroad.

Legal Differences in the Global Business Environment

All U.S. companies that conduct business in other countries must be familiar with U.S. law, international law, and the laws of the specific countries where they plan to trade or do business. For example, all companies doing international business must comply with the 1978 Foreign Corrupt Practices Act. This U.S. law outlaws actions such as bribing government officials in other nations to approve deals. It does, however, allow certain payments, including small payments to officials for expediting routine government actions.

Exhibit 3.5

Checklist for Doing Business Abroad

Use this checklist as a starting point when investigating a foreign culture.

UNDERSTAND SOCIAL CUSTOMS

✓ How do people react to strangers? Are they friendly? Hostile? Reserved?

✓ How do people greet each other? Should you bow? Nod? Shake hands?

✓ How are names used for introductions?

✓ What are the attitudes toward touching people?

✓ How do you express appreciation for an invitation to lunch or dinner or to someone's home? Should you bring a gift? Send flowers? Write a thank-you note?

✓ How, when, or where are people expected to sit in social or business situations?

✓ Are any phrases, facial expressions, or hand gestures considered rude?

✓ How close do people stand when talking?

✓ How do you attract the attention of a waiter? Do you tip the waiter?

✓ When is it rude to refuse an invitation? How do you refuse politely?

✓ What are the acceptable patterns of eye contact?

✓ What gestures indicate agreement? Disagreement? Respect?

✓ What topics may or may not be discussed in a social setting? In a business setting?

✓ How is time perceived?

✓ What are the generally accepted working hours?

✓ How do people view scheduled appointments?

LEARN ABOUT CLOTHING AND FOOD PREFERENCES

✓ What occasions require special clothing? What colors are associated with mourning? Love? Joy?

✓ Are some types of clothing considered taboo for one sex or the other?

✓ What are the attitudes toward human body odors? Are deodorants or perfumes used?

✓ How many times a day do people eat?

✓ How are hands or utensils used when eating?

✓ What types of places, food, and drink are appropriate for business entertainment?

✓ Where is the seat of honor at a table?

ASSESS POLITICAL PATTERNS

✓ How stable is the political situation? Does it affect businesses in and out of the country?

✓ How is political power manifested? Military power? Economic strength?

✓ What are the traditional government institutions?

LEARN ABOUT ECONOMIC AND BUSINESS INSTITUTIONS

✓ Is the society homogeneous?

✓ What minority groups are represented?

✓ What languages are spoken?

✓ Do immigration patterns influence workforce composition?

- ✓ What are the primary resources and principal products?
- ✓ What vocational/technological training is offered?
- ✓ What are the attitudes toward education?
- ✓ Are businesses generally large? Family controlled? Government controlled?
- ✓ Is it appropriate to do business by telephone? By fax? By e-mail?
- ✓ Do managers make business decisions unilaterally, or do they involve employees?
- ✓ How are status and seniority shown in an organization? In a business meeting?
- ✓ Must people socialize before conducting business?

APPRAISE THE NATURE OF ETHICS, VALUES, AND LAWS

- ✓ Is money or a gift expected in exchange for arranging business transactions?
- ✓ What ethical or legal issues might affect business transactions?
- ✓ Do people value competitiveness or cooperation?
- ✓ What are the attitudes toward work? Toward money?
- ✓ Is politeness more important than factual honesty?
- ✓ What qualities are admired in a business associate?

Critics of this U.S. law complain that payoffs are a routine part of world trade, so forbidding U.S. companies to follow suit cripples their ability to compete. Others counter that U.S. exports haven't been affected by this law and that companies can conduct business abroad without violating antibribery rules. Regardless of whether they agree or disagree with the law, some companies have had to forgo opportunities as a result of it. For example, a U.S. power-generation company recently walked away from a $320 million contract in the Middle East because government officials demanded a $3 million bribe. The contract went to a Japanese company instead.[31]

Forms of International Business Activity

Once a company decides to operate in the global marketplace, it must decide on the level of involvement it is willing to undertake and develop strategies for marketing its products internationally. Five common forms of international business activities are *importing and exporting, licensing, franchising, strategic alliances and joint ventures*, and *foreign direct investment*. Each has a varying degree of ownership, financial commitment, and risk.

Importing and Exporting

Importing, the buying of goods or services from a supplier in another country, and **exporting**, the selling of products outside the country in which they are produced, have existed for centuries. In the last few decades, however, the increased level of these activities has caused the economies of the world to become tightly linked.

Exporting, one of the least risky forms of international business activity, permits a firm to enter a foreign market gradually, assess local conditions, then fine-tune its product to meet the needs of foreign consumers. In most cases, the firm's financial exposure is limited to market research costs, advertising costs, and the costs of either establishing a direct sales and distribution system or hiring intermediaries. Such intermediaries include *export management companies*, which are domestic firms that specialize in performing international marketing services on a commission basis, and *export trading companies*, which are general trading firms that will buy your products for resale over-

importing
Purchasing goods or services from another country and bringing them into one's own country

exporting
Selling and shipping goods or services to another country

seas as well as perform a variety of importing, exporting, and manufacturing functions. Still another alternative is to use foreign distributors.

Working through a foreign distributor with connections in the target country is often helpful to both large and small companies because such intermediaries can provide you with the connections, expertise, and market knowledge you will need to conduct business in a foreign country.[32] In addition, many countries now have foreign trade offices to help importers and exporters interested in doing business within their borders. Other helpful resources include professional agents, local businesspeople, and the International Trade Administration of the U.S. Department of Commerce. This trade organization offers a variety of services, including political and credit-risk analysis, advice on entering foreign markets, and financing tips.

International Licensing

licensing
Agreement to produce and market another company's product in exchange for a royalty or fee

Licensing is another popular approach to international business. License agreements entitle one company to use some or all of another firm's intellectual property (patents, trademarks, brand names, copyrights, or trade secrets) in return for a royalty payment. Underwear manufacturer Jockey licenses the rights to use the Jockey name to certain foreign manufacturers of women's active wear, sleepwear, and slippers. Jockey licenses its products in more than 120 countries but is careful that all such arrangements add value to the Jockey name.[33]

Many firms choose licensing as an approach to international markets because it involves little out-of-pocket cost. A firm has already incurred the costs of developing the intellectual property to be licensed. Pharmaceutical firms, for instance, routinely use licensing to enter foreign markets. Once a pharmaceutical firm has developed and patented a new drug, it is often more efficient to grant existing local firms the right to manufacture and distribute the patented drug in return for royalty payments. Israel's Teva Pharmaceutical Industries, for example, has a license to manufacture and market Merck's pharmaceutical products in Israel. This arrangement saves Merck the expense of establishing its own Israeli salesforce.[34] Of course, licensing agreements are not restricted to international business. A company can also license its products or technology to other companies in its domestic market.

International Franchising

strategic alliance
Long-term relationship in which two or more companies share ideas, resources, and technologies in order to establish competitive advantages

Some companies choose to expand into foreign markets by *franchising* their operation. International franchising is among the fastest-growing forms of international business activity today. Under this arrangement, a franchisor enters into an agreement whereby the franchisee obtains the rights to duplicate a specific product or service—perhaps a restaurant, photocopy shop, or video rental store—and the franchisor obtains a royalty fee in exchange. Holiday Inn Worldwide has used this approach to reach customers in over 65 countries. So have KFC, McDonald's, and scores of others. Smaller companies have also found that franchising is a good way for them to enter the global marketplace.[35] By franchising its operations, a firm can minimize the costs and risks of global expansion and bypass certain trade restrictions. (The advantages and disadvantages of franchising in general will be discussed in detail in Chapter 4.)

In the last few years, China's major cities have sprouted numerous franchises and outlets of familiar U.S. names, including McDonald's, Pizza Hut, and Starbucks.

International Strategic Alliances and Joint Ventures

A **strategic alliance** is a long-term partnership between two or more companies to jointly develop, produce, or sell products in the global marketplace. To reach their individual but complementary goals, the companies typically share ideas, expertise, resources, technologies, investment costs, risks, management, and profits.

Strategic alliances are a popular way to expand one's business globally. When Starbucks ventures overseas, the company partners with locals.[36] The

China's Counterfeit Economy

The vast economy in the People's Republic of China has come alive in recent years, with the communist government embracing many principles of free-market economics. The quality of Chinese products has already risen dramatically, and many of the world's best-known companies now rely on Chinese manufacturers to build some of their products for them.

Unfortunately, the Chinese manufacturing phenomenon is not limited to legitimate products. China also produces more counterfeit products than any other nation—everything from autos to aircraft parts, beer to razor blades, soap to shampoo, TVs to toilets. Nearly half of the world's 14 billion batteries are produced in China. But most of them are fake versions of Panasonic, Gillette, and other big brands. Bikes with names that include Yamaha zip along the roads from Beijing to Tibet, but Yamaha didn't make a lot of them. Procter & Gamble (P&G) claims counterfeiters sell $150 million of fake P&G products annually. More than 90 percent of all music CDs sold in China are pirated copies, joining $168 million worth of pirated movies on DVD, according to industry experts. Microsoft has invested several billion dollars in China but has yet to generate a nickel of profit, since more than 90 percent of the application software sold in the country is counterfeit.

Most counterfeiters work at small to midsized factories, but many stay at home, doing things like filling Head & Shoulders bottles with concoctions from large vats in their living rooms or translating subtitles for pirated movies. Overall, the amount of China's manufacturing base that is dependent on illegal knockoffs is estimated to be 10 percent to 30 percent—and growing.

Raids do occur daily, but even the government's efforts aren't cracking down on the number of counterfeiters. Local officials are hesitant to stop the pirates because they create millions of jobs. "Entire villages live off counterfeiting. If you suddenly throw these people out of work, you'll have riots," says one spokesperson for a leading private anti-counterfeiting agency. Shutting down the fakes at Yiwu—China's largest wholesale distribution center, where it is estimated that 80 percent of the consumer goods sold are counterfeits—would cripple the city's economy because many hotels, restaurants, and businesses cater to the trade.

The sale of fake or pirated products is not limited to the Chinese market, either; these items are exported around the globe—to Europe, Russia, the Middle East. Unilever says that fake Dove soap is making its way from China into Europe. Bose, a maker of high-end audio systems, is finding Chinese fakes in overseas markets. These exports are made possible by the growing sophistication of Chinese manufacturing. Ten years ago, China's knockoffs were below Western standards. Now, many fake Duracell batteries look so genuine that Gillette has to send them to a forensics lab to analyze them.

So what are pirated brand owners to do? For the most part, companies hope to encourage greater government enforcement, but it's a tough task. Although U.S. sunglasses maker Oakley has gotten Chinese authorities to close counterfeiters' factories, new ones pop up in their place. Officials have confiscated and destroyed millions of DVDs and CDs, but the counterfeiters continue to churn them out in ever greater numbers.

Some multinationals are shutting down or shrinking some product lines in China because these products are overrun by counterfeits. But China's market is so vast and promising, few companies are willing to pull out entirely. Given the magnitude of the problem and the number of people who are dependent on this shadow economy, the situation won't be solved anytime soon, if ever.

Questions for Critical Thinking
1. Honda recently set up a joint venture to make and sell motorcycles with a Chinese company that used to produce Honda knockoffs. Why would Honda do this?
2. How might product counterfeiting in China affect consumers in the United States?

benefits of this form of international expansion include ease of market entry, shared risk, shared knowledge and expertise, and synergy. Companies that form a strategic alliance with a foreign partner can often compete more effectively than if they entered the foreign market alone. Consider the strategic alliance established by American Airlines, British Airways, Cathay Pacific Airways, Qantas, and others. Named *oneworld*, this partnership makes global travel easier for consumers. Benefits include integrated frequent-flyer programs, common airport lounges, and more efficient ticketing among member carriers so that a change of airlines is transparent when booking international flights.[37]

A **joint venture** is a special type of strategic alliance in which two or more firms join together to create a new business entity that is legally separate and distinct from its parents. In some countries, foreign companies are prohibited from owning facilities outright or from investing in local business. Thus, establishing a joint venture with a local

joint venture
Cooperative partnership in which organizations share investment costs, risks, management, and profits in the development, production, or selling of products

partner may be the only way to do business in that country. In other cases, foreigners may be required to move some of their production facilities to the country to earn the right to sell their products there. For instance, the Chinese government would not allow Boeing to sell airplanes in China until the company agreed to move half of the tail-section production for its 737s to Xian.[38]

Foreign Direct Investment

Exporting, licensing, franchising, and strategic alliances allow a firm to enter the global marketplace without investing in foreign factories or facilities. However, many firms prefer to enter international markets through ownership and control of assets in foreign countries.

The most comprehensive form of international business is a wholly owned operation run in another country, without the financial participation of a local partner. Many U.S. firms conduct business this way, as do companies based in other countries. These operations vary in form, size, and purpose. Some are started from scratch; others are acquired from local owners. Some are small sales offices; others are full-scale manufacturing facilities. Some are set up to exploit the availability of raw materials; others take advantage of low wage rates; still others minimize transportation costs by choosing locations that give them direct access to markets in other countries. In almost all cases, at least part of the workforce is drawn from the local population.

multinational corporations (MNCs)
Companies with operations in more than one country

foreign direct investment (FDI)
Investment of money by foreign companies in domestic business enterprises

Companies with a physical presence in numerous countries are called **multinational corporations** (**MNCs**). Since 1969, the number of multinational corporations in the world's 14 richest countries has more than tripled, from 7,000 to 24,000.[39] Some multinational corporations increase their involvement in foreign countries by establishing **foreign direct investment** (**FDI**). That is, they either establish production and marketing facilities in the countries where they operate or purchase existing foreign firms, as Wal-Mart did in the late 1990s when it acquired large retail stores in Germany and Great Britain and later converted them into Wal-Mart supercenters. Such foreign direct investment constitutes the highest level of international involvement. Moreover, it carries much greater economic and political risk and is more complex than any other form of entry in the global marketplace.[40]

The U.S. Commerce Department reports that foreign direct investment in the United States has been rising steadily over the past few years.[41] In addition to the United States, areas such as the Chinese Economic Area (China, Hong Kong, and Taiwan), South Korea, Singapore, Thailand, Malaysia, Indonesia, Vietnam, India, South Africa, Turkey, and Brazil are attractive spots for foreign investment. Labeled *big emerging markets*, these countries make up 70 percent of the world's land, 85 percent of the world's population, and 99 percent of the anticipated growth in the world's labor force.[42] As such, they have been identified by the U.S. International Trade Administration as having the greatest potential for a large increase in U.S. exports over the next two decades.

Strategic Approaches to International Markets

Choosing the right form of business to pursue is only one of many decisions that companies need to make when moving into other countries. Virtually everything you learn about in this course, from human resources to marketing to financial management, needs to be reconsidered carefully when going international. Some of the most important decisions involve products, customer support, pricing, promotion, and staffing:

- **Products.** The primary dilemma regarding products is whether to *standardize* the product, selling the same product everywhere in the world, or to *customize* the product to accommodate the lifestyles and habits of local target markets. Customization seems like an obvious choice, but it can increase costs and operational complexity, so the decision to customize is not automatic. The degree of customization can also vary. A company may change only the product's name or packaging, or it can modify the product's components, size, and functions. Of course, understanding a country's regulations, culture, and local competition plays into the decisions. Disney learned this the hard way, after losing $1 billion in the first year after it opened the Euro Disney theme park outside of Paris. "When we first launched Euro Disney there was the belief that it was enough to be Disney," says Euro Disney CEO Jay Rasulo. "Now we realize that our guests need to be welcomed on the basis of their own culture and travel habits."[43] The company made numerous changes to accommodate local preferences, from offering wine with meals to renaming the facility, and now Disneyland Paris is Europe's leading tourist attraction.[44]

Even with the worldwide power of the Disney brand, the company learned that it needed to adapt its products and services to the local tastes of the European market.

- **Customer support.** Cars, computers, and other products that require some degree of customer support add another layer of complexity to international business. Many customers are reluctant to buy foreign products that don't offer some form of local support, whether it's a local dealer, a manufacturer's branch office, or a third-party organization that offers support under contract to the manufacturer.

- **Promotion.** Advertising, public relations, and other promotional efforts also present the dilemma of standardization versus customization. As you'll see in Chapter 12, consistency is one of the keys to successful promotion, making sure the audience receives the same message from all sources, time after time. However, after years of trying to build global brands, many U.S. companies are putting new emphasis on crafting customized messages for each country. As Martin Sorrell, head of the UK advertising conglomerate WPP, puts it, "One size doesn't fit all. Consumers are more interesting for their differences rather than their similarities."[45]

- **Pricing.** Even a standardized strategy adds costs, from transportation to communication, and customized strategies add even more costs. Before moving into other countries, businesses need to make sure they can cover all these costs and still be able to offer competitive prices.

- **Staffing.** Depending on the form of business a company decides to pursue in international markets, staffing questions can be major considerations. Many companies find that a combination of U.S. and local personnel works best, mixing company experience with local knowledge and connections. In Latin American markets, U.S. companies such as Home Depot, Payless, and Marriott have been successful transferring Spanish-speaking employees, many of whom are immigrants from Latin America, back to the region to establish and manage facilities.[46]

Given the number and complexity of the decisions to be made, you can see why successful companies plan international expansion with great care.

TERRORISM'S IMPACT ON THE GLOBAL BUSINESS ENVIRONMENT

In the global marketplace, the problems of one country can greatly affect world economics. The September 11, 2001, terrorist attacks on the World Trade Center in New York City and the Pentagon in Washington, D.C., were targeted at the U.S. population and the free-market system, but economically the attacks knew no borders. When U.S. consumers stop buying—even if for only a short period of time—the world feels the impact.

To get a perspective of how important U.S trade is to the world economies, consider the following: Each day U.S. Customs processes about 38,000 trucks and railcars, 16,000 containers on 600 ships, and 2,600 aircraft, most of which are filled with foreign goods brought into the United States.[47] Foreign trade, which accounted for 20 percent of

U.S. economic activity a decade ago, now accounts for almost 30 percent. U.S. exports alone have been responsible for a third of the 20 million jobs created since 1986.[48] And while the 2,500 largest U.S. companies sold about 12 percent of their goods and services outside the United States in 1980, that figure has tripled in the past two decades.[49]

In the wake of September 11, some U.S. businesses, including such high-profile firms as Merrill Lynch, Morgan Stanley, Charles Schwab, Home Depot, Ford Motor Company, and Gateway Computers, pulled back or canceled their global expansion plans, but many other companies did not.[50] In fact, a United Nations survey the following year showed that 70 percent of respondents expected investment and employment in their foreign operations to rise in the near term.[51]

KFC, with 5,000 U.S. restaurants and 6,000 abroad, is one of the companies that didn't slow its international plans. In all, KFC has restaurants in more than 80 countries, including Indonesia, Saudi Arabia, Japan, Australia, Egypt, Mexico, Malaysia, and Swaziland. In China, where KFC has more than 500 restaurants, it is opening about 10 new stores a month. KFC plans to open more than 1,000 stores a year overseas for the foreseeable future. As the company's CEO David Novak sees it, KFC's long-standing presence in so many countries makes it an accepted part of the landscape and therefore less likely to be a major target of terrorism. "We're going to have some radical situations, but not to the extent we think it's going to alter our business plan."[52] "We're still on a fast track overseas, in fact it's one of the keys to our company's growth," adds the vice president of marketing.[53]

World trade has certainly become more complicated in the wake of September 11 and subsequent terror attacks in other countries, with tighter airport security, longer delays at borders, cargo restrictions, and higher transport costs. Every container entering the United States at the Mexican border must now be opened and inspected. As a result, cargo-laden trucks now take up to seven hours to cross, compared with one or two hours before the attacks. Similarly, where a cargo jet could make five stops a day before the attacks, now it makes four.[54] Such delays force companies to inventory more spare parts and increase their manufacturing and operating costs.

Security concerns have raised costs in other ways as well. Joseph Coleman, CEO of RiteCheck Financial Service Centers, a small chain of check-cashing stores in New York, estimates he now spends an extra $100,000 a year to comply with the record-keeping provisions of the USA Patriot Act (a set of antiterrorism laws passed in the wake of September 11).[55] Beefing up security also costs money, whether it's the small, private police force that Federal Express set up to guard the company's operations or more routine items such as increased background checks on new employees, vulnerability assessments by security consultants, or backup facilities for corporate computer systems.[56]

In spite of these costs and obstacles, most businesses have too much riding on globalization to give up on it now. For multinationals such as Whirlpool, globalization is the key to their future. And some even believe that rather than deterring globalization, the terrorist attacks could accelerate it.[57] The more countries cooperate against terrorism, the more the world begins to see itself as one place.

Summary of Learning Objectives

1 **Discuss why nations trade.**

Nations trade to obtain raw materials and goods that are unavailable to them or too costly to produce. International trade benefits nations by increasing a country's total output, offering lower prices and greater variety to its consumers, subjecting domestic oligopolies and monopolies to competition, and allowing companies to expand their markets and achieve production and distribution efficiencies.

2 **Explain why nations restrict international trade, and list four forms of trade restrictions.**

Nations restrict international trade to boost local economies, to shield domestic industries from head-to-head competition with overseas rivals, to save specific jobs, to give weak or new industries a chance to grow strong, and to protect a nation's security. The four most commonly used forms of trade restrictions are tariffs (taxes, surcharges, or duties levied against imported goods), quotas (limitations on the amount of a particular good that can be imported), embargoes (the banning of imports and exports of certain goods), and sanctions (politically motivated embargoes).

3 **Highlight three protectionist tactics that nations use to give their domestic industries a competitive edge.**

From time to time countries give their domestic producers a competitive edge by imposing restrictive import standards, such as requiring special licenses or unusually high product standards, by subsidizing certain domestic producers so they can compete more favorably in the global marketplace, and by dumping or selling large quantities of a product at a lower price than it costs to produce the good or at a lower price than the good is sold for in its home market.

4 **Explain how trading blocs affect trade.**

Trading blocs are regional groupings of countries within which trade barriers have been removed. These alliances ease trade among bloc members and strengthen barriers for nonmembers. Critics of trading blocs fear that as members become more protective of their regions, those not in the bloc could suffer. Proponents see them as a way to help smaller or younger nations compete with producers in more-developed nations. The four most powerful trading blocs today are the Association of Southeast Asian Nations (ASEAN), the Mercosur, the North American Free Trade Agreement (NAFTA), and the European Union (EU).

5 **Highlight the opportunities and challenges of conducting business in other countries.**

Conducting business in other countries can provide such opportunities as increased sales, operational efficiencies, exposure to new technologies, and consumer choices. At the same time, it poses challenges such as the need to learn unique laws, customs, and ethical standards. Furthermore, it exposes companies to the risks of political and economic instabilities, volatile currencies, international trade relationships, and the threat of global terrorism.

6 **List five ways to improve communication in an international business relationship.**

To improve international communication, learn as much as you can about the culture and customs of the people you are working with; keep an open mind and avoid stereotyping; anticipate misunderstandings and guard against them by clarifying your intent; adapt your style to match the style of others; and learn how to show respect in other cultures.

7 **Identify five forms of international business activity.**

Importing and exporting, licensing, franchising, strategic alliances and joint ventures, and foreign direct investment are five of the most common forms of international business activity. Each provides a company with varying degrees of control and entails different levels of risk and financial commitment.

8 **Discuss terrorism's impact on globalization.**

Terrorism could prompt companies to withdraw from the global marketplace and focus more on doing business within their national borders. But the likelihood of moving in that direction is remote. Most multinational organizations have too much at stake to move backward; they see globalization as the key to their future. Global terrorism, however, does pose new challenges to world trade. Tighter security, border crossing delays, cargo restrictions, and higher transportation costs are having an impact on the free flow of goods in the global marketplace. These obstacles are forcing some companies to rethink their inventory and manufacturing strategies.

Behind **the Scenes**

Doing Everybody's Wash—Whirlpool's Global Lesson

David Whitwam's timing couldn't have been worse. Just as the company was planting its feet in international markets, economic turmoil hit Asia and Europe. Wildly fluctuating foreign exchange rates wreaked havoc in Asia, where Whirlpool had participated in several joint ventures. Fortunately, less than 5 percent of Whirlpool's sales came from Asia, so the company was not seriously hurt. Still, ongoing global economic woes contributed to Whirlpool's multimillion-dollar losses overseas.

The global economic crisis forced Whitwam to fine-tune his expansion plans. Whirlpool dropped one joint venture in China (costing the company $350 million) and rearranged others as weak economic conditions and intense competition drove appliance prices down and sapped profits. "The thing we misjudged was how rapidly Chinese manufacturers could improve their quality," notes Whitwam.

In Brazil, where Whirlpool had long been profitable, a currency crisis coupled with inflation worries slowed appliance sales to a trickle. Still, Whitwam remained committed to the market. Anticipating future growth opportunities in this emerging market, Whirlpool invested hundreds of millions of dollars to modernize operations, cut costs, and solidify its position as the country's market leader in refrigerators, room air conditioners, and washers.

David Whitwam's global strategy, however, was not widely copied by rivals. As Whirlpool continued to expand in Europe, Latin America, and Asia, the company's major competitor, Maytag, was selling its European and Australian businesses to refocus on the lucrative North American market. Nevertheless, Whitwam was willing to ride out the storm, even as global economic troubles dragged on.

Whitwam expedited Whirlpool's entry into foreign markets by focusing less on manufacturing its own products overseas and more on developing licensing arrangements and strategic alliances with other companies. For example, Whirlpool formed strategic alliances with Tupperware to work jointly on marketing, branding, and product development in Europe, Africa, and the Middle East.

Whirlpool also kept things simple by developing basic appliance models that used about 70 percent of the same parts. For instance, feature-rich German appliances were combined with efficient, low-cost Italian technologies to produce a "world washer." Then Whirlpool modified the machines for local preferences. Front-loading washing machines were scaled down for European homes, as were refrigerators for India. Despite their widely different exteriors and sizes, the appliances had plenty of common parts and designs.

In less than a decade, Whitwam transformed Whirlpool from essentially a U.S. company into the world's leading manufacturer of major home appliances. With more than a dozen major brands sold in 170 countries, international sales now account for about 45 percent of the company's $11 billion annual revenue. Moreover, the outlook for growth in the global appliance industry looks promising. Still, Whitwam understands that doing business in the global marketplace is fraught with risk; conditions can change at the drop of a baht, ruble, or dollar.[58]

Critical Thinking Questions

1. What did Whirlpool find to be the advantages and disadvantages of doing business around the world?
2. How did global expansion affect Whirlpool's products?
3. Should Whirlpool be concerned about a currency devaluation in a country where it sells few appliances?

LEARN MORE ONLINE

Find out how Whirlpool is faring with its global strategy. Go to Chapter 3 of this text's website at www.prenhall.com/bovee, and click on the Whirlpool hotlink to read the latest news releases about Whirlpool's financial performance, international operations, and plans for expansion. How are Whirlpool's sales doing outside the United States? Where is the company strongest? Where is it struggling? What changes, if any, is the company making to its global strategy? ■

Key Terms

absolute advantage (65)
balance of payments (65)
balance of trade (65)
comparative advantage
    theory (65)
dumping (68)
economies of scale (65)
embargo (67)
euro (72)

exchange rate (72)
exporting (77)
foreign direct investment (FDI) (80)
free trade (68)
importing (77)
joint venture (79)
licensing (78)
multinational corporations
    (MNCs) (80)

protectionism (67)
quotas (67)
strategic alliance (78)
tariffs (67)
trade deficit (65)
trade surplus (65)
trading blocs (70)

Test Your Knowledge

Questions for Review

1. How can a company use a licensing agreement to enter world markets?
2. What two fundamental product strategies do companies choose between when selling their products in the global marketplace?

3. What is the balance of trade, and how is it related to the balance of payments?
4. What is dumping, and how does the United States respond to this practice?
5. What is a floating exchange rate?

Questions for Analysis

6. Why would a company choose to work through intermediaries when selling products in a foreign country?

7. How do companies benefit from forming international joint ventures and strategic alliances?

8. What types of situations might cause the U.S. government to implement protectionist measures?

9. How do tariffs and quotas protect a country's own industries?

10. **Ethical Considerations.** Should the U.S. government more closely regulate the practice of giving trips and other incentives to foreign managers to win their business? Is this bribery?

Questions for Application

11. Suppose you own a small company that manufactures baseball equipment. You are aware that Russia is a large market, and you are considering exporting your products there. What steps should you take? Who might be able to give you assistance?

12. Because your Brazilian restaurant caters to Western businesspeople and tourists, much of the food you buy is imported from the United States. Lately, the value of the real (Brazil's currency) has been falling relative to the dollar. This change makes your food imports much more costly, and it negatively affects your profitability. You have three options; which one will you choose? (a) Raise menu prices across the board. (b) Accept only U.S. dollars from customers. (c) Try to purchase more of your food items locally. Please explain your selection.

13. **Integrated.** Review the theory of supply and demand discussed in Chapter 1. Using this theory, explain how a country's currency is valued and why governments sometimes adjust the values of their currency.

14. **Integrated.** You just received notice that a large shipment of manufacturing supplies you have been waiting for has been held up in customs for two weeks. A local business associate tells you that you are expected to give customs agents some "incentive money" to see that everything clears easily. How will you handle this situation? Evaluate the ethical merits of your decision by answering the questions outlined in Exhibit 2.3.

Practice Your Knowledge

Sharpening Your Communication Skills

Languages never translate on a word-for-word basis. When doing business in the global marketplace, choose words that convey only their most specific denotative meaning. Avoid using slang or idioms (words that can have meanings far different from their individual components when translated literally). For example, if a U.S. executive tells an Egyptian executive that a certain product "doesn't cut the mustard," chances are that communication will fail.

Team up with two other students and list 10 examples of slang (in your own language) that would probably be misinterpreted or misunderstood during a business conversation with someone from another culture. Next to each example, suggest other words you might use to convey the same message. Make sure the alternatives mean exactly the same as the original slang or idiom. Compare your list with those of your classmates.

Building Your Team Skills

In today's interdependent global economy, fluctuations in a country's currency can have a profound effect on the flow of products across borders. The U.S. steel industry, for example, has been feeling intense competition from an influx of Korean, Brazilian, and Russian steel imports. After the currencies of those countries plummeted in value, the price of steel products exported to the United States dropped as well, making U.S. steel much more expensive by comparison.

Fueled by low prices, steel flooded into the United States, hurting sales of U.S. steel. Over the course of several months, the volume of steel imports nearly doubled. Stung, U.S. steelmakers slashed production and laid off more than 10,000 U.S. workers. U.S. trade officials charge that the cheap imported steel is being dumped, and they are considering protectionist measures such as imposing quotas on steel imports.[59]

With your team, brainstorm a list of at least four additional ways the United States might handle this situation. Once you have your list, consider the probable effect of each option on these stakeholders:

- U.S. businesses that buy steel
- U.S. steel manufacturers
- U.S. businesses that export to Korea, Brazil, or Russia
- Employees of U.S. steel manufacturers

On the basis of your analysis and discussion, which option will your team recommend? Select a spokesperson to explain your selection and your team's reasoning to the other teams. Compare your recommendation with those of your classmates.

Expand Your Knowledge

Discovering Career Opportunities

If global business interests you, consider working for a U.S. government agency that supports or regulates international trade. For example, here are the duties performed by an international trade specialist at the International Trade Administration of the U.S. Department of Commerce: "The incumbent will assist senior specialists in coordination and support of government trade programs and events; perform research and analysis of trade data and information on specific topics or issues within a larger project or assignment; and disseminate trade information and materials on government products/services to U.S. businesses and associations. Incumbent will attend meetings and engage in other activities for developmental purposes. As a condition of employment, applicants must be available for reassignment and relocation within the United States."[60]

1. On the basis of this description, what education and skills (personal and professional) would you need to succeed as an international trade specialist? Why? How does this job description fit your qualifications and interests?

2. Given their duties, where would you expect international trade specialists to be situated or transferred? Would you be willing to move to another city or state for this type of position?

3. What sources would you contact to locate trade-related jobs with government agencies such as the International Trade Administration?

Developing Your Research Skills

Companies involved in international trade have to watch the foreign exchange rates of the countries in which they do business. Use your research skills to locate and analyze information about the value of the Japanese yen relative to the U.S. dollar. As you complete this exercise, make a note of the sources and search strategies you used.

1. How many Japanese yen does one U.S. dollar buy right now? Find yesterday's foreign exchange rate for the yen in the *Wall Street Journal* or on the Internet. (Note: One Internet source for foreign exchange rates is www.xrates.com.)

2. Investigate the foreign exchange rate for the yen against the dollar over the past month. Is the dollar growing stronger (buying more yen) or growing weaker (buying fewer yen)?

3. If you were a U.S. exporter selling to Japan, how would a stronger dollar be likely to affect demand for your products? How would a weaker dollar be likely to affect demand?

SEE IT ON THE WEB

For live links to the websites that follow, go to this text's website at www.prenhall.com/bovee. When you log on, select Chapter 3, then select "Featured Websites," click on the URL of the website you wish to visit, review the website, and answer the following questions:

1. What is the purpose of this website?

2. What kinds of information does this website contain? Please be specific.

3. How is the information provided at this website useful for businesspeople? Consumers?

4. How did you expand your knowledge of conducting business in the global environment by reviewing the material at this website? What new things did you learn about this topic?

Navigating Global Business Differences

In today's global marketplace, knowing as much as possible about your international customers' business practices and customs could give you a strategic advantage. To help you successfully conduct business around the globe, navigate the resources at the U.S. Government Export Portal. Start at www.export.gov, then click on "Market Research," then "Country Information—Quick Reference (TIC)." Click anywhere on the world map to learn more about each country. www.export.gov

Going Global

Have you ever thought about getting into the world of exporting? Where would you go for information and help? Many small and large companies have gotten valuable export assistance from online material such as the *Basic Guide to Exporting*, offered by the U.S. Department of Commerce. Visit www.export.gov, click on "The Export Basics," then click on "Basic Guide to Exporting" for a wealth of information about export procedures; foreign markets, industries, companies, and products; export financing; unfair trade practices; trade statistics; and more. www.export.gov

Banking on the World Bank

The World Bank plays an important role in today's fast-changing, closely meshed global economy. Do you know what this organization of five closely associated institutions does? Do you know who runs the bank, where the bank gets its money, and where the money goes? Learn how this organization's programs and financial assistance help poorer nations as well as affluent ones. Log on to the World Bank website and find out why global development is everyone's challenge. www.worldbank.org

Companion Website

Learning Interactively

Go to the Companion Website at www.prenhall.com/bovee. For Chapter 3, take advantage of the interactive "Study Guide" to test your knowledge of the chapter. Get instant feedback on whether you need additional studying.

Also, visit this site's "Study Hall," where you'll find an abundance of valuable resources that will help you succeed in this course.

Video **Case**

Entering the Global Marketplace: Lands' End and Yahoo!

LEARNING OBJECTIVES

The purpose of this video is to help you:

1. Understand the different reasons that businesses undertake international expansion.
2. Identify the financial and marketing issues of selling goods and services internationally.
3. Recognize the influence of culture on business decisions in an international firm.

SYNOPSIS

Yahoo! is an Internet company headquartered in Santa Clara, California, with offices around the world. The company's service offerings have expanded from a search engine and web directory to a wide array of content and e-commerce offerings. Yahoo! now counts more than 200 million users worldwide. Lands' End began in 1963 by selling sailing equipment by catalog. Today the publicly owned firm is one of the largest apparel brands in the United States, with a variety of catalogs and a high-volume e-commerce site. This video segment shows how these two very different companies approached the same goal: expansion into international business. You will see how each copes with cultural, financial, monetary, and marketing differences as well as differences in language and method of payment. See whether you can identify those areas in which each firm chose to adapt to the needs and expectations of the international marketplace, and where it maintained its original product or policy.

Discussion Questions

1. *For analysis:* Compare the different reasons why Lands' End and Yahoo! decided to expand internationally.
2. *For analysis:* How did Lands' End succeed in establishing itself in the United Kingdom and Japan?
3. *For application:* In addition to hiring local employees in countries such as France and China, how could Yahoo! help educate U.S. employees about the nuances of doing business in these countries?
4. *For application:* How should Lands' End alter its online marketing efforts in countries that have different expectations of personal modesty?
5. *For debate:* Both Yahoo! and Lands' End expect their employees to behave in an ethical manner in all business dealings. However, experienced managers recognize that definitions of ethical behavior can vary from country to country. Should both companies demand a consistent ethical code in all cases across all regions of the world? Why or why not?

ONLINE EXPLORATION

Visit Yahoo!'s website (www.yahoo.com) and explore some of the features and functions that appeal to you. Then select one of the international sites listed at the bottom of the Yahoo! homepage and compare it to the U.S. site. Identify the changes that have been made to suit the particular country's language and customs, and observe what elements of the site have *not* been changed. What do you think is the motivation behind the design and content choices Yahoo! made in the overseas site? Do you think it is successful in its market?

E-Business in Action

THE BIGGEST AUDIENCE IN THE WHOLE WIDE WORLD WIDE WEB

As signs of progress go, it's not one that will make anybody happy, but it's a sign of progress nonetheless: The Peoples' Republic of China is now the world's number two receiver of junk e-mail, second only to the United States. The dubious distinction goes hand in hand with China's rapid rise as an online market. More than 80 million Chinese residents were online in 2004, and that number is expected to reach 150 or 200 million by 2006. At that point, China will have more Internet users than the United States (and, presumably, more spam).

The game company Kingsoft is a good example of how rapidly Chinese consumers are embracing new online offerings. After attempting to sell software to consumers for years, the company gave up and shifted to the Internet, starting with an action game called Sword Online. Within six months, Kingsoft had signed up 1.7 million customers and has plans to keep growing into a technology leader. Forecasters expect the online game market in China to surpass $800 million by 2007.

Internet + Mobile Phones = Profits

The marriage of the Internet and wireless technology promises to be another hot business across China. The country already has twice as many mobile phone subscribers as the United States, and online portals now deliver a variety of information and entertainment services to phone users—news, games, dating services, even voice greeting cards featuring NBA star Yao Ming. The wireless multimedia market alone jumped from $200 million in 2001 to $3 billion in 2004. Kingsoft is among the companies developing phone games that combine movies, voice, and data.

Multimedia phone services proved to be an enormous blessing for China's leading web portals, which include Sina, Sohu, and NetEase. (A web portal is a multifaceted website such as www.yahoo.com, which provides a variety of information and entertainment offerings, along with site directories, search engines, and other services.) Because advertising opportunities in China were so minuscule to begin with, Sina and the other Chinese portals avoided a misstep that hobbled many U.S. e-commerce companies during the early days of the Internet boom—trying to support themselves by selling online advertising. That business model never really took off in the United States and, in fact, proved to be the financial undoing of many promising young companies that invested millions of dollars in the untested hope that ad dollars would show up sooner or later. In contrast, the Chinese portals are already profitable, thanks to wireless content services.

Rapid Evolution

This sizzling growth is a far cry from just a few years ago, when the Chinese government generally viewed e-commerce as a threat to its tight control over the economy and consumer behavior. Now, the country's leadership is intent on making China a global technology leader, showing strengths in both networking and wireless technologies. In rapid succession, the country is evolving from a low-cost manufacturer to a high-quality manufacturer and is on its way to being a technical innovator as well. As Robert Mao, CEO of greater China operations for networking giant Nortel, put it, China is now "part of the leading edge."

This isn't to say that growth is easy, by any means. Peggy Lu, head of DangDang.com, which roughly models itself after Amazon.com, faced the challenge of selling products online without a financial feature that marketers in many countries take for granted—credit cards (most Chinese citizens don't have them yet). To get around this hurdle, Lu's company accepts money orders and lets customers pay in cash when products are delivered.

Internet entrepreneurs such as Lu are becoming role models for a new generation who see that they can get ahead on their own initiative, without relying on official connections. In an economy under tight state control, "people used to think you could only get rich with stocks or smuggling," says one Chinese CEO. "Now, with the Internet, they know they can get rich using their intelligence."

Freedom to Profit, Not Freedom of the Press

Does all this free-market fervor mean that China's communist government is relaxing its control over the country's citizens? Hardly. Site operators are forbidden to publish information about Falun Gong, an outlawed religious group, or to raise the call for political reform, for instance. Moreover, the government has been known to demand free advertising space on portal sites.

Web logs, or blogs, the newest online rage in the United States, also come under close scrutiny in China. In 2004, for instance, the government shut down two blogs for carrying content it deemed objectionable—rumored to be discussions relating to the 1989 crackdown on a student protest in Beijing's Tiananmen Square. A year earlier, officials blocked access to Blogspot, a popular site in the United States that helps people build their own blogs.

In addition, Internet cafés, popular with students and travelers all over the world, can also prompt government crackdowns. Officials recently banned the establishment of any new Internet cafés close to primary or middle schools or within residential buildings, out of fear that illegal online content might corrupt young minds.

Building a Bubble?

In spite of the technical and political challenges, the World Wide Web is in China to stay. And the Internet economy may have taken a while to catch a spark in China, but it's been on fire ever since. In fact, market watchers liken the frantic growth to the dot-com boom in the United States in the late 1990s. Stock prices for China's leading Internet companies are growing as fast as their markets, leading some to worry that the bubble will soon burst, as the dot-coms did in the United States a few years ago. However, executives such as NetEase's Ted Sun insist things are different in China. Not only are the companies already making money, but they tend not to be saddled by much debt and

they run their operations in a much more frugal manner than their U.S. counterparts did.

Speaking of U.S. Internet firms, where do such giants as Yahoo! and AOL show up in the list of China's most popular online sites? Not much more than a blip on the radar screen, actually. Yahoo! China ranks a distant fourth in popularity, behind Sina, Sohu, and NetEase. As one investor put it, "Everybody thought AOL was going to take over the world. They didn't." Experts and users both say that foreign-owned sites don't yet seem to have a good feel for the Chinese market. With the world's largest Internet population in their sights, though, you can bet that the world's leading Internet companies aren't about to ignore China's vast online market.

Questions for Critical Thinking

1. What advantages do U.S. e-commerce companies have over their Chinese counterparts? What disadvantages?
2. Why is a country's infrastructure an important factor in e-commerce development and success?
3. How might government control of information affect the growth of e-commerce in China?

BUSINESS PlanPro Exercises

Conducting Business in the Global Economy

Review Appendix D, "Your Business Plan" (on pages 416–417), to learn how to use Business PlanPro Software so you can complete these exercises.

THINK LIKE A PRO

Objective: By completing these exercises you will become acquainted with the sections of a business plan that address forms of competition, company and product/service descriptions, and the economic outlook for the related industry. You will use the sample business plan for Adventure Excursions Unlimited (listed as Travel Agency–Adventure Sports in the Sample Plan Browser) in this exercise. Use the table of contents to move from section to section as you explore the plan and answer these questions.

1. What products and services does Adventure Excursions provide? Will the company compete on the basis of

price, speed, quality, service, or innovation to gain a competitive advantage?
2. What is the economic outlook for the travel industry? What competition does Adventure Excursions face?
3. How does Adventure Excursions plan to use the Internet?

CREATE YOUR OWN BUSINESS PLAN

Now start a new plan for your own business. Answering the following questions will help you think about different aspects of your business plan. Enter your answers in the appropriate sections of the new business plan.

What information should you include about your product or service when creating a business plan? Describe in detail the product or service your company will provide. Indicate whether you will compete on price, speed, quality, service, or innovation. What are some of the things you should discuss about your competition in a business plan? In what industry will you compete? What is the economic outlook for that industry? What kinds of competition do you expect to face?

Part 2
Starting and Organizing a Business

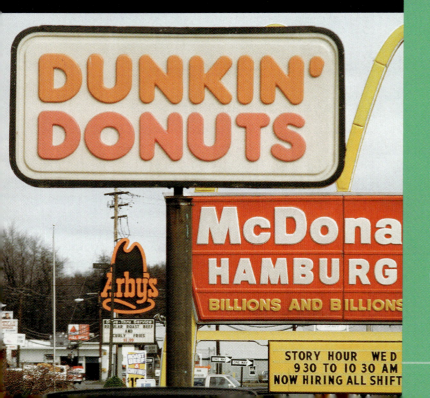

Chapter 4
Selecting the Optimum Form of Business Ownership and Exploring Business Combinations

LEARNING OBJECTIVES
After studying this chapter, you will be able to

1 List five advantages and four disadvantages of sole proprietorships

2 List five advantages and two disadvantages of partnerships

3 Explain the differences between common and preferred stock from a shareholder's perspective

4 Highlight the advantages and disadvantages of public stock ownership

5 Cite four advantages and three disadvantages of corporations

6 Delineate the three groups that govern a corporation and describe the role of each

7 Identify six main synergies companies hope to achieve by combining their operations

Behind the Scenes

Growing Pains at Kinko's

www.kinkos.com

Paul Orfalea knew he would run a big company someday. He just never envisioned Kinko's as that dream. At 22, Orfalea borrowed enough money to open a copying service near the University of California, Santa Barbara. The store was so small that he had to wheel the single copier onto the sidewalk to make room for customers. Nevertheless, it met the needs of local college students.

By 1995 (some 25 years later), Kinko's—named after Orfalea's reddish, curly hair—had grown into a chain of 815 stores operating in five countries. But Kinko's wasn't managed as a single entity. Instead, the business consisted of 130 separate partnerships, each operating groups of stores. Even though Orfalea retained a majority interest in each partnership, the partners were free to operate their stores as they saw fit. As a result, not all Kinko's were the same. And that was a problem. Some reinvested their earnings in high-tech equipment while others cashed in their profits. This meant that traveling customers would find color copiers and high-speed Internet access at spruced-up outlets in one city and dilapidated storefronts with little more than black-and-white copy machines in another.

Kinko's ad hoc management structure was hobbling its growth. Orfalea knew that to succeed in a high-tech marketplace, all Kinko's stores would have to look alike and offer comparable services. Moreover, with more and

Kinko's, once known simply as the leading chain of printing and copy shops, has recast itself for the work-obsessed digital age.

more people working at home, in cars, in airports, or in other remote locations, the stores would have to invest in expensive equipment such as digital printers, high-speed copiers, fast Internet connections, and even videoconferencing equipment to service the growing needs of these virtual workers. Such services, of course, would require lots of money and a shift in focus for many Kinko's partners.

Seeking financial acumen and managerial expertise, Orfalea selected private investors Clayton, Dublier & Rice (CD&R) in 1997 to help turn things around. Orfalea sold one-third of his partnership interests to the leveraged-buyout firm for $220 million. Meanwhile, CD&R organized a massive "roll-up" whereby individual partnerships swapped their interests for shares of stock in the new private Kinko's corporation. This structure allowed CD&R to centralize all management functions.

Now CD&R's challenge was to harness, not destroy, Kinko's entrepreneurial culture—the engine of its success. But how? What programs could management implement to keep the new private shareholders motivated? What new services could they offer to attract the growing customer base of business travelers and home-office workers? How could they convince 23,000 co-workers at 900 Kinko's branches worldwide that changing to a corporate structure would provide the operating efficiencies and funds the shops would need to survive and thrive?[1] ■

CHOOSING A FORM OF BUSINESS OWNERSHIP

As Paul Orfalea knows, one of the most fundamental decisions you must make when starting a business is selecting a form of business ownership. This decision can be complex and have far-reaching consequences for owners, employees, and customers. Picking the right ownership structure involves knowing your long-term goals and how you plan to achieve them. Your choice also depends on your desire for ownership and your tolerance for risk. Furthermore, as your business grows, chances are you may change the original form you selected, as Orfalea did.

The three most common forms of business ownership are sole proprietorship, partnership, and corporation. Each form has its own characteristic internal structure, legal status, size, and fields to which it is best suited. Each has key advantages and disadvantages for the owners. Exhibit 4.1 contrasts the characteristics of the three forms of business ownership.

Exhibit 4.1 **Characteristics of the Forms of Business Ownership**

The "best" form of ownership depends on the objectives of the people involved in the business.

STRUCTURE	OWNERSHIP RULES AND CONTROL	TAX CONSIDERATIONS	LIABILITY EXPOSURE	EASE OF ESTABLISHMENT AND TERMINATION
Sole proprietorship	One owner has complete control.	Profits and losses flow directly to the owners and are taxed at individual rates.	Owner has unlimited personal liability for business debts.	Easy to set up but leaves owner's personal finances at risk. Owner must generally sell the business to get his or her investment out.
General partnership	Two or more owners; each partner is entitled to equal control unless agreement specifies otherwise.	Profits and losses flow directly to the partners and are taxed at individual rates. Partners share income and losses equally unless the partnership agreement specifies otherwise.	Personal assets of any operating partner are at risk from business creditors.	Easy to set up. Partnership agreement recommended but not required. Partners must generally sell their share in the business to recoup their investment.
Limited partnership	Two or more owners; the general partner controls the business; limited partners don't participate in the management.	Same as for general partnership.	Limited partners are liable only for the amount of their investment.	Same as for general partnership.
Corporation	Unlimited number of shareholders; no limits on stock classes or voting arrangements. Ownership and management of the business are separate. Shareholders in public corporations are not involved in daily management decisions; in private or closely held corporations, owners are more likely to participate in managing the business.	Profits and losses are taxed at corporate rates. Profits are taxed again at individual rates when they are distributed to the investors as dividends.	Investor's liability is limited to the amount of his or her investment.	Expense and complexity of incorporation vary from state to state; can be costly from a tax perspective. In a public corporation, shareholders may trade their shares on the open market; in a private corporation shareholders must find a buyer for their shares to recoup their investment.

Sole Proprietorships

A **sole proprietorship** is a business owned by one person (although it may have many employees), and it is the easiest and least expensive form of business to start. Many farms, retail establishments, and small service businesses are sole proprietorships, as are many home-based businesses (such as caterers, consultants, and computer programmers). Chances are, many of the local businesses you frequent around your college campus are sole proprietorships.

Advantages of Sole Proprietorships

A sole proprietorship has many advantages, starting with ease of establishment. All you have to do to launch a sole proprietorship is obtain necessary licenses, start a checking account for the business, and open your doors. Another advantage is the satisfaction of working for yourself. As a sole proprietor, you can make your own decisions, such as which hours to work (beware the old joke that working for yourself means you get to choose which 80 hours you work every week), whom to hire, what prices to charge, whether to expand, and whether to shut down. You also get to keep all the after-tax profits, and, depending on your filing status and taxable income, you may be obligated to pay less as a sole proprietor, compared to what you would pay as a corporation (although you are also obligated to pay self-employment tax as a sole proprietor).

As a sole proprietor, you also have the advantage of privacy; you do not have to reveal your performance or plans to anyone. Although you may need to provide financial information to a banker if you need a loan, and you must provide certain financial information when you file tax returns, you do not have to prepare any reports for outsiders as you would if the company were a public corporation.

Disadvantages of Sole Proprietorships

One major drawback of a sole proprietorship is the proprietor's **unlimited liability**. From a legal standpoint, the owner and the business are one and the same. Any legal damages or debts incurred by the business are the owner's responsibility. As a sole proprietor, you might have to sell personal assets, such as your home, to satisfy a business debt. And if someone sues you over a business matter, you might lose everything you own if you do not have the proper types and amount of business insurance.

In some cases, the sole proprietor's independence can also be a drawback because it means that the business depends on the talents and managerial skills of one person. If problems crop up, the sole proprietor may not recognize them or may be too proud to seek help, especially given the high cost of hiring experienced managers and professional consultants. Other disadvantages include the difficulty of a single-person operation obtaining large sums of capital and the limited life of a sole proprietorship. Although some sole proprietors pass their business on to their heirs as part of their estate, the owner's death may mean the demise of the business. And even if the business does transfer to an heir, the founder's unique skills may have been crucial to the successful operation of the business.

Partnerships

If starting a business on your own seems a little intimidating, you might decide to share the risks and rewards of going into business with a partner. In that case, you would form a **partnership**—a legal association of two or more people as co-owners of a business for profit. You and your partners would share the profits and losses of the business and perhaps the management responsibilities. Your partnership might remain a small, two-person operation or it might have multiple partners, like Kinko's did.

Partnerships are of two basic types. In a **general partnership**, all partners are considered equal by law, and all are liable for the business's debts. For instance, when accounting firm Laventhol and Horwath plunged into bankruptcy, the partners had to dig into their own pockets to satisfy creditors.[2] To guard against personal liability exposure, some organizations choose to form a **limited partnership**. Under this type of

sole proprietorship
Business owned by a single individual

unlimited liability
Legal condition under which any damages or debts attributable to the business can also be attached to the owner because the two have no separate legal existence

partnership
Unincorporated business owned and operated by two or more persons under a voluntary legal association

general partnership
Partnership in which all partners have the right to participate as co-owners and are individually liable for the business's debts

limited partnership
Partnership composed of one or more general partners and one or more partners whose liability is usually limited to the amount of their capital investment

Technologies That Are Revolutionizing Business

Groupware
Groupware is an umbrella term for systems that let people communicate, share files, present materials, and work on documents simultaneously.

How it's changing business
Groupware is changing the way employees interact with one another—and even the way businesses work together. In fact, groupware is changing the way many companies are structured. *Shared workspaces* are "virtual offices" that give everyone on a team access to the same set of resources and information: databases, calendars, project plans, archived instant messages and e-mails, reference materials, and team documents. These workspaces (which are typically accessible through a web browser) let you and your team organize your work files into a collection of electronic folders, making it easy for geographically dispersed team members to access shared files anytime, anywhere. Employees no longer need to be in the same office or even in the same time zone. They don't even need to be employees. Groupware makes it easy for companies to pull together partners and temporary contractors on a project-by-project basis.

Groupware is often integrated with web-based meeting systems that combine instant messaging, shared workspaces, videoconferencing, and other tools such as *virtual whiteboards* that let teams collaborate in real time.

Where you can learn more
Log on to www.zdnet.com, click on "Tech Update," then "Software Infrastructure," then "Groupware."

partnership one or more persons act as *general partners* who run the business, while the remaining partners are passive investors (that is, they are not involved in managing the business). These partners are called *limited partners* because their liability (the amount of money they can lose) is limited to the amount of their capital contribution. Many states now recognize *limited liability partnerships* (LLPs) in which all partners in the business are limited partners and have only limited liability for the debts and obligations of the partnership. The limited liability partnership was invented to protect members of partnerships from being wiped out by claims against their firms. Most states restrict LLPs to certain types of professionals such as attorneys, physicians, dentists, and accountants.[3] Of the three forms of business ownership, partnerships are the least common (see Exhibit 4.2).

Advantages of Partnerships
Proprietorships and partnerships have some of the same advantages. Like proprietorships, partnerships are easy to form. Partnerships also provide the same potential tax advantages as proprietorships.

However, in a couple of respects, partnerships are superior to sole proprietorships, largely because there's strength in numbers. When you have several people putting up their money, you can start a more ambitious enterprise. In addition, the diversity of skills that good partners bring to an organization leads to innovation in products, services, and processes, which improves your chances of success.[4] The partnership form of ownership also broadens the pool of capital available to the business. Not only do the partners' personal assets support a larger borrowing capacity but the ability to obtain

Exhibit 4.2

Popular Forms of Business Ownership

The most popular form of business ownership is sole proprietorship, followed by corporations, then partnerships.

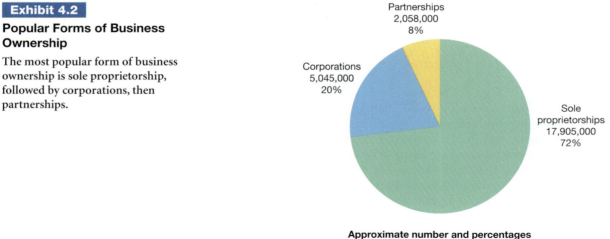

Approximate number and percentages of existing firms in the United States

financing increases because general partners are legally responsible for paying off the debts of the group. Finally, by forming a partnership you increase the chances that the organization will endure, because new partners can be drawn into the business to replace those who die or retire. For example, even though the original partners of the accounting firm KPMG Peat Marwick (founded in 1897) died many years ago, the company continues.

Disadvantages of Partnerships

Except in limited liability partnerships, at least one member of every partnership must be a general partner. All general partners have unlimited liability. Thus, if one of the firm's partners makes a serious business or professional mistake and is sued by a disgruntled client, all general partners are financially accountable. At the same time, general partners are responsible for any debts incurred by the partnership.

Another disadvantage of partnerships is the potential for interpersonal problems. Difficulties often arise because each partner wants to be responsible for managing the organization. Electing a managing partner to lead the organization may diminish the conflicts, but disagreements are still likely to arise. Moreover, the partnership may have to face the question of what to do with unproductive partners. And if a partner wants to leave the firm, conflicts can arise over claims on the firm's profits and on capital the partner invested. Provisions for handling the departure and addition of partners are usually covered in the partnership agreement.

Partnership Agreement

A *partnership agreement* is a written document that states all the terms of operating the partnership by spelling out the partners' rights and responsibilities. Although the law does not require a written partnership agreement, it is wise to work with a lawyer to develop one. One of the most important features of such an agreement is to address sources of conflict that could result in battles between partners. The agreement spells out such details as the division of profits, decision-making authority, expected contributions, and dispute resolution. Moreover, a key element of this document is the buy/sell agreement, which defines the steps a partner must take to sell his or her partnership interest or what will happen if one of the partners dies.

Corporations

A **corporation** is a legal entity, distinct from any individual persons, with the power to own property and conduct business. Regardless of how many owners a corporation has (some have thousands of owners), the law generally treats the corporation the same way it treats an individual person. The modern corporation evolved in the 19th century when large sums of capital were needed to build railroads, steel mills, and manufacturing plants. Such endeavors required so much money that no single individual or group of partners could hope to raise it all. The solution was to sell *shares* in the business to numerous investors, who would get a cut of the profits in exchange for their money. These investors got a chance to vote on certain issues that might affect the value of their investment, but they were not involved in managing day-to-day operations. The investors were protected from the risks associated with such large undertakings by having their liability limited to the amount of their investment.

It was a good solution, and the corporation quickly became a vital force in the nation's economy. As rules and regulations developed to define what corporations could and could not do, corporations acquired the legal attributes of people. Like you, a corporation can receive, own, and transfer property; make contracts; sue; and be sued. Unlike the case with sole proprietorships and partnerships, a corporation's legal status and obligations exist independently of its owners.

corporation
Legally chartered enterprise having most of the legal rights of a person, including the right to conduct business, to own and sell property, to borrow money, and to sue or be sued; owners of the corporation enjoy limited liability

Volkswagen executives address shareholders at the company's annual meeting.

shareholders
Owners of a corporation

stock certificate
Document that proves stock ownership

common stock
Shares whose owners have voting rights and have the last claim on distributed profits and assets

dividends
Distributions of corporate assets to shareholders in the form of cash or other assets

preferred stock
Shares that give their owners first claim on a company's dividends and assets after paying all debts

private corporation
Company owned by private individuals or companies

public corporation
Corporation that actively sells stock on the open market

Business BUZZ

Painting the tape:
Unscrupulous attempts to generate interest in a stock, such as by splitting a large purchase into multiple small purchases to create the illusion that many investors are interested in the stock

Ownership

The corporation is owned by its **shareholders**, who are issued shares of stock in return for their investments. These shares are represented by a **stock certificate**, and they may be bequeathed or sold to someone else. As a result, the company's ownership may change drastically over time while the company and its management remain intact (as long as the company is economically sound). The corporation's unlimited life span, combined with its ability to raise capital, gives it the potential for significant growth.

Common Stock   Most stock issued by corporations is **common stock**. Owners of common stock have voting rights and get one vote for each share of stock they own. They can elect the company's board of directors in addition to voting on major policies that will affect ownership—such as mergers and acquisitions. Besides conferring voting privileges, common stock frequently pays **dividends**, payments to shareholders from the company's profits. Dividends can be paid in cash or stock (called *stock dividends*). They are declared by the board of directors but their payment is not mandatory. For example, some companies, especially young or rapidly growing ones, pay no dividends. Instead, they reinvest their profits in new product research and development, equipment, buildings, and other assets so they can grow and earn future profits.

In addition to dividends, common shareholders can earn a return on their investment. If shareholders sell their stock in good times for more than they paid for it, they stand to pocket a handsome gain. But because the value or price of a company's common stock is subject to many economic variables besides the company's own performance, common-stock investments are risky and shareholders may not get any profit at all.

Preferred Stock   In contrast to common stock, **preferred stock** does not usually carry voting rights. It does, however, give preferred shareholders the right of first claim on the corporation's assets (in the form of dividends) after all the company's debts have been paid. This right is especially important if the company ever goes out of business. Moreover, preferred shareholders get their dividends before common shareholders do. The amount of preferred dividend is usually set (or fixed) at the time the preferred stock is issued and can provide investors with a source of steady income. Like common stock, however, dividends on preferred stock may be omitted in times of financial hardship. Still, most preferred stock is *cumulative preferred stock*, which means that any unpaid dividends must be paid before dividends are paid to common shareholders.

Public Versus Private Ownership   The ownership of corporations can be arranged in several different ways, which occasionally leads to some confusion about terminology. The stock of a **private corporation** such as Kinko's is held by only a few individuals or companies and is not publicly traded. By withholding their stock from public sale, the owners retain complete control over their operations and ownership. Such famous companies as Hallmark and Hyatt Hotels have opted to remain private corporations (also referred to as *closed corporations* or *closely held companies*). These companies finance their operating costs and growth from either company earnings or other sources, such as bank loans. Doctors, lawyers, and some other professionals often join forces in a special type of private corporation called a *professional corporation*. As with other private corporations, shares in these professional corporations are not available to the public.

In contrast, the stock of a **public corporation** is held by and available for sale to the general public (including not only individual investors but also mutual funds, nonprofit organizations, and other companies); thus, the company is said to be *publicly held* or *publicly traded*. Whenever you hear discussions about "corporations," people are nearly always talking about public corporations. These are the stocks you see listed in the newspaper stock tables and on various websites that offer investing information (you'll learn about these in Chapter 14).

As you'll read in Chapter 5, the primary reason for "going public" is to help finance the enterprise. In addition to providing a ready supply of capital, public ownership has other advantages and disadvantages. Among the advantages are increased liquidity, enhanced visibility, and the establishment of an independent market value for the company. Moreover, having a publicly traded stock gives companies flexibility to use such stock to acquire other firms. This was one of the primary reasons UPS decided to sell 10 percent of its stock to the public in 1999, after nearly a century of remaining a privately held organization.[5] Nevertheless, selling stock to the public also has distinct disadvantages: (1) The cost of going public is high (ranging from $50,000 to $500,000), (2) the filing requirements with the SEC (Securities and Exchange Commission) are burdensome, (3) ownership control is reduced, (4) management must be ready to handle the administrative and legal demands of heightened public exposure, and (5) the value of the company's stock becomes subject to external forces beyond the company's control.

Advantages of Corporations

No other form of business ownership can match the success of the corporation in bringing together money, resources, and talent; in accumulating assets; and in creating wealth. As it grows, a corporation gains from a diverse labor pool, greater financing options, and expanded research-and-development capabilities. The corporation has certain inherent qualities that make it the best vehicle for reaching those objectives. One such quality is limited liability. Although a corporate entity can assume tremendous liabilities, it is the corporation that is liable and not the private shareholders. Take Johannes Schwartlander, who ran his San Francisco marble and granite business as a sole proprietorship for seven years. When the company began to grow, Schwartlander decided to incorporate to protect himself. "When we had so many employees and started installing marble panels 10 stories up, I realized that if five years later something fell down, I would be responsible," he says.[6] Incorporation also protects him from personal liability should his business go bankrupt.

In addition to limited liability, corporations that sell stock to the general public have the advantage of **liquidity**, which means that investors can easily convert their stock into cash by selling it on the open market. This option makes buying stock in a corporation attractive to many investors. In contrast, liquidating the assets of a sole proprietorship or a partnership can be difficult. Moreover, shareholders of public corporations can easily transfer their ownership by selling their shares to someone else. Thus, corporations tend to be in a better position than proprietorships and partnerships to make long-term plans, with their unlimited life span and funding available through the sale of stock. As they grow, corporations can benefit from the diverse talents and experience of a large pool of employees and managers. Moreover, large corporations are often able to finance projects internally.

Keep in mind that a company need not be large to incorporate. Most corporations, like most businesses, are relatively small, and most small corporations are privately held. The big ones, however, are *really* big. The 500 largest corporations in the United States, as listed by *Fortune* magazine, have combined sales of over $7.4 trillion.[7] Wal-Mart, the largest U.S. company, employs more than 1.2 million people, which is greater than the population of Detroit, Michigan.[8]

Disadvantages of Corporations

Corporations are not without some disadvantages. The paperwork and costs associated with incorporation can be burdensome, particularly if you plan to sell stock. The complexity varies from state to state, but regardless of where you live, it is wise to consult an attorney and an accountant before incorporating. In addition, corporations are taxed twice. They must pay federal and state corporate income tax on the company's profits, and individual shareholders must pay income taxes on their share of the company's profits received as dividends.

Avis has never paid cash dividends to shareholders. The company believes that shareholders are best served by reinvesting profits back into the company to foster long-term growth.

liquidity
The level of ease with which an asset can be converted to cash

Hyatt's owners, the Pritzker family, have opted to retain control of their enterprise because they appreciate the long-term value of doing so. That status also has a profound effect on the way Hyatt runs its 212 hotels and resorts worldwide. Public companies, which have an eye trained on the stock price, tend to overlook the long-term effects of decisions in favor of short-term gains. But Hyatt general managers have the freedom from concern about quarterly earning reports and stock prices. This gives them a certain entrepreneurial attitude that other hotel managers might not enjoy.

S corporation
Corporation with no more than 75 shareholders that may be taxed as a partnership; also known as a subchapter S corporation

limited liability companies (LLCs)
Organizations that combine the benefits of S corporations and limited partnerships without the drawbacks of either

subsidiary corporations
Corporations whose stock is owned entirely or almost entirely by another corporation

parent company
Company that owns most, if not all, of another company's stock and that takes an active part in managing that other company

holding company
Company that owns most, if not all, of another company's stock but does not actively participate in the management of that other company

Another drawback pertains to publicly owned corporations. As mentioned earlier, such corporations are required by the government to publish information about their finances and operations. Disclosing financial information increases the company's vulnerability to competitors and to those who might want to take over control of the company against the wishes of the existing management. Entrepreneurs who've spent years building companies can even be kicked out of the company if enough other shareholders think it's time for a leadership change. Disclosure also increases the pressure on corporate managers to achieve short-term growth and earnings targets in order to satisfy shareholders and to attract potential investors. Some cite such earnings pressure as the driving force behind the aggressive accounting practices recently adopted by some corporations, as Chapter 13 discusses.

Special Types of Corporations

Certain types of corporations enjoy special privileges provided they adhere to strict guidelines and rules. One special type of corporation is known as the **S corporation** (or subchapter S corporation). An S corporation distinction is made only for federal income tax purposes; otherwise, in terms of legal characteristics, it is no different from any other corporation. Basically, the owners receive the tax advantages of a partnership while they raise money through the sale of stock. In addition, income and tax deductions from the business flow directly to the owners, who are taxed at individual income tax rates, just as they are in a partnership. Corporations seeking "S" status must meet certain criteria: (1) They must have no more than 75 investors, none of whom may be nonresident aliens; (2) they must be a domestic (U.S.) corporation; and (3) they can issue only one class of common stock, which means that all stock must share the same dividend and liquidation rights (but may have different voting rights).[9]

Limited liability companies (LLCs) are flexible business entities that combine the tax advantages of a partnership with the personal liability protection of a corporation. Furthermore, LLCs are not restricted in the number of shareholders they can have, and members' participation in management is not restricted as it is in limited partnerships. Members of an LLC normally adopt an operating agreement (similar to a partnership agreement) to govern the entity's operation and management. These agreements generally are flexible and permit owners to structure the allocation of income and losses any way they desire, as long as certain tax rules are followed. In addition, the agreements can be designed to meet the special needs of owners, such as special voting rights, management controls, and buyout options. The only limit to what can be done is the owners' imagination.[10] The advantages of LLCs over other forms have made them quite popular in recent years. In New Hampshire, for instance, new LLCs are forming at four times the rate of regular corporations.[11] Although LLCs are favored by many small companies, they are by no means limited to small firms. Some fair-sized and well-known firms have gone the LLC route, including BMW of North America, Segway (makers of the high-tech Segway Human Transporter), Freightliner (trucks, fire engines, and other vehicles), and CMP Media (a leading publisher of professional journals and websites).

Some corporations are not independent entities; that is, they are owned by a single entity. **Subsidiary corporations**, for instance, are partially or wholly owned by another corporation known as a **parent company**, which supervises the operations of the subsidiary. A **holding company** is a special type of parent company that owns other companies for investment reasons and usually exercises little operating control over those subsidiaries.

To further complicate matters, corporations can also be classified according to where they do business. An *alien corporation* operates in the United States but is incorporated in another country. A *foreign corporation*, sometimes called an *out-of-state*

Exhibit 4.3 **Corporate Governance**

In theory the shareholders of a corporation own the business, but in practice they elect others to run it.

corporation, is incorporated in one state (frequently the state of Delaware, where incorporation laws are lenient) but does business in several other states where it is registered. And a *domestic corporation* does business only in the state where it is chartered (incorporated).

Corporate Governance

Although a corporation's common shareholders own the business, they are rarely involved in managing it, particularly if the corporation is publicly traded. Instead, the common shareholders elect a board of directors to represent them, and the directors, in turn, select the corporation's top officers, who actually run the company (see Exhibit 4.3). *Corporate governance* has come under close scrutiny in recent years, with critics and regulators claiming that a number of corporate officials in companies such as Enron and WorldCom have failed to uphold their obligations to shareholders.

The center of power in a corporation often lies with the **chief executive officer (CEO)**. Together with the chief financial officer (CFO) and the chief operating officer (COO), the CEO is responsible for establishing company policies, managing corporate direction, and making the big decisions that will affect the company's growth and competitive position, as Chapter 6 discusses in detail. Keep in mind that the chief executive officer may also be the chairman of the board, the president of the corporation, or both. Moreover, because corporate ownership and management are separate, the owners may get rid of the managers (in theory, at least) if the owners vote to do so.

chief executive officer (CEO)
Person appointed by a corporation's board of directors to carry out the board's policies and supervise the activities of the corporation

Shareholders Shareholders of a corporation can be individuals, other companies, nonprofit organizations, pension funds, and mutual funds. All shareholders who own voting shares are invited to an annual meeting to choose directors, select an independent accountant to audit the company's financial statements, and attend to other business. Those who cannot attend the annual meeting in person vote by **proxy**, signing and returning a slip of paper that authorizes management to vote on their behalf. Because shareholders elect the directors, in theory they are the ultimate governing body of the corporation. In practice, however, most individual shareholders in large corporations—where the shareholders may number in the millions—usually accept the recommendations of management.

proxy
Document authorizing another person to vote on behalf of a shareholder in a corporation

Typically, the more shareholders a company has, the less tangible the influence each shareholder has on the corporation. However, some shareholders have more influence than others. In recent years, *institutional investors,* such as pension funds, insurance companies, mutual funds, and college endowment funds, have accumulated an increasing number of shares of stock in U.S. corporations. As a result, these large institutional investors are playing a more powerful role in governing the corporations in which they own substantial shares, especially with regard to the election of a company's board of directors.[12] For instance, as the largest public pension fund in the country, California Public Employees Retirement System (CalPERS) is one of those institutions with enough influence to get the attention of major corporations. One of its recent moves was withholding its votes for three board members of the Safeway grocery chain, citing several years of poor financial results.[13] Furthermore, at companies such as Avis and United Airlines, employees are major shareholders and so have a significant voice in how the company is run.

board of directors
Group of people, elected by the shareholders, who have the ultimate authority in guiding the affairs of a corporation

Board of Directors The **board of directors** in a corporation represents the shareholders and is responsible for declaring dividends, guiding corporate affairs, reviewing long-term strategic plans, selecting corporate officers, and overseeing financial performance. Depending on the size of the company, the board might have anywhere from 3 to 35 directors, although 15 to 25 is the typical range for traditional corporations and perhaps 5 to 10 for smaller, newer corporations. The board has the power to vote on major management decisions, such as building a new factory, hiring a new president, or buying a new subsidiary. The board's actual involvement in running a corporation varies from one company to another. Some boards are strong and independent and serve as a check on the company's management. Others act as a "rubber stamp," simply approving management's recommendations.

At most large corporations, boards are composed exclusively of directors from outside the company, with only the CEO and a senior executive or two from inside the organization. This arrangement helps ensure that the board provides diligent and independent oversight.[14] But the debate over the optimal number of inside versus outside directors continues. On the one hand, too many insiders can give management too much power over a group whose function is to protect shareholders' rights and investments. On the other hand, outside directors are at a serious information disadvantage. Thus, they must rely largely on the CEO's portrayal of the firm's condition and prospects. Moreover, many outside directors are selected for their accomplishments and stature and are often exceedingly busy. Most are top executives at other companies and typically work 50 to 70 hours per week, travel extensively, and incur a lot of stress in their jobs. Many also serve on the boards of several large companies.

To compensate directors for their time and contributions, most large companies pay their directors a sizable fee and issue them stock options—the right to purchase a set number of shares of stock at a specific price (see Chapter 9). Some think compensation in the form of company stock aligns the directors' interests with those of other stockholders and is the most effective way to get outside directors to vigorously represent the shareholder. Evidence shows that companies in which directors own large amounts of stock and take an active role in guiding the company usually outperform those with more passive boards. Nonetheless, critics of this practice claim that directors with excessive stockholdings could compromise their independent decision making by placing too much focus on a company's short-term stock performance.

Recent debacles involving lack of oversight or even unethical behavior by corporate directors are shedding new light on the importance of director independence, integrity, performance, and compensation. When directors profit from consulting fees or other business activities as a result of their company board positions, they are open to charges of conflict of interest. Such was the case at Enron, where one outside director received hundreds of thousands of dollars in consulting fees and another director headed a cancer institute that received more than $1 million in Enron donations.[15] At WorldCom, which collapsed in bankruptcy after $11 billion in fraudulent accounting was uncovered, a court-appointed investigator concluded that the company's board was so passive and poorly informed that it routinely approved management decisions while knowing little or nothing about them. In one instance, the board approved a $6 billion acquisition of another company during a 35-minute conference call—with no documents to review. And without even knowing it had done so, the board gave two top executives the authority to borrow unlimited amounts of money from the company. Investigators assert that if the board had questioned WorldCom's growing debt load, it could've stopped or at least slowed the company's descent into bankruptcy.[16]

Every Home Depot director must make formal visits to at least 20 stores each year to gain hands-on knowledge of the company's operation.

In the past few years, court rulings and increased attention from investors have increased the pressure on boards to perform. For instance, a judge in Delaware, corporate home to more than half of the *Fortune 500* and some 400,000 U.S. corporations overall, recently allowed shareholders to sue Disney's board for allegedly failing to uphold their responsibilities to the company and the shareholders. This was only a single shareholder lawsuit, but it signals a change in the way courts view the responsibility of corporate boards.[17] The Sarbanes-Oxley Act, passed in the wake of the Enron and WorldCom scandals, also raised the standards of financial responsibility for both executives and board members. This new level of scrutiny will not only protect shareholders but will also help corporations. Studies show that well-governed corporations tend to be more successful, too.[18]

UNDERSTANDING BUSINESS COMBINATIONS

Companies have been combining in various configurations since the early days of business. Joining two companies is a complex process because it involves every aspect of both companies. For instance, executives have to agree on how the combination will be financed and how the power will be transferred and shared. Marketing departments need to figure out how to blend advertising campaigns and sales forces. Incompatible information systems often need to be rebuilt or replaced in order to operate together seamlessly. And companies must deal with layoffs, transfers, and changes in job titles and work assignments.

Mergers and Acquisitions

Businesses can combine through either mergers or acquisitions. The two terms are often discussed together, usually with the shorthand phrase "M & A," or used interchangeably (although they are technically different). In fact, sometimes an acquisition will be announced to the public and to employees as a merger to help the acquired company save face.[19] The business intentions and outcomes of a merger or acquisition are usually the same, although the legal and tax ramifications can be quite different, depending on the details of the transaction.

In a **merger**, two companies join to form a single entity. Traditionally, mergers took place between companies of roughly equal size and stature, but mergers between companies of vastly different sizes is common today. Companies can merge by either pooling their resources or through a purchase of the assets of one company by the other.[20] Although it's not strictly a merger, a **consolidation**, in which two companies create a new, third entity that then purchases the two original companies, is often lumped together with the other two merger approaches.[21] (Note that businesspeople and the media often use "consolidation" in a more general sense, to describe any combination of two or more companies.)

In an **acquisition**, one company simply buys a controlling interest in the voting stock of another company. Unlike the real or presumed marriage of equals in a merger, the buyer is definitely the dominant player in an acquisition. In most acquisitions, the selling parties agree to be purchased; management is in favor of the deal and encourages shareholders to vote in favor of it as well. Since buyers frequently offer shareholders more than their shares are currently worth, sellers often have a motivation to sell. However, in a minority of situations, a buyer attempts to acquire a company against the wishes of management. In these **hostile takeovers**, the buyer tries to convince enough shareholders to go against management and vote to sell.

Buyers can offer sellers cash, stock in the acquiring company, or a combination of the two. Another option involves debt. A **leveraged buyout (LBO)** occurs when one or more individuals purchase a company's publicly traded stock by using borrowed funds. The debt is expected to be repaid with funds generated by the company's operations and, often, by the sale of some of its assets. For an LBO to be successful, a company must

merger
Combination of two companies in which one company purchases the other and assumes control of its property and liabilities

consolidation
Combination of two or more companies in which the old companies cease to exist and a new enterprise is created

acquisition
Form of business combination in which one company buys another company's voting stock

hostile takeovers
Situations in which an outside party buys enough stock in a corporation to take control against the wishes of the board of directors and corporate officers

leveraged buyouts (LBO)
Situation in which individuals or groups of investors purchase companies primarily with debt secured by the company's assets

have a reasonably priced stock and easy access to borrowed funds. Unfortunately, in many cases, the acquiring company must make huge interest and principle payments on the debt, which then depletes the amount of cash that the company has for operations and growth.

Whether it's technically a merger or an acquisition, the combination can take one of several forms (usually all referred to as mergers for simplicity's sake):

- A *vertical merger* occurs when a company purchases a complementary company at a different level in the "value chain," often when a company purchases one of its suppliers or one of its customers. For instance, a car manufacturer and a windshield manufacturer would be a vertical merger since the two companies complement each other in the creation of automobiles.

- A *horizontal merger* involves two similar companies at the same level, such as a combination of two car manufacturers, two windshield manufacturers, two banks, or two retail chains. Because these mergers are often between two competitors, regulators review them closely to make sure the combined firm won't have monopoly power.

- In a *conglomerate merger*, the two firms offer dissimilar products or services, often in widely different industries.[22] Conglomeration was a popular strategy in the 1950s and 1960s, based on the hope that by diversifying into a variety of markets at once, the company could survive market downturns in one or a few of them. However, the stock prices of conglomerates often didn't live up to the hope, and the strategy's popularity declined in the 1970s.[23]

- A *market extension merger* combines firms that offer similar products and services in different geographic markets. For instance, Bank of America, which already had a strong presence in the West and Southeast, gained an instant presence in the Northeast when it acquired FleetBoston in 2004.[24]

- Companies pursue a *product extension merger* when they need to round out a product line. This approach is common in the computer industry, where larger customers expect suppliers to provide a wide range of goods and services. If a company doesn't have the time or resources to develop all the products, it will try to buy someone else who has already developed the missing pieces.

Advantages of Mergers and Acquisitions

Companies pursue mergers and acquisitions for a wide variety of reasons: They might hope to reduce costs by eliminating redundant resources; increase their buying power as a result of their larger size; increase revenue by cross-selling products to each other's customers; increase market share by combining product lines to provide more comprehensive offerings; eliminate manufacturing overcapacity; or gain access to new expertise, systems, and teams of employees who already know how to work together. Often these advantages are grouped under umbrella terms such as *economies of scale, efficiencies*, or *synergies*, which generally mean that the benefits of working together will be greater than if each company continued to operate independently.

The recent combination of two computer companies, HP and Compaq, illustrates both the challenges of a complex acquisition and the advantages of combining two large organizations successfully. The numbers were staggering: 145,000 employees, factories and offices in 160 countries, and 163 product lines, many of which overlapped. In addition, mergers and acquisitions in the technology industry are particularly difficult because these firms depend so heavily on the brainpower of individual scientists, engineers, and other specialists. Executives need to pay special attention to employee retention so that good people don't get frustrated and leave.[25]

Fortunately for HP and Compaq, the managers involved in the merger could learn from experience. Compaq had acquired another large technology company, Digital Equipment, just a few years earlier—and took so long to weave the two firms together that Dell Computer took advantage of Compaq's distraction to shoot past and become the number one personal computer company in the United States. To avoid repeating that mistake, the HP/Compaq transition team followed a rigorous, four-step process to avoid delays:[26]

Hewlett-Packard's CEO Carly Fiorina oversaw one of the most complex corporate mergers in history when HP acquired Compaq.

1. Establish a "decision factory" staffed by key personnel from both firms who had the insight and authority to make the difficult decisions ahead.

2. Use an approach they called "adopt-and-go," in which the team assessed everything from factory locations and products to sales staffs and the company name, and decided whether to keep the HP element or the Compaq element, rather than trying to keep both pieces alive. This was a painful process, to be sure; numerous products were jettisoned, along with facilities, suppliers, internal systems, managerial positions, and 18,000 jobs.

3. Stay focused on the business. The company kept creating new products and supporting customers throughout the nearly two years it took them to combine.

4. Enforce deadlines. The painful, complex process can create all kinds of distractions—HP even wound up in court, sued by a major shareholder who was against the merger. Through it all, the transition team kept the process on schedule.

HP CEO Carly Fiorina took a lot of heat from the press, employees, and some investors when she first announced her intention to acquire Compaq. But she was convinced that the computer market was changing rapidly and that only a few large, global players would survive. To be one of them, HP had to expand its product offerings and reduce its costs. At least in terms of cost reductions, the HP/Compaq merger is clearly a success. The company reduced costs by more than $3 billion a year and did so a year ahead of schedule.[27]

Disadvantages of Mergers and Acquisitions

Despite the promise of economies of scale and success stories such as HP, studies of merged companies show that 65 to 85 percent of these deals fail to actually achieve promised efficiencies.[28] One such study even found that the profitability of acquired companies on average declined.[29] As one expert put it, if you combine two lumbering companies, you get one that runs worse, not better.[30]

Part of the problem with mergers is that companies often borrow immense amounts of money to acquire a firm, and the loan payments on this corporate debt gobble up cash needed to run the business. Moreover, managers must help combine the operations of the two entities, pulling them away from their normal day-to-day responsibilities. Another obstacle that companies face when combining forces is that they tend to underestimate the difficulties of merging two cultures.

As you'll read in Chapter 6, a company's culture is a general term that describes the way people in a given organization approach the day-to-day business of running a company. Culture includes not only management style and practices but also the way people dress, how they communicate, and whether they punch a time clock. *Culture clash* occurs when two joining companies have different beliefs about what is really important, how to make decisions, how to supervise people, how to communicate, and so on (see "DaimlerChrysler: Merger of Equals or Global Fender Bender?"). Experts note that in too many deals the acquiring company imposes its values and management systems on the acquired company without any regard to what worked well there.

Learning from Business Blunders

Oops: The deal was a sure sign that the digital revolution was reshaping the world economy: New-school Internet upstart America Online (AOL) was acquiring old-school publishing and cable TV titan Time Warner, a company with five times AOL's revenues. Sadly, the deal of the century didn't take long to turn into one of the biggest business blunders of all time, destroying $200 billion in shareholder wealth and throwing tens of thousands of people out of work.

What You Can Learn: Perhaps more than anything else, the AOL Time Warner deal is a painful reminder that mergers and acquisitions are extremely complicated, difficult, and prone to failure, even under the best of circumstances. In the perfect storm of the AOL Time Warner deal, failure was virtually guaranteed. Corporate egos clashed as the buttoned-down Time Warner crew and the free-spirited AOL crew failed to harmonize. The purchase was made with hyperinflated dot-com stock that was ripe for a collapse (as most new economy stocks were at the time). And the success of the deal was predicated on the unproven assumption that advertisers would flock en masse to online media outlets, which didn't happen.

Current Trends in Mergers and Acquisitions

Every year, a few megadeals catch everyone's attention, but in reality, several thousand mergers and acquisitions occur every year in the United States, and thousands more take place in other countries. As Exhibit 4.4 shows, merger activity tapered off through the 1970s, during the waning years of the conglomeration age. The 1980s saw a brief surge in activity but nothing like the boom of the late 1990s, which was fueled by the rapid price increases in dot-com and other technology stocks. Tens of thousands of mergers and acquisitions took place during this period, including a number of huge deals in such major industries as news and entertainment media (AOL and Time Warner), automobiles (Chrysler and Daimler-Benz), oil (Exxon and Mobil), and banking (Travelers and Citicorp).[31] However, when the stocks that financed so much of this activity cooled or collapsed, the number of mergers and acquisitions fell off rapidly as well. Then as the stock market began to show signs of recovery in 2003 and 2004, deal activity began to pick up again.

The number of deals can vary widely from year to year, based on both general economic conditions (such as the health of the stock market) and the dynamics of specific industries. For instance, when a new industry or business model emerges, the market often fills up quickly with more suppliers than the number of customers can support. The stronger players then frequently acquire smaller, weaker players, reducing the number of suppliers left in the market.

Given the less-than-stellar record of mergers and acquisitions (see "Hey, Wanna Lose a Few Billion? We Have a Sure Deal for You"), one might be tempted to ask why so many deals continue to happen, year in and year out. In some cases, the managers involved believe that the potential advantages outweigh the risks. In others cases, executives believe they need to combine companies in order to stay competitive in a changing marketplace. This belief drives a lot of mergers and acquisitions in telecommunications, banking, energy, media, and transportation, for instance. As one economist put it, "If you don't play the game as a global company, you're going to wind up a niche player."[32]

Mergers and Acquisitions Involving U.S. Companies

Rising stock prices during the dot-com boom of the late 1990s fueled a surge in merger-and-acquisition activity among U.S. companies, which fell off quickly when those stock prices collapsed.

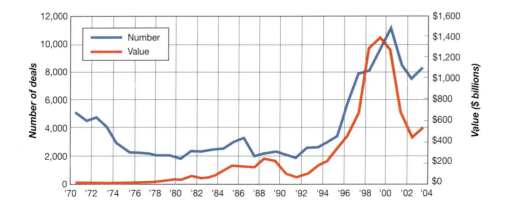

DaimlerChrysler: Merger of Equals or Global Fender Bender?

On paper, it seemed like a perfect fit. The German automaker Daimler-Benz and the U.S. automaker Chrysler were both doing well, but each had strengths that would complement the other's weaknesses. Daimler's engineering was legendary, and it was strong in technology. Chrysler excelled at new-product design and development. Complementary products and geographical mix would allow them to challenge rivals around the world. Moreover, anticipated synergies would save the combined operation $3 billion annually. Optimism was running high when the $36 billion merger was announced in May 1998, creating the world's third-largest automaker.

Charged with excitement and curious about each other's cars and culture, the two companies began the integration process. But fundamental differences in managerial, operational, and decision-making styles made the transition difficult. For example, a German decision would work its way through the bureaucracy for final approval at the top. Then it was set in stone. By contrast, the Americans valued consensus building and shared decision making. Moreover, they allowed midlevel employees to proceed on their own initiative, sometimes without waiting for executive-level approval.

Turf battles also bogged down the combination process. Managers from both sides spent more time defending their way of doing things than promoting the integration of systems. Issues that should have been resolved by managers were bumped up to the company's board of directors. Differences in salary levels and management perks fueled an undercurrent of tension. The Americans earned two, three, and in some cases four times as much as their German counterparts. But the expenses of U.S. workers were tightly controlled compared with those of the German system. Daimler-Benz employees thought nothing of flying to Paris or New York for a half-day meeting, then capping the visit with a fancy dinner and a night in an expensive hotel. The Americans blanched at such extravagances.

Within months, the stock price fell to half its post-merger peak. Friction led to the departure of talented Chrysler midlevel managers and of several top Chrysler executives—including Chrysler's president Thomas Stallkamp, who had played an instrumental role in orchestrating the merger. Soon the management board was scaled down from 17 members to 13 (8 Germans and 5 Americans), and the reality became clear: Daimler executives were indeed running the show. A joke making the rounds in Chrysler offices said it all:

Q: How do you pronounce "DaimlerChrysler"?
A: "Daimler." The "Chrysler" is silent.

The merger of equals turned out to be anything but. For all intents and purposes, Daimler-Benz had acquired Chrysler, and an American icon had lost its independence. And shareholders lost once again: By 2004, the company's market value had plunged by $46 billion.

Critical Thinking Questions

1. What prevented DaimlerChrysler from achieving the promised synergies?
2. Which of these stakeholders benefited the most from the merger: the original Chrysler shareholders or the new DaimlerChrysler shareholders? Explain your answer.

Merger and Acquisition Defenses

Every corporation that sells stock to the general public is potentially vulnerable to takeover by any individual or company that buys enough shares to gain a controlling interest, although as mentioned earlier, most takeovers are friendly acquisitions welcomed by the acquired company. A hostile takeover can be launched in one of two ways: by tender offer or by proxy fight. In a *tender offer*, the buyer, or *raider*, as this party is sometimes called, offers to buy a certain number of shares of stock in the corporation at a specific price. The price offered is generally more, sometimes considerably more, than the current stock price so that shareholders are motivated to sell. The raider hopes to get enough shares to take control of the corporation and to replace the existing board of directors and management. In a *proxy fight*, the raider launches a public relations battle for shareholder votes, hoping to enlist enough votes to oust the board and management.

Proxy fights are tough to win. The insiders have certain advantages: They can get in touch with shareholders, and they can use money from the corporate treasury in their campaign. Walter Hewlett, son of Hewlett-Packard (HP) co-founder William Hewlett, faced this uphill battle when he launched a five-month proxy fight against HP's proposed $19.4 billion acquisition of Compaq. Hewlett, whose family foundation and trusts

Hey, Wanna Lose a Few Billion? We Have a Sure Deal for You

If you were about to make a multi-billion-dollar deal but statistics suggested you had an 80 percent chance of failure, would you go for it? Sure you would, if you work in the slightly wacky world of corporate mergers and acquisitions.

Studies consistently show that the vast majority of mergers and acquisitions fail to meet their primary goal of increasing shareholder value. During the deal-crazy period from 1995 to 2000, for instance, businesses around the world bought and sold each other to the tune of more than $12 trillion. Guess how much all that deal making increased shareholder value? It *decreased* net value by at least $1 trillion—that's more financial destruction than even the dotcom crash managed to generate. In many cases, the only people who win in these deals are the shareholders in acquired companies, when eager buyers shell out more for shares than they're really worth.

How can so many otherwise talented people keep making so many mistakes? Although no one answer applies to every situation, experts cite these common mistakes:

- Companies often rush into deals in search of synergies but then fail to develop them. Once the merger is done, management doesn't follow through to make sure that the computer programmers, sales representatives, engineers, and others responsible for carrying out the details are able to cut costs and boost revenues according to plan.
- Companies pay excessively high premiums for the companies they acquire. According to one expert, any time an acquiring company pays a premium of 25 percent or more over the trading price of the acquired company's stock, the acquiring company is exposing itself and its shareholders to substantial risk.

- Companies are unable to reconcile differences in corporate cultures. A successful merger requires more than respecting each partner's differences. Procedures must be established to settle disputes and to integrate workforces and product lines strategically.

Without question, some mergers and acquisitions are beneficial to companies and shareholders in both the short term and the long term. As HP and Compaq showed, synergies and cost-efficiencies are possible. However, managers need to approach mergers and acquisitions with caution by answering these questions: Will the regulatory environment change? How will competitors respond? Do the expected gains justify the up-front costs and disruption to business operations? Will the cultures, systems, processes, and product lines of the two companies blend well? Executives will continue to believe they can beat the odds and craft successful deals, but without seeking honest answers to these questions first, they're likely to only find themselves adding to the depressing statistics about mergers and acquisitions.

Critical Thinking Questions

1. If you were on the board of directors at a company and the CEO announced plans to merge with a competitor, what types of questions would you want answered before you gave your approval?
2. If a CEO has the opportunity to merge with or acquire another company and is reasonably certain that the transaction will benefit shareholders, is the CEO obligated to pursue the deal? Why or why not?

---

owned 5.7 percent of HP's shares, hoped to kill the largest technology merger in history, arguing that it was too expensive and too risky. Following a narrow victory margin for HP, Hewlett refused to concede. He sued HP, alleging that the company had engaged in "improper means" to secure votes that resulted in a "slim but sufficient" majority vote.[33] HP's board prevailed.

Corporate boards and executives have devised a number of schemes to defend themselves against unwanted takeovers:

- *The poison pill.* This plan, triggered by a takeover attempt, makes the company less valuable in some way to the potential raider; the idea is to discourage the takeover from actually happening. A good example is a special sale of newly issued stock to current stockholders at prices below the market value of the company's existing stock. Such action increases the number of shares the raider has to buy, making the takeover more expensive. Many shareholders believe that poison pills are bad for a company, because they can entrench weak management and discourage takeover attempts that would improve company value.[34]

- *The golden parachute.* This method is designed to benefit a company's top executives by guaranteeing them generous compensation packages if they ever leave or are forced out after a takeover. These packages often total millions of dollars for each executive and therefore make the takeover much more expensive for the acquiring company. Thus, a golden parachute has an effect similar to that of a poison pill.

- *The shark repellent.* This tactic is more direct; it is simply a requirement that stockholders representing a large majority of shares approve of any takeover attempt. Of course, such a plan is viable only if the management team has the support of the majority of shareholders.

- *The white knight.* This tactic uses a friendly buyer to take over the company before a raider can. White knights usually agree to leave the current management team in place and to let the company continue to operate in an independent fashion. Starwood Lodging Trust, a large hotel investment firm, used this tactic to block the hostile takeover attempt of ITT by Hilton Hotels.[35]

Sometimes a group of investors is able to take a publicly traded company off the open market by purchasing all of the company's stock. This tactic is known as "taking the company private." Descendants of Levi Strauss, for example, borrowed $3 billion to buy back all the shares of Levi's stock so that the family could maintain control of the company.[36]

Although companies such as Levi Strauss may go private to thwart unwanted takeovers, this is a radical action. First, stockholders must be willing to sell, and second, buyers must have enough cash on hand to repurchase all the company's stock. Moreover, going private eliminates the firm's ability to raise future capital by selling authorized shares to the public, so it's not a move that many corporations make.

Strategic Alliances and Joint Ventures

Chapter 3 discussed strategic alliances and joint ventures from the perspective of international expansion, defining a strategic alliance as a long-term partnership between companies to jointly develop, produce, or sell products, and a joint venture as a special type of strategic alliance in which two or more firms jointly create a new business entity that is legally separate and distinct from its parents. In many situations, a strategic alliance or a joint venture is preferable to a merger or acquisition.

Many strategic alliances are driven by the realization that no single company can offer customers everything they need. RadioShack's strategic alliances with Verizon Wireless and Sprint PCS is one good example of how companies benefit from entering into such arrangements. "Our strategic alliances and innovative store-within-a-store concepts with Sprint PCS and Verizon Wireless helped make RadioShack the single largest retailer of wireless phones," says RadioShack's CEO, Leonard Roberts. Meanwhile, Sprint PCS and Verizon Wireless benefit from the strategic alliance by building on RadioShack's household name and existing customer base. Customers can view and purchase wireless phones and sign up for national, regional, and local services offered by these partners at any of the 4,000-plus RadioShack locations.[37]

Strategic alliances can accomplish many of the same goals as a merger, consolidation, or acquisition without requiring a painstaking process of integration.[38] They can help a company gain credibility in a new field, expand its market presence, gain access to technology, diversify offerings, and share best practices without forcing the partners to become fast friends for life. If the arrangement does not work out or its usefulness expires, the partners can simply go their separate ways.

Companies can also form joint ventures to accomplish the same benefits enjoyed by strategic alliances. Joint ventures are similar to partnerships except that they are formed for a specific, limited purpose. For instance, America Online, Philips Electronics, and Direct TV formed a joint venture to develop and offer an interactive service that lets customers access the Internet via their TV sets. Like strategic alliances, joint ventures have many advantages. They allow companies to use each other's complementary strengths that might otherwise take too long to develop on their own, and they allow companies to share what may be the substantial cost and risk of starting a new operation.[39]

Summary of Learning Objectives

1 List five advantages and four disadvantages of sole proprietorships.

Sole proprietorships have five advantages: (1) They are easy to establish, (2) they provide the owner with control and independence, (3) the owner reaps all the profits, (4) profits are taxed at individual rates, and (5) the company's plans and financial performance remain private. The four main disadvantages of a sole proprietorship are (1) the company's financial resources are usually limited, (2) management talent may be thin, (3) the owner is liable for the debts and damages incurred by the business, and (4) the business may cease when the owner dies.

2 List five advantages and two disadvantages of partnerships.

In addition to being easy to establish and having profits taxed at individual rates, partnerships offer a greater ability to obtain financing, longevity, and a broader base of skills. The two main disadvantages of partnerships are unlimited liability for general partners and the potential for personality and authority conflicts.

3 Explain the differences between common and preferred stock from a shareholder's perspective.

Common shareholders can vote and can share in the company's profits through discretionary dividends and adjustments in the market value of their stock. In other words, they can profit from their investment if the value of the stock rises above the price they paid for it, or they can lose money if the value of the stock falls below the price they paid for it. In contrast, preferred shareholders cannot vote, but they can get a fixed return (dividend) on their investment and a priority claim on assets after creditors.

4 Highlight the advantages and disadvantages of public stock ownership.

Public stock ownership offers a company increased liquidity, enhanced visibility, financial flexibility, and an indepen-dently established market value for the stock. The disadvantages of public stock ownership are high costs, burdensome filing requirements, loss of ownership control, heightened public exposure, and loss of direct control over the market value of the company's stock.

5 Cite four advantages and three disadvantages of corporations.

Because corporations are a separate legal entity, they have the power to raise large sums of capital, they offer the shareholders protection from liability, they provide liquidity for investors, and they have an unlimited life span. In exchange for these advantages, businesses pay large fees to incorporate, and they are taxed twice on company profits—corporations pay tax on profits and individuals pay tax on dividends (distributed corporate profits). Finally, if publicly owned, corporations must adhere to strict government reporting requirements.

6 Delineate the three groups that govern a corporation and describe the role of each.

Shareholders are the basis of the corporate structure. They elect the board of directors, who in turn elect the officers of the corporation. The corporate officers carry out the policies and decisions of the board. In practice, the shareholders and board members have often followed the lead of the chief executive officer. However, some board members are more active than others. This is especially true of young dot-com corporations that appoint directors for their management expertise and industry connections.

7 Identify six main synergies companies hope to achieve by combining their operations.

By combining their operations, companies hope to eliminate redundant costs, increase their buying power, increase their revenue, improve their market share, eliminate manufacturing overcapacity, and gain access to new expertise and personnel.

Behind **the Scenes**

Restructuring Kinko's Partnerships to Duplicate Success

Plunking down $214 million in exchange for a 30 percent share of Kinko's, Clayton, Dublier & Rice rolled the 130 individual partnerships into a single privately held corporation and centralized all management functions. The firm replaced Kinko's founder and chief executive, Paul Orfalea, with Joseph Hardin, Jr., the former CEO of Wal-Mart's Sam's

Club discount supermarket chain. Orfalea moved into the position of chairman of the board, where he assumed the role of chief idea person. The original partners needed some time to adjust to the new corporate structure—after all, they were accustomed to being their own bosses. But eventually they came around. Besides, they realized that having a private equity stake in Kinko's could be worth a sizable fortune if the company went public some day.

To recruit and motivate managers to make the many changes that would help Kinko's grow, Hardin used an instrument called "phantom stock." Essentially a bookkeeping device, fictional shares are awarded to those responsible for helping the company reach certain financial and market share benchmarks. Here's how it works: Once a year Kinko's uses outside consultants to determine what these phantom shares would sell for if they were publicly traded. For example, the first 120,000 shares of Kinko's phantom stock were awarded to managers and higher-level employees for meeting company goals. The phantom shares were priced at $70 each, which means that if the company were to go public at $300 per share, managers could purchase an equivalent number of real company shares at $70 per share, sell them for $300 each, and make a tidy profit of $230 per share.

Now Hardin had everyone working in the same direction. The store managers lobbied aggressively for new equipment and expanded their services to include on-site computer rentals, document binding and finishing, custom printing, passport photos, mailing services (including overnight delivery drop-off), videoconference facilities, and more. In addition, the company launched Kinkonet, a proprietary document distribution and print network that allows customers to transmit information from one Kinko's site to another. Now customers can pick up finished projects at any location, eliminating shipping costs or the inconvenience of lugging boxes on an airplane. Furthermore, they can go into any of the 1,100 Kinko's stores in such far-flung places as Australia, Japan, South Korea, or the United Kingdom and find the same equipment, supplies, and services, making it possible for small-business owners and travelers to rely on Kinko's as their office away from home.

Restructuring the partnerships helped turn Kinko's into the world's leading provider of document solutions and business services. The public stock offering many partners hoped for never happened, however, and Orfalea and other shareholders accused CD&R of preventing them from cashing out their shares. Rather than taking the company public, CD&R began buying up partners' shares of stock, first reaching 40 percent ownership, then paying an additional $175 million to acquire 73 percent ownership in 2003 under new CEO Gary Kusin. CD&R's investment paid off—in a major way—when Federal Express purchased the entire Kinko's operation in early 2004 for $2.4 billion. Although some analysts were surprised at the price tag, FedEx sees the acquisition as an opportunity to expand its retail presence and compete more effectively with arch-rival UPS, which recently expanded *its* retail presence with the acquisition of Mailboxes Etc.[40]

Critical Thinking Questions

1. Why is it important for all Kinko's stores to have the same equipment and offer the same services?
2. Why did Kinko's change its structure from individual partnerships to a single corporate entity?
3. What effect might all these ownership issues have on the operation of individual Kinko's stores? Explain your answer.

LEARN MORE ONLINE

Go to Chapter 4 of this text's website at www.prenhall.com/bovee, and click on the Kinko's hotlink to learn about the company's many services. Why does Kinko's provide extensive information on how to prepare documents, brochures, posters, presentations, and more? Read about Kinko's partnership in education. How does this program bring more business to Kinko's? Who might benefit from a service such as Kinkonet? ■

Key Terms

acquisition (101)
board of directors (100)
chief executive officer (CEO) (99)
common stock (96)
consolidation (101)
corporation (95)
dividends (96)
general partnership (93)
holding company (98)
hostile takeovers (101)

leveraged buyouts (LBO) (101)
limited liability companies
  (LLCs) (98)
limited partnership (93)
liquidity (97)
merger (101)
parent company (98)
partnership (93)
preferred stock (96)
private corporation (96)

proxy (99)
public corporation (96)
S corporation (98)
shareholders (96)
sole proprietorship (93)
stock certificate (96)
subsidiary corporations (98)
unlimited liability (93)

Test Your Knowledge

Questions for Review

1. What are the three basic forms of business ownership?
2. What is the difference between a general and a limited partnership?
3. What is a closely held corporation, and why do some companies choose this form of ownership?
4. What is the role of a company's board of directors?
5. What is culture clash?

Questions for Analysis

6. Why is it advisable for partners to enter into a formal partnership agreement?
7. To what extent do shareholders control the activities of a corporation?
8. How might a company benefit from having a diverse board of directors that includes representatives of several industries, countries, and cultures?
9. Why do so many mergers fail?
10. **Ethical Considerations.** Your father sits on the board of directors of a large, well-admired public company. Yesterday, while looking for an envelope in his home office, you stumbled on a confidential memorandum. Unable to resist the temptation to read the memo, you discovered that your father's company is talking with another publicly traded company about the possibility of a merger, with Dad's company being the survivor. Dollar signs flashed in your mind. Should the merger occur, the value of the other company's stock is likely to soar. You're tempted to log on to your E*Trade account in the morning and place an order for 1,000 shares of that company's stock. Better still, maybe you'll give a hot tip to your best friend in exchange for the four Dave Matthews Band tickets your friend has been flashing in your face all week. Would either of those actions be unethical? Explain your answer.

Questions for Application

11. Suppose you and some friends want to start a business to take tourists on wilderness backpacking expeditions. None of you has much extra money, so your plan is to start small. However, if you are successful, you would like to expand into other types of outdoor tours and perhaps even open up branches in other locations. What form of ownership should your new enterprise take, and why?
12. Selling antiques on the Internet has become more successful than you imagined. Overnight your website has grown into a full-fledged business—now generating some $200,000 in annual revenue. It's time to think about the future. Several competing online antique dealers have approached you with a proposal to merge their website with yours to create the premier online antique store. The money sounds good, but you have some concerns about joining forces. What might they be? What other growth options should you consider before joining forces with another business?
13. **Integrated.** Chapter 3 discussed international strategic alliances and joint ventures. Why might a U.S. company want to enter into those types of arrangements instead of merging with a foreign concern?
14. **Integrated.** You've developed considerable expertise in setting up new manufacturing plants, and now you'd like to strike out on your own as a consultant who advises other companies. However, you recognize that manufacturing activity tends to expand and contract at various times during the business cycle (see Chapter 1). Do you think a single-consultant sole proprietorship or a small corporation with a half dozen or more consultants would be better able to ride out tough times at the bottom of a business cycle?

Practice Your Knowledge

Sharpening Your Communication Skills

You have just been informed that your employer is going to merge with a firm in Germany. Because you know very little about German culture and business practices, you think it might be a good idea to do some preliminary research—just in case you have to make a quick trip overseas. Using the Internet or library sources, find information on German culture and customs and prepare a short report discussing such cultural differences as German social values, decision-making customs, concepts of time, use of body language, social behavior and manners, and legal and ethical behavior.

Building Your Team Skills

Directors often have to ask tough questions and make difficult decisions, as you will see in this exercise. Imagine that the president of your college or university has just announced plans to retire. Your team, playing the role of the school's board of directors, must decide how to choose a new president to fill this vacancy next semester.

First, generate a list of the qualities and qualifications you think the school should seek in a new president. What background and experience would prepare someone for this key position? What personal characteristics should the new president have? What questions would you ask to find out how each candidate measures up against the list of credentials you have prepared?

Now list all the stakeholders that your team, as directors, must consider before deciding on a replacement for the retiring president. Of these stakeholders, whose opinions do you think are most important? Whose are least important? Who will be directly and indirectly affected by the choice of a new president? Of these stakeholders, which should be represented as participants in the decision-making process?

Select a spokesperson to deliver a brief presentation to the class summarizing your team's ideas and the reasoning behind your suggestions. After all the teams have completed their presentations, discuss the differences and similarities among credentials proposed by all the teams for evaluating candidates for the presidency. Then compare the teams' conclusions about stakeholders. Do all teams agree on the stakeholders who should participate in the decision-making process? Lead a classroom discussion on a board's responsibility to its stakeholders.

Expand Your Knowledge

Discovering Career Opportunities

Are you best suited to working as a sole proprietor, as a partner in a business, or in a different role within a corporation? For this exercise, select three businesses with which you are familiar: one run by a single person, such as a dentist's practice or a local landscaping firm; one run by two or three partners, such as a small accounting firm; and one that operates as a corporation, such as Target.

1. Write down what you think you would like about being the sole proprietor, one of the partners, and the corporate manager or an employee in the businesses you have selected. For example, would you like having full responsibility for the sole proprietorship? Would you like being able to consult with other partners in the partnership before making decisions? Would you like having limited responsibility when you work for other people in the corporation?

2. Now write down what you might dislike about each form of business. For example, would you dislike the risk of bearing all legal responsibility in a sole proprietorship? Would you dislike having to talk with your partners before spending the partnership's money? Would you dislike having to write reports for top managers and shareholders of the corporation?

3. Weigh the pluses and minuses you have identified in this exercise. In comparison, which form of business most appeals to you?

Developing Your Research Skills

Review recent issues of business newspapers or periodicals (print or online editions) to find an article or series of articles illustrating one of the following business developments: merger, acquisition, consolidation, hostile takeover, or leveraged buyout.

1. Explain in your own words what steps or events led to this development.

2. What results do you expect this development to have on (a) the company itself, (b) consumers, (c) the industry the company is part of? Write down and date your answers.

3. Follow your story in the business news over the next month (or longer, as your instructor requests). What problems, opportunities, or other results are reported? Were these developments anticipated at the time of the initial story, or did they seem to catch industry analysts by surprise? How well did your answers to question 2 predict the results?

SEE IT ON THE WEB

For live links to the websites that follow, go to this text's website at www.prenhall.com/bovee. When you log on, select Chapter 4, then select "Featured Websites," click on the URL of the website you wish to visit, and review the website to complete these exercises. Explore these chapter-related websites, review their content, and answer the following questions for each website you visit:

1. What is the purpose of this website?

2. What kinds of information does this website contain? Please be specific.

3. How is the information provided at this website useful for businesspeople? Consumers?

4. How did you expand your knowledge of forms of business ownerships and business combinations by reviewing the material at this website? What new things did you learn about this topic?

Choose a Form of Ownership

Which legal form of ownership is best suited for a new business? Answering this question can be a challenge—especially if you're not familiar with the attributes of sole proprietorships, partnerships, and corporations. That's where Nolo Self-Help Centers can help. Because there's no right or wrong choice for everyone, your job is to understand how each legal structure works and then pick the one that best meets your needs. Start your research by browsing the small-business law center at Nolo. Be sure to check out the FAQs and Legal Encyclopedia. www.nolo.com

rate performance. You can search the list by ranking, by industry, by company name, or by CEO. And to help you identify the largest international corporations, there's a special Global 500 list as well. www.fortune.com

Follow the Fortunes of the Fortune 500

Quick! Name the largest corporation in the United States, as measured by annual revenues. Give up? Just check *Fortune* magazine's yearly ranking of the 500 largest U.S. companies. For years, General Motors has topped the list with its $170 billion-plus in annual revenues, but now Wal-Mart has taken over with over $200 billion in annual revenues. The Fortune 500 not only ranks corporations by size but also offers brief company descriptions along with industry statistics and additional measures of corpo-

Build a Great Board

Want a great board of directors? This inc.com guide contains the best resources for entrepreneurs who are ready to recruit outside directors for their boards. Find out how to recruit board members and how to persuade top-notch people to come on board. Once you've selected your members, learn how to maximize your board's impact and resolve conflicts among board members. Check out one expert's five practical tips for good nuts-and-bolts boardsmanship. www.inc.com/guides/growth/20672.html

Companion Website

Learning Interactively

Go to the Companion Website at www.prenhall.com/bovee. For Chapter 4, take advantage of the interactive "Study Guide" to test your knowledge of the chapter. Get instant feedback on whether you need additional studying.

Also, visit this site's "Study Hall," where you'll find an abundance of valuable resources that will help you succeed in this course.

Video **Case**

Doing Business Privately: Amy's Ice Creams

LEARNING OBJECTIVES

The purpose of this video is to help you:

1. Distinguish among the types of corporations.
2. Consider the advantages and disadvantages of incorporation.
3. Understand the role that shareholders play in a privately held corporation.

SYNOPSIS

Amy's Ice Creams, based in Austin, Texas, is a privately held corporation formed in 1984 by Amy Miller and owned by Miller and a small group of family members and friends. At the outset, one of the most important decisions Miller faced was choosing an appropriate legal ownership structure for the new business. Fueled by the founder's dedication to creating happy ice cream memories for customers, Amy's has continued to evolve and grow. The company now operates 11 stores and rings up close to $3.5 million in annual sales. Applying for a job is an adventure in creativity, and Miller welcomes employees' suggestions for new flavors and new promotions to keep sales growing.

Discussion Questions

1. *For analysis:* How does Amy's Ice Creams differ from a publicly held corporation?
2. *For analysis:* What are some of the particular advantages of corporate ownership for a firm such as Amy's Ice Creams?
3. *For application:* How well do you think Amy's is working to ensure its continued survival and success? Looking ahead to future growth, what marketing, financial, or other suggestions would you make?
4. *For application:* What are some of the issues that Amy Miller may have to confront because her 22 investors are family members and friends?
5. *For debate:* Should Amy's Ice Creams become a publicly held corporation? Support your chosen position.

ONLINE EXPLORATION

Find out what is required to incorporate a business in your state. You might begin by searching the CCH Business Owner's Toolkit site at www.toolkit.cch.com. If you were going to start a small business, would you choose to incorporate or choose a different form of legal organization? List the pros and cons that incorporation presents for the type of business you would consider.

Chapter 5

Starting and Financing a Small Business

Behind the Scenes

Why Is Papa John's Rolling in Dough?

www.papajohns.com

As a high school student working at a local pizza pub, John Schnatter liked everything about the pizza business. "I liked making the dough; I liked kneading the dough; I liked putting the sauce on; I liked putting the toppings on; I liked running the oven," recalls Schnatter. Obsessed with perfect pizza topping placement and bubble-free melted cheese, Schnatter knew that something was missing from national pizza chains: a superior-quality traditional pizza delivered to the customer's door. And his dream was to one day open a pizza restaurant that would fill that void.

Schnatter worked his way through college making pizzas, honing the techniques and tastes that would someday become Papa John's trademark. Shortly after graduating from Ball State University with a business degree, he faced his first business challenge. His father's tavern was

Papa John's opened its first restaurant in 1985. Today it is the fastest growing pizza company in the United States.

$64,000 in debt and failing. So Schnatter sold his car to buy some used restaurant equipment, knocked out a broom closet in the back of his father's tavern, and began selling pizzas to the tavern's customers. Soon the pizza became the tavern's main attraction and helped turn the failing business around. Schnatter officially opened the first Papa John's restaurant and set about expanding.

But Schnatter needed a recipe for success. With Little Caesar's promoting deep discounts and Domino's emphasizing fast delivery, Papa John's needed a fresh approach to compete successfully with the big chains. If you were John Schnatter, how would you grow a small pizza operation into one that could compete with national players? Would you franchise your concept? Would you remain a private enterprise or go public? Would you expand overseas? Where would you focus your efforts?[1] ∎

UNDERSTANDING THE WORLD OF SMALL BUSINESS

Many small businesses start out like Papa John's: with an entrepreneur, an idea, and a drive to succeed. In fact, the United States was originally founded by people involved in small businesses—the family farmer, the shopkeeper, the craftsperson. Successive waves of immigrants carried on the tradition, launching restaurants and laundries, providing repair and delivery services, and opening newsstands and bakeries. This trend continued for decades, until improvements in transportation and communication enabled large producers to manufacture goods at low costs and pass the savings on to consumers. Many smaller businesses could not compete with larger retailers on price, so scores of them closed their doors, and big business emerged as the primary economic force. The trend toward bigness continued for several decades, then it reversed.

The 1990s were a golden decade for entrepreneurship in the United States. Entrepreneurs launched small companies in droves to fill new consumer needs. Many took advantage of Internet technologies to gain a competitive edge. Some succeeded; others failed. But the resurgence of small businesses helped turn the U.S. economy into the growth engine for the world.

Business BUZZ

Social entrepreneur:
Someone who applies entrepreneurial business skills and experience to a social or charitable cause

Defining just what constitutes a small business is surprisingly tricky because *small* is a relative term. For example, a manufacturing firm with 500 employees might be considered small if it competes against much larger companies, but a retail establishment with 500 employees might be classified as big when compared with its competitors.

The U.S. Small Business Administration (SBA) defines a **small business** as a firm that (a) is independently owned and operated, (b) is not dominant in its field, (c) is relatively small in terms of annual sales, and (d) has fewer than 500 employees (although the agency's exact standards vary from industry to industry, adjusting for the competitive makeup of each industry). By this definition, the United States is home to approximately 23 million small businesses. The SBA reports that 80 percent of all U.S. companies have annual sales of less than $1 million and that about 60 percent of the nation's employers have fewer than five workers.[2]

small business
Company that is independently owned and operated, is not dominant in its field, and meets certain criteria for the number of employees and annual sales revenue

Economic Roles of Small Businesses

Small businesses are the cornerstone of the U.S. economy. They bring new ideas, processes, and vigor to the marketplace. They generate about half of private sector output,[3] and they fill niche markets that are often not served by large businesses. Here are just some of the important roles small businesses play in the economy:

- *They provide jobs.* Small businesses employ about half of the private-sector workforce in this country and create 75 percent of new jobs.[4]

- *They introduce new products.* The National Science Foundation estimates that 98 percent of the nation's "radical" new-product developments spring from small firms, a staggering percentage given the fact that small companies spend considerably less on research and development than large companies do.[5]

- *They supply the needs of large corporations.* Many small businesses act as distributors, servicing agents, and suppliers to large corporations. For instance, the 160 employees of Parallax inspect nuclear power plants, implement safety procedures, and clean up hazardous and nuclear waste at power plants and weapons complexes across the nation. Seventy percent of Parallax's business comes from large corporations such as Westinghouse and Lockheed Martin. Not bad for a company launched out of the founder's home with $10,000 in personal savings.[6]

- *They inject a considerable amount of money into the economy.* Small businesses spend $2.2 trillion annually, just a bit less than the $2.6 trillion spent by big companies.[7]

- *They take risks that larger companies sometimes avoid.* Entrepreneurs play a significant role in the economy as risk takers, the people willing to try new and unproven ideas.

- *They provide specialized goods and services.* When Mike Woods tried to teach his son how to read, he couldn't find any toys on the market that helped teach phonics. So he left his job as a partner in a big law firm and started LeapFrog. The company's initial product was the Phonics Disk, a toy that teaches children shapes, sounds, and pronunciation of letters and words. The company has since expanded with dozens of award-winning products and more than 1,000 employees worldwide.[8]

Characteristics of Small Businesses

Small businesses are of two distinct types: lifestyle businesses and high-growth ventures. Roughly 80 to 90 percent are modest operations with little growth potential (although some have attractive income potential for the solo businessperson). The self-employed consultant working part-time from a home office, the corner florist, and the family-owned neighborhood pizza parlor fall into the category of *lifestyle businesses*—firms built around the personal and financial needs of an individual or a family.[9] Lifestyle businesses aren't designed to grow into large enterprises.

In contrast to lifestyle businesses, some firms are small simply because they are new. Many companies—such as FedEx, Microsoft, and Papa John's—start out as small

Recuperating from a broken ankle while vacationing in Lake Tahoe, Perry Klebahn decided to try out a pair of snowshoes he found in a friend's closet. Today his company, Atlas Snow-Shoe, sells high-end snowshoes in more than 1,000 stores across the United States, ringing up annual sales of about $12 million.

entrepreneurial firms but quickly outgrow their small-business status. These *high-growth ventures* are usually run by a team rather than by one individual, and they expand rapidly by obtaining a sizable supply of investment capital and by introducing new products or services to a large market. But expanding from a small firm into a large enterprise is no easy task; there's a world of difference between the two.

The typical small business has few products or services, focuses on a narrow group of customers, and remains in close contact with its markets. In addition, most small-business owners work with limited resources and tend to be more innovative.

Limited Resources

Small companies tend to have limited resources, so owners and employees must perform a variety of job functions in order to get the work done. Being a jack-of-all-trades is not for everyone, however (see Exhibit 5.1). When Bob Hammer and Sue Crowe purchased Blue Jacket Ship Crafters, a mail-order model-ship-kit manufacturer, they quickly learned that running a small company was not like running Motorola, where the two had been senior managers for the better part of their careers. It took a lot more work and time than they had imagined. Even Crowe admits, "You will put in more money than you thought you would, you will take out a lot less, and you will work harder than you did when you were making a six-figure salary at your large corporation."[10] Many executives who leave the corporate world to start a small business have trouble adjusting to the daily grind of entrepreneurship. They miss the support services, conveniences, and fringe benefits they enjoyed in large corporations.[11]

Innovation

Small businesses also tend to be more open-minded and willing to try new things than big businesses. Case studies show that being small can stimulate innovation: (1) Small businesses can make decisions faster, (2) the owners are more accessible, and (3) employees have a greater opportunity for individual expression. Putting an idea into action in big companies often means filing formal proposals, preparing research reports, and attending lots of meetings. A manager at Microsoft once quit out of frustration with the company's laborious decision-making process at the time. It took 10 meetings and three months to act on his suggestion to add a feature to Hot Mail (the company's free Internet e-mail service) that would quickly take 40 million users to Microsoft's MSN website. In contrast, it took only 30 minutes to write the software to implement the feature.[12]

To compete with small companies, many big companies now divide their organizations into smaller, independent work units. Xerox, AT&T, Du Pont, Motorola, Hewlett-Packard, and others have launched their own small enterprises to keep new ideas from falling through the cracks. Run by *intrapreneurs*—people who create innovation of any kind

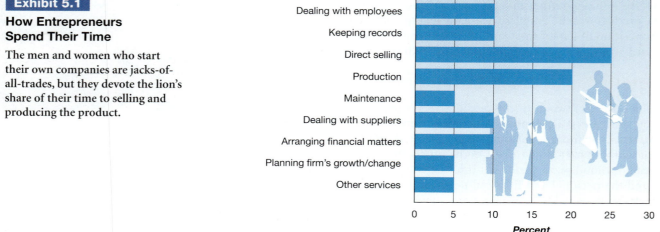

Exhibit 5.1

How Entrepreneurs Spend Their Time

The men and women who start their own companies are jacks-of-all-trades, but they devote the lion's share of their time to selling and producing the product.

David Competes with Goliath Online

The Internet continues to change business in many ways, and one of the most profound changes is the way it helps small companies compete against much larger firms. You may not have the plush offices or fancy retail space of a large company in the physical world, but you can look just as impressive in the online world. Follow these tips to create a powerful online presence:

■ *Present a professional corporate image.* Be sure to provide a corporate profile that tells people something about your company in order to remove their fear of the unknown. Include news releases or articles about your business so that customers can see how well known or successful you are in your industry. Make sure your material is accurate, interesting, and related to your products. Identify the key benefits of your product (include product details on a secondary page). Check out other websites for inspiration—especially your competitors' sites—and decide what you like or dislike about their appearance. Think of ways to distinguish your site.

■ *Don't forget the basics.* Always give visitors a person to call and a place to send for information. Be sure to list your postal and e-mail addresses and phone and fax numbers. And remember, because the Internet is international, list the nation(s) where your company or its dealers are located.

■ *Make your website easy to use.* Web surfers have a short attention span, and large companies spend a significant amount of time and money making their sites easy to use. Give users a clear and obvious pathway through your site, and be sure to have several people test the navigation before you go live. Review other sites to see which terms are in common use. For instance, most

sites now put company background information on a page entitled "About Us" so many web surfers expect to see such a page. Check out several of the many books now available on effective website design.

■ *Anticipate your customers' needs.* Plan ahead. By including answers to frequently asked questions, you'll address many common concerns. Remember, users tend to provide both frank and useful input, but only if you ask them for it. So be sure to include an active customer feedback mechanism such as e-mail, open feedback forms, or structured survey forms. However, if you invite e-mail, be sure to respond to incoming messages. Customers get frustrated quickly if they think their messages are falling into a black hole. Also, don't require people to register before they can see your site or access useful information; most will simply click away to one of your competitors.

■ *Promote your website.* Be sure to list with numerous search engines and online industry directories. Stay on top of the latest developments in online promotion, such as sponsored listings on search engines. Seek out related but noncompetitive companies that might attract the same customers you want to attract, then offer to link to each others' sites. Make sure your URL is included in all your advertising, signs, business cards, letterhead, and anywhere else potential customers might see it.

Questions for Critical Thinking

1. Why do web surfers have a short attention span?
2. If you're a tiny company competing against much larger firms, should you play up or play down your size? Explain your answer.

within an organization (think of them as entrepreneurs inside a large organization)—these ventures get funding and support from the parent organization. Nevertheless, some intrapreneurial ventures continue to face giant obstacles because the parent corporation burdens them with strict reporting requirements and formal procedures.[13]

Factors Contributing to the Increase in the Number of Small Businesses

Three factors are contributing to the increase in the number of small businesses today: technological advances, an increase in the number of businesses owned by women and minorities, and corporate downsizing and outsourcing.

E-Commerce and the Internet

E-commerce technologies have spawned thousands of new business ventures in recent years—both firms that create the technology and firms that use it. ShippingSupply.com is one such firm. Karen Young, a collector of knickknacks, founded this small business

Sue Calloway is among the growing number of women entrepreneurs starting a small business. Calloway started S.C.R.U.B.S. to provide carefree hospital clothing to doctors and nurses. Her whimsical designs help brighten hospital settings, easing patients' anxieties.

when she was looking for affordable packing and shipping materials for her mail-order items. On a whim, Young decided to market bubble wrap, plastic foam, and shipping tubes, which she purchased direct from manufacturers, to eBay sellers. Today, ShippingSupply.com has eight full-time employees, occupies 7,000 square feet of warehouse space, and has over 35,000 customers in its database.[14]

E-commerce makes it possible for small companies such as ShippingSupply.com to compete on a level playing field with larger ones. Small businesses can use the Internet to communicate with customers and suppliers all over the world—any time of the day—and to access the types of resources and information that were previously available only to larger firms. The Internet also makes it easier to start a small home-based business. With the Internet and online resources, accountants, writers, lawyers, and consultants can set up shop at home—or on the web. Millions of home-based businesses exist in the United States and millions of employees of other businesses work at home via telecommuting technologies.[15] Some predict that as much as half the workforce soon may be involved in full- or part-time home-based businesses.[16]

Rise in Number of Businesses Owned by Women and Minorities

Small-business growth is also being fueled by women and minorities who want alternatives to traditional employment. Women now own more than 10 million U.S. businesses—and one of every 11 women in the country owns a business. Moreover, businesses owned by women are increasing both revenue and employment faster than the national average.[17]

As Exhibit 5.2 shows, women are starting small businesses for a number of reasons. Some choose to run their own companies so they can enjoy a more flexible work arrangement; others start their own business because of barriers to corporate advancement, known as the *glass ceiling*. Josie Natori is a perfect example of such a scenario. By her late twenties, Natori was earning six figures as the first female vice president of investment banking at Merrill Lynch. But Natori knew that her chances of further advancement were slim in the male-dominated financial world. So she started her own lingerie line. Today, Natori is the owner of a multi-million-dollar fashion empire that sells elegant lingerie and evening wear.[18]

Between 1987 and 1997, the number of firms owned by minorities grew 168 percent—more than triple the 47 percent rate of U.S. businesses overall.[19] Minorities now own 15 percent of all U.S. businesses, double the number of a decade ago.[20] Part of this growth is attributed to firms that do a better job of marketing to specific segments of the population.

Exhibit 5.2

Women Starting Businesses

More than half of all women business owners started their own businesses because they had an entrepreneurial idea or wished to further advance their careers.

What women with companies less than a decade old say is the main reason they started a business:

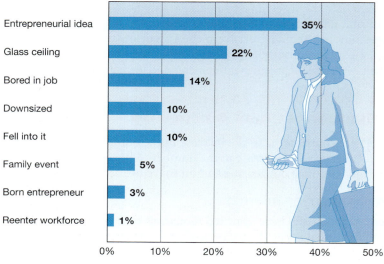

Entrepreneurial idea	35%
Glass ceiling	22%
Bored in job	14%
Downsized	10%
Fell into it	10%
Family event	5%
Born entrepreneur	3%
Reenter workforce	1%

0%   10%   20%   30%   40%   50%

For instance, Hispanic-owned businesses have been doing better than the economy as a whole in recent years, thanks in large part to their success at marketing to the growing Hispanic-American population.[21]

Downsizing and Outsourcing

Contrary to popular wisdom, business start-ups often soar when the economy sours. During hard times, many companies downsize or lay off talented employees, who then have little to lose by pursuing self-employment. In fact, several well-known companies were started during recessions. Tech titans William Hewlett and David Packard joined forces in Silicon Valley in 1938 during the Great Depression. Bill Gates started Microsoft during the 1975 recession. And the founders of Sun Microsystems, Compaq Computer, Adobe Systems, Silicon Graphics, and Lotus Development started their companies in 1982—in the midst of a recession and high unemployment.[22]

To make up for layoffs of permanent staff, some companies **outsource** or subcontract special projects and secondary business functions to experts outside the organization. Others turn to outsourcing as a way to permanently eliminate entire company departments. Regardless of the reason, the increased use of outsourcing provides opportunities for smaller businesses to service the needs of larger enterprises.

outsource
Subcontracting work to outside companies

STARTING A SMALL BUSINESS

As many as 800,000 new small businesses are started each year.[23] Could you or should you join the thousands of entrepreneurs who start new businesses every year? What qualities would you need? What tasks would you have to perform to get started?

Characteristics of Entrepreneurs

Contrary to what you might expect, most entrepreneurs are not glamorous adventurers; instead, they are often ordinary people like John Schnatter who have a good idea. But even Schnatter knows it takes more than a good idea to launch a successful business. Most entrepreneurs have these qualities in common:

- They are highly disciplined.
- They like to control their destiny.
- They listen to their intuitive sense.
- They relate well to others.
- They are eager to learn whatever skills are necessary to reach their goal.
- They learn from their mistakes.
- They stay abreast of market changes.
- They are willing to exploit new opportunities.
- They seldom follow trends (rather, they spot and interpret trends).
- They are driven by ambition.
- They think positively.
- They prefer the excitement and potential rewards of risk taking over security.[24]
- Most cite making money as a secondary reason for starting their own business, not the primary reason.[25]

Kate Spade offers a good case study in the qualities required of a successful entrepreneur. When she quit her job as accessories editor for *Mademoiselle* and launched her own handbag company in 1991, even her mother said she had gotten cocky. Priced at $100 to $400, Spade's nylon bags weren't cheap, and she had a tough time getting them into trade shows because she didn't "do leather." But Spade's instincts were better than the stylemakers'. On an impulse the night before her first trade show, Spade ripped the

Technologies That Are Revolutionizing Business

Social network applications

Social networking sounds like the time you spend wandering around a party trying to meet people, but it's actually a new category of technology that is changing the way many professionals communicate. Social network applications, which can be either stand-alone software products or websites, help identify potential business connections by indexing e-mail and instant messaging address books, calendars, and message archives. For instance, you might find that the sales lead you've been struggling to contact at a large customer is a golf buddy of one of your suppliers or a relative of your child's soccer coach.

How they're changing business

One of the biggest challenges small-business owners face is finding the right people and making those connections, whether you're looking for a new employee, an investor, a potential customer, or anyone else who might be important to the future of your business. With social network applications, businesspeople can reach more people than they could ever hope to reach via traditional, in-person networking.

Where you can learn more

Visit the websites of LinkedIn (www.linkedin.com), Ryze (www.ryze.com), and Spoke (www.spoke.com) to learn more about their products. To find other products and information about social network applications, enter "business networking" or "social networking" in your favorite search engine.

labels "kate spade new york" from the inside of her bags and stitched them on the outside, sewing until her fingers got puffy. Good move. Upscale retailer Barneys ordered 18 of her bags, and *Vogue* decided to feature them on the glossy's accessories page. It wasn't long before Julia Roberts and Gwyneth Paltrow (who saw the bags in fashion magazines) had them on their shoulders. Nevertheless, the company didn't become profitable until 1996, when Saks and Neiman Marcus each ordered 3,000 bags for all their stores. Then in 1999 Neiman Marcus purchased a majority stake in the company. Since its inception, Kate Spade has added shoes, accessories, and more to the company's product line.[26]

Entrepreneurs such as Kate Spade start with relatively small sums of money and operate informally from their homes, at least for a while.[27] Most have diverse backgrounds in terms of education and business experience. Some come from companies unlike the ones they start; others use their prior knowledge and skills—such as editing, telemarketing, public relations, or selling—to start their own businesses. Still others have less experience but an innovative idea or a better way of doing something. Like Kate Spade and John Schnatter, they find an overlooked corner of the market, exploit a demographic trend unnoticed by others, or meet an unsatisfied consumer need through better service or a higher-quality product. Moreover, they often plan and develop their product quickly, while the rest of the business world ponders whether a market for the product exists.

Importance of Preparing a Business Plan

Getting started in a new business requires a lot of work (see Exhibit 5.3), not the least of which is planning. Although many successful entrepreneurs claim to have done little formal planning, even the most intuitive of them have *some* idea of what they're trying to accomplish and how they hope to do it. In other words, even if they haven't produced a formal printed document, chances are they've thought through the big questions, which is just as important. Jeff Bezos, founder of Amazon.com, planned the world's first online bookstore in the backseat of his car as his wife drove them from New York to Seattle. As Bezos and other entrepreneurs know, planning is essential for success. No amount of hard work can turn a bad idea into a profitable one: The health-food store in a meat-and-potatoes neighborhood and the child-care center in a retirement community are probably doomed from the beginning.

Planning forces you to think ahead. Before you rush in to supply a product, you need to be sure that a market exists. You must also try to foresee some of the problems that might arise and figure out how you will cope with them. For instance, what will you do if one of your suppliers suddenly goes out of business? Can you locate another supplier quickly? What if the neighborhood starts to change—even for the better? An influx of wealthier neighbors may cause such a steep increase in rent that your business must move. Also, tough competition may move into the neighborhood along with the fatter pocket-

✓ Choose a business name, verify the right to use it, and register it.

✓ Reserve a corporate name if you will be incorporating.

✓ Register a domain name for your website.

✓ Register or reserve state or federal trademarks.

✓ Apply for a patent if you will be marketing an invention.

✓ Write a business plan.

✓ Choose a location for the business.

✓ File partnership or corporate papers.

✓ Get any required business licenses or permits.

✓ Have business phone lines installed.

✓ Check into business insurance needs.

✓ Apply for a sales tax number.

✓ Apply for an employer identification number if you will have employees.

✓ Open business bank account(s).

✓ Have business cards and stationery printed.

✓ Purchase equipment and supplies.

✓ Order inventory.

✓ Order signage.

✓ Order fixtures.

✓ Print brochures and other sales literature.

✓ Send out publicity releases.

✓ Call everyone you know and tell them you are in business.

books. Do you have an alternative location staked out? What if styles suddenly change? Can you switch quickly from, say, hand-painted crafts to some other kind of artwork?

One of the first steps you should take toward starting a new business is to develop a **business plan**, a written document that summarizes an entrepreneur's proposed business venture, communicates the company's goals, highlights how management intends to achieve those goals, and shows how consumers will benefit from the company's products or services. Preparing a business plan serves two important functions: First, it guides the company operations and outlines a strategy for turning an idea into reality; second, it helps persuade lenders and investors to finance your business. In fact, without a business plan, many investors won't even grant you an interview. Keep in mind that sometimes the greatest service a business plan can provide an entrepreneur is the realization that "the concept just won't work." Discovering this on paper can save you considerable time and money.

business plan
A written document that provides an orderly statement of a company's goals and a plan for achieving those goals

As important as planning is, it's equally important to monitor the market and be ready to adjust once you start moving. You don't want to be so locked into your plan that you fail to see changes in the market or new opportunities along the way.

Small-Business Ownership Options

Once you've done your research and planning, if you decide to take the risk, you can get into business for yourself in three ways: Start from scratch, buy an existing business, or obtain a franchise. Roughly two-thirds of business founders begin **start-up companies**;

start-up companies
New ventures

Learning from Business Blunders

Oops: Carol Skonberg's company, Swasko Jewels, made sterling silver charms that dinner guests could wrap around the stems of their wineglasses to prevent confusion over which glass belongs to whom. Not a life-and-death problem, to be sure, but one of the things people would readily pay a few dollars to avoid, she figured. Her hunch proved correct, and she soon convinced 90 retailers in her home state of Texas to carry the products. Sales looked promising—then quickly plummeted as competitors with similar products but more aggressive marketing appeared out of nowhere. Skonberg and her business partner disbanded the company soon after.

What You Can Learn: According to small-business experts, Skonberg made several common rookie mistakes. The first was believing she had a unique product. It's not unusual for more than one company to come up with the same solution to a given problem. The second mistake was failing to investigate legal protection earlier. Although she couldn't patent her designs (jewelry usually can't be patented), she could've come up with a catchy brand name and eye-catching logo, then trademarked those. The third—and probably biggest—mistake was not being prepared to go nationwide quickly. Two competitors did expand rapidly, signing up sales reps around the country and getting into catalogs with wide distribution. The story has a happy ending, though. Skonberg learned from her experience and tried again, this time with a jewelry company called HipIce that makes chains that drape off beltlines. So far, so good.

that is, they start from scratch rather than buy an existing operation or inherit the family business. Starting a business from scratch has many advantages and disadvantages (see Exhibit 5.4); in many cases it can be the most difficult option.

Another way to go into business for yourself is to buy an existing business. This approach tends to reduce the risks—provided, of course, that you check out the company carefully. When you buy a business, you generally purchase an established customer base, functioning business systems, a proven product or service, and a known location. You don't have to go through the challenging period of building a reputation, establishing a clientele, finding suppliers, and hiring and training employees. In addition, financing an existing business is often much easier than financing a new one; lenders are reassured by the company's history and existing assets and customer base. With these major details already settled, you can concentrate on making improvements.

Still, buying an existing business is not without disadvantages. For one thing, the business may be overpriced. For another, inventories and equipment may be obsolete. Furthermore, the location may no longer be satisfactory, the previous owner may have created ill will, your personality may clash with those of existing managers and employees, and outstanding bills owed by customers may be difficult to collect. Keep in mind that no matter how fast you learn and how much investigating you do, you're likely to find that the challenges of running an existing business are far greater than you anticipated.[28]

The Franchise Alternative

An alternative to buying an existing business is to buy a **franchise** in somebody else's business. This approach enables the buyer to use a larger company's trade name and sell its products or services in a specific territory. In exchange for this right, the **franchisee** (the small-business owner who contracts to sell the goods or services) pays the

franchise
Business arrangement in which a small business obtains rights to sell the goods or services of the supplier (franchisor)

franchisee
Small-business owner who contracts for the right to sell goods or services of the supplier (franchisor) in exchange for some payment

Exhibit 5.4

Weighing the Advantages and Disadvantages of Starting a New Business

Owning a business has many advantages, but you must also consider the potential drawbacks.

Advantages	Disadvantages
+ Control over your own destiny	− Uncertainty of income
+ Ability to reach your full potential	− Risk of losing your entire investment
+ Unlimited profits	− Long hours and hard work
+ Recognition for your efforts	− Complete responsibility
+ Doing what you enjoy	− High levels of stress

Blueprint for an Effective Business Plan

Even for a small firm, the business plan still requires a great deal of thought. For example, before you open your doors (or open your virtual doors online), you have to make important decisions about personnel, marketing, facilities, suppliers, and distribution. A written business plan forces you to think about those issues and develop programs that will help you succeed. If you are starting out on a small scale and using your own money, your business plan may be relatively informal. But at a minimum, you should describe the basic concept of the business and outline its specific goals, objectives, and resource requirements. A formal plan, suitable for use with banks or investors, should cover these points:

■ *Summary.* In one or two pages, summarize your business concept. Describe your product or service and its market potential. Highlight some things about your company and its owners that will distinguish your firm from the competition. Summarize your financial projections and the amount of money investors can expect to make on their investment. Be sure to indicate how much money you will need and for what purpose.

■ *Mission and objectives.* Explain the purpose of your business and what you hope to accomplish.

■ *Company and industry.* Give full background information on the origins and structure of your venture and the characteristics of its industry.

■ *Products or services.* Give a complete but concise description of your product or service, focusing on its unique attributes. Explain how customers will benefit from using your product or service instead of those of your competitors.

■ *Market and competition.* Provide data that will persuade the investor that you understand your target market and can achieve your sales goals. Be sure to identify the strengths and weaknesses of your competitors.

■ *Management.* Summarize the background and qualifications of the principals, directors, and key management personnel in your company. Include résumés in the appendix.

■ *Marketing strategy.* Provide projections of sales and market share, and outline a strategy for identifying and contacting customers, setting prices, providing customer services, advertising, and so forth. Whenever possible, include evidence of customer acceptance, such as advance product orders.

■ *Design and development plans.* If your product requires design or development, describe the nature and extent of what needs to be done, including costs and possible problems.

■ *Operations plan.* Provide information on the facilities, equipment, and labor needed.

■ *Overall schedule.* Forecast development of the company in terms of completion dates for major aspects of the business plan.

■ *Critical risks and problems.* Identify all negative factors and discuss them honestly.

■ *Financial projections and requirements.* Include a detailed budget of start-up and operating costs, as well as projections for income, expenses, and cash flow for the first three years of business. Identify the company's financing needs and potential sources.

■ *Exit strategy.* Explain how investors will be able to cash out or sell their investment, such as through a public stock offering, sale of the company, or a buyback of the investors' interest. When covering these points, keep in mind that your audience wants short, concise information—not lengthy volumes—and realistic projections for growth.

Questions for Critical Thinking

1. What details should you know about your business before writing a business plan?

2. Why is it important to identify critical risks and problems in a business plan?

---

franchisor (the supplier) an initial fee (and often monthly royalties as well). Franchises are a factor of rising importance in the U.S. economy. The International Franchise Association estimates that 1,500 franchising systems in the United States do business through more than 320,000 retail outlets.[29] U.S. franchises sell more than $1 trillion of goods and services every year.[30]

franchisor
Supplier that grants a franchise to an individual or group (franchisee) in exchange for payments

Types of Franchises

Franchises are of three basic types. A *product franchise* gives you the right to sell trademarked goods, which are purchased from the franchisor and resold. Car dealers and gasoline stations fall into this category. A *manufacturing franchise,* such as a soft-drink bottling plant, gives you the right to produce and distribute the manufacturer's

Prospective Subway franchisees must attend company training classes and pass a final exam before they can own a Subway sandwich shop.

products, using supplies purchased from the franchisor. A *business-format franchise* gives you the right to open a business using a franchisor's name and format for doing business. Fast-food chains such as Papa John's, KFC, Taco Bell, and Pizza Hut typify this form of franchising.

How to Evaluate a Franchise

How do you protect yourself from a poor franchise investment? The best way is to study the opportunity carefully before you commit. Since 1978 the Federal Trade Commission has required franchisors to disclose information about their operations to prospective franchisees. By studying this information, you can determine the financial condition of the franchisor and ascertain whether the company has been involved in lawsuits with franchisees. Before signing a franchise agreement, it's also wise to consult an attorney. Exhibit 5.5 suggests some points to consider as you study the package of information on the franchise.

Nevertheless, some people find out too late that franchising isn't the best choice for them. They make a mistake common among prospective franchisees—buying without really understanding the day-to-day business. Often, prospects simply don't get beyond the allure of the successful name or concept—or the mistaken notion that a franchise brings instant success. "People go into a sub shop at the noon hour and see the cash register opening and closing," says the president of Franchise Solutions. "What they don't see is having to get there at 4 A.M. to bake the bread." Buying a franchise is much like buying any other business: It requires analyzing the market, finding capital, choosing a site, hiring employees, and buying equipment. The process also includes an element not found in other businesses—evaluating the franchisor.[31]

One of the best ways to evaluate a prospective franchisor is by talking to other franchisees. At a minimum, you should find out what other franchisees think of the opportunity. If they had it to do over again, would they still invest? You might even want to spend a few months working for someone who already owns a franchise you're interested in. Fabiola Garcia did. She worked at a 7-Eleven evenings and swing shifts, learning all aspects of the business as part of the screening and training process for prospective 7-Eleven franchise owners. This was in addition to a two-week special session at headquarters, where Garcia learned the franchisor's administrative procedures.[32]

Exhibit 5.5

Ten Questions to Ask Before Signing a Franchise Agreement

A franchise agreement is a legally binding contract that defines the relationship between the franchisee and the franchisor. Because the agreement is drawn up by the franchisor, the terms and conditions generally favor the franchisor. Before signing the franchise agreement, be sure to consult an attorney.

1. What does the initial franchise fee cover? Does it include a starting inventory of supplies and products?

2. How are the periodic royalties calculated and when are they paid?

3. Are all trademarks and names legally protected?

4. Who provides and pays for advertising and promotional items?

5. Who selects the location of the business?

6. Is the franchise assigned an exclusive territory?

7. If the territory is not exclusive, does the franchisee have the right of first refusal on additional franchises established in nearby locations?

8. Is the franchisee required to purchase equipment and supplies from the franchisor or other suppliers?

9. Under what conditions can the franchisor and/or the franchisee terminate the franchise agreement?

10. Can the franchise be assigned to heirs?

Nevertheless, as Jim and Laura White discovered, evaluating a franchise means more than assessing the current operation. What the market will be like tomorrow is just as important an issue to address. For example, when the Whites opened their Body Shop franchise in 1994, they expected to earn a comfortable living on their $300,000 investment. Instead, the outlet lost money every year. What they hadn't taken into account was that less than a year after the Whites' Body Shop opened, Bath & Body would come into the same mall. So did Crabtree & Evelyn, followed a year later by Garden Botanika (these chains sell products that compete directly with Body Shop's, and each of the stores was bigger than the Whites').[33]

Advantages of Franchising

Why is franchising so popular? For one thing, when you invest in a franchise, you know you are getting a viable business, one that has "worked" many times before. If the franchise is well established, you get the added benefit of instant name recognition, national advertising programs, standardized quality of goods and services, and a proven formula for success. Buying a franchise also gives you instant access to a support network and in many cases a ready-made blueprint for building a business. For an initial investment (from a few thousand dollars to upward of a million, depending on the franchise), you get services such as site-location studies, market research, training, and technical assistance, as well as assistance with building or leasing your structure, decorating the building, purchasing supplies, and operating the business during your initial ownership phase. Some franchisors also assist franchisees in financing the initial investment.

Disadvantages of Franchising

Although franchising offers many advantages, it is not the ideal vehicle for everyone. First, owning a franchise is no guarantee of wealth. Even though it may be a relatively easy way to get into business, not all franchises are hugely profitable. Some franchisees barely survive, in fact. One of the biggest disadvantages of franchising is the monthly payment, or royalty, that must be turned over to the franchisor. Royalties are not necessarily bad as long as the franchisee gets ongoing assistance in return. Royalty fees vary from nothing at all to 20 percent of sales. Papa John's, for example, charges franchisees a monthly royalty fee of 4 percent of net sales.[34]

Another drawback of franchises is that many allow individual operators little independence. Franchisors can prescribe virtually every aspect of the business, down to the details of employee uniforms and the color of the walls. Furthermore, when a chain loses its cutting edge in the marketplace, being stuck with a franchise can be painful. By contrast, if independent retailers run into trouble with their product lines, they can change suppliers or perhaps switch rapidly to a whole new line of business. Franchisees can't. They're usually bound by contracts to sell only authorized products, often at a price set by the franchisor.

Although franchisors can make important decisions without consulting franchisees, the days of franchisors' exercising such control are ending. In many cases the relationship between franchisor and franchisee is becoming more of a joint venture. Some franchisors are rewriting contracts to become less dictatorial, says the CEO of U.S. Franchise Systems. Newer contracts offer stock options, automatic contract renewals, and empowerment through franchise advisory boards. Great Harvest Bread, for instance, promotes innovation among its franchisees. Owners are free to run their bakeries as they see fit, on just one condition: They must share what they learn along the way with other franchise owners.[35] Some franchisors are giving franchisees a voice in how advertising funds are used. Moreover, legislative proposals are being considered that would require franchisors to meet certain criteria (something like an accreditation) before they can sell a franchise in the United States.[36]

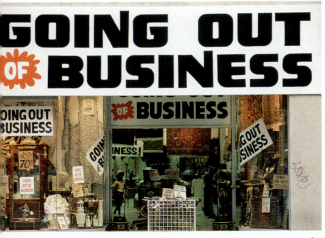

Starting a business is a risky venture with no guarantee of success.

Why New Businesses Fail

Even if you carefully evaluate a prospective franchisor or write a winning business plan, you have no guarantee of success. In fact, you may have heard some depressing statistics about the number of new businesses that fail. Some reports say your chances of succeeding are only one in three; others claim that the odds are even worse, stating that 85 percent of all new business ventures fail within 10 years. Actual statistics, however, show otherwise. Among all companies that close their doors, only about one in seven actually fails—that is, goes out of business leaving behind unpaid debts.[37] Moreover, the true failure rate is much lower if you remove those operations that business analysts say aren't "genuine businesses." For instance, a freelance writer who writes one article for a magazine and then stops writing would be counted as a failed business under the traditional measurement (which is based on tax returns).[38]

Businesses can fail for any number of reasons, as Exhibit 5.6 suggests. Lack of management skills, experience, and proper financing are among the top 10 reasons for failure. So is uncontrolled growth. Growth forces changes throughout the organization that affect every aspect of the business operation. In general, growing companies need to install more sophisticated systems and processes. They must staff positions that never existed and learn how to delegate responsibilities and control. They must hire experienced managers. And they must stay focused.

When growth is too rapid, it can force so much change that things spin out of control. And nothing can kill a successful business faster than chaos.[39] Doug and Jill Smith learned this the hard way. With a 50 percent increase in sales in one year alone, their company, Buckeye Beans & Herbs, was spinning out of control. They needed more people to take the orders, fill them, package the product, and so on. It took them a while to realize they weren't running a little mom-and-pop operation anymore. "We just couldn't do it all, and we didn't have the people in place yet," note the Smiths, who eventually got things back on the right track.[40]

Besides growing too rapidly, another mistake entrepreneurs make is to stray too far from the original product or market. Take Lifeline Systems, a provider of personal-response systems for the elderly. Fewer than 10 years after it was founded, the company went public and was distributing its monitoring devices in more than 700 hospitals across the United States. Fearing that its focus was too small, the company diversified by introducing a new version of its monitoring device that could be used by children and college students in emergencies. It sold these devices to drug, electronics, and department stores at roughly half the price of the original model. But the mass-market strategy found few buyers. Worse, it alienated the company's hospital customers, whose demand for the original product was already falling as a result of slashed hospital budgets. Lifeline began reporting losses. When a new CEO was hired to turn things around, one of the first things he did was undo the company's diversification efforts and restore the company's original focus.[41]

Exhibit 5.6

Why New Businesses Fail

Experts have identified these 10 reasons as the most likely causes of new business failure.

1. Management incompetence
2. Lack of industry experience
3. Inadequate financing
4. Poor business planning
5. Unclear or unrealistic goals
6. Failure to attract and keep target customers
7. Uncontrolled growth
8. Inappropriate location
9. Poor inventory and financial controls
10. Inability to make the entrepreneurial transition

Even when signs of failure begin to surface, some entrepreneurs don't pull the plug fast enough. Jeff Schwarz worked three years without drawing a salary and used up $100,000 of his personal savings before closing his photography business, Remarkable Moments.[42] Keep in mind that failure isn't always the end of the world. Many presidents of big, successful companies, including Fred Smith of FedEx, can spin long tales about how failure got them where they are today or how failure was a valuable learning experience.[43] Moreover, many sources of small-business assistance exist to help you plan your new business and overcome these obstacles.

Sources of Small-Business Assistance

Many local business professionals are willing to serve as mentors and can help you avoid the pitfalls of business. A number of smaller companies assemble advisory boards to help them review plans and decisions. Some executives meet regularly in small groups to analyze each other's progress month by month. As a small-business owner, you may also turn to small-business resources such as the Service Corps of Retired Executives (SCORE—a resource partner of the SBA), incubators, and the Internet. These resources can help you evaluate your business idea, develop a business plan, locate start-up funding sources, and promote your business more effectively.

SCORE

Some of the best advice available to small businesses costs little or nothing. It's delivered by SCORE's 12,000 volunteers. These men and women are working and retired executives and active small-business owners who offer advice and one-to-one counseling sessions on topics such as developing a business plan, securing financing, and managing business growth. Every year, SCORE counselors help some 400,000 U.S. businesses.[44]

Whether you use a SCORE counselor or find a private mentor, having someone to bounce your ideas off of or help you create a five-year financial forecast can increase the chances of your business's survival, as Lynelle and John Lawrence discovered. Owners of the Mudhouse Café in Charlottesville, Virginia, the Lawrences used a SCORE representative to help them prepare a detailed business plan and obtain financing. "There's no way we would be here without SCORE," confesses the couple.[45]

Incubators

Incubators are centers that provide "newborn" businesses with just about everything a company needs to get started—office space, expert advice, legal and accounting services, clerical services, marketing support, contacts, and more.[46] Some incubators are open to businesses of all types; others specialize in a specific industry or product. An incubator's goal is to convert "tenant" firms into "graduates," so most incubators set limits—from 18 months to five years—on how long a company can stay in the nest.[47]

Studies show that firms that start out in incubators typically increase sales by more than 400 percent from the time they enter until the time they leave.[48] Furthermore, 8 out of 10 businesses nurtured in incubators succeed. For instance, a Milwaukee, Wisconsin, business incubator gave Yolanda Cross the chance to move her catering-related business from her home into a more professional setting, where it has flourished.[49]

The Internet

The Internet is another source of small-business assistance. Sonja Edmond, owner of Heavenly Bounty Giftbaskets, a handcrafted gift-basket business, had to look no further than her computer screen when she needed help. Although she enjoyed making gift baskets as a hobby, she wasn't sure whether a viable market existed to support a home-based business. So she posted a price-setting question on CompuServe's Working

incubators
Facilities that house small businesses during their early growth phase

After a friend referred John and Lynelle Lawrence to SCORE, counselor Joe Geller (right) helped the couple through each stage of preparation for their Mudhouse Café in Charlottesville, Virginia.

from Home and Handcrafts forum. Within 24 hours, her e-mail box was flooded with answers from forum members, who "convinced me I could do this," she says. Edmond struck a resource gold mine: Not only did she find the encouragement she needed to plunge into entrepreneurship, she also got valuable business leads and advice on licensing her product.[50]

FINANCING A NEW BUSINESS

Once you've decided to go into business for yourself, you will probably need some money to get started. Depending on the type of business, you may need to hire employees, purchase inventory, and acquire assets such as land, production facilities, and equipment before you can generate revenue.

Where can firms obtain the money they need to launch and operate a new business? Most new businesses turn to private financing sources, such as family, friends, and loans from banks, finance companies, or other commercial lenders. As the start-up grows, owners can raise additional funds by selling shares of stock to the public. For instance, in 1993—eight years after John Schnatter opened his first restaurant—Papa John's raised over $40 million by selling company stock to the public.[51]

As you can imagine, financing an enterprise is a complex undertaking. The process begins by assessing the firm's financing needs and determining whether funds are needed for the short or the long term. You must also assess the cost of obtaining financing, and you must weigh the advantages and disadvantages of financing through debt or equity, taking into consideration the firm's special needs and circumstances. In short, choosing the right sources of financing can be just as important as choosing the right location. Your decision will affect your company's *capital structure*—the mix of debt and equity—forever.

Length of Term

Financing can be either short-term or long-term. *Short-term financing* is any financing that will be repaid within one year, whereas *long-term financing* is any financing that will be repaid in a period longer than one year. The primary purpose of short-term debt financing is to ensure that a company maintains its liquidity, or its ability to meet financial obligations (such as rent), as they become due. By contrast, long-term financing is used to acquire long-term assets such as buildings and equipment or to fund a start-up and expansion via any number of growth options.

Cost of Capital

In general, a company wants to obtain money at the lowest cost and least amount of risk. However, lenders and investors want to receive the highest possible return on their investment, also at the lowest risk. A company's *cost of capital*, the average rate of interest it must pay on its financing, depends on three main factors: the risk associated with the company, the prevailing level of interest rates, and management's selection of funding vehicles. Obviously, the more financially solid a company is, the less risk investors face. However, time also plays a vital role. Because a dollar will be worth less tomorrow than it is today, lenders need to be compensated for waiting to be repaid. As a result, long-term financing generally costs a company more than short-term financing.

Regardless of how financially solid a company is, the cost of money will vary over time because interest rates fluctuate. Companies must take such interest rate fluctuations into account when making financing decisions. For instance, a company planning to finance a short-term project when interest rates are 8.5 percent would want to reevaluate the project if interest rates rose to, say, 10 percent a few months later. Even though companies try to time their borrowing to take advantage of drops in interest rates, this option is not always possible. A firm's need for money doesn't always coincide with a period of favorable rates. At times, a company may be forced to borrow when rates are high and then renegotiate the loan when rates drop. Sometimes projects must be put on hold until interest rates become more affordable.

Debt Versus Equity Financing

Debt financing refers to what people normally think of as a loan. A creditor agrees to lend money to a debtor in exchange for repayment, with accumulated interest, at some future date. Loans can be secured or unsecured. **Secured loans** are those backed by something of value, known as *collateral*, which may be seized by the lender if the borrower fails to repay the loan. The most common types of collateral are accounts receivable, inventories, and property such as marketable securities, buildings, and other assets. **Unsecured loans** are ones that require no collateral. Instead, the lender relies on the general credit record and the earning power of the borrower.

Equity financing is achieved by selling shares of a company's stock. Whenever a corporation offers its shares of ownership, or **stock**, to the public for the first time, the company is said to be *going public*. The initial shares offered for sale are the company's **initial public offering (IPO)**. Going public is an effective method of raising needed capital, but it can be an expensive and time-consuming process with no guarantee you'll get the amount of money you need. Public companies must file a variety of statements with regulatory agencies, pay fees, and prepare audited financial statements, as Chapter 13 points out.

When choosing between debt and equity financing, you should weigh the advantages and disadvantages of each (see Exhibit 5.7). In addition to considering whether the financing is for the short or the long term and assessing the cost of the financing, such as interest, fees, and other charges, you must also evaluate your desire for ownership control. Two of the biggest benefits of debt financing are (1) the lender does not gain an

secured loans
Loans backed up with something of value that the lender can claim in case of default, such as a piece of property

unsecured loans
Loans requiring no collateral but a good credit rating

stock
Shares of ownership in a corporation

initial public offering (IPO)
Corporation's first offering of stock to the public

Exhibit 5.7	**Debt Versus Equity**	

When choosing between debt and equity financing, companies evaluate the characteristics of both types of funding.

CHARACTERISTIC	DEBT	EQUITY
Maturity	**Specific:** Specifies a date by which it must be repaid.	**Nonspecific:** Specifies no maturity date.
Claim on income	**Fixed cost:** Company must pay interest on debt held by bondholders and lenders before paying any dividends to shareholders. Interest payments must be met regardless of operating results.	**Discretionary cost:** Shareholders may receive dividends after creditors have received interest payments; however, company is not required to pay dividends.
Claim on assets	**Priority:** Lenders have prior claims on assets.	**Residual:** Shareholders have claims only after the firm satisfies claims of lenders.
Influence over management	**Little:** Lenders are creditors, not owners. They can impose limits on management only if interest payments are not received.	**Varies:** As owners of the company, shareholders can vote on some aspects of corporate operations. Shareholder influence varies, depending on whether stock is widely distributed or closely held.

ownership interest in the business, and (2) a firm's obligations are limited to repaying the loan. By contrast, equity financing involves an exchange of money for a share of business ownership: It allows firms to obtain funds without pledging to repay a specific amount of money at a particular time, but in exchange for this benefit the firm must give up some ownership control.

Private Financing Sources

Most new companies obtain start-up capital from personal assets, from family and friends, or from strategic partners or customers. Another source of private financing is big business. Companies such as Coca-Cola and Procter & Gamble fund young companies in exchange for stock or exclusive rights to future products. By working with start-ups, larger companies hope to hasten product development and infuse their own operations with more of the entrepreneurial spirit.[52]

Bank loans are another source of private financing, but obtaining such financing can be difficult for most start-ups. For one thing, banks consider start-ups risky so they shy away from lending money to new businesses. For another, the risk inherent in some start-ups justifies higher interest rates than banks are allowed to charge by law. Consequently, most banks will finance a start-up only if they can obtain payment guarantees from other financially sound parties or to the extent that the business has marketable collateral, such as buildings and equipment, to back the loan.[53]

In addition to friends, corporate financing, and bank loans, other sources of private financing assistance include venture capitalists, angel investors, credit cards, and the SBA.

Venture Capitalists

venture capitalists
Investment specialists who provide money to finance new businesses or turnarounds in exchange for a portion of the ownership, with the objective of making a considerable profit on the investment; also called VCs

Venture capitalists are investment specialists who raise pools of capital from large private and institutional sources (such as pension funds) to fund ventures that have a high, rapid growth potential and a need for large amounts of capital. Venture capitalists, or VCs as they're called in entrepreneurial circles, do not simply lend money to a small business as a bank would. Instead, they provide money and management expertise in return for a sizable ownership interest in the business. Once the business becomes profitable, venture capitalists reap the reward by selling their interest to other long-term investors for a sizable profit. Because they usually risk a considerable amount of money, most VCs are quite selective when it comes to investing. Of the 600,000 or so businesses that started up in 2000, for instance, only some 5,000 received venture-capitalist funding.[54]

The flow of money from VCs slowed dramatically after the dot-com fallout at the end of the 1990s. VCs invested $106 billion in 2000 but only $13 billion in 2003.[55] In addition to being more selective, venture capitalists are also becoming more aggressive in their oversight and management of firms they've already funded. For instance, they are shutting down firms that show little promise and pumping extra cash into those they think can survive. VCs are also scrutinizing business plans more skeptically. Applicants must now show real revenue, real customers, and a clear path to profits.[56] Still, most venture-capitalist firms will finance only firms that need $10 million or more.[57] If you're looking for less, you'll probably need to find an angel instead.

Angel Investors

Comfortable with risks that scare off many banks, *angel investors* put their own money into start-ups with the goal of eventually selling their interest for a large profit. These wealthy individuals are willing to loan smaller amounts of money than are VCs and to stay involved with the company for a longer period of time.

Start-ups that seek out angels typically have spent their first $50,000 to $100,000 and are now looking for the next $250,000 to grow their business.[58] In addition to providing financing, angels can be a great source of business expertise and credibility. High-profile angels include such experts as Bill Gates (chairman of Microsoft), Marc Andresseen (founder of Netscape), and others.[59]

Credit Cards

According to one recent study, one-third of businesses with fewer than 20 employees use credit cards to finance their new business ventures.[60] Many people turn to credit cards because credit card companies don't care how borrowers spend the money just as long as they pay the bill. Others use credit cards because they are the only source of funding available to them. But with higher interest rates than almost any other type of funding, credit cards are a risky way to finance a business, as Jorge de la Riva discovered. He used personal credit cards to start up his industrial wholesale business—an experience he calls "playing with the tiger." As de la Riva put it, "You can make it work only if you have a definite plan to pay back the debt."[61] Unfortunately, many do not.

Small Business Administration Assistance

If your business doesn't fit the profile of high-powered venture-capital start-ups, or you can't find an angel, you might be able to qualify for a bank loan backed by the SBA. To get an SBA-backed loan, you apply to a regular bank, which actually provides the money; the SBA guarantees to repay up to 80 percent of the loan if you fail to do so. The average SBA-backed loan is about $100,000; the upper limit is $1 million with a 75 percent guarantee.[62] Guaranteed loans provided by the SBA launched FedEx, Intel, and Apple Computer. These three now pay more annual taxes to the federal government than the entire yearly cost of running the SBA.[63] In addition to operating its loan guarantee program, the SBA provides a limited number of direct loans to women, veterans, and minorities.[64]

Aspiring entrepreneurs like Karla Brown, who might not qualify for regular bank loans, can apply for SBA microloans to make their dreams come true.

From the businessperson's standpoint, SBA-backed loans are especially attractive because most have longer repayment terms than conventional bank loans—nine years as opposed to two or three. A longer repayment term translates into lower monthly payments. Unfortunately, demand for SBA loans vastly outstrips the agency's budget.[65] Nevertheless, Karla Brown is one of the lucky ones. With plenty of perseverance and a $19,000 microloan from the SBA, Brown was able to start her business, Ashmont Flowers Plus. The SBA microloan program began in 1992 to help people realize the American dream—to own a business and be self-sufficient. Microloans range from $100 to $25,000, with the average loan of $10,000 paid back over four years.[66]

Another option for raising money is one of the investment firms created by the Small Business Administration. Small Business Investment Companies (SBICs) and Minority Enterprise Small Business Investment Companies (MESBICs), which finance minority-owned businesses, are similar in operation to venture-capital firms, but they tend to make smaller investments and are willing to consider businesses that VCs may not want to finance.[67]

Summary of Learning Objectives

1 Highlight the major contributions small businesses make to the U.S. economy.

Small businesses bring new ideas, processes, and vigor to the marketplace. They generate about half of private sector output and provide about 75 percent of all new jobs and employ over half of the private nonfarm U.S. workforce. Small businesses introduce new goods and services, provide specialized products, and supply the needs of large corporations. Additionally, they spend almost as much as big businesses in the economy each year.

2 Identify the key characteristics (other than size) that differentiate small businesses from larger ones.

In general, small businesses tend to sell fewer products and services to a more targeted group of customers. They have closer contact with their customers and many tend to be more open-minded and innovative because they have less to lose than established companies. Small-business owners generally make decisions faster and give employees more opportunities for individual expression and authority.

Because they have limited resources, however, small-business owners often must work harder and perform a variety of job functions.

3 Discuss three factors contributing to the increase in the number of small businesses.

One factor is the advancement of technology and the Internet, which makes it easier to start a small business, compete with larger firms, or work from home. A second factor is the increase in the number of women and minorities who are interested in becoming entrepreneurs. Third, corporate downsizing and outsourcing have made self-employment or small-business ownership a more attractive and viable option.

4 Cite the key characteristics common to most entrepreneurs.

Successful entrepreneurs are highly disciplined, intuitive, innovative, ambitious individuals who are eager to learn and like to set trends. They prefer excitement and are willing to take risks to reap the rewards. Few start businesses for the sole purpose of making money.

5 List three ways of going into business for yourself.

You can start a new company from scratch, you can buy a going concern, or you can invest in a franchise. Each option has its advantages and disadvantages when it comes to cost, control, certainty, support, and independence.

6 Identify four sources of small-business assistance.

One source for small-business assistance is SCORE—an organization staffed by retired executives and active small-business owners who provide counseling and mentoring for free. Incubators are another source. They provide facilities, business resources, and all types of start-up support. The Internet is an excellent resource for product and market research, business leads, advice, and contacts. And many small-business owners try to take advantage of mentors and advisory boards.

7 Highlight several factors you should consider when evaluating financing options and discuss the principal sources of small-business private financing.

When assessing financing options, you should consider the cost and risk of capital and the firm's special needs and circumstances. You should also weigh the length of term for which financing is needed and the advantages and disadvantages of debt versus equity financing, including impact on ownership control. Bank loans are a principal source of private financing. Family and friends are another. Other alternatives include big businesses, venture capitalists, angel investors, and credit cards. Finally, the Small Business Administration, though not an actual source, can assist entrepreneurs by guaranteeing small bank loans up to 80 percent of the amount borrowed.

Behind the Scenes

Papa John's Piping Hot Performance

John Schnatter did a remarkable job of expanding from a single pizza store he started in his father's tavern. Three years after Schnatter opened his first Papa John's, he expanded outside the Louisville, Kentucky, area. He was no novice. He knew the grass roots of the pizza business, he had an intuitive grasp on what customers wanted, and he knew how to make pizzas taste a little bit better than the competition's. Moreover, he had the qualities of an entrepreneur: driven, intense, willing to make things happen, visionary, and very competitive.

John Schnatter used franchising to grow the business. Today about 75 percent of Papa John's are franchised; the rest are company owned. He was encouraged by Kentucky Fried Chicken, Long John Silvers, Chi Chi's, and other Kentucky-born restaurants that had successfully taken their franchised restaurants national. Schnatter thought, "What the heck, maybe I could do it too." But to keep growth under control, Papa John's didn't just move into an area and open up 200 stores. Schnatter grew the stores one at a time—spending up to six months to a year assessing an area's potential.

It wasn't long before Papa John's began grabbing business from such giants as Pizza Hut, Little Caesar's, and delivery king Domino's. Then in 1999 Papa John's made its European debut by acquiring Perfect Pizza Holdings, a 205-unit delivery and carryout pizza chain in the United Kingdom. The acquisition gave Papa John's instant access to proven sites that would have been difficult to obtain. Besides the real estate, Perfect Pizza had a good management team that Schnatter could fold into his organization.

Today, Papa John's has vaulted past Little Caesar's to become the nation's third-largest pizza chain. The company now boasts roughly 3,000 stores in 49 states and 15 international markets. Annual sales have mushroomed to nearly

$2 billion. In spite of its tremendous growth, Schnatter insists on maintaining the highest-quality standards. He does so by keeping things simple. About 95 percent of the restaurants are takeout only. The menu is simple—just two types of pizza, thin crust or regular—no exotic toppings, no salads, no sandwiches, and no buffalo wings. Owners are trained to remake any pies that rate less than 8 on the company's 10-point scale. If a pizza has cheese with a single air bubble or the crust is not golden brown, out the offender goes. Schnatter's attention to product quality has earned the company awards. For four consecutive years, Papa John's was voted number one in customer satisfaction among all fast-food restaurants in the American Consumer Satisfaction Index.

To keep things in order, Schnatter visits four to five stores a week, often unannounced. He also trains managers how to forecast product demand. Stores project demand one to two weeks in advance. They factor in anything from forthcoming promotions to community events to the next big high school football game. If a big game is on TV, Schnatter wants to make sure the store owners are ready for the surge in deliveries.

Still, like many companies today, Papa John's faces new challenges. It's becoming increasingly difficult to grow the company's share of the pie. Although Americans consume pizza at a rate of 350 slices a second, the pizza industry is stagnant and highly competitive. Growth generally comes at the expense of a competitor's existing business. Moreover, to keep profitability in line, Schnatter has scaled back company expansion plans and even closed some unprofitable outlets. But Schnatter is determined to succeed. And if one strength rises above the others in Schnatter's path to success, it's his ability to recruit and retain the right people. "There's nothing special about John Schnatter except the people around me," Schnatter says. "They make me look better" and they make Papa John's what it is—committed to its heritage of making a superior-quality, traditional pizza.[68]

Critical Thinking Questions

1. What steps did John Schnatter take to turn Papa John's into a successful pizza chain?
2. If you were drafting Papa John's initial business plan, what would you need to know about the competition?
3. Why would Papa John's rely on franchising to grow its concept?

LEARN MORE ONLINE

Visit the Papa John's website by going to Chapter 5 of this text's website at www.prenhall.com/bovee and clicking on the Papa John's hotlink. Read about the Papa John's franchise system. What kind of assistance does Papa John's provide to new franchisees? What are the minimum requirements for new franchisees? About how much does it cost to open a Papa John's restaurant? ■

Key Terms

business plan (121)
franchise (122)
franchisee (122)
franchisor (123)
incubators (127)

initial public offering (IPO) (129)
outsource (119)
secured loans (129)
small business (115)
start-up companies (121)

stock (129)
unsecured loans (129)
venture capitalists (130)

Test Your Knowledge

Questions for Review

1. What are two essential functions of a business plan?
2. What are the advantages of buying a business rather than starting one from scratch?
3. What are the advantages and disadvantages of owning a franchise?
4. What are the key reasons for most small-business failures?
5. What is a business incubator?

Questions for Analysis

6. Why is writing a business plan an important step in starting a new business?

7. Why is it important to establish a time limit for a new business to generate a profit?
8. What things should you consider when evaluating a franchise agreement?
9. What factors should you consider before selecting financing alternatives for a new business?
10. **Ethical Considerations:** You're thinking about starting your own hot dog and burger stand. You've got the perfect site in mind, and you've analyzed the industry and all the important statistics. It looks as if all systems are go. Uncle Pete is even going to back you on this one. You really understand the fast-food market. In fact, you've become a regular at a competitor's operation (down the road) for

over a month. The owner thinks you're his best customer. He even wants to name a sandwich creation after you. But you're not there because you love Frannie's fancy fries. No, you're actually spying. You're learning everything you can about the competition so you can outsmart them. Is this behavior ethical? Explain your answer.

Questions for Application

11. Briefly describe an incident in your life in which you failed to achieve a goal you set for yourself. What did you learn from this experience? How could you apply this lesson to a future experience as an entrepreneur?

12. Lack of industry experience is one of the most common reasons for failure of new businesses. If you wanted to start a new business that provides catering and other services for corporate events (office parties, executive retreats, public open houses, and so on), how might you gain the experience needed to succeed in such a venture?

13. **Integrated.** Entrepreneurs are one of the five factors of production as discussed in Chapter 1. Review that material plus Exhibit 1.2 (Rags to Riches), and explain why entrepreneurs are an important factor for economic success.

14. **Integrated.** Pick a local small business or franchise that you visit frequently and discuss whether that business competes on price, speed, innovation, convenience, quality, or any combination of those factors. Be sure to provide some examples.

Practice Your Knowledge

Sharpening Your Communication Skills

Effective communication begins with identifying your primary audience and adapting your message to your audience's needs. This is true even for business plans. One of the primary reasons for writing a business plan is to obtain financing. With that in mind, what do you think are the most important things investors will want to know? How can you convince them that the information you are providing is accurate? What should you assume investors know about your specific business or industry?

Building Your Team Skills

The 10 questions shown in Exhibit 5.5 cover major legal issues you should explore before plunking down money for a franchise. In addition, however, there are many more questions you should ask in the process of deciding whether to buy a particular franchise.

With your team, think about how to investigate the possibility of buying a Papa John's franchise. First, brainstorm with your team to draw up a list of sources (such as printed sources, Internet sources, and any other suitable sources) where you can locate basic background information about the franchisor. Also list at least two sources you might consult for detailed information about buying and operating a Papa John's franchise. Next, generate a list of at least 10 questions any interested buyer should ask about this potential business opportunity.

Choose a spokesperson to present your team's ideas to the class. After all the teams have reported, hold a class discussion to analyze the lists of questions generated by all the teams. Which questions were on most teams' lists? Why do you think those questions are so important? Can your class think of any additional questions that were not on any team's lists but seem important?

Expand Your Knowledge

Discovering Career Opportunities

Would you like to own and operate your own business? Whether you plan to start a new business from scratch or buy an existing business or a franchise, you will need certain qualities to be successful. Start your journey to entrepreneurship by reviewing this chapter's section on entrepreneurs and by studying Exhibit 5.3. Now you are ready to delve deeper into the career opportunities of owning and running a small business.

1. Which of the entrepreneurial characteristics mentioned in the chapter and in Exhibit 5.3 describe you? Which of those characteristics can you develop more fully in advance of running your own business?

2. Using library sources, find a self-test on entrepreneurial qualities or use the entrepreneurial test at the website www.onlinewbc.gov/docs/starting/test.html. Analyze the test's questions. Which of the characteristics discussed in this chapter are mentioned or suggested by the questions included in the test?

3. Answer all the questions in the self-test you have selected. Which questions seem the most critical for entrepreneurial success? How did you score on this self-test and on the questions you think are most critical? Before you go into business for yourself, which characteristics will you need to work on?

Developing Your Research Skills

Scan issues of print or online editions of business journals or newspapers for articles describing problems or successes faced by small businesses in the United States. Clip or copy three or more articles that interest you and then answer the following questions.

1. What problem or opportunity does each article present? Is it an issue faced by many businesses, or is it specific to one industry or region?

2. What could a potential small-business owner learn about the risks and rewards of business ownership from reading these articles?

3. How might these articles affect someone who is thinking about starting a small business?

SEE IT ON THE WEB

For live links to the websites that follow, go to this text's website at www.prenhall.com/bovee. When you log on, select Chapter 5, then select "Featured Websites," click on the URL of the website you wish to visit, review the website, and answer the following questions:

1. What is the purpose of this website?

2. What kinds of information does this website contain? Please be specific.

3. How is the information provided at this website useful for businesspeople? Consumers?

4. How did you expand your knowledge of starting and financing a small business by reviewing the material at this website? What new things did you learn about this topic?

Guide Your Way to Small-Business Success

Inc.com has an outstanding selection of articles and advice on buying, owning, and running a small business that you won't want to miss. If you're considering a franchise, the tools and tips at this site will help you find your ideal business. Concerned about financing? Check out the articles on raising start-up capital, finding an angel, or attracting venture capital. You can also find information on how to create or spruce up a website, set up your first office, develop entrepreneurial savvy, and overcome burnout. Running a small business is no easy feat, so get a head start by reading the Inc.com guides online. www.inc.com/guides

Start a Small Business

Thinking about starting your own business? The U.S. Small Business Administration (SBA) website puts you in touch with a wealth of resources to assist you in your start-up. Perhaps you would like some professional business counseling, financial assistance, or advice on developing a business plan. Starting a new business or buying an existing one can be an overwhelming process. But you can increase your chances of success by taking your first steps with the SBA's Startup Kit. So log on to find out if entrepreneurship is for you. Then do your research and discover some of the secrets of success. www.sba.gov

Learn the ABCs of IPOs

Taking a company public is not for the faint of heart. But like a Broadway opening, a successful debut can launch a relatively unknown company into stardom—or allow it to quietly disappear from the public eye. Even today's largest corporations were at some point small start-ups looking for public financing. Which company is the next AOL, Xerox, or Microsoft? How do IPOs work? How does a young company play the IPO game? You can find the answer to these questions and more by checking out the Beginners Guide to IPOs at Hoover's IPO Central. www.hoovers.com (click on IPO Central)

Companion Website

Learning Interactively

Go to the Companion Website at www.prenhall.com/bovee. For Chapter 5, take advantage of the interactive "Study Guide" to test your knowledge of the chapter. Get instant feedback on whether you need additional studying.

Also, visit this site's "Study Hall," where you'll find an abundance of valuable resources that will help you succeed in this course.

Video **Case**

Managing Growth at Student Advantage

LEARNING OBJECTIVES

The purpose of this video is to help you:

1. See how a company is successfully making the transition away from being a small business.

2. Understand some of the pitfalls of growing beyond a small, entrepreneurial organization.

3. Recognize how important partnerships with established companies can be for many small businesses.

SYNOPSIS

Many students are familiar with the Student Advantage discount card, saving them up to 50 percent on everyday purchases on and off campus, including air and ground transportation. Keeping pace with the growing consumer base among high school and college students, Student Advantage, Inc. has successfully implemented an aggressive growth strategy. Working with hundreds of colleges, universities, and campus organizations, and more than 15,000 merchant locations, the company reaches customers offline through the Student Advantage Membership and online through its website. Eleven acquisitions in its first ten years of existence have taught this company and its young CEO, Ray Sozzi, that communication is the key to growing beyond a small business without losing the original entrepreneurial vision.

Discussion Questions

1. *For analysis:* Even though Student Advantage may have started as a small company, it was clearly created with an eye on growth, rather than as a lifestyle business designed to support one family. In a company that must partner with dozens of other companies and provide ser-

vices to more than a million customers, what are the risks of growing quickly?

2. *For analysis:* Based on what you learned in the video, what steps did Student Advantage take to avoid the potential problems of a high-growth strategy based on frequent acquisitions?

3. *For analysis:* How does the "buddy system" help Student Advantage integrate employees from acquired companies?

4. *For application:* Student Advantage's corporate lawyer made a strong case for a go-slow approach to growing internationally. Given the millions of students in other countries who might want to use the company's services—and who might find other alternatives before Student Advantage becomes available in their respective countries—why would it be wise to grow slowly and carefully, rather than jumping into new markets quickly, before competitors can spring up?

5. *For debate:* One of the Student Advantage executives describes the challenge of growing into the job without the benefit of previous managerial or executive experience. What are the pros and cons of bringing in experienced outside managers to help a small company, versus giving existing employees the opportunity to grow into managerial jobs?

ONLINE EXPLORATION

Visit Student Advantage's website at www.studentadvantage.com. Based on the types of services you see, what sort of companies does Student Advantage seek out as partners? How does the company promote its services to students? How does the website try to appeal to student lifestyle concerns, such as summer vacation or spring break?

E-Business in Action

THE RISE, FALL, AND RISE OF DOT-COMS

On April 8, 1999, Craig Winn, founder of Value America, became a dot-com billionaire. Investors flocked to his idea of a "Wal-Mart" of the Internet, where shoppers could order jars of caviar along with their gas barbecues or desktop computers. The company served as a go-between: It transmitted customer orders immediately to manufacturers, who would ship the merchandise directly to buyers. Value America's IPO was a success. The stock closed the first day at $55 a share, valuing the three-year-old profitless company at $2.4 billion.

Running on Empty

Twelve months later, Value America filed for Chapter 11 bankruptcy protection, and the price of the company's stock had fallen to 72 cents. The cyberstore was supposed to harness every efficiency promised by the Internet: no inventory, no shipping costs, no warehouse, no physical store. But like many Internet entrepreneurs, Winn tried to do too much too soon. Company computers crashed, customers waited to get their orders filled, returned merchandise piled up in the halls of the company's offices, and discounting and advertising drained the company's cash, wiping out any chance of profitability.

Instant Paper Billions

Value America's rise and fall is symbolic of an era of unbridled optimism. For much of the 1990s, U.S. businesses and their investors displayed an appetite for risk that would have been considered reckless just a few years earlier. A raging bull market, free-flowing capital, and technological advances created so many opportunities at the turn of the millennium that it was sometimes difficult to separate a calculated risk from a wild grab at the brass ring.

Just about any dot-com company that wanted to hawk wares over the Net found plenty of eager investors hoping to reap huge profits from the dot-com craze. The web was like a vast, underdeveloped prairie; web entrepreneurs even used the word "landgrab" to describe their mad attempts at capturing market share—at any cost. The new-economy boom led many to believe that the rules of business had changed. Venture capitalists, flush with wealth from skyrocketing stock prices, threw too many millions at inexperienced entrepreneurs with untested ideas and unproven technology. Enthusiastic investors raced to claim a stake in the new frontier at Internet speed. Most went in with their eyes wide shut,

driving stock prices even higher—which gave VCs that much more money to throw at new businesses.

The Lights Go Out

Like a thrill ride at an amusement park, however, the whole affair soon screeched to a halt. Entrepreneurs learned the hard way that successfully launching a public company was much different from successfully running one. Cyberspace got crowded. New dot-coms went unnoticed. Desperate to get consumers' attention and business, e-tailers spent lavishly on advertising. Some pumped out discount offers and free-shipping promises—hemorrhaging cash and piling up losses. This turn of events prompted investors to take a second look and change their minds—overnight. Profits, it seemed, mattered after all. Many investors watched in shock as dot-com stock prices fell through the floor.

Some, of course, had predicted the dot-com fallout. History, they said, would repeat itself. After all, from 1855 to 1861, the number of start-up telegraph companies in the United States shrank by 87 percent—from 50 to 6. The Internet, they predicted, would not escape a shakeout of its own. Why did the dot-coms run out of steam? Experts now cite these reasons:

- *Poor management.* Many dot-coms were founded by people with little or no experience running a business. Some entrepreneurs were in such a rush to go public they forgot one small detail: They needed a sound business plan. They were more attracted by the potential to get rich than by the need to create a company "built to last." Craig Winn's business background, for instance, consisted mainly of leading another public company into bankruptcy. His technology experience? None. Only during a period of a seeming suspension of the "rules of business" could someone with Winn's background amass the funds to launch such a risky venture.

- *Unrealistic goals.* Many dot-com start-ups were dedicated to achieving the impossible—launching companies in weeks and attracting millions of customers in months. But the evolution of consumers was far slower than most people predicted. People were not ready to buy mortgages and new cars in volume over the Internet. In fact, most Internet firms found that hoped-for volume simply wasn't there. Take online grocers, for example. Buying groceries online requires consumers to make a big change in the way they shop for basic household goods. Moreover, to build up a base of customers from scratch, the newcomers had to spend heavily on advertising and other types of marketing. Webvan, for instance, spent 25 to 35 percent of its revenue on advertising, compared with an average of about 1 percent spent by traditional grocers. Another unrealistic goal, and one that doomed a number of dot-coms, was the assumption that a herd of advertisers would migrate from television and other traditional venues as soon as enough websites attracted enough "eyeballs."

■ *Going public too soon.* Venture capitalists, eager to back the next AOL or Amazon, tossed huge sums of money at companies that had barely a prayer of prospering. In many cases, the VCs took the dot-coms public way too soon. Instead of waiting the customary four to five years, dot-coms were taken public in two years or less—long before the company or its management could prove consistent performance to the public. Nonetheless, investors overlooked business fundamentals and continued to scoop up these stocks, driving prices into the stratosphere.

■ *Fighting the laws of supply and demand.* Demand-driven start-ups are born to fulfill existing needs of consumers or businesses. By contrast, supply-driven start-ups are born in the mind of the entrepreneur with little more than a gut feeling that someone will eventually need or want the company's product or service. Thus, supply-driven start-ups leave the company with the enormous task of establishing a new market rather than participating in an existing one. Moreover, with relatively low barriers to entry in many cases, other dot-coms could easily copy a good idea.

■ *Extravagant spending.* Companies spent recklessly to lure customers with special promotions and silly marketing campaigns—no matter the cost. For instance, drkoop.com, an online health site, burned through three-quarters of the $84 million it raised in an IPO in less than one year. Losses, of course, were excused as necessary in the pursuit of new customers. Some dot-coms even began to act like conventional retailers—building costly warehouses and adding staff—to compete. Webvan officials argued in the company's early stages that the centers, which could handle up to 8,000 orders a day (many times more than a traditional warehouse) would give it a big cost advantage over its bricks-and-mortar competitors. But it never gained the sales volume to take full advantage of the efficiencies, and so its profit margins trailed those of large traditional grocers. After chewing through $830 million in start-up and IPO funds, Webvan filed for bankruptcy protection.

■ *Locked out of cash.* Most dot-coms were started with venture capital. When they burned through that money,

they had to find new funding or go public. For many, neither happened. As the dot-com failure rate grew, investors forced companies to cut costs vigorously, look for merger candidates, postpone or scrap their plans to go public, find a buyer at any price, or simply close up shop.

As quickly as they'd jumped on the bandwagon, investors, the press, and the general public turned on the whole idea of dot-coms. VCs and individual investors licked their wounds and looked for safer places to invest whatever money they had left. Workers who had been lured away from big-company jobs with the dream of IPO riches tried to return. Most people seemed to write it off as some big, crazy experiment that went wildly wrong.

Internet entrepreneurs learned a lot during the dot-com boom, everything from fundamentals of supply and demand (when there's no demand, there's not much point in having supply) to the truth about those traditional business models they once scoffed at as outmoded (there's a reason those models have been in use for years . . . they work!). Online companies learned how hard it was to compete in businesses that often had razor-thin profit margins, such as retailing, and how hard it was to change consumer habits.

A Funny Thing Happened on the Way to the Trash Heap

A year or two after the bleakest point of the dot-com story, an amazing thing began to happen: Some of the dot-coms started to succeed. Amazon.com became a multi-billion-dollar retailer that started to turn a profit on its massive investment in e-commerce. eBay reinvented the world of flea markets and auctions on its way to becoming the most popular shopping site in the world and continues to show strong profits. Yahoo! attracts more than 200 million visitors a month to its global network of web portals. Google has become a household name, synonymous with searching online. And old-school retailers such as Wal-Mart and manufacturers such as Dell learned from dot-com mania and now harness the Internet successfully themselves. So while the dot-com party certainly got out of control in the late 1990s, it seems there were some ideas worth celebrating after all.

Critical Thinking Questions

1. Why did so many dot-com businesses fail at the beginning of the 21st century?

2. How did the attitude of dot-com investors change? Why did it change?

3. If you had the opportunity to invest in a dot-com business today, what questions would you ask before investing your money?

BUSINESS PlanPro Exercises

Starting and Organizing a Small Business

Review Appendix D, "Your Business Plan" (on pages 416–417), to learn how to use Business PlanPro Software so you can complete these exercises.

THINK LIKE A PRO

Objective: By completing these exercises you will become acquainted with the sections of a business plan that address forms of ownership, financing the enterprise, and the franchising alternative. You will use the sample business plan for Pegasus Sports (listed as Inline Skating Products in the Sample Plan Browser) in this exercise.

1. What form of ownership does Pegasus currently use? What are the advantages of selecting that form of ownership? What change in ownership form is Pegasus planning to make?

2. How is Pegasus financing its start-up operations? Has the company gone public (or does the plan indicate it wants to go public)?

3. Would you recommend that Pegasus use franchising to grow its business? Explain your answer.

CREATE YOUR OWN BUSINESS PLAN

Think about your own business. What form of ownership will you choose? Why? How much start-up money will you need? How will you finance your start-up costs? Where will you obtain the money you will need to grow your business? Enter your answers in the appropriate sections of your business plan.

Part 3

Managing a Business

Chapter 6

Understanding the Functions and Roles of Management

LEARNING OBJECTIVES
After studying this chapter, you will be able to

1 Define the four basic management functions

2 Outline the tasks involved in the strategic planning process

3 Explain the purpose of a mission statement

4 List the benefits of setting long-term goals and objectives

5 Cite three leadership styles and explain why no one style is best

6 Clarify how total quality management (TQM) is changing the way organizations are managed

7 Identify and explain the three types of managerial skills

Behind **the Scenes**

Nokia: A Finnish Fable

www.nokia.com

For more than a century, the Finnish corporation Nokia produced everything from diapers and toilet paper to tires and rubber boots. But all that changed during the early 1990s when a global recession threw the company into a tailspin. More than 125 years of profitable operations came to a sudden standstill when Nokia's customers stopped buying its products. The collapse of the Soviet Union, Finland's chief trading partner, made matters worse. Moreover, Nokia's struggling mobile phone division couldn't keep up with the mass production techniques used by competitors. By the time Jorma Ollila was appointed CEO in 1992, the company was losing $80 million a year.

Challenged to come up with a survival plan, Ollila took a gigantic gamble. He believed that people have a tendency to get complacent and that it takes a push to tap into their strongest instincts—those that guide success. Ollila and several colleagues concluded that mobile phones were about to move from business markets to

After Jorma Ollila took charge of Nokia in 1992, the company began to report one success story after another.

consumer markets. So he ditched Nokia's multiple interests and gave the company a single, new focus: wireless telecommunications. He beefed up research and development, and soon the company developed a line of phones with stylish features to meet the mood of the market.

While rivals stumbled, Nokia came up with the best products, the best manufacturing logistics, and the best brand name in telecom. Still, Ollila knew that transforming a manufacturer of pulp, paper, chemicals, and rubber into a mobile-phone leader would require much more than just shedding its old skin and developing innovative products. If you were Jorma Ollila, what management skills would you use to lead Nokia into a promising but different future? Would you assume an autocratic leadership style, or would you opt for a more hands-off approach? How would you transform your vision into reality? What goals would you establish to transform the stodgy Finnish conglomerate into a mobile phone industry leader?[1] ■

THE FOUR BASIC FUNCTIONS OF MANAGEMENT

Jorma Ollila knows that when managers possess the right combination of vision, skill, experience, and determination, they can lead an organization to success. Ollila also knows that not everyone is equipped to be an effective manager. So he focuses on finding the right managers to help him turn his vision into reality. In this chapter we explore the four basic functions that **management** entails: planning, organizing, leading, and controlling resources (land, labor, capital, and information) to efficiently reach a company's goals (see Exhibit 6.1).[2] And we highlight the skills required of effective managers.

In the course of performing the four management functions, managers play a number of **roles** that fall into three main categories:

- *Interpersonal roles.* Managers perform ceremonial obligations; provide leadership to employees; build a network of relationships with bosses, peers, and employees; and act as liaison to groups and individuals both inside and outside the company (such

management
Process of coordinating resources to meet organizational goals

roles
Behavioral patterns associated with or expected of certain positions

Exhibit 6.1   The Four Basic Functions of Management

Some managers, especially those in smaller organizations, perform all four managerial functions. Although these functions tend to occur in a somewhat progressive order, sometimes they occur simultaneously, and often the process is ongoing.

Planning → Organizing → Leading → Controlling

as suppliers, competitors, government agencies, consumers, special-interest groups, and interrelated work groups).

- *Informational roles.* Managers spend a fair amount of time gathering information by questioning people both inside and outside the organization. They also distribute information to employees, other managers, and outsiders.

- *Decisional roles.* Managers use the information they gather to encourage innovation, to resolve unexpected problems that threaten organizational goals (such as reacting to an economic crisis), and to decide how organizational resources will be used to meet planned objectives. They also negotiate with many individuals and groups, including suppliers, employees, and unions.[3]

Being able to move among these roles while performing the four basic management functions is just one of the many skills that managers must possess. But these functions are not discrete; they overlap and influence one another. Let's examine them in detail.

The Planning Function

Planning is the primary management function, the one on which all others depend. Managers engaged in **planning** develop strategies for success, establish goals and objectives for the organization, and translate their strategies and goals into action plans. To develop long-term strategies and goals, managers must be well informed on a number of key issues and topics that could influence their decisions. A closer look at the strategic planning process will give you a clearer idea of the types of information managers need to help them plan for the company's future.

Understanding the Strategic Planning Process

Strategic plans outline the firm's long-range (two to five years) organizational goals and set a course of action the firm will pursue to reach its goals. These long-term goals encompass eight major areas of concern: market standing, innovation, human resources, financial resources, physical resources, productivity, social responsibility, and financial performance.[4] A good strategic plan answers: Where are we going? What is the environment? How do we get there?

To answer these questions and establish effective long-term goals, managers require extensive amounts of information. For instance, managers must study budgets, production schedules, industry and economic data, customer preferences, internal and external data, competition, and so on. Managers use this information to set a firm's long-term course of direction during a process called *strategic planning*, which consists of six steps: developing a clear vision, creating a mission statement, developing forecasts, analyzing the competition, establishing goals and objectives, and developing action plans.

planning
Establishing objectives and goals for an organization and determining the best ways to accomplish them

strategic plans
Plans that establish the actions and the resource allocation required to accomplish strategic goals; they're usually defined for periods of two to five years and developed by top managers

When Wendelin Wiedeking took over as CEO of Porsche in 1992, the company was racing toward record losses of $150 million. Few people believed that Wiedeking could get Porsche back on track. But Wiedeking had a clear vision for the company—one that adopted lean and efficient Japanese production systems at Porsche. Thanks to Wiedeking's vision and leadership, Porsche is back in the fast lane. By the turn of the century, it was racking up some of the highest profit margins of any manufacturer in the automobile industry.

Develop a Clear Vision   Most organizations are formed in order to realize a **vision**—a realistic, credible, and attainable view of the future that grows out of and improves on the present.[5] Henry Ford envisioned making affordable transportation available to every person. Fred Smith (founder of FedEx) envisioned making FedEx an information company (besides being a transportation company). Bill Gates (chairman of Microsoft) envisioned empowering people through great software, anytime, anyplace, and on any device. And Jorma Ollila was able to see, before others, that mobile phones would fill an important need in the consumer market. Without such visionaries, who knows how the world would be different. Thus, developing a clear vision is a critical task in the strategic planning process. But having a vision alone is no guarantee of success; it must also be communicated to others, executed, and modified as conditions change.

vision
A viable view of the future that is rooted in but improves on the present

Translate the Vision into a Meaningful Mission Statement   To transform vision into reality, managers must define specific organizational goals, objectives, and philosophies. A starting point is to write a company **mission statement**, a brief document that defines why the organization exists, what it seeks to accomplish, and the principles that the company will adhere to as it tries to reach its goals (see Exhibit 6.2). Put differently, a mission statement communicates what the company is, what it does, and where it's headed. Typical components of a mission statement include the company's product or service; primary market; fundamental concern for survival, growth, and profitability; managerial philosophy; and commitment to quality and social responsibility.

mission statement
A statement of the organization's purpose, basic goals, and philosophies

Another important function of a mission statement is to bring clarity of focus to members of the organization. A mission statement helps employees understand how their role is tied to the organization's greater purpose. Thus, it should inspire and guide employees and managers in such a way that they can understand the firm's vision and identify with it. Furthermore, the statement must be congruent with the organization's core values. Managers should use it to assess whether new project proposals are within the scope of the company's mission.[6]

Consider Edge Learning Institute, an employee-training firm based in Tempe, Arizona. Edge executives were considering mass-marketing their training videos

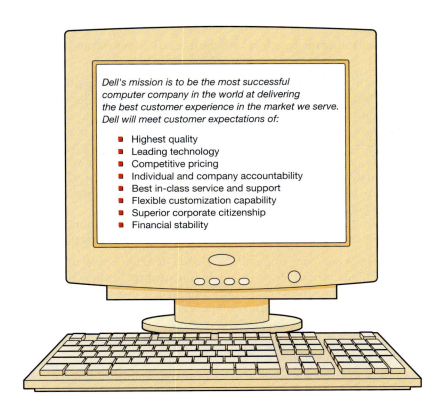

Dell's mission is to be the most successful computer company in the world at delivering the best customer experience in the market we serve. Dell will meet customer expectations of:

- Highest quality
- Leading technology
- Competitive pricing
- Individual and company accountability
- Best in-class service and support
- Flexible customization capability
- Superior corporate citizenship
- Financial stability

Exhibit 6.2

Mission Statement

The mission statement for Dell Computer embodies the firm's high standards for quality and customer service.

through television "infomercials." However, they realized that doing so would be contrary to the company's mission of using "the human touch when providing individuals and organizations with information." So they decided instead to expand Edge's reach by developing a network of franchises that follow the company's training methods.[7]

Develop Forecasts   To develop forecasts, managers must make a number of educated assumptions about future trends and events and modify those assumptions once new information becomes available. Some managers rely on expert forecasts such as those found in *Industry Week*'s "Trends and Forecasts," *Business Week*'s "Survey of Corporate Performance," and Standard & Poor's *Earnings Forecast* as a foundation for their projections. However, these sources may not always include key variables specific to an individual company or industry. Therefore, managers must also develop their own forecasts.

Managerial forecasts fall under two broad categories: *quantitative forecasts*, which are typically based on historical data or tests and that involve complex statistical computations, and *qualitative forecasts*, which are based on intuitive judgments or consumer research. Statistically analyzing the cycles of economic growth and recession over several decades to predict when the economy will take a downward turn is an example of quantitative forecasting. Making predictions about sales of a new product on the basis of experience and consumer responses to a survey is an example of qualitative forecasting. Neither method is foolproof, but both are valuable tools, enabling managers to fill in the unknown variables that inevitably crop up in the planning process.

Analyze the Competition   All business decisions take place within a competitive context, so understanding who your competitors are and how you stack up against them is a critical part of planning. Managers can assess their competition by asking five questions:[8]

- Who are our competitors, both our current competitors and any who might join the market in the future?
- What are their strengths and weaknesses?
- What strategies and tactics have they employed in the past?
- What strategies and tactics are they likely to employ in the future, particularly in response to moves we might make?
- How will their future moves affect both the industry in general and our company in particular?

Analyzing your own company is just as important as analyzing competitors. Many managers use a technique known as *SWOT analysis*, which identifies strengths, weaknesses, opportunities, and threats. Strengths and weaknesses are your internal capabilities, whereas opportunities and threats are an assessment of the external markets in which you compete. Conducting SWOT analysis of competitors is a helpful exercise as well. In addition to analyzing their strengths and weaknesses as you would normally do in competitive analysis, put yourself in their shoes and try to identify the opportunities and threats they're likely to perceive in the marketplace. If you can see the world as they see it, you have a better chance of predicting their future behavior.

With insight into its own capabilities and those of its competitors, a company can then work to gain a competitive edge through at least one of three strategies:

- *Differentiation.* A company using differentiation develops a level of service, a product image, unique product features (including quality), or new technologies that distinguish its product from competitors' products. Volvo, for instance, stresses the safety of its cars. Caterpillar Tractor emphasizes product durability.
- *Cost leadership.* Businesses that pursue this strategy aim to become the low-cost leader in an industry by producing or selling products more efficiently and economically than competitors. Cost leaders have a competitive advantage by reaching buyers whose primary purchase criterion is price. Wal-Mart is a typical industry cost leader.

■ *Focus.* When using a focus strategy, companies concentrate on a specific regional market or consumer group, such as the Southwest United States or drivers of economy cars. This type of strategy enables organizations to develop a better understanding of their customers and to tailor their products specifically to customer needs.[9] Examples of focused strategies include Abercrombie and Fitch (high-end apparel for young adults) and Williams-Sonoma (quality cookware and appliances for serious cooks).

Many firms gain a competitive advantage by excelling in two of these areas at once, such as Toyota's efforts to excel at both quality (a differentiation strategy) and lower cost. However, pursuing more than one strategic focus at a time can be risky if it leads to mediocre efforts across the board.[10]

Establish Company Goals and Objectives   As mentioned earlier, establishing goals and objectives is the key task in the planning process. Although these terms are often used interchangeably, a **goal** is a broad, long-range accomplishment that the organization wishes to attain in typically five or more years, whereas an **objective** is a specific, short-range target designed to help reach that goal. For Nokia, a goal might be to increase market share of mobile phone sales in the United States by 25 percent over the next five years, and an objective might be to sell 500,000 mobile phones to U.S. customers by year-end. To be effective, organizational goals and objectives should be specific, measurable, relevant, challenging, attainable, and time limited. For example, it is better to state "increase our sales by 25 percent over the next five years" than "substantially increase our sales."

Setting appropriate goals has many benefits: It increases employee motivation, establishes standards for measuring individual and group performance, guides employee activity, and clarifies management's expectations. By establishing organizational goals, managers set the stage for the actions needed to achieve those goals. If actions aren't planned, the chances of reaching company goals are slim.

goal
Broad, long-range target or aim

objective
Specific, short-range target or aim

Develop Action Plans   Once managers have established a firm's long-term strategic goals and objectives, they must then develop a plan of execution. **Tactical plans** lay out the actions and the allocation of resources necessary to achieve specific, short-term objectives that support the company's broader strategic plan. Tactical plans typically focus on departmental goals and cover a period of one to three years. Their limited scope permits them to be changed more easily than strategic plans. **Operational plans** designate the actions and resources required to achieve the objectives of tactical plans. Operational plans usually define actions for less than one year and focus on accomplishing a firm's specific objectives, such as developing a strategic partnership with another company.

Keep in mind that many highly admired CEOs have stumbled not because they didn't have strategies for success, but because they didn't execute their strategies or deliver on their commitments. That's because developing a strategy or vision is less than half the battle. It's executing it that counts. In today's information age, strategies quickly become public property. Everyone knows Dell's direct business model, for example, yet few companies, if any, have successfully copied its execution.

tactical plans
Plans that define the actions and the resource allocation necessary to achieve tactical objectives and to support strategic plans; they're usually defined for a period of one to three years and developed by middle managers

operational plans
Plans that lay out the actions and the resource allocation needed to achieve operational objectives and to support tactical plans; they're usually defined for less than one year and developed by first-line managers

Planning for a Crisis

No matter how well a company plans for its future, any number of problems can arise to threaten its existence. An ugly fight for control of a company, a product failure, a breakdown in routine operations (as a result of fire, for example), or an environmental accident could develop into a serious and crippling crisis. Managers can help a company survive these setbacks through **crisis management**, a plan for handling such unusual and serious problems.

The goal of crisis management is to keep the company functioning smoothly both during and after a crisis. Successful crisis management requires comprehensive contin-

crisis management
System for minimizing the harm that might result from some unusually threatening situations

When New York State Attorney General Eliot Spitzer began to investigate questionable business practices within the mutual fund industry, a number of financial firms found themselves scrambling to implement crisis management plans.

organizing
Process of arranging resources to carry out the organization's plans

management pyramid
Organizational structure comprising top, middle, and lower management

top managers
Those at the highest level of the organization's management hierarchy; they are responsible for setting strategic goals, and they have the most power and responsibility in the organization

middle managers
Those in the middle of the management hierarchy; they develop plans to implement the goals of top managers and coordinate the work of first-line managers

gency plans in addition to speedy, open communication with all who are affected by the crisis. Experts suggest setting up a crisis communications team with a knowledgeable spokesperson to handle the many requests for information that arise during a crisis. The individuals selected should be able to remain honest and calm when a crisis hits. Moreover, top managers should be visible in the hours immediately following the crisis to demonstrate that the company will do whatever is necessary to control the situation as best it can, find the cause, and prevent a future occurrence.[11]

Ford and Bridgestone/Firestone were criticized for not taking these actions when reports started surfacing about the faulty tires manufactured by Bridgestone/Firestone and fitted on Ford Explorer sport utility vehicles. When the vehicles were driven at high speed, the treads separated from the tires, causing the cars to roll over and injuring— even killing—passengers. Although both Ford and Firestone eventually recalled 6.5 million tires, both companies paid the price for making serious mistakes in handling the crisis. Some say that Firestone's reputation may be damaged beyond repair.[12]

The Organizing Function

Organizing, the process of arranging resources to carry out the organization's plans, is the second major function of managers. During the organizing stage, managers think through all the activities that employees carry out (from programming the organization's computers to mailing its letters), as well as all the facilities and equipment employees need in order to complete those activities. They also give people the ability to work toward organizational goals by determining who will have the authority to make decisions, to perform or supervise activities, and to distribute resources.

The organizing function is particularly challenging because most organizations undergo constant change. Long-time employees leave, and new employees arrive. Equipment breaks down or becomes obsolete, and replacements are needed. The public's tastes and interests change, and the organization has to reevaluate its plans and activities. Shifting political and economic trends can lead to employee cutbacks—or perhaps expansion. Long-time competitors take unexpected actions, and new competitors enter the market. Every week the organization faces new situations, so management's organizing tasks are never finished. Consider Microsoft. The company continually challenges itself by asking: "Are we making what customers want and working on products and technologies they'll want in the future? Are we staying ahead of all our competitors? What don't our customers like about what we do, and what are we doing about it? Are we organized most effectively to achieve our goals?"[13]

The organizing function will be discussed in detail in Chapter 7. In this chapter, however, we will discuss the three levels of a corporate hierarchy—top, middle, bottom—commonly known as the **management pyramid** (see Exhibit 6.3). In general, **top managers** are the upper-level managers who have the most power and who take overall responsibility for the organization. An example is the chief executive officer (CEO). Top managers establish the structure for the organization as a whole, and they select the people who fill the upper-level positions. Top managers also make long-range plans, establish major policies, and represent the company to the outside world at official functions and fundraisers.

Middle managers have similar responsibilities but usually for just one division or unit. They develop plans for implementing the broad goals set by top managers, and they coordinate the work of first-line managers. In traditional organizations, managers at the middle level are plant managers, division managers, branch managers, and other similar positions, all reporting to top-level managers. But in more innovative management structures, middle managers often function as team leaders who are expected to supervise and lead small groups of employees in a variety of job functions. Similar to consultants, they must understand every department's function, not just their own area of expertise. Furthermore, they are granted decision-making authority previously reserved for only high-ranking executives.[14]

JetBlue: Making Tough Management Decisions in Tough Times

David Neeleman knew that he was entering dangerous territory. When he launched JetBlue Airways in February 2000, he was determined to succeed in an industry where a number of other ambitious entrants had failed: Kiwi International, People Express, and Tower Air, to name a few. With $130 million from private investors, Neeleman hoped to fill a niche left empty by the big air carriers—all-coach leather seats, seat-back satellite TV, excellent service, candor about delays, and more. Still, nothing could have prepared Neeleman for the events of September 11 or for their impact on the airline industry. Overnight, Neeleman had to operate the most ambitious start-up in U.S. aviation on pure instinct.

JetBlue's management developed a crisis strategy that bucked the industry trend. From company headquarters, nine miles from ground zero, Neeleman vowed not to lay off any of the airline's 2,000 employees, even though its planes were flying mostly empty. Then, while rivals scaled back flights and postponed deliveries of new planes, JetBlue expanded services to new markets and ordered additional planes. It was a daring move, indeed. Not only did the newcomer have an all-important instinct for survival, but its innovative strategies were paying off as well. JetBlue posted profits while others posted losses.

How did JetBlue beat the odds? To begin with, Neeleman based the airline at New York's JFK airport, an international gateway that is crowded only a few hours per day. This location allows JetBlue to bypass congested and delay-plagued La Guardia Airport. Then, to keep costs down, it adopted Southwest Airlines' point-to-point service—flying busy routes between some 20 secondary airports. Moreover, JetBlue pays its nonunion workforce far less than major carriers do and keeps pilots happy by granting them stock options and promoting first officers to captains relatively quickly. The company also reduces training and maintenance costs by flying only one type of aircraft—factory-fresh, state-of-the-art Airbus A320s, each with ample amounts of legroom. And it saves fuel by configuring all planes with emergency overwater equipment so its flights can swing out over the ocean to avoid congestion on popular East Coast routes.

JetBlue's innovative strategic flight plan has gained altitude even during turbulent times. Still, critics note that it's one thing to execute a smooth takeoff; it's another to go public and expand cross-country. JetBlue plans to add 60 jetliners in five years to an existing fleet of 23. Of course, only time will tell whether JetBlue can outfox the major carriers, which have historically grounded newcomers. Neeleman knows the risks are high. But as he sees it, where there's chaos, there's opportunity.

Questions for Critical Thinking

1. How would you describe JetBlue's strategic plan?
2. How might JetBlue's decisions regarding employees after the September 11 crisis affect customer service and customer satisfaction?

At the bottom of the management pyramid are **first-line managers** (or *supervisory managers*). They oversee the work of operating employees, and they put into action the plans developed at higher levels. Positions at this level include supervisor, department head, and office manager.[15] Even though more managers are at the bottom level than at the top, as illustrated in Exhibit 6.3, today's leaner companies tend to have fewer levels, flattening the organizational structure, as Chapter 7 points out.

first-line managers

Those at the lowest level of the management hierarchy; they supervise the operating employees and implement the plans set at the higher management levels; also called supervisory managers

Exhibit 6.3

The Management Pyramid

Separate job titles are used to designate the three basic levels in the management pyramid.

The Leading Function

Leading—the process of influencing and motivating people to work effectively and willingly toward company goals—is the third basic function of management. Leading becomes even more challenging in today's business environment, where individuals who have different backgrounds and unique interests, ambitions, and personal goals are melded into a productive work team. Managers with good leadership skills have greater success in influencing the attitudes and actions of others, both through the demonstration of specific tasks and through the manager's own behavior and spirit. Furthermore, effective leaders are good at *motivating,* or giving employees a reason to do the job and to put forth their best performance (see Chapter 9).

What makes a good leader? When early researchers studied leadership, they looked for specific characteristics, or *traits,* common to all good leaders. At the time, they were unable to prove any link between particular traits and leadership ability. However, researchers found that leaders who have specific traits, such as decisiveness and self-confidence, are likely to be more effective.[16] Additional studies have shown that managers with strong interpersonal skills and high emotional quotients (EQs) tend to be more effective leaders. The characteristics of a high EQ include:[17]

- *Self-awareness.* Self-aware managers have the ability to recognize their own feelings and how they, their job performance, and other people are affected by those feelings. Moreover, managers who are highly self-aware know where they are headed and why.
- *Self-regulation.* Self-regulated managers have the ability to control or reduce disruptive impulses and moods. They can suspend judgment and think before acting. Moreover, they know how to utilize the appropriate emotion at the right time and in the right amount.
- *Motivation.* Motivated managers are driven to achieve beyond expectations—their own and everyone else's.
- *Empathy.* Empathetic managers thoughtfully consider employees' feelings, along with other factors, in the process of making intelligent decisions.
- *Social skill.* Socially skilled managers tend to have a wide circle of acquaintances, and they have a knack for finding common ground with people of all kinds. They assume that nothing important gets done by one person alone and have a network in place when the time for action comes.

Keep in mind that these traits alone do not define a leader. Different leadership traits are appropriate under different leadership situations.[18]

Adopting an Effective Leadership Style

Leadership style is the way a manager uses authority to lead others. Every manager, from the baseball coach to the university chancellor, has a definite style, although an individual's style might vary over time and from situation to situation. Management theorists have identified quite a variety of leadership styles; the major styles include *autocratic, democratic, laissez-faire, contingent,* and *situational.*

Autocratic leaders make decisions without consulting others. "My way or the highway" summarizes this style, which tends to go with traditional, hierarchical organizational structures. Although autocratic leadership can be highly effective when quick decisions are necessary, it does little to empower employees or encourage innovation. Al Dunlap, past CEO of Sunbeam, demonstrated an extreme form of autocratic leadership style to try to turn the failing household appliance maker around. True to his word, Dunlap turned Sunbeam inside out and upside down—and nearly destroyed the company with his "chainsaw" management style—crushing employee morale and creating unbearable stress by exerting excruciating pressure on his staff. As Dunlap liked to brag, "I don't get heart attacks, I give them."[19]

In contrast, **democratic leaders** delegate authority and involve employees in decision making. Even though their approach can lead to slower decisions, soliciting input from people familiar with particular situations or issues may result in better decisions. As more companies adopt the principles of teamwork, democratic leadership continues to gain in popularity. For example, managers at Rhone-Poulenc, the U.S. subsidiary of France's leading chemical and pharmaceutical manufacturer, gradually made the transition from autocratic to democratic leadership as the organization moved from a hierarchical structure to a team-based environment. CEO Peter Neff says, "I don't look over people's shoulders anymore. . . . My role now is to enable people to do the best they know how to do." For Neff, this means acting as an opportunity seeker, coach, facilitator, motivator, and mentor rather than as a controller or problem solver.[20]

The third leadership style, laissez-faire, is sometimes referred to as free-rein leadership. The French term *laissez-faire* can be translated as "leave it alone," or more roughly as "hands off." **Laissez-faire leaders** take the role of consultant, encouraging employees' ideas and offering insights or opinions when asked. The laissez-faire style may fail if workers pursue goals that do not match the organization's. However, the style has proven effective in some situations. Managers at Hewlett-Packard's North American distribution organization adopted a laissez-faire style when they were given nine months to reorganize their order-fulfillment process. The managers eliminated all titles, supervision, job descriptions, and plans, and they made employees entirely responsible for the project. At first there was chaos. However, employees soon began to try new things, make mistakes, and learn as they went. In the end, the team finished the reorganization ahead of schedule, reduced product delivery times from 26 days to 8 days, and cut inventory by 20 percent. Moreover, the employees experienced a renewed sense of challenge, commitment, and enjoyment in their work.[21]

More and more businesses are adopting democratic and laissez-faire leadership as they reduce the number of management layers in their corporate hierarchies and increase the use of teamwork. However, experienced managers know that no one leadership style works every time. In fact, new research shows that leaders with the best results do not rely on only one leadership style; instead they adapt their approach to match the requirements of the particular situation.[22] Adapting leadership style to current business circumstances is called **contingency leadership**. One of the more important contingency styles is **situational leadership**, in which leaders adapt their style based on the readiness of employees to accept the changes or responsibilities the manager wants them to accept.[23] You can think of leadership styles as existing along a continuum of possible leadership behaviors, as suggested by Exhibit 6.4.

Aside from these styles, leaders also differ in the degree to which they try (or need) to reshape their organizations. **Transactional leaders** tend to focus on meeting established goals, making sure employees understand their roles in the organization, making sure the correct resources are in place, and so on. In contrast, some leaders can "take it up a notch," inspiring their employees to perform above and beyond the everyday, expected responsibilities of their jobs. These **transformational leaders** can reshape the destinies of their organizations by inspiring employees to see the world in new ways, to find creative solutions to business challenges, to rise above self-interest, and to create new levels of success for the company as a whole.[24] Well-known transformational leaders include Jeff Bezos of Amazon.com and Bill Gates of Microsoft, both of whom have inspired thousands of employees to feats that have changed entire industries. But many other leaders have transformational qualities in less spectacular ways. Mary Cadigan, a manager at the mortgage lender Fannie Mae, faced the huge task of moving the company's data center—including 577 computer servers and 365 miles of cable—to a new location, without disrupting business and without the luxury of paying anyone extra to do it. Over the course of 13 weekends, including all-nighters on Fridays, she inspired hundreds of people to work long hours on their own time for the good of the organization (she did eventually convince the company to give the team bonuses). Through her energy, compassion, sense of humor, and attention to employee needs, she led a team to success in a seemingly impossible challenge.[25]

Meg Whitman, CEO of eBay, is a perfect example of a democratic leader. She attributes much of eBay's success to involvement of employees and managers in decision making. "I'm really proud of what we've created at eBay, but I haven't done it alone," says Whitman. "It really has been our management team and the people that come to eBay and build our community. It's a partnership."

laissez-faire leaders
Leaders who leave the actual decision making up to employees

contingency leadership
Adapting the leadership style to what is most appropriate, given current business conditions

situational leadership
A variation on contingency leadership in which the manager adapts his or her style based on the readiness of employees to accept changes or task responsibilities

transactional leaders
Managers who focus on meeting established goals, making sure current business operations run smoothly

transformational leaders
Managers who can reshape the destinies of their organizations by inspiring employees to rise above self-interest and create new levels of success for the company as a whole

Continuum of Leadership Behavior

Leadership style occurs along a continuum, ranging from boss-centered to employee-centered. Situations that require managers to exercise greater authority fall toward the boss-centered end of the continuum. Other situations call for a manager to give workers leeway to function more independently.

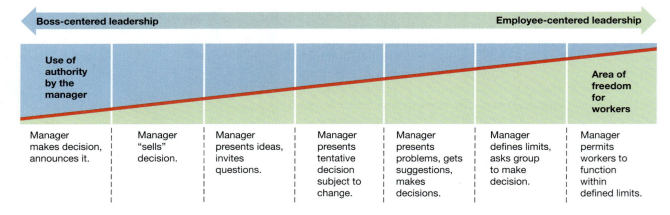

Boss-centered leadership — Employee-centered leadership

Use of authority by the manager — Area of freedom for workers

| Manager makes decision, announces it. | Manager "sells" decision. | Manager presents ideas, invites questions. | Manager presents tentative decision subject to change. | Manager presents problems, gets suggestions, makes decisions. | Manager defines limits, asks group to make decision. | Manager permits workers to function within defined limits. |

Coaching and Mentoring

Managers can provide effective leadership by coaching and mentoring their employees. On a winning sports team, the coach focuses on helping all team members perform at their highest potential. In a similar way, *coaching* managers strive to bring out the best in their employees.

coaching

Helping employees reach their highest potential by meeting with them, discussing problems that hinder their ability to work effectively, and offering suggestions and encouragement to overcome these problems

Coaching involves taking the time to meet with employees, discussing any problems that may hinder their ability to work effectively, and offering suggestions and encouragement to help them find their own solutions to work-related challenges.

This process requires keen powers of observation, sensible judgment, and both a willingness and an ability to take appropriate action. However, just as a sports coach cannot play the game for team members, a coaching manager must step back and let employees perform when it's "game time." Coaching managers develop a solid game plan and empower their team to carry it out. If the team gets behind, the manager offers encouragement to boost morale. And when team members are victorious, the manager recognizes and praises their outstanding achievement.[26] Tom Gegax, cofounder of Tires Plus stores, has been using internal coaches in his organization for years. "People are more willing to take feedback from a coach than from a boss because so many of us have been coached before," says Gegax.[27]

mentor

Experienced manager or employee with a wide network of industry colleagues who can explain office politics, serve as a role model for appropriate business behavior, and help other employees negotiate the corporate structure

Acting as a mentor is similar to coaching, but mentoring also emphasizes helping employees understand how the organization works. A **mentor** is usually an experienced manager or employee who can help guide other employees through the corporate maze. Mentors have a deep knowledge of the business and a useful network of industry colleagues. In addition, they can explain office politics, serve as a role model for appropriate business behavior, and provide valuable advice about how to succeed within the organization.

Your mentor won't necessarily be your boss. Relationships with mentors often develop informally between the individuals involved. However, some companies have established formal mentoring programs. In the program at Xerox, women employees can spend a few hours every month discussing work or career issues with any of the participating women executives.[28] Mentoring offers benefits for both parties: The less-experienced employee gains from the mentor's advice and ideas; the mentor gains new networking contacts, in addition to personal satisfaction.

Managing Change

Another important function of leaders is managing the process of change. The stimulus for change can come from any direction, both inside and outside the organization. Internally, a shift in strategy might require changes to the structure of the organization and to the jobs of many people within the company. In others cases, managers might identify a need to improve performance or fix organizational weaknesses. For instance, when Rick Wagoner took over as CEO of General Motors, he inherited problems that had been growing for decades, including factory productivity that lagged far behind Japanese competitors, a pension program for GM retirees that was underfunded by as much as $23 billion, a bureaucratic corporate hierarchy, and bland products. To start to solve these problems, Wagoner had to institute an array of changes, including bringing in executives from other companies to instituting rigorous financial controls.[29]

Outside the organization, changes can come from many directions, in many flavors. Some develop over time and are relatively easy to prepare for, such as shifts in demographics. For instance, if your company markets exclusively to teenagers and you observe that birthrates have been declining, you know it won't be too many years before your market will start to shrink. Other times, you know that change is heading your way but you can't reliably predict the effects it will have on your organization. This is often the case with new competitors, new technologies, new regulations, and shifts in political influence. Still other changes come without warning, such as natural disasters and terrorist attacks. Leaders in these situations often need to institute decisive and dramatic changes.

Change presents a major leadership challenge for one simple reason: Most people don't like it. They may fear the unknown, they may be unwilling to give up current habits or benefits, they may believe that the change is bad for the organization, or they may not trust the motives of the people advocating change.[30] As a result, many—perhaps most—change initiatives fail, according to one recent study.[31] To improve the chances of success when the organization needs to change, managers can follow these steps:[32]

1. **Identify what needs to change.** Changes can involve the structure of the organization, technologies and systems, or people's attitudes, beliefs, skills, or behaviors.[33]

2. **Identify the forces acting for and against the change.** By understanding these forces, managers can work to amplify the forces that will facilitate the change and remove or diminish the negative forces. For instance, if uncertainty is one of the forces working against the change, education and communication may help reduce these forces and thereby reduce resistance to the change.

3. **Choose the approach, or combination of approaches, best suited to the situation.** Managers can institute change through a variety of techniques, including communication, education, participation in the decision making, negotiation with groups opposed to the change, visible support from top managers or other opinion leaders, or coercive use of authority (usually recommended only for crisis situations). Helping people understand the need for change is often called *unfreezing* existing behaviors.

4. **Reinforce changed behavior and monitor continued progress.** Once the change has been made, managers need to reinforce new behaviors and make sure old behaviors don't creep back in. This effort is commonly called *refreezing* new behaviors.

In many industries and markets, change now appears to be a constant aspect of business, making change management a vital skill for leaders at all levels of the organization.

Building a Strong Organizational Culture

Strong leadership is a key element in establishing a productive *organizational culture*—the set of underlying values, norms, and practices shared by members of an organization. When you visit an organization, observe how the employees work, dress, communicate, address each other, and conduct business. Each organization has a special way of doing things. In corporations, this force is often referred to as **corporate culture**.

A company's culture influences the way people treat and react to each other and to customers and suppliers. It shapes the way employees feel about the company and the work they do; the way they interpret and perceive the actions taken by others; the expectations they have regarding changes in their work or in the business; and their ability to lead, be

corporate culture
A set of shared values and norms that support the management system and that guide management and employee behavior

How Much Do You Know About the Company's Culture?

Before you accept a job at a new company, it's a good idea to learn as much as possible about the company's culture. Use this list of questions to guide you in your investigation.

COMPANY VALUES

- Is there a compelling vision for the company?
- Is there a mission statement supporting the vision that employees understand and can implement?
- Do employees know how their work relates to this vision?
- Is there a common set of values that bind the organization together?
- Do officers/owners follow these values, or is there a gap between what they say and what they do?

PEOPLE

- How are people treated?
- Is there an atmosphere of civility and respect?
- Is teamwork valued and encouraged, with all ideas welcomed?
- Are employee ideas acknowledged, encouraged, and acted upon?
- Are employees given credit for their ideas?
- Is there a positive commitment to a balance between work and life?
- Is there a commitment from top management to support working parents?

COMMUNITY INVOLVEMENT

- Is the company involved in the community?
- Is there a corporate culture of service?

- Is there a stated policy of community involvement by the company and its employees?

COMMUNICATION

- Is there open communication?
- Do officers/owners regularly communicate with all levels?
- Are the customer service and financial results widely distributed?
- Is there meaningful two-way communication throughout the organization?
- Are employee surveys on workplace issues conducted and published? Are employees asked for input on solutions?
- Is there an open-door policy for access to management?

EMPLOYEE PERFORMANCE

- How are personnel issues handled?
- Is employee feedback given regularly?
- Are employee evaluations based on agreed-upon objectives that have been clearly communicated?
- Are employees asked to provide a summary of their accomplishments for placement into their evaluations?

Questions for Critical Thinking

1. How might a job candidate find the answers to these questions?
2. Why is it important to learn about the company's culture before accepting a job?

---

productive, and choose the best course of action. For example, TechTarget, an interactive media company in Massachusetts, has established a culture that emphasizes employee responsibility and accountability. Rather than defining working hours, vacation time, and other standard policies, TechTarget lets employees decide when they come to work and how much vacation to take, as long as they meet their agreed-upon performance objectives.[34]

Positive cultures create an environment that encourages employees to make ethical decisions for the good of the company and its customers. At companies with legendary corporate cultures, such as Nordstrom and Southwest Airlines, employees routinely go the extra mile to make sure customers are treated well. In contrast, negative, dysfunctional cultures can lead employees to make decisions that are bad for customers, bad for the company—and even unethical or illegal.

Corporate cultures are established and maintained through the countless actions and decisions of leaders, year after year. When Southwest Airlines employees saw former CEO Herbert Kelleher emphasizing fun, teamwork, and sacrificing for the common good, they followed suit. However, as the company has grown and the airline industry has come under considerable cost pressures, even Southwest's culture is starting to show signs of wear and tear. The company is now taking steps to reinvigorate the culture through better communication, but some longtime employees are wondering if the magic of the early days is gone.[35]

The Controlling Function

Controlling is the fourth basic managerial function. In management, **controlling** means monitoring a firm's progress toward meeting its organizational goals and objectives, resetting the course if goals or objectives change in response to shifting conditions, and correcting deviations if goals or objectives are not being attained.

The Control Cycle

Managers strive to maintain a high level of **quality**—a measure of how closely goods or services conform to predetermined standards and customer expectations. Many firms control for quality through a four-step cycle that involves all levels of management and all employees (see Exhibit 6.5). In the first step, top managers set **standards**, or criteria for measuring the performance of the organization as a whole. At the same time, middle and first-line managers set departmental quality standards so they can meet or exceed company standards. Establishing control standards is closely tied to the planning function and depends on information supplied by employees, customers, and other external sources. Examples of specific standards might be "Produce 1,500 circuit boards monthly with less than 1 percent failures."

In the second step of the control cycle, managers assess performance, using both quantitative (specific, numerical) and qualitative (subjective) performance measures. In the third step, managers compare performance with the established standards and search for the cause of any discrepancies. If the performance falls short of standards, the fourth step is to take corrective action, which may be done by either adjusting performance or reevaluating the standards. If performance meets or exceeds standards, no corrective action is taken. As Exhibit 6.5 shows, if everything is operating smoothly, controls permit managers to repeat acceptable performance. If results are below expectations, controls help managers take any necessary action.

For example, suppose Nokia does not reach its objective of selling 500,000 mobile phones to U.S. customers by year-end. With proper control systems in place, managers will evaluate why this objective was not reached. Perhaps they will find that a shortage of parts created manufacturing delays. Or perhaps the market where sales were targeted

controlling
Process of measuring progress against goals and objectives and correcting deviations if results are not as expected

quality
A measure of how closely a product conforms to predetermined standards and customer expectations

standards
Criteria against which performance is measured

Exhibit 6.5   **The Control Cycle**

The control cycle has four basic steps: (1) On the basis of strategic goals, top managers set the standards by which the organization's overall performance will be measured. (2) Managers at all levels measure performance. (3) Actual performance is compared with the standards. (4) Appropriate corrective action is taken (if performance meets standards, nothing other than encouragement is needed; if performance falls below standards, corrective action may include improving performance, establishing new standards, changing plans, reorganizing, or redirecting efforts).

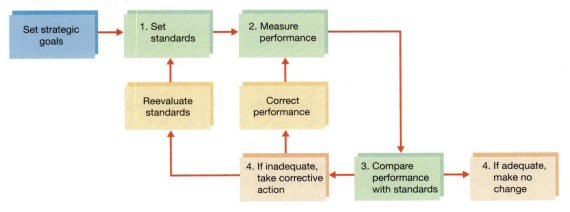

Learning from Business Blunders

Oops: When the worst blackout in North American history shut off electrical power to 50 million people in the eastern United States and Canada and drained up to $10 billion from the U.S. and Canadian economies in the summer of 2003, both countries discovered just what a complicated managerial challenge the power industry faces. Electrical suppliers and customers are connected via a complex grid of transmission lines that ensure continued power even as supply and demand ebb and flow in various parts of the grid. Every power station has automatic controls that prevent the grid from drawing too much power, which can happen when demand rises across the grid or when other stations reduce the power they make available to the grid. The system can usually respond to localized power shortages by managing availability, but power station operators need to know what's going on to make these decisions.

Believe it or not, a few trees triggered this economic disaster. Three high-voltage lines in Ohio, owned by power company FirstEnergy, shorted out when they came into contact with trees that should have been trimmed but weren't. Then FirstEnergy's monitoring facility didn't detect the problem because its computer system wasn't operating properly and employees weren't trained adequately. Because the company didn't respond to its own problems or alert other power generators, a surge of unmet demand for electricity began to roll through the grid—which triggered automatic protection systems at other stations across the grid and continued to amplify the problem until it rolled all the way to the East Coast.

What You Can Learn: The 2003 blackout yielded several key business lessons: (1) Monitoring and control, based on reliable data, are essential to the operation of every business; (2) unless they are detected and dealt with quickly, relatively small mistakes can mushroom into huge problems—moreover, complex systems need vigorous, constant scrutiny; (3) employee training and system maintenance are crucial—managers can't just assume that people or systems will work properly; (4) when various independent business entities are connected (either literally connected, as in the power industry, or financially connected, as in banking, for instance), problems can spread quickly. The bottom line: Know yourself—and your business partners.

became saturated with cell phones made by competitors. Regardless, management will search for the cause of the discrepancies before modifying the company's objectives or trying a different approach to achieve the company's long-term goals. Control methods are examined in greater detail in Chapter 8.

Total Quality Management

The controlling function is an important part of total quality management, which is sometimes referred to as *total quality control*. In the past, *control* often meant those little sticky tags attached to new items that say, "inspected by #47." Companies would inspect finished products and rework or discard items that didn't meet quality standards. Today, this inspection step is only one small part of the total control process.

Total quality management (TQM) is both a management philosophy and a strategic management process that focuses on delivering the optimum level of quality to customers by building quality into every organizational activity (see Exhibit 6.6). Total quality management draws its ideas, principles, and tools from psychology, sociology, statistics, management, and marketing. The goal of TQM is to create an environment that encourages people to grow as individuals and to learn to bring about continuous and breakthrough improvements. Companies that adopt TQM create a value for all stakeholders—customers, employees, owners, suppliers, and the community.[36] In many industries, adopting some form of TQM has become mandatory in order to meet international quality standards (see Chapter 8). The four key elements of TQM are employee involvement, customer focus, benchmarking, and continuous improvement.

total quality management (TQM)
Comprehensive, strategic management approach that builds quality into every organizational process as a way of improving customer satisfaction

participative management
Sharing information with employees and involving them in decision making

- *Employee involvement.* Total quality management involves every employee in quality assurance. Workers are trained in quality methods and are empowered to stop a work process if they feel that products or services are not meeting quality standards. Managers also encourage employees to speak up when they think of better ways of doing things. This approach exemplifies a **participative management** style—the sharing of information at all levels of the organization (also known as *open-book management*). By directly involving employees in decision making, companies increase employees' power in an organization and improve the flow of information between employees and managers. At Borg-Warner Automotive (BWA), manufacturer of highly engineered components and systems for vehicle engines and transmissions, participatory management is ingrained in the company's culture. The product emphasis there is high tech and the workforce emphasis is high involvement. Management understands that people are the true drivers of improvement.[37]

1. **Create constancy of purpose for the improvement of goods and services.**

    The organization should constantly strive to improve quality, productivity, and consumer satisfaction to improve performance today and tomorrow.

2. **Adopt a new philosophy to reject mistakes and negativism.**

    Customers, managers, and employees all need to change their attitudes toward unacceptable work quality and sullen service.

3. **Cease dependence on mass inspection.**

    Instead of inspecting products after production to weed out bad quality, improve the process to build in good quality.

4. **End the practice of awarding business on price alone.**

    Create long-term relationships with suppliers who can deliver the best quality.

5. **Improve constantly and forever the system of production and service.**

    Improvement is not a onetime effort; managers must lead the way to continuous improvement of quality, productivity, and customer satisfaction.

6. **Institute training.**

    Train all organization members to do their jobs consistently well.

7. **Institute leadership.**

    Managers must provide the leadership to help employees do a better job.

8. **Drive out fear.**

    Create an atmosphere in which employees are not afraid to ask questions or to point out problems.

9. **Break down barriers between units.**

    Ensure that people in organizational departments or units do not have conflicting goals and are able to work as a team to achieve overall goals.

10. **Eliminate slogans, exhortations, and targets for the workforce.**

    These alone cannot help anyone do a better job, and they imply that employees could do better if they tried harder; instead, management should provide methods for improvement.

11. **Eliminate numerical quotas.**

    Quotas count only finished units, not quality or methods, and they generally lead to defective goods, wasted resources, and demoralized employees.

12. **Remove barriers to pride in work.**

    Most people want to do a good job but are prevented from doing so by misguided management, poor communication, faulty equipment, defective materials, and other barriers that managers must remove to improve quality.

13. **Institute a vigorous program of education and retraining.**

    Both managers and employees have to be educated in the new quality methods.

14. **Take action to accomplish the transformation.**

    With top-management commitment, have the courage to make the changes throughout the organization that will improve quality.

Exhibit 6.6

Total Quality Management

These 14 points, based on the work of W. Edwards Deming, can help managers improve their goods and services through total quality management.

- *Customer focus.* Focusing on the customer simply means finding out what customers really want and then providing it. This approach requires casting aside assumptions about customers and relying instead on accurate research. It also requires developing long-term relationships with customers, as Chapter 11 discusses in detail.

- *Benchmarking.* This element of TQM involves comparing your company's processes and products against the standards of the world's best companies and then working to match or exceed those standards. This process entails rating the manufacturing process, product development, distribution, and other key functions against those of acknowledged leaders; analyzing how those role models achieve their outstanding results; and then applying that knowledge to make quality improvements. Among the world-class organizations frequently cited as benchmarks for production are Toyota, IBM, and Hewlett-Packard; for distribution, L.L. Bean and FedEx; and for customer service, American Express and Nordstrom.[38]

- *Continuous improvement.* This key feature of TQM requires an ongoing effort to reduce defects, cut costs, slash production and delivery times, and offer customers innovative products. Improvements are often small, incremental changes that add up to greater competitiveness over the long run. Because responsibility for such improvement often falls on employees, it becomes management's job to provide employee incentives that will motivate them to want to improve. Geon, a manufacturer of polyvinyl chloride (PVC) resins, motivates its employees through two programs. The first links employee bonuses to improvements in productivity, quality, and manufacturing. In recent years, employees have received an average bonus of 11 percent of their annual salaries through the program. The second program is a success-sharing plan tied to sales gains and stock price. This plan pays out millions of dollars in stock each year. Both initiatives have helped Geon produce 20 percent more PVC resin with 25 percent less manufacturing capacity, putting the company in a much better financial position.[39]

Although many U.S. companies are enjoying greater success as a result of total quality initiatives, a recent study of the largest U.S. companies indicates that such initiatives have fallen short of expectations in a large number of companies. However, the fact that total quality principles played a significant role in propelling Japanese businesses from postwar ruins to pillars of innovation and productivity suggests that much can be gained from the process. What may be lacking in the United States is a firm commitment to TQM. Many companies have jumped on the TQM bandwagon hoping for a quick boost in performance without really thinking about how to make total quality a part of their long-term strategy. Such companies often fail to provide the necessary managerial and financial support for the programs. In about half of the firms studied, less than 40 percent of workers and less than 80 percent of management teams were sufficiently knowledgeable about TQM philosophy, concepts, and tools.[40] Experts agree that the entire organization—from the bottom all the way up to the CEO—must be actively and visibly involved for TQM to work. Companies that make a halfhearted commitment should not expect dramatic improvements.[41]

At the same time, pursuing TQM is not necessarily a prerequisite for success. Many successful companies do not have TQM programs.[42] However, no business that operates in a competitive environment can expect long-term success unless managers strive to meet customers' needs, improve processes, lower costs, and empower employees in one way or another.

Jenny J. Ming, president of Old Navy, oversees everything from store operations to marketing and advertising. Her passion for fashion has helped drive the company's record growth. So has her ability to communicate effectively with others. Ming recognizes that people's needs change as quickly as the latest fashion trend. So when communicating with others, she takes extra care to focus on her audience's special needs and differing backgrounds.

MANAGEMENT SKILLS

Managers rely on a number of skills to perform their functions and maintain a high level of quality in their organizations. These skills can be classified into three basic categories: *interpersonal, technical,* and *conceptual.* As managers rise through the organization's hierarchy, they may need to strengthen their abilities in one or more of these skills; fortunately, managerial skills can usually be learned.[43] Such managers may also need to de-emphasize skills that helped them in lower-level jobs. For instance, staying closely involved with project details is often a plus for a first-line supervisor, but it can lead to serious performance issues for a higher-level manager.[44]

Interpersonal Skills

The various skills required to communicate with other people, work effectively with them, motivate them, and lead them are **interpersonal skills**. Because managers mainly get things done through people at all levels of the organization, they use good interpersonal skills in countless situations. Encouraging employees to work together toward common goals, interacting with employees and other managers, negotiating with partners and suppliers, developing employee trust and loyalty, and fostering innovation—all these activities require interpersonal skills.

Communication, or exchanging information, is the most important and pervasive interpersonal skill that managers use. Effective communication not only increases the manager's and the organization's productivity but also shapes the impressions made on colleagues, employees, supervisors, investors, and customers. Communication allows you to perceive the needs of these stakeholders (your first step toward satisfying them), and it helps you respond to those needs.[45] Moreover, as the workforce becomes more and more diverse, managers will need to adjust their interactions with others, communicating in a way that considers the different needs, backgrounds, and experiences of people.

Technologies That Are Revolutionizing Business

Business intelligence systems

One of the maddening ironies of contemporary business is that many decision makers are awash in data but starved for true information and insights. *Business intelligence* (BI) systems aim to harness all that data and turn it into the information and insights that managers need.

The good news is that a number of companies now offer solutions to this problem. The bad news is there's a dizzying array of terminology in use today. The wide range of technologies that fall under the BI umbrella include *executive information systems* (a general term for systems that present top managers with vital operational information), *decision support systems* (which collect and analyze data, then model various scenarios to let managers study the likely outcomes of the decisions they face), and a variety of other systems and tools. You'll also encounter such terms as *online analytical processing (OLAP)* and *business analytics* (data analysis tools that help managers discover trends and relationships in operating data), *performance metrics* (systems that measure and report on progress toward organizational goals), and *executive dashboards* (specialized webpages that present performance metrics in easy-to-read formats).

How they're changing business

Business intelligence systems are helping managers and professionals in many industries grapple with both strategic and tactical problems. For instance, Boeing tracks the staggeringly complex process of custom-building each of its aircraft, and DaimlerChrysler analyzes millions of owner contact records to learn more about customer needs and expectations.

Where you can learn more

Because business intelligence is a broad term that describes a variety of approaches, technologies, and specific products, you can expect to find a wide range of information. Start with Business Intelligence.com, www.businessintelligence.com, then try several of the leading vendors, including Cognos, www.cognos.com; Business Objectives, www.businessobjects.com; and Hyperion, www.hyperion.com.

---

interpersonal skills
Skills required to understand other people and to interact effectively with them

Technical Skills

A person who knows how to operate a machine, prepare a financial statement, program a computer, or pass a football has **technical skills**; that is, the individual has the knowledge and ability to perform the mechanics of a particular job. Technical skills are most important at lower organizational levels because managers at these levels work directly with employees who are using the tools and techniques of a particular specialty, such as automotive assembly or computer programming. Still, 21st-century managers must have a strong technology background. They must find new computer applications that can complete daily work routines faster or provide more accurate information sooner.

Managers at all levels use **administrative skills**, which are the technical skills necessary to manage an organization. Administrative skills include the abilities to make

technical skills
Ability and knowledge to perform the mechanics of a particular job

administrative skills
Technical skills in information gathering, data analysis, planning, organizing, and other aspects of managerial work

schedules, gather information, analyze data, plan, and organize. Managers often develop such skills through education and then improve them by working in one or more functional areas of an organization, such as accounting or marketing.[46] Project-management skills are becoming an increasingly important administrative skill. Managers must know how to start a project or work assignment from scratch, map out each step in the process to its successful completion, develop project costs and timelines, and establish checkpoints at key project intervals.

Exhibit 6.7

Greatest Management Decisions Ever Made

Great decisions change things. Here are some of the greatest management decisions made in the last 100 years.

Coca-Cola

During WWII, Robert Woodruff, president of Coca-Cola, committed to selling bottles of Coke to members of the armed services for a nickel a bottle. Customer loyalty never came cheaper.

Diners Club

In 1950, when Frank McNamara found himself in a restaurant with no money, he came up with the idea of the Diners Club Card. The first credit card changed the nature of buying and selling throughout the world.

Holiday Inn

When the Wilson family of Memphis went on a motoring vacation, they discovered it was not much fun staying in motels that were either too expensive or too slovenly. So Kemmons Wilson built his own. The first Holiday Inn opened in Memphis in 1952.

Honda

When Honda arrived in America in 1959 to launch its big motorbikes, customers weren't keen on their problematic performance. However, they did admire the little Supercub bikes Honda's managers used. So Honda bravely changed direction and transformed the motorbike business overnight.

Weight Watchers

When Jean Nidetch was put on a diet by the Obesity Clinic at New York Department of Health, she invited six dieting friends to meet in her apartment every week. In 1961 she started Weight Watchers and helped create the diet industry.

CNN

Ted Turner launched the Cable News Network in 1980. No one thought a 24-hour news network would work, but CNN has become a fixture in global news media.

Sony

Sony chief Akito Morita noticed that young people liked listening to music wherever they went. So in 1980 he and the company developed what became the Walkman, the forerunner of all portable music players.

Tylenol

When Johnson & Johnson pulled Tylenol from store shelves in 1982 after capsules were found to be poisoned, the company put customer safety before corporate profit. And it provided a lesson in media openness.

Dell

In 1984 Michael Dell decided to sell PCs direct and built to order. Now everybody in the industry is trying to imitate Dell Computer's strategy.

Amazon.com

With relentless focus on the mundane, behind-the-scenes details, such as warehousing, packaging, and shipping, Jeff Bezos proved that large-scale e-commerce can work.

Conceptual Skills

Managers need **conceptual skills** to see the organization as a whole, in the context of its environment, and to understand how the various parts interrelate. Conceptual skills are especially important to top managers. These managers are the strategists who develop the plans that guide the organization toward its goals. Managers such as Jorma Ollila use their conceptual skills to acquire and analyze information, identify both problems and opportunities, understand the competitive environment in which their companies operate, develop strategies, and make decisions.

A key managerial activity requiring conceptual skills is **decision making**, a process that has five distinct steps: (1) recognizing the need for a decision; (2) identifying, analyzing, and defining the problem or opportunity; (3) generating alternatives; (4) selecting an alternative and implementing it; and (5) evaluating the results. Managers monitor the results of decisions over time to see whether the chosen alternative works, whether any new problem or opportunity arises because of the decision, and whether a new decision must be made. Exhibit 6.7 lists some classic business decisions that created fortunes and launched entire industries.[47]

Keep in mind that a company's managerial structure defines the way decisions are made. Today's flatter organizations, for example, allow information to flow more freely among all levels of the organization, and they push decision making down to lower organizational levels. As Chapter 7 discusses in detail, more and more organizations are empowering their employees and teams by giving them increasing discretion over work-related issues.[48]

conceptual skills
Ability to understand the relationship of parts to the whole

decision making
Process of identifying a decision situation, analyzing the problem, weighing the alternatives, choosing an alternative and implementing it, and evaluating the results

Summary of Learning Objectives

1 Define the four basic management functions.

The four management functions are (1) planning—establishing objectives and goals for the organization and translating them into action plans; (2) organizing—arranging resources to carry out the organization's plans; (3) leading—influencing and motivating people to work effectively and willingly toward company goals; and (4) controlling—monitoring progress toward organizational goals, resetting the course if goals or objectives change in response to shifting conditions, and correcting deviations if goals or objectives are not being attained.

2 Outline the tasks involved in the strategic planning process.

The strategic planning process begins with a clear vision for the company's future. This vision is then translated into a mission statement so it can be shared with all members of the organization. Next, managers develop forecasts about trends that affect their industry and products; then they analyze the competition—paying close attention to their strengths and weaknesses so they can use this information to gain a competitive edge. With an eye on the company's vision and mission as well as on competition, managers establish company goals and objectives. Finally, they translate these goals and objectives into action plans.

3 Explain the purpose of a mission statement.

A mission statement defines why the organization exists, what it does, what it hopes to achieve, and the principles it will abide by to meet its goals. It is used to bring clarity of focus to members of the organization and to provide guidelines for the adoption of future projects.

4 List the benefits of setting long-term goals and objectives.

Goals and objectives establish long- and short-range targets that help managers fulfill the company's mission. Setting appropriate goals increases employee motivation, establishes standards by which individual and group performance can be measured, guides employee activity, and clarifies management's expectations.

5 Cite three leadership styles and explain why no one style is best.

Three leadership styles are autocratic, democratic, and laissez-faire (also called free-rein). Each may work best in a different situation: autocratic when quick decisions are needed, democratic when employee participation in decision making is desirable, and laissez-faire when fostering creativity is a priority. Good leaders are flexible enough to respond with the best approach for the situation.

6 Clarify how total quality management (TQM) is changing the way organizations are managed.

Total quality management is both a management philosophy and a management process that focuses on delivering quality to customers. TQM redirects management to focus on four key elements: (1) Employee involvement includes team building and soliciting employee input on decisions. (2) Customer focus involves gathering customer feedback and then acting on that feedback to better serve customers. (3) Benchmarking involves measuring the company's standards against the standards of industry leaders. (4) Continuous improvement requires an ongoing commitment to reducing defects, cutting costs, slashing production and delivery times, and offering customers innovative products.

7 Identify and explain the three types of managerial skills.

Managers use (1) interpersonal skills to communicate with other people, work effectively with them, and lead them; (2) technical skills to perform the mechanics of a particular job; and (3) conceptual skills (including decision making) to see the organization as a whole, to see it in the context of its environment, and to understand how the various parts interrelate.

Behind **the Scenes**

Nokia's Secret

Nokia's Jorma Ollila was on a mission. From the time Ollila was appointed CEO in 1992, he wanted to transform a company that once made toilet paper, tires, and rubber boots into a world-class mobile telecommunications company. He wanted the company to produce wireless phones that shaped new markets. But how?

Ollila created a culture that encouraged innovation and, above all, one where employees were not afraid to make mistakes. He used a democratic, hands-off leadership style to empower employees. He demolished hierarchies that prevented the company from listening to customers and employees and reorganized the company into decision-making teams. Then he challenged employees to learn and to speak their minds. He even hosted a series of annual meetings known as the Nokia Way to give employees the opportunity to determine Nokia's priorities. Finally, he relied on management to translate these priorities into a strategic plan for the company.

Nokia shipped its first new stylish phones in 1993. Management had hoped to sell 400,000 phones; instead, the company sold 20 million. The competition was caught flat-footed. What was Nokia's secret? To begin with, Nokia stayed in touch with consumers' needs. It produced a constant stream of different model phones that appealed to specific market segments, encouraging consumers to upgrade their existing phones to take advantage of new technologies and cool designs. Nokia also engineered its phones so that the same models could be adapted to the varying frequencies and mobile phone standards around the world.

Innovation became Nokia's lifeblood. The company had created the first digital phone for global system mobile communications networks, the first mobile phone specially designed for Asian customers (with a large full-graphics display and Asian language interfaces), the first mobile phones with user-changeable covers and changeable ringing tones, and the first mobile phones with a unique short-message chat function. Bottom line: Nokia made cell phones that worked well and looked great. By late 1998, Nokia was pumping out new models every 35 days. Such innovations helped Nokia capture 30 percent of the global mobile phone market, rolling over rivals Motorola and Ericsson to become the biggest mobile phone supplier in the world.

To keep the company on track, Nokia continually monitored its goals. For example, if annual growth of a specific mobile phone fell below 25 percent, the company shifted its focus to other mobile phone product lines with more growth potential. Still, management was careful not to analyze data to death. "We're pretty determined about timeliness and about getting things done," says Ollila. "Somebody has to take the responsibility and say, 'O.K, this is it. This is what we are going to do.' Otherwise you just have a lot of fun in discussing things and nobody takes the ball and carries it."

Of course, nobody does a better job of carrying the ball than Jorma Ollila. Recently voted *IndustryWeek*'s CEO of the year, Ollila helped transform Nokia into the leading maker of mobile phones. But with over 50,000 employees and global sales approaching $40 billion, his company now faces different challenges. Mobile phone sales account for over 80 percent of the company's revenues and demand is shrinking. In Europe, just about everybody who wants an ordinary cell phone has one. Moreover, competition is intensifying as rivals such as Motorola and Ericsson aggressively roll out cool phones to match Nokia's. That leaves Ollila and Nokia with a new problem: how to keep growing as the industry matures.

"This isn't a business where you do one big strategic thing right and you're set for the next five years," says Ollila. "It's a big orchestration task." And, if any cell phone maker can thrive, Nokia can. In fact, Jorma Ollila is a man with a mission. While other high-tech industry executives are obsessed with wiring the planet, he is intent on creating the mobile information society—bringing people, words, data, and the Internet together anywhere and anytime without wires.

But big question marks loom. What will it take to convince consumers to surf the web via their mobile phones? When will technological improvements make such wireless communications efficient? Will new products such as phones embedded with digital cameras take off? And can Nokia continue to move faster than rivals? Ollila claims

Nokia is ready to lead the industry with the next generation of wireless phones. But only time will tell whether this company can repeat its stunning performance.[49]

Critical Thinking Questions

1. Why did Jorma Ollila transform Nokia, and how did he do it? (*Hint:* In your discussion be sure to mention organizational culture, leadership style, mission, and vision.)
2. How does Nokia stay ahead of its competitors?
3. What new challenges does Nokia face today?

LEARN MORE ONLINE

Go to Chapter 6 of this text's website at www.prenhall.com/bovee, and click on the hotlink to Nokia's website. Review the website to answer these questions: How has Nokia achieved global success? What are Nokia's future goals? ■

Key Terms

administrative skills (157)
autocratic leaders (148)
coaching (150)
conceptual skills (159)
contingency leadership (149)
controlling (153)
corporate culture (151)
crisis management (145)
decision making (159)
democratic leaders (148)
first-line managers (147)
goal (145)
interpersonal skills (157)

laissez-faire leaders (149)
leading (148)
management (141)
management pyramid (146)
mentor (150)
middle managers (146)
mission statement (143)
objective (145)
operational plans (145)
organizing (146)
participative management (154)
planning (142)
quality (153)

roles (141)
situational leadership (149)
standards (153)
strategic plans (142)
tactical plans (145)
technical skills (157)
transactional leaders (149)
transformational leaders (149)
top managers (146)
total quality management
   (TQM) (154)
vision (143)

Test Your Knowledge

Questions for Review

1. What is management? Why is it so important?
2. What is forecasting, and how is it related to the planning function?
3. What is the goal of crisis management?
4. What are some common characteristics of effective leaders?
5. Why are interpersonal skills important to managers at all levels?

Questions for Analysis

6. Is the following statement an example of a strategic goal or an objective? "To become the number-one retailer of

computers and computer accessories in terms of revenue, growth, and customer satisfaction." Explain your answer.
7. How do the three levels of management differ?
8. Why are coaching and mentoring effective leadership techniques?
9. How are the four main elements of total quality management related to the goal of delivering quality to customers?
10. **Ethical Considerations.** When an organization learns about a threat that could place the safety of its workers or its customers at risk, is management obligated to immediately inform these parties of the threat? Explain your answer.

Questions for Application

11. What are your long-term goals? Develop a set of long-term career goals for yourself and several short-term objectives that will help you reach those goals. Make sure your goals are specific, measurable, and time limited.

12. Do you have the skills it takes to be an effective manager? Find out by taking the Keirsey Temperament Sorter II personality test at www.keirsey.com.

13. **Integrated.** Using Dell Computer's mission statement in Exhibit 6.2 as a model and the material you learned in Chapter 2, develop a mission statement for a socially responsible company such as Patagonia or Ben & Jerry's.

14. **Integrated.** What is the principal difference between a business plan (as discussed in Chapter 5) and a strategic plan?

Practice Your Knowledge

Sharpening Your Communication Skills

As the manager of Richter's Restaurant Supply, you see a huge potential for selling company products on the Internet to customers around the world. Your company already has a website but it's geared to U.S. sales only. Before you propose your ideas to senior management, however, you're going to do your homework. Studies show that companies selling in the global marketplace benefit by modifying their websites to accommodate cultural differences. For instance, a mailbox with a raised flag has no meaning in many foreign countries.

Your task is to review the websites of several leading global companies and take notes on how they adapt their websites for global audiences. Once you've gathered your notes, write a short memo to management highlighting (via bullet points) some of the ways these leaders make their websites effective for a global audience.

Building Your Team Skills

A good mission statement should define the organization's purpose and ultimate goals and outline the principles that are to guide managers and employees in working toward those goals. Using library sources such as annual reports or Internet sources such as organizational websites, locate mission statements from one nonprofit organization, such as a school or a charity, and one company with which you are familiar.

Bring these statements to class and, with your team, select four mission statements to evaluate. How many of the mission statements contain all five of the typical components (product or service; primary market; concern for survival, growth, and profitability; managerial philosophy; commitment to quality and social responsibility)? Which components are most often absent from the mission statements you are evaluating? Which components are most often included? Of the mission statements your team is analyzing, which is the most inspiring? Why?

Now assume that you and your teammates are the top management team at each organization or company. How would you improve these mission statements? Rewrite the four mission statements so that they cover the five typical components, show all organization members how their roles are related to the vision, and inspire commitment among employees and managers.

Summarize your team's work in a written or oral report to the class. Compare the mission statement that your team found the most inspiring with the statements that other teams found the most inspiring. What do these mission statements have in common? How do they differ? Of all the inspiring mission statements reported to the class, which do you think is the best? Why? Does this mission statement inspire you to consider working for or doing business with this organization?

Expand Your Knowledge

Discovering Career Opportunities

If you become a manager, how much of your day will be spent performing each of the four basic functions of management? This is your opportunity to find out. Arrange to shadow a manager (such as a department head, a store manager, or a shift supervisor) for a few hours. As you observe, categorize the manager's activities in terms of the four management functions and note how much time each activity takes. If observation is not possible, interview a manager in order to complete this exercise.

1. How much of the manager's time is spent on each of the four management functions? Is this the allocation you expected?

2. Ask whether this is a typical workday for this manager. If it isn't, what does the manager usually do differently? During a typical day, does this manager tend to spend most of the time on one particular function?

3. Of the four management functions, which does the manager believe is most important for good organizational performance? Do you agree?

Developing Your Research Skills

Find two articles in business journals or newspapers (print or online editions) that profile two senior managers who lead a business or a nonprofit organization.

1. What experience, skills, and business background do the two leaders have? Do you see any striking similarities or differences in their backgrounds?

2. What kinds of business challenges have these two leaders faced? What actions did they take to deal with those challenges? Did they establish any long-term goals or objectives for their company? Did the articles mention a new change initiative?

3. Describe the leadership strengths of each person as they are presented in the articles you selected. Is either leader known as a team builder? Long-term strategist? Shrewd negotiator? What are each leader's greatest areas of strength?

SEE IT ON THE WEB

For live links to the websites that follow, go to this text's website at www.prenhall.com/bovee. When you log on, select Chapter 6, then select "Featured Websites," click on the URL of the website you wish to visit, review the website, and answer the following questions:

1. What is the purpose of this website?

2. What kinds of information does this website contain? Please be specific.

3. How is the information provided at this website useful for businesspeople? Consumers?

4. How did you expand your knowledge of management by reviewing the material at this website? What new things did you learn about this topic?

Become a Better Manager

ManagementFirst.com can help you become a better manager. Focused on management theory and practice, this website is a management portal that explores in-depth management issues including leadership, time management, training, strategy, knowledge management, personal development, customer relationship management, and more. Each channel provides lengthy articles, advice, and a collection of carefully annotated links. Log on today and join ManagementFirst.com to become information rich and well organized. Learn why knowledge management is important. Discover what emotional intelligence is all about. And find out why companies form strategic alliances. www.managementfirst.com

Linking to Organizational Change

Looking for more information on every aspect of organizational change management? You'll find a comprehensive collection of links on the website of the Management Assistance Program for Nonprofits. This is the place to access articles, discussion groups, and other resources related to organizational change in businesses and in not-for-profit organizations. Start with the overview, which sets the stage for browsing the many links devoted to exploring management and employee perspectives on the challenges and goals of managing change. www.managementhelp.org/org_chng/org_chng.htm

Learn from the Best—and the Worst

Every year, *BusinessWeek* magazine profiles the managers who've done the best and worst jobs of leading their respective companies. See who the magazine's editors and reporters select each year, and find out what they've done. www.businessweek.com/magazine (then click on "Special Reports" and look for "The Best and the Worst Managers of the Year").

Companion Website

Learning Interactively

Go to the Companion Website at www.prenhall.com/bovee. For Chapter 6, take advantage of the interactive "Study Guide" to test your knowledge of the chapter. Get instant feedback on whether you need additional studying.

Also, visit this site's "Study Hall," where you'll find an abundance of valuable resources that will help you succeed in this course.

Video **Case**

Creative Management: Creative Age Publications

LEARNING OBJECTIVES

The purpose of this video is to help you:

1. Understand how and why managers set organizational goals.
2. Identify the basic skills that managers need to be effective.
3. Discuss how corporate culture can affect an organization.

SYNOPSIS

Creative Age Publications uses creativity in managing its beauty-industry publications. With offices or franchised operations in Europe, Japan, Russia, and other countries, the company has expanded rapidly—thanks to sound management practices. One of the company's goals is to avoid overtaxing its management team by growing slowly in the near future. The CEO is working toward delegating most or all of the decisions to her management team rather than making these decisions herself. As Creative Age's managers moved up through the ranks, they honed their technical skills as well as their skills in working with others. "Having heart" is a major part of the company's culture—an important element that, in the CEO's opinion, many companies lack.

Discussion Questions

1. *For analysis:* How does global growth affect Creative Age's emphasis on the management skill of interacting well with other people?
2. *For analysis:* How does moving Creative Age's managers up through the ranks help them develop their conceptual skills?
3. *For application:* How would you suggest that the CEO spread Creative Age's culture throughout its global offices?
4. *For application:* How might the CEO manage Creative Age's growth through the process of controlling?
5. *For debate:* Do you agree with the CEO's policy of allowing managers and employees to work on any company magazine they choose? Support your position.

ONLINE EXPLORATION

Visit Creative Age's website www.creativeage.com and follow the link to *NailPro* magazine. Scan the magazine's homepage and then click on the About Us link to read more about the magazine and its parent company. Why would Creative Age call attention to each magazine's goals and market rather than focusing on the parent company? How might Creative Age use a corporate website to communicate with other people and organizations that affect its ability to achieve its goals?

Chapter 7

Organizing and Working in Teams

Behind **the Scenes**

Reinventing the Retail Experience at The Container Store

www.containerstore.com

Let's face it: frontline jobs in retail sometimes don't have the greatest reputation. From an employee's perspective, these sales positions often combine low pay with high stress, leading to rapid burnout and frequent turnover. From a customer's perspective, frontline retail employees in some stores seem to fall into two categories: poorly trained and poorly motivated rookies or aggressive staffers who seem more intent on getting their commissions than helping customers.

What if you wanted to put a new face on retailing? What if you wanted shopping to be a pleasant, welcome experience for both employees and customers? Too much to ask for, perhaps?

This is the challenge Garrett Boone and Kip Tindell set for themselves when they opened the first Container Store in Dallas, Texas. The chain, which continues to expand and now numbers more than 30 locations across the country,

Effective team communication behind the scenes is key to creating positive customer experiences at The Container Store.

carries a staggering array of products that help customers organize their lives. Store employees are expected to help customers solve every storage problem imaginable, from sweaters to DVDs to rubber stamps to tax records, with a variety of boxes, baskets, hangers, hooks, closet organizers, and more. The Container Store, which certainly lives up to its motto, "Contain Yourself," offers some sort of storage solution for every room in the house, from the kitchen to the garage to the home office.

If you were in Boone and Tindell's shoes, what steps would you take to break out of the retail rut and create a company that is satisfying for both customers and employees? How would you attract the best and the brightest employees and pull off a minor miracle in retailing—hanging on to them year after year? How would you organize the staffs in your stores? How much information would you share with them, and how would you communicate it?[1] ▪

DESIGNING AN EFFECTIVE ORGANIZATION STRUCTURE

organization structure
Framework enabling managers to divide responsibilities, ensure employee accountability, and distribute decision-making authority

As Garrett Boone and Kip Tindell can tell you, a company's **organization structure** has a dramatic influence on the way employees and managers make decisions, communicate, and accomplish important tasks. This structure helps the company achieve its goals by providing a framework for managers to divide responsibilities, effectively distribute the authority to make decisions, coordinate and control the organization's work, and hold employees accountable for their work. In some organizations, this structure is a relatively rigid vertical hierarchy (a group of people organized by rank or authority), such as the management pyramid described in Chapter 6. In other organizations, teams of employees and managers from across levels and functions work together to make decisions and achieve the organization's goals.[2]

organization chart
Diagram showing how employees and tasks are grouped and where the lines of communication and authority flow

When managers design the organization's structure, they use an **organization chart** to provide a visual representation of how employees and tasks are grouped and how the lines of communication and authority flow. Exhibit 7.1 shows the organization

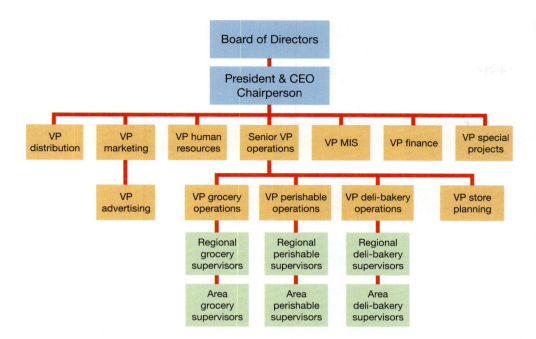

Exhibit 7.1

Organization Chart for Food Lion Grocery Store Chain

Many organization charts look like this one, for Food Lion. The traditional model of an organization is a pyramid in which numerous boxes form the base and lead up to fewer and fewer boxes on higher levels, ultimately arriving at one box at the top. A glance at Food Lion's organization chart reveals who has authority over whom, who is responsible for whose work, and who is accountable to whom.

chart for a grocery store chain. An organization chart depicts the official design for accomplishing tasks that lead to achieving the organization's goals, a framework known as the **formal organization**. Every company also has an **informal organization**—the network of interactions that develop on a personal level among workers. Sometimes the interactions among people in the informal organization parallel their relationships in the formal organization, but often interactions transcend formal boundaries. Crossing formal boundaries can help establish a more pleasant work environment, but it can also undermine formal work processes and hinder a company's ability to get things done.[3]

How do companies design an organization structure, and which organization structure is the most effective? In the past, organizations were designed around management's desire to control workers, with everything set up in a hierarchy. Today, however, more and more companies are designing organization structures around the customers' needs for fast decisions. As this chapter will discuss later, companies are eliminating layers of management, or flattening their organization structures, to give more decision-making authority to employees who deal directly with customers. In fact, as management guru Peter Drucker sees it, "There is no such thing as one right organization. Each has distinct strengths, distinct limitations, and specific applications."[4] In other words, today's managers require a toolbox full of organization structures so they can select the right tool for each specific task. To identify the best structure for their organizations, managers need to identify job responsibilities, define the chain of command, and organize the workforce in a way that maximizes effectiveness and efficiency.

formal organization
A framework officially established by managers for accomplishing tasks that lead to achieving the organization's goals

informal organization
Network of informal employee interactions that are not defined by the formal structure

Identifying Job Responsibilities

The nature of the work employees are expected to do is a critical aspect of the organization decision. Management must first decide on the optimal level of **work specialization**, sometimes referred to as the *division of labor*—the degree to which organizational tasks are broken down into separate jobs.[5] Few employees have the skills to perform every task a company needs. Therefore, work specialization can improve organizational efficiency by enabling each worker to perform tasks that are well defined and that require specific skills. The notion of specialization dates to 1776, when Scottish economist Adam Smith found that if each of 10 workers went through every step needed to

work specialization
Specialization in or responsibility for some portion of an organization's overall work tasks; also called division of labor

make a pin, the entire group could make 200 pins a day. However, if each worker performed only a few steps and no one made a pin from start to finish, the same 10 workers could make 48,000 pins a day. When employees concentrate on the same specialized tasks, they can perfect their skills and perform their tasks more quickly.

Work specialization continues to be a prominent feature in business organizations, from the various responsibilities along an automobile assembly line to an accounting firm in which various staff members specialize in different aspects of taxation. In addition to aligning skills with job tasks, specialization prevents overlapping responsibilities and communication breakdowns. For instance, in business-to-business markets, the ongoing relationship between a supplier and a customer can sometimes involve dozens or even hundreds of employees. To ensure efficient communication, *relationship managers* (frequently senior salespeople) are often put in charge of the relationship on both sides. Other employees will communicate back and forth, to be sure, but significant issues, such as contract negotiations and schedule updates, are usually left to these two people.

However, organizations can overdo specialization. If a task is defined too narrowly, employees may become bored with performing the same limited, repetitious job over and over. They may also feel unchallenged and alienated. An overemphasis on specialization can also lead employees to focus so intently on their own responsibilities they reduce their contribution to the organization's overall success. As you'll see later in the chapter, many companies are adopting a team-based approach to give employees a wider range of work experiences and responsibilities.

Defining the Chain of Command

Once the various jobs and their individual responsibilities have been identified, the next step is defining the **chain of command**, the lines of authority that connect the various groups and levels within the organization. The chain of command helps organizations function smoothly by making two things clear: who is responsible for each task, and who has the authority to make official decisions.

All employees have a certain amount of **responsibility**—the obligation to perform the duties and achieve the goals and objectives associated with their jobs. As they work toward the organization's goals, employees must also maintain their **accountability**, their obligation to report the results of their work to supervisors or team members and to justify any outcomes that fall below expectations. Managers ensure that tasks are accomplished by exercising **authority**, the power to make decisions, issue orders, carry

chain of command
Pathway for the flow of authority from one management level to the next

responsibility
Obligation to perform the duties and achieve the goals and objectives associated with a particular position

accountability
Obligation to report results to supervisors or team members and to justify outcomes that fall below expectations

authority
Power granted by the organization to make decisions, take actions, and allocate resources to accomplish goals

out actions, and allocate resources to achieve the organization's goals. Authority is vested in the positions that managers hold, and it flows down through the management pyramid. **Delegation** is the assignment of work and the transfer of authority and responsibility to complete that work.[6]

Look again at Exhibit 7.1. The senior vice president of operations delegates responsibilities to the vice presidents of grocery operations, perishable operations, deli-bakery operations, and store planning. These department heads have the authority to make certain decisions necessary to fulfill their roles, and they are accountable to the senior VP for the performance of their respective divisions. In turn, the senior VP is accountable to the company CEO.

The simplest and most common chain-of-command system is known as **line organization** because it establishes a clear line of authority flowing from the top down, as Exhibit 7.1 depicts. Everyone knows who is accountable to whom, as well as which tasks and decisions each is responsible for. However, line organization sometimes falls short because the technical complexity of a firm's activities may require specialized knowledge that individual managers don't have and can't easily acquire. A more elaborate system called **line-and-staff organization** was developed out of the need to combine specialization with management control. In such an organization, managers in the chain of command are supplemented by functional groupings of people known as *staff*, who provide advice and specialized services but who are not in the line organization's overall chain of command (see Exhibit 7.2).

Span of Management

The number of people a manager directly supervises is called the **span of management** or *span of control*. When a large number of people report directly to one person, that person has a wide span of management. This situation is common in **flat organizations** with relatively few levels in the management hierarchy. Sun Microsystems, Visa, and Oticon (a hearing-aid manufacturer in Denmark) are all companies that have flat organizations. British Petroleum (BP) is also amazingly flat and lean for an organization with $148 billion in revenues and 107,000 employees. At BP there is no level between the general managers of the business units and the group of nine operating executives who oversee the businesses.[7]

In contrast, **tall organizations** have many hierarchical levels, typically with fewer people reporting to each manager than is the case in a flat organization. In these organizations, the span of management is narrow (see Exhibit 7.3). General Motors traditionally had a tall organization structure with as many as 22 layers of management. Under tall organization structures, employees who want to institute a change must ask a supervisor, who in turn must ask a manager, who in turn must ask another manager at the

delegation
Assignment of work and the authority and responsibility required to complete it

line organization
Chain-of-command system that establishes a clear line of authority flowing from the top down

line-and-staff organization
Organization system that has a clear chain of command but that also includes functional groups of people who provide advice and specialized services

span of management
Number of people under one manager's control; also known as span of control

flat organizations
Organizations with a wide span of management and few hierarchical levels

tall organizations
Organizations with a narrow span of management and many hierarchical levels

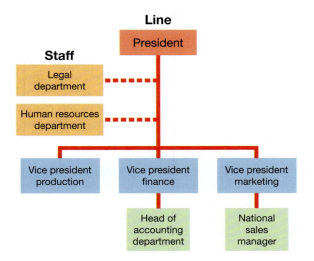

Exhibit 7.2

Simplified Line-and-Staff Structure

A line-and-staff organization divides employees into those who are in the direct line of command (from the top level of the hierarchy to the bottom) and those who provide staff (or support) services to line managers at various levels. Staff report directly to top management.

| Exhibit 7.3 | **Tall Versus Flat Organizations** |

A tall organization, such as the U.S. Army's, has many levels with a narrow span of management at each level so that relatively few people report to each manager on the level above them. In contrast, a flat organization, such as the Catholic Church, has relatively few levels with a wide span of management so that more people report to each manager.

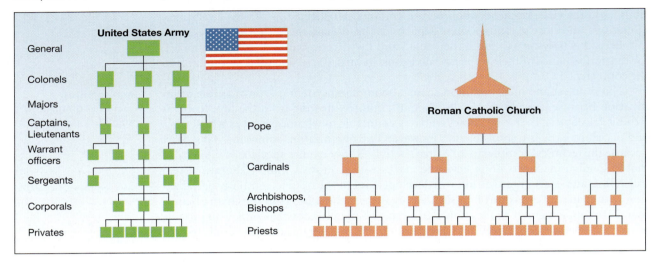

next level up, and so on. To reduce the time it takes to make decisions, many companies are now flattening their organization structures by removing layers of management and by delegating increased responsibilities and authority to middle managers, work teams, and individual employees.[8] However, these changes must be considered with care, since flatter organizations can increase the demand on individual managers.

No formula exists for determining the ideal span of management. How well people work together is more important than the number of people reporting to one person. Still, several factors affect the number of people a manager can effectively supervise, including the manager's personal skill and leadership ability, the skill of the workers, the motivation of the workers, and the nature or complexity of the job. In general, employees who are highly skilled or who are trained in many work tasks don't require as much supervision as employees who are less skilled.

Centralization Versus Decentralization

Organizations that focus decision-making authority near the top of the chain of command are said to be centralized. **Centralization** can benefit a company by utilizing top management's experience and broad view of organizational goals. It can also help companies coordinate large undertakings more efficiently, and it can accelerate decisions that might otherwise get bogged down in discussions and disagreements. Both line organizations and line-and-staff organizations tend to be centralized.

However, the trend in business today is toward decentralization. **Decentralization** pushes decision-making authority down to lower organizational levels—such as department heads—while control over essential companywide matters remains with top management. Implemented properly, decentralization can stimulate responsiveness because decisions don't have to be referred up the hierarchy.[9] For instance, to accelerate the development of new drugs, the pharmaceutical giant GlaxoSmithKline recently divided the 15,000 scientists in its research-and-development lab into six smaller labs, each with independent responsibility to pursue products in a specific area, such as heart disease or cancer.[10]

However, decentralization does not work in every situation or in every company. At times, strong authority from the top of the chain of command may be needed to keep the organization focused on immediate goals. In other cases, a company may need strong central decision making to coordinate efforts on complex projects or to present a

centralization
Concentration of decision-making authority at the top of the organization

decentralization
Delegation of decision-making authority to employees in lower-level positions

unified image to customers. Managers should select the level of decision making that will most effectively serve the organization's needs given the individual circumstances.[11]

Organizing the Workforce

The decisions regarding job responsibilities, span of management, and centralization versus decentralization provide the insights managers need to choose the best organization structure. The arrangement of activities into logical groups that are then clustered into larger departments and units that form the total organization is known as **departmentalization**.[12] The choice must involve both the *vertical structure*—how many layers the chain of command is divided into from the top of the company to the bottom—and the *horizontal structure*—how the various business functions and work specialties are divided across the company. For instance, looking back at Exhibit 7.1, you can see that Food Lion divides the chain of command into six vertical layers from the board of directors down to the area supervisors, and the operations group is departmentalized into four horizontal subgroups.

Variations in the vertical and horizontal designs of the organization can produce an almost endless array of structures—some flat, some wide; some simple and clear; others convoluted and complex. For instance, a retailer such as Wal-Mart is likely to duplicate a single organization structure across all of its stores, whereas a large high-technology firm might use one structure in its hardware division, a different structure in its software division, and a third structure in its sales and support division, since the nature of these activities differs widely. Two similar companies in the same industry may decide to organize in different ways, based on their unique competitive strengths and weaknesses, company history, and the preferences of the owners or top executives.

Within this endless variety of structure possibilities, most designs fall into one of five types: functional, divisional, matrix, network, or hybrids that combine features of two or more types. Keep in mind that large companies often combine structure choices at different levels in the organization. For example, a company might first divide into divisions, then use a functional structure within each of those divisions.

Functional Structures

The **functional structure** groups employees according to their skills, resource use, and job requirements. Common functional departments include marketing and sales, human resources, operations, finance and accounting, and research and development, with each department working independently of the others.[13] As depicted in Exhibit 7.1, functional departmentalization is highly centralized.

Splitting the organization into separate functional departments offers several advantages: (1) Grouping employees by specialization allows for the efficient use of resources and encourages the development of in-depth skills, (2) centralized decision making enables unified direction by top management, and (3) centralized operations enhance communication and the coordination of activities within departments. Despite these advantages, functional departmentalization can create communication barriers between departments, thereby slowing response to change, hindering effective planning for products and markets, and overemphasizing work specialization (which alienates

---

Learning from Business Blunders

Oops: In an attempt to accelerate innovation by decentralizing decision making, telecommunication equipment maker Lucent Technologies split its three operating divisions into 11 largely independent business units. Unfortunately, the move toward decentralization apparently made matters worse, slowing decision making, creating new communication and control issues, and adding another layer of cost and complexity to the organizational structure. Experts say the reorganization played a significant role in a decline that saw the company lose money every quarter for more than three years and shed more than 100,000 jobs. (To be fair, just about everybody in the telecommunication business has been hammered in recent years, but Lucent's losses were extraordinarily painful.)

What You Can Learn: Decentralization works only if the various units of a company can truly work independently. However, Lucent makes extremely complex systems that require close coordination across many groups within the company to be successful. After the failed experiment in decentralization, the company has become more efficient by becoming even more centralized than it was before.

---

departmentalization
Grouping people within an organization according to function, division, matrix, or network

functional structure
Grouping workers according to their similar skills, resource use, and expertise

Business BUZZ

Stovepipe organization:
A rigid organization structure in which each group functions independently, without communicating and collaborating with other groups; sometimes referred to as a *silo organization*

employees).[14] Moreover, employees may become too narrowly focused on departmental goals and lose sight of larger company goals. For instance, the research-and-development departments in some companies have been criticized for designing new products then "throwing them over the wall" to manufacturing and marketing, leaving those other departments to figure out what to do with the new products. Firms that use functional structures often try to counter these weaknesses by using *cross-functional teams* to coordinate efforts across functional boundaries, as you'll see later in the chapter.

Divisional Structures

divisional structure
Grouping departments according to similarities in product, process, customer, or geography

The **divisional structure** establishes self-contained departments that encompass all the major functional resources required to achieve their goals—such as research and design, manufacturing, finance, and marketing.[15] These departments are typically formed according to similarities in product, process, customer, or geography. In some companies, these divisions operate with great autonomy, almost as multiple small companies within a larger company.

product divisions
Divisional structure based on products

- *Product divisions.* Many organizations use a structure based on **product divisions**—grouping around each of the company's products or family of products. The logic behind this organizational structure is that each department can manage all the activities needed to develop, manufacture, and sell a particular product or product line.

process divisions
Divisional structure based on the major steps of a production process

- *Process divisions.* **Process divisions**, also called *process-complete* departments, are based on the major steps of a production process. For example, a table-manufacturing company might have three divisions, one for each phase of manufacturing a table. Astra/Merck, a company that markets antiulcer and antihypertension drugs, is organized around six process divisions, including drug development and distribution.[16]

customer divisions
Divisional structure that focuses on customers or clients

- *Customer divisions.* The third approach, **customer divisions**, concentrates activities on satisfying specific groups of customers. For example, Acer America, manufacturer of computer equipment, restructured into six customer-centric divisions to facilitate the fulfillment of the company's mission—to provide customers with the highest level of quality, reliability, and support (see Exhibit 7.4).[17]

geographic divisions
Divisional structure based on location of operations

- *Geographic divisions.* **Geographic divisions** enable companies spread over a national or an international area to respond more easily to local customs, styles, and product preferences. For example, Quaker Oats has two main geographic divisions: (1) U.S. and Canadian Grocery Products and (2) International Grocery Products. Each division is further subdivided to allow the company to focus on the needs of customers in specific regions.

Divisional structures offer both advantages and disadvantages. First, because divisions are self-contained, they can react quickly to change, making the organization more flexible. In addition, because each division focuses on a limited number of products, processes, customers, or locations, divisions can offer better service to customers. Moreover, top managers can focus on problem areas more easily, and managers can gain valuable experience by dealing with the various functions in their divisions. However,

Exhibit 7.4   Customer Division Structure

Acer America's organizational structure supports the company's mission to be more customer focused.

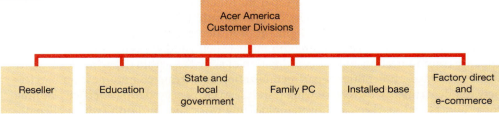

divisional departmentalization can also increase costs by duplicating the use of resources such as facilities and personnel. Furthermore, poor coordination between divisions may cause them to focus too narrowly on divisional goals and neglect the organization's overall goals. Finally, divisions may compete with one another for resources and customers, causing rivalries that hurt the organization as a whole.[18]

Matrix Structures

A **matrix structure** is an organizational design in which employees from functional departments form teams to combine their specialized skills (see Exhibit 7.5). This structure allows the company to pool and share resources across divisions and functional groups. The matrix may be a permanent feature of the organization's design, or it may be established to complete a specific project. For instance, the tool and appliance manufacturer Black & Decker shifted to a matrix organization in the early 1990s. Departments such as mechanical design, electrical engineering, and model shop assigned employees with specific technical skills to work on product-development projects in such categories as saws, cordless appliances, and woodworking.[19]

The matrix structure can help big companies function like smaller ones by allowing teams to devote their attention to specific projects or customers without permanently reorganizing the company's structure. But matrix structures are not without drawbacks. One problem of a matrix structure is that team members usually continue to report to their functional department heads as well as to a project team leader. Another drawback is that authority tends to be more ambiguous and up for grabs, creating power struggles and other interpersonal conflicts. Black & Decker realized this problem soon after implementing its matrix organization. The manager with the most authority was always the functional department head, and the project team did not really hold any control. The company has since redesigned its organization structure, which is now based on product divisions that employ teams of people from many functional areas.[20]

In a matrix organization, excellent communication and coordination are necessary to avoid conflicts. In addition, companies may find it difficult to coordinate the tasks of diverse functional specialists so that projects are completed efficiently.[21] However, because it facilitates the pooling of resources across departments, a matrix organization can also enable a company to respond better to changes in the business environment.

Network Structures

A **network structure** stretches beyond the boundaries of the company to connect a variety of partners and suppliers that perform selected tasks for a headquarters organization. Also called a *virtual organization*, the network organization can *outsource* engineering, marketing, research, accounting, production, distribution, or other functions. That is, the organization hires other organizations under contracts to handle one or more of those functions. In fact, companies such as Nike, Liz Claiborne, and Dell Computer sell hundreds of millions of dollars' worth of products even though they outsource most of

matrix structure
Structure in which employees are assigned to both a functional group and a project team (thus using functional and divisional patterns simultaneously)

network structure
Structure in which individual companies are connected electronically to perform selected tasks for a small headquarters organization

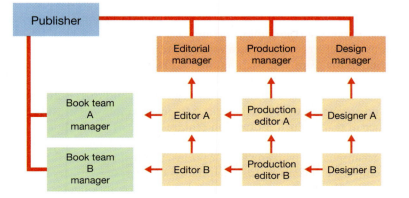

Exhibit 7.5

Matrix Structure

In a matrix structure, each employee is assigned to both a functional group (with a defined set of basic functions, such as production management) and a project team (which consists of members of various functional groups working together on a project, such as bringing out a new consumer product).

their manufacturing. As these companies have learned, the network approach is especially appropriate for international operations, allowing every part of the business to draw on resources no matter where in the world they may be.[22]

The biggest advantage of the network structure is its flexibility. Companies hire whatever services are needed and then change them once they are no longer needed. The limited hierarchy required to manage a network organization also permits the company to make decisions and react to change quickly. Additional advantages are that the organization can continually redefine itself, and a lean structure usually means employees have greater job variety and satisfaction. However, the network approach lacks hands-on control, because the functions are not in one location or company. Also, if one company in the network fails to deliver, the headquarters organization could suffer or even go out of business. Finally, strong employee loyalty and team spirit are less likely to develop, because the emotional connection between the employee and the organization is weak.[23]

Hybrid Structures

hybrid structure
Structure designs that combine elements of functional, divisional, matrix, and network organizations

Some companies find it most effective to adopt a **hybrid structure**, combining various elements from the four standard types of structure. For example, employees from various departments or functions can be grouped around a few companywide, cross-functional core processes, and they are responsible for an entire core process from beginning to end. Employees who create new product designs, for instance, work with engineers and marketing personnel to make sure the designs can be manufactured and marketed successfully. A typical core process group might include staff from finance, research and development, manufacturing, and customer service. All core processes lead to one objective: creating and delivering something of value to the customer.

In another example of hybrid design, Xerox organized its business operations around five core processes based on five types of products. The core processes are supported by two companywide operations: technology management and customer service. This way, researchers are not constrained by specific markets, and customers face only one customer service representative even if they buy different product types.[24]

By now you can see that whether it uses a traditional, tall structure or an innovative horizontal or hybrid organization, every organization must coordinate activities and communication among its employees. Without such coordination, functional departments would be isolated from one another, and they would be unable to align their objectives.[25] No matter what the structure, teamwork is crucial to every organization's success.

WORKING IN TEAMS

While the vertical chain of command is a tried-and-true method of organizing for business, it is limited by the fact that decision-making authority is often located high up the management hierarchy and real-world feedback from customers is usually located at or near the bottom of the hierarchy. Companies that organize vertically may become slow to react to change, and high-level managers may overlook many great ideas for improvement that originate in the lower levels of the organization. To combat these issues, many organizations work to involve employees from all levels and functions of the organization in the decision-making process, using a variety of team formats in day-to-day operations.

Even though the team approach has many advantages, shifting to a team structure often requires a fundamental shift in the organization's culture. Teams must also have clear goals that are tied to the company's strategic goals, and their outcomes need to be measured and compared with benchmarks. Moreover, employees must be motivated to work together in teams. Such motivation requires extensive training and a compensation system that is based, at least in part, on team performance. This last objective is sometimes accomplished by using stock options, profit sharing, performance bonuses, and other employee incentives, as Chapter 10 discusses. For instance, Wainwright Industries, a manufacturer of automotive and aerospace components, sets aside 25 percent of profits every year and splits this amount equally. This means the chairman, plant manager, punch-press operator, custodian, and everyone else in the organization gets the same amount.[26]

What Is a Team?

A **team** is a unit of two or more people who work together to achieve a goal. Teams differ from work groups in that work groups interact primarily to share information and to make decisions to help one another perform within each member's area of responsibility. In other words, the performance of a work group is merely the summation of all group members' individual contributions.[27] By contrast, the members of a team have a shared mission and are collectively responsible for their work. By coordinating their efforts, team members generate a positive synergy and achieve a level of performance that exceeds what would have been accomplished if members had worked individually.[28]

At Microsoft, almost all work is completed in teams. Two factors that have made Microsoft teams so successful are clear goals and strong leadership.[29] Although the team's goals may be set by either the team or upper management, it is the job of the team leader to make sure the team stays on track to achieve those goals. Team leaders are often appointed by senior managers, but sometimes they emerge naturally as the team develops. Westinghouse Hanford, an electric power company, also uses teams. As one employee notes, by using teams, "we come up with better ideas, work more cohesively and find better ways to solve problems." All of these factors help companies become more flexible and respond more quickly to the challenges of the competitive global workplace.[30]

Types of Teams

The type, structure, and composition of individual teams within an organization depend on the organization's strategic goals and the objective for forming the team. The five most common forms of teams are *problem-solving teams, self-managed teams, functional teams, cross-functional teams,* and *virtual teams.* Such classifications are not exclusive. For example, a problem-solving team may also be self-managed and cross-functional. Similarly, some teams are established on an informal basis. That is, they are designed to encourage employee participation but do not become part of the formal organization structure.

Problem-Solving Teams

The most common type of informal team is the **problem-solving team**. Also referred to as *quality circles,* problem-solving teams usually consist of 5 to 12 employees from the same department who meet voluntarily to find ways of improving quality, efficiency, and the work environment. Any recommendations they come up with are then submitted to management for approval.[31] Land Rover, a manufacturer of luxury sport-utility vehicles, was able to save millions of dollars, improve productivity, and sell more vehicles by using problem-solving teams.[32] If such teams are able to successfully contribute to the organization, as Land Rover's were, they may evolve into formal teams, a change that represents a fundamental shift in the way the organization is structured.

Self-Managed Teams

Self-managed teams take problem-solving teams to the next level. As the name implies, **self-managed teams** manage their own activities and require minimum supervision. Typically, they control the pace of work and determination of work assignments. Fully self-managed teams select their own members. As you might imagine, many managers are reluctant to embrace self-managed teams because it requires them to give up significant control.

A modular office layout such as this one at Continental Packaging Products encourages an open communication climate and the sharing of information among employees.

team
A unit of two or more people who share a mission and collective responsibility as they work together to achieve a goal

problem-solving team
Informal team of 5 to 12 employees from the same department who meet voluntarily to find ways of improving quality, efficiency, and the work environment

self-managed teams
Teams in which members are responsible for an entire process or operation

Mervyn's Calls SWAT Team to the Rescue

The situation is tense. The stakes are high. Time is short. So whom do you call for help if you're an executive at Mervyn's California facing the Christmas rush or the loss of a key manager? You call the company's SWAT team, of course.

Mervyn's is a department store chain with 32,000 employees and 264 locations in 14 states. Its SWAT team consists of 19 managers who race from division to division, usually at a moment's notice, to help with the kinds of crises that inevitably erupt in a high-pressure retail environment. SWAT team members must have experience in at least one specific discipline: buying, merchandising, or advertising. Assignments are as short as a week or as long as six months. Even though SWAT team members don't travel around in armored vehicles, life on the team can be pretty hectic.

This group of highly trained people can be deployed anywhere in the company's buying divisions, at any time, wherever they are needed. They can perform jobs quickly and efficiently, without a long learning curve. They help the company manage its unpredictable staffing needs, meet the requirements of its erratic markets, and seize unanticipated opportunities.

Originally created as an experiment to fill in for vacancies created by managers working flextime or on family leave, Mervyn's SWAT team has become something bigger. It has become an effective vehicle for moving talent around the company. SWAT team members aren't just good at learning fast; they're good at sharing what they've learned in other departments. And because team members have had a lot of exposure to various areas in the company, they're the most valued and highly sought-after employees in the organization.

It's no surprise that the team's biggest problem is turnover: Members are frequently hired away for full-time positions by managers whom they've impressed. In fact, joining the SWAT team has become a high-priority career tactic for young people who want to move up or for veterans who want a change of pace.

Questions for Critical Thinking

1. How could Mervyn's parent company, Target, use the SWAT team concept to benefit all its stores—Target, Dayton's, Hudson's, and Marshall Fields? (*Hint:* Think about the benefits of cross-functional teams.)
2. How does Mervyn's benefit from using the SWAT team concept on both a short-term and a long-term basis?

At SEI Investments, administrator for $121 billion in investor assets, the defining unit of operation is the self-managed team. Finding itself indistinguishable from other competitors, SEI took a wrecking ball to the traditional corporate pyramid and formed 140 self-managed teams to speed up reaction time, innovate more quickly, and get closer to the customer. Some SEI teams are permanent, designed to serve big customers or important markets; others are temporary—they come together to solve a problem and disband when their work is done. This flexible team structure is supported by having all office furniture on wheels so that teams can easily create their own work areas. In fact, employees move their desks so often that SEI has created software to map every employee's location.[33]

Functional Teams

functional teams
Teams whose members come from a single functional department and that are based on the organization's vertical structure

Functional teams, or *command teams*, are organized along the lines of the organization's vertical structure and thus may be referred to as *vertical teams*. They are composed of managers and employees within a single functional department. For example, look again at Exhibit 7.1. Functional teams could be formed in Food Lion's marketing, human resources, and finance departments. The structure of a vertical team typically follows the formal chain of command. In some cases, the team may include several levels of the organizational hierarchy within the same functional department.[34]

Cross-Functional Teams

cross-functional teams
Teams that draw together employees from different functional areas

In contrast to functional teams, **cross-functional teams**, or *horizontal teams*, draw together employees from various functional areas and expertise. In many cross-functional teams, employees are cross-trained to perform a variety of tasks. At Pillsbury the most experienced workers can handle 23 different jobs.[35] Cross-functional teams have many benefits: (1) They facilitate the exchange of information between employees, (2) they generate ideas for how to best coordinate the organizational units that are represented, (3) they encourage new solutions for organizational problems, and (4) they aid the development of new organizational policies and procedures.[36]

To develop its 777 airplane, Boeing used hundreds of "design-build" teams that integrated design engineers and production workers to develop the new model.[37] Cross-functional teams have also become a way of life at Harley-Davidson. At the heart of Harley's organization structure are three cross-functional teams called circles—the Create Demand Circle, the Produce Product Circle, and the Provide Support Circle. Each circle includes design engineers, purchasing professionals, manufacturing personnel, marketing personnel, and others. The cross-functional circles are responsible for every motorcycle produced by Harley—from product conception to final design. Within each circle, the leadership role moves from person to person, depending on the issue being addressed.[38]

Executives at Harley-Davidson know that the best way to improve product quality and reliability is to create an environment where everyone takes responsibility for the company's present and future.

In addition to permanent circles such as the ones used at Harley-Davidson, cross-functional teams can take on a number of formats:

- *Task forces.* A **task force** is a type of cross-functional team formed to work on a specific activity with a completion point. Several departments are usually involved so that all parties who have a stake in the outcome of the task are able to provide input. However, once the goal has been accomplished, the task force is disbanded.[39] Saint Francis Hospital in Tulsa, Oklahoma, established a task force to find ways to reduce the cost of supplies. The team members came from many departments, including surgery, laboratory, nursing, financial planning, administration, and food service. The team not only helped the hospital save money by curbing supply waste but also generated excitement among hospital employees about working together for common goals.[40]

task force
Team of people from several departments who are temporarily brought together to address a specific issue

- *Special-purpose teams.* Like task forces, **special-purpose teams** are created as temporary entities to achieve specific goals. However, special-purpose teams are different because they exist outside the formal organization hierarchy. Such teams remain a part of the organization but have their own reporting structures, and members view themselves as separate from the normal functions of the organization. A special-purpose team might be used to develop a new product when complete creative freedom is needed. By operating outside the formal organization, the team would be able to test new ideas and new ways of accomplishing tasks.[41]

special-purpose teams
Temporary teams that exist outside the formal organization hierarchy and are created to achieve a specific goal

- *Committees.* In contrast to a task force, a **committee** usually has a long life span and may become a permanent part of the organization structure. Committees typically deal with regularly recurring tasks. For example, a grievance committee may be formed as a permanent resource for handling employee complaints and concerns. Because many committees require official representation in order to achieve their goals, committee members are sometimes selected on the basis of their titles or positions rather than their personal expertise.

committee
Team that may become a permanent part of the organization and is designed to deal with regularly recurring tasks

Virtual Teams

Virtual teams are groups of physically dispersed members who work together to achieve a common goal. Virtual team members communicate using a variety of technological formats and devices such as company intranets, e-mail, electronic meeting software, and teleconferencing or videoconferencing. Occasionally, they may meet

virtual teams
Teams that use communication technology to bring geographically distant employees together to achieve goals

Don't Leave Home: American Express's Virtual Environment

"Don't leave home without it!" sends a powerful message about the dangers of traveling without an American Express card tucked into your pocket. Millions of customers heed that advice each day, making American Express Company the world's largest travel agency and a leading provider of financial services. But providing a seamless network of services for customers around the globe requires effective teamwork from all employees, whether they're working from the New York headquarters or telecommuting from home in Los Angeles. David House makes sure that his employees have everything they need to work together and contribute to the company's success—even if they don't leave home to go to work.

As president of American Express Global Establishment Services, the division that recruits new American Express merchants, House encourages his staff members to work together to achieve their goals. But uniting employees in sales offices across the country demands more than a few rousing pep talks. To build a successful team, House uses technology to promote communication within his division. He provides every employee with access to the company's highly efficient computer network. He offers employees the opportunity to work from home, eliminating the time, expense, and stress of daily commutes to the office. He even provides employees with computer training, software and

hardware setup, and selection and delivery of office furniture to complete their virtual office environment.

Nevertheless, House knows that effective teams need more than equipment to produce quality work. They need to communicate. House's telecommuters conduct virtual meetings with colleagues around the world, taking advantage of e-mail and videoconferencing to brainstorm and collaborate on projects. Several units in House's division use a buddy system that requires remote workers to chat with on-site colleagues by phone every morning, covering topics from new customers to office politics. Other telecommuters report to a local or regional office several times each week, meeting with co-workers for specific purposes.

House's knack for developing and using virtual teams at American Express has indeed paid off. Not only do virtual teams save the company time and travel costs, but they have increased employee productivity and improved customer satisfaction rates. Moreover, by using virtual teams, House has reduced the number of field offices from 85 to 7, resulting in additional cost savings for the company.

Questions for Critical Thinking

1. How does American Express support virtual teams?
2. How do American Express telecommuters stay in touch with the company and with each other?

face-to-face, particularly when they start working together, to help establish and maintain rapport.

The biggest advantage of virtual teams is that members are able to work together even if they are thousands of miles and several time zones apart. At Texas Instruments, for instance, microchip engineers in India, Texas, and Japan are able to pool ideas, design new chips, and collaboratively debug them—even though they're separated by 8,000 miles and 12 time zones.[42]

Although virtual teams can overcome the barriers of time and distance, they do present special communication challenges. For instance, people communicating in person rely heavily on *nonverbal cues*, such as facial expressions and body language, to ascertain the true meaning of what is being said. Since virtual teams rely so heavily on electronic communication, these cues are sometimes lost, resulting in misunderstandings or bruised emotions. Close proximity also helps in-person teams resolve technical questions and other issues. In addition, much of the cooperative nature of in-person teams is often formed in nonwork settings, such as when teams meet for lunch or participate in volunteer activities together. To overcome these obstacles, virtual teams need people who possess strong project- and time-management skills, the ability to use electronic communication and collaboration technologies, the ability to work across cultures, and heightened interpersonal awareness.[43]

In many cases, virtual teams are as effective as teams that function under a single roof—and in some cases, they are even more effective. At British Petroleum, for example, virtual teams link workers in the Gulf of Mexico with teams working in the eastern Atlantic and around the globe. By using a virtual team network, the company has decreased the number of helicopter trips to offshore oil platforms, has avoided refinery shutdowns because technical experts at other locations were able to handle problems remotely, and has experienced a significant reduction in construction rework, among other benefits.[44] The manufacturing company American Standard has used webconferencing and videoconferencing to cut product development time by as much as two-thirds.[45]

Advantages and Disadvantages of Working in Teams

Even though teams can play a vital role in helping an organization reach its goals, they are not appropriate for every situation. Managers must weigh both the advantages and the disadvantages of teams when deciding whether to use them.[46]

One of the biggest advantages of teams is that the interaction of the participants leads to higher-quality decisions based on the combined expertise of the group. Moreover, teams lead to increased acceptance of a solution. Team members who participate in making a decision are more likely to enthusiastically support the decision and encourage others to accept it.[47] Another big advantage is that teams have the potential to unleash vast amounts of creativity and energy in workers. Motivation and performance are often increased as workers share a sense of purpose and mutual accountability. Teams can also fill the individual worker's need to belong to a group. Furthermore, they can reduce boredom, increase feelings of dignity and self-worth, and reduce stress and tension between workers. Teams also empower employees to bring more knowledge and skill to the tasks they perform and thereby often lead to greater efficiency and cost reduction. Organizational flexibility is another key benefit of using teams in the workplace. Such flexibility means employees are able to exchange jobs, workers can be reallocated as needed, managers can delegate more authority and responsibility to lower-level employees, and the company can meet changing customer needs more effectively.

In short, using teams can add up to more satisfied employees performing higher-quality work that helps the organization achieve its goals. Studies of individual industries show that companies using teamwork to organize, plan, and control activities enjoy greater productivity, increased profits, fewer defects, lower employee turnover, less waste, and even increased market value.[48] Consider the results these companies achieved by using employee teams: Kodak halved the amount of time it takes to move a new product from the drawing board to store shelves; Tennessee Eastman, a division of Eastman Chemical, increased labor productivity by 70 percent; Texas Instruments increased revenues per employee by over 50 percent; and Ritz-Carlton Hotels jumped to the top of the J. D. Power and Associates consumer survey of luxury hotels.[49]

Although teamwork has many advantages, it also has a number of potential disadvantages. For one thing, power within the organization sometimes becomes realigned with teams. Successful teams mean that fewer supervisors are needed and usually fewer middle and frontline managers. Adjusting to their changing job roles, or even to the loss of their jobs, is understandably difficult for many people. Another potential disadvantage is **free riders**—team members who don't contribute their fair share to the group's activities because they aren't being held individually accountable for their work. The free-ride attitude can lead to the nonfulfillment of certain tasks. Still another drawback to teamwork is the high cost of coordinating group activities. Aligning schedules, arranging meetings, and coordinating individual parts of a project can eat up a lot of time and money. Moreover, a team may develop *groupthink*, a situation in which pressures to conform to the norms of the group cause members to withhold contrary or unpopular opinions. Groupthink can hinder effective decision making because some possibilities will be overlooked.[50]

free riders
Team members who do not contribute sufficiently to the group's activities because members are not being held individually accountable for their work

Characteristics of Effective Teams

Team size is one factor that contributes to a team's overall effectiveness. The optimal size for teams is generally thought to be between 5 and 12 members. Teams smaller than 5 may be lacking in skill diversity and may, therefore, be less effective at solving problems.

Teams of more than 12 may be too large for group members to bond properly or communicate efficiently and may discourage some members from sharing their ideas. Larger groups are also prone to disagreements and factionalism because so many opinions must be considered, thus making the team leader's job more difficult. Moreover, studies have shown that turnover and absenteeism are higher in larger teams because members tend to feel that their presence makes less of a difference.

For a team to be successful over time, it must also be structured to accomplish its task and to satisfy its members' needs for social well-being. Effective teams usually fulfill both requirements with a combination of members who assume one of four roles: task specialist, socioemotional role, dual role, or nonparticipator. People who assume the *task-specialist role* focus on helping the team reach its goals. In contrast, members who take on the *socioemotional role* focus on supporting the team's emotional needs and strengthening the team's social unity. Some team members are able to assume *dual roles*, contributing to the task and still meeting members' emotional needs. These members often make effective team leaders. At the other end of the spectrum are members who are *nonparticipators*, contributing little to reaching the team's goals or to meeting members' emotional needs. Exhibit 7.6 outlines the behavior patterns associated with each of these roles.

Other characteristics of effective teams include the following:[51]

- *Clear sense of purpose.* Team members clearly understand the task at hand, what is expected of them, and their role on the team.
- *Open and honest communication.* The team culture encourages discussion and debate. Team members speak openly and honestly, without the threat of anger, resentment, or retribution. They listen to and value feedback from others. As a result, all team members participate.
- *Creative thinking.* Effective teams encourage original thinking, considering options beyond the usual.
- *Focus.* Team members get to the core issues of the problem and stay focused on key issues.
- *Decision by consensus.* All decisions are arrived at by consensus. No easy, quick votes are taken.

Of course, learning effective team skills takes time and practice, so many companies now offer employees training in building their team skills. At Saturn, for example, every

Exhibit 7.6   **Team Member Roles**

Team members assume one of these four roles. Members who assume a dual role often make effective team leaders.

Task specialist role	**Dual role**	
• Focuses on task accomplishment over human needs	• Focuses on task and people	
• Important role, but if adopted by everyone, team's social needs won't be met	• May be a team leader	
	• Important role, but not essential if members adopt task specialist and socioemotional roles	
Nonparticipator role	**Socioemotional role**	
• Contributes little to either task or people needs of team	• Focuses on people needs of team over task	
• Not an important role—if adopted by too many members, team will disband	• Important role, but if adopted by everyone, team's tasks won't be accomplished	

High / Low — Member task behavior

Low / High — Member social behavior

team member goes through a minimum of 92 hours of training in problem solving and people skills. Saturn teaches team members how to reach a consensus point they call "70 percent comfortable but 100 percent supportive." At that level of consensus, everybody supports the solution.[52] For a brief review of characteristics of effective teams, see Exhibit 7.7.

BUILD A SENSE OF FAIRNESS IN DECISION MAKING

✓ Encourage debate and disagreement without fear of reprisal

✓ Allow members to communicate openly and honestly

✓ Consider all proposals

✓ Build consensus by allowing team members to examine, compare, and reconcile differences

✓ Avoid quick votes

✓ Keep everyone informed

✓ Present all the facts

SELECT TEAM MEMBERS WISELY

✓ Involve stakeholders

✓ Limit team size to the minimum number of people needed to accomplish the task at hand

✓ Select members with a diversity of views

✓ Select creative thinkers

MAKE WORKING IN TEAMS A TOP MANAGEMENT PRIORITY

✓ Recognize and reward individual and group performance

✓ Provide ample training opportunities for employees to develop interpersonal, decision-making, and problem-solving skills

✓ Allow enough time for the team to develop and learn how to work together

MANAGE CONFLICT CONSTRUCTIVELY

✓ Share leadership

✓ Encourage equal participation

✓ Discuss disagreements

✓ Focus on the issues, not the people

✓ Keep things under control

STAY ON TRACK

✓ Make sure everyone understands the team's purpose

✓ Communicate what is expected of team members

✓ Stay focused on the core assignment

✓ Develop and adhere to a schedule

✓ Develop rules and obey norms

Exhibit 7.7

Characteristics of Effective Teams

Effective teams practice these good habits.

Five Stages of Team Development

Developing an effective team is an ongoing process. Like the members who form them, teams grow and change as time goes by. You may think that each team evolves in its own way. However, research shows that teams typically go through five definitive stages of development, nicknamed forming, storming, norming, performing, and adjourning.[53]

- *Forming.* The forming stage is a period of orientation and breaking the ice. Members get to know each other, determine what types of behaviors are appropriate within the group, identify what is expected of them, and become acquainted with each other's task orientation.

- *Storming.* In the storming stage, members show more of their personalities and become more assertive in establishing their roles. Conflict and disagreement often arise during the storming stage as members jockey for position or form coalitions to promote their own perceptions of the group's mission.

- *Norming.* During the norming stage, these conflicts are resolved, and team harmony develops. Members come to understand and accept one another, reach a consensus on who the leader is, and reach agreement on what each member's roles are.

- *Performing.* In the performing stage, members are really committed to the team's goals. Problems are solved, and disagreements are handled with maturity in the interest of task accomplishment.

- *Adjourning.* Finally, if the team has a limited task to perform, it goes through the adjourning stage after the task has been completed. In this stage, issues are wrapped up and the team is dissolved.

cohesiveness
A measure of how committed the team members are to their team's goals

As the team moves through the various stages of development, two things happen. First, the team develops a certain level of **cohesiveness**, a measure of how committed the members are to the team's goals. The team's cohesiveness is reflected in meeting attendance, team interaction, work quality, and goal achievement. Cohesiveness is influenced by many factors, although the two primary factors are competition and evaluation. If a team is in competition with other teams, cohesiveness increases as the team strives to win. In addition, if a team's efforts and accomplishments are recognized by the organization, members tend to be more committed to the team's goals. Strong team cohesiveness generally results in high morale. Moreover, when cohesiveness is coupled with strong management support for team objectives, teams tend to be more productive.

norms
Informal standards of conduct that guide team behavior

The second thing that happens as teams develop is the emergence of **norms**—informal standards of conduct that members share and that guide their behavior. Norms define what is acceptable behavior. They also set limits, identify values, clarify what is expected of members, and facilitate team survival. Norms can be established in various ways: from early behaviors that set precedents for future actions, from significant events in the team's history, from behaviors that come to the team through outside influences, and from a leader's or member's explicit statements that have an impact on other members.[54]

Team Conflict

By now you can see that being an effective team member requires many skills. However, none is more important than the ability to handle *conflict*—the antagonistic interactions resulting from differences in ideas, opinions, goals, or ways of doing things. Conflict can be both constructive and destructive to a team's effectiveness. Conflict is constructive if it increases the involvement of team members and results in the solution to a problem. Conflict is destructive if it diverts energy from more important issues, destroys the morale of teams or individual team members, or polarizes or divides the team.[55]

Causes of Team Conflict

Team conflicts can arise for a number of reasons. First, teams and individuals may feel they are in competition for scarce or declining resources, such as money, information, and supplies. Second, team members may disagree about who is responsible for a specific task; this type of disagreement is usually the result of poorly defined responsibilities and job boundaries. Third, poor communication can lead to misunderstandings and misperceptions about other team members or other teams. In addition, intentionally withholding information can undermine trust among members. Fourth, basic differences in values, attitudes, and personalities may lead to clashes. Fifth, power struggles may result when one party questions the authority of another or when people or teams with limited authority attempt to increase their power or exert more influence. Sixth, conflicts can arise because individuals or teams are pursuing different goals.[56]

For example, a British cardboard-manufacturing company switched from a hierarchical, functionally oriented organization to a team-based structure with the hope of empowering employees and reducing scrap. However, once they got started, the teams realized that the company had many problems to solve. Conflicts resulted when team members couldn't agree on which problems to tackle first.[57]

Solutions to Team Conflict

Each team member has a unique style of dealing with conflict, but the members' styles are primarily based on how competitive or cooperative team members are when a conflict arises. Depending on the particular situation, the same individual may use one of several styles, which include avoidance, defusion, and confrontation.[58] *Avoidance* may involve ignoring the conflict in the hope that it will subside on its own, or it may even involve physically separating the conflicting parties. *Defusion* may involve several actions, including downplaying differences and focusing on similarities between team members or teams, compromising on the disputed issue, taking a vote, appealing to a neutral party or higher authority, or redesigning the team. *Confrontation* is an attempt to work through the conflict by getting it out in the open, which may be accomplished by organizing a meeting between the conflicting parties.

People in team settings can ususally resolve conflict and get what they want if they are willing to work together. In many cases, the resolution process is an exchange of opinions and information that gradually leads to a mutually acceptable solution.

These three styles of conflict resolution come into play after a conflict has developed, but team members and team leaders can take several steps to prevent conflicts. First, by establishing clear goals that require the efforts of every member, the team reduces the chance that members will battle over their objectives or roles. Second, by developing well-defined tasks for each member, the team leader ensures that all parties are aware of their responsibilities and the limits of their authority. And finally, by facilitating open communication, the team leader can ensure that all members understand their own tasks and objectives as well as those of their teammates. Keep in mind that communication builds respect and tolerance, and it provides a forum for bringing misunderstandings into the open before they turn into full-blown conflicts.

Productive Team Meetings

Meetings are the primary communication venue for business teams, whether they take place in formal conference rooms or on the Internet in *virtual meetings*. Well-run meetings can help you solve problems, develop ideas, and identify opportunities. Much of your workplace communication will take place in small-group meetings; therefore, your ability to contribute to the company and to be recognized for those contributions will depend on your meeting participation skills.

Unfortunately, many meetings are unproductive. In a recent study, senior and middle managers reported that only 56 percent of their meetings were actually productive and that 25 percent of them could have been replaced by a phone call or a memo.[59] The three most frequently reported problems with meetings are getting off the subject, not having an agenda, and running too long.[60] Given such demoralizing statistics and the high cost of meetings—which can run hundreds or thousands of dollars an hour in lost work time and travel expenses—it's no wonder that companies are focusing on making their team meetings more productive. Companies can make better use of valuable meeting time by following these steps:

- **Clarify the purpose of the meeting.** Although many meetings combine purposes, most focus on one of two types: *Informational meetings* involve sharing information and perhaps coordinating action. *Decision-making meetings* involve persuasion, analysis, and problem solving. They often include a brainstorming session, followed by a debate on the alternatives. Moreover, decision-making meetings require that each participant be aware of the nature of the problem and the criteria for its solution. Whatever your purpose, make sure it is clear and clearly communicated to all participants.

- **Select participants carefully.** With a clear purpose in mind, it's easier to identify the right participants. If the session is purely informational and one person will do most of the talking, you can invite a large group. For problem-solving and decision-making meetings, invite only those people who are in a direct position to help the meeting reach its objective. The more participants, the more comments and confusion you're likely to get, and the longer the meeting will take. However, make sure you invite all the key decision makers, or your meeting will fail to satisfy its purpose.

- **Establish a clear agenda.** The success of any meeting depends on the preparation of the participants. Distribute a carefully written agenda to participants, giving them enough time to prepare as needed. A productive agenda answers three key questions: (1) What do we need to do in this meeting to accomplish our goals? (2) What issues will be of greatest importance to all participants? (3) What information must be available in order to discuss these issues?[61] In addition to improving productivity, this level of agenda detail shows respect for participants and the other demands on their time.

- **Keep the meeting on track.** A good meeting draws out the best ideas and information the group has to offer. Good leaders occasionally guide, mediate, probe, stimulate, and summarize, but mostly they encourage participants to share. Experience will help you recognize when to be dominant and press the group forward and when to step back and let people talk. If the meeting lags, you'll need to ask questions to encourage participation. Conversely, there will be times when you have no choice but to cut off discussion in order to stay on schedule.

- **Follow agreed-upon rules.** Business meetings run the gamut from informal to extremely formal, complete with detailed rules for speaking, proposing new items to discuss, voting on proposals, and so on. The larger the meeting, the more formal you'll need to be to maintain order. Whatever system of rules you employ, make sure everyone is clear about the expectations.

- **Encourage participation.** As the meeting gets under way, you'll discover that some participants are too quiet and others are too talkative. The quiet participants might be shy, they might be expressing disagreement or resistance, or they might be answering e-mail or instant messages on their laptop computers. Draw them out by asking for their input on issues that particularly pertain to them. For the overly talkative, simply say that time is limited and others need to be heard from.

- **Close effectively.** At the conclusion of the meeting, verify that the objectives have been met; if not, arrange for follow-up work

Effective teams know how to keep meetings on track while ensuring full participation from everyone involved.

as needed. Either summarize the general conclusion of the discussion or list the actions to be taken. Make sure all participants agree on the outcome and give people a chance to clear up any misunderstandings.

Summary of Learning Objectives

1 Discuss the function of a company's organization structure.

An organization structure provides a framework through which a company can coordinate and control the work, divide responsibilities, distribute authority, and hold employees accountable. An organization chart provides a visual representation of this framework.

2 Explain the concepts of accountability, authority, and delegation.

Accountability is the obligation to report work results to supervisors or team members and to justify any outcomes that fall below expectations. Authority is the power to make decisions, issue orders, carry out actions, and allocate resources to achieve the organization's goals. Delegation is the assignment of work and the transfer of authority and responsibility to complete that work.

3 Define five major types of organization structure.

Companies can organize in four primary ways: by function, which groups employees according to their skills, resource use, and expertise; by division, which establishes self-contained departments formed according to similarities in product, process, customer, or geography; by matrix, which assigns employees from functional departments to interdisciplinary project teams and requires them to report to both a department head and a team leader; and by network, which connects separate companies that perform selected tasks for a headquarters organization. In addition, many companies now combine elements of two or more of these designs into hybrid structures.

4 Describe the five most common forms of teams.

The five most common forms of teams are (1) problem-solving teams, which seek ways to improve a situation and then submit their recommendation to management; (2) self-managed teams, which manage their own activities and seldom require supervision; (3) functional teams, which are composed of employees within a single functional department; (4) cross-functional teams, which draw together employees from various departments and expertise in a number of formats such as task forces, special-purpose teams, and committees; and (5) virtual teams, which bring together employees from distant locations.

5 Highlight the advantages and disadvantages of working in teams.

Teamwork has the potential to increase creativity, motivation, performance, and satisfaction of workers and thereby can lead to greater company efficiency, flexibility, and cost savings. The potential disadvantages of working in teams include the difficulties of managing employees' changing roles, the possibilities of free riders and groupthink, and the costs and time needed to coordinate members' schedules and project parts.

6 List the characteristics of effective teams.

Effective teams have a clear sense of purpose, communicate openly and honestly, build a sense of fairness in decision making, think creatively, stay focused on key issues, manage conflict constructively, and select team members wisely by involving stakeholders, creative thinkers, and members with a diversity of views. Moreover, effective teams have an optimal size of between 5 and 12 members.

7 Review the five stages of team development.

Teams typically go through five stages of development. In the forming stage, team members become acquainted with each other and with the group's purpose. In the storming stage, conflict often arises as coalitions and power struggles develop. In the norming stage, conflicts are resolved and harmony develops. In the performing stage, members focus on achieving the team's goals. In the adjourning stage, the team dissolves upon completion of its task.

8 Highlight six causes of team conflict and three styles of conflict resolution.

Conflict can arise from competition for scarce resources; confusion over task responsibility; poor communication and misinformation; differences in values, attitudes, and personalities; power struggles; and goal incongruity. Conflict can be resolved by avoiding it and hoping that it will go away; by defusing it—downplaying team member differences or focusing on member similarities; or by confronting it and working hard to resolve the issues at hand.

Behind **the Scenes**

Teaming Up for Success at The Container Store

The Container Store was not started with a modest goal. Founders Garrett Boone and Kip Tindell set out to become the "best retail store in the United States." Judging by feedback from customers and employees, they just might have succeeded.

As millions of frustrated consumers know all too well, though, delivering great customer service in retail environments isn't easy. The Container Store does it with strong company values, respect for employees, and a structure that promotes teamwork over individual competition. The company's values flow from the idea that people are its greatest asset because they are the key to exceptional service. The notion that "people are our greatest asset" is repeated often in the business world, and often without substance to back it up, but The Container Store goes to extraordinary lengths to practice what it preaches.

When selecting new employees, for instance, the company engages in a comprehensive interviewing and selection process to find the perfect person for each position, driven by the belief that one great person equals three good ones. Most employees are college educated, almost half come from employee referrals, and most have been customers of the store. They are also self-motivated, team-oriented, and passionate about customer service.

Those traits are enhanced by extensive employee development: New full-time employees receive 235 hours of training in their first year and 160 hours per year after that. In comparison, most retailers give new workers less than 10 hours of training per year. As a result, Container Store employees feel extremely confident in their ability to help customers, and positive feedback from customers continues to build that confidence.

The Container Store also pays three to four times minimum wage, offering wages as much as 50 to 100 percent above those of other retailers. The financial security builds loyalty and helps keep annual turnover around 20 percent, a fraction of the typical turnover rates in the industry. What's more, salespeople are not paid commissions, unlike retail staffs in many other companies. Without the constant pressure to "make the numbers," it's easier for employees to take their time with customers, using their creative instincts and extensive training to design complete solutions to customers' storage problems. By not paying commissions, The Container Store also helps employees sense that they're all part of a team, rather than being in competition with one another.

That emphasis on teamwork is reinforced twice a day, before opening and after closing, through a meeting called "the huddle." Similar to a huddle in football, it helps to give everyone a common purpose: set goals, share information, boost morale, and bond as a team. Morning sessions feature spirited discussions of sales goals and product applications and may include a chorus of "Happy Birthday" for celebrating team members. Evening huddles include more team building and friendly competitions such as guessing the daily sales figures. Tindell believes that full, open communication with employees takes courage but says, "The only way that people feel really, really a part of something is if they know everything." Team-building efforts are further encouraged by participation in community outreach activities, such as school supply drives for local schools, and through purely recreational activities dreamed up by the employees on the Fun Committee.

The Container Store also differs dramatically from many retail establishments in the way it embraces part-time employees. These workers are essential at the busiest times, such as evenings and holiday seasons, but they are treated as second-class citizens in some companies. Not at The Container Store. To begin with, the company refers to them as "prime-time" employees, not part-time, since these staffers are most valuable in those prime-time rush periods. And these people also receive extensive training and are treated as equal members of the team at each store. As one prime-timer in Houston puts it, "Everyone is treated as an important human being. I don't feel like a part-time employee at all—I feel like a professional. They make belonging easy and a source of pride."

By aligning its corporate values with its management practices and its organization structure, The Container Store paves the way for its employees to deliver great customer service. And by frequently astonishing its employees with enlightened leadership, the company sets a strong example for the people in blue aprons who are expected to astonish customers every day.

People outside the company are starting to notice, too. The Container Store has become a consistent winner in such nationwide forums as the annual Performance Through People Award, presented by Northwestern University, and *Fortune* magazine's annual list of The 100 Best Companies to Work For.[62]

Critical Thinking Questions

1. Based on what you've learned about the way The Container Store employees interact with customers, do you think that the company emphasizes centralized or decentralized decision making? Explain your answer.

2. How might the company's emphasis on teamwork affect accountability and authority?
3. What effect might a change to commission-based compensation have on the team structure at The Container Store?

LEARN MORE ONLINE

Effective teamwork and communication have helped The Container Store earn consistent acclaim as one of the best companies to work for in the United States. Go to Chapter 7 of this text's website at www.prenhall.com/bovee and click on the "Best Places to Work" hotlink. Read through the profiles of recent winners. How have the winners improved quality or customer satisfaction through better teamwork? What role does communication play in their success? How does the structure of the organization help the company succeed? ■

Key Terms

accountability (168)	formal organization (167)	organization structure (166)
authority (168)	free riders (179)	problem-solving team (175)
centralization (170)	functional structure (171)	process divisions (172)
chain of command (168)	functional teams (176)	product divisions (172)
cohesiveness (182)	geographic divisions (172)	responsibility (168)
committee (177)	hybrid structure (174)	self-managed teams (175)
cross-functional teams (176)	informal organization (167)	span of management (169)
customer divisions (172)	line organization (169)	special-purpose teams (177)
decentralization (170)	line-and-staff organization (169)	tall organizations (169)
delegation (169)	matrix structure (173)	task force (177)
departmentalization (171)	network structure (173)	team (175)
divisional structure (172)	norms (182)	virtual teams (177)
flat organizations (169)	organization chart (166)	work specialization (167)

Test Your Knowledge

Questions for Review

1. Why is organization structure important?
2. What are the characteristics of tall organizations and flat organizations?
3. What are the advantages and disadvantages of work specialization?
4. What are the advantages and disadvantages of functional departmentalization?
5. What are the advantages and disadvantages of working in teams?

Questions for Analysis

6. Why would you expect a manager of a group of nuclear physicists to have a wide span of management?
7. How can a virtual organization reduce costs?
8. What can managers do to help teams work more effectively?
9. How can companies benefit from using virtual teams?
10. **Ethical Considerations.** You were honored that you were selected to serve on the salary committee of the employee negotiations task force. As a member of that committee, you reviewed confidential company documents listing the salaries of all department managers. You discovered that managers at your level are earning $5,000 more than you, even though you've been at the company the same amount of time. You feel that a raise is justified on the basis of this confidential information. How will you handle this situation?

Questions for Application

11. You are the leader of a cross-functional work team whose goal is to find ways of lowering production costs. Your team of eight employees has become mired in the storming stage. They disagree on how to approach the task, and they are starting to splinter into factions. What can you do to help the team move forward?
12. Your warehouse operation is currently functioning at capacity. To accommodate anticipated new business, your company must either build a major addition to your current warehouse operation or build a new warehouse that

would be located at a distant site. As director of warehouse operations, you would like several people to participate in this decision. Should you form a task force, a committee, or a special-purpose team? Explain your choice.

13. **Integrated.** One of your competitors has approached you with an intriguing proposition. The company would like to merge with your company. The economies of scale are terrific. So are the growth possibilities. There's just one issue to be resolved. Your competitor is organized under a flat structure and uses lots of cross-functional teams. Your company is organized under a traditional tall structure that is departmentalized by function. Using your knowledge about culture clash, what are the likely issues you will encounter if these two organizations are merged?

14. **Integrated.** Chapter 6 discussed several styles of leadership, including autocratic, democratic, and laissez-faire. Using your knowledge about the differences in these leadership styles, which style would you expect to find under the following organization structures: (a) tall organization—departmentalization by function; (b) tall organization—departmentalization by matrix; (c) flat organization; (d) self-directed teams?

Practice Your Knowledge

Sharpening Your Communication Skills

Write a brief memo to your instructor describing a recent conflict you had with a peer at work or at school. Be sure to highlight the cause of the conflict and steps you took to resolve it. Which of the three conflict-resolution styles discussed in this chapter did you use? Did you find a solution that both of you could accept?

Building Your Team Skills

What's the most effective organization structure for your college or university? With your team, obtain a copy of your school's organization chart. If this chart is not readily available, gather information by talking with people in administration, then draw your own chart of the organization structure.

Analyze the chart in terms of span of management. Is your school a flat or a tall organization? Is this organization structure appropriate for your school? Does decision making tend to be centralized or decentralized in your school? Do you agree with this approach to decision making?

Finally, investigate the use of formal and informal teams in your school. Are there any problem-solving teams, task forces, or committees at work in your school? Are any teams self-directed or virtual? How much authority do these teams have to make decisions? What is the purpose of teamwork in your school? What kinds of goals do these teams have?

Share your team's findings during a brief classroom presentation, then compare the findings of all teams. Is there agreement on the appropriate organization structure for your school?

Expand Your Knowledge

Discovering Career Opportunities

Whether you're a top manager, first-line manager (supervisor), or middle manager, your efforts will impact the success of your organization. To get a closer look at what the responsibilities of a manager are, log on to the Prentice Hall Student Success SuperSite at www.prenhall.com/success. Click on Majors Exploration, and select "management" in the drop-down box. Then scroll down and read about careers in management.

1. What can you do with a degree in management?

2. What is the future outlook for careers in management?

3. Follow the link to the American Management Association website, and click on Research. Then scroll down and click on Administrative Professionals Current Concerns Survey. According to the survey, what has affected administrative professionals most recently? On which five tasks do managers spend most of their time?

Developing Your Research Skills

Although teamwork can benefit many organizations, introducing and managing team structures can be a real challenge. Search past issues of business journals or newspapers (print or online editions) to locate articles about how an organization has overcome problems with teams.

1. Why did the organization originally introduce teams? What types of teams are being used?

2. What problems did each organization encounter in trying to implement teams? How did the organization deal with these problems?

3. Have the teams been successful from management's perspective? From the employees' perspective? What effect has teamwork had on the company, its customers, and its products?

SEE IT ON THE WEB

For live links to the websites that follow, go to this text's website at www.prenhall.com/bovee. When you log on, select Chapter 7, then select "Featured Websites," click on the URL of the website you wish to visit, review the website, and answer the following questions:

1. What is the purpose of this website?

2. What kinds of information does this website contain? Please be specific.

3. How is the information provided at this website useful for businesspeople? Consumers?

4. How did you expand your knowledge of organizing and working in teams by reviewing the material at this website? What new things did you learn about these topics?

Build Teams in the Cyber Age

Let Teamworks, the Virtual Team Assistant, help you build a more effective team, resolve team conflict, manage projects, solve team problems, be a team leader, encourage team feedback, and teach with teams. Each of the site's nine information modules contains background information, self-assessment vehicles, skill development exercises, and links to helpful resources. Log on now and increase your effectiveness as a team member by learning more about why teams work, the stages of team development, tips for communicating with team members during a project, and some creative problem-solving techniques. www.vta.spcomm.uiuc.edu

Be Direct

If you want to learn more about building effective teams, you can read many excellent books on the subject. But you might be surprised by just how much information on team building you can find on the Internet. One good starting point is the Self-Directed and Self-Managed Work Teams page. This site's designers are passionate about teamwork, and they want to make it easier for people to work effectively in teams. Read the Frequently Asked Question (FAQs) about self-managed teams. Then explore some of the links to discover more about teams and teamwork. www.mapnp.org/library/grp_skll/slf_drct/slf_drct.htm

Resolve Conflict Like a Pro

The field of conflict resolution has been growing very quickly and includes practices such as negotiation, mediation, arbitration, international peace building, and more. Learn more about each of these topics along with basic information about conflict resolution by visiting CRInfo. Be sure to check out the web resources, where you'll find links to communication and facilitation skills, consensus building, and more. Find out why BATNA is important. Discover what a mediator does. Learn how to conduct effective meetings. And don't leave without testing your knowledge of common negotiation terms. www.crinfo.org

Companion Website

Learning Interactively

Go to the Companion Website at www.prenhall.com/bovee. For Chapter 7, take advantage of the interactive "Study Guide" to test your knowledge of the chapter. Get instant feedback on whether you need additional studying.

Also, visit this site's "Study Hall," where you'll find an abundance of valuable resources that will help you succeed in this course.

Video **Case**

Juicing Up the Organization: Nantucket Nectars

LEARNING OBJECTIVES

The purpose of this video is to help you:

1. Recognize how growth affects an organization's structure.
2. Discuss why businesses organize by departmentalization.
3. Understand how flat organizations operate.

SYNOPSIS

Tom Scott and Tom First founded Nantucket Nectars in 1989 with an idea for a peach drink. In the early days, the two ran the entire operation from their boat. These days, Nantucket Nectars has more than 130 employees split between headquarters in Cambridge, Massachusetts, and several field offices. As a result, management has developed a more formalized organization structure to keep the business running smoothly. The company relies on cross-functional teams to handle special projects such as the implementation of new accounting software. These strategies have helped Nantucket Nectars successfully manage its rapid growth.

Discussion Questions

1. *For analysis:* What type of organization is in place at Nantucket Nectars?
2. *For analysis:* How would you describe the top-level span of management at Nantucket Nectars?

3. *For application:* Nantucket Nectars may need to change its organization structure as it expands into new products and new markets. Under what circumstances would some form of divisional departmentalization be appropriate for the firm?
4. *For application:* Assume that Nantucket Nectars is purchasing a well-established beverage company with a tall structure stressing top-down control. What are some of the problems that management might face in integrating the acquired firm into the existing organization structure of Nantucket Nectars?
5. *For debate:* Assume that someone who is newly promoted into a management position at Nantucket Nectars cannot adjust to delegating work to lower-level employees. Should this new manager be demoted? Support your chosen position.

ONLINE EXPLORATION

Visit the Nantucket Nectars site at www.juiceguys.com and follow the links to read about the company and its products. Then use your favorite search engine to find recent news about the company (which is formally known as Nantucket Allserve). Has it been acquired by a larger company or has it acquired one or more smaller firms? What are the implications for the chain of command, decision making, and organization structure of Nantucket Nectars?

Chapter 8

Producing Quality Goods and Services

LEARNING OBJECTIVES

After studying this chapter, you will be able to

1 Explain what production and operations managers do

2 Identify key tasks involved in designing a production process

3 Discuss the role of computers and automation technology in production

4 Explain the strategic importance of managing inventory

5 Distinguish among JIT, MRP, and MRP II inventory management systems

6 Highlight the differences between quality control and quality assurance

7 Describe the supply chain and explain how companies today are managing their supply chains

Behind the Scenes

Harley-Davidson Goes Full Throttle

www.harley-davidson.com

From the earliest days of motorized transportation, cycle enthusiasts looked to Harley-Davidson for the thrill of its high-performance, heavyweight motorcycles—until the company hit a deep pothole in the 1970s. Cutting costs to battle stiff competition from imports, Harley let production quality slip and fell behind on product design and development. Its big-iron cruisers and long-distance touring bikes were heavy, chrome laden, and expensive. They leaked oil and vibrated excessively. Some customers even joked that they should buy two Harleys—one to ride and one for parts. Tired of tolerating frequent breakdowns, motorcycle buyers turned to the smooth-riding imports. Harley's market share tumbled.

Over the next two decades, Harley rebuilt its production processes from the ground up, putting more emphasis on quality than on quantity. By the early 1990s, the company had quality firmly under control. With its reputation mended, demand rebounded so strongly that dealers reported long waiting lists of riders eager to climb back on a Harley—which by now had become an inspiring turnaround story in addition to being an American icon. Management responded to the surge of orders by carefully ratcheting up annual motor-

Chief Executive Jeffrey Bleustein is taking Harley-Davidson into the future.

cycle production while maintaining quality. But products were snapped up as quickly as they could be cranked out.

By 1995, annual production had reached the 100,000 mark and projections indicated a strong increase in demand for the coming years. So with every reason to celebrate, why was Harley-Davidson planning a major retooling of the motorcycle manufacturing production processes?

Harley's top managers wanted to rev up output and expand sales in Europe, Scandinavia, Australia, Japan, and other global markets without cutting back on domestic distribution. They set an ambitious companywide goal: to be able to produce 200,000 motorcycles annually by 2003, the company's centennial. But meeting this goal would require a top-to-bottom revamping of the entire production process. Not only was Harley's 84-year-old distribution warehouse cramped and outdated, but its equipment was decades old.

Facing such a deadline, what could CEO Jeff Bleustein and his top managers do to wring much more efficiency out of the production process without sacrificing quality? How could they apply technology to improve the company's production process? How could the company work hand in hand with its suppliers to meet Harley's centennial goal?[1] ■

UNDERSTANDING PRODUCTION AND OPERATIONS MANAGEMENT

As managers of Harley-Davidson know, the extremely competitive nature of the global business environment requires companies to produce high-quality goods and services in the most efficient way possible. Few defects, fast production, low costs, excellent customer service, broad market reach, innovative products and processes, less waste, and high flexibility are all objectives that improve quality by adding value to the good or service being produced. Companies pursue these objectives to maintain a competitive advantage.[2] Moreover, managers understand that the level of quality that a company aspires to in the production of goods and services affects its long-term ability to address the needs of its customers, its employees, and its shareholders.

Like most aspects of business, production tends to get more complex and technologically advanced with each passing year. To get a sense of what production means today and how it might affect your career, it's important to first clarify what production really is, explain how it fits in the value chain, identify the unique challenges of service production, understand the difference between mass production and customization, and explore the impact that outsourcing is having on businesses and employers all over the world.

What Is Production?

To many people, the term *production* suggests images of factories, machines, and assembly lines staffed with employees making automobiles, computers, furniture, motorcycles, or other tangible goods. That's because in the past people used the terms *production* and *manufacturing* interchangeably. With the growth in the number of service-based businesses and their increasing importance to the economy, however, the term **production** is now used to describe the transformation of resources into goods and services that people need or want. The broader term **production and operations management (POM)**, or simply *operations management*, refers to all the activities involved in producing a firm's goods and services.

Like other types of management, POM involves the basic functions of planning, organizing, leading, and controlling. It also requires careful consideration of a company's goals, the strategies for attaining those goals, and the standards against which results will be measured. In both manufacturing and service organizations, the production and operations manager is the person responsible for performing these functions. One of the principal responsibilities of the production and operations manager is to design and oversee an efficient conversion process—one that lowers costs by optimizing output from each resource used in the process. These resources include money, materials, inventories, people, buildings, and time.

production
Transformation of resources into goods or services that people need or want

production and operations management (POM)
Coordination of an organization's resources for the manufacture of goods or the delivery of services

The Value Chain and the Conversion Process

Every business, from neighborhood coffeehouses to motorcycle manufacturers, tries to create value by transforming inputs (such as labor, information, and raw materials) into outputs (goods and services that customers want to purchase). This transformation, often called the *conversion process*, is at the core of the company's **value chain**, which includes all the business functions necessary to support the transformation process—marketing, accounting, human resources, and so on.

This transformation concept applies to tangible goods and intangible services. An airline, for example, uses such processes as booking flights, flying airplanes, maintaining equipment, and training crews to transform tangible and intangible inputs such as the plane, pilot's skill, fuel, time, and passengers into the delivery of customers to their destinations. For a clothing manufacturer to produce a jacket, inputs such as cloth, thread, and buttons are transformed by the seamstress into the finished product (see Exhibit 8.1).

Conversion is of two basic types. An **analytic system** breaks raw materials into one or more distinct products, which may or may not resemble the original material in form and function. In meatpacking, for example, a steer is divided into hide, bone, steaks, and so on. A **synthetic system** combines two or more materials to form a single product. For example, in steel manufacturing, iron is combined with small quantities of other minerals at high temperatures to make steel.

value chain
All of the functions required to transform inputs into outputs (goods and services), along with the business functions that support the transformation process

analytic system
Production process that breaks incoming materials into various component products and divisional patterns simultaneously

synthetic system
Production process that combines two or more materials or components to create finished products; the reverse of an analytic system

Exhibit 8.1
The Conversion Process
Production of goods or services is basically a process of conversion. Inputs (the basic ingredients) are transformed (by the application of labor, equipment, and capital) into outputs (the desired product or service).

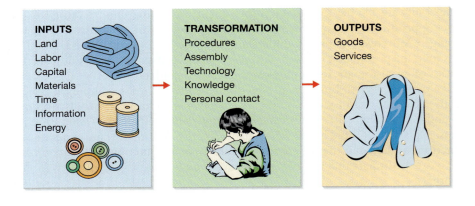

INPUTS
Land
Labor
Capital
Materials
Time
Information
Energy

TRANSFORMATION
Procedures
Assembly
Technology
Knowledge
Personal contact

OUTPUTS
Goods
Services

The Unique Challenges of Service Delivery

The conversion processes for services and goods are similar in terms of *what* is done, transforming inputs into outputs, but the two differ in *how* the processes are performed (see Exhibit 8.2). That's because the production of goods results in a tangible output—something you can see or touch, such as a jacket, motorcycle, desk, or bicycle—while the production of a service results in an intangible act. Most of the concepts associated with goods manufacturing apply to services as well, although service providers do face some unique issues:[3]

- Customers are usually involved in—and can affect the quality of—the service delivery. Personal trainers can instruct clients in the proper way to work out, but if the clients don't follow directions, the result will be unsatisfactory.

- Unlike goods, which can usually be built ahead of time and stored in inventory until customers buy them, most services are consumed at the same time they are produced. For instance, if a 200-seat airline flight takes off half empty, those 100 sales opportunities are lost forever; they can't be stored in inventory for later sale. This attribute can have a dramatic impact on the way service businesses are managed, from staffing (making sure enough people are on hand to help with peak demands) to pricing (using discounts to encourage people to buy services when they are available). Note that some technology-based services don't have to deal with this constraint. Online data backup services, for example, are available whenever customers want to use them.

- Services are usually people-intensive, whether it's manual skills (carpentry, landscaping) or intellectual or creative energy skills (advertising, freelance writing). Much of the investment in e-commerce in recent years has been aimed at offering services that don't require as much human activity to compete, such as Amazon.com in online retailing.

- Customers often dictate when and where services are delivered. The equipment and food ingredients used in a restaurant can be produced just about anywhere, but the restaurant itself needs to be located close to customers and be open when customers want to eat.

- Service quality can be more subjective than goods quality. If you create a pair of scissors, for instance, both you and the customer can measure and agree on the hardness of the steel, the sharpness of the blades, the smoothness of the action, and so on. If you create a haircut using those scissors, however, you and the customer might disagree on the attractiveness of the style or the quality of the salon experience.

With the majority of workers in the United States now involved in the service sector, managers in thousands of companies need to pay close attention to these factors when designing service-delivery systems.

Exhibit 8.2   **Input-Transformation-Output Relationships for Typical Systems**

Both goods and services undergo a conversion process, but the components of the process vary to accommodate the differences between tangible and intangible outputs.

SYSTEM	REPRESENTATIVE INPUTS	TRANSFORMATION COMPONENTS	TRANSFORMATION FUNCTION	TYPICAL DESIRED OUTPUT
Hospital	Patients, medical supplies	Physicians, nurses, equipment	Health care	Healthy individuals
Restaurant	Hungry customers, food	Chef, waitress, environment	Well-prepared and well-served food	Satisfied customers
Automobile factory	Sheet steel, engine parts	Tools, equipment, workers	Fabrication and assembly of cars	High-quality cars
College or university	High school graduates, books	Teachers, classrooms	Impart knowledge and skills	Educated individuals
Department store	Shoppers, stock of goods	Displays, salesclerks	Attract shoppers, promote products, fill orders	Sales to satisfied customers

Mass Production, Mass Customization, and Customized Production

Both goods and services can be created through mass production, mass customization, or fully customized production, depending on the nature of the product and the desires of target customers. In **mass production**, identical goods or services are created, usually in large quantities, such as when Sony churns out 10,000 identical Walkman CD players. Although not normally associated with services, mass production is what American Airlines is doing when it offers hundreds of opportunities for passengers to fly from, say, Dallas to Chicago every day—every customer on these flights gets the exact same service at the same time.

At the other extreme is **customized production**, sometimes called *batch-of-one production* in manufacturing, in which the producer creates a unique good or service for each customer. If you order a piece of furniture from a local craftsperson, for instance, you can specify everything from the size and shape to the types of wood and fabric used. Or you can hire a charter pilot to fly you wherever you want, whenever you want. Both products are customized to your unique requirements.

Mass production has the advantage of economies of scale, but it frequently can't deliver the unique goods and services that today's customers demand. On the other hand, fully customized production can offer uniqueness but usually at a much higher price. An attractive compromise in many cases is **mass customization**, in which part of the product is mass produced, then the remaining features are customized for each buyer. For instance, it would cost you a small fortune to have someone build you a unique car from scratch, but you can partially customize any manufacturer's model to your needs and tastes by choosing from the available options for engines, colors, seat coverings, stereos, and so on. The manufacturer can mass produce the basic elements of the car, then partially customize it based on your selections.

Technology continues to increase the options for mass customization. For instance, Meridian Golf mass customizes golf clubs in 1,100 different combinations. Customers are fitted by swinging a

mass production
Production of uniform products in large quantities

customized production
Production of individual goods and services for individual customers

mass customization
Producing partially customized goods and services by combining mass production techniques with individual customization

Individual craftspeople often engage in customized production, creating a unique product for each customer.

club on a special in-store platform where computers measure 14 aspects of their golf swing. Thanks to such mass customization, Meridian Golf boasts a 99.5 percent customer satisfaction rate.[4]

Outsourcing

Chapter 5 introduced the concept of outsourcing as a source of opportunity for small businesses. Nearly every aspect of a business has the potential to be outsourced, from product design and manufacturing to human resources to marketing and sales. For instance, some companies choose to focus on design and hand some or all of the manufacturing duties off to companies that specialize in that phase of the value chain. DaimlerChrysler's Smart car is a good example of this process. Just about everything in Smartville, the production center where the Smart car is assembled, is relegated to suppliers—from inventorying nuts and bolts on the assembly line to delivering cars to dealers in Europe and out to Japan. Over half the 1,900 people working in Smartville aren't even on the manufacturer's payroll. The biggest suppliers are right on-site, building most of the car in the form of large modules—body, doors, rear section with engine, and so on. Conveyors link major suppliers' plants directly to the assembly building where the cars are bolted together. Suppliers carry much of the cost of work-in-progress inventory, since they don't get paid until the car comes off the line and is accepted for sale by inspectors—about every 90 seconds, which is quick time for the auto industry. Meanwhile, DaimlerChrysler hopes to incorporate what it has learned about suppliers, modules, pay-on-build, and new technologies into its global operation. "We are getting more and more into learning from others," says one Smart car plant manager. "We take good things in other places and install them at our plant."[5]

Outsourcing all or part of the manufacturing function has several potential advantages. For one thing, it allows companies to redirect the capital and resources spent on manufacturing to new product research and development, marketing, and customer service. For another, many contract manufacturers are industry specialists with state-of-the-art facilities and production efficiencies that would be costly to duplicate on an individual scale. In the electronics industry, a number of contract electronic manufacturers (CEMs) now produce all or parts of many products that bear other companies' names. For instance, Solectron, one of the largest of these CEMs, assembles everything from pagers and printers to computers and television decoding boxes for some of the biggest brand names in electronics, including Hewlett-Packard, Cisco, IBM, and Lucent.[6] In some cases, the CEM provides additional services beyond the manufacturing function, including inventory management, delivery, and after-sales service.[7]

With all its potential financial and technical advantages, however, outsourcing is not without critics or controversy. For a broader look at the implications of outsourcing, see "Offshoring: Profits, Yes, but at What Cost?"

In automotive manufacturing circles, the way the Smart car is built has attracted as much attention as the vehicle. Outsourcing the manufacturing function integrates the Smart car supply chain to the maximum.

DESIGNING THE PRODUCTION PROCESS

When Jeff Bleustein and his management team at Harley-Davidson set out to return Harley to a competitive position, they learned that the way an organization designs its operations can dramatically affect a company's ability to deliver quality products. Designing an effective production process is one of the key responsibilities of production and operations managers. It involves six important tasks: identifying the supply chain, forecasting demand, planning for capacity, choosing a facility location, designing a facility layout, and scheduling work.

Establishing the Supply Chain

The value chain and the conversion process that it incorporates rely on supplies at every step of the way. Next time you visit a coffeehouse, whether it's a local independent or a chain such as Starbucks, take a second to look around at all the goods and services

Offshoring: Profits, Yes, But at What Cost?

Few business issues in recent years have generated the emotional intensity that outsourcing has stirred up. Outsourcing has been going on for about as long as businesses have existed, but it has become a hot topic as the outsourcing movement expands from mostly lower-paying assembly positions to higher-paying technical and professional positions.

When companies outsource any function in the value chain, they often eliminate the jobs associated with that function as well. And, increasingly, those jobs aren't going across the street to another local company but rather around the world, a variation on outsourcing known as *offshoring*. HP, IBM, Dell, Microsoft, and Accenture are among the many U.S. technology firms that have already moved thousands of technical jobs to India, which has a large pool of educated workers willing to work for far less than U.S. workers are typically paid.

Proponents say that offshoring is crucial to the survival of many U.S. companies and that it saves other U.S. jobs. Plus, offshoring helps raise the standard of living in other countries and thereby expands opportunities for U.S. companies to export their products.

Opponents say that companies are selling out the U.S. middle class in pursuit of profits and starting a trend that can only harm the country. When jobs in engineering, medicine, scientific research, architecture, and law can move overseas, they ask, what jobs are going to be left in the United States? Their anger isn't helped when terminated U.S. employees are forced to train their own overseas replacements, an apparently common practice.

Uncertainty is only fueling the controversy, because nobody can be entirely certain just how far the offshoring trend will go or what impact it will have on employees, communities, or companies themselves. Estimates vary widely about the number of jobs that have moved or could move to other countries. Moreover, aside from cases in which a particular job was moved to another country, it's often difficult to identify the specific reasons why one country gained jobs or another lost jobs. The emergence of new technology, the phasing out of old technology, shifts in consumer tastes, changes in business strategies, and other factors can all create and destroy jobs.

Moreover, traditional economic theory suggests that outsourcing lower-level jobs to countries with lower wages is good for U.S. companies because it frees up money and employees to work on more valuable activities. To some degree, this did in fact happen when many U.S. manufacturing jobs moved overseas in previous decades. However, when those more valuable activities themselves started to move overseas, quite a few people began to question the theory.

Some economists continue to assert that short-term pains will lead to long-term gains—that the jobs lost this time around will once again be replaced by other jobs. Here again, though, there's more uncertainty: no one has yet identified what those jobs are going to be. Paul Craig Roberts, a former assistant treasury secretary, says the traditional economists are wrong because they're using 200-year-old assumptions about comparative advantage (see Chapter 3) that don't apply to a highly mobile, information-based economy. With companies trying to reduce costs wherever possible but workers trying to protect as many jobs as possible, offshoring promises to be a hot topic for years to come—not only for businesses and employees but for governments and society as a whole.

Questions for Critical Thinking

1. Some economists have suggested "wage insurance" to help workers whose income declines after their high-paying jobs go overseas. Do you agree? Why or why not? If you do agree, who should pay for the insurance, taxpayers or the companies that offshore jobs?
2. Will global labor markets eventually balance out, with workers in comparable positions all over the world making roughly the same wages? Explain your answer.

---

required to operate such a business. Even for a relatively simple business such as a coffeehouse, the list is long: the many different types of coffee beans, flavor additives, chocolate shavings, sugar, sweetener, cream, half-and-half, cow's milk, soy milk, cinnamon, water, electricity, workers' aprons, maintenance for espresso machines, coffee cups, lids, place mats, napkins, stirrers, and so on. And that doesn't include all the goods and services that aren't directly involved in making coffee, such as accounting software to pay taxes and print paychecks, heating, security systems, advertising, phone service, window washers, paint, rest room supplies and furniture repair. Now just imagine what it must be like to supply Boeing with the 6 million parts that make up a single 747.[8]

A company's ability to deliver quality products and services is often tied to the dynamics of its suppliers. One faulty part, one late shipment, can send rippling effects through the production system and can even bring operations to a grinding halt. When a surge of orders for new Boeing 747s stepped up demand for parts, for instance, Boeing's suppliers were caught flat-footed. "We had $25,000 engine mounts that couldn't be finished because we were waiting for $40 nuts and bolts," noted one Boeing supplier. As a result, promised aircraft delivery dates were delayed and Boeing suffered huge losses. To avoid such problems in the future, Boeing now works hand in hand with its suppliers to refine products and delivery schedules.[9]

supply chain
The collection of suppliers and systems that provide all of the materials and supplies required to create finished products and deliver them to final customers

The collection of suppliers and systems that provide all the various materials required to make a finished product is called the **supply chain**. (*Supply chain* and *value chain* are sometimes used interchangeably, but it's helpful to distinguish the supply chain as the part of the overall value chain that acquires and manages the goods and services needed to produce whatever it is the company produces and then deliver it to the final customer. Everyone in the company is part of the value chain, but not everyone is involved in the supply chain.[10]) The supply chain begins with the provider of raw materials and ends with the company that produces the finished product that is delivered to the final customer. The members of the supply chain vary according to the nature of the operation and type of product but typically include suppliers, manufacturers, distributors, and retailers. For example, if the finished product is a wood table, the supply chain going backward would include the retail store where it was sold, the shipping company that delivered it to the retail store, the furniture manufacturer, the hardware manufacturer, and the lumber company that acquired the wood from the forest.[11]

Before a company can produce a single product, it must first create a supply chain. Managers need to identify which materials and other supplies they need, who can supply them, where they should be stored, and a host of other variables. When TiVo, the maker of the popular personal video recorders that capture television programming, started up several years ago, executives figured they needed to get products on the market as quickly as possible. They established a supply chain almost overnight by outsourcing manufacturing, distribution, retailer recruiting, public relations, advertising, and customer support.[12]

production forecasts
Estimates of how much of a company's goods and services must be produced in order to meet future demand

Supply-chain decisions might not sound as glamorous as high-level corporate strategy or innovative e-commerce, but they are every bit as crucial to a company's success. For instance, the public face of Amazon.com is a website that has all the hallmarks of a leading-edge Internet company; behind the scenes, though, are some of the world's most sophisticated warehouses and supply-chain technologies. In fact, more than a few dot-com pioneers in the 1990s learned to their dismay just how important supply chains are when their razzle-dazzle web company ideas faltered because of nuts-and-bolts supply-chain problems.

Forecasting Demand

A smooth-running supply chain can provide the inputs a company needs, but managers need to figure out how much to buy. And to make that decision, they need to forecast demand for the goods they'll be manufacturing or the services they'll be delivering. Using customer feedback, sales orders, market research, past sales figures, industry analyses, and educated guesses about the future behavior of the economy and competitors, operations managers prepare **production forecasts**, estimates of future demand for the company's products. For example, after years of experience, operation managers for Carnival's Elation Cruise Line can now forecast that a one-week Caribbean cruise will require some 10,000 pounds of meat, 10,080 bananas, and 41,600 eggs.[13] These estimates are then used to plan, budget, and schedule the use of resources. Of course, many factors in the business environment cannot be predicted or controlled with certainty. For this reason, managers must regularly review and adjust their forecasts to account for these uncertainties.

Planning for Capacity

Once product demand has been estimated, management must determine the company's capacity to produce the goods or services. The term *capacity* refers to the volume of manufacturing or service capability that an organization can handle. For example, a

Many new cruise ships have elegant restaurants, boutiques, luxury spas, high-tech fitness rooms, conference and meeting rooms, theaters, playrooms, ice-skating rinks, and even rock-climbing walls. With passenger counts of 2,600 and upward, forecasting customer demand for food, supplies, and entertainment is no easy task.

doctor's office with only one examining room limits the number of patients the doctor can see each day. And a cruise ship with 750 staterooms limits the number of passengers that the ship can accommodate in any given week. Similarly, a beverage bottling plant with only one conveyor belt and one local warehouse limits the company's ability to manufacture beverage products.

Capacity planning is a long-term strategic decision that establishes the overall level of resources needed to meet customer demand. The neighborhood convenience store needs to consider traffic volume throughout the day and night in order to plan staffing levels appropriately. At the other extreme of complexity, when managers at Boeing plan for the production of an airliner, they have to consider not only the staffing of thousands of people but also factory floor space, material flows from hundreds of suppliers, internal deliveries, cash flow, tools and equipment, and dozens of other factors. Because of the potential impact on finances, customers, and employees, capacity planning involves some of the most difficult decisions that managers have to make. As noted earlier, service businesses have a particular challenge in this respect because they usually can't create their products ahead of time; they need to match capacity and demand simultaneously.

capacity planning
A long-term strategic decision that determines the level of resources available to an organization to meet customer demand

Top management uses long-term capacity planning to make significant decisions about an organization's ability to produce goods and services, such as expanding existing facilities, constructing new facilities, or phasing out unneeded ones. Such decisions entail a great deal of risk, for two reasons: (1) Large shifts in demand are difficult to predict accurately, and (2) long-term capacity decisions can be difficult to undo. For example, if a new facility is built to produce a new product that then fails or if demand for a popular product suddenly declines, the company will find itself with expensive excess capacity. Managers must decide what they should do with this excess capacity. If they keep it, they might try to find an alternate use for this space. If they eliminate it and demand picks up again, the company will have to forgo profits because it is unable to meet customer demand.[14]

Choosing a Facility Location

One long-term issue that management must resolve early when designing the production process for goods and services is the location of production facilities. The goal is to choose a location that minimizes costs while increasing operational efficiencies and product quality. To accomplish this goal, management must consider such regional costs as land, construction, labor, local taxes, energy, and local living standards. As noted earlier in the outsourcing discussion, the dramatic differences in labor costs (not just for semiskilled employees, but for a wide range of professional positions as well) around the world makes labor a particularly important decision.

For many industries, location decisions also depend heavily on transportation costs, which cover the shipping of supplies and finished goods. Moreover, companies that sell a lot of products overseas must be able to arrange for efficient air or water transportation. Finally, companies must consider raw materials costs. For example, the location of a coal-based power plant must be chosen to minimize the cost of distributing electrical power to customers and to minimize the cost of shipping coal to the plant.

Location considerations may be different for some service organizations. Although they may also take regional costs into consideration, the main objective for many service firms is to locate where profit potential is greatest. Unlike manufacturing operations, in which low production costs are an important consideration, services tend to focus on more customer-driven factors.[15] Because they often require one-on-one contact with customers, service organizations such as gas stations, restaurants, department stores, and charities

Whenever transportation costs are a major expense in the production of a product or service, access to railroads and other means of transport becomes an important consideration.

must locate where their target market is large and sustainable. Therefore, market research often plays a central role in site selection. However, for service companies that reach customers primarily by telephone, mail, or the Internet, proximity to customers is less of a consideration.

Support from local communities and governments often plays a key role in location decisions as well. To provide jobs and expand their income and sales tax bases, many governments offer companies generous packages of financial relief, from reduced property taxes to free land. When the South Korean automaker Kia recently explored locations for building its first factory in Europe (partly to avoid the European Union's high import duties on cars), Slovakia made the most attractive offer, outbidding Poland, the Czech Republic, and Hungary.[16]

Designing a Facility Layout

Once a site has been selected, managers must turn their attention to *facility layout*, the arrangement of production work centers and other elements (such as materials, equipment, and support departments) needed to process goods and services. Layout includes the efforts involved in selecting specific locations for each department, process, machine, support function, and other activity required for the operation or service. The need for a new layout design can occur for a number of reasons besides new construction; for instance, a new process or method might become available, the volume of business might change, a new product or service may be offered, an outdated facility may be remodeled, the mix of goods or services offered may change, or an existing product or service may be redesigned.[17]

Facility layout affects the amount of on-hand inventory, the efficiency of materials handling, the utilization of equipment, and the productivity and morale of employees. In goods manufacturing, the primary concern is the efficient movement of resources and inventory. In the production of services, facility layout controls the flow of customers through the system and influences the customer's satisfaction with the service.[18] In both services and goods operations, the major goals of a good layout design are to minimize materials-handling costs, reduce bottlenecks in moving material or people, provide flexibility, provide ease of supervision, use available space effectively and efficiently, reduce hazards, and facilitate coordination and communications wherever appropriate.[19] Four typical facility layouts are the *process layout, product layout, cellular layout*, and *fixed-position layout* (see Exhibit 8.3).[20]

A **process layout**, also called a *functional layout*, concentrates everything needed to complete one phase of the production process in one place. Specific functions, such as drilling or welding, are performed in one location for different products or customers (see Exhibit 8.3A). The process layout is often used in machine shops as well as in service industries. For example, a medical clinic might dedicate one room to X rays, another room to routine examinations, and still another to outpatient surgery.

An alternative to the process layout is the **product layout**, also called the *assembly-line layout*, in which the main production process occurs along a line, and products in progress move from one workstation to the next. Materials and subassemblies of component parts may feed into the main line at several points, but the flow of production is continuous. Automotive and personal-computer manufacturers are just two of many industries that typically use this layout (see Exhibit 8.3B).

Some production of services is also organized by product. For example, when you go to your local department of motor vehicles to get a driver's license, you usually go through a series of steps administered by several people: registering, taking a written or computerized test, having an eye exam, paying a cashier, and getting your picture taken. You emerge from this system a licensed driver (unless, of course, you fail one of the tests).

A **cellular layout** groups dissimilar machines into work centers (or cells) to process parts that have similar shapes and processing requirements (see Exhibit 8.3C). Arranging work flow by cells can improve the efficiency of a process layout while main-

process layout
Method of arranging a facility so that production tasks are carried out in separate departments containing specialized equipment and personnel

product layout
Method of arranging a facility so that production proceeds along a line of workstations

cellular layout
Method of arranging a facility so that parts with similar shapes or processing requirements are processed together in work centers

| Exhibit 8.3 | **Types of Facility Layouts** |

Facility layout is often determined by the type of product an organization is producing.

(A) Process layout: Typically, a process layout is used for an organization producing made-to-order products. A process layout is arranged according to the specialized employees and materials involved in various phases of the production process.

(B) Product layout: A product layout is used when an organization is producing large quantities of just a few products. In a product or assembly-line layout, the developing product moves in a continuous sequence from one workstation to the next.

(C) Cellular layout: A cellular layout works well in organizations that practice mass customization. In a cellular layout, parts with similar shapes or processing requirements are processed together in work centers, an arrangement that facilitates teamwork and flexibility.

(D) Fixed-position layout: A fixed-position layout requires employees and materials to be brought to the product and is used when the product is too large to move.

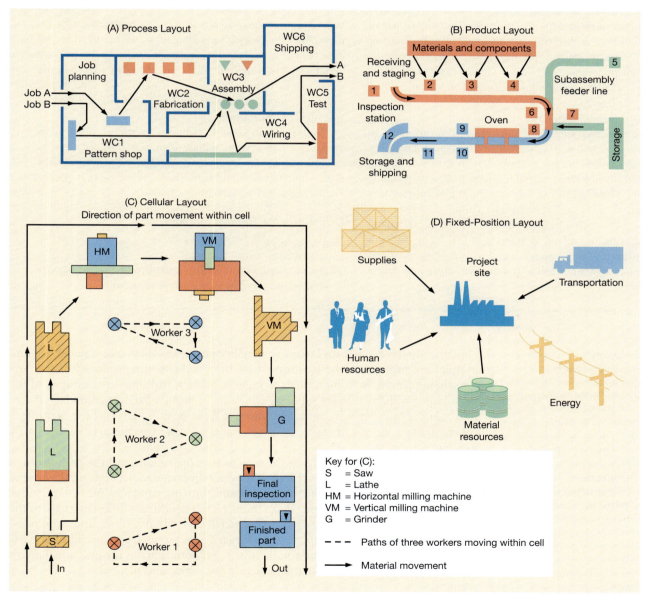

taining its flexibility. At the same time, grouping smaller numbers of workers in cells facilitates teamwork and joint problem solving. Employees are also able to work on a product from start to finish, and they can move between machines within their cells, thus increasing the flexibility of the team. Cellular layouts are commonly used in computer chip manufacture and metal fabricating.[21]

A Bike That Really Travels

When bike industry veteran Hanz Scholz decided to pedal across Europe in 1987, his vision of packing a folding bike in a suitcase when it was time to board a plane or train soon began to fade. Scholz was disappointed by the quality of folding bikes available. So he set out to build his own: one compact enough to fit into a large suitcase but high quality enough to tackle steep hills and long, rugged stretches.

Five years later, the first commercial orders for Scholz's Bike Friday were rolling in. Unlike its fold-up predecessors—often one-size-fits-all models available in retail stores—all Bike Fridays are custom-made by manufacturer Green Gear Cycling to meet the rider's size and component/color preference. The bike fits into a car trunk, a tight storage space, or an optional suitcase to travel on a plane like regular baggage.

Green Gear's operations are as distinctive as its product. The relatively small company ($3 million in sales, 30 employees, 17,000 square feet of production space) uses advanced manufacturing principles adopted from Toyota Motor and other large manufacturers. Built individually, each Bike Friday begins its life as a bundle of tubes, components, and other structures. These elements are processed through a build-to-order, flow-manufacturing configuration organized in a series of cells. The cells are designed so that any one cell can do some of the work of the previous or next cell if production runs behind or ahead.

Once work on a bike has begun, it flows through the process without hesitation at any point. "It works like a track relay with a transition area," says Scholz. "We've set up everything with single-process-specific tools so there is no process changeover time. The flow motto is 'touch it once, do it now.'" When a quality problem is discovered, the operator switches on a red light and all procedures stop until the production cell is adjusted to eliminate the problem.

Operating in a one-at-a-time flow system rather than in batches maximizes the chances for continuous improvement. "For us, every bike is a batch, so we have 150 to 200 chances per month to make process improvements," says Scholz. "A small manufacturer operating in a large-batch mode can be put out of business if it ruins just one. If you can make improvements as you find them, you can survive as a small manufacturer."

Today, Green Gear Cycling builds about 2,000 bikes annually. At an average selling price of $1,700, Bike Friday commands a premium price. "We give people what they want, when they want it," says Scholz. "If you do that, people are willing to pay you for it."

Questions for Critical Thinking

1. What are the advantages of using a cellular layout to manufacture Bike Fridays?
2. Does Green Gear Cycling mass produce or mass customize folding bikes? Explain your answer.

---

fixed-position layout
Method of arranging a facility so that the product is stationary and equipment and personnel come to it

Finally, the **fixed-position layout** is a facility layout in which labor, materials, and equipment are brought to the location where the good is being produced or the customer is being served. Buildings, roads, bridges, airplanes, and ships are examples of the types of large products that are typically constructed using a fixed-position layout (see Exhibit 8.3D). Many service companies also use fixed-position layouts; for example, a plumber goes to a job site bringing the tools, material, and expertise needed to repair a broken pipe.

routing
Specifying the sequence of operations and the path the work will take through the production facility

Routing is the task of specifying the sequence of operations and the path through the facility that the work will take. The way production is routed depends on the type of product and the layout of the plant. A table-manufacturing company, for instance, uses a process layout because it has three departments, each handling a different phase of the table's manufacture and each equipped with specialized tools, machines, and employees. Department 1 cuts wood into tabletops and legs. These pieces are then sent to department 2, where holes are drilled and rough finishing is done. Finally, the individual pieces are routed to department 3, where the tables are assembled and painted.

Scheduling Work

scheduling
Process of determining how long each production operation takes and then setting a starting and ending time for each

In any production process, managers must use **scheduling**—determining how long each operation takes and setting a starting and ending time for each. A master schedule, often called a *master production schedule (MPS)*, is a schedule of planned completion of items. In services such as a doctor's office, the appointment book serves as the master schedule.

When a job has relatively few activities and relationships, many production managers keep the process on schedule with a **Gantt chart**. Developed by Henry L. Gantt in the early 1900s, the Gantt chart is a bar chart showing the amount of time required to accomplish each part of a process. It allows managers to see at a glance whether the process is in line with the schedule they had planned (see Exhibit 8.4).

For more complex jobs, the **program evaluation and review technique (PERT)** is helpful. It is a planning tool that helps managers identify the optimal sequencing of activities, the expected time for project completion, and the best use of resources within a complex project. To use PERT, the manager must (1) identify the activities to be performed, (2) determine the sequence of activities, (3) establish the time needed to complete each activity, (4) diagram the network of activities, (5) calculate the longest path through the network that leads to project completion, and (6) refine the network's timing or use of resources as activities are completed. The longest path through the network is known as the **critical path** because it represents the minimum amount of time needed to complete the project.

In place of a single time projection for each task, PERT uses four figures: an *optimistic* estimate (if things go well), a *pessimistic* estimate (if they don't go well), a *most likely* estimate (how long the task usually takes), and an *expected* time estimate—an average of the other three estimates.[22] The expected time is used to diagram the network of activities and determine the length of the critical path.

Consider the manufacture of shoes in Exhibit 8.5. At the beginning of the process, three paths deal with heels, soles, and tops. All three processes must be finished before the next phase (sewing tops to soles and heels) can be started. However, one of the three paths—the tops—takes 33 days, whereas the other two take only 18 and 12 days. The shoe tops, then, are on the critical path because they will delay the entire operation if they fall behind schedule. In contrast, soles can be started up to 21 days after starting the tops without slowing down production. This free time in the soles schedule is called *slack time* because managers can choose to produce the soles anytime during the 33-day period required by the tops.

Included in the scheduling process is the **dispatching** function, or the issuing of work orders to department supervisors. These orders specify the work to be done and the schedule for its completion. Work orders also inform department supervisors of their operational priorities and the schedule they must maintain.

Of course, once the schedule has been set and the orders dispatched, a production manager cannot just sit back and assume that the work will get done correctly and on time. Even the best scheduler may misjudge the time needed to complete an operation, and production may be delayed by accidents, mechanical breakdowns, or supplier problems. Therefore, the production manager needs a system for handling delays and pre-

Gantt chart
Bar chart used to control schedules by showing how long each part of a production process should take and when it should take place

program evaluation and review technique (PERT)
A planning tool that managers of complex projects use to determine the optimal order of activities, the expected time for project completion, and the best use of resources

critical path
In a PERT network diagram, the sequence of operations that requires the longest time to complete

dispatching
Issuing work orders and schedules to department heads and supervisors

---

Exhibit 8.4   **A Gantt Chart**

A chart like this one enables a production manager to immediately see the dates on which production steps must be started and completed if goods are to be delivered on schedule. Some steps may overlap to save time. For instance, after three weeks of cutting table legs, cutting tabletops begins. This overlap ensures that the necessary legs and tops are completed at the same time and can move on together to the next stage in the manufacturing process.

ID	Task Name	Start Date	End Date	Duration	2005
1	Make legs	8/1/05	8/28/05	28d	
2	Cut tops	8/22/05	8/28/05	7d	
3	Drill	8/29/05	9/4/05	6d	
4	Sand	9/5/05	9/11/05	7d	
5	Assemble	9/12/05	9/25/05	14d	
6	Paint	9/19/05	9/25/05	7d	

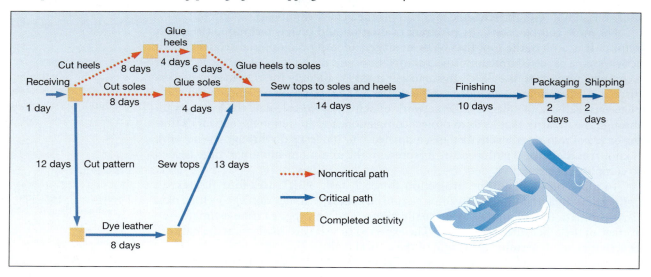

Exhibit 8.5   **PERT Diagram for Manufacturing Shoes**

In the manufacture of shoes, the critical path involves receiving, cutting the pattern, dyeing the leather, sewing the tops, sewing the tops to soles and heels, finishing, packaging, and shipping—a total of 61 days.

venting a minor disruption from growing into chaos. A successful system is based on good communication between the employees and the production manager.

Suppose a machine breakdown causes department 2 of a manufacturing company to lose half a day of drilling time. If the schedule is not altered to direct other work to department 3 (the next department), the employees and equipment in department 3 will sit idle for some time. However, if department 2 informs the production manager of its machine problem right away, the production manager can immediately reschedule some fill-in work for department 3.

IMPROVING PRODUCTION THROUGH TECHNOLOGY

Today, more and more companies are taking advantage of new production technologies to improve their efficiency and productivity. Two of the most visible advances in production technology are computers and **robots**—programmable machines that work with tools and materials to perform various tasks. Although industrial robots may seem exotic, they are actually quite common and are really nothing more than smart tools. Industrial robots can easily perform precision functions as well as repetitive, strenuous, or hazardous tasks.[23] When equipped with machine vision, or electronic eyes, robots can place doors on cars in precise locations, cull blemished vegetables from frozen-food processing lines, check the wings of aircraft for dangerous ice buildup, make sure that drug capsules of the right color go into the correct packages before they are shipped to pharmacies, and even assist with surgery.[24]

In addition to robots, other major developments in manufacturing automation include computer-aided design and engineering, computer-aided manufacturing, computer-integrated manufacturing, flexible manufacturing systems, and electronic data interchange.

Computer-Aided Design and Computer-Aided Engineering

Computer-aided design (CAD) applies advanced computer graphics and mathematical modeling to the design of products, helping designers create better products in less time. A related technology, **computer-aided engineering (CAE)**, lets engineers use computer-generated three-dimensional images and computerized calculations to test products.

robots
Programmable machines that can complete a variety of tasks by working with tools and materials

Business BUZZ

Biomimicry: Using nature as an inspiration for design ideas and manufacturing methods; for instance, the design of Velcro was inspired by the way burrs stick to clothing fabrics

computer-aided design (CAD)
Use of computer graphics and mathematical modeling in the development of products

computer-aided engineering (CAE)
Use of computers to test products without building an actual model

With CAE, engineers can subject proposed products to changing temperatures, various stresses, and even simulated accidents without ever building preliminary models. Moreover, the *virtual reality* capability of today's computers allows designers to see how finished products will look and operate before physical prototypes are built.

Using computers to assist in design and engineering saves time and money because revising computer designs is much faster than revising hand-drafted designs and building physical models. In fact, computer technology allows companies to perfect a product or abandon a bad idea before production even begins. The result is better overall product quality. For example, when Boeing engineers designed the 777 airplane, they corrected problems and tried out new ideas entirely on their computer screens. Digitally preassembling the 3 million parts of the 777 allowed Boeing to exceed its goals for reducing errors, changes, and rework.[25]

Computer-Aided Manufacturing and Computer-Integrated Manufacturing

The use of computers to control production equipment is called **computer-aided manufacturing (CAM)**. In a CAD/CAM system, computer-aided design data are converted automatically into processing instructions for production equipment to manufacture the part or product. This integration of design and production can increase the output, speed, and precision of assembly lines, as well as make customized production much easier.[26] In addition, the latest CAD/CAM software allows company departments to share designs and data over intranets and the Internet, enabling geographically dispersed departments to work together on complex projects.[27] For example, Ford uses a CAD/CAM/CAE system it calls C3P to develop new vehicle prototypes, dramatically improving engineering efficiency and reducing prototyping costs.[28]

The highest level of computerization in operations management is **computer-integrated manufacturing (CIM)**, in which all the elements of production—design, engineering, testing, production, inspection, and materials handling—are integrated into one automated system. Computer-integrated manufacturing is not a specific technology but rather a strategy that uses technology for organizing and controlling a factory. Its role is to link the people, machines, databases, and decisions involved in each step of producing a good.[29]

Flexible Manufacturing Systems

Advances in design technology have been accompanied by changes in the way the production process is organized. Traditional automated manufacturing equipment is *fixed* or *hard-wired*, meaning it is capable of handling only one specific task. Although fixed

---

Technologies That Are Revolutionizing Business

Nanotechnology

Think small. Really small. Think about manufacturing products a molecule or even a single atom at a time. That's the scale of nanotechnology, a rather vague term that covers a wide range of supertiny research and engineering efforts.

How it's changing business

Nanotechnology is just starting to make a ripple on the front lines of business, but the research projects now in the pipeline could have dramatic impact in the next decade or two. The potential uses of nanotechnology range from the practical—smart materials that can change shape and heal themselves, superstrong and superlight materials for airplanes, smart medical implants, and ultrasmall computers—to the somewhat wilder—food-growing machines and microscopic robots that could travel through your body to cure diseases and fix injuries. (Like any new technology with lots of promise, nanotechnology also suffers from lots of hype.)

Also, although they're slightly larger than the generally accepted scale of nanotechnology, *microelectromechanical systems (MEMS)* are already having a major impact in some industries. These tiny machines (pumps, valves, and so on), some no bigger than a grain of pollen, are used in the nozzles of ink-jet printers, air bag sensors, and ultraprecise miniature laboratory devices. MEMS are a $4 billion industry today, and that's expected to double by 2007.

Where you can learn more

Hundreds of companies and universities are involved with nanotechnology, so you can find information all over the web. For starters, try IBM (www.research.ibm.com/pics/nanotech), *Small Times* magazine (www.smalltimes.com), and Nanotechnology Now (www.nanotech-now.com). Not everyone supports nanotechnology research, by the way; check out the Center for Responsible Nanotechnology (www.crnano.org) or search Google for "molecular assembler" or "grey goo."

---

computer-aided manufacturing (CAM)
Use of computers to control production equipment

computer-integrated manufacturing (CIM)
Computer-based systems, including CAD and CAM, that coordinate and control all the elements of design and production

Flexible manufacturing systems make it easy to switch production from one type of product to another.

setup costs
Expenses incurred each time a producer organizes resources to begin producing goods or services

flexible manufacturing system (FMS)
Production system using computer-controlled machines that can adapt to various versions of the same operation

electronic data interchange (EDI)
Use of information systems that transmit documents such as invoices and purchase orders between computers, thereby lowering ordering costs and paperwork

XML
A standardized web language that goes beyond basic HTML, defining content or data, in addition to displaying formatting

automation is efficient when one type or model of good is mass produced, a change in product design requires extensive equipment changes. Such adjustments may involve high **setup costs**, the expenses incurred each time a manufacturer begins a production run of a different type of item. In addition, the initial investment for fixed automation is high because specialized equipment is required for each of the operations involved in making a single item. Only after much production on a massive scale can a company recoup the cost of that specialized equipment. For example, Harley-Davidson invested $4.8 million in fixed manufacturing equipment to make a particular motorcycle—only to dismantle the operation when the product faded.[30]

An alternative to a fixed manufacturing system is a **flexible manufacturing system (FMS)**. Such systems link numerous programmable machine tools by an automated materials-handling system of conveyors known as automatic guided vehicles (AGVs). These driverless computer-controlled vehicles move materials from any location on the factory floor to any other location. Changing from one product design to another requires only a few signals from a central computer. Each machine changes tools automatically, making appropriate selections from built-in storage carousels that can hold more than 100 tools. In addition, the sequence of events involved in building an item can be completely rearranged.[31] This flexibility saves both time and setup costs. Moreover, producers can outmaneuver less agile competitors by moving swiftly into profitable new fields. Flexible manufacturing, sometimes called *agile manufacturing*, also allows producers to adapt their products quickly to changing customer needs.[32] For instance, a flexible manufacturing system at Porsche allows 11 different versions of the Porsche 911 to be assembled on the same line.[33]

Flexible manufacturing systems are particularly suited for *job shops*, such as small machine shops, which make dissimilar items or produce at so irregular a rate that repetitive operations won't help. As a $10 million manufacturer of precision metal parts, Cook Specialty is one such operation that competes with larger manufacturers through flexible manufacturing. Cook used to make only certain products, such as basketball hoops and display racks. Now the company has transformed its production facilities so that it is capable of manufacturing custom-engineered medical instruments and precision parts for high-tech equipment. Technical innovations for these devices advance rapidly, but Cook is able to adapt its production facilities to keep up with the changes. In fact, almost one-third of the products Cook manufactures each year are new.[34]

Electronic Data Interchange

Have you ever had difficulty getting a digital camera to talk to your computer or getting two computers to share files? Multiply that frustration by a few million and you'll have a sense of what it can be like trying to convince the various computers in a complex supply chain to cooperate with one another. To meet this challenge, many businesses rely on **electronic data interchange (EDI)**, a method of electronic communication that simplifies data transfer between computers in a supply chain (think of it as automated e-mail between computers instead of human beings). For instance, when a manufacturer needs more parts from a certain supplier, the manufacturer's inventory software can send an electronic request to the supplier's product database, which then fills the order and sends an electronic invoice back to the manufacturer's accounting system. Roughly one-third of all business documents now travel back and forth electronically using EDI.[35]

EDI has been in use since the 1960s, and like many designs from that era, various companies came up with different and often incompatible schemes. In contrast, the Internet and the World Wide Web are built on universal standards, making them accessible to anyone who follows these standard conventions. One of the newest web standards, a language called **XML**, which stands for *eXtensible Markup Language*, can accomplish the computer-to-computer communication that EDI has been handling for years. (As you read in Appendix A, HTML is the basic language for controlling *how* text and graphics are displayed on webpages. XML takes that to another level by also controlling *what* is displayed. Instead of predefining the content, as you have to do with HTML, XML lets you redefine information "on the fly," which means computers can access each other's databases to get whatever information they need.) Because EDI and XML can solve the same problems, supply chain managers in many companies are now faced with the dilemma of which technology to use. XML promises to be less expensive and easier to implement, but EDI is firmly entrenched in thousands of companies around the world. As a result, XML will likely be used in most new systems, but some companies will continue to invest in EDI, and both schemes will coexist in the supply chain for years to come.[36]

MANAGING AND CONTROLLING THE PRODUCTION PROCESS

During the production design phase, operations managers establish the supply chain, forecast demand, plan for capacity, choose facility locations, design facility layouts and configurations, and develop production schedules and sequences. With the process in place, now it's time to "flip the switch" and start producing goods and services. Two major responsibilities at this point are coordinating the supply chain and assuring product quality.

Today's supply chains often span the globe, pulling in parts and materials from multiple countries.

Coordinating the Supply Chain

By now you have a sense of how many pieces must fit together—in the right place, at the right time—for successful production. Unfortunately, you can't just pile up huge quantities of everything you might eventually need because **inventory**, the goods and materials kept in stock for production or sale, costs money to purchase and store. On the other hand, not having an adequate supply of inventory can delay production and result in unhappy customers. That's why more and more companies are changing the way they purchase and handle the materials they use to produce goods and services.

Purchasing is the acquisition of the raw materials, parts, components, supplies, and finished products required to produce goods and services. The goal of purchasing is to make sure that the company has all of the materials it needs, when it needs them, at the lowest possible cost. To accomplish this goal, a company must always have enough supplies on hand to cover a product's **lead time**—the period that elapses between placing the supply order and receiving materials. This balancing act is the job of **inventory control**, which tries to determine the right quantities of supplies and products to have on hand, then tracks where those items are.

Simply controlling what's in inventory is not enough for many companies, however, and over the years, operations specialists have developed several approaches to coordinating the supply chain, including *just-in-time systems*, *material requirements planning*, *manufacturing resource planning*, and *supply-chain management*.

Just-in-Time Systems

Just-in-time (JIT) systems are designed to have only the right amounts of materials arrive at precisely the times they are needed. Because supplies arrive just as they are needed, and no sooner, inventories are theoretically eliminated and waste is reduced.

Reducing stocks of parts to practically nothing also encourages factories to keep production flowing smoothly, from beginning to end, without any holdups. And a constant production flow requires good teamwork. On the other hand, JIT exposes a company to greater risks, as a disruption in the flow of raw materials from suppliers can slow or stop the production process. Shortly after the September 11, 2001, terrorist attacks,

inventory
Goods kept in stock for the production process or for sales to final customers

purchasing
Acquiring the raw materials, parts, components, supplies, and finished products needed to produce goods and services

lead time
Period that elapses between the ordering of materials and their arrival from the supplier

inventory control
System for determining the right quantity of various items to have on hand and keeping track of their location, use, and condition

just-in-time (JIT) system
Continuous system that pulls materials through the production process, making sure that all materials arrive just when they are needed with minimal inventory and waste

for instance, Toyota Motor Corp. came within 15 hours of halting production of its Sequoia sport-utility vehicle at its Princeton, Indiana, plant. One of its suppliers was waiting for steering sensors normally imported by plane from Germany, but the planes weren't flying.[37] Transportation slowdowns since 9/11 are forcing many industrial operators to stockpile more parts, components, and materials.

A JIT system also places a heavy burden on suppliers because they must be able to meet the production schedules of their customers. For instance, an increasingly strong demand for electronic and computer components at the beginning of the 21st century left many electronic equipment manufacturers battling one another for computer chips and other components. "Just-in-time has become just-in-trouble," says the chief financial officer of one electronics company.[38]

Thus, to be effective, JIT systems must be designed to include multifunctional teamwork, flexible manufacturing, small-batch production, strict production control, quick setups, consistent production levels, preventive maintenance, and reliable supplier networks. Furthermore, poor quality simply cannot be tolerated in a stockless manufacturing environment because one defective part can bring production to a halt. In other words, JIT cannot be implemented without a commitment to total quality control.[39] When all of these factors work in sync, the manufacturer achieves *lean production*; that is, it can do more with less.[40]

In those cases where it is difficult for manufacturers and suppliers to coordinate their schedules, JIT may not work. For example, shoemaker Allen-Edmonds cannot get its principal raw material whenever it wants because calfskin hides come on the market only at certain times each year.[41] Additional product factors can also affect JIT: seasonality (popularity during specific seasons such as winter), perishability, and unusual handling characteristics such as size or weight.

JIT concepts can also be used to reduce inventory and cycle time for service organizations. For instance, Koley's Medical Supply manages inventory for hospitals using what it calls "stockless distribution." Rather than making large, general deliveries to the stockroom, the company delivers specific items in just the right quantities to the various floors and rooms in the hospital. Doing so isn't always easy: At one hospital, Koley's has to make deliveries to 168 individual receiving points. But the system creates value for Koley's customers, such as Bishop Clarkson Memorial Hospital in Omaha, Nebraska, which reduced its annual inventory costs from $500,000 to just $7,000.

Material Requirements Planning

material requirements planning (MRP)
Method of getting the correct materials where they are needed, on time, and without carrying unnecessary inventory

Material requirements planning (MRP) is another inventory-control technique that helps a manufacturer get the correct materials where they are needed, when they are needed, and without unnecessary stockpiling. Managers use computer programs to calculate when certain materials will be required, when they should be ordered, and when they should be delivered so that storage costs will be minimal. These systems are so effective at reducing inventory levels that they are used almost universally in both large and small manufacturing firms.

perpetual inventory
System that uses computers to monitor inventory levels and automatically generate purchase orders when supplies are needed

A more automated form of material requirements planning is the **perpetual inventory** system, in which computers monitor inventory levels and automatically generate purchase orders when supplies fall below a certain level. The price scanners found at the checkout counters of many stores are part of perpetual inventory systems. Every time a product is purchased, the scanner deletes that particular item from the computer system's inventory data. When inventory of the product reaches a predetermined level, the system generates an order for more. Often, the store's system is linked to the supplier's own computer system, which enables the order to be placed with virtually no human involvement.

Manufacturing Resource Planning

The MRP systems on the market today are made up of various modules, including inventory control, purchasing, customer order entry, production planning, shop-floor control, and accounting. With the addition of more and more modules that focus on capacity

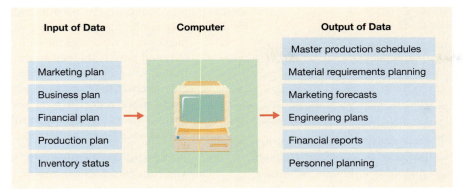

Exhibit 8.6

MRP II

An MRP II computer system gives managers and workers in every department easy access to data from all other departments, which in turn makes it easier to generate—and adhere to—the organization's over-all plans, forecasts, and schedules.

planning, marketing, and finance, an MRP system evolves into a **manufacturing resource planning (MRP II)** system.

Because it draws together all departments, an MRP II system produces a company-wide game plan that allows everyone to work with the same numbers (see Exhibit 8.6). Employees can now draw on data, such as inventory levels, back orders, and unpaid bills, once reserved for only top executives. Moreover, the system can track each step of production, allowing managers throughout the company to consult other managers' inventories, schedules, and plans. In addition, MRP II systems are capable of running simulations (models of possible operations systems) that enable managers to plan and test alternative strategies.[42] Many companies have extended the MRP II concept to include functions outside of manufacturing, such as accounting and sales, an approach known as **enterprise resource planning (ERP)**.

Supply-Chain Management

Whereas MRP II and ERP seek to incorporate more functions with the business, **supply-chain management (SCM)**, focuses on the movement and coordination of goods, services, information, and capabilities all the way through the supply chain, from raw materials to finished products delivered to the final consumer.[43] SCM combines business procedures and policies with a comprehensive software solution that integrates the various elements of the supply chain into a cohesive system, even if the supply chain involves a wide variety of outside suppliers and distribution partners. (ERP and SCM are similar in many respects, and the terminology in the industry can be rather confusing; for instance, vendors of ERP software are adding modules that handle SCM tasks.[44])

Although SCM sounds like basic inventory control on the surface, it has the potential to have a much more profound strategic impact on companies, in three important ways:[45]

- **Manage risks.** SCM can help companies manage the complex risks involved in a supply chain, risks that include everything from cost and availability to health and safety issues.

- **Manage relationships.** It can also coordinate the numerous relationships in the supply chain and help managers focus their attention on the most important company-to-company relationships. For instance, General Motors buys massive quantities of both steel and aluminum, but the nature of the two markets puts a higher priority on GM's relationship with its aluminum supplier, Alcan. GM uses SCM to forge a close relationship with Alcan, including stabilizing prices in ways that help both companies.

- **Manage trade-offs.** Finally, SCM helps managers address the many trade-offs in the supply chain. These trade-offs can be a source of conflict within the company, and SCM helps balance the competing interests of the various functional areas. This holistic view helps managers balance both capacity and capability along the entire chain. For instance, to deliver a complex, multiple-computer system to a customer,

manufacturing resource planning (MRP II)
Computer-based system that integrates data from all departments to manage inventory and production planning and control

enterprise resource planning (ERP)
A comprehensive database system that expands beyond the production function to include other groups such as sales and accounting

supply-chain management (SCM)
An approach to coordinating and optimizing the flow of goods, services, information, and capabilities throughout the entire supply chain, including outside business partners

Sun Microsystems used to consolidate all the components at a staging facility, then repackage the entire system and have it shipped to the customer. After analyzing the time and cost involved, the company realized it made more sense to have Federal Express take care of the consolidation, in addition to the shipping.[46]

Successful applications of SCM can yield increased sales, cost savings, inventory reductions, improved quality, accelerated delivery time, and improved customer service.[47] In fact, the potential of SCM is so great that businesses now spend roughly $20 billion a year on SCM software and related technology. Unfortunately, nearly half the companies in one recent survey said they were disappointed in their SCM efforts. Some experts pin the blame on the approach people take to SCM, not on the concept itself. To ensure success, managers need to view SCM at a strategic level, look at trade-offs across the entire supply chain, and make sure that the various groups in the chain have the training and tools required to cooperate effectively.[48]

Assuring Product Quality

Besides maintaining optimal inventory levels, companies today must produce high-quality goods and services as efficiently as possible. In almost every industry you can name, this global challenge has caused companies to re-examine their definition of quality and re-engineer their production processes. Just as Harley-Davidson was able to re-establish itself as the worldwide leader, many other U.S. companies are following in Harley's footsteps by setting new standards for quality. In some industries, quality is literally a matter of life and death. Nearly 100,000 deaths in the United States every year are attributed to medical errors; in Canada, a quarter of all patients who seek medical care wind up getting another illness as a result of medical mistakes.[49]

Maintaining high quality standards is not an easy task because the production of complex goods and services is not simply a matter of adding part A to part B to part C and so forth until a product emerges ready to ship. For example, the Mercedes M-Class sport-utility vehicle is assembled from subunits built by 65 major suppliers and many other smaller ones.[50] Making sure that all the pieces are put together in the proper sequence and at the proper time requires large-scale planning and scheduling. The same is true for the production of complex services.

quality control
Routine checking and testing of a finished product for quality against an established standard

quality assurance
System of policies, practices, and procedures implemented throughout the company to create and produce quality goods and services

The traditional means of maintaining quality is called **quality control**—measuring quality against established standards after the good or service has been produced and weeding out any defects. A more comprehensive approach is **quality assurance**, a system of companywide policies, practices, and procedures to ensure that every product meets preset quality standards. Quality assurance includes quality control as well as doing the job right the first time by designing tools and machinery properly, demanding quality parts from suppliers, encouraging customer feedback, training employees, empowering them, and encouraging them to take pride in their work. As discussed in Chapter 6, total quality management takes things to an even a higher level by building quality into every activity within an organization.

Companies approach quality assurance in various ways. As a builder of sheet-metal components and electromechanical assemblies, Trident Precision Manufacturing empowers workers to make decisions on the shop floor, and it spends 4.7 percent of payroll on employee training.[51] High-end computer maker Sequent Computer Systems has a "customer process engineering manager" whose primary responsibility is to continually communicate with customers and identify any recurring problems. These companies know that eliminating only one inefficiency, such as a defect or an excessively complex process, can reduce total product costs because less money is spent on inspection, complaints, and product service.[52]

Statistical Quality Control and Continuous Improvement

Quality assurance also includes the now widely used concept of **statistical quality control (SQC)**, in which all aspects of the production process are monitored so that managers can see whether the process is operating as it should. The primary tool of SQC is **statistical process control (SPC)**, which involves taking samples from the process periodically and plotting observations of the samples on a *control chart*. A large enough sample provides a reasonable estimate of the entire process. By observing the random fluctuations graphed on the chart, managers and workers can identify whether such changes are normal or whether they indicate that some corrective action is required in the process. In this way, SPC can prevent poor quality.[53]

Statistical quality control is not limited to goods-producing industries. For example, financial services provider GE Capital uses statistical control methods to make sure the bills it sends to customers are correct. The company's use of SQC lowers the cost of making adjustments while improving customer satisfaction.[54]

In addition to using SQC, companies can empower each employee to continuously improve the quality of goods production or service delivery. The Japanese word for continuous improvement is *kaizen*. Japanese manufacturers learned long before many U.S. manufacturers that continuous improvement is not something that can be delegated to one or a few people. Instead, it requires the full participation of every employee. This means encouraging all workers to spot quality problems, halt production when necessary, generate ideas for improvement, and adjust work routines as needed.[55]

Global Quality Standards

Companies that choose to do business in Europe may have to leap an extra quality hurdle. Many manufacturers and service providers in Europe require that suppliers comply with standards set by the International Organization for Standardization (ISO), a non-government entity based in Geneva, Switzerland. Recently revised into a family of quality-management-system standards and guidelines known collectively as **ISO 9000**, such standards are voluntary by definition. Companies may choose to comply with these standards and, if met, promote their certification to gain recognition for their quality achievements.

In the past, ISO 9000 standards applied mostly to products that have health and safety-related features. However, the newer ISO 9001 and ISO 9004 standards maintain a greater focus on customer satisfaction, user needs, and continuous improvement.[56] The standards are recognized in over 100 countries, and about one-fourth of the world's corporations insist that all their suppliers be ISO certified.[57]

ISO standards help companies become *world-class manufacturers*, a term used to describe the level of quality and operational effectiveness that puts a company among the top performers in the world. Some companies view ISO standards as a starting point to achieving other national quality awards such as Japan's Deming Prize, a highly regarded industrial quality award, or the U.S. Malcolm Baldrige National Quality Award, which honors the quality achievements of U.S. companies (see Exhibit 8.7). Of course, even if an organization doesn't want to actually apply for an award, it can improve quality by measuring its performance against an award's standards and working to overcome any problems uncovered by this process.

It takes more than a quality mix to produce perfect Krispy Kreme doughnuts all the time. To ensure consistent quality, Krispy Kreme supplies its stores with everything they need to produce premium doughnuts—including the production machinery and equipment.

statistical quality control (SQC)
Monitoring all aspects of the production process to see whether the process is operating as it should

statistical process control (SPC)
Use of random sampling and control charts to monitor the production process

ISO 9000
A collection of global standards set by the International Organization for Standardization establishing a minimum level of acceptable quality

Criteria for the Malcolm Baldrige National Quality Award

The Malcolm Baldrige National Quality Award is given annually to companies that demonstrate an outstanding commitment to quality. Named after former Secretary of Commerce Malcolm Baldrige, the awards are given to companies in each of four categories: manufacturing, services, small businesses, and universities and hospitals. This chart lists the criteria on which companies are judged for the award.

✓ **Leadership.** Have senior leaders clearly defined the company's values, goals, and ways to achieve the goals? Is the company a model "corporate citizen"?

✓ **Information and analysis.** Does the company effectively use data and information to support customer-driven performance excellence and marketplace success?

✓ **Strategic planning.** How does the company develop strategies and business plans to strengthen its performance and competitive position?

✓ **Human resources development and management.** How does the company develop the full potential of its workforce? How are its human resource capabilities and work systems aligned with its strategic and business plans?

✓ **Process management.** How does the company design, manage, and improve key processes, such as customer-focused design and product and service delivery?

✓ **Business results.** How does the company address performance and improvement in key business areas—product and service quality, productivity and operational effectiveness, supply quality, and financial performance indicators linked to these areas?

✓ **Customer focus and satisfaction.** How does the company determine requirements, expectations, and preferences of customers? What are its customer satisfaction results?

Summary of Learning Objectives

1 Explain what production and operations managers do.

Production and operations managers design and oversee an efficient conversion process—the sequence of events that convert resources into goods and services. To do this, they must coordinate a firm's resources and optimize output from each resource. Additionally, production and operations managers perform the four basic functions of planning, organizing, leading, and controlling, but the focus of these activities is the production of a company's goods and services.

2 Identify key tasks involved in designing a production process.

Managers must first prepare production forecasts, or estimates of future demand for the company's products. Next they must consider capacity, which is a business's volume of manufacturing or service delivery. The next step is to find a facility location that minimizes regional costs (land, construction, labor, local taxes, leasing, energy), transportation costs, and raw materials costs. Once a location has been selected, managers need to consider facility layout—the arrangement of production work centers and other facilities (such as material, equipment, and support departments) needed for the processing of goods and ser-

vices. Finally, managers must develop a master production schedule.

3 Discuss the role of computers and automation technology in production.

Computers and automation technology improve the production process in several ways: (1) Robots perform repetitive or mundane tasks quickly and with great precision; (2) CAD and CAE systems allow engineers to design and test virtual models of products; (3) CAM systems easily translate CAD data into production instructions; (4) CIM systems link the people, machines, databases, and decisions involved in each step of producing a good; and (5) flexible manufacturing systems (FMSs) reduce setup costs and time by linking programmable, multifunctional machine tools through a computer network and an automated materials-handling system.

4 Explain the strategic importance of managing inventory.

The goods and materials kept in stock for production or sale make up inventory, which must be managed to minimize costs and ensure that the right supplies are in the right place at the right time. Having too much inventory is costly and increases the risk that products will become obsolete. Having too little inventory can result in production delays and unfilled orders.

5 Distinguish among JIT, MRP, and MRP II inventory management systems.

Just-in-time (JIT) systems reduce waste and improve quality by producing only enough to fill orders when they are due, thus eliminating finished-goods inventory. Furthermore, under the JIT system, parts or materials are ordered only when they are needed, thus eliminating supplies inventories. Material requirements planning (MRP) and perpetual inventory systems are used to determine when materials are needed, when they should be ordered, and when they should be delivered. A more advanced system is manufacturing resource planning (MRP II), which brings together data from all parts of a company (including financial, design, and engineering departments) to better manage inventory and production planning and control.

6 Highlight the differences between quality control and quality assurance.

Quality control focuses on measuring finished products against a preset standard and weeding out any defects. On the other hand, quality assurance is a system of company-wide policies, practices, and procedures that build quality into a product and ensure that each product meets quality standards.

7 Describe the supply chain and explain how companies today are managing their supply chains.

The supply chain consists of all companies involved in making a finished product. The members of the chain vary according to the nature of the operation and the type of product but typically include suppliers, manufacturers, distributors, and retail outlets. Today, more and more companies are working closely with their supply chains to be more responsive to the changing needs of their customers. To do this, companies are reducing the number of firms in their supply chain, developing long-term relationships with remaining members, and sharing information with them. Some companies are even involving members of their supply chain in the design and production processes.

Behind **the Scenes**

Harley-Davidson Revs Its Engines Toward Higher Output and Productivity

During the 1970s, when attractive new imports were roaring into the U.S. motorcycle market, Harley-Davidson suffered a serious quality crisis. It took the company almost two decades to figure out how to maintain high quality standards while boosting output. But incorporating continuous improvement methods into the company's manufacturing processes eventually paid off. By the mid-1990s, Harley had won back market share and was selling $2 billion in motorcycles, parts, and accessories to loyal fans all over the world. Still, CEO Jeff Bleustein was anything but complacent. Eyeing the projected increase in domestic demand and the huge sales potential of markets outside North America, he was determined to overhaul the production process for higher output and productivity.

One key target was the company's inefficient supply chain. Nearly 1,000 suppliers provided Harley with raw materials, parts, and components. The head of purchasing soon narrowed the supplier list to just 425 and streamlined purchasing through a web-based supply system. These steps strengthened supplier commitment and helped purchasing get more mileage out of the company's $1 billion yearly supply budget. The company also centralized purchasing and inventory into a single supply management department and in doing so improved Harley's buying power. Next, all purchasing agents were required to complete a training course in structured materials planning and buying, capped by testing and formal certification.

The distribution warehouse was another key target. Crowded, old, and inefficient, the warehouse was simply inadequate. After some analysis, the company decided to build a gigantic new distribution center in a Milwaukee suburb with state-of-the-art technology to track and control the inbound and outbound movement of items. This new distribution center doubled productivity and sliced fulfillment time for orders from 12 days to 2.

In the race to boost output and productivity, Harley invested $650 million in new production facilities and manufacturing equipment. One new plant, equipped with a sophisticated materials management system, could produce motorcycles 30 percent more efficiently than the older plant. Advanced technology was integrated throughout the production process, including a computer-aided design (CAD) system accessible to employees in many departments. Harley also allowed selected suppliers to access the CAD system so they could collaborate on product development.

Although Bleustein was investing heavily to expand capacity and update facilities and systems, the improvements were expected to shave $40 million from overall production and inventory costs. Output and productivity soared, as did sales around the world. Harley was soon selling 243,000 bikes a year and had surpassed its production goal. What proved to be disastrous economic times for hundreds of companies didn't faze Harley. At a time when automakers were whacking at their profit margins, Harley sold every bike it made, and dealers often charged $2,000 to $4,000 *above* the sticker price.

Despite its success, Harley is headed for a nasty spill if it doesn't navigate its generational speed bump. The median age of a Harley buyer is 46, and the company has failed to attract younger riders who prefer the speedy, more technically advanced machines from Honda, Yamaha, and BMW. To attract younger buyers Bleustein is pushing his company into places it has never gone, with products such as the V-Rod, its first small, inexpensive bike in more than 20 years. And the company is revving up demand by teaching young people—especially women—how to ride a motorcycle through an instructional program called Rider's Edge.

While bikers continue to gawk at their Harleys, Bleustein is going hog wild to make sure the company lasts another century. "We don't need new customers today, we don't need them tomorrow. But we may 10 years from now," says Bleustein. So he constantly warns employees against his twin fears, complacency and arrogance: "We have to pretend 10 fiery demons are chasing us all the time," says Bleustein—a mighty task, even for a company that caters to Hells Angels.[58]

Critical Thinking Questions

1. Why would Harley allow employees in the purchasing department as well as selected suppliers access to information in the CAD system used for new product design and development?
2. How do you think reducing the time needed to fulfill parts orders would affect Harley's inventory costs?
3. What new challenges does Harley-Davidson face?

LEARN MORE ONLINE

Visit the Harley-Davidson website by clicking on the hotlink at Chapter 8 of this text's website at www.prenhall.com/bovee. Locate the section with company and investor information, and read the company's latest annual report. Then look at the current and historical production and sales statistics posted on the site. How many motorcycles did Harley produce in the most recent quarter? In the most recent year? What is the output trend? Now review the demographic profile of a Harley-Davidson customer. How is the typical Harley-Davidson customer changing? ■

Key Terms

analytic system (193)
capacity planning (199)
cellular layout (200)
computer-aided design (CAD) (204)
computer-aided engineering (CAE) (204)
computer-aided manufacturing (CAM) (205)
computer-integrated manufacturing (CIM) (205)
critical path (203)
customized production (195)
dispatching (203)
electronic data interchange (EDI) (206)
enterprise resource planning (ERP) (209)
fixed-position layout (202)
flexible manufacturing system (FMS) (206)

Gantt chart (203)
inventory (207)
inventory control (207)
ISO 9000 (211)
just-in-time (JIT) system (207)
lead time (207)
manufacturing resource planning (MRP II) (209)
mass customization (195)
mass production (195)
material requirements planning (MRP) (208)
perpetual inventory (208)
process layout (200)
product layout (200)
production (193)
production and operations management (POM) (193)
production forecasts (198)

program evaluation and review technique (PERT) (203)
purchasing (207)
quality assurance (210)
quality control (210)
robots (204)
routing (202)
scheduling (202)
setup costs (206)
statistical process control (SPC) (211)
statistical quality control (SQC) (211)
supply chain (198)
supply-chain management (SCM) (209)
synthetic system (193)
value chain (193)
XML (206)

Test Your Knowledge

Questions for Review

1. What is the conversion process?
2. What is mass customization?
3. What factors need to be considered when selecting a site for a production facility?
4. Why is an effective system of inventory control important to every manufacturer?
5. Why might a company want to outsource its manufacturing function?

Questions for Analysis

6. Why is capacity planning an important part of designing operations?
7. How do JIT systems go beyond simply controlling inventory?
8. Why have companies moved beyond quality control to quality assurance?
9. How can supply chain management (SCM) help a company establish a competitive advantage?
10. **Ethical Considerations.** How does society's concern for the environment affect a company's decisions about facility location and layout?

Questions for Application

11. Assume you are the production manager for a small machine shop that manufactures precision parts for industrial equipment. How can you use CAD, CAE, CAM, CIM, FMS, and EDI or XML to manufacture better parts more easily?
12. If your final product requires several unique subunits that are all produced with different machinery and in differing lengths of time, what facility layout will you choose and why?
13. **Integrated.** Review the discussion of franchises in Chapter 5. From an operational perspective, why is purchasing a franchise such as Wendy's or Jiffy Lube an attractive alternative for starting a business?
14. **Integrated.** Review the discussion of corporate cultures in Chapter 6. What things could you learn about a company's culture by observing the layout and design of its production facility? Discuss both goods and services operations.

Practice Your Knowledge

Sharpening Your Communication Skills

As the newly hired manager of Campus Athletics—a shop featuring athletic wear bearing logos of colleges and universities—you are responsible for selecting the store's suppliers. Merchandise with team logos and brands can be very trendy. When a college team is hot, you've got to have merchandise. You know that selecting the right supplier is a task that requires careful consideration, so you have decided to host a series of selection interviews. Think about all the qualities you would want in a supplier, and develop a list of interview questions that will help you assess whether that supplier possesses those qualities.

Building Your Team Skills

Facility layout is one of the most critical decisions production managers must make. In this exercise, you and your team are playing the role of production managers for the following companies, some producing a specific good and some producing a specific service:

- Mountain Dew—soft drinks
- H&R Block—tax consultation
- Bob Mackie—custom-made clothing
- Burger King—fast food
- Boeing—commercial jets
- Massachusetts General Hospital—medical services
- Hewlett-Packard—personal computers
- Toyota—sport-utility vehicles

For each company on the list, discuss and recommend a specific facility layout, referring to Exhibit 8.3 for an overview of the four layouts. Why does your team believe the recommended layout is best suited to the product or service each company produces? How would the recommended layouts affect the movement of resources and inventory for the manufacturers on the list? How would the layouts affect customer interaction for the service providers on the list?

Expand Your Knowledge

Discovering Career Opportunities

Whether you prefer to work with products or services, many possible careers await you in production and operations. From input to transformation to output, companies are looking for resourceful, results-oriented employees able to meet the demands of ever-changing schedules and specifications. Start your research by scanning the help-wanted classified and display ads in your local newspaper and in the *Wall Street Journal*; also check help-wanted ads in business magazines such as *Industry Week*. Go online and search the production and manufacturing jobs listed in America's Job Bank, www.ajb.org, or Monster, www.monster.com.

1. As you read through these want ads, note all the production-related job titles you find. How many of these jobs include quality or technology (or both) among the duties and responsibilities?

2. Select two job openings that interest you. Reread the ads for those jobs to find out what kind of work experience and educational background are required. What further preparation will you need to qualify for these jobs?

3. Assume you have the qualifications for the two jobs you have selected. What keywords should you include on your electronic résumé to show the employers that you are a good job candidate?

Developing Your Research Skills

Seeking increased efficiency and productivity, a growing number of producers of goods and services are applying technology to improve the production process. Find an article in business journals or newspapers (print or online edition) that discusses how one company used CAD, CAE, robots, XML, or other technological innovations to refit or reorganize its production operations.

1. What problems led the company to rethink its production process? What kind of technology did it choose to address these problems? What goals did the company set for applying technology in this way?

2. Before adding the new technology, what did the company do to analyze its existing production process? What changes, if any, were made as a result of this analysis?

3. How did technology-enhanced production help the company achieve its goals for financial performance? For customer service? For growth or expansion?

SEE IT ON THE WEB

For live links to the websites that follow, go to this text's website at www.prenhall.com/bovee. When you log on, select Chapter 8, then select "Featured Websites," click on the URL of the website you wish to visit, review the website, and answer the following questions:

1. What is the purpose of this website?

2. What kinds of information does this website contain? Please be specific.

3. How is this information provided at this website useful for businesspeople? Consumers?

4. How did you expand your knowledge of operations management by reviewing the material at this website? What new things did you learn about this topic?

Step Inside ISO Online

The International Organization for Standardization (ISO) is a worldwide federation of national standards bodies from some 130 countries, one from each country. Established in 1947, ISO is a nongovernmental organization with the following mission: to promote the development of standardization and related activities in the world with a view to facilitating the international exchange of goods and services and to developing cooperation in the spheres of intellectual, scientific, technological, and economic activity. Step inside ISO Online and take a closer look at how ISO standards are developed, why international standardization is needed, and what fields are covered by ISO standards. www.iso.ch

Make Quality Count

In today's competitive business environment, companies have to be concerned about the quality of their goods and services. For information and advice, many turn to the American Society for Quality (ASQ). There you can find out about ISO 9000 and the Malcolm Baldrige Award. Find out who Malcolm Baldrige was and why the award was established. Discover how winning companies are selected, which companies have won the award, and how the award differs from ISO 9000. Follow the links to other quality-related websites. At the ASQ, quality is only a click away. www.asq.org

Follow This Path to Continuous Improvement

The business of manufacturing is more complex than ever before. Today's operations managers must address the conflicting needs of customers, suppliers, employees, and shareholders. Discover why many operations managers turn to *Industry Week* magazine to stay on top of trends, technologies, and strategies to help drive continuous improvement throughout their organization. Log on to this magazine's website and read about the world's best-managed companies. Find out which manufacturing plants have won awards. Check out the surveys and special industry reports. Take a peek at the factories of the future. Don't leave without browsing the current articles or reviewing the glossary of manufacturing terms. www.industryweek.com

Companion Website

Learning Interactively

Go to the Companion Website at www.prenhall.com/bovee. For Chapter 8, take advantage of the interactive "Study Guide" to test your knowledge of the chapter. Get instant feedback on whether you need additional studying.

Also, visit this site's "Study Hall," where you'll find an abundance of valuable resources that will help you succeed in this course.

Video Case

Managing Production Around the World: Body Glove

LEARNING OBJECTIVES

The purpose of this video is to help you:

1. Recognize the production challenges faced by a growing company.
2. Understand the importance of quality in the production process.
3. Discuss how and why a company may shift production operations to other countries and other companies.

SYNOPSIS

Riding the wave of public interest in water sports, Body Glove began manufacturing wet suits in the 1950s. The founders, dedicated surfers and divers, came up with the idea of making the wet suits from neoprene, offering more comfortable insulation than the rubber wet suits of the time. The high costs of neoprene and labor were major considerations in Body Glove's eventual decision to have its wet suits made in Thailand. The company's constant drive for higher quality was also a factor. Now company management can focus on building Body Glove's image as a California-lifestyle brand without worrying about inventory and other production issues. In licensing its brand for a wide range of goods and services—from cell phone cases to flotation devices, footwear, resorts, and more—Body Glove has created a network of partners around the world.

Discussion Questions

1. *For analysis:* Even though Body Glove makes its wet suits in Thailand, why must its managers continually research how U.S. customers use its products?
2. *For analysis:* Which aspects of product quality would wet suit buyers be most concerned about?
3. *For application:* When deciding whether to license its name for a new product, what production issues might Body Glove's managers research in advance?
4. *For application:* How might Body Glove's Thailand facility use forecasts of seasonal demand to plan production?
5. *For debate:* Should the products that Body Glove does not manufacture be labeled to alert buyers that they are produced under license? Support your chosen position.

ONLINE EXPLORATION

Visit the Body Glove website www.bodyglove.com and follow the links to read the Body Glove story and see the variety of products sold under the Body Glove brand. Also look at the electronics products, including the cell phone cases. Then browse the contacts listing to find out which U.S. and international companies have licensed the Body Glove brand for various products. How do these licensed products fit with the Body Glove brand image? What challenges might Body Glove face in coordinating its work with so many different companies and licensed products?

E-Business in Action

WHATEVER HAPPENED TO B2B EXCHANGES?

Of all the innovative ideas that bubbled up in the heady days of the dot-com boom, online business-to-business (B2B) exchanges seemed like one of the few that actually made economic sense. The idea behind these exchanges was to bring buyers and sellers together in huge online trading hubs where purchasing, selling, and other supply-chain transactions for the entire industry could take place under one virtual roof—it would all be fast, efficient, and good for just about anybody. This wasn't some crazy dot-com scheme, like giving people free computers in return for watching online advertising. This sounded like a real business opportunity, complete with paying customers.

It sounded so good, in fact, that some 37,000 B2B exchanges opened for business by the end of 2000, serving just about every industry imaginable. Some were run by independent third parties; others were set up by industry players who joined forces to form new ventures. The two most common types of B2B exchanges are *buyer exchanges* and *supplier exchanges*. Buyer exchanges are marketplaces formed by large groups of buyers (even competitors) who purchase similar items. By joining forces and aggregating demand for a product, they can achieve economies of scale that are not possible individually. Supplier exchanges are formed by suppliers who band together to create marketplaces to sell their goods online. These groups of suppliers typically sell complementary products, offering buyers one-stop shopping for most of their needs.

Another Dot-Com Dream Up in Smoke

B2B exchanges promised to save members billions of dollars annually in reduced supply-chain costs and to transform overnight the way companies bought and sold. Unfortunately, nearly all of them went out of business—95 percent of them by one estimate—and only a few of the survivors have serious backing from major global corporations. Among the casualties: small exchanges such as Foodusa.com, which tried to link slaughterhouses, distributors, and brokers of beef and poultry, and big exchanges such as PetroCosm, an online buying site formed by Chevron and Texaco for the petroleum industry, and Zoho.com, a B2B marketplace formed by Starwood Hotels for the hotel industry. These start-ups learned that the path to B2B prosperity was full of unanticipated roadblocks:

- *Member rivalry.* For large, public B2B exchanges to work effectively, competitors must be willing to expose business processes—processes that often give them a competitive advantage. Some companies were concerned that participation in public exchanges would put sales information and other critical data in the hands of customers and competitors. For instance, using a public exchange to purchase goods could tip a company's hand to competitors who were monitoring buying patterns, giving them valuable competitive information.

- *Supplier resistance.* It was easy to see how buyers would benefit by joining forces, but suppliers worried that online marketplaces, auctionlike pricing, and easy access to cheaper goods would drive down the prices of their goods. Many refused to join.

- *Customer resistance.* Many companies were unwilling to dump the network of suppliers they'd built up over the years and make all their purchases through a new, unfamiliar exchange. Larger companies such as Dell, Intel, and Wal-Mart, for example, already get the best prices possible from suppliers and have no plans to join the public marketplaces that operate in their industry. Moreover, many manufacturers have long-term buying contracts and didn't see how the exchanges would get them lower prices or offer additional benefits. As a result, the anticipated droves of customers never showed up.

- *Incompatible systems.* One of the biggest challenges facing B2B exchanges was the need to seamlessly blend the operating systems used by exchange members. This included dozens of software packages, accounting systems, data management systems, and manufacturing schedules. Different customs, languages, and laws from country to country further complicated the endeavors. For the truly giant endeavors, such as Covisint.com, set up by the major U.S. automakers, this proved an insurmountable hurdle. As one participant put it, "Relationship behavior is more important than people thought."

To Be or Not To Be?

Despite these roadblocks, a few public B2B exchanges are making progress, such as exchanges for health-care supplies (Broadlane.com), steel and metals (e-Steel.com), chemicals (ChemConnect.com), and shipping (LevelSeas.com).

The real news, however, might be in a new generation of B2B exchanges based on the concept of "one-to-many." Instead of having many buyers and many sellers in the exchange, this new format connects a single buyer with multiple sellers. For instance, IBM Canada has a private B2B exchange with a number of travel-related suppliers, including American Express, Air Canada, Hertz, and Delta

Hotels. Because the suppliers don't compete with one another, and there's only one buyer to coordinate technology with, the system works quite well.

Are the mighty public B2B exchanges a thing of the past, though? Some observers believe the economic benefits are still there, if only people would cooperate. Until that glorious day arrives, private exchanges such as IBM Canada's and smaller public exchanges in niche markets will keep the dream alive.

Questions for Critical Thinking

1. Why would a buyer want to participate in a B2B exchange?

2. Would sellers ever have any incentive to participate? Explain your answer.

3. Why does a private B2B exchange such as IBM Canada's work?

BUSINESS PlanPro Exercises

Managing a Business

Review Appendix D, Your Business Plan (on pages 416–417), to learn how to use Business PlanPro Software so you can complete these exercises.

THINK LIKE A PRO

Objective: By completing these exercises you will become acquainted with the sections of a business plan that address a company's mission, goals and objectives, and management team. You will use the sample business plan for JavaNet (listed as Internet Cafe in the Sample Plan Browser) in this exercise.

1. Evaluate JavaNet's mission statement. Does it summarize why the organization exists, what it seeks to accomplish, and the principles that the company will adhere to as it tries to reach its goals? How might you improve this mission statement?

2. Evaluate JavaNet's objectives. Are they clearly stated? Are they measurable? Do they seem realistic? Which objectives might need some refining?

3. Assess the risks facing JavaNet. How do you expect these threats to affect the company's ability to compete?

4. Read about the company's management structure and personnel plan. What challenges might JavaNet face as a result of its chosen structure and personnel plan?

CREATE YOUR OWN BUSINESS PLAN

Return to the plan you are creating for your own business. List your company's goals and objectives, and be sure they are clearly stated and measurable. How will you reach these goals and objectives? What might prevent you from achieving them? What information should you include about your management team? Should you mention the team's weaknesses in addition to its strengths? Why?

Part 4

Managing Employees

Chapter 9

Motivating Today's Workforce and Handling Employee-Management Relations

LEARNING OBJECTIVES

After studying this chapter, you will be able to

1 Compare Maslow's hierarchy of needs and Herzberg's two-factor theory, then explain their application to employee motivation

2 Explain why expectancy theory is considered by some to be the best description of employee behavior

3 Discuss three staffing challenges employers are facing in today's workplace

4 Explain the challenges and advantages of a diverse workforce

5 Discuss three popular alternative work arrangements companies are offering their employees

6 Cite three options unions can exercise when negotiations with management break down

7 Cite three options management can exercise when negotiations with a union break down

Behind **the Scenes**

Learning the Art of Motivation at Atlas Container

www.atlascontainer.com

In some businesses, motivation almost seems to be a natural part of the job. Investment bankers and venture capitalists thrive on the thrill of the deal. Management consultants fly to fashionable cities around the world, deliver inspirational talks to rapt audiences, and get interviewed by popular business magazines. Senior executives in many industries make million- or billion-dollar decisions and enjoy the perks that come with power. Scientists and engineers pursue the joy of discovery and the satisfaction of designing products that improve the lives of millions of people.

But what if your job was all about cardboard? What if you came to work every day facing the prospect of converting giant rolls of corrugated paper into cardboard boxes? Hundreds, thousands, millions of boxes—one box after another, day after day after day? It's difficult, noisy, sweaty work in an industry that rarely makes headlines and never involves glamorous business trips. Plus, it's in a no-growth business populated mostly by small companies offering few of the opportunities and benefits that major corporations can use to motivate their employees. Other than the need to earn a paycheck, how could you possibly get excited about a job like this?

Now imagine that you're a manager in such a firm, and it's *your* responsibility to motivate people who come

Atlas Container shook up an old-school industry by applying enlightened motivational strategies that gave employees a real stake in the success of the company.

to work every day to make cardboard boxes. Such was the challenge facing brothers Peter and Paul Centenari when they purchased Atlas Container, a small producer of cardboard packaging based in Severn, Maryland. When they bought the company, these well-connected, Harvard Business School graduates were investment bankers, not industrialists, and their goal was to buy a small company, apply their financial smarts to grow it into a slightly larger company, then resell it at a tidy profit. "Seven years and out," that was the plan according to Paul, who serves as the company's CEO.

A funny thing happened on the way to the auction block, however. For starters, the brothers stumbled badly, mismanaging a profitable business into a financial mess. Then somehow during the painful process of learning how to run the business and return it to fiscal health, they got excited about the box business and decided to keep the company rather than sell it. But these brothers weren't going to run just any old company; they wanted to redefine what it meant to be an employee and what it meant to be a manager. They wanted people to be excited about making cardboard boxes. If you were Paul Centenari, how would you motivate employees in this gritty, nonglamorous business? How would you encourage them to exceed beyond even their own expectations?[1] ∎

UNDERSTANDING HUMAN RELATIONS

Peter and Paul Centenari know that employees who maintain high **morale** or a positive attitude toward both their job and organization perform better.[2] But they also know that cultivating high morale is an ongoing challenge, in good times and bad. Morale is particularly challenging when the economy is depressed or a specific industry is in upheaval. Declining stock values, plummeting sales, and workforce cutbacks can result

morale
Attitude an individual has toward his or her job and employer

human relations
Interaction among people within an organization for the purpose of achieving organizational and personal goals

in employee turnover, unscheduled absenteeism, and waning morale—all of which can negatively affect a company's productivity and bottom line.[3]

In organizations, the goal of **human relations**—interactions among people within the organization—is to balance the diverse needs of employees with those of management and other stakeholders in the organization. For instance, to maintain productivity and customer satisfaction, employers must ensure that employees stay motivated and satisfied. But they must also remain competitive in the marketplace to ensure the organization's long-term success. Of course, achieving this balance becomes increasingly difficult as companies face many staffing and demographic challenges, as you'll see in this chapter. Chapter 10 then takes a closer look at what human resources managers do, explaining the details of the hiring process, employee compensation, and specific employee benefits. As you'll also see in both chapters, management approaches to all of these challenges have evolved over time, and even today, various companies and managers sometimes take different approaches to these challenges; there is rarely one right answer that fits every situation.

MOTIVATING EMPLOYEES

Both common sense and formal research suggest that motivated employees are a key to success in every business. You've probably experienced this as a consumer yourself. For instance, when an employee in a retail store seems motivated to make sure you're a satisfied customer, you're likely to keep returning to that store—and to encourage friends and family to shop there as well. Conversely, when employees just don't seem to care, the effect on customers can be just as dramatic in the negative direction, leading to the decline or even collapse of the business.

In fact, making sure that employees are motivated is one of the most important challenges facing every manager. It's also one of the most complex; human beings are complicated creatures to begin with, and today's demanding business environment makes the challenge that much greater. You can start to appreciate the challenge by first exploring what motivation is, then by considering some of the many theories proposed over the years to explain motivation in the workplace.

What Is Motivation?

motivation
Force that moves someone to take action

Motivation is the combination of forces that moves individuals to take certain actions and avoid others in pursuit of individual objectives. The notion of movement is vital here; motivational strategies have little value if they don't translate into action that helps the business enterprise. As you'll see in the following section, a diverse range of theories has attempted to explain motivation. However, every theory or motivational approach needs to consider three key steps:

1. **Need.** The employee senses a need of some sort, from the basic need to earn enough money to buy food to a need for recognition or self-respect. We are all born with certain needs but can acquire other needs as we grow up, such as a need for achievement, a need for power, or a need to affiliate with compatible friends and colleagues.[4]

2. **Action.** To fulfill the need, the employee engages in actions or behaviors that he or she believes will result in the need being satisfied.

3. **Outcome.** The employee observes the outcome of the action (sometimes called the *reward*) and determines whether the effort was worthwhile. Actions that result in positive outcomes are likely to be repeated; those that result in negative outcomes are less likely to be repeated.

These three steps are an extremely simplified look at the complex issue of motivation, but even from this simple model you can start to grasp the challenges involved. For instance, what if two or more needs conflict, leading to incompatible actions? It's hard to balance the need to relax and have fun with the need to generate enough money to pay the rent. Or what if an employee's need for recognition motivates him or her to work hard in the hopes of getting a promotion, but thanks to a tough economy, the company isn't growing and can't offer the promotion? Or what if top management doesn't notice the hard work—or worse yet, credits it to someone else? Think about these three steps the next time you encounter an employee in action. Maybe that customer service representative who wouldn't take the time to help you actually started the job full of desire to help people but soon learned that management rewarded productivity more than customer satisfaction.

Before moving into specific theories, it's important to consider the role of money as a motivator, since it's a central issue for most employees. Money obviously plays a critical role in most everyone's work life, but it is not the ultimate motivator for many people because money often can't compensate for the lack of other satisfying factors. In other words, it's important but not enough to truly motivate people toward peak performance. Today, employees also expect to be treated fairly and want the opportunity to pursue satisfying work. They want to balance their careers and their family lives. "There's an increasing interest in people finding meaning in their lives and in their work," notes Don Kuhn, the executive director of the International University Consortium for Executive Education. "People are no longer content with income alone. They are looking for personal satisfaction."[5] They want to be part of something they can believe in, something that confers meaning on their work and on their lives. They want to be motivated.[6]

Satisfied, motivated employees tend to be more productive and more effective, leading to higher rates of customer satisfaction and repeat business.

Theories of Motivation

Motivation has been a topic of interest to managers and researchers for more than a hundred years. A number of theories have evolved over the years, some that describe *what* motivates people and others that describe *how* they go about fulfilling their needs. No single theory offers a complete and proven picture of the motivation puzzle, but each can offer some perspective.

One of the earliest motivational researchers, Frederick W. Taylor, a machinist and engineer from Philadelphia, studied employee efficiency and motivation late in the 19th century. He is credited with developing **scientific management**, an approach that sought to improve employee efficiency through the scientific study of work. In Taylor's view, people were motivated almost exclusively by money, so he set up pay systems that rewarded employees when they were productive. Under Taylor's piecework system, for example, employees who just met or fell short of the quota were paid a certain amount for each unit produced. Those who produced more were paid a higher rate for *all* units produced, not just for those that exceeded the quota; this pay system gave employees a strong incentive to boost productivity.

Although money has always been a powerful motivator, scientific management fails to take into account other motivational elements, such as opportunities for personal satisfaction or individual initiative. Thus, scientific management can't explain why someone still wants to work even though that person's spouse already makes a good living or why a successful executive will take a hefty pay cut to serve in government. Therefore, other researchers have looked beyond money to discover what else motivates people. The most widely recognized theories include Maslow's hierarchy of needs, Herzberg's two-factor theory, Theory X and Theory Y, Theory Z, equity theory, and expectancy theory.

scientific management
Management approach designed to improve employees' efficiency by scientifically studying their work

Maslow's Hierarchy of Needs

In 1943 psychologist Abraham Maslow proposed the theory that behavior is determined by a variety of needs. He organized these needs into five categories and then arranged the categories in a hierarchy. As Exhibit 9.1 shows, the most basic needs are at the bottom of this hierarchy and the more advanced needs are toward the top. In Maslow's hierarchy, all of the requirements for basic survival—food, clothing, shelter, and the like—

Exhibit 9.1

Maslow's Hierarchy of Needs

According to Maslow, needs on the lower levels of the hierarchy must be satisfied before higher-level needs can be addressed.

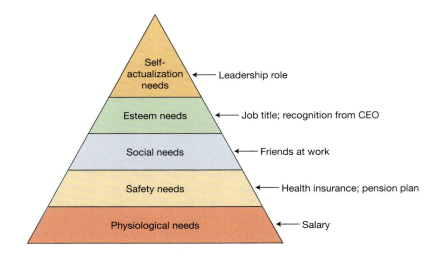

fall into the category of *physiological needs*. These basic needs must be satisfied before the person can consider higher-level needs such as *safety needs, social needs* (the need to give and receive love and to feel a sense of belonging), and *esteem needs* (the need for a sense of self-worth and integrity).

At the top of Maslow's hierarchy is *self-actualization*—the need to become everything one can become. This need is also the most difficult to fulfill. Employees who reach this point work not only to make money or to impress others but also because they feel their work is worthwhile and satisfying in itself. Self-actualization needs partially explain why some people make radical career changes or strike out on their own as entrepreneurs.

Although Maslow's hierarchy is a convenient way to classify human needs, it would be a mistake to view it as a rigid sequence. A person need not completely satisfy each level of needs before being motivated by a higher need. Indeed, at any one time, most people are motivated by a combination of needs.

Herzberg's Two-Factor Theory

In the 1960s Frederick Herzberg and his associates asked accountants and engineers to describe specific aspects of their jobs that made them feel satisfied or dissatisfied. They found that two entirely different sets of factors were associated with satisfying and dissatisfying work experiences: *hygiene factors* and *motivators* (see Exhibit 9.2). What Herzberg called **hygiene factors** are associated with *dissatisfying* experiences. The potential sources of dissatisfaction include working conditions, company policies, pay, and job security. Management can decrease worker dissatisfaction by improving hygiene factors, but such improvements seldom increase satisfaction. On the other hand, managers can help employees feel more motivated and, ultimately, more satisfied by paying attention to **motivators** such as achievement, recognition, responsibility, and other personally rewarding factors.[7] Herzberg's theory is related to Maslow's hierarchy of needs: The motivators closely resemble the higher-level needs, and the hygiene factors resemble the lower-level needs.

According to Herzberg's model, managers need to focus on removing dissatisfying elements (such as unpleasant working conditions or low pay) and adding satisfying elements (such as interesting work and professional recognition). The specific areas to address vary from one situation to the next. A skilled, well-paid, middle-aged employee may be motivated to perform better if motivators are supplied. However, a young, unskilled worker who earns low wages or an employee who is insecure will probably still need the support of strong hygiene factors to reduce dissatisfaction before the motivators can be effective.

hygiene factors
Aspects of the work environment that are associated with dissatisfaction

motivators
Factors of human relations in business that may increase motivation

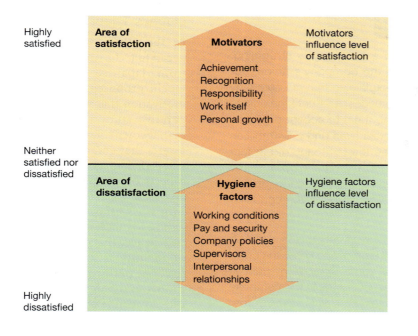

Highly satisfied	**Area of satisfaction**	**Motivators** — Motivators influence level of satisfaction
		Achievement Recognition Responsibility Work itself Personal growth
Neither satisfied nor dissatisfied		
	Area of dissatisfaction	**Hygiene factors** — Hygiene factors influence level of dissatisfaction
		Working conditions Pay and security Company policies Supervisors Interpersonal relationships
Highly dissatisfied		

Exhibit 9.2

Two-Factor Theory

Hygiene factors such as working conditions and company policies can influence employee dissatisfaction. On the other hand, motivators such as opportunities for achievement and recognition can influence employee satisfaction.

McGregor's Theory X and Theory Y

In the 1960s psychologist Douglas McGregor identified two radically different sets of assumptions that underlie most management thinking, which he classified as *Theory X* and *Theory Y* (see Exhibit 9.3). According to McGregor, **Theory X**-oriented managers believe that employees dislike work and can be motivated only by the fear of losing their jobs or by *extrinsic rewards* such as money, promotions, and tenure. This management style emphasizes physiological and safety needs and tends to ignore the higher-level needs in Maslow's hierarchy. In contrast, **Theory Y**-oriented managers believe that employees like work and can be motivated by working for goals that promote creativity or for causes they believe in. Thus, Theory Y-oriented managers seek to motivate employees through *intrinsic rewards*.

The assumptions behind Theory X emphasize authority; the assumptions behind Theory Y emphasize growth and self-direction. It was McGregor's belief that, although some employees need the strong direction demanded by Theory X, those who are ready to realize their social, esteem, and self-actualization needs will not work well under Theory X assumptions.[8]

Theory X

Managerial assumption that employees are irresponsible, are unambitious, and dislike work and that managers must use force, control, or threats to motivate them

Theory Y

Managerial assumption that employees like work, are naturally committed to certain goals, are capable of creativity, and seek out responsibility under the right conditions

THEORY X	THEORY Y
1. Employees inherently dislike work and will avoid it whenever possible.	1. Employees like work and consider it as natural as play and rest.
2. Because employees dislike work, they must be threatened with punishment to achieve goals.	2. People naturally work toward goals they are committed to.
3. Employees will avoid responsibilities whenever possible.	3. The average person can learn to accept and even seek responsibility.
4. Employees value security above all other job factors.	4. The average person's intellectual potential is only partially realized.

Exhibit 9.3

Theory X and Theory Y

McGregor proposed two distinct views of human nature: The assumptions of Theory X are basically negative, whereas those of Theory Y are basically positive.

Learning from Business Blunders

Oops: In a move that is not unusual when a company is struggling, American Airlines CEO Donald Carty asked the company's unions for $1.8 billion in wage and benefit concessions, explaining that the company was on the edge of bankruptcy. His plea was successful—until the unions learned that at the same time Carty was asking them to accept pay cuts, he had arranged generous bonuses for top executives and a $40 million plan that would protect their pensions in case the company did in fact slide into bankruptcy. Union leader John Ward expressed what many union members probably felt: "It's the equivalent of an obscene gesture from management." The unions agreed to the pay cuts on the condition that Carty resign, which he did.

What You Can Learn: The American Airlines pay situation was a classic example of equity theory in action. When most employees know the company is in trouble, they're willing to accept some short-term pain in exchange for keeping their jobs, but they expect everyone in the company to suffer equally. (In contrast to Carty's actions, executives in several other companies in recent financial trouble have reduced or even eliminated their own salaries, and a few have even given back bonuses previously earned.)

Ouchi's Theory Z

In the 1980s, when U.S. businesses began to feel a strong competitive threat from Japanese companies, William Ouchi proposed another approach to motivation that was based on his comparative study of Japanese and U.S. management practices. His **Theory Z** asserts that employees are more motivated if managers involve them in all aspects of company decision making, give them greater responsibility for their own work efforts, and treat them like family. Managers who adopt these practices believe that employees with a sense of identity and belonging are more likely to perform their jobs conscientiously and will try more enthusiastically to achieve company goals.[9]

Equity Theory

Equity theory contributes to the understanding of motivation by suggesting that employee satisfaction depends on the perceived ratio of inputs to outputs. If you work side by side with someone, doing the same job and giving the same amount of effort, only to learn that your colleague earns more money, would you be satisfied in your work and motivated to continue working hard? You perceive a state of *inequity*, so you probably won't be happy with the situation. In response, you might ask for a raise, decide not to work as hard, try to change perceptions of your efforts or their outcomes, or simply quit and find a new job; any one of these steps could bring your perceived input/output ratio back into balance.[10] In the aftermath of large-scale layoffs in many sectors of the economy in the past few years, many of the employees left behind feel a sense of inequity in being asked to shoulder the work of those who left, without getting paid more for the extra effort.[11] Equity also plays a central role in many unionizing efforts, whenever employees feel they aren't getting a fair share of corporate profits or are being asked to shoulder more than their fair share of hardships (see "Learning from Business Blunders").

Expectancy Theory

Expectancy theory, considered by many experts to offer the best available explanation of employee motivation, links an employee's efforts with the outcome he or she expects from that effort. Like equity theory, expectancy theory focuses less on the specific forces that motivate employees and more on the process they follow to seek satisfaction in their jobs. Expectancy theory expands on earlier theories in several important ways, including linking effort to performance and linking rewards to individual goals (see Exhibit 9.4). The effort employees will put forth depends on (1) their expectations about their own ability to perform, (2) their expectations about the rewards that the organization will give in response to that performance, and (3) the attractiveness of those rewards relative to their individual goals.[12]

Imagine that you're a carpenter assigned to a home remodeling project. If you don't think you have the skills necessary to do an absolutely perfect job on the kitchen cabinets (maybe you specialize in framing, not finish work), or you do have the skills but you don't think your boss will reward you for putting in the extra effort, or you don't know what level of performance is expected from you, your motivation may suffer. Or perhaps you do have the skills and the boss will recognize your efforts with a cash bonus, but

Theory Z
Human relations approach that emphasizes involving employees at all levels and treating them like family

equity theory
A theory that suggests employees base their level of satisfaction on the ratio of their inputs to the job and the outputs or rewards they receive from it

expectancy theory
Suggests that the effort employees put into their work depends on expectations about their own ability to perform, expectations about the rewards that the organization will give in response to that performance, and the attractiveness of those rewards relative to their individual goals

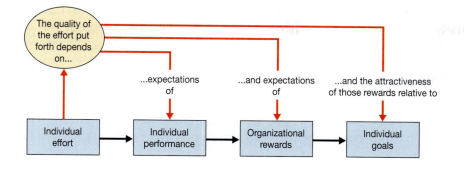

Expectancy Theory

Expectancy theory suggests that employees base their efforts on expectations of their own performance, expectations of rewards for that performance, and the value of those rewards.

you'd rather receive an extra day off to spend with your family. Expectancy theory points out several areas in which motivation can suffer and so gives managers more insight into how to successfully motivate employees.

Motivational Strategies

Once managers have some idea of what motivates—or de-motivates—employees, they can devise policies and procedures that attempt to keep workforce morale at a productive level. Even in professions that have a reputation for poorly motivated workers, creative and committed managers can foster environments that motivate employees and contribute to business success. For example, the pay-television industry (both cable and satellite) is infamous for poor service when customers phone in with problems or questions. In a recent survey by the American Customer Satisfaction Index, three large cable companies, AT&T, Charter Communications, and Comcast, scored customer satisfaction ratings that were "among the lowest ever recorded, across all companies and all industries." And yet, Directv, which competes in the same industry—and even uses the same outsourcing firm that some of its competitors use—earns significantly higher customer satisfaction scores with a motivational strategy that emphasizes seven key points:[13]

- Encouraging enthusiasm for the products the company sells
- Listening to employees' complaints and suggestions
- Giving workers the tools they need and the authority to make decisions
- Making the job seem cool (including inviting celebrities into the customer service center)
- Keeping workers busy (for instance, computer-based training lessons pop up on their screens when they don't have customer calls to answer)
- Giving them some leeway in working with customers, rather than following rigid procedures
- Helping employees reach personal goals (such as offering tuition reimbursement)

Being good to employees is good for Directv's business, too: Higher customer satisfaction scores translate to greater customer loyalty. The range of motivational decisions managers face is almost endless, from redesigning jobs to make them more interesting to offering recognition programs for high achievers. You'll read more about some of these decisions later in this chapter, in the section on alternative work arrangements, and about others in Chapter 10, in the sections on compensation and benefits. Whether it's a basic award program for salespeople or an entirely new way to structure the workforce, though, every motivational strategy needs to consider two critical aspects: setting goals and reinforcing behavior.

Setting Goals

As mentioned earlier, successful motivation involves action. To be successful, that action needs to be directed toward a meaningful goal. Accordingly, **goal-setting theory** suggests the idea that goals can motivate employees. The process of setting goals is often

goal-setting theory
Motivational theory suggesting that setting goals can be an effective way to motivate employees

management by objectives (MBO)
A motivational approach in which managers and employees work together to structure personal goals and objectives for every individual, department, and project to mesh with the organization's goals

embodied in the technique known as **management by objectives (MBO)**, a company-wide process that empowers employees and involves them in goal setting and decision making. This process consists of four steps: setting goals, planning actions, implementing plans, and reviewing performance (see Exhibit 9.5). Because employees at all levels are involved in all four steps, they learn more about company objectives and feel that they are an important part of the companywide team. Furthermore, they understand how even their small job function contributes to the organization's long-term success.

One of the key elements of MBO is a collaborative goal-setting process. Together, a manager and employee define the employee's goals, the responsibilities for achieving those goals, and the means of evaluating individual and group performance so that the employee's activities are directly linked to achieving the organization's long-term goals. Jointly setting clear and challenging—but achievable—goals can encourage employees to reach higher levels of performance.

Reinforcing Behavior

reinforcement theory
A motivational approach based on the idea that managers can motivate employees by influencing their behaviors with positive and negative reinforcement

Employees in the workplace, like human beings in all aspects of life, tend to repeat behaviors that create positive outcomes. **Reinforcement theory** suggests that managers can motivate employees by controlling or changing their actions through **behavior modification**. Managers systematically encourage those actions that are desirable by providing pleasant consequences and discourage those that are not by providing unpleasant consequences.

behavior modification
Systematic use of rewards and punishments to change human behavior

Positive reinforcement offers pleasant consequences (such as a gift, praise, public recognition, bonus, dinner, or trip) for completing or repeating a desired action. Experts recommend the use of positive reinforcement because it emphasizes the desired behavior rather than the unwanted behavior. By contrast, *negative reinforcement* allows people to avoid unpleasant consequences by behaving in the desired way. For example, fear of losing a job (unpleasant consequences) may move an employee to finish a project on time (desired

Exhibit 9.5

Management by Objectives

The MBO process has four steps. This cycle is refined and repeated as managers and employees at all levels work toward establishing goals and objectives, thereby accomplishing the organization's strategic goals.

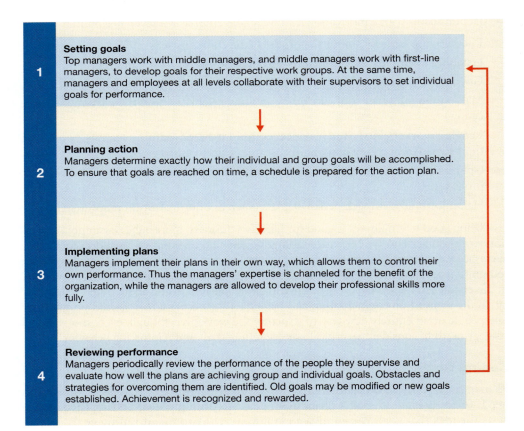

1 Setting goals
Top managers work with middle managers, and middle managers work with first-line managers, to develop goals for their respective work groups. At the same time, managers and employees at all levels collaborate with their supervisors to set individual goals for performance.

2 Planning action
Managers determine exactly how their individual and group goals will be accomplished. To ensure that goals are reached on time, a schedule is prepared for the action plan.

3 Implementing plans
Managers implement their plans in their own way, which allows them to control their own performance. Thus the managers' expertise is channeled for the benefit of the organization, while the managers are allowed to develop their professional skills more fully.

4 Reviewing performance
Managers periodically review the performance of the people they supervise and evaluate how well the plans are achieving group and individual goals. Obstacles and strategies for overcoming them are identified. Old goals may be modified or new goals established. Achievement is recognized and rewarded.

behavior). Such negative motivation, however, is much less effective than encouraging an individual's own sense of direction, creativity, and pride in doing a good job.

Managers and the organizations they represent in today's global economy take a variety of approaches to motivation, some more enlightened than others. However, all these managers face the challenge of motivating a workforce that is diverse, dynamic, and at times demanding, as you'll see in the following section.

KEEPING PACE WITH TODAY'S WORKFORCE

Today's managers lead the efforts of diverse groups of individuals and recognize that all employees have interests and obligations outside of work, such as family, volunteer activities, and hobbies. Addressing employees' many needs becomes even more critical in a work environment plagued with a number of staffing challenges.

Staffing Challenges

If you ask business leaders what their biggest challenges are today, you will most likely get these answers: finding, attracting, and keeping talented people; rightsizing their workforces; and satisfying employees' desire for a work-life balance.[14] Finding and keeping good workers is especially difficult for small-company owners, who often trail bigger companies in salary, benefits, job security, and other criteria that lead workers to choose one company over another.

Shortage of Skilled Labor

A close look at Appendix E confirms that many of today's growing occupations require specialized skills or training, whereas the shrinking occupations involve activities that require fewer skills or ones that are increasingly being automated. In fact, nearly all jobs today require computer literacy. Machinists, for example, need computer skills to operate sophisticated equipment. Telemarketers must know how to keyboard. Even package delivery involves data entry. But finding technology-literate employees is a challenge for many companies today.

Some companies are revamping rigid pay systems to make it easier for employees to move laterally and enhance their skills. Others are installing new career-development programs to help employees plan their career moves. Managers at International Paper, for example, sit down with every employee once a year to discuss his or her career desires, separate from the annual performance review.[15] Still others are instituting educational programs to attract and keep skilled employees. Cisco Systems, a manufacturer of computer networking equipment, runs its own Networking Academy. This in-house vocational program teaches students how to build and manage the computer-server networks the company sells. Cisco hopes that eventually the students will return to the company for permanent jobs.[16]

UPS took a particularly creative approach with its staffing challenge when Louisville, Kentucky, could not supply the 6,000 additional employees the company needed for its growing $6 billion air-freight business. Rather than moving its main U.S. air hub from Louisville to another location, UPS partnered with the city of Louisville to attract new employees to the area. Together they built "UPS University" and special dormitories so student-workers could sleep during the day, attend classes taught by professors from the University of Louisville at night, and then work the UPS graveyard shift (from 11:30 P.M. to 3:30 A.M.) and still have time to study. With over 15,000 employees in Louisville alone, UPS is now Kentucky's largest employer.[17]

Rightsizing

The increasing demand for educated workers and the continuing conversion from a manufacturing-based economy to a service-based economy (as discussed in Chapter 1) are also forcing many companies to realign their workforces into business growth

Union official John Drueke said his "heart just dropped" after learning about the closing of Life Savers' Holland, Michigan, plant. The plant employed 600 workers and was the city's third-largest taxpayer. The company shifted production to Québec, citing high U.S. sugar prices as the major factor behind the relocation.

areas, a practice generally known as *rightsizing*. Although rightsizing often involves *downsizing*—reducing the workforce, sometimes by thousands of employees in a single move—companies often add other workers even while they eliminate some jobs. Such was the case at Hewlett-Packard when the company shed marketing jobs but added new positions in consulting and sales. "In many cases, companies are trying to upgrade their talent," says one human resources expert.[18] In a few cases, companies are simply trying to reduce costs, as Circuit City recently did when it dismissed 3,900 of its highest-paid (and most-experienced) salespeople in a single day. Losing a competitive battle with Best Buy and other electronics retailers, the company believed the move was "the best thing long-term."[19]

Employee Loyalty As you can imagine, rightsizing is a contributing factor to declining employee loyalty. Devastated by the lack of job security, employees quickly learn to "do what's best for me," as Exhibit 9.6 shows. For some, that means putting job security and a long-term financial future ahead of finding challenging work. Public affairs specialist Yara Lizarraga didn't even consider looking for another job when her employer Agilent Technologies asked her to take a 10 percent pay cut. "If I said it didn't hurt, I'd be lying," says Lizarraga. "But I'm just so grateful to have a job."[20]

Like Lizarraga, today's employees have more realistic expectations. They recognize that the old idea of a paternal company taking care of employees has, for the most part, died. Hardworking, loyal employees no longer expect to advance quickly up the organizational hierarchy. They realize that companies are going to do whatever they have to do to succeed and to survive. And this may mean manufacturing in South America, eliminating layers of management, closing down plants, or cutting salaries and perks.[21] Even the Japanese tradition of lifetime employment is under attack. After years of severe economic recession and intense global competition, Japanese companies are realizing that unconditional loyalty is becoming too expensive to justify. To remain competitive, many of these firms are chipping away at their seniority-based management system and are forcing executives to perform or go—bringing Japan a little closer to the U.S. model.[22]

Employee Burnout Rightsizing is also putting pressure on remaining employees to work longer hours. When 3M spun off its data-storage and medical-imaging divisions, for example, some employees began putting in 80-hour weeks. One 3M customer service consultant summed up the feelings of many employees when he said, "I always perceived work to be a means to an end, but not *the* end."[23] Others are working longer hours just to keep up. "It seems like you work, work, work," says one Michigan chemist.[24]

Exhibit 9.6

The Committed Employee—Then and Now

Employee loyalty isn't what it used to be. A recent survey confirms that even today's most valuable and committed workers often put career development and life and family issues ahead of company goals. This chart illustrates this shift in workforce commitment.

CHARACTERISTIC	THEN	NOW
Attachment to employer	Long-term	Near-term
Readiness to change jobs	Not interested	Not looking (but will listen)
Priorities on the job	The firm and its goals	Personal life and career goals
Devotion to employer goals	Follows orders	Buys in (usually)
Effort on the job	Meets expectations	Exceeds expectations
Motto	Always faithful	Seize the day

On average, workers are putting in 260 more hours a year now than they did a decade ago—many without overtime pay.[25] Such long hours can lead to employee *burnout,* which is characterized by emotional exhaustion, depersonalization, and lower levels of achievement. Severe burnout or stress may even lead to clinical depression.[26] Other sources of employee burnout are job insecurity, technological advancements, and information overload:

- *Job insecurity.* Workers anxious about job security feel they have to put in extra hours or risk being seen as expendable. What once were considered crisis-mode workloads have now become business as usual. These extra hours, which don't always bring extra pay, can leave employees feeling burned out and resentful.[27]

- *Technological advancements.* New technology allows employees to work from home, but being wired to the office 24 hours a day can add extra pressure. Employees feel compelled to answer that voice mail or e-mail whatever the hour. "We have all these great tools to save our time," notes one career expert. "Instead, it just extends our week. We're never out of touch anymore."[28]

- *Information overload.* Managers claim they're unable to handle the vast amounts of information they now receive. In fact, more information has been produced in the last 30 years than the previous 5,000, and the total quantity of printed material is doubling every 5 years, and accelerating.[29]

How does burnout affect the ability of workers to do their jobs? "When you feel under stress, you find your mental wheels spinning and you work mechanically rather than creatively," says one human resources expert. "The tasks that normally would take a few minutes sit unfinished for days because you lose the capacity to prioritize and you put off larger, important projects that take more energy and concentration."[30]

Quality of Work Life

A recent survey by jobtrack.com found that 42 percent of all job seekers identified work-life issues as the most important consideration in their choice of a new job. For some employees the primary work-life issue is caring for an elderly parent; for others it's child care, rising college tuition costs, or a desire to return to school part-time.[31] Regardless, achieving a work-life balance is especially difficult when both parents work or in situations where downsizing and restructuring have left remaining employees with heavier workloads than in the past.

To help employees balance the demands of work and family, businesses are offering child-care assistance, family leave, flexible work schedules, telecommuting, and other solutions that are explored later in this chapter and in Chapter 10. Many, such as Hewlett-Packard, are also focusing on improving the **quality of work life (QWL)**, the environment created by work and job conditions.[32] Hewlett-Packard is addressing the fundamental problems of how much time a job really demands and how to build a life beyond work by encouraging employees to set leisure goals and focus on developing their personal lives. As Hewlett-Packard knows, an improved QWL benefits both the individual and the organization. Employees gain the chance to use their specialized abilities, improve their skills, and balance their lives. The organization gains a more motivated and loyal employee.[33]

Two common ways of improving QWL are through **job enrichment**, which reduces specialization and makes work more meaningful by expanding each job's responsibilities, and **job redesign**, which restructures work to provide a better fit between employees' skills and their jobs. Quality of work life can be improved in other ways, too. Like Hewlett-Packard, many organizations are providing their employees with a number of benefits designed to help them balance their work with personal responsibilities. Pepsi has an on-site dry cleaning drop-off at its New York headquarters, and American Banker's Insurance Group and Hewlett-Packard have sponsored schools at company sites that allow employees to visit their children during lunchtime and after school. All of these measures can improve employees' lives by freeing up their time and by making work a more enjoyable place to be.[34]

quality of work life (QWL)
Overall environment that results from job and work conditions

job enrichment
Reducing work specialization and making work more meaningful by adding to the responsibilities of each job

job redesign
Designing a better fit between employees' skills and their work to increase job satisfaction

Chuckle While You Work

Lighten up. Let loose. Laugh a little. Experts are now advising managers to make company-sponsored fun a fundamental part of work. That's because after experiencing a decade of restructuring, downsizing, and reengineering, employees could use a laugh or two. In fact, a recent survey of 1,300 corporate managers showed that more than 60 percent disagreed with the statement "I have fun at work these days."

"Because we spend more of our waking hours working than doing anything else, fun should be a very fundamental part of work," notes one expert on human behavior. In fact, workplace fun is increasingly important because today's jobs are more insecure and more competitive than they once were. Furthermore, camaraderie is diminishing as employees spend more and more time relating to machines than to each other, eat lunch at their desks, or work from home.

Although traditional business wisdom says that people having fun on the job are probably slacking off, studies show that a happy workforce is also a productive one. For one thing, a little wisecracking and laughs can go a long way toward relieving stress. Moreover, fun can raise a company's bottom line by improving health, reducing absenteeism, boosting morale, building teamwork, releasing creativity, improving productivity, and increasing enthusiasm. So while the pursuit of fun may seem frivolous to the serious-minded, more and more companies are beginning to see the value of a good hearty laugh or a little giggle now and then.

At Sprint, company-sponsored fun days encourage employees to wear clothes backward and to go on a photo safari with disposable cameras, taking candid photos of other employees. At Lands' End—voted as one of the best places to work—employees can participate in the company's "Cruise Room," where workers can enjoy calypso music and fruit punch on their breaks. Other companies have organized employee costume parties, hosted goofy birthday celebrations, and sponsored fun-filled weekends at hotels. These companies and others recognize that if work is fun, people will want to come to work. As George Zimmer, CEO of the Men's Wearhouse and a major advocate of trying to make work more enjoyable, puts it, "If the employees are happy and make the stores fun, then that will make it fun for the customers. If they're happy, business will follow, and shareholders will be happy. It all starts with the employees and making it fun for them. Why does work have to be dull?"

Questions for Critical Thinking

1. Under which level of Maslow's hierarchy of needs would you place having fun at work?
2. Would a manager who promoted workplace fun be Theory X- or Theory Y-oriented?

Demographic Challenges

The workforce is always in a state of demographic change, whether from a shift in global immigration patterns or from the changing balance of age groups within a country's population. The companies that are most successful at managing and motivating their employees take great care to (1) understand the diversity of their workforces and (2) establish programs and policies that both embrace that diversity and help employers take full advantage of diversity's benefits.

Workforce Diversity

Today's workforce is diverse in race, gender, age, culture, family structures, religion, sexual orientation, mental and physical ability, and educational backgrounds. Smart business leaders recognize the competitive advantages of diverse workforces: They bring a broader range of viewpoints and ideas, they help companies understand and identify with diverse markets, and they enable companies to tap into the broadest possible pool of talent. Diversity is simply a fact of life for all companies—even if it's nothing more than a mix of men and women of various ages working together.

Differences in everything from religion to ethnic heritage to geography and military experience enrich the workplace, but all create managerial challenges for businesses throughout the world. Today's increasingly diverse workforce brings with it a wide range of skills, traditions, backgrounds, experiences, outlooks, and attitudes toward work—all of which can affect employee behavior on the job. Supervisors face the challenge of communicating with these diverse employees, motivating them, and fostering cooperation and harmony among them. Teams face the challenge of working together closely, and companies are challenged to coexist peacefully with business partners and with the community as a whole. Some of the most important diversity issues include the globalization of the workforce, the aging of the U.S. workforce, gender equality, and sexual harassment.

The Globalization of the Workforce   For many companies, both large and small, managing the workforce is now an international challenge, whether it involves offshoring work to other countries (see Chapter 8), hiring employees to establish operations in other countries, or hiring workers who have immigrated to the United States from other countries. The United States has been a nation of immigrants from the beginning, and that trend continues today. The western and northern Europeans who made up the bulk of immigrants during the nation's early years now share space with people from across Asia, Africa, Eastern Europe, and other parts of the world. By 2010 recent immigrants will account for half of all new U.S. workers.[35] Nor is this pattern of immigration unique to the United States: Workers from Africa, Asia, and the Middle East are moving to Europe in search of new opportunities, while workers from India, the Philippines, and Southeast Asia contribute to the employment base of the Middle East.[36] This international, intercultural nature of the workforce yields a number of important benefits, including cost advantages, specialized talents, and local market knowledge, but it often gives managers a more complex employee base to supervise and motivate.

The Aging U.S. Workforce   Against this backdrop of global immigration and outsourcing, the workforce within the United States is aging. The baby boom generation, which currently dominates the middle and upper tiers of the workforce, is nearing retirement age and triggering a host of age-related issues. Perhaps the most important of these is when boomers will actually retire. Reversing a long-term trend toward earlier and earlier retirement, employment rates among older workers have recently increased, along with the number of people who plan to continue working well into their 60s, 70s, and even 80s.[37] Economists cite a number of reasons: the desire to stay active longer, rising healthcare costs (complicated by the number of employers who've canceled insurance coverage for their retired employees), reductions in company pension plans, and individual retirement savings that took a beating during the stock market decline in 2000 through 2002. A number of employers are happy to hire older workers, too, citing greater flexibility in work hours and pay, lower rates of absenteeism, lower turnover, and the ability to train younger workers.[38]

Although older workers are making some employment gains, the workplace is not always a welcoming environment. Even though the 1967 Age Discrimination in Employment Act (ADEA) makes workers over 40 a protected class, charges of age discrimination filed with the Equal Employment Opportunity Commission (EEOC) are on the rise.[39] Older workers continue to battle perceptions that they aren't as adaptable, as open to new technology, or as adept at learning new skills as their younger colleagues.[40]

sexism
Discrimination on the basis of gender

Gender Equality   One of the most significant diversity issues is gender equality, avoiding **sexism** by assuring equal opportunities and commensurate pay for women in the workforce. On average, women in the United States earn roughly 25 percent less than men.[41] Moreover, even though women now hold 46 percent of executive, administrative, and managerial positions (up from 34 percent in 1983), they hold only 13.6 percent of the seats on the boards of Fortune 500 companies.[42] With laws against employment discrimination and a society that is much more supportive of women in professional roles than it was just a few decades ago, why do these gaps still exist? Analysts point to a variety of reasons, including levels of education and job training, occupational choices, the need to juggle

The number of U.S. workers over 65 has been growing in recent years, creating both opportunities and challenges for managers.

Too Many Workers? Not for Long

One of the biggest challenges all managers face is trying to juggle short-term reality with long-term predictions. It's hard to keep one eye on the things you need to do today and another on the changes that could affect your business in the future—particularly when tomorrow promises to be radically different from today.

With the economy still reeling from a recession, the nation engaged in an ongoing argument about offshoring, and millions of employees worried about their jobs, talk of a labor shortage seems almost far-fetched. As they struggle to reduce their workforces, many managers find it hard to believe that they're going to be facing the exact opposite problem in just a few years, that they'll be struggling to find enough qualified workers. Similarly, workers who have been downsized surely find it hard to believe that they'll be hot commodities a few years from now.

The reason is simple demographics: The huge baby boom generation (those born between 1946 and 1964) ballooned the workforce during the 1980s and 1990s, but by 2010, many of those workers will be retired, and the generations coming behind them aren't nearly large enough to fill the empty slots the boomers will leave behind. Declining college enrollment in high-tech fields and a rise in the number of young mothers who choose not to work outside the home further complicate the situation. Moreover, if college tuitions continue to rise and financial aid continues to shrink, the ranks of college graduates may not grow as rapidly as in the past.

But while a labor shortage presents tremendous hurdles for employers, it brings opportunity for employees. A slower-growing workforce could indeed shift the balance of power to workers, forcing employers to hike wages, add day-care centers, increase flexible work hours, provide more training, and develop innovative ways to attract and retrain existing employees. Moreover, older workers could suddenly take on value as a skilled pool of labor. Bottom line: Employers that refit the work environment to appeal to both young and old, experienced and inexperienced, native and immigrant, will end up in the best position. And forward-thinking employers realize that they need to address the problem now, before they're left shorthanded. For instance, Cigna Systems is retraining workers for such jobs as database administrators, which are likely to face severe talent shortages, teaming younger workers with older colleagues before that experience walks out the door into retirement. Stratus Technologies continues to offer its new hires attractive wages and benefits, even though it could pay them less in a tough job market. The company figures that employers who squeeze employees during tough times aren't creating enough loyalty to hang on to those workers when job opportunities start to grow again.

Questions for Critical Thinking

1. Why do experts predict a skilled-labor shortage in the near future?
2. What can employers do to prepare for a future skilled-labor shortage?

---

glass ceiling
Invisible barrier attributable to subtle discrimination that keeps women out of the top positions in business

the heavy demands of both career and parenthood, and the fact that whenever anyone leaves the workforce for extended periods to care for family, the absence can limit long-term career prospects, and more women than men choose to be stay-at-home parents. However, the U.S. General Accounting Office suggests that such factors explain only about 55 percent of the wage difference between men and women and attributes the remaining 44 percent to unequal treatment. The lack of opportunities to advance into the top ranks is often referred to as the **glass ceiling**, implying that women can see the top but can't get there. Note that the glass ceiling can also be a concern for minorities, for many of the same reasons that have slowed women's career progress.

Companies that do treat women equally are discovering that it's not only the right thing to do but also better for business. Studies suggest a strong correlation between gender diversity in managerial ranks and financial success. From 1996 to 2000, for instance, companies in the Fortune 500 that had the highest percentage of women as senior executives significantly outperformed those that had the lowest percentage.[43] However, it's important to note this is a correlation, not necessarily a causation; managing gender diversity successfully may be just one of many things that successful companies manage well.[44]

sexual harassment
Unwelcome sexual advance, request for sexual favors, or other verbal or physical conduct of a sexual nature within the workplace

Sexual Harassment   The EEOC defines **sexual harassment** as either an obvious request for sexual favors with an implicit reward or punishment related to work, or the more subtle creation of a sexist environment in which employees are made to feel uncomfortable by off-color jokes, lewd remarks, and posturing. Even though male employees may also be targets of sexual harassment and both male and female employees may experience same-sex harassment, sexual harassment of female employees by male colleagues continues to make up the majority of reported cases.

In a recent survey 21 percent of women and 7 percent of men reported being sexually harassed at work.[45] To put an end to sexual harassment, many companies are now enforcing strict harassment policies. To be effective, the policy must be in writing, must be communicated to all employees, and must be enforced.[46] This means that the company must train all employees on the policy, and the company must have clear procedures for reporting such behavior—including allowing employees access to management other than their supervisors. Without such policies, companies can be held indirectly responsible for a harasser's actions even when top managers had no idea that such practices were going on.[47]

Diversity Initiatives

Whether they address diversity under legal or social pressure or recognize the advantages of embracing diversity, many companies have implemented *diversity initiatives*, formal policies, procedures, and training programs to promote successful management of diverse workforces. Such initiatives range from long-term commitments to hiring more women, company-sponsored networking and career planning for women, diversity training and workshops, and mentoring programs designed to help female employees move more quickly through the ranks. Pitney Bowes's long-term commitment to diversity, for instance, has resulted in women holding 5 of the top 11 jobs at the company. Patagonia boasts that women now hold more than half of the company's top-paying jobs and almost 60 percent of managerial jobs. And the appointment of Carly Fiorina to CEO of Hewlett-Packard (HP) was hailed by many as a milestone for women. With women accounting for more than a quarter of HP's managers, it seems that the glass ceiling at this company has been shattered.[48]

Although encouraging sensitivity to employee differences is an important first step, a company stands to benefit most when it incorporates its employees' diverse perspectives into the organization's work. This assimilation enables the company to uncover new opportunities by rethinking primary tasks and redefining markets, products, strategies, missions, business practices, and even cultures. Consider the small public-interest law firm of Dewey & Levin. In the mid-1980s the firm had an all-white legal staff. Concerned about its ability to serve ethnically diverse populations, the firm hired a Hispanic female attorney. She introduced Dewey & Levin to new ideas about what kinds of cases to take on, and many of her ideas were pursued with great success. Hiring more minority women brought even more fresh perspectives. The firm now pursues cases that the original staff members would never have considered because they would not have understood the link between the issues involved in the cases and the firm's mission.[49] In short, diversity can be an asset, and one of the challenges of corporate human relations is to make the most of this asset.

Alternative Work Arrangements

To meet today's staffing and demographic challenges, many companies are adopting alternative work arrangements. Three of the most popular arrangements are flextime, telecommuting, and job sharing. Many organizations find that a mix of these arrangements and other employee benefits works better than a one-size-fits-all approach.[50]

Flextime

An increasingly important alternative work arrangement, **flextime** is a scheduling system that allows employees to choose their own hours, within certain limits. For instance, a company may require everyone to be at work between 10:00 A.M. and 2:00 P.M., but employees may arrive or depart whenever they want as long as they work a total of 8 hours every day. Another popular flextime schedule is to work four 10-hour days each

flextime
Scheduling system in which employees are allowed certain options regarding time of arrival and departure

Exhibit 9.7

9-to-5 Not for Everyone

For many full-time employees and independent contractors, their degree of job satisfaction is closely linked to the availability of these job conditions or attributes.

Full-time, permanent employees and independent contractors who say these are "extremely important" in job satisfaction

	Full-time	Independent
Ability to work from home	15%	44%
Flexible work schedule	40%	62%
Freedom from office politics	44%	60%
Believing in what they do	72%	83%
Making right amount of money	50%	46%
Work they find challenging	55%	59%

week, taking one prearranged day off. Of course, flextime is more feasible in businesses that do not have to maintain standard customer service hours. For this reason, it is not usually an option for employees on production teams, in retail stores, or in many offices where employees have to be on hand to assist customers or answer calls.

The sense of control employees get from arranging their own work schedules is motivating for many (see Exhibit 9.7). Companies have found that flextime reduces turnover, enables the company to adapt to business cycles, allows operation of a round-the-clock business, and helps maintain morale and performance after re-engineering or downsizing. Still, flextime is not without drawbacks. They include supervisors who feel uncomfortable and less in control when employees are coming and going and co-workers who resent flextimers because they assume that people who work flexible hours don't take their jobs seriously enough.[51]

Telecommuting

telecommuting
Working from home while staying connected to the office through a variety of telecommunication products and services

Telecommuting, or *telework*—working from home or another location using computers and telecommunications equipment to stay in touch with colleagues, suppliers, and customers—provides another dimension of flexibility. Defining the precise number of telecommuters in the United States is difficult, since some surveys include people who work from home as infrequently as once a month. However, telecommuting has clearly become a major element in the work life of U.S. employees. More than 20 million U.S. employees now work from home at least part of the time; about a quarter of these work at home every day or nearly every day.[52] Some two-thirds of Fortune 1000 companies now offer telecommuting arrangements to at least some of their employees.[53] Telecommuting is on the rise around the world, too; Europe is now home to 20 million teleworkers as well.[54]

Companies such as AT&T, IBM, and Lucent Technologies provide employees with laptops, dedicated phone lines, software support, fax-printer units, help lines, and full technical backup at the nearest corporate facility. Some even provide employees who work at home with a generous allowance for furnishings and equipment to be used at their discretion.[55] Still, some company operations clearly are not designed for telecommuting. For example, a printer who runs giant color presses can't run the presses from home. But for the kinds of jobs that can be performed from remote sites, telecommuting helps meet employees' needs for flexibility while boosting their productivity as much as 20 percent.[56]

Telecommuting offers many advantages. For one thing, it can save the company money by eliminating offices people don't need,

GeniusBabies.com, seller of educational toys, allows workers such as Michelle Donahue-Arpas to telecommute so she can spend more time with her daughter.

consolidating others, and reducing related overhead costs.[57] Telecommuting also enables a company to hire talented people in distant areas without requiring them to relocate. This benefit expands the company's pool of potential job candidates because employees who have an employed spouse, children in school, or elderly parents to care for are reluctant to move.[58] Employees also like telecommuting because they can set their own hours, reduce job-related expenses such as commuting costs, and spend more time with their families. Telecommuting can also raise outputs and morale by disconnecting employees from unproductive environments in the office, such as noisy working conditions.

Telecommuting does have potential limitations. One of the most commonly expressed concerns is work-life balance, with employees struggling to shut down their work lives so they can participate in their home lives. Some managers struggle with a perceived loss of control over employees they can't see. Others are concerned that people working at home will slack off (although some studies show that telecommuters actually work *more* hours, not fewer) or that telecommuting could cause resentment among office-bound colleagues or weaken company loyalty.[59] Some companies find that the lack of face-to-face communication hinders decision making,

---

Technologies That Are Revolutionizing Business

Telecommuting technologies

In simplest form, telecommuting doesn't require much more than a computer, a telephone, and access to the Internet and e-mail. However, most corporate employees need a more comprehensive connection to their offices, with such features as secure access to confidential files, groupware (see Chapter 4), and web-based virtual meetings that let people communicate and share information over the Internet. Some of the other technologies you'll encounter in telecommuting include broadband Internet connections (cable, DSL, or satellite), some form of file access (including shared workspaces), security (including user authentication and access control), Internet-based telephones, and wireless networking.

How they're changing business

When they're used successfully, telecommuting technologies can reduce real estate costs, put employees closer to customers, reduce traffic and air pollution in congested cities, give companies access to a wide range of independent talent, and let employees work in higher-salary jobs while living in lower-cost areas of the country. In the future, these technologies have the potential to change business so radically they could even influence the design of entire cities. With less need to pull millions of workers into central business districts, business executives, urban planners, and political leaders have the opportunity to explore such new ideas as *telecities*—virtual cities populated by people and organizations who are connected technologically, rather than physically.

Where you can learn more

Start with the International Telework Association and Council, www.telecommute.org. Companies that supply hardware, software, and services for telecommuting often have information as well; see Cisco (www.cisco.go/teleworker), ATT (www.att.com/telework), and AgilQuest (www.agilquest.com) for examples.

---

in spite of the best technology available. Accel, a venture-capital firm based in London, has cut down on its use of telecommuting because "we were becoming dysfunctional," in the words of one partner.[60]

To see if employees are truly compatible with this style of working, and to prepare them and their managers for the transition, Merrill Lynch requires prospective telecommuters to submit a detailed proposal that covers when and how they're going to work at home and even what their home office will look like. Next, they participate in a series of meetings. Finally, they spend two weeks in a simulation lab that lets employees and their managers experience the change. Once at home, telecommuters are required to document their at-home working hours and submit weekly progress reports.[61]

Job Sharing

Job sharing, which lets two employees share a single full-time job and split the salary and benefits, has been slowly gaining acceptance as a way to work part-time in a full-time position. According to a recent survey by Hewitt Associates (a firm specializing in employee benefits), 37 percent of employers offer job-sharing arrangements to their employees.[62] But such arrangements are usually offered to people who already work for the company and who need to cut back their hours. Rather than lose a good employee or have to find and train someone new, the company finds a way to split responsibilities.

job sharing
Splitting a single full-time job between two employees for their convenience

WORKING WITH LABOR UNIONS

Although they work toward common goals in most cases, managers and employees do face an inherent conflict over resources: Managers, as representatives of company ownership, want to minimize the costs of operating the business, whereas employees want to maximize salaries and ensure good benefits and safe, pleasant working conditions. If employees believe they are not being treated fairly or don't have a voice in how the company is run, one option they can consider is joining **labor unions**, organizations that seek to protect employee interests by negotiating with employers for better wages and benefits, improved working conditions, and increased job security.

The history of labor-management relationships is long, complex, and often hostile. Unions can trace their history back nearly a thousand years, to early guilds in Europe that gave craftspeople bargaining power over merchants. In the United States, the Industrial Revolution in the second half of the 1800s and the Great Depression of the 1930s were formative events in the history of unionization. Responding to worker complaints about unsafe working conditions, long hours (60- and even 80-hour weeks were common), child labor, and other concerns, unions gained a strong foothold in the United States. At the peak of unionization in the 1950s, about a third of the U.S. workforce belonged to unions. Unions have played an important and lasting role in U.S. employee-management relations and are largely responsible for the establishment of worker's compensation, child-labor laws, overtime rules, minimum-wage laws, severance pay, and more. Employees are most likely to turn to unions if they are deeply dissatisfied with their current job conditions, if they believe that unionization can be helpful in improving those conditions, and if they are willing to overlook negative stereotypes that have surrounded unions in recent years.[63]

One advantage of joining labor unions is that it gives employees stronger bargaining power. By combining forces, union employees can put more pressure on management than they could as individuals. Still, not all employees support labor unions. Some believe that unions stifle individual initiative and are not necessary to ensure fair treatment from employers. Moreover, companies that have most successfully resisted unionization seem to have adopted participative management styles and an enhanced sense of responsibility toward employees. In addition, some of the most egregious management abuses that unions initially rallied against, such as forcing children to work long hours, are now prohibited by law.

Like many companies today, Marriott International has recognized that the primary reasons employees consider unionizing is because they feel they are not treated well by management. To demonstrate to workers that they are valued, Marriott offers its employees stock options, social-service referral networks, day care, training classes, and opportunities for advancement. As a result, Marriott's employee turnover is well below that of most companies, and its employees' enthusiasm is high.[64]

But even the best working conditions are no guarantee that employees won't seek union representation. For instance, although Starbucks is renowned for its generous employee benefit programs and supportive work environment, employees of stores in Vancouver, British Columbia, organized and successfully bargained for higher wages.[65]

The Collective Bargaining Process

As long as a union has been recognized as the exclusive bargaining agent for a group of employees, its main job is to negotiate employment contracts with management. In a process known as **collective bargaining**, union and management negotiators work together to forge the human resources policies that will apply to the unionized employees—and other employees covered by the contract—for a certain period, usually three years.

Most labor contracts are a compromise between the desires of union members and those of management. The union pushes for the best possible deal for its members, and management tries to negotiate agreements that are best for the company (and the shareholders, if a corporation is publicly held). Exhibit 9.8 illustrates the collective bargaining process.

---

labor unions
Organizations of employees formed to protect and advance their members' interests

collective bargaining
Process used by unions and management to negotiate work contracts

| Exhibit 9.8 | The Collective Bargaining Process |

Contract negotiations go through the four basic steps shown here.

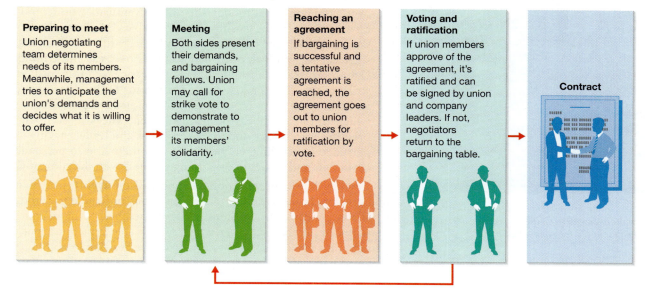

Preparing to meet
Union negotiating team determines needs of its members. Meanwhile, management tries to anticipate the union's demands and decides what it is willing to offer.

Meeting
Both sides present their demands, and bargaining follows. Union may call for strike vote to demonstrate to management its members' solidarity.

Reaching an agreement
If bargaining is successful and a tentative agreement is reached, the agreement goes out to union members for ratification by vote.

Voting and ratification
If union members approve of the agreement, it's ratified and can be signed by union and company leaders. If not, negotiators return to the bargaining table.

Contract

Meeting and Reaching an Agreement

When the negotiating teams made up of representatives of the union and management sit down together, they state their opening positions and each side discusses its position point by point. In a cooperative atmosphere, the real issues behind the demands gradually come to light. For example, management may begin by demanding the right to determine the sizes of work crews when all it really wants is smaller work crews; the union, however, wants to protect the jobs of its members and keep crew sizes as large as possible but may agree to certain reductions in exchange for, say, higher pay. After many stages of bargaining, each party presents its package of terms, and any gaps between labor and management demands are then dealt with.

If negotiations reach an impasse, outside help may be needed. The most common alternative is **mediation**—bringing in an impartial third party to study the situation and make recommendations for resolution of the differences. Mediators are generally well-respected community leaders whom both sides will listen to. However, mediators can only offer suggestions, and their solutions are not binding. When a legally binding settlement is needed, the negotiators may submit to **arbitration**—a process in which an impartial referee listens to both sides and then makes a judgment by accepting one side's view. In *compulsory arbitration*, the parties are required by a government agency to submit to arbitration; in *voluntary arbitration*, the parties agree on their own to use arbitration to settle their differences.

mediation
Process for resolving a labor-contract dispute in which a neutral third party meets with both sides and attempts to steer them toward a solution

arbitration
Process for resolving a labor-contract dispute in which an impartial third party studies the issues and makes a binding decision

Exercising Options When Negotiations Break Down

The vast majority of management-union negotiations are settled without the need for either side to take further action. However, negotiations occasionally reach an impasse, and neither side is willing to compromise. Both labor and management are able to draw on many powerful options when negotiations or mediation procedures break down.

Labor's Options Strikes and picket lines are perhaps labor's best-known tactics, but other options are also used.

- *Strike.* The most powerful weapon that organized labor can use is the **strike**, a temporary work stoppage aimed at forcing management to accept union demands. The basic idea behind the strike is that, in the long run, it costs management more in lost

strike
Temporary work stoppage by employees who want management to accept their union's demands

When contract talks broke down between grocery workers and major grocery chains in Southern California in late 2003, the result was a strike that lasted four and a half months.

picketing
Strike activity in which union members march before company entrances to persuade nonstriking employees to walk off the job and to persuade customers and others to cease doing business with the company

boycott
Union activity in which members and sympathizers refuse to buy or handle the product of a target company

strikebreakers
Nonunion workers hired to replace striking workers

lockouts
Management tactics in which union members are prevented from entering a business during a strike in order to force union acceptance of management's last contract proposal

earnings to resist union demands than to give in. A 15-day strike by UPS drivers cost the company $750 million in lost revenue, and a 54-day strike at General Motors (GM) cost the automaker over $2 billion. Even though the union eventually won temporary reprieves on the closing of unprofitable GM plants, the settlement agreement failed to directly address important issues, such as GM's push to open new factories overseas and trim its U.S. workforce. As a result, some observers pegged this costliest strike in decades as a lose-lose situation for both the company and the union.[66] An essential part of any strike is **picketing**, in which union members positioned at entrances to company premises march back and forth with signs and leaflets, trying to persuade nonstriking employees to join them and to persuade customers and others to stop doing business with the company.

- *Boycott.* A less direct union weapon is the **boycott**, in which union members and sympathizers refuse to buy or handle the product of a target company. Millions of union members form an enormous bloc of purchasing power, which may be able to pressure management into making concessions. One of the best-known boycotts was the grape boycott organized by Cesar Chavez in the early 1970s. To pressure California growers into accepting the United Farm Workers (UFW) as the bargaining agent for previously unorganized farm laborers, he and his colleagues persuaded an estimated 17 million people in the United States to stop buying grapes. Eventually, the California legislature passed the country's first law guaranteeing farmworkers the right to hold union elections.[67]

- *Publicity.* Increasingly, labor is pressing its case by launching publicity campaigns, often called *corporate campaigns*, against the target company and companies affiliated with it. These campaigns might include sending investors alerts that question the firm's solvency, staging rallies during peak business hours, sending letters to charitable groups questioning executives' motives, handing out leaflets that allege safety and health-code violations, and stimulating negative stories in the press.

Labor's other options include *slowdowns*, in which employees continue to do their jobs but at a slow enough pace to disrupt operations, and *sickouts*, in which employees feign illness and stay home.

Management's Options   From its side, management can use a number of legal methods to pressure unions when negotiations stall:

- *Strikebreakers.* When union members walk off their jobs, management can legally replace them with **strikebreakers**, nonunion workers hired to do the jobs of striking workers. (Union members brand them as "scabs.") For example, when over 2,000 union workers struck at the *Detroit News* and *Detroit Free Press* newspapers, management kept the presses rolling by hiring 1,400 replacement workers. Although the strike caused both papers to lose customers, advertisers, and profits, the papers persevered for 19 months until the union gave in. By that time, many temporary replacements had been hired permanently, an action that management is legally permitted to take if it's necessary to keep a business going.[68]

- *Lockouts.* The U.S. Supreme Court has upheld the use of **lockouts**, in which management prevents union employees from entering the workplace, in order to pressure the union to accept a contract proposal. A lockout is management's counterpart to a strike. It is a preemptive measure designed to force a union to accede to management's demands. Lockouts are legal only if the union and management have come to an impasse in negotiations and the employer is defending a legitimate bargaining position. During a lockout, the company may hire temporary replacements as long as it has no antiunion motivation and negotiations have been amicable.[69]

■ *Injunctions.* An **injunction** is a court order prohibiting union workers from taking certain actions. Management used this weapon without restriction in the early days of unionism, when companies typically sought injunctions to order striking employees back to work on the grounds that the strikers were interfering with business. Today, injunctions are legal only in certain cases. For example, the president of the United States has the right, under the Taft-Hartley Act, to obtain a temporary injunction to halt a strike deemed harmful to the national interest, such as a wide-scale transportation strike.

injunction
Court order prohibiting certain actions by striking workers

The Labor Movement Today

In certain industries, including transportation, retailing, and manufacturing, unions remain a significant force in employee-management relations in the United States. But their membership continues to decline. Unions now represent only 13.5 percent (16.3 million) of workers in the United States (down from 20 percent in 1983 and 35 percent in the 1950s).[70] One key reason for the decrease in union membership is the shift from a manufacturing-based economy to one dominated by service industries, which tend to appeal less to unions. Another factor contributing to the decline is the changing nature of the labor force. Women, young workers, and highly skilled workers have been harder to organize with traditional methods, as have workers in less hierarchical organizations.[71] True to the often combative nature of the relationship, each side blames organized labor's decline on the other. Some business leaders say unions don't have anything relevant to offer today's workers, while union leaders say managers use every tactic they can think of, both legal and illegal, to thwart unionization efforts.[72]

Meanwhile, some labor leaders have recognized that their own inertia is partly to blame for the unions' decline, and they are taking corrective measures. Even though unions are sticking to their traditional causes—good wages, safe conditions, and benefits—progressive labor leaders are pursuing new workplace issues such as job security, increasing health-care costs, labor involvement in management decisions, child care, and more job training.[73]

What does the future hold for unions? It is difficult to make predictions, but two key issues highlight the continuing complexity of union-management relations:

■ **Health-care costs.** By just about any measure, health-care costs in the United States are spiraling out of control, climbing much faster than the general inflation rate. These costs have become a major point of contention in labor negotiations, with employers saying that employees need to pay a larger share of health-care costs and employees saying they can't afford to. In 2003, union workers at three grocery store chains went on strike to protest an employer plan to share health-care costs. Further complicating the issue is the growing national dominance of Wal-Mart, the nation's largest private employer and a company famous—or infamous, depending on whose side you're on—for cutting costs to the bone. Wal-Mart pays its workers less than other chains and charges employees so much for health insurance that many say they can't afford it. Even though Wal-Mart workers are not unionized, the company is such a dominant force in retail that many competitors feel they have no choice but to cut their own operating costs in order to survive.[74]

■ **International competition.** In industries that face vigorous international competition, such as autos, steel, and aircraft, some union and business leaders are trying to work more cooperatively than they have in years past. In the steel industry, for instance, union leaders have made significant concessions and even helped arrange the consolidation of three battered steel companies in the hopes of competing more effectively with overseas suppliers.[75]

Both health-care costs and international competition are staggeringly complex challenges with no clear solutions, but attempts to solve them may well influence the progress of unions in the coming years.

Business BUZZ

Wal-Mart effect: Used to describe any of several business phenomena that some observers attribute to Wal-Mart's massive presence in the economy—both positive (such as holding inflation in check and boosting productivity) and negative (driving other companies into bankruptcy and driving down wages), depending on one's perspective

Summary of Learning Objectives

1 Compare Maslow's hierarchy of needs and Herzberg's two-factor theory, then explain their application to employee motivation.

Maslow's hierarchy organizes individual needs into five categories and proposes that the individual must satisfy the most basic needs before being able to address higher-level needs. Based on the assumption that employees want to "climb to the top" of Maslow's pyramid, managers should provide opportunities to satisfy those higher-level needs. Herzberg's two-factor theory covers the same general set of employee needs but divides them into two distinct groups. His theory suggests that hygiene factors—such as working conditions, company policies, and job security—can influence employee dissatisfaction, but an improvement in these factors will not motivate employees. Only motivational factors such as recognition and responsibility can improve employee performance.

2 Explain why expectancy theory is considered by some to be the best description of employee behavior.

Expectancy, which suggests that the effort employees put into their work depends on expectations about their own ability to perform, expectations about the rewards that the organization will give in response to that performance, and the attractiveness of those rewards relative to their individual goals, is considered a good model because it considers the linkages between effort and outcome. For instance, if employees think a linkage is "broken," such as having doubts that their efforts will yield acceptable performance or worries that they will perform well but no one will notice, they're likely to put less effort into their work.

3 Discuss three staffing challenges employers are facing in today's workplace.

A shortage of skilled labor, rightsizing the workforce, and an increasing employee desire to balance work and life responsibilities are making it difficult for employers to find and keep talented people. The factors contributing to these staffing challenges are the increasing use of technology in the workplace, a robust U.S. economy, the conversion of a manufacturing-based economy to a service-based economy, a general mismatch between employee job skills and job demands, declining employee loyalty, and increasing employee burnout.

4 Explain the challenges and advantages of a diverse workforce.

Smart business leaders recognize diverse workforces bring a broader range of viewpoints and ideas, they help companies understand and identify with diverse markets, and they enable companies to tap into the broadest possible pool of talent. Supervisors face the challenge of communicating with these diverse employees, motivating them, and fostering cooperation and harmony among them. Teams face the challenge of working together closely, and companies are challenged to coexist peacefully with business partners and with the community as a whole.

5 Discuss three popular alternative work arrangements companies are offering their employees.

To meet today's staffing and demographic challenges, companies are offering their employees flextime (the ability to vary their work hours), telecommuting (the ability to work from home or another location), and job sharing (the ability to share a single full-time job with a co-worker).

6 Explain the two steps unions take to become the bargaining agent for a group of employees.

First, unions distribute authorization cards to employees, which designate the union as the bargaining agent, and if at least 30 percent (but usually a majority) of the target group sign the cards, the union asks management to recognize it. Second, if management is unwilling to do so, the union asks the National Labor Relations Board to sponsor a certification election. If a majority of the employees vote in favor of being represented by the union, the union becomes the official bargaining agent for the employees.

7 Cite three options unions can exercise when negotiations with management break down.

Unions can conduct strikes, organize boycotts, and use publicity to pressure management into complying with union proposals. A strike is a temporary work stoppage, which the union hopes will cost management enough in lost earnings so that management will be forced to accept union demands. A boycott is a union tactic designed to pressure management into making concessions by convincing sympathizers to refuse to buy or handle the product of the target company. A negative publicity campaign against the target company is a pressure tactic designed to smear the reputation of the company in hopes of gaining management's attention.

8 Cite three options management can exercise when negotiations with a union break down.

To pressure a union into accepting its proposals, management may continue running the business with strikebreakers (nonunion workers hired to do the jobs of striking workers), institute a lockout of union members by preventing union employees from entering the workplace, or seek an injunction against a strike or other union activity.

Behind **the Scenes**

Giving Employees a Voice at Atlas Container

By their own admission, Peter and Paul Centenari did not get off to a good start. When the brothers purchased Atlas Container, their plan was to grow the Severn, Maryland, packaging company, then sell it for a nice profit. Trouble is, these two young investment bankers didn't know much about the container business. Before long, they'd pushed the profitable, debt-free company to the brink of bankruptcy. "Basically, we drove it into the ground. We were thinking like investment bankers," Paul explained. Costs spun out of control and operational efficiency plummeted.

While they were learning to think like manufacturers, the situation got even worse. At one point, paper supplies shrank across the industry, and no one would sell the struggling company the paper it needed to feed its box-making machinery. The brothers had to go all the way to Puerto Rico to find a supplier.

Step by step, the Centenaris managed to climb back to profitability, and the experience gave them plenty of time to think about what kind of company they wanted to have. They started to enjoy their work, and the idea of managing a company built on respect for employees began to form. Their management philosophy would grow to include four pillars: employee stock ownership, open-book management, continuous learning, and giving employees a voice in the decisions that affect their work and their future. As the company explains to customers in its promotional materials, "We believe there is a direct correlation between employee empowerment and customer satisfaction. We also believe if they are encouraged to think like owners, they will act accordingly."

These four pillars are not unique in the business world, of course, but the way Atlas implements them is highly unusual. Employee stock ownership is fairly common, but open-book management is still a novelty for most companies. The Centenaris believe their employees can make better decisions and involve themselves more deeply in the company if they know everything there is to know about the company's financial health. Open-book management is supported with financial training for everyone in the company, so they know what the numbers mean and how they all contribute to those results. Even machine operators on the production line can analyze and discuss the company's financial data like practiced accountants. Moreover, each is empowered to take action whenever he or she can to increase revenues or lower the cost of doing business. Unlike many companies, where employees can see a connection between what they do every day and the company's overall health, Atlas employees know exactly how their work affects the company's bottom line. Paul explains that, "If you can somehow create a line of sight from what they do every day and how it affects the financial statement, you're going to create a passionate workforce that wants to make a difference and a profit."

The final pillar, employee involvement, is what truly sets Atlas apart. Rather than making decisions in a closed room, then handing them over to the employees to implement, the Centenaris let the employees vote on everything from health insurance plans to new production machinery—a level of employee involvement that is almost unheard of. The employees even outvoted the owners in the purchase of some major new equipment. Like the best democracies, voting works best when the people are truly informed, and Atlas's commitment to training and open-book management ensures that the employees know what they're talking about when they cast their votes.

And the results speak for themselves. In a ferociously competitive industry with practically no overall growth, Atlas manages to increase its sales 20 to 25 percent a year through both acquisitions and strong customer service (its on-time delivery is in the 90 to 95 percent range, well above the industry average of 75 percent). Costs are kept under control, too; employees are careful with the company's money because it's their money, too. Plus, with workforce morale higher than it is in many competitive firms, turnover is much lower—about 15 percent a year, compared to 50 percent for the industry. That keeps continuity and customer satisfaction high and costs low as well.

Financial success helps the company offer generous benefits to its employees, even to funding tutoring services for employees' children. Helping employees not only gives the brothers personal satisfaction, but Paul explains that, "The more we give, the more we get." It's enough to get employees excited to come to work, even in the tough business of making cardboard boxes.[76]

Critical Thinking Questions

1. Why does involving employees in decision making help raise their morale?
2. What are the challenges involved in giving employees the opportunity to vote on major business decisions?
3. What problems might Atlas run into as it continues to acquire other companies and instill its management style in those new facilities?

LEARN MORE ONLINE

Visit the Atlas Container website by clicking on the hotlink at Chapter 9 of this text's website at www.prenhall.com/bovee. Explore the company, product, and employment information on the site. How does Atlas Container describe itself? How does the company try to distinguish itself from its competitors? What kind of people is the company looking to hire? ■

Key Terms

arbitration (239)
behavior modification (228)
boycott (240)
collective bargaining (238)
equity theory (226)
expectancy theory (226)
flextime (235)
glass ceiling (234)
goal-setting theory (227)
human relations (222)
hygiene factors (224)
injunction (240)

job enrichment (231)
job redesign (231)
job sharing (237)
labor unions (238)
lockouts (240)
management by objectives (MBO) (228)
mediation (239)
morale (221)
motivation (222)
motivators (225)
picketing (240)

quality of work life (QWL) (231)
reinforcement theory (228)
scientific management (223)
sexism (233)
sexual harassment (234)
strike (239)
strikebreakers (240)
telecommuting (236)
Theory X (225)
Theory Y (225)
Theory Z (226)

Test Your Knowledge

Questions for Review

1. What is the goal of human relations?
2. What is rightsizing?
3. What are the principal causes of employee burnout?
4. What is the glass ceiling?
5. What is quality of work life, and how does it influence employee motivation?

Questions for Analysis

6. Why do managers often find it difficult to motivate employees who remain after downsizing?
7. How can diversity initiatives benefit a company?
8. What are some of the advantages and disadvantages of alternative work arrangements?
9. Why do employees choose to join labor unions? Why do they not join labor unions?

10. **Ethical Considerations.** You've got a golf game scheduled for Sunday afternoon, and you've worked all weekend to write a proposal to be presented Monday morning. The proposal is more or less finished, but a few more hours of work would make it polished and persuasive. Do you cancel the game?

Questions for Application

11. Some of your talented and hardworking employees come to you one day and say they do not feel challenged. They expected to be able to diversify their skills more and take on greater responsibility than they now have. How do you respond?
12. Assume you are the plant manager for a company that manufactures tires for cars and light trucks. To compete more economically in the global market, the company is seriously considering closing the plant within the next

year and moving manufacturing operations to Southeast Asia. Upon hearing about the possible plant closing, the union votes to launch a strike in one week if its demands for job security aren't met. Because of a recent surge in orders, the company is not in a position to close the plant yet. What are your options as you continue to negotiate with union representatives? Which option would you choose and why?

13. **Integrated.** How do economic concepts such as profit motive and competitive advantage (see Chapter 1) affect today's workforce?

14. **Integrated.** Why is it difficult for small businesses to allow employees to telecommute, share jobs, and work flexible hours?

Practice Your Knowledge

Sharpening Your Communication Skills

As the director of public relations for a major airline, your job is to prepare news releases should the pilots decide to strike. This is a challenging task because many people will be affected by the strike. Being a good communicator, you know that one of the first things you must do before preparing a message is to analyze the audience. Think about an airline strike and answer these questions briefly to practice this important communication technique:

1. What groups of people do you think would be interested in the information about the airline strike?

2. What do you think each of these groups would want to know about most?

3. How might they react to the information you will provide? Summarize your answers to these three questions in a short memo to your instructor.

Building Your Team Skills

Debate the pros and cons of telecommuting for an accounting, computer programming, or graphics design firm. Break into groups of four students, with two students taking the employees' pro side and the other two taking management's con side. As you prepare for this debate, consider the following factors: employee motivation, staffing challenges, quality of work life, costs, control, and feasibility.

During your team's debate, let one side present its arguments while the other side takes notes on the major points. After both sides have completed their presentations, discuss all the supporting points and try to reach a consensus as to whether or not your firm will support telecommuting. Draft a one-page statement outlining your team's conclusion and reasoning, and then share it during a class discussion.

Compare your team's conclusion and reasoning with those of other teams. Do most teams believe telecommuting is a good or bad idea? What issues do most teams agree on? What issues do they disagree on?

Expand Your Knowledge

Discovering Career Opportunities

Is an alternative work arrangement such as flextime, job sharing, or telecommuting in your career future? This exercise will help you think about whether these work arrangements fit into your career plans.

1. Look at the list of possible business careers in Appendix E. Of the careers that interest you, which seem best suited to flextime? To job sharing? To telecommuting?

2. Select one of the careers that seems suited to telecommuting. What job functions do you think could be performed at home or from another remote location?

3. Thinking about the same career, do you think it would be possible to split the job's responsibilities with a co-worker under a job-sharing arrangement? What issues, if any, might you need to resolve first?

Developing Your Research Skills

Select one or two articles from recent issues of business journals or newspapers (print or online editions) that relate to employee motivation or morale.

1. What is the problem or trend discussed in the article(s), and how is it influencing employee attitudes or motivation?

2. Is this problem unique to this company, or does it have broader implications? Who is affected by it now, and who do you think might be affected by it in the future?

3. What challenges and opportunities does this situation present to the company or industry? The employees? Management?

SEE IT ON THE WEB

For live links to the websites that follow, go to this text's website at www.prenhall.com/bovee. When you log on, select Chapter 9, then select "Featured Websites," click on the URL of the website you wish to visit, review the website, and answer the following questions:

1. What is the purpose of this website?
2. What kinds of information does this website contain? Please be specific.
3. How is the information provided at this website useful for businesspeople? Consumers?
4. How did you expand your knowledge of motivation and employee-management relations by reviewing the material at this website? What new things did you learn about these topics?

Working Hard on the Web

Frustrated workers and managers now have a place to go to voice their opinions, commiserate with others, and get advice on how to motivate employees. The place is Hard@Work, a website created "to reduce the oversupply of fear and alienation in the workplace by meeting the pent-up demand for constructive communication about what's happening on the job." Visitors can hang around the "Water Cooler" to chat with others about work issues and careers; play "Stump the Mentor," which offers suggestions for handling sticky work situations; or dig into the "Rock Pile," which features realistic case studies. Hard@Work offers something for workers and job seekers alike. www.hardatwork.com

Learn the Language of Equal Opportunity

The Equal Employment Opportunity Commission (EEOC) offers an extensive array of information online for both employees and employers. Explore the categories of employment discrimination and learn how the government defines each type. Learn more about the employment laws that employers are expected to follow, or see the steps employees can take when they feel they have been discriminated against. www.eeoc.gov

Spreading the Union Message

Of all the websites devoted to union causes, the AFL-CIO's site offers perhaps the most extensive collection of statistics, information, and commentaries on union issues and programs. The site is designed to educate members and prospective members about union activities and campaigns. Topics include union membership campaigns, safety and family issues, and much more. The AFL-CIO also maintains online directories with the e-mail addresses of members of Congress plus sample letters to encourage communication with legislators. Browse this site to get the latest on union initiatives as well as information about trends in the labor movement today. www.aflcio.org

Companion Website

Learning Interactively

Go to the Companion Website at www.prenhall.com/bovee. For Chapter 9, take advantage of the interactive "Study Guide" to test your knowledge of the chapter. Get instant feedback on whether you need additional studying.

Also, visit this site's "Study Hall," where you'll find an abundance of valuable resources that will help you succeed in this course.

Video **Case**

Keeping Labor–Management Relations on Track: Witt Firm

LEARNING OBJECTIVES

The purpose of this video is to help you:

1. Recognize the kinds of issues that are negotiated between company managers and labor unions.

2. Understand the role of arbitration in resolving an impasse between labor and management.

3. Discuss how company management and union leadership view the advantages and disadvantages of using arbitration.

SYNOPSIS

Helen Witt is an arbitrator with 30 years of experience in making decisions about contentious issues that affect relations between employers and unionized employees. Railroads and their unions—such as the Burlington Northern Santa Fe and the United Transportation Union—often turn to arbitrators such as Witt when they are at odds over benefits, job security, compensation, or other issues. Railroad management and union leaders acknowledge the importance of working together for mutual benefit. When they cannot agree, however, they may use arbitration to have a third party, such as Helen Witt, listen to each side's case and decide how to resolve the dispute.

Discussion Questions

1. *For analysis:* Why is the relationship between company management and union leadership "very much like a marriage," in the words of Helen Witt?
2. *For analysis:* Why should top management of a company and its unions try to agree in advance on the methods to be used in resolving disputes?

3. *For application:* What kinds of disputes might arise between the Burlington Northern Santa Fe Railroad and the United Transportation Union?
4. *For application:* Under what circumstances might the railroad and its union choose mediation rather than arbitration to resolve their differences?
5. *For debate:* Should a railroad such as the Burlington Northern Santa Fe invite one or more union representatives to become a member of its board of directors? Support your chosen position.

ONLINE EXPLORATION

Visit the website of the United Transportation Union www.utu.org and read the latest news about union activities on the homepage. Also follow the About UTU link to read more about the union's background and the links about benefits such as the Discipline Income Protection Program. What issues are currently in the forefront of the UTU's activities? How do its members stand to benefit from the UTU's involvement? Has the UTU recently participated in any arbitration cases? If so, what were the issues and what was the outcome?

Chapter 10

Managing Human Resources

Behind **the Scenes**

Brewing Up People Policies for Chainwide Success

Hiring, training, and compensating a diverse workforce of 40,000 employees worldwide would be a difficult task for any company. But it was an especially daunting challenge in an industry whose annual employee turnover rate approached 300 percent. It was even more of a challenge for a company that was striving to open a new store every day, despite a tight labor market, an uncertain global economy, and increasingly intense competition.

By offering benefits to all employees (including part-timers), Starbucks attracts and keeps quality employees.

This was the high-pressure situation facing Starbucks Coffee Company in the 1990s, when CEO Howard Schultz set a torrid pace for global expansion. Starbucks wanted to perk past $1 billion in yearly sales and spread its gourmet coffee across more continents. Already, the rich aroma of fresh-brewed espresso was wafting through neighborhoods all over North America, with new stores planned for the United Kingdom, Japan, even China. But Schultz and his management team knew that good locations and top-quality coffee were just part of the company's formula for success.

To keep up with this ambitious schedule of new store openings, Starbucks had to find, recruit, and train 700 new employees every month, no easy feat "when there is a shortage of labor and few people want to work behind a retail counter," as Schultz noted. Moreover, Starbucks's employees had to deliver consistently superior customer service in every store and every market. In other words, Starbucks's employees (known internally as *partners*) had to do more than simply pour coffee—they had to believe passionately in the product and pay attention to all the details that can make or break the retail experience for the chain's 10 million weekly customers.

Schultz knew it would take more than good pay and company benefits to motivate and inspire employees. But what? If you were a member of Schultz's management team, how would you attract, train, and compensate a diverse workforce? What human resources policies and practices would you implement to motivate employees to give topnotch service?[1] ■

UNDERSTANDING WHAT HUMAN RESOURCES MANAGERS DO

As Starbucks's Howard Schultz knows, hiring the right people to help a company reach its goals and then overseeing their training and development, motivation, evaluation, and compensation is critical to a company's success. These activities are known as **human resources management (HRM)**, which encompasses all the tasks involved in acquiring, maintaining, and developing an organization's human resources. Because of the accelerating rate at which today's workforce, economy, corporate cultures, and legal environment are being transformed, the role of HRM is increasingly viewed as a strategic one.[2]

Human resources (HR) managers must figure out how to attract qualified employees from a shrinking pool of entry-level candidates; how to train less-educated, lower-skilled employees; how to keep experienced employees when they may have few oppor-

human resources management (HRM)
Specialized function of planning how to obtain employees, oversee their training, evaluate them, and compensate them

tunities for advancement; and how to adjust the workforce equitably when rightsizing is necessary. They must also retrain employees to cope with increasing automation and computerization, manage increasingly complex (and often expensive) employee benefits programs, shape workplace policies to address changing workforce demographics and employee needs (as discussed in Chapter 9), and cope with the challenge of meeting government regulations in hiring practices and equal opportunity employment (see Exhibit 10.1).

Exhibit 10.1 **Major Employment Legislation**

Here are a few of the most significant sets of laws that affect employer-employee relations in the United States.

CATEGORY	LEGISLATION	HIGHLIGHTS
Labor and unionization	National Labor Relations Act, also known as the Wagner Act	Establishes the right of employees to form, join, and assist unions and the right to strike; prohibits employers from interfering in union activities
	Labor-Management Relations Act, also known as the Taft-Hartley Act	Expands union rights, gave employers free speech rights to oppose unions, gave the president the right to impose injunctions against strikes
	Labor-Management Reporting and Disclosure Act, also known as the Landrum-Griffin Act	Gives union members the right to nominate and vote for union leadership candidates
	State right-to-work laws	Gives individual employees the right to choose not to join a union
	Fair Labor Standards Act	Establishes minimum wage and overtime pay for nonexempt workers; sets strict guidelines for child labor
	Immigration Reform and Control Act	Prohibits employers from hiring illegal immigrants
Workplace safety	State workers' compensation acts	Require employers (in most states) to carry either private or government-sponsored insurance that provides income to injured workers
	Occupational Health and Safety Act	Empowers the Occupational Health and Safety Administration (OSHA) to set and enforce standards for workplace safety
Employee benefits	Employee Retirement Income Security Act	Governs the establishment and operation of private pension programs
	Consolidated Omnibus Budget Reconciliation Act (usually known by the acronym COBRA)	Requires employers to let employees or their beneficiaries buy continued health insurance coverage after employment ends
	Federal Unemployment Tax Act and similar state laws	Requires employers to fund programs that provide income for qualified unemployed persons
	Social Security Act	Provides a level of retirement, disability, and medical coverage for employees and their dependents; jointly funded by employers and employees

Exhibit 10.2

The Functions of the Human Resources Department

Human resources departments are responsible for these six important functions.

1. Planning for staffing needs
2. Recruiting and hiring
3. Training and development
4. Appraising performance
5. Administering compensation and benefits
6. Overseeing changes in employment status

In short, human resources managers and staff members help keep the organization running smoothly at every level by planning for a company's staffing needs, recruiting and hiring employees, training and developing employees and managers, appraising employee performance, and retaining valuable employees. (Note that in most organizations, HR shares these responsibilities with other functional departments. For instance, to train new accountants, HR will typically coordinate with the accounting department to provide the content expertise for training classes.) The HR staff also administers compensation and employee benefits and oversees changes in employment status (promotion, reassignment, termination or resignation, and retirement). This chapter explores each of these human resources responsibilities, beginning with planning (see Exhibit 10.2).

PLANNING FOR A COMPANY'S STAFFING NEEDS

One of the six functions of the human resources staff members is to plan for a company's staffing needs. Proper planning is critical because a miscalculation could leave a company without enough employees to keep up with demand, resulting in customer dissatisfaction and lost business. Yet if a company expands its staff too rapidly, profits may be eaten up by payroll or the firm may have to lay off people who were just recruited and trained at considerable expense. The planning function consists of two steps: (1) forecasting supply and demand and (2) evaluating job requirements (see Exhibit 10.3).

Exhibit 10.3 **Steps in Human Resources Planning**

Careful attention to each phase of this sequence helps ensure that a company will have the right human resources when it needs them.

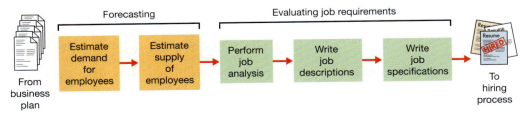

Forecasting Supply and Demand

Planning begins with forecasting *demand*, the numbers and types of employees who will be needed at various times. HR managers consider a number of variables when estimating demand, including (1) predicted sales of the company's goods and services; (2) the expected *turnover rate*, the percentage of the workforce that leaves every year; (3) the current workforce's skill level, relative to the company's future needs; (4) impending strategic decisions that might affect the number and type of workers needed; (5) changes in technology or other business factors that could affect the number and type of workers needed; and (6) the company's current and projected financial status.[3] Juggling all these variables in a dynamic business environment can get so complex that many HR managers, particularly in larger companies, rely on computer models to help predict workforce demands.

In addition to overall workforce levels, every company has a number of employees and managers who are considered so critical to the company's ongoing operations that HR managers work with top executives to identify potential replacements in the event any of these people need to be replaced, a process known as **succession planning**. These plans can cover owners, senior executives, researchers, top sales staff, and other vital members of the organization.[4] A **replacement chart** identifies these key employees and lists potential replacements, along with any current vacancies in key positions and other planning details (such as the number of years before the CEO is expected to retire, for instance).

With some idea of future workforce demands, the HR staff then tries to estimate the *supply* of available employees. In many cases, that supply is within the company already—perhaps just needing training to fill future requirements. Starbucks may well find that the assistant manager at an existing store can be promoted to manage the new store and that one of the current employees can be moved up to assistant manager.

To ensure a steady supply of experienced employees for new opportunities and to maintain existing operations, successful companies focus heavily on **employee retention**, the degree to which they are able to keep desired employees. A good way to understand the retention challenge is to review Herzberg's two-factor theory from Chapter 9. Both hygiene factors (dissatisfiers) and motivators contribute to retention efforts. For instance, both better pay (removing a dissatisfier) and the opportunity to lead a new project (adding a motivator) are steps that could increase employee retention. The steps employers take also fluctuate with the economy. In contrast to the onsite massage therapists, free espresso, game rooms, and other, sometimes frivolous offerings from the 1990s, many employers now emphasize more meaningful work-life benefits that help employees balance their work and home lives, including flexible work schedules, telecommuting, and career planning assistance.[5]

If existing employees cannot be tapped for new positions, the HR team must determine how to find people outside the company who have the necessary skills. In addition to hiring permanent employees, either part time or full time, companies have several other options for meeting workforce needs, including temporary employees and outsourcing.

Temporary Employees

More and more businesses try to save money and increase flexibility by augmenting their core workforces with temporary employees, or "temps," whose schedules can be rearranged to suit the company's needs. As a result, this segment of the labor force has increased by leaps and bounds in recent years.[6] The temporary ranks include computer systems analysts, human resource managers, accountants, doctors, and even CEOs, with technical fields making up the fastest-growing segment of temporary employment.

Companies are incorporating temporary workers in long-term plans, whereas 15 years ago they used temps to fill occasional vacancies. The use of temps is an excellent recruiting technique because it allows companies to try out employees before hiring

---

succession planning
Workforce planning efforts that identify possible replacements for specific employees, usually senior executives

replacement chart
A planning tool that identifies the most vital employees in the organization and any available information related to their potential replacement

employee retention
Efforts to keep current employees

them permanently. Thus, what often begins as a temp assignment can turn into multiyear employment. Some 29 percent of workers employed by temp agencies remain on the job assignment for one year or more, according to the Bureau of Labor Statistics. Many of these "permatemps" hold high-prestige, high-skilled technology jobs at leading firms. In fact, they often do the same work as the company's permanent employees, but because they are temps, they do not qualify for the benefits enjoyed by regular workers. However, some permatemps have sued companies, saying that they are, in fact, full-time employees and as such deserve employee benefits.[7] Moreover, the guidelines for determining whether a worker is an employee or an independent contractor are complicated and not always clear but have significant tax repercussions for both the worker and the company.[8]

A special category of foreign temporary workers has generated its own controversy in recent years as well. Usually known as "H1-B" workers for the type of *work visa* they've been granted by the U.S. government, these workers are allowed to work in the United States for three years and one three-year extension (a similar program, H2-B, lets lower-skilled workers in the country for up to 10 months). The pur-

Technologies That Are Revolutionizing Business

Assistive technologies

The term *assistive technologies* covers a broad range of devices and systems that help people with disabilities perform activities that might otherwise be difficult or impossible. These include technologies that help people communicate orally and visually, interact with computers and other equipment, and enjoy greater mobility, along with numerous other specific functions.

How they're changing business

Assistive technologies create a vital link for thousands of employees with disabilities, giving them the opportunity to pursue a greater range of career paths and giving employers access to a broader base of talent. With the United States heading for a potentially serious shortage of workers in a few years, the economy will benefit from everyone who can make a contribution, and assistive technologies will be an important part of the solution.

Where you can learn more

AssistiveTech.net, www.assistivetech.net, is a great place to search for the many categories of assistive technologies now available; it also provides links to a variety of other sites. The Business Leadership Network, www.usbln.com, "recognizes and promotes best practices in hiring, retraining, and marketing to people with disabilities." For a look at the government's efforts to promote these technologies, visit the National Institute on Disability and Rehabilitation Research, www.ed.gov/about/offices/list/osers/nidrr. If you'd like to explore a career in assistive technologies, visit the Rehabilitation Engineering and Assistive Technology Society of North America, www.resna.org. Technology companies such as IBM and Microsoft also devote significant resources to developing assistive technologies and making information technology more accessible.

pose of the H1-B program is to give U.S. companies, primarily in high technology, access to people with specific talents that may be in short supply in the United States at any particular time.[9] Many U.S. companies claim that they need H1-B workers to remain competitive, but some U.S. employees complain that the program is allowing in more foreign workers than it was designed for and that some companies may be manipulating the program to replace high-paid native employees with less-expensive foreign workers.[10]

Outsourcing

Just as companies can opt to outsource parts of the production function (Chapter 8), they can also use outsourcing as a way to meet staffing throughout the organization without hiring permanent employees. Some companies outsource an entire function, such as sales or human resources, whereas others outsource selected jobs or projects. In general, outsourcing is used to take advantage of outside expertise, to increase flexibility, or to benefit from the cost-efficiencies offered by firms that specialize in a single business function. Many companies even outsource work to former employees who've set themselves up as independent contractors or started companies that perform the same functions they used to perform for employers.[11]

Outsourcing has many advantages: It gives companies access to new resources and world-class capabilities; it shares the risk of getting the work done; and it frees company resources for other purposes. Still, outsourcing has its share of risks, including loss of control, greater dependency on suppliers, and loss of in-house skills. Some companies have also experienced work delays, unhappy customers, and labor union battles as a result of outsourcing.[12]

Evaluating Job Requirements

The second step of the planning function is to evaluate job requirements. If you were the owner of a small business, you might have a good grasp of the requirements of all the jobs in your company. However, in large organizations where hundreds or thousands of employees are performing a wide variety of jobs, management needs a more formal and objective method of evaluating job requirements. That method is called **job analysis**.

To obtain the information needed for a job analysis, the human resources staff asks employees or supervisors several questions: What is the purpose of the job? What tasks are involved in the job? What qualifications and skills are needed to do it effectively? In what kind of setting does the job take place? Is there much public contact involved? Does the job entail much time pressure? Sometimes they obtain job information by observing employees directly. Other times they ask employees to keep daily diaries describing exactly what they do during the workday.

Once job analysis has been completed, the human resources staff develops a **job description**, a formal statement summarizing the tasks involved in the job and the conditions under which the employee will work. In most cases, the staff will also develop a **job specification**, which identifies the type of personnel a job requires, including the skills, education, experience, and personal attributes that candidates need to possess[13] (see Exhibit 10.4).

job analysis
Process by which jobs are studied to determine the tasks and dynamics involved in performing them

job description
Statement of the tasks involved in a given job and the conditions under which the holder of the job will work

job specification
Statement describing the kind of person who would be best for a given job—including the skills, education, and previous experience that the job requires

Exhibit 10.4

Job Description and Specification

A well-written job description and specification tells potential applicants what to expect from the job and what employers will expect from them.

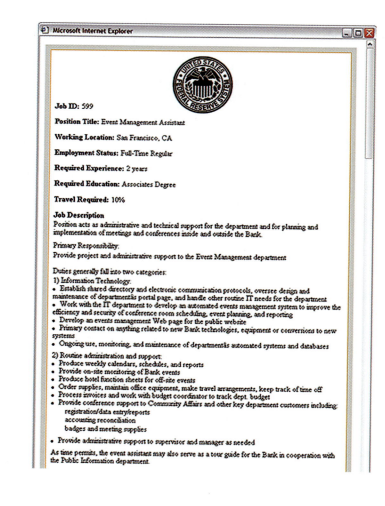

Microsoft Internet Explorer

Job ID: 599

Position Title: Event Management Assistant

Working Location: San Francisco, CA

Employment Status: Full-Time Regular

Required Experience: 2 years

Required Education: Associates Degree

Travel Required: 10%

Job Description
Position acts as administrative and technical support for the department and for planning and implementation of meetings and conferences inside and outside the Bank.

Primary Responsibility:
Provide project and administrative support to the Event Management department

Duties generally fall into two categories:
1) Information Technology:
• Establish shared directory and electronic communication protocols, oversee design and maintenance of department's portal page, and handle other routine IT needs for the department
• Work with the IT department to develop an automated events management system to improve the efficiency and security of conference room scheduling, event planning, and reporting
• Develop an events management Web page for the public website
• Primary contact on anything related to new Bank technologies, equipment or conversions to new systems
• Ongoing use, monitoring, and maintenance of department's automated systems and databases

2) Routine administration and support:
• Produce weekly calendars, schedules, and reports
• Provide on-site monitoring of Bank events
• Produce hotel function sheets for off-site events
• Order supplies, maintain office equipment, make travel arrangements, keep track of time off
• Process invoices and work with budget coordinator to track dept. budget
• Provide conference support to Community Affairs and other key department customers including:
    registration/data entry/reports
    accounting reconciliation
    badges and meeting supplies

• Provide administrative support to supervisor and manager as needed

As time permits, the event assistant may also serve as a tour guide for the Bank in cooperation with the Public Information department.

RECRUITING, HIRING, AND TRAINING NEW EMPLOYEES

Having forecast a company's supply and demand for employees and evaluated job requirements, the human resources manager's next step is to match the job specification with an actual person or selection of people. This task is accomplished through **recruiting**, the process of attracting suitable candidates for an organization's jobs. One recent study shows that companies with excellent recruiting and retention policies provide a nearly 8 percent higher return to shareholders than those that don't.[14]

Recruiters are specialists on the human resources staff who are responsible for locating job candidates. They use a variety of methods and resources, including internal searches, newspaper and Internet advertising, public and private employment agencies, union hiring halls, college campuses and career offices, trade shows, corporate "head-hunters" (outside agencies that specialize in finding and placing employees), and referrals from employees or colleagues in the industry (see Exhibit 10.5). One of the fastest-growing recruitment resources for both large and small businesses is the Internet. Today, many companies recruit online through their websites in addition to using popular online recruiting services, as the special feature "E-Business in Action" at the end of this part discusses.

recruiting
Process of attracting appropriate applicants for an organization's jobs

The Hiring Process

After exploring at least one—but usually more—of the available recruitment channels to assemble a pool of applicants, the human resources department may spend weeks and sometimes months on the hiring process. Most companies go through the same basic stages in the hiring process as they sift through applications to come up with the person (or persons) they want.

The first stage is to select a small number of qualified candidates from all of the applications received. Finalists may be chosen on the basis of a standard application form that all candidates fill out or on the basis of a résumé—a summary of education, experience, and personal data compiled by each applicant (see "Preparing Your Résumé" in Appendix E for further details). Sometimes both sources of information are used. Many organizations now use *applicant tracking systems* to help them quickly sort through résumés and identify the most attractive candidates for each job; the systems contain résumés submitted electronically and paper résumés that have been scanned in. These systems not only help companies filter through thousands of résumés, they can also help HR professionals analyze the efficiency of the entire recruiting process.[15]

The second stage in the hiring process is to interview each candidate to clarify qualifications and to fill in any missing information (see "Interviewing with Potential Employers"

Exhibit 10.5   **How Employers and Job Seekers Approach the Recruiting Process**

Studies show that employers prefer to fill job openings with people from within their organization or from an employee's recommendation. Placing want ads is often viewed as a last resort. In contrast, typical job seekers begin their job-search process from the opposite direction (starting with reading a newspaper or Internet ads).

Employers →

| Look for someone inside the organization | Rely on networking contacts and personal recommendations | Hire an employment agency or search firm | Review/send unsolicited résumés | Place/read a newspaper or an Internet ad |

← **Job Seekers**

in Appendix E for further details). Another goal of the interview is to get an idea of the applicant's personality and ability to work well with others. A growing number of companies, from the Woman & Infants Hospital of Rhode Island to delivery giant UPS, realize that the right attitude can be as vital as job experience or technical qualifications.[16] Depending on the type of job at stake, candidates may also be asked to take a test or a series of tests.

After the initial prescreening interviews comes the third stage, when the best candidates may be asked to meet with someone in the human resources department who will conduct a more probing interview. For higher-level positions, candidates may go through a series of interviews with managers, potential co-workers, and the employees who will make up the successful candidate's staff. Sometimes this process can take weeks. When Southwest Airlines had to fill 4,200 job openings in one year, the company interviewed nearly 80,000 people. For many positions, candidates undergo a rigorous interview process that can take as long as six weeks before they are hired. Southwest wants to make sure that new employees will fit in with the company's culture. The payback: low turnover and high customer satisfaction.[17]

After all the interviews have been completed, the process moves to the final stages. In the fourth stage, the department supervisor evaluates the candidates, sometimes in consultation with a higher-level manager, the human resources department, and staff. During the fifth stage, the employer checks the references of the top few candidates. The employer may also research the candidates' education, previous employment, and motor vehicle records. A growing number of employers are also checking candidates' credit histories, a practice that is drawing criticism as a violation of privacy.[18] In the sixth stage, the supervisor selects the most suitable person for the job. Now the search is over—provided the candidate accepts the offer.

Background Checks

In response to concerns about workplace violence, unethical business behavior, and other problems, many companies are taking a closer look at job candidates. For instance, more than 1 million physical assaults and thousands of homicides occur at work each year. Violence can not only harm employees and customers, hurt productivity, and lead to expensive lawsuits and higher health-care costs, but employers can also be found liable if they fail to screen applicants adequately. This means that companies need to be especially careful about negligent hiring.[19]

As Exhibit 10.6 shows, employers conduct a variety of background checks on job applicants, including verifying all educational credentials and previous jobs, accounting for any large time gaps between jobs, and checking references. Background checks are particularly important for jobs in which employees are in a position to harm others

Exhibit 10.6

Checking Out New Hires

Today's employers are scrutinizing new employees more closely.

Percentage of employers that perform background checks

Employment verification	86%
Criminal records check	81%
Drug screen	78%
Reference checks	70%
Education verification	70%
Motor vehicle records	56%

or handle large amounts of cash, for instance. Roughly 80 percent of U.S. employers conduct criminal background checks, and a third now conduct credit checks. These checks can prevent serious hiring errors—according to one firm that does criminal background checks for employers, 9 percent of its searches uncover felony records that applicants failed to disclose—although some applicants and privacy advocates have expressed concerns about both invasion of privacy and the chance of errors in both criminal and credit histories.[20]

Hiring and the Law

Federal and state laws and regulations govern many aspects of the hiring process. In particular, employers must be careful to avoid discrimination in the wording of their application forms, in interviewing, and in testing. Employers must also respect the privacy of applicants. Consider the dilemma this situation presents for employers.

On the one hand, asking questions about unrelated factors such as citizenship, marital status, age, and religion violates the Equal Employment Opportunity Commission's regulations because such questions may lead to discrimination. In addition, employers are not allowed to ask questions about whether a person has children, whether a person owns or rents a home, what caused a physical disability, whether a person belongs to a union, whether a person has ever been arrested, or when a person attended school. The exception is when such information is related to a bona fide occupational qualification for the specific job.

Learning from Business Blunders

Oops: In late October 2003, federal agents raided 61 Wal-Mart locations in 21 states, rounding up 250 to 300 illegal aliens who worked for companies that Wal-Mart hired to clean its stores at night. The public and regulators would probably overlook one or two instances of this nature, but Wal-Mart has made quite a few headlines in recent years, with several cases of illegal aliens working for cleaning contractors and multiple accusations of violating child labor laws and overtime laws, discriminating against women, and locking employees in stores at night (the company claims this policy was intended to protect employees in high-crime areas, but some employees have complained they couldn't get out of the building when they were sick or injured, when hurricanes hit in Florida, or when their wives went into labor). In all of these cases, Wal-Mart defended itself by saying that any wrong actions taken on the part of employees or outside firms are against company policy.

What You Can Learn: Managing a company as large as Wal-Mart is a complex task, to be sure, and mistakes are bound to happen. Big companies are also big targets, so based on numbers alone, Wal-Mart is going to attract more complaints and more lawsuits than smaller employers. Moreover, Wal-Mart wasn't accused of hiring illegal aliens itself (whether or not Wal-Mart knew its contractors hired illegal aliens is a point of dispute). However, in the court of public opinion, such distinctions are often lost on many people. In addition, the public and government officials aren't always going to accept the defense that company policy forbids all these wrong actions and that the problems were caused by a few rogue managers acting on their own. When mistakes are repeated or occur in multiple places throughout the company, people get suspicious. As Jeffrey Garten, dean of the Yale School of Management, recently wrote in reference to Wal-Mart's troubles, "For me, there is too much smoke for there not to be a fire." In addition to clearly communicating explicit policies that forbid illegal activity, managers also need to review the culture of the organization to see if it is intentionally or unintentionally promoting bad behavior. For instance, if a supervisor picks up the message to "cut costs or you'll lose your job," even if it's never expressed in those exact words, he or she might be sorely tempted to cut ethical or legal corners.

On the other hand, employers must also obtain sufficient information about employees to avoid becoming the target of a negligent-hiring lawsuit. Moreover, the Immigration Reform and Control Act (passed in 1986) forbids almost all U.S. companies from hiring illegal aliens. The act also prohibits discrimination in hiring on the basis of national origin or citizenship status. This creates a difficult situation for employers who must try to determine their applicants' citizenship, so they can verify that the newly hired are legally eligible to work, without asking questions that violate the law. As you can imagine, striking the balance can be quite a challenge.

Testing

One much-debated aspect of the hiring process is testing—using not only the tests that prospective employers give job applicants but any devices that can evaluate employees when making job decisions. Tests are used to gauge abilities, intelligence, interests, and sometimes even physical condition and personality.

Yasuko Ishikawa, a Delta Air Lines flight attendant, was fired after a random urine test showed her sample had been tampered with. So Ishikawa took her case to court. The jury found that the lab conducting the drug test was negligent and awarded Ishikawa $400,000. Delta also offered to reinstate her.

Many companies rely on preemployment testing to determine whether applicants are suited to the job and whether they'll be worth the expense of hiring and training. Companies use three main procedures: job-skills testing, psychological testing, and drug testing. Job-skills tests are the most common type, designed to assess competency or specific abilities needed to perform a job. Psychological tests usually take the form of questionnaires. These tests can be used to assess overall intellectual ability, attitudes toward work, interests, managerial potential, or personality characteristics—including dependability, commitment, and motivation. People who favor psychological testing say that it can predict how well employees will actually perform on the job. However, critics say that such tests are ineffective and potentially discriminatory.

Drug and alcohol testing is one of the most controversial issues in business today. Some employers believe such testing is absolutely necessary to maintain workplace safety, whereas others view it as an invasion of employee privacy and a sign of disrespect. Even within a single industry, you can find widely divergent opinions on the subject. Computer maker Dell tests every employee, whereas rival HP doesn't test anyone. Some companies test only applicants but not current employees.[21] Nationwide, nearly half of all companies now require applicants to undergo drug and alcohol testing, and this percentage is expected to rise for two reasons: (1) to cut the costs (approximately $100 billion a year) and the reduced productivity associated with drug abuse and (2) to reduce the number of accidents (substance abusers have two to four times as many accidents as other employees, and drug use is linked to 40 percent of industrial fatalities).[22] Moreover, companies are liable for negligent hiring practices if an employee harms an innocent party on the job. Thus, drug testing will probably increase, even though the direct financial payback of these programs is unclear.[23]

Training and Development

Even the best applicants rarely begin a job knowing everything they need to know or possessing all the skills they need to have in order to succeed in a specific position, company, or industry. Moreover, with the pace of change in everything from government regulations to consumer tastes to technology, knowledge and skills need to be constantly updated. Consequently, the most successful companies place a heavy emphasis on employee training and development efforts, for everyone from entry-level workers to the CEO. Overall, U.S. companies now spend some $50 billion a year on training.[24]

Most companies begin the training process as soon as new employees join the workforce. These **orientation** programs usually include information about company background and structure, equal opportunity practices, safety regulations, standards of employee conduct, company culture, employee compensation and benefit plans, work times, and other topics that newly hired employees might have questions about.[25] Orientation programs help new employees understand their role in the organization and feel more comfortable.

At Intel, for instance, all new hires participate in a six-month "integration" curriculum. Day One begins when new hires receive a packet at their home. The packet contains material about the company's culture and values, along with some forms to fill out. During the first month, all new hires attend a class called "Working at Intel," a formal eight-hour introduction to the company's corporate culture. At the end of the six-month period, each new hire participates in a two-hour structured question-and-answer session in which an executive reviews the employee's transition into Intel and then asks a final long-term question: "What do you think it will take to succeed at Intel?"[26]

Training and other forms of employee development continue throughout the employee's career in most cases. Many HR departments maintain a **skills inventory**, which identifies both the current skill levels of all the employees and the skills the com-

orientation
Session or procedure for acclimating a new employee to the organization

skills inventory
A list of the skills a company needs from its workforce, along with the specific skills that individual employees currently possess

Click and Learn: E-Training Today's Employees

Employers from automakers and software firms to hospitals and pharmaceutical companies are turning to computers to train today's employees. Electronic training, or e-learning, uses computers and live or recorded webcasts, web-based self-paced tutorials, and other forms of electronic media such as CD-ROMs to instruct employees on new products, customer service, sales techniques, and more.

Dell Computer expects 90 percent of its learning solutions to be totally or partially technology enabled. General Motors University uses interactive satellite broadcasts to teach salespeople the best way to highlight features on new cars. Pharmaceutical companies such as Merck use live interactive Internet classes to instruct sales reps on the latest product information rather than fly them to a conference center. And IBM has moved online virtually all the content of the first three phases of management training for its first-line managers—eliminating the need to send them to offsite locations over the course of a training period that stretched out over six months.

As these companies have learned, e-training has many benefits:

- *Reduced costs.* Much of the cost savings comes from reduced travel expenses and time savings. Intel has saved over $1 million annually by using e-training programs. "If we save our 70,000 employees just 20 minutes a year, that alone is $1 million in savings," says one Intel training manager.
- *Increased productivity.* "Our salesforce can't come in for three-day conferences anymore," says one Black & Decker vice president. "But they still need to understand the company's new products and features." So the company has instituted online training courses—which means the company's 700-person salesforce can spend a combined 12,000 more days a year with customers.

- *Individualized pace.* E-learning allows you to learn at your own pace—skipping over material you already know and spending more time learning material that meets your specific needs.
- *Increased consistency.* Companies can create one set of instructional materials that is used consistently by everyone in the organization. Thus, all employees are learning the same thing—regardless of their location.

Like many other Internet-related efforts in recent years, e-learning saw a rapid rise followed by a period of rethinking, when corporate trainers moved past the "gee-whiz" factor and took a more objective look at what training technology really could—and couldn't—offer. They began to appreciate the value of e-learning but also realized it wasn't the solution to every training challenge and that impressive technology was no substitute for good instructional planning. As a result, many companies now emphasize *blended learning*, which is a combination of delivery methods. Wendy O'Brien of 3Com, a computer networking firm based in Massachusetts, says her team examines the content and audience of each training effort, along with parameters such as budgets and deadlines, before they choose a delivery method. By combining the best available methods in each individual case, 3Com maintains the focus on the learner, rather than on the technology, while still using e-learning to its fullest potential.

Questions for Critical Thinking

1. Why is e-learning an increasingly popular training approach for companies?
2. How might an economic slowdown or global terrorism affect e-learning?

pany needs in order to succeed. Depending on the industry, some of the most common subjects for ongoing training include problem solving, new products, sales, customer service, safety, sexual harassment, supervision, quality, strategic planning, communication, time management, and team building.[27]

Tires Plus is a good example of a company that invests heavily in employee training to become more competitive. Some 1,700 employees spend a total of 60,000 hours annually attending formal training programs at Tires Plus University. The company also offers special training programs to develop inexperienced but promising workers into mechanics and managers. While training programs cost Tires Plus more than $3 million a year, they help the company retain talented workers and fill leadership positions—a small price to pay in today's competitive market.[28] Southwest Airlines is another company that offers its employees training through its "University for People." Employees can choose courses that will help them to do their jobs more effectively and be more flexible in the tasks they can perform.[29]

A growing number of companies now use a variety of web-based and computer-based tools to train employees.

performance appraisal
Evaluation of an employee's work according to specific criteria

In addition, companies also use a variety of methods to deliver training. Self-paced, computer-based training (see "Click and Learn: E-Training Today's Employees") is gaining momentum, but the majority of training courses in most companies still involve an instructor, either in person in a classroom or long distance via videoconferencing or webcasting.[30] Many training efforts incorporate a combination of approaches, such as an initial instructor-led class followed by self-paced training via workbooks or web-based courses.

APPRAISING EMPLOYEE PERFORMANCE

How do employees (and their managers) know whether they are doing a good job? How can they improve their performance? What new skills should they learn? Most human resources managers attempt to answer these questions by developing **performance appraisals** to objectively evaluate employees according to set criteria. Well-designed appraisals promote both fairness and improvement by focusing on job-related performance standards.

The ultimate goal of performance appraisals is not to judge employees but rather to improve their performance. Thus, experts recommend that performance reviews be an ongoing discipline—not just a once-a-year event linked to employee raises. Periodic performance evaluations are especially important in today's project-driven, results-oriented workplace. Employees need fast feedback so they can correct their deficiencies in a timely manner.

Most companies require regular written evaluations of each employee's work. To ensure objectivity and consistency, firms generally use a standard company performance appraisal form to evaluate employees. The evaluation criteria are in writing so that both employee and supervisor understand what is expected and are therefore able to determine whether the work is being done adequately. Written evaluations also provide a record of the employee's performance, which may protect the company in cases of disputed terminations. An increasing number of companies now conduct evaluations online, using password-protected websites to record and analyze information.[31]

The specific measures of employee performance vary widely by job, company, and industry. Most jobs are evaluated in several areas, including tasks specific to the position, contribution to the company's overall success, and interaction with colleagues and customers. A production-line technician might be evaluated on such factors as work quality, productivity, innovation and problem solving, teamwork, job knowledge, and reliability. In contrast, the production manager might be evaluated on the basis of communication skills, people management, leadership, teamwork, recruiting and employee development, delegation, financial management, planning, and organizational skills.[32]

Many performance appraisals require the employee to be rated by several people (including more than one supervisor and perhaps several co-workers). This practice further promotes fairness by correcting for possible biases. One appraisal format that moves the review process from a one-dimensional perspective to a multidimensional format is the *360-degree review*. Designed to provide employees with a broader range of perspectives, the 360-degree review solicits feedback from colleagues above, below, and around the employee to provide observations of the person's performance in several skill and behavioral categories. This means that employees rate the performance of their superiors as well as that of their peers.[33]

One of the biggest problems with any employee appraisal system is finding a way to measure productivity. In a production job, the person who types the most pages of acceptable copy or who assembles the most defect-free microprocessors in a given amount of time is clearly the most productive. But how does an employer evaluate the productivity of a registration clerk at a hotel, a programming manager at a large television station, or a research scientist? Although the organization's overall productivity can be measured (number of rooms booked per night, number of viewers per hour, number of patents or new products), often the employer can't directly relate the results to any one employee's efforts.

Evaluating productivity becomes an even greater challenge in organizations where employees work in teams. Some companies, such as Con-Way Transportation Services, meet this challenge by having teams evaluate themselves. About every three months a neutral facilitator leads a discussion in which team members rate team performance on a 1 to 5 scale for 31 criteria, which can include customer satisfaction, the ability to meet goals, employee behavior toward co-workers and customers, job knowledge, motivation, and skills. During the meetings, members discuss the team's performance. Individual performance is also discussed, but only in the context of the team. Each person creates two columns on a sheet of paper, one labeled "strengths" and the other "something to work on." Team members self-assess and then pass the list around the room so other team members can add their comments.[34]

In addition to formal, periodic performance evaluations, many companies evaluate some workers' performance continuously, using **electronic performance monitoring (EPM)**, sometimes called *computer activity monitoring*. For instance, customer service and telephone sales representatives are often evaluated by the number of calls they complete per hour and other variables. Newer software products extend this monitoring capability, from measuring data input accuracy to scanning for suspicious words in employee e-mails. As you can imagine, EPM efforts can generate controversy in the workplace, elevating employee stress levels and raising concerns about invasion of privacy.[35]

electronic performance monitoring (EPM)
Real-time, computer-based evaluation of employee performance

ADMINISTERING COMPENSATION AND EMPLOYEE BENEFITS

Pay and benefits are of vital interest to all employees, of course, and these subjects also consume considerable time and attention in HR departments. In many companies, payroll is the single biggest expense in the entire company, and the cost of benefits, particularly health care, continues to climb. Consequently, **compensation**, the combination of direct payments such as wages or salary and indirect payments through employee benefits, is one of the HR manager's most significant responsibilities.

compensation
Money, benefits, and services paid to employees for their work

Salaries and Wages

Most employees receive the bulk of their compensation in the form of **salary**, if they receive a fixed amount per year, or **wages**, if they are paid by the unit of time (hourly, daily, or weekly) or by the unit of output (often called "getting paid by the piece" or "piecework"). The Fair Labor Standards Act, introduced in 1938 and amended many times since then, sets specific guidelines that employers must follow when administering salaries and wages, including setting a minimum wage and paying overtime for time worked beyond 40 hours a week. However, most professional and managerial employees are considered exempt from these regulations, meaning, for instance, their employers don't have to pay them for overtime. Although the potential for long hours with no extra pay is a disadvantage of being exempt (some professionals and executives sometimes work as many as 50, 60, or even 70 hours a week), these employees often enjoy other advantages, such as higher pay and more flexibility in setting their own schedules. The distinction between *exempt employees* and *nonexempt employees* is based on job responsibilities and pay level. In general, salaried employees are exempt, although there are many exceptions to this.[36]

Both wages and salaries are, in principle, based on the contribution of a particular job to the company. Thus, a sales manager, who is responsible for bringing in sales revenue, is paid more than a secretary, who handles administrative tasks but doesn't

salary
Fixed cash compensation for work, usually by yearly amount; independent of the number of hours worked

wages
Cash payment based on the number of hours the employee has worked or the number of units the employee has produced

sell or supervise. However, pay often varies widely by position, industry, and location. Among the best-paid employees in the world are chief executive officers of large U.S. corporations.

Compensation has become a hot topic in recent years, at both ends of the pay scale. At the low end, for instance, many businesses, employees, and unions are wrestling with the downward pressure on wages and benefits exerted by Wal-Mart's enormous presence in the economy. With a million and a half employees (1 out of every 20 new jobs in this country is at Wal-Mart), the company's cost-conscious strategy indirectly affects thousands of people who've never worked there. In addition to offering lower wages than many traditional grocery and retail stores, Wal-Mart squeezes every possible penny out of operating costs and is quick to import goods from China and other lower-cost countries when U.S. suppliers can't meet its cost demands. As a result, many companies now feel forced to lower their own costs in order to compete. For instance, as Safeway, Albertson's, and other grocery stores try to compete with Wal-Mart, these retailers feel they have no choice but to pay their employees less and offer fewer benefits (see Chapter 9). Consumers, particularly low-income shoppers, benefit from Wal-Mart's lower prices, and their patronage benefits Wal-Mart's stockholders, but some critics charge that Wal-Mart employees who can't afford the company's health insurance and those who are on food stamps are increasing the burden on taxpayers.[37] Lower wages also mean Wal-Mart employees themselves are able to spend less on consumer goods and services, and consumer spending is a major factor in the strength of the U.S. economy. As one researcher puts it, "You can't have every company adopt a Wal-Mart strategy. It isn't sustainable." Given Wal-Mart's aggressive growth and continuing popularity with shoppers, this issue is likely to dominate compensation discussions for years.

Not all of Wal-Mart's competitors are following the "race to the bottom," as some people call it. For example, Wegmans and Costco are two retail chains that are succeeding with a markedly different approach to compensation. Wegmans, which offers most employees free health-care coverage and higher wages than Wal-Mart, follows the belief that "If we take care of our employees, they will take care of our customers," in the words of vice president Karen Shadders. Costco, which competes with Wal-Mart's Sam's Club chain of superstores, also offers higher wages and better benefits—and yet still generates better financial results than Sam's Club. Costco attributes much of its success to satisfied, motivated employees who are more productive and more eager to help customers.[38]

At the upper end of the pay scale, executive compensation, and the pay of CEOs in particular, has generated its own brand of controversy. CEOs typically receive complex compensation packages that include a base salary plus a wide range of benefits and bonuses, including *golden handshakes* when they join a company and *golden parachutes* when they leave. In 2002, the average compensation package for CEOs of the 100 largest U.S. public companies was around $15 million. Part of the controversy stems from the widening compensation gap between CEOs and their employees. A second aspect of the controversy can be the disparity between results and compensation. For instance, Walt Disney CEO Michael Eisner is credited with saving the company in the early 1980s, but during the five-year period from 1998 to 2003, Disney shareholder value dropped 41 percent while Eisner's compensation package totaled more than $700 million. It is important to note that comparing compensation packages is difficult because they are so complex, and some include potential income that executives haven't actually received yet, but critics still find the numbers staggering. The boards of directors who grant these packages generally defend them as necessary to retain key executives, but critics respond that many other CEOs earn far less and don't leave in search of greener pastures.[39]

Incentive Programs

incentives
Cash payments to employees who produce at a desired level or whose unit (often the company as a whole) produces at a desired level

To encourage employees to be more productive, innovative, and committed to their work, many companies provide managers and employees with **incentives**, cash payments linked to specific individual, group, and companywide goals; overall productivity; and company success. In other words, achievements, not just activities, are made the basis for payment. The success of these programs often depends on how closely incentives are linked to actions within the employee's control:

- *Bonuses.* For both salaried and wage-earning employees, one type of incentive compensation is the **bonus**, a payment in addition to the regular wage or salary. As an incentive to reduce turnover during the year, some firms pay an annual year-end bonus, amounting to a certain percentage of each employee's wages. Other cash bonuses are tied to company performance.

- *Commissions.* In contrast to bonuses, **commissions** are a form of compensation that pays employees a percentage of sales made. Used mainly for sales staff, they may be either the sole compensation or an incentive payment in addition to a regular salary.

- *Profit sharing.* Employees may be rewarded for staying with a company and encouraged to work harder through **profit sharing**, a system in which employees receive a portion of the company's profits. Depending on the company, profits may be distributed quarterly, semiannually, or annually.

Thanks to Jamba Juice's management incentives, such as bonuses and paid sabbaticals, employee turnover at the company is substantially below the industry average.

These incentive programs are so popular in today's workplace that many employees consider their financial value as part of their overall salary package.

Employee Benefits and Services

Companies also regularly provide **employee benefits**—elements of compensation other than wages, salaries, and incentives. For example, Starbucks offers medical and dental insurance, vacation and holiday pay, stock options, discounts on Starbucks products, adoption assistance, domestic partner benefits, and support resources for child care and elder care. The benefits package is available to employees who work more than 20 hours a week, helping Starbucks attract and retain good people at every level.[40]

Companies may offer employee benefits either as a preset package—that is, the employee gets whatever insurance, paid holidays, pension plan, and other benefits the company sets up—or as flexible benefits, recognizing that people have different priorities and needs at different stages of their lives. Flexible plans allow employees to pick their benefits—up to a certain dollar amount—to create a benefits package tailored to their individual needs. Moreover, they smooth out imbalances in benefits received by single employees and workers with families.[41] An employee with a young family might want extra life or health insurance, for example, and might feel no need for a pension plan, whereas a single employee might choose to "buy" an extra week or two of vacation time by giving up some other benefit.

The benefits most commonly provided by employers are insurance, retirement benefits, employee stock-ownership plans, stock options, and family benefits. In the following sections, we will explore how these benefits and services are undergoing considerable change to meet the needs of today's workforce.

Insurance

Employers can offer a range of insurance to their employees, including life, health, dental, vision plans, disability, and long-term-care insurance. Although employers are under no general legal obligation to provide insurance coverage (except in union contracts, for instance), most mid- to large-size companies now offer some level of insurance coverage. However, perhaps no other issue illustrates the challenging economics of business today than health insurance. With insurance premiums and other costs rising faster than employers can raise their own prices, many companies are searching for ways to reduce the financial impact. They're taking a variety of steps, including forcing employees to pick up more of the cost, capping or reducing coverage for retired employees, auditing employees' health claims more carefully, inquiring into employees' health and habits

bonus
Cash payment, in addition to regular wage or salary, that serves as a reward for achievement

commissions
Employee compensation based on a percentage of sales made

profit sharing
The distribution of a portion of the company's profits to employees

employee benefits
Compensation other than wages, salaries, and incentive programs

more closely, dropping spouses from insurance plans, or firing employees who are so sick or disabled that they are no longer able to work. At the same time, however, workers' earnings aren't increasing fast enough to cover these new expenses, either. The tension is likely to continue, prompting calls for more government intervention, spurring unionizing efforts, and even pitting healthy employees against their less-healthy colleagues.[42]

Health-care costs are also changing the way some employers structure their workforces, as more companies hire part-time and temporary workers, who typically receive few company benefits. Nonetheless, some companies, such as Starbucks, continue to provide attractive benefit packages because doing so discourages employee turnover. Starbucks's CEO Howard Schultz figures that recruiting, interviewing, and training a new employee costs more than two years of medical coverage for an employee who stays with the company.[43]

Retirement Benefits

Social Security was created by the federal government following the Great Depression of the 1930s to provide basic support to those who could not accumulate the retirement money they would need later in life. Today, nearly everyone who works regularly is eligible for Social Security payments during retirement. This income is paid for by the Social Security tax, part of which is withheld by the employer from employees' wages and part of which is paid by the employer. If you are self-employed, you pay the full tax amount. As Chapter 1 noted, however, the Social Security system is severely underfunded, leading some employees to worry whether they'll get the retirement benefits they expect to receive.

retirement plans
Company-sponsored programs for providing retirees with income

In addition to Social Security from the federal government, many employers offer **retirement plans**, which are designed to provide continuing income after the employee retires. Employees at most midsized and large firms are offered some form of retirement benefits, although the types of coverage and amounts available have been changing significantly in recent years.[44] These plans are regulated by the Employees' Retirement Income Security Act of 1974 (ERISA), which established a federal agency to insure the assets of pension plans, along with newer laws that address specific types of retirement plans.

pension plans
Generally refers to traditional, defined benefit retirement plans

Company-sponsored retirement plans can be categorized as either *defined benefit plans*, in which the company specifies how much it will pay employees upon retirement, or *defined contribution plans*, in which companies specify how much they will put into the retirement fund (by matching employee contributions, for instance), without guaranteeing any specific payouts during retirement. Although both types are technically **pension plans**, when most people speak of pension plans, they are referring to traditional defined benefit plans, in which employers promise to pay their employees a benefit upon retirement based on the employee's retirement age, final average salary, and years of service.[45] In the past, most U.S. employers that offered retirement plans offered these defined benefit plans, but today fewer than 50 percent still do. Moreover, many of these plans are now in serious financial trouble. To meet their current and future obligations to employees, pension fund managers invest some of the company's cash and assume those investments will grow enough to cover future retirement needs. However, dramatic stock market losses in recent years have left many plans underfunded, some by billions of dollars, forcing those companies to redirect cash from other purposes. For instance, Delphi Automotive, a large auto parts manufacturer, has had to divert $600 million a year from expansion and hiring plans in order to cover gaps in its pension plan.[46]

Defined contribution plans are similar to savings plans that provide a future benefit based on annual employer contributions, voluntary employee matching contributions, and accumulated investment earnings. Employers can choose from several different types of defined contribution plans, the most common of which is known as a *401(k) plan*. In a 401(k) plan, employees contribute a percentage of their pretax income, and employers often match that amount or some portion of it. In addition to the money their employers invest, employees enjoy tax reductions based on their annual contributions to the fund.[47] Unfortunately, stock market declines, reductions in company contributions, and accounting scandals have reduced the attractiveness of 401(k) plans in the eyes of many employees, particularly in the all-too-common situation where employees invested most of their 401(k) fund in their own employer's stock. Enron employees alone lost an estimated $1 billion of retirement savings when that stock collapsed.[48]

Some 8 million U.S. employees are now enrolled in another type of defined benefit plan known as an **employee stock-ownership plan (ESOP)**, in which a company places a certain amount of its stock in trust for some or all of its employees, with each employee entitled to a certain share. These plans allow employees to later purchase the shares at a fixed price. If the company does well, the ESOP may provide a substantial employee benefit. In addition to potential retirement benefits, an ESOP also provides a means for employees to have a representative on the board of directors, a situation now found in more than 300 U.S. corporations.[49]

Stock Options

A related method for tying employee compensation to company performance is the stock option plan. **Stock options** grant employees the right to purchase a set number of shares of the employer's stock at a specific price, called the *grant* or *exercise price*, during a certain time period. Options typically "vest" over five years, at a rate of 20 percent annually. This means that at the end of one year employees can purchase up to 20 percent of the shares in the original grant, at the end of two years 40 percent, and so on. If the stock's market price exceeds the exercise price, the option holder can exercise the option and sell the stock at a profit. If the stock's price falls below the exercise price, the options become worthless, at least temporarily (such options are often referred to as being "under water").

Stock options can be a win-win situation for employers and employees. From the employer's perspective, stock options cost little, provide long-term incentives for good people to stay with the company, and encourage employees to work harder because they have a vested interest in the company doing well. From the employee's perspective, stock options can generate a handsome profit if the stock's market price exceeds the grant price. But stock options lose their appeal when the stock does not perform as expected.

Options are particularly common in executive compensation packages, where they offer an incentive for effective corporate management. They were also quite popular in the technology boom in the 1980s and 1990s, when start-ups would frequently lure new employees with low salaries but thousands of stock option shares. In the cases where those stocks enjoyed healthy growth, some employees became quite wealthy. Practically an entire generation of Microsoft employees earned enormous sums of money this way. However, employees in many other companies, particularly in dot-coms in the late 1990s, saw their dreams of stock-option riches turn to dust as stock prices collapsed. Stock options have also come under attack from regulators and financial reformers in recent years, who claim they can tempt executives into decisions that boost stock prices in the short term but harm the company in the long term. In a sign of what could be a major shift in compensation strategies, Microsoft announced in 2003 that it would stop awarding employees with stock options.[50]

Family Benefits

The Family Medical and Leave Act (FMLA), signed into law in 1993, requires employers with 50 or more workers to provide up to 12 weeks of unpaid leave per year for childbirth, adoption, or the care of oneself, a child, a spouse, or a parent with serious illness.[51] Many employees can't afford to take extended periods of time off without pay, but at least the law creates the opportunity for those who can.

Day care is another important family benefit, especially for two-career couples. Ford Motor Company, for instance, is opening more than a dozen centers providing employees with 24-hour child care—part of a sweeping plan to provide family related services in more than 30 locations around the United States. "Not only will [the centers] attract and retain the best, but the workforce, when they're at work, don't have to worry about their children and where they are," says one company spokesperson.[52] Today, only 10 percent of companies provide day-care facilities on the premises, but 86 percent of companies

Charles Prestwood is one of the many former Enron employees whose retirement savings were virtually wiped out when the company's stock collapsed. The value of his Enron stock plunged from $1.3 million to just $8,000.

employee stock-ownership plan (ESOP)
Program enabling employees to become partial owners of a company

stock options
Contract allowing the holder to purchase or sell a certain number of shares of a particular stock at a given price by a certain date

CEO Jim Goodnight of SAS Institute (a software development firm) takes a snack break with children at the company's on-site day-care center.

surveyed by Hewitt & Associates offer some form of child-care assistance. Types of assistance include dependent-care spending accounts and resource and referral (R&R) services, which help employees find suitable child care. Firms estimate that they save anywhere from $2.00 to $6.75 in lost productivity and employee absenteeism for every $1.00 they spend on R&R programs.[53]

A related family issue is care for aging parents. An estimated 50 percent of employers offer some form of elder-care assistance, ranging from referral services that help find care providers to dependent-care allowances. Some companies will even agree to move elderly relatives when they transfer an employee to another location.[54]

Other Employee Benefits

Although sometimes overlooked, paid holidays, sick pay, premium pay for working overtime or unusual hours, and paid vacations are important benefits. Companies handle holiday pay in various ways. To provide incentives for employee loyalty, most companies grant employees longer paid vacations after they've been with the organization for a prescribed number of years. Some companies let employees buy additional vacation time or sell unused days back to the employer. Sick-day allowances also vary from company to company and from industry to industry. Some U.S. companies have begun offering paid-time-off banks that combine vacation, personal use, and sick days into one package. Employees can then take a certain number of days off each year for whatever reason necessary, with no questions asked.[55]

Among the many other benefits that companies sometimes offer are sabbaticals, tuition loans and reimbursements, professional development opportunities, personal computers, financial counseling and legal services, assistance with buying a home, paid expenses for spouses who travel with employees, employee assistance programs, nap time, and wellness programs. Typical wellness programs include health screenings, health and wellness education programs, and fitness programs. Children's clothier OshKosh B'Gosh, for example, provides wellness education classes in nutrition, heart disease, cancer, diabetes, prescription medication, and others.[56] Wellness programs have been reported to reduce absenteeism, health-care costs, sickness, and work-related accidents.[57]

employee assistance programs (EAPs)
Company-sponsored counseling or referral plans for employees with personal problems

According to the U.S. Labor Department, 48 percent of all employers with more than 100 workers now offer **employee assistance programs (EAPs)**. EAPs offer private and confidential counseling to employees who need help with issues related to drugs, alcohol, finances, stress, family, and other personal problems. Studies by the National Council on Alcoholism and Drug Dependence (NCADD) show that the average annual cost for EAP services runs from $12 to $20 per employee. However, these services save between $5 and $16 for each dollar spent as a result of improved safety and productivity, as well as reduced employee turnover.[58]

Benefits such as company cars, paid country club memberships, free parking, and expanded casual dress days are often referred to as *perks* (short for *perquisite*). In a tight job market companies offer perks to attract the best managers.[59] "But recruitment perks only go so far," says one compensation expert. "Organizations must offer the total work experience to attract talent." And to keep talent from leaving, they must offer workers challenging jobs and training, more family-related benefits, and better management supervision.[60]

OVERSEEING CHANGES IN EMPLOYMENT STATUS

Business BUZZ

Warm-chair attrition: A situation in which employees have mentally checked out from their current jobs but are waiting for the economy to improve before finding better jobs

attrition
Loss of employees for reasons other than termination

Of course, providing competitive compensation and good employee benefits is no guarantee that employees will stay with the company. Every company experiences some level of **attrition**, when employees leave for reasons other than termination, including retirement, new job opportunities, long-term disability, or death. Virtually all companies also find themselves with the need to terminate employment of selected workers from time

Should Employees Pay to Keep Their Jobs?

When the economy is booming, job seekers tend to be in the driver's seat, and hiring managers will try signing bonuses, stock options, and other perks—doing whatever it takes to recruit and retain employees. However, when the economy heads south, negotiating power shifts back to employers, who sometimes have more workers than they can afford.

Facing a weakened economy, some companies immediately lay off employees. Others, recognizing that human capital is their most important asset, try to limit or avoid layoffs so they won't lose experienced talent and have to hastily rehire when the economy recovers. But maintaining huge payroll costs—which can account for as much as two-thirds of most companies' expenses—is a challenge during an economic downturn. So some companies freeze wages or cut pay across the surviving workforce to distribute the pain more equitably.

Salary and benefit cuts "are the last thing you want to do in a down economy," warn some human resources experts. "It's never good to take away from the people you want to keep." In fact, many companies that imposed widespread pay cuts in past recessions say they would never do it again. The cuts generated millions in savings. But worker morale—and productivity—plummeted. These experts argue that it would be better for companies to lay off their least-productive workers so they can afford to keep more-

productive employees. Not so, say others, who maintain that you can't have good morale unless all employees have confidence that a company will treat them fairly, which for some employees means avoiding layoffs at all costs, even if they have to swallow a pay cut.

The debate continues over which approach is the lesser of two evils: widespread layoffs or limited layoffs combined with across-the-board pay and benefits cuts for those who survive. From a company perspective, hiring and firing and then rehiring is an exercise they'd rather not repeat. But maintaining high payroll costs in poor economic times is also something they can't afford. From an employee's perspective, finding a new job in a recession is extremely difficult, so some are willing to pay to keep their jobs. But here's the twist: If employees feel they are being exploited by companies that are using an economic downturn to take back some of their hard-earned gains in the past decade or so, they will be the first to bolt when the economy strengthens.

Questions for Critical Thinking

1. What are management's staffing options in a declining economy?
2. Debate the options you just identified. Which options do your classmates prefer? Why? Do you agree?

to time. Whatever the reason, when a vacancy occurs, companies must go to the trouble and expense of finding a replacement, whether from inside or outside the company. Overseeing changes in employment status is another responsibility of the human resources department.

Promoting and Reassigning Employees

As Exhibit 10.5 shows, many companies prefer to look within the organization to fill job vacancies. In part, this "promote from within" policy allows a company to benefit from the training and experience of its own workforce. This policy also rewards employees who have worked hard and demonstrated the ability to handle more challenging tasks. In addition, morale is usually better when a company promotes from within because employees see that they can advance.

However, a potential pitfall of internal promotion is that a person may be given a job beyond his or her competence. A common practice is for someone who is good at one kind of job to be made a manager. Yet managing often requires a completely different set of skills. Someone who consistently racks up the most sales in the company, for example, is not necessarily a good candidate for sales manager. If the promotion is a mistake, the company not only loses its sales leader but also risks losing the employee altogether. People who can't perform well in a new job generally become demoralized and lose confidence in the abilities they do have. At the very least, support and training are needed to help promoted employees perform well.

Terminating Employees

termination
Act of getting rid of an employee
through layoff or firing

A company invests time, effort, and money in each new employee it recruits and trains. This investment is lost when an employee is removed by **termination**—permanently laying off the employee because of cutbacks or firing the employee for poor performance or other reasons. Many companies facing a downturn in business have avoided large-scale layoffs by cutting administrative costs (curtailing travel, seminars, and so on), freezing wages, postponing new hiring, implementing job-sharing programs, or encouraging early retirement. However, sometimes a company has no alternative but to reduce the size of its workforce, leaving the human resources department to handle layoffs and their resulting effects on both the terminated and the remaining employees.

layoffs
Termination of employees for
economic or business reasons

Layoffs are the termination of employees for economic or business reasons unrelated to employee performance. Companies are free to make layoffs in any manner they choose, just as long as certain demographic groups are not disproportionately affected. But as Michael Dell puts it, making cuts "is one of the hardest, most gut-wrenching decisions you can make as a leader." Layoffs are "an admission that we screwed up" by overhiring, admits Dell. If there's a lesson, says Dell, it's that "when things heat up quite a bit, we should take some pause"[61]

To help ease the pain of layoffs, many companies provide laid-off employees with job-hunting assistance. *Outplacement* aids such as résumé-writing courses, career counseling, office space, and secretarial help are offered to laid-off executives and blue-collar employees alike. Moreover, outplacement centers offer courses and tests to help employees decide what types of jobs are best suited for them.[62]

Terminating employment by firing an employee is a complex subject with many legal ramifications, and the line between a layoff and a firing can be blurry. For instance, many employees would be surprised to learn that every state except Montana supports the concept of *at-will employment*, meaning that companies are free to fire nearly anyone they choose. Exceptions to this vary from state to state, but in general, employers cannot discriminate in firing (such as by firing someone because he or she is of a certain race or a certain age), nor can they fire employees for whistle-blowing, filing a worker's compensation claim, or testifying against the employer in harassment or discrimination lawsuits.[63] If the employee believes any of these principles have been violated, he or she can opt to file a *wrongful discharge* lawsuit against the employer. In addition, employers must abide by the terms of an employment contract, if one has been entered into with the employee (these are much more common for executives than they are for lower-level employees). In spite of the leeway provided by at-will employment, many employers offer written assurances that they will terminate employees only *for cause*, which usually includes such actions as committing crimes or violating company policy.

Retiring Employees

As Chapter 9 discussed, the U.S. population is aging rapidly. For the business community, an aging population presents two challenges. The first is to give job opportunities to people who are willing and able to work but who happen to be past the traditional retirement age. Many older citizens are concerned about their ability to live comfortably on fixed retirement incomes. Others simply prefer to work. For several decades, many companies and industries had **mandatory retirement** policies that made it necessary for people to quit working as soon as they turned a certain age. Then, in 1967, the Age Discrimination in Employment Act outlawed discrimination against anyone between the ages of 40 and 65. In 1986 Congress amended the act to prohibit mandatory retirement for most employees. As a corollary, employers are also forbidden to stop benefit contributions or accruals because of age.

mandatory retirement
Required dismissal of an employee
who reaches a certain age

The second challenge posed by an aging workforce is to find ways to encourage older employees to retire early if the company needs to balance its workforce. One method a company may use is to offer older employees financial incentives to resign, such as enhanced retirement benefits or onetime cash payments. Inducing employees to depart by offering them financial incentives is known as a **worker buyout**. This method

worker buyout
Distribution of financial incentives
to employees who voluntarily
depart; usually undertaken in order
to reduce the payroll

can be a lot more expensive than firing or laying off employees, but it has several advantages: The morale of the remaining employees is preserved because they feel less threatened about their own security, younger employees see increased chances for promotion, and the risk of age-discrimination lawsuits is minimized.

Summary of Learning Objectives

1 List six main functions of human resources departments.

Human resources departments plan for a company's staffing needs, recruit and hire new employees, train and develop employees, appraise employee performance, administer compensation and employee benefits, and oversee changes in employment status.

2 Cite eight methods recruiters use to find job candidates.

Recruiters find job candidates by (1) promoting internal candidates, (2) advertising in newspapers and on the Internet, (3) using public and private employment agencies, (4) contacting union hiring halls, (5) recruiting at college campuses and career placement offices, (6) attending trade shows, (7) hiring corporate "headhunters," and (8) soliciting referrals from employees or colleagues in the industry.

3 Identify the six stages in the hiring process.

The stages in the hiring process are (1) narrowing down the number of qualified candidates, (2) performing initial screening interviews, (3) administering a series of follow-up interviews, (4) evaluating candidates, (5) conducting reference checks, and (6) selecting the right candidate.

4 Discuss how companies incorporate objectivity into employee performance appraisals.

Employee performance appraisals are an effective way to inform employees if they are doing a good job and how they can improve their performance. To ensure objectivity and fairness, most firms use a standard, companywide format, provide a written record of appraisals for future reference, and solicit several perspectives by engaging superiors, peers, and colleagues at different levels in the organization in the review process.

5 Highlight five popular employee benefits.

The two most popular employee benefits are insurance (health, life, disability, and long-term care) and retirement benefits, such as pension plans that help employees save for later years. Employee stock-ownership plans and stock options, two additional benefits, allow employees to receive or purchase shares of the company's stock and thus obtain a stake in the company. Family benefits programs, also popular, include maternity and paternity leave, child-care assistance, and elder-care assistance.

6 Describe four ways an employee's status may change, and discuss why many employers like to fill job vacancies from within.

An employee's status may change through promotion or through reassignment to a different position, through termination (removal from the company's payroll), through voluntary resignation, or through retirement. Employers like to fill vacancies created from such changes by promoting from within for these reasons: The employee has been trained by the company and knows the ropes; it boosts employee morale; and it sends a message to other employees that good performance will be rewarded.

Behind **the Scenes**

Perking Up the Perfect Blend at Starbucks

On the fast track toward global growth, the Starbucks chain transformed the ordinary cup of coffee into a wide variety of taste choices for millions of coffee lovers. Along the way, the company's astonishing success encouraged competitors to join the fray. Now expansion-minded companies such as The Second Cup, Seattle's Best Coffee, and Barnie's were turning up the heat in the upscale coffee category. To stay on top, Starbucks managers had to ensure that their stores provided the best service along with the best coffee—which meant attracting, training, and compensating a diverse and dedicated workforce.

Guided by the company mission statement, CEO Howard Schultz and his managers designed a variety of human resources programs to motivate Starbucks partners (employees). First they raised employees' base pay. Next management bucked the trend in the industry by offering full medical, dental, life insurance, and disability insurance benefits to every partner who worked at least 20 hours per week. These partners were also eligible for paid vacation days and retirement savings plans, benefits not commonly available to part-time restaurant workers. Finally, Starbucks invested in its workforce by providing new hires with 24 hours of training about the finer points of coffee brewing as well as the company's culture and values.

But the most innovative benefit brewed up by management was its Bean Stock, a program offering stock options not just to upper-echelon managers but to all partners who worked 20 or more hours per week. "We established Bean Stock in 1991 as a way of investing in our partners and creating ownership across the company," explained Bradley Honeycutt, vice president of human resource services. "It's been a key to retaining good people and building loyalty." For those who wanted to enlarge their financial stake in Starbucks, management devised a program that permitted partners to buy company stock at a discount. Owning a piece of the company motivated employees to take customer service to an even higher level of excellence. "We do everything we possibly can to get our customers to come back," says Schultz.

To help partners better balance their work and family obligations—another priority for Starbucks—the human resources department designed a comprehensive work-life program featuring flexible work schedules, access to employee assistance specialists, and referrals for child-care and elder-care support. The company also encouraged employees to become involved in their local communities, and it honored employees whose achievements exemplified the company's values. Finally, to encourage open communication and employee feedback, good or bad, management began holding a series of open forums in which company performance, results, and plans were openly discussed. Employees were encouraged to share ideas. "There is a tremendous amount of sharing in the company," notes Schultz. "It makes everybody think like an owner."

While most CEOs say that people are their most important asset, Starbucks lives that idea every day by giving people a stake in the outcome and treating them with respect and dignity. In all, putting employees first has helped Starbucks expand by attracting an energetic, committed workforce and keeping turnover to a minimal 60 percent, much lower than the industry average.[64]

Critical Thinking Questions

1. Why do Starbucks human resources managers need to be kept informed about any changes in the number and timing of new store openings planned for the coming year?
2. Why does Starbucks offer benefits to its part-time labor force?
3. How does Starbucks liberal employee-benefits program motivate its employees?

LEARN MORE ONLINE

Go to Chapter 10 of this text's website at www.prenhall.com/bovee, and click on the hotlink to get to the Starbucks website. Then visit the site's job section to see how Starbucks presents its HR policies to potential employees. Browse the pages that discuss working at Starbucks. Read about company culture, diversity, benefits, and learning and career development. Why would Starbucks post information about company culture in this section of the website? Why would job candidates be interested in learning about the culture as well as the employee benefits and training at Starbucks? ∎

Key Terms

attrition (266)
bonus (263)
commissions (263)
compensation (261)
electronic performance monitoring (EPM) (261)
employee assistance programs (EAPs) (266)
employee benefits (263)
employee retention (252)
employee stock-ownership plan (ESOP) (265)

human resources management (HRM) (249)
incentives (262)
job analysis (254)
job description (254)
job specification (254)
layoffs (268)
mandatory retirement (268)
orientation (258)
pension plans (264)
performance appraisal (260)

profit sharing (263)
recruiting (255)
replacement chart (252)
retirement plans (264)
salary (261)
skills inventory (259)
stock options (265)
succession planning (252)
termination (268)
wages (261)
worker buyout (268)

Test Your Knowledge

Questions for Review

1. What do human resources managers do?
2. What are some strategic staffing alternatives that organizations use to avoid overstaffing and understaffing?
3. What is the purpose of conducting a job analysis? What are some of the techniques used for gathering information?
4. What are the three types of preemployment tests administered by companies, and how is each of these tests used to assist with the hiring decision?
5. What functions do orientation programs serve?

Questions for Analysis

6. How do incentive programs encourage employees to be more productive, innovative, and committed to their work?
7. Why do some employers offer comprehensive benefits even though the costs of doing so have risen significantly in recent years?
8. What are the advantages and disadvantages of 401(k) retirement plans?
9. The 1986 Immigration Reform and Control Act forbids companies to hire illegal aliens but at the same time prohibits discrimination in hiring on the basis of national origin or citizenship status. How can companies satisfy both requirements of this law?

10. **Ethical Considerations.** Corporate headhunters have been known to raid other companies of their top talent to fill vacant or new positions for their clients. Is it ethical to contact the CEO of one company and lure him or her to join the management team of another company?

Questions for Application

11. If you were on the human resources staff at a large health-care organization that was looking for a new manager of information systems, what recruiting method(s) would you use and why?
12. Assume you are the manager of human resources at a manufacturing company that employs about 500 people. A recent cyclical downturn in your industry has led to financial losses, and top management is talking about laying off workers. Several supervisors have come to you with creative ways of keeping employees on the payroll, such as exchanging workers with other local companies. Why might you want to consider this option? What other options exist besides layoffs?
13. **Integrated.** Of the five levels in Maslow's hierarchy of needs, which is satisfied by offering salary? By offering health-care benefits? By offering training opportunities? By developing flexible job descriptions?
14. **Integrated.** What are some of the human resources issues managers are likely to encounter when two companies (in the same industry) merge?

Practice Your Knowledge

Sharpening Your Communication Skills

A visit to CCH's SOHO Guide at www.toolkit.cch.com can help you reduce your legal liability whether you are laying off or firing a single employee or are contemplating a companywide reduction in your workforce. Log on to the website and scroll down to the CCH Small Business Guide, then click on Table of Contents. Scroll down to People Who Work for You, and click on Firing and Termination to find out the safest way to fire someone from a legal standpoint before it's too late. Learn why it's important to document disciplinary actions. Then use the information at this website to write a short memo to your instructor summarizing how to set up a

termination meeting and what you should say and do at the meeting when you fire an employee.

Building Your Team Skills

Team up with a classmate to practice your responses to interview questions. Use the list of common interview questions provided in Appendix E, and take turns posing and responding to those questions. Which questions did you find most difficult to answer? What insights did you gain about your strengths and weaknesses by answering those questions? Why is it a good idea to rehearse your answers before going to an interview?

Expand Your Knowledge

Discovering Career Opportunities

If you pursue a career in human resources, you'll be deeply involved in helping organizations find, select, train, evaluate,

and retain employees. You have to like people and be a good communicator to succeed in HR. Is this field for you? Using your local Sunday newspaper, the *Wall Street Journal*, and online sources such as Monster Board (www.monster.com), find ads seeking applicants for positions in the field of human resources.

1. What educational qualifications, technical knowledge, or specialized skills are applicants for these jobs expected to have? How do these requirements fit with your background and educational plans?

2. Next, look at the duties mentioned in the ad for each job. What do you think you would be doing on an average day in these jobs? Does the work in each job sound interesting and challenging?

3. Now think about how you might fit into one of these positions. Do you prefer to work alone, or do you enjoy teamwork? How much paperwork are you willing to do? Do you communicate better in person, on paper, or by phone? Considering your answers to these questions, which of the HR jobs seems to be the closest match for your personal style?

Developing Your Research Skills

Locate one or more articles in business journals or newspapers (print or online editions) that illustrate how a company or industry is adapting to changes in its workforce. (Examples include retraining, literacy or basic-skills training, flexible benefits, and benefits aimed at working parents or people who care for aging relatives.)

1. What changes in the workforce or employee needs caused the company to adapt? What did the company do to respond to these changes? Was the company's response voluntary or legally mandated?

2. Is the company alone in facing these changes, or is the entire industry trying to adapt? What are other companies in the industry doing to adapt to the changes?

3. What other changes in the workforce or in employee needs do you think this company is likely to face in the next few years? Why?

SEE IT ON THE WEB

For live links to the websites that follow, go to this text's website at www.prenhall.com/bovee. When you log on, select Chapter 10, then select "Featured Websites," click on the URL of the website you wish to visit, review the website, and answer the following questions:

1. What is the purpose of this website?

2. What kinds of information does this website contain? Please be specific.

3. How is the information provided at this website useful for businesspeople? Consumers?

4. How did you expand your knowledge of human resources management by reviewing the material at this website? What new things did you learn about this topic?

Explore the Latest Workforce Management Ideas

Visit *Workforce Management* online to see what management leaders are thinking about month by month (requires registration to read most articles, but it's free). The Community Center hosts a number of forums in which you can read questions, answers, and commentary from working HR managers. The Research Center lists a wide range of topics to explore in the HRM field. www.workforce.com

Digging Deeper at the Bureau of Labor Statistics

By now you're probably aware that the U.S. government has an agency for almost every purpose. Many of these agencies gather facts and statistics on trends in the United States, and the Bureau of Labor Statistics is no exception. When you need to research detailed information about national or regional employment conditions—such as wages, unemployment, productivity, and benefits—point your web browser to this site: www.bls.gov.

Maximizing Your Earning Potential

You know you should be making more money. So now what? Log on to Salary.com to find out what you are worth. Then maximize your earning potential by exploring the basics of negotiation. Sharpen your skills so you can get the job, salary, and benefits you want. Contemplating a move? Use the cost-of-living wizard to find out if it makes economic sense. You may even want to prepare for your next performance review by taking one of the site's self-tests. Finally, don't leave without learning how to manage your take-home pay or getting some facts about tuition assistance. Many companies will reimburse you for your career course work. But you may not get it if you don't ask. www.salary.com

Companion Website

Learning Interactively

Go to the Companion Website at www.prenhall.com/bovee. For Chapter 10, take advantage of the interactive "Study Guide" to test your knowledge of the chapter. Get instant feedback on whether you need additional studying.

Also, visit this site's "Study Hall," where you'll find an abundance of valuable resources that will help you succeed in this course.

Video Case

Channeling Human Resources at Showtime

LEARNING OBJECTIVES

The purpose of this video is to help you

1. Identify the many ways in which human resource managers can actively develop employees
2. Appreciate the role of mentoring in employee development
3. Understand how a performance appraisal system can be designed and administered

SYNOPSIS

Showtime Networks Inc. (SNI), which is a wholly owned subsidiary of media conglomerate Viacom, operates the premium television networks Showtime, The Movie Channel (TMC), Flix, and Showtime Event Television. It also operates the premium network Sundance Channel, a joint venture with Robert Redford and Universal Studios. One of the biggest challenges at SNI, as anywhere, is attracting, retaining, and motivating a committed workforce. Demographic changes, work and family issues, and increasing diversities of age, race, and lifestyle call forth the dedication and creativity of its human resource staff. This video introduces various Showtime executives who discuss the company's human resource policies and challenges. The firm is a leader in creating a broad training and career development program that serves many different kinds of employee needs. It also uses a performance appraisal system that employees have helped design and has a formal program for encouraging mentoring.

Discussion Questions

1. *For analysis:* Among the organizational changes recently made at Showtime are the combining of the legal and the human resource departments and the appointment of one particular human resource manager to each SNI division. Comment on the advantages or disadvantages of these changes.
2. *For analysis:* Is Showtime doing a good job of offering its employees chances to develop and improve their skills? Can you suggest additional programs it could undertake to achieve this goal?
3. *For analysis:* Do you think the performance appraisal system at Showtime is an effective one? Why or why not?
4. *For application:* Could you apply Showtime's approach to a company with only three or four employees? Why or why not?
5. *For debate:* Do companies have a responsibility, beyond their own business needs, to mentor and develop employees? Why or why not?

ONLINE EXPLORATION

Visit the online job board of Showtime's parent company Viacom at http://jobhuntweb.viacom.com/Viacom/main/jobhome_viacom.asp (online applications for all Viacom companies is handled through this central site). Consider the information available on this site and the manner in which it is presented. Does Viacom sound like the sort of company you'd like to work for? Why or why not? What advice would you give the company to improve recruiting of college graduates, if any?

E-Business in Action

JOB RECRUITING MOVES ONLINE

In just the past few years, e-cruiting (recruiting over the Internet) has become an integral part of the recruiting strategy for companies of all sizes. Companies have discovered that the Internet is a fast, convenient, and inexpensive way to find prospective job candidates. And job candidates are finding that the Internet is a convenient way to gather company information, search for job vacancies, and post résumés on both high-volume career websites such as Monster, Yahoo! HotJobs, and CareerBuilder (also known as job boards) and on more focused websites such as Dice (for high-tech jobs) and InternshipPrograms.com (for intern opportunities).

The Traditional Path Versus E-Cruiting

Before the advent of the Internet, recruiting followed a traditional path: When a company had exhausted internal possibilities, it would "announce" a job opening to the marketplace (through a classified ad, an executive recruiter, employee referral incentives, a job fair, or other medium), and recruiters made endless rounds of cold telephone calls to identify potential job candidates. Then, after a lengthy process of sorting through faxed and mailed résumés, someone from human resources called the most promising candidates and interviewed them.

This process, however, is expensive and inefficient. For one thing, communication by regular mail is slow. By the time a phone call is made or snail mail is received, a good candidate may have accepted another job. Plus, the cost of placing classified ads in newspapers is high, so most ads contain brief job descriptions and appear for only a few days or weeks. Furthermore, the traditional process operates mostly in one direction. Most applicants do not place ads announcing their availability—although some job seekers do send unsolicited letters with résumés.

Thanks to the Internet, however, the recruiting process is changing. Companies are using the Internet to search for résumés of promising candidates, take online applications, accept electronic résumés, conduct interviews, and administer tests. Recruiters at Amazon.com, for example, post ads on job boards and actively search the web for résumés. "To be a recruiter at Amazon.com, you have to like the thrill of the hunt," says Amazon's manager of technical recruiting. Amazon's recruiters sort through hundreds of candidates they consider for every position by using a tool to presort and categorize résumés. Like Amazon, many companies now advertise job vacancies on their company websites and on third-party job boards. From entry-level position to CEO, no job is outside the Internet's reach.

Benefits and Drawbacks of E-Cruiting

In comparison to traditional recruiting methods, the benefits of Internet recruiting are many:

- *Speed.* The Internet allows job seekers to search for jobs quickly, from any place and at any time, and to communicate via e-mail with potential employers. Companies can also save time in the hiring process by using the Internet to become a 24-hour, seven-days-a-week recruiter and give applicants quick responses to their queries. Determined nocturnal headhunters can snap up hot résumés posted on the Internet before dawn and contact candidates immediately by e-mail. Some companies report receiving responses and résumés only minutes after posting a job opening.

- *Reach.* The Internet allows employers to contact a broader selection of applicants more quickly, target specific types of applicants more easily, and reach highly skilled applicants more efficiently. Some company websites bring in thousands of résumés in one week, a volume that would be far too cumbersome to manage through traditional means.

- *Cost savings.* Electronic ads typically cost much less than traditional print ads, career fairs, and open houses. Moreover, processing electronic application forms is more efficient than processing paper forms. Intelligent automated search agents can filter or prescreen potential applicants and find résumés that match job descriptions and specific employer criteria.

Of course, e-cruiting is not without drawbacks. The biggest complaint voiced by companies is that the Internet produces more job applicants than ever before. The number of résumés one company received went from 6,000 to 24,000 annually after going online. The increased volume of résumés makes it more difficult to cull promising candidates from unqualified ones. "People will send their résumé because it's very simple to cut and paste. But, they're no way qualified for the position," notes one HR director. And online recruiting will probably never replace employers' favorite methods of finding new hires: their own workforces or referrals from current employees.

The Future of E-Cruiting

In spite of these drawbacks, the future of e-cruiting looks promising. In addition to the big three (Monster, Yahoo! HotJobs, and CareerBuilder), thousands of other job boards now try to match employers and employees in specific areas. Some of these specialty boards include HireDiversity.com, Vets4Hire, and Attorneyjobs. For instance, Maureen Kelleher, a recruiting director for Ernst & Young, uses a group of 20 specialty boards to find more-experienced professionals. She says that Monster is fine for lower-tier jobs but not for more senior positions. (To learn more about specialty job boards, visit www.careerxroads.com.)[65]

Questions for Critical Thinking

1. How are job seekers and employers using the Internet in the recruiting process?

2. What are the benefits and drawbacks of Internet recruiting?

3. What steps would you take to make your résumé stand out among the thousands that are transmitted electronically? (*Hint:* Think of content.)

BUSINESS PlanPro Exercises

Managing Human Resources and Employee Relations

Review Appendix D, Your Business Plan (on pages 416–417), to learn how to use Business PlanPro Software so you can complete these exercises.

THINK LIKE A PRO

Objective: By completing these exercises you will become acquainted with the sections of a business plan that address staffing the enterprise and managing employees. You will use the sample business plan for Sagebrush Sam's (listed as Restaurant—Steak Buffet in the Sample Plan Browser) in this exercise.

1. What do the mission statement and keys to success sections say about Sagebrush Sam's approach to employee relations? Why are good relations with employees so important to the success of this type of business?

2. What workforce challenges is Sagebrush Sam's likely to encounter as it grows?

3. What are the company's estimates for manager and employee compensation, and how do these estimates change over the years covered by the plan?

4. According to the business plan, Sagebrush Sam's will need a director of store operations when it has more than five units. How might the company recruit a manager with the appropriate experience and background for this position?

CREATE YOUR OWN BUSINESS PLAN

The success of your business depends on hiring, training, and motivating the right employees. Answer these questions as you continue developing your own business plan. How many employees will your business require? Of these, how many will be managers? How will you motivate your staff? Will you pay them a salary or a commission? Will you offer alternative work arrangements? If so, which ones? Will you use part-time and temporary employees? Will you provide your employees with benefits? Which ones?

Part 5
Developing Marketing Strategies to Satisfy Customers

Chapter 11
Developing Product and Pricing Strategies

LEARNING OBJECTIVES
After studying this chapter, you will be able to

1 Explain what marketing is and describe the four utilities created by marketing

2 Explain why and how companies learn about their customers

3 Outline the three steps in the strategic marketing planning process

4 Define market segmentation and cite six factors used to identify segments

5 Highlight the four stages in the life cycle of a product and the marketing focus of each stage

6 Discuss the functions of packaging and labeling

7 Identify four ways of expanding a product line and discuss two risks that product-line extensions pose

8 List seven factors that influence pricing decisions and cite five common pricing methods

Behind the Scenes

Flying High with Adobe Acrobat

www.adobe.com

Back when the World Wide Web was little more than a research collection hosted at a nuclear energy lab in Switzerland and few people outside of the technology business had e-mail addresses, software engineers at Adobe Systems in San Jose, California, were inventing a technological breakthrough that would change the way millions of people send and receive information. Although still in their infancy, electronic documents were already showing great promise. Sending reports, spreadsheets, and other files via e-mail or downloading them from the growing number of websites was a fast and convenient way to share information—but it suffered from a host of problems. If the person you were sending a file to didn't have the same type of computer and same software setup as you (this was before Microsoft Office became the standard software in most businesses), chances are he or she wouldn't be able to view the file at all. And even if that person did have the right software, the appearance of documents and other files depended on the availability of specific fonts and other design variables, so documents that looked perfect on one computer often turned into jumbled rubbish on a different computer. In addition, many users wanted a way to prevent recipients from modifying the content of a document, either accidentally or intentionally (changing the wording of a contract, for instance).

As those problems were brewing, Adobe was inventing the perfect solution. Its new Acrobat software and portable document format (PDF) meant that people could "freeze" the content and design of their files after creating them. These self-contained PDF files could redisplay themselves perfectly on any computer with the

Adobe's Acrobat Reader is an important link in a software system used by millions of computer owners.

Acrobat software. To encourage the widespread use of the PDF approach, Adobe split Acrobat into two products, the main product to create PDF files and a less-expensive *reader* to view files.

Because computer users needed only the Adobe Reader to view newsletters, reports, manuals, and other formatted files, Acrobat became the ideal software for sharing documents over the Internet. Heralded as the "Most Significant Technology" at the computer-industry Comdex trade show when it was introduced in 1992, Acrobat indeed promised to change the way companies communicate.

In spite of its potential, the product got off to a slow start. For one thing, the concept of electronic documents wasn't yet a high priority for most businesses. For another, many companies were struggling to get existing—and widely disparate—computer networks to talk to each other and to get their employees connected to the burgeoning World Wide Web. Adobe seemed to be one step ahead of the market. Moreover, people who were publishing electronic material had no way of knowing whether their target audiences would own a copy of the Acrobat Reader or would be willing to pay $50 for the software just to view electronic documents.

Since its founding a decade earlier, Adobe had relied mainly on trade shows and word-of-mouth in the graphic design community to promote its software programs. But now Acrobat needed a different marketing strategy—one that would capture the imagination of people far beyond its core market before competitors caught on. If you were a member of Adobe's management team, what marketing strategies would you develop to turn Acrobat's promise into profits?[1] ■

WHAT IS MARKETING?

Your experiences as a consumer may not have given you lots of insights into accounting, production, and other business functions, but you already know a lot about marketing. Companies have been targeting you as a customer since you were a young child, and if you're now a young adult about to enter your professional career, thousands of companies would like to get a piece of your paycheck. You've been on the receiving end of plenty of marketing tactics—contests, advertisements, displays of merchandise, price markdowns, and product giveaways, to name but a few. However, marketing involves much more than displays, commercials, and contests. In fact, a lot of planning and execution is needed to develop a new product such as Acrobat software, set its price, get it into stores, and convince people to buy it.

Think about all the decisions you would have to make if you worked at Adobe Systems, for example. How many software packages would you need to sell in order to be profitable? Which types of customers would purchase your software products? How would you attract new customers? How would you price and promote the software? What would you do if another software company offered an equally attractive product at a lower price? These are just a few of the many marketing decisions that all companies make in order to be successful.

The American Marketing Association (AMA) defines **marketing** as planning and executing the conception, pricing, promotion, and distribution of ideas, goods, and services to create exchanges that satisfy individual and organizational objectives.[2] With respect to products, marketing involves all decisions related to determining a product's characteristics, price, production specifications, market-entry date, distribution, promotion, and sales. With respect to customers, marketing involves understanding customers' needs and their buying behavior, creating consumer awareness, providing **customer service**—which is everything a company does to satisfy its customers—and maintaining relationships with customers long after the sales transaction is complete (see Exhibit 11.1).

Most people, of course, think of marketing in connection with selling tangible goods for a profit (the term *product* refers to any "bundle of value" that can be exchanged in a marketing transaction). But marketing applies to services, nonprofit organizations, people, places, and causes, too. Politicians always market themselves. So do places (such as Paris or Poland) that want to attract residents, tourists, and business investment. **Place marketing** describes efforts to market geographical areas ranging from neighborhoods to entire countries. **Cause-related marketing** promotes a

marketing
Process of planning and executing the conception, pricing, promotion, and distribution of ideas, goods, and services to create and maintain relationships that satisfy individual and organizational objectives

customer service
Efforts a company makes to satisfy its customers to help them realize the greatest possible value from the products they are purchasing

place marketing
Marketing efforts to attract people and organizations to a particular geographical area

cause-related marketing
Identification and marketing of a social issue, cause, or idea to selected target markets

Exhibit 11.1

What Is Marketing?

Each of the core marketing concepts—needs, wants, demands, products, services, value, satisfaction, quality, exchanges, transactions, relationships, and markets—builds on the ones before it.

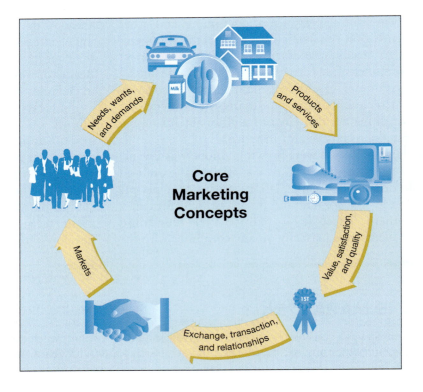

Core Marketing Concepts

Needs, wants, and demands · Products and services · Value, satisfaction, and quality · Exchange, transaction, and relationships · Markets

cause or a social issue—such as physical fitness, cancer awareness, recycling, or highway safety.

The Role of Marketing in Society

Take another look at the AMA definition of marketing. Notice that marketing involves an exchange between two parties—the buyer and the seller—both of whom seek some level of satisfaction from the transaction. This definition suggests that marketing plays an important role in society by helping people satisfy their needs and wants and by helping organizations determine what to produce.

The breast cancer awareness campaign attracts millions of marketing dollars from companies such as Kellogg's that want to associate with the cause in consumers' minds.

Needs and Wants

To survive, people need food, water, air, shelter, and clothing. A **need** represents a difference between your actual state and your ideal state. You're hungry and you don't want to be hungry; you need to eat. Needs create the motivation to buy products and are therefore at the core of any discussion of marketing.

Your **wants** are based on your needs but are more specific. Producers do not create needs, but they do shape your wants by exposing you to alternatives. For instance, when you need some food, you may want a Snickers bar or an orange. One of the fundamental goals of marketing is to create perceptions of products that encourage customers to want those specific brands as solutions to their basic needs.[3]

Exchanges and Transactions

When you participate in the **exchange process**, you trade something of value (usually money) for something else of value, whether you're buying an airline ticket, a car, or a college education. When you make a purchase, you cast your vote for that item and encourage the producer of that item to make more of it. In this way, supply and demand are balanced, and society obtains the goods and services that are most satisfying.

When the exchange actually occurs, it takes the form of a **transaction**. Party A gives Party B $1.29 and gets a medium Coke in return. A trade of values takes place. Most transactions in today's society involve money, but money is not necessarily required. Bartering, which predates the use of cash, is making a comeback thanks to the Internet. The dot-com boom, which saw many cash-poor start-ups pay for goods and services with company stock instead of cash, seemed to open many eyes to the possibility of trading goods and services. A number of online exchanges now facilitate bartering using a trade credit system; members trade everything from office space to website design.[4]

The Four Utilities

To encourage the exchange process, marketers enhance the appeal of their products and services by adding **utility**, something of value to customers (see Exhibit 11.2). When organizations change raw materials into finished goods, they are creating **form utility** desired by consumers. For example, when Nokia combines plastic, computer chips, and other materials to make digital phones, the company is providing form utility. In other cases, marketers try to make their products available when and where customers want to buy them, creating **time utility** and **place utility**. Overnight couriers such as Airborne Express create time utility, whereas coffee carts in office buildings and ATM machines in shopping malls create place utility. The final form of utility is **possession utility**—the satisfaction that buyers get when they actually possess a product, both legally and physically. First Union Mortgage, for example, creates possession utility by offering loans that allow people to buy homes they could otherwise not afford.

need
Difference between a person's actual state and his or her ideal state; provides the basic motivation to make a purchase

wants
Things that are desirable in light of a person's experiences, culture, and personality

exchange process
Act of obtaining a desired object from another party by offering something of value in return

transaction
Exchange between parties

utility
Power of a good or service to satisfy a human need

form utility
Customer value created by converting raw materials and other inputs into finished goods and services

time utility
Customer value added by making a product available at a convenient time

place utility
Customer value added by making a product available in a convenient location

possession utility
Customer value created when someone takes ownership of a product

Exhibit 11.2

Examples of the Four Utilities

The utility of a good or service has four aspects, each of which enhances the product's value to the consumer.

UTILITY	EXAMPLE
Form utility	Kettle Valley's Fruit Snack bars provide the nutritional value of real fruit in a form that offers greater convenience and longer storage life.
Time utility	LensCrafters has captured a big chunk of the market for eyeglasses by providing on-the-spot, one-hour service.
Place utility	By offering convenient home delivery of the latest fashion apparel and accessories, the Delia*s catalog and website have become favorites of teenaged girls.
Possession utility	RealNetworks, producer of software for listening to music from the Internet, allows customers to download and install its programs directly from the company's website.

The Marketing Concept

marketing concept
Approach to business management that stresses customer needs and wants, seeks long-term profitability, and integrates marketing with other functional units within the organization

The underlying philosophy that guides all marketing decisions and activities is known as the **marketing concept**, the idea that companies should stress customers' needs and wants while seeking long-term profitability and coordinating their own marketing efforts to achieve the company's long-term goals. These customer-focused companies modify their marketing strategies and product offerings to satisfy customers' changing needs and wants. From an organizational point of view, this also requires treating the marketing function as more than an isolated department. To be truly customer focused, the entire company needs to embrace the marketing concept.[5]

Understanding Today's Customers

To implement the marketing concept, companies must have good information about what customers want. This is a challenge because today's customers, both individual consumers and organizational buyers, are a diverse and demanding group, with little patience for marketers who do not understand them or will not adapt business practices to meet their needs. They expect goods and services to be delivered faster and more conveniently. And most have no qualms about switching to competitors if their demands are not met. Armed with facts, prices, data, product reviews, advice, how-to guides, and databases, today's customers are informed, which places them in an unprecedented position of control.[6]

Home buyers, for example, use real estate websites to gain more control of the house-hunting process. Home descriptions, room dimensions, photographs, virtual tours, property tax information, and school and town information are all provided on websites—making it possible for customers to do their research online before setting foot in the real estate office.[7] The same is true for car buyers. They research online, then walk into car dealerships holding detailed reports that disclose the dealer's invoice cost, dealer rebates, and other purchasing incentives.[8] Today's customers are indeed calling the shots, which is why it becomes increasingly important for businesses to understand how buyers think and what they want.

As part of the marketing concept, successful companies tend to invest heavily in customer service. This instant messaging system from InstantService is an example of the latest tools that companies can use to improve customer service.

The Consumer Decision Process Think about several purchase decisions you've made recently or might make in the near future. What sort of process did you follow to arrive at the specific choice you made in each case? Classical economics suggests that you'd follow the rational process in Exhibit 11.3, first recognizing a need, gathering information, identifying alternative solutions, then making your choice from those alternatives. How often do you make decisions like

The Rational Model of Buyer Decisions

In the classic, rational model of buyer behavior, customers work through several steps in logical order before making a purchase decision. However, new research shows that most consumer decisions are less rational and more subconscious than the classical model suggests.

that? Or do you sometimes buy on impulse, like the $125 pair of basketball shoes that you saw in a shop window and purchased a few seconds later, or the pair of black pants you bought because they were on sale, even though you already own 19 pairs of black pants? The classical, rational model serves as a helpful starting point, but researchers now realize that consumer behavior tends to be far less logical and far more complicated (and more interesting) than this model suggests.

Even in situations in which consumers gather lots of information and appear to be making a well-thought-out, rational decision, they often are acting more on gut feel and emotional response. For instance, you might see some hot new car drive past on the street, and in that split second—before you even start "thinking" about it—you've already decided to buy one just like it. Sure, you'll gather brochures, do research on the Internet, test-drive other models, and so on, but chances are you're not really evaluating alternatives. Instead, your rational, conscious brain is just looking for evidence to support the decision that your emotional, semiconscious brain has already made.

Moreover, we consumers make all kinds of decisions that are hard to explain by any rational means; does anybody really "need" 50 pairs of shoes or a car that can go 160 miles an hour? Sometimes we buy food that we know isn't healthy (sure tastes good) or furniture that isn't comfortable (sure looks good next to that expensive painting we don't like). We might spend two weeks gathering data on $200 MP3 players, then choose a college with $20,000 tuition because our best friends are going there. Sometimes we buy things for no apparent reason other than the fact that we have money in our pockets. At one time or another, all consumers suffer from **cognitive dissonance**, which occurs when our beliefs and behaviors don't match. A common form of this is *buyer's remorse*, when we make a purchase then regret doing so—sometimes immediately after the purchase.

This isn't to say that many purchases aren't rational or that consumers don't try to make rational decisions most of the time. But a significant portion of consumer decisions don't follow a strictly logical, conscious sequence. In fact, new research suggests that 95 percent of the decision-making process is subconscious and that sensory cues can play a much larger role than objective information plays.[9] You can start to understand why so many decisions seem mysterious from a rational point of view if you consider all the influences that affect purchases:

- *Culture.* The cultures (and subgroups within cultures) that people belong to shape their values, attitudes, and beliefs and influence the way they respond to the world around them. Understanding culture is therefore an increasingly important step in international business and in marketing to diverse populations within a country such as the United States.

- *Social class.* In addition to being members of a particular culture, people also perceive themselves as members of a certain social class—be it upper, middle, lower, or somewhere in between. In general, members of various classes pursue different activities, buy different goods, shop in different places, and react to different media—or at least like to believe they do.

cognitive dissonance
Tension that exists when a person's beliefs don't match his or her behaviors; a common example is *buyer's remorse*, when someone regrets a purchase immediately after making it

Learning from Business Blunders

Oops: On the surface, it looked like Hallmark Cards did about everything you're supposed to do. Its researchers, monitoring the demographic bulge of the baby boom generation, created the Time of Your Life product line to appeal specifically to people reaching the 50-year milestone in life. Their careful customer research showed that while boomers might be aging, they don't want to think of themselves as old. In response, the product line featured youthful, healthy images of people in the prime of life. The products were displayed in a special Time of Your Life section in Hallmark stores. Great idea? Hallmark has succeeded with other product lines aimed at specific groups of customers, such as Mahogany (African-American themes) and Tree of Life (Jewish themes). Time of Your Life sounded like another winner, but the product line was a flop.

What You Can Learn: While the products themselves may have been right on the mark in terms of customer wants and needs, the final piece of the puzzle—the retail presentation—put people off. Boomers who didn't want to think of themselves as old weren't about to shop in the "old people's" section of the card store. Marketers need to consider the entire consumer experience; a mistake at any stage can doom the entire effort.

- *Reference groups.* A reference group consists of people who have a good deal in common: family members, friends, co-workers, sports enthusiasts, music lovers, computer buffs. Individuals are members of many such reference groups, and they use the opinions of the appropriate group as a benchmark when they buy certain types of goods or services. Anyone who remembers high school is an expert in peer pressure; it's a stage in life when reference groups can have profound influence on individual behavior.

- *Situational factors.* These factors include events or circumstances in people's lives that are more circumstantial but that can influence buying patterns. Such factors might include having a coupon, being in a hurry, celebrating a holiday, being in a bad mood, and so on. If you've ever practiced "retail therapy" to cheer yourself up, you know all about situational factors.

- *Self-image.* Many consumers tend to believe that "you are what you buy," so they make or avoid choices that support their desired self-image. Marketers capitalize on people's need to express their identity through their purchases by emphasizing the image value of goods and services (see "Learning from Business Blunders"). That's why professional athletes and musicians frequently appear as product endorsers—so that consumers will incorporate part of these celebrities' public image into their own self-image.

Even from this brief introduction to consumer behavior and some reflection on our own decisions as a consumer, you can start to understand why marketers spend vast sums of money trying to understand what makes people tick.

The Organizational Customer Decision Process In a sense, the purchasing behavior of organizations (which includes businesses, nonprofit organizations, and governments) is easier to understand because it's more clearly driven by economics and influenced less by subconscious, emotional factors. Here are some of the significant ways in which organizational purchasing differs from consumer purchasing:[10]

- *An emphasis on economic payback and other rational factors.* Most organizational purchases are carefully evaluated for financial impact, technical compatibility, reliability, and so forth. Businesses and other organizations don't always make the best choices, of course, but their choices are usually based on a more rational analysis of needs and alternatives. However, some business-to-business marketers make the mistake of assuming that customer emotions play little or no role in the purchase decision, forgetting that organizations don't make decisions, people do. Fear of change, fear of failure, excitement over new technologies, and the pride of being associated with world-class suppliers are just a few of the emotions that can influence organizational purchases.

- *A formal buying process.* From office supplies to new factories, most organizational purchases follow a formal buying process, particularly in government agencies and in mid- to large-size companies. In fact, the model in Exhibit 11.3 is a better representation of organizational purchasing than it is of consumer purchasing, although organizational purchasing often includes additional steps such as establishing budgets, analyzing potential suppliers, and requesting proposals.

- *The participation and influence of multiple people.* Except in the very smallest businesses, where the owner may make all the purchasing decisions, the purchase process usually involves a number of people. This team can include end users, technical experts, the manager with ultimate purchasing authority, and a professional purchasing agent (whose job includes researching suppliers, negotiating prices, and evaluating supplier performance).

- *Closer relationships between buyers and sellers.* Close and long-lasting relationships between buyers and sellers are common in organizational purchasing. For example, a company might use the same advertising agency, accounting firm, and raw material suppliers for years or even decades. In some cases, employees from the seller even have offices inside the buyer's facility to promote close interaction.

Marketing Research and Customer Databases

Many companies obtain information about customers' changing needs by engaging in **marketing research**—the process of gathering and analyzing information about customers, markets, and related marketing issues. Popular marketing research tools include personal observations, customer surveys, experiments, telephone or personal interviews, studies of small samples of the consumer population, and focused interviews of 6 to 10 people (called *focus groups*). Thanks to their low costs and rapid delivery of results, online surveys have become quite popular in recent years, although they do suffer from the potential flaw of not representing a true cross section of the population.[11]

Another way to learn about customer preferences is to gather and analyze all kinds of customer-related data. **Database marketing** is the process of recording and analyzing customer interactions, preferences, and buying behavior for the purpose of contacting and transacting with customers. Capital One, for example, has become a leading credit card company by collecting extensive records on millions of consumers and using that information to plan its marketing strategies. Every credit card transaction, Internet sale, and frequent-buyer purchase leaves behind a trail of information that retailers can use to their advantage. Frequent-shopper card programs, good for a wealth of discounts at checkout, have convinced customers to share some of the most intimate details about their lives. For instance, customer grocery purchases reveal preferences for everything from hygiene products to junk food to magazines.

Once companies gather data about customers, they enter this information into customer databases to remember customer preferences and priorities and to make the customer's experience more personal and compelling. Allstate, for example, uses database marketing to amass huge amounts of data about applicants (credit reports, driving records, claims histories) in order to swiftly price a customer's insurance policy.[12] Ritz Carlton records all customer requests, comments, and complaints in a worldwide database that now contains individual profiles of more than 500,000 guests. By accessing these profiles, employees at any Ritz Carlton hotel can accommodate the individual tastes of its customers from anywhere in the world.[13]

Building Relationships with Customers

Another way that companies remain customer focused is by building long-term, satisfying relationships with key parties—customers, suppliers, distributors—to retain their long-term business. This practice, commonly referred to as **relationship marketing**, focuses on establishing a learning relationship with each customer. Thus, the relationship between customer and company does not end with the sales transac-

marketing research
The collection and analysis of information for making marketing decisions

database marketing
Process of building, maintaining, and using customer databases for the purpose of contacting customers and transacting business

relationship marketing
A focus on developing and maintaining long-term relationships with customers, suppliers, and distributors for mutual benefit

Online research tools, such as this survey system from Zoomerang, help marketers learn more about their customers.

Your Right to Privacy Versus the Marketing Databases

Are all the details of your personal life really private? Consider this: Your bank knows your account balance, your credit history, your Social Security number, and, increasingly, when and where you might be shopping for new loans or other financial products. Government agencies know how much money you made last year, the kind of car you own, and how many parking tickets you've received. Credit agencies know to whom you owe money and how much. This list goes on and on, from video stores to insurance companies. Plus every time you register online, or even click on a website, all sorts of data are being collected about you. By depositing "cookies" on your hard drive, web marketers can follow your path and track the sites you visit.

Of course, there's nothing unethical about collecting data or maintaining a database. The ethical problems arise when marketers buy, borrow, rent, or exchange information, usually without your knowledge or permission. Who should have the right to see your records? The answer depends on where you live. In Europe, strict privacy regulations prevent companies from using data about individuals without asking permission and explaining how the data will be used. But in the United States and most other countries, marketers can easily buy information about who you are, where you live, how much you earn, and what you buy—for as little as a nickel.

Many web marketers post privacy policies showing how they use personal data. Moreover, a 1999 law requires U.S. companies to send privacy policies to customers once a year—offering customers the opportunity to "opt out," which, if elected, prohibits companies from selling customer information to unrelated firms. But as privacy advocates note, companies are still allowed to share data with subsidiaries and with companies they purchase, merge with, affiliate with, and so on.

As you can imagine, the consumer's right to privacy is an ongoing debate—one that has intensified and taken on new dimensions since the September 11, 2001, terrorist attacks. Privacy advocates argue that people should have the right to be left alone, whereas marketers argue that they should have the right to freedom of speech—the right to inform customers about their offers. Thus, the ultimate dilemma: Do a marketer's needs and freedom of speech outweigh the consumer's right to privacy? What's your opinion?

Questions for Critical Thinking

1. Should a marketer selling long-distance telephone service be allowed to see your telephone records without your knowledge or permission?
2. Should web marketers be required to conspicuously post their privacy policies and ask consent before collecting and using visitors' personal data?

---

customer relationship management (CRM)
A computer-based method for collecting information and coordinating activities related to a company's interactions with each of its customers

tion; instead, it is viewed as an ongoing process.[14] Moreover, the relationship gets smarter with each customer interaction—you learn something about your customer and you change your product or service to meet the customer's needs. To help manage customer information and coordinate multiple interactions between the company and its customers, many companies have turned to **customer relationship management (CRM)** systems.

Maintaining long-term relationships with customers has many benefits:[15]

- Acquiring a new customer can cost up to five times as much as keeping an existing one.
- Long-term customers buy more, take less of a company's time, bring in new customers, and are less price-sensitive.
- Satisfied customers are the best advertisement for a product.
- Firms perceived to offer superior customer service find that they can charge as much as 10 percent more than their competitors.
- Research shows that dissatisfied customers may tell as many as 20 other people about their bad experiences.

But keeping customers satisfied in an environment where they have more product information available than ever before is a challenge. So some companies try to gain a competitive edge by differentiating the customer experience—making it more personal and compelling.

One-to-one marketing involves individualizing a firm's marketing efforts for a single customer to accommodate the specific customer's needs. Starbucks lets you order coffee drinks in more than 19,000 individualized varieties, for instance.[16] Industrial and technology companies have been customizing multi-million-dollar systems and facilities for the unique demands of individual buyers for years, but thanks to e-commerce and mass customization in more and more industries, consumers can now customize everything from makeup and shoes to cars and furniture.[17] The four key steps to putting an effective one-to-one marketing program in place are (1) identifying your customers, (2) differentiating among them, (3) interacting with them, and (4) customizing your product or service to fit each individual customer's needs.[18]

PLANNING YOUR MARKETING STRATEGIES

By now you can see why successful marketing rarely happens without carefully analyzing and understanding your customers. Once you have learned about your customers, you're ready to begin planning your marketing strategies.

Strategic marketing planning is a process that involves three steps: (1) examining your current marketing situation, (2) assessing your opportunities and setting your objectives, and (3) developing a marketing strategy to reach those objectives (see Exhibit 11.4). The

Exhibit 11.4   The Strategic Marketing Planning Process

Strategic marketing planning comprises three steps: (1) examining your current marketing situation, (2) assessing your opportunities and setting objectives, and (3) developing your marketing strategy.

Examine Current Marketing Situation
- Review past and current performance
- Evaluate competition
- Examine internal strengths and weaknesses
- Analyze external environment

Assess Opportunities and Set Objectives
- Assess product and market opportunities
- Set specific and measurable objectives

Develop Marketing Strategy
- Segment market
- Choose target market
- Position product
- Develop marketing mix

purpose of strategic marketing planning is to help you identify and create a competitive advantage, something that sets you apart from your rivals and makes your product more appealing to customers.[19] Most companies record the results of their planning efforts in a document called the *marketing plan*. Here's a closer look at the three steps in the process.

Step 1: Examining Your Current Marketing Situation

Examining your current marketing situation includes reviewing your past performance (how well each product is doing in each market where you sell it), evaluating your competition, examining your internal strengths and weaknesses, and analyzing the external environment.

Reviewing Performance

Unless you're starting a new business, your company has a history of marketing performance. Maybe sales have slowed in the past year; maybe you've had to cut prices so much that you're barely earning a profit; or maybe sales are going quite well and you have money to invest in new marketing activities. Reviewing where you are and how you got there is critical, because you will want to repeat your successes and learn from your past mistakes.

Evaluating Competition

In addition to reviewing past performance, you must also evaluate your competition. If you own a Burger King franchise, for example, you need to watch what McDonald's and Wendy's are doing. You also have to keep an eye on Taco Bell, KFC, Pizza Hut, and other restaurants in addition to paying attention to any number of ways your customers might satisfy their hunger—including fixing a sandwich at home. Furthermore, you need to watch the horizon for competitors that do not yet exist, such as the next big food craze. For instance, when low-carbohydrate diets caught on recently, established food companies such as Kraft and General Mills found themselves suddenly losing business to competitors they'd never heard of before, such as Atkins Nutritionals.[20]

Examining Internal Strengths and Weaknesses

Successful marketers try to identify both sources of competitive advantage and areas that need improvement. They look at such things as management, financial resources, production capabilities, distribution networks, managerial expertise, and promotional capabilities. This step is important because you can't develop a successful marketing strategy if you don't know your strengths as well as your limitations. On the basis of your internal analysis, you will be able to decide whether your business should (1) limit itself to those opportunities for which it possesses the required strengths or (2) challenge itself to reach higher goals by acquiring and developing new strengths.

Understanding your strengths and weaknesses is especially important when evaluating the merits of global expansion. Selling products overseas requires not only managerial expertise and financial resources but also the ability to adjust your operation to different cultures, customs, legal requirements, and product specifications. Even selling on the Internet requires technological expertise and commitment as well as a thorough understanding of customer buying behavior.

Analyzing the External Environment

Marketers must also analyze a number of external environment factors when planning their marketing strategies. These factors include:

- *Economic conditions.* Marketers are greatly affected by trends in interest rates, inflation, unemployment, personal income, and savings rates. In tough times, consumers put off buying expensive items such as major appliances, cars, and homes. They cut back on travel, entertainment, and luxury goods. Conversely, when the economy is good, consumers open their wallets and satisfy their pent-up demand for higher-priced goods and services.

- *Natural environment.* Changes in the natural environment can affect marketers, both positively and negatively. Interruptions in the supply of raw materials can upset even the most carefully conceived marketing plans. Floods, droughts, and cold weather can affect the price and availability of many products as well as the behavior of target customers.

- *Social and cultural trends.* Planners also study the social and cultural environment to determine shifts in consumer values. If social trends are running against a product, the producer might need more advertising to educate consumers about the product's benefits or alter the product to make it more appealing. For example, when beef consumption fell out of favor, marketers used ads to educate consumers on the benefits of including more beef in their diet.

- *Laws and regulations.* Like every other function in business today, marketing is controlled by laws at the local, state, national, and international levels. From product design to pricing to advertising, virtually every task you'll encounter in marketing is affected in some way by laws and regulations. For example, the Nutritional Education and Labeling Act of 1990 forced marketers to put standardized nutritional labels on food products. Although this regulation cost manufacturers millions of dollars, it was a bonanza for food-testing laboratories.

- *Technology.* When technology changes, so must your marketing approaches. Encyclopaedia Britannica presents a classic case of how changing technology can turn an industry upside down—almost overnight. The 235-year-old publisher cruised into the 1990s with record sales of its flagship product, an encyclopedia set that cost over $1,400, weighed 118 pounds, and consumed four and a half feet of shelf space. But then along came CD-ROMs and the Internet, which enabled much cheaper—and sometimes free—solutions from competitors. Even though most of these alternatives couldn't deliver the comprehensive quality of Britannica, they quickly ate into the company's sales. After a stumble or two, including the common misstep of trying to support a site through advertising revenue, Britannica now has 200,000 paid subscribers online.[21] Marketers must not only keep on top of today's external environment, they must also think about tomorrow's changes. Car manufacturers, for example, are responding to increasing consumer and governmental pressure to reduce emissions by producing hybrid gas-and-electric vehicles.

Step 2: Assessing Your Opportunities and Setting Your Objectives

Once you've examined your current marketing situation, you're ready to assess your marketing opportunities and set your objectives. Successful companies are always on the lookout for new marketing opportunities, which can be classified into four options: selling more of your existing products in current markets (market penetration), creating new products for your current markets (new product development), selling your existing products in new markets (geographic expansion), and creating new products for new markets (diversification).[22] These four options are listed in order of increasing risk; trying new products in unfamiliar markets is usually the riskiest choice of all.

With opportunities in mind, you are ready to set your marketing objectives. A common marketing objective is to achieve a certain level of **market share**, which is a firm's portion of the total sales within a market. Objectives must be specific and measurable. Establishing a goal to "increase sales in the future" is not a good objective; it doesn't say by how much or by what date. On the other hand, a goal to "increase sales 25 percent by the end of next year" provides a clear target and a reference against which progress can be measured. Objectives should also be challenging enough to be motivating. As CEO Mitchell Leibovitz of the Pep Boys auto parts chain says, "If you want to have ho-hum performance, have ho-hum goals."[23] Whatever objectives you set, be sure all employees know and understand what the organization wants to accomplish. Every Ritz Carlton employee, for example, attends a daily 15-minute meeting in which managers reiterate the hotel chain's business goals and commitment to customer service.[24]

market share
A firm's portion of the total sales in a market

Step 3: Developing Your Marketing Strategy

Using your current marketing situation and your objectives as your guide, you're ready to move to the third step. This is where you develop your **marketing strategy**, which consists of dividing your market into *segments* and *niches*, choosing your *target markets* and the *position* you'd like to establish in those markets, and then developing a *marketing mix* to help you get there.

Dividing Markets into Segments

A **market** contains all the customers or businesses that might be interested in a product and can pay for it. Most companies subdivide the market in an economical and feasible manner by identifying *market segments*, or homogeneous groups of customers within a market that are significantly different from each other. This process is called **market segmentation**; its objective is to group customers with similar characteristics, behavior, and needs. Each of these market segments can then be targeted by offering products that are priced, distributed, and promoted differently.

The goal of market segmentation is to understand why certain customers buy what they buy so that you can sell them your products and services by targeting their needs. Here are five factors marketers frequently use to identify market segments:

- *Demographics.* When you segment a market using **demographics**, the statistical analysis of a population, you subdivide your customers according to characteristics such as age, gender, income, race, occupation, and ethnic group. Be aware, however, that according to recent studies, demographic variables are poor predictors of behavior. For instance, not all American men aged 35 to 44 making $100,000 per year buy a Mercedes. In fact, some don't even buy a luxury car, and those who do may not purchase such cars for the same reasons.[25]

- *Geographics.* When differences in buying behavior are influenced by where people live, it makes sense to use **geographic segmentation**. Segmenting the market into different geographical units such as regions, cities, counties, or neighborhoods allows companies to customize and sell products that meet the needs of specific markets. For instance, car rental agencies stock more four-wheel-drive vehicles in mountainous and snowy regions than they do in the South.

- *Psychographics.* Whereas demographic segmentation is the study of people from the outside, **psychographics** is the analysis of people from the inside, focusing on their psychological makeup, including attitudes, interests, opinions, and lifestyles. Psychographic analysis focuses on why people behave the way they do by examining such issues as brand preferences, media preferences, reading habits, values, and self-concept.

- *Geodemographics.* Dividing markets into distinct neighborhoods by combining geographical and demographic data is the goal of **geodemographics**. One of the geodemographic systems, developed by Claritas Corporation, divided the United States into 40 neighborhood types, with labels such as "Blue Blood Estates" and "Old Yankee Rows." This system, known as PRIZM, uses postal ZIP codes for the geographic segmentation part, making it easy to use specialized marketing programs to reach people in targeted neighborhoods. Responding to changes in the U.S. population, Claritas and other geodemographic researchers continue to devise new breakdowns that include such clusters as "Bright Lites, Li'l City" (child-free professional couples living in upscale communities near big cities) and "Young Digerati" (ethnically diverse and technically sophisticated young urbanites).[26]

- *Behavior.* Markets can also be segmented according to customers' knowledge of, attitude toward, use of, or response to products or product characteristics. This approach is known as **behavioral segmentation**. Many web-based companies ask first-time visitors to fill out a personal profile so they can gear product recommendations and even display customized webpages that appeal to certain behavioral segments.

---

marketing strategy
Overall plan for marketing a product

market
People or businesses who need or want a product and have the money to buy it

market segmentation
Division of a total market into smaller, relatively homogeneous groups

demographics
Study of statistical characteristics of a population

geographic segmentation
Categorization of customers according to their geographical location

psychographics
Classification of customers on the basis of their psychological makeup

geodemographics
Method of combining geographical data with demographic data to develop profiles of neighborhood segments

behavioral segmentation
Categorization of customers according to their relationship with products or response to product characteristics

Questionable Marketing Tactics on Campus

Alarmed by how quickly college students can bury themselves in debt and fed up with aggressive sales tactics, a growing number of universities are banning or restricting credit card marketing on campus.

College administrators complain that students are bombarded with credit card offers from the moment they step on campus as freshmen. Marketers have shown up on campuses unannounced and without permission to hawk cards in dorms and other areas. They stuff applications into bags at college bookstores. They entice students to apply for cards and take on debt with free T-shirts, music CDs, and promises of an easy way to pay for spring break vacations. Some yell at students to get their attention and follow them through hallways to make a sale. And they even get student organizations to work for them so that friends pressure friends.

College students are, of course, a prized target for the credit card industry because consumers tend to be loyal to their first credit card. And even though college students often have little or no income, they are not considered high-risk borrowers because parents generally bail them out if they get into trouble. As a result, an estimated 80 percent of full-time college students now have a credit card in their own name. But only about half of those students pay their bills in full each month, and the number who usually make just the minimum payment is rising. The average balance carried is now $3,000, and 10 percent of students carry balances of $8,000 or more.

Many young people can't even keep up with the minimum payment. In fact, it is estimated that in one year 150,000 people younger than 25 will declare personal bankruptcy. That means for 150,000 young people, their first significant financial event as an adult will be to declare themselves a failure—a failure that will complicate their lives for years. And for each one who goes into bankruptcy, there are dozens just behind them, struggling with credit card bills—like Katy Spivak, for instance. Within her first three years at college, Spivak ran up $9,000 in credit card debt—forcing her to work two part-time jobs just to pay off her credit card bills.

While some universities have banned credit card marketers from campus to protect students from their own potentially destructive credit practices, many students say it's paternalistic for schools to do so. After all, marketers don't give up. They just move across the street or to other locations frequented by students, such as spring break vacation hot spots. Moreover, credit cards have almost become a necessity in modern consumer life in recent years, since so many businesses require them as security or identification even when you don't use them for purchasing.

Questions for Critical Thinking

1. Should credit card companies be prohibited from soliciting on college campuses? Why or why not?
2. Why do credit card companies target students even though they have little or no income?

- *Usage.* An increasingly popular way to segment e-commerce customers is by Internet usage patterns. Companies are finding that categorizing web users by their session length, time per page, category concentration, and so on helps define the types of marketing that are best suited for each user type.[27]

When you segment your market, you end up with several customer groups, each representing a potentially productive focal point for marketing efforts. However, keep in mind that marketers also segment customers using multiple variables in order to produce more narrowly defined target groups known as *microsegments*, or *niches*.[28] A typical marketing niche might be young adult tennis players. Members of this niche would be interested in tennis products such as rackets, shoes, and tennis wear.

Choosing Your Target Markets

Once you have segmented your market, the next step is to find appropriate target segments or **target markets** to focus your efforts on. Deciding exactly which segment to target—and when—is not an easy task. Sometimes the answer will be obvious, such as when you lack the necessary technological skills or financial power to enter a particular market segment. At other times, you'll have the resources to compete in several segments but not enough resources to compete in all of them. In general, marketers use a variety of criteria to narrow their focus to a few suitable market segments. These criteria can include size of segment, competition in the segment, sales and profit potential, compatibility with company resources and strengths, costs, growth potential, and risks.[29]

target markets
Specific customer groups or segments to whom a company wants to sell a particular product

Targeting is such a critical part of strategic marketing that missteps can be costly, as Motorola found out. The company stayed focused on the traditional cell phone market segment long after rivals Nokia and Ericsson had expanded into the digital phone segment. Furthermore, Motorola didn't respond when it was asked to develop digital phones for AT&T's digital network. By the time Motorola began to work on digital phones, its competitors had grabbed market share and brand loyalty in that fast-growing segment.[30]

Exhibit 11.5 diagrams three popular strategies for reaching target markets. Companies that practice *undifferentiated marketing* (or mass marketing) ignore differences among buyers and offer only one product or product line to satisfy the entire market. This strategy, which concludes that all buyers have similar needs that can be served with the same standardized product, was more popular in the past than it is today. Henry Ford, for instance, sold only one car type (the Model T Ford) and in one color (black) to the entire market.

By contrast, companies that manufacture or sell a variety of products to several target customer groups practice *differentiated marketing*. General Motors, for instance, manufactures a car for every personality, and Nike produces a shoe for every athlete. Differentiated marketing is a popular approach, but it requires substantial resources because you have to tailor products, prices, promotional efforts, and distribution arrangements for each customer group.

When company resources are limited, *concentrated marketing* may be the best marketing strategy. You acknowledge that different market segments exist and you choose to target just one. Southwest Airlines, for instance, began its operation by originally concentrating on servicing the submarket of intrastate, no-frills commuters.[31] The biggest advantage of concentrated marketing is that it allows you to focus all your time and resources on a single type of customer. The strategy can be risky, however, because you've staked your company's fortune on just one segment.

Exhibit 11.5

Market-Coverage Strategies

Three alternative market-coverage strategies are undifferentiated marketing, differentiated marketing, and concentrated marketing.

1. Undifferentiated marketing

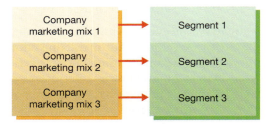

2. Differentiated marketing

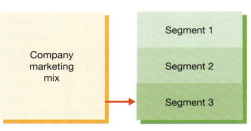

3. Concentrated marketing

Positioning Your Product

Once a company has decided which segments of the market it will enter, it must then decide what position it wants to occupy in those segments. **Positioning** your product is the act of designing your company's offering and image so that it occupies a meaningful and distinct competitive position in your target customers' minds.

Even though consumers position products with or without the help of marketers, marketers do not want to leave their product's position to chance. Instead, they choose positions that will give their products the greatest advantage in selected target markets.[32] They can position their products on specific product features or attributes (such as size, ease of use, style, performance, quality, durability, or design), on the services that accompany the product (such as convenient delivery, lifetime customer support, or installation methods), on the product's image (such as reliability or sophistication), on price (such as low cost or premium), on category leadership (such as the leading online bookseller), and so forth. For example, BMW and Porsche associate their products with performance, Mercedes Benz with luxury, and Volvo with safety. Organizing products and services into categories based on the perceived position helps consumers simplify the buying process. Instead of test-driving all cars, for instance, they may focus on those they perceive to be high-performance vehicles.

Developing the Marketing Mix

After you've segmented your market, selected your target market, and positioned your product, your next task is to develop a marketing mix. A firm's **marketing mix** (often called the *four Ps*) consists of product, price, place (or distribution), and promotion (see Exhibit 11.6).

Products   The most basic marketing-mix element is *product*, which covers the product itself plus brand name, design, packaging, services, quality, and warranty. From a marketing standpoint, **product** is anything offered for the purpose of satisfying a want or a need in a marketing exchange. If you were asked to name three popular products off the top of your head, you might think of Doritos tortilla chips, the Mini Cooper, and Gatorade drinks. You might not think of the Boston Celtics, Disney World, and *Gilmore Girls*. That's because we tend to think of products as *tangible* objects, or things that we

positioning
Using promotion, product, distribution, and price to differentiate a good or service from those of competitors in the mind of the prospective buyer

marketing mix
The four key elements of marketing strategy: product, price, distribution (place), and promotion

product
Good or service used as the basis of commerce

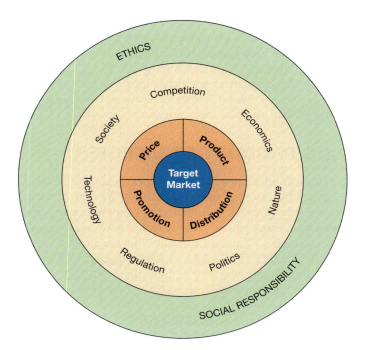

Exhibit 11.6

Positioning and the Marketing Environment

When positioning products for target markets, you need to consider the four marketing-mix elements plus the external environment.

can actually touch and possess. Basketball teams, amusement parks, and television programs provide an *intangible* service for our use or enjoyment, not for our ownership; nevertheless, these and other services are products just the same. In fact, broadly defined, products can be persons, places, physical objects, ideas, services, and organizations. No matter what it is, every product possesses a number of *features* or *attributes* (what the product is or does) that create *benefits* (what it does for the customer). High-technology companies that create complex products face a recurring challenge in this respect; they need to keep one eye on the technology and the features and one eye on customer needs and benefits.[33]

price
The amount of money charged for a product or service

Pricing **Price**, the amount of money customers pay for the product (including any discounts), is the second major component of a firm's marketing mix. As Adobe Systems knows, developing a product's price is one of the most critical decisions a company must make, because price is the only element in a company's marketing mix that produces revenue—all other elements represent cost. Thus, setting a product's price not only determines the amount of income your company will generate from sales of that product but also can differentiate the product from competition. As you can imagine, determining the right price is not an easy task. If a company charges too much, it will generate fewer sales, as Adobe Systems discovered with its Acrobat product. If it charges too little, it will sacrifice potential profits.

Distribution or Place Place (which is commonly referred to as *distribution*) is the third marketing-mix element. It covers the organized network of firms that move goods and services from the producer to the consumer. This network is also known as *marketing channels* or **distribution channels**. A company's channel decisions directly affect all other marketing decisions. For instance, a company's pricing depends on whether it uses mass merchandisers or high-quality specialty stores. And a firm's sales-force and advertising decisions depend on how much training, motivation, and support the dealers need.[34]

distribution channels
Systems for moving goods and services from producers to customers; also known as marketing channels

promotion
Wide variety of persuasive techniques used by companies to communicate with their target markets and the general public

Promotional Strategies **Promotion**, the fourth marketing-mix element, includes all the activities the firm undertakes to communicate and promote its products to the target market. Among these activities are advertising, personal selling, public relations, and sales promotion. Promotion may take the form of direct, face-to-face communication or indirect communication through such media as television, radio, magazines, newspapers, direct mail, billboards, bus ads, the Internet, and other channels. Of the four components in a firm's marketing mix, promotion is perhaps the one most often associated with marketing. Although it is no guarantee of success, promotion does have a profound impact on a product's performance in the marketplace.

The remainder of this chapter takes a closer look at what's involved in developing product and pricing strategies. Then Chapter 12 discusses the steps involved in developing a firm's distribution and promotional strategies.

DEVELOPING PRODUCT STRATEGIES

Why does General Motors offer a product in nearly every category from economy cars to SUVs, whereas Aston Martin offers only a handful of models, all of which are ultra-expensive sports cars? Why does L.L. Bean sell casual and outdoor clothing from head to toe but not tuxedos or evening gowns? Why is Nokia now an electronics company and not a paper or tire company? Why can't you buy a burger and fries at Starbucks or fettuccine Alfredo at McDonald's? The answers to these questions might seem obvious to consumers, but every company needs to address these product strategy questions at some point—and sometimes over and over again as managers try to increase sales and maintain competitiveness.

Product strategies are among the most difficult and important decisions managers need to make, since products can take months or years and millions of dollars to develop and introduce to the marketplace. Most companies have survived the occasional flop, but few can survive a sustained series of product mistakes. To maximize the chances of success, companies should follow a clear process for developing new products:[35]

1. *Generate new ideas.* New product ideas can come from a variety of sources, including customers, salespeople, research engineers, and even competitors. Some consumer products companies employ thousands of teenagers to report back on what's hot and what's not all over the world.[36] Of course, many "new" product ideas are simply improvements to or variations on existing products, but even those slight alterations can generate big revenues.

2. *Develop and screen product concepts.* Many of these ideas need to be explored further and expanded into viable product concepts, then managers need to screen these concepts to see which are compatible with the company's overall strategy and resources and which stand the best chance of success in the marketplace.

3. *Develop marketing strategies.* At this stage, marketing specialists can craft a preliminary marketing plan that identifies potential customers, pricing options, distribution channels, and other variables.

4. *Analyze business potential.* With a clearer idea of what the product will be and who might buy it, financial experts can then compare the cost of designing and manufacturing the product (or delivering the service) with the price the company hopes to charge for it. If the *business case* doesn't look compelling at this stage, most companies will either drop the idea or find ways to improve it.

5. *Design and develop the products.* If the product idea makes financial sense, the next step is to devote time and resources to completing the design and getting it ready for production. Depending on the product, this could take anywhere from a few years to many years. As you can imagine, companies that are fast and efficient at this stage have a considerable advantage over their competitors.

6. *Test market.* Have you ever seen a new menu item show up in your favorite fast-food restaurant only to disappear a few weeks later? Chances are the company was *test marketing* it, trying to gauge marketplace reaction before investing in widespread marketing efforts.

7. *Commercialize.* When the chances of success look good, the company then ramps up production and markets the product on the wide scale.

This process doesn't guarantee success, of course, but it does improve the chances. Conversely, cutting corners on any of these seven steps can dramatically increase the chance of failure.

Types of Products

The nature of the product influences the way it should be created and marketed; for instance, Boeing can't develop a new airplane in the same way that Charles Schwab develops a new financial service. Although some products are predominantly tangible and others are mostly intangible, most products fall somewhere between those two extremes. When you buy software such as Adobe's Acrobat, for example, you get service features along with the product—such as product updates, customer assistance, and so on. The *product continuum* indicates the relative amounts of tangible and intangible components in a product (see Exhibit 11.7). Education is a product at the intangible extreme, whereas salt and shoes are at the tangible extreme. TGI Friday's restaurants fall in the middle because they involve both tangible (food) and intangible (service) components.

Service products have some special characteristics that affect the way they are marketed. As we have seen, *intangibility* is one fundamental characteristic, as you read in Chapter 8. You can't usually show a service in an ad, demonstrate it before customers buy, mass produce it, or give customers anything tangible to show for their purchase. Services marketers often compensate for intangibility by using tangible symbols or by adding tangible components to their products. Prudential Insurance, for example, uses the Rock of Gibraltar as a symbol of stability, and its ads invite you to get "your piece of the rock."

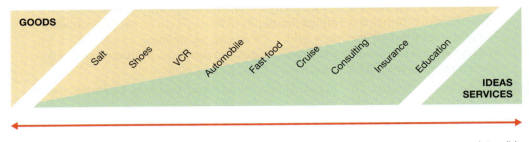

Exhibit 11.7 **The Product Continuum**

Products contain both tangible and intangible components; predominantly tangible products are categorized as goods, whereas predominantly intangible products are categorized as services.

Another unique aspect of service products is *perishability*. Because services cannot usually be created in advance or held in storage until people are ready to buy, services are time sensitive. For instance, if airlines don't sell seats on a particular flight, once the flight takes off an unsold seat can never produce revenue. Hotel rooms, movie theater seats, and restaurants are similar. For this reason, many services try to shift customer demand by offering discounts or promotions during slow periods.

Another way that marketers categorize products is by use. Both organizations and consumers use many of the same products, but they use them for different reasons and in different ways. Individual consumers or households generally purchase smaller quantities of goods and services for personal use. Products that are primarily sold to consumers are known as *consumer products*. Consumer products can be classified into four subgroups, depending on how people shop for them:

- *Convenience products* are the goods and services that people buy frequently, without much conscious thought, such as toothpaste, dry cleaning, film developing, and photocopying.

- *Shopping products* are fairly important goods and services that people buy less frequently: a stereo, a computer, a refrigerator, or a college education. Such purchases require more thought and comparison shopping to check on price, features, quality, and reputation.

- *Specialty products* include CK perfume, Armani suits, and Suzuki violin lessons—particular brands that the buyer especially wants and will seek out, regardless of location or price. Specialty products are not necessarily expensive, but they are products that customers go out of their way to buy and rarely accept substitutes for. Even through a recent recession, the Danish firm Bang & Olufsen fared well selling its world-renowned home entertainment gear, which includes $20,000 TV sets and $8,000 speakers.[37]

- *Unsought goods* are products that people do not normally think of buying, such as life insurance, cemetery plots, and new products they must be made aware of through promotion.[38]

By contrast, *organizational products*, or products sold to firms, are generally purchased in large quantities and are not for personal use. Two categories of organizational products are expense items and capital items. *Expense items* are relatively inexpensive goods and services that organizations generally use within a year of purchase. Examples are pencils and printer cartridges. *Capital items*, by contrast, are more expensive organizational products and have a longer useful life. Examples include desks, photocopiers, and computers.

Aside from dividing products into expense and capital items, organizational buyers and sellers often classify products according to their intended usage.

- *Raw materials* such as iron ore, crude petroleum, lumber, and chemicals are used in the production of final products.

- *Components* such as spark plugs and printer cartridges are similar to raw materials. They also become part of the manufacturer's final products.

- *Supplies* such as pencils, nails, and lightbulbs that are used in a firm's daily operations are considered expense items.

- *Installations* such as factories, power plants, airports, production lines, and semi-conductor fabrication machinery are major capital projects.

- *Equipment* includes less-expensive capital items such as desks, telephones, and fax machines that are shorter-lived than installations.

- *Business services* range from simple and fairly risk-free services such as landscaping and cleaning to complex services such as management consulting and auditing.

The Product Life Cycle

Regardless of a product's classification, few products last forever. Most products go through a **product life cycle**, passing through four distinct stages in sales and profits: introduction, growth, maturity, and decline (see Exhibit 11.8). As the product passes from stage to stage, various marketing approaches become appropriate.

The product life cycle can describe a product class (gasoline-powered automobiles), a product form (sports-utility vehicles), or a brand (Ford Explorer). Product classes and forms tend to have the longest life cycles, whereas specific brands tend to have shorter life cycles. The amount of time that a product remains in any one stage depends on customer needs and preferences, economic conditions, the nature of the product, and the marketer's strategy. Still, the proliferation of new products, changing technology, globalization, and the ability to quickly imitate competitors is hurtling product forms and brands through their life cycles much faster today. The pace is so frenetic that in the words of GTE's president Kent Foster, "Companies are marketing products that are still evolving, delivered to a market that is still emerging, via technology that is changing on a daily basis."[39]

Consider electronics, where product life is now a matter of months: Panasonic replaces its consumer electronic products with new models every 90 days.[40] Why? Smart companies know that if they don't keep innovating, competitors who do will capture the business. Such was the case with Polaroid, a company that failed to properly respond to digital technology. One by one, Polaroid customers defected to digital cameras or other technologies, and in 2001 Polaroid filed for Chapter 11 bankruptcy protection. Many experts predict that the company will never emerge but will use the court's protection to sell off company assets.[41]

Introduction

The first stage in the product life cycle is the *introductory stage*, during which producers launch a new product and stimulate demand. In this stage, companies typically spend heavily on conducting research-and-development efforts to create the new product, on

product life cycle
Four basic stages through which a product progresses: introduction, growth, maturity, and decline

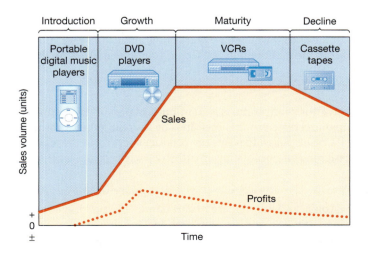

Exhibit 11.8

The Product Life Cycle

Most products and product categories move through a life cycle similar to the one represented by the curve in this diagram. However, the duration of each stage varies widely from product to product.

developing promotions to build awareness of the product, and on establishing the distribution system to get the product into the marketplace. Every product—from personal computers to digital cameras—gets its start in this stage. The producer makes little profit during the introduction; however, these start-up costs are a necessary investment if the new product is to succeed.

Growth

After the introductory stage comes the *growth stage*, marked by a rapid jump in sales and, usually, an increase in the number of competitors and distribution outlets. As competition increases, so does the struggle for market share. This situation creates pressure to introduce new product features and to maintain large promotional budgets and competitive prices. In fact, marketing in this stage is so expensive that it can drive out smaller, weaker firms. With enough growth, however, a firm can often produce and deliver its products more economically than in the introduction phase. Thus, the growth stage can reap handsome profits for those who survive.

Maturity

During the *maturity stage*, the longest in the product life cycle, sales begin to level off or show a slight decline. Most products are in the maturity stage of the life cycle where competition increases and market share is maximized—making further expansion difficult. Because the costs of introduction and growth have diminished in this stage, most companies try to keep mature products alive so they can use the resulting profits to fund development of new products. Some companies extend the life of a mature product by modifying the product's characteristics to improve the product's quality and performance. Keebler, for instance, has extended the life of its popular cookies by selling them in convenient miniversions. Packaged in resealable cans, the minicookies are sold at convenience stores to appeal to consumers on the run.[42] Like Keebler, the Dean Food Company introduced new single-serving plastic bottles called Chugs to help turn around a long-term decline in chocolate milk consumption. Chugs not only increased sales for the product but it brought new life to the entire chocolate milk category.[43]

Decline

Although maturity can be extended for many years, most products eventually enter the *decline stage*, when sales and profits slip and then fade away. Declines occur for several reasons: changing demographics, shifts in popular taste, product competition, and advances in technology. When a product reaches this point in the life cycle, the company must decide whether to keep it and reduce the product's costs to compensate for declining sales or discontinue it and focus on developing newer products. General Motors, for instance, recently put an end to the Oldsmobile brand after more than 100 years. "The decision was long overdue," notes one marketing expert. Sales of Olds have been declining for over a decade, and the brand has lost its identity.[44] Sometimes an entire product category begins to decline, which is currently happening to film-based cameras as digital cameras gain widespread acceptance. Eastman Kodak, which has been selling film cameras for more than a century, decided to phase out most of them in 2004, citing continued losses on the product line.[45]

Product Identities

Creating an identity for your products is an important part of developing effective product strategies. Companies create product identities by assigning their products a **brand** identity—a unique name or design that sets the product apart from those offered by competitors—and by designing and producing an attractive package and label for the product.

Branding

Jeep, Levi's 501, Apple, and Acrobat are **brand names**, the portion of a brand that can be spoken, including letters, words, or numbers. McDonald's golden arches symbol is an example of a **brand mark**, the portion of a brand that cannot be expressed verbally. The

---

brand
A name, term, sign, symbol, design, or combination of these used to identify the products of a firm and to differentiate them from competing products

brand names
Portion of a brand that can be expressed orally, including letters, words, or numbers

brand mark
Portion of a brand that cannot be expressed verbally

choice of a brand name and any associated brand marks can be a critical success factor. A well-known brand name, for instance, can generate more sales than an unknown name. As a result, manufacturers zealously protect their names.

Brand names and brand symbols may be registered with the Patent and Trademark Office as trademarks. As Appendix B explains, a **trademark** is a brand that has been given legal protection so that its owner has exclusive rights to its use. Keep in mind, however, that when a name becomes too widely used it no longer qualifies for protection under trademark laws. Cellophane, kerosene, linoleum, escalator, zipper, shredded wheat, and raisin bran are just a few of the many brand names that have passed into public domain, much to their creators' dismay.

Sometimes companies, such as Warner Brothers, *license* or sell the rights to specific well-known names and symbols—such as Looney Tunes cartoon characters—to manufacturers that use the licensed items to help sell products. In fact, 65 percent of Fortune 500 companies have licensing agreements. Licensing can be a terrific source of revenue. General Mills alone has more than 1,200 licensing agreements that cover everything from clothes to cologne and generate annual revenues of $1.1 billion.[46]

Brand names may be owned by manufacturers, retailers, wholesalers, and a variety of business types. Brands offered and promoted by a national manufacturer, such as Procter & Gamble's Tide detergent and Pampers disposable diapers, are called **national brands**. **Private brands** are not linked to a manufacturer but instead carry a wholesaler's or a retailer's brand. DieHard batteries and Kenmore appliances are private brands sold by Sears. As an alternative to branded products, some retailers also offer **generic products**, which are packaged in plain containers that bear only the name of the product. Generic products can cost up to 40 percent less than brand-name products because of uneven quality, plain packaging, and lack of promotion. Yet generic goods have found a definite market niche, as a look at your local supermarket shelves will confirm.

Co-branding is another way to strengthen brands and products. **Co-branding** occurs when two or more companies team up to closely link their names in a single product. Two examples of successful co-branding include Kellogg's Pop Tarts made with Smucker's jam and Nabisco Cranberry Newtons filled with Ocean Spray cranberries. Co-branding can help companies reach new audiences and tap the equity of particularly strong brands.[47] Moreover, it can help change a product's image. In an attempt to associate the Kodak brand with the output side of digital photography, the company has been co-branding its name with all things digital. For instance, the Kodak name sits above Lexmark's logo on an ink-jet printer that is optimized for printing on photo paper, and it's all over the websites of companies that trumpet their use of Kodak processing and papers.[48]

Packaging

Another way that marketers create an identity for their products is through packaging. Most products need some form of packaging to protect the product from damage or tampering and to make it convenient for customers to purchase. In some cases, packaging is an essential part of the product itself, such as microwave popcorn or toothpaste in pump dispensers. Besides function, however, packaging plays an important role in a product's marketing strategy. Packaging makes products easier to display, facilitates the sale of smaller products, serves as a means of product differentiation, and enhances the product's overall appeal and convenience.

Companies spend a lot of money on packaging to attract consumer attention and to promote a product's benefits through the package's shape, composition, and design. Gatorade's ergonomically designed bottle, Quaker Oats cereal in bags, Hidden Valley Ranch Dressing's "Easy-Squeeze" inverted bottle, Coca-Cola's 12-can refrigerator pack, and Mentadent toothpaste's two-chamber package with pump are examples of innovative packaging with strong consumer appeal.

Labeling

Labeling is an integral part of packaging. Whether the label is a separate element attached to the package or a printed part of the container, it serves to identify a brand. Labels also provide grading information about the product and information about

trademark
Brand that has been given legal protection so that its owner has exclusive rights to its use

national brands
Brands owned by the manufacturers and distributed nationally

private brands
Brands that carry the label of a retailer or a wholesaler rather than a manufacturer

generic products
Products characterized by a plain label, with no advertising and no brand name

co-branding
Partnership between two or more companies to closely link their brand names together for a single product

Linking a brand to a popular entertainer or athlete is a common method of generating interest in a brand name. The Discovery Channel boosted the visibility of its brand when it signed an endorsement deal with cyclist Lance Armstrong.

Universal Product Codes (UPCs)
A bar code on a product's package that provides information read by optical scanners

product line
A series of related products offered by a firm

product mix
Complete list of all products that a company offers for sale

ingredients, operating procedures, shelf life, or risks. The labeling of foods, drugs, cosmetics, and many health products is regulated under various federal laws, which often require disclosures about potential dangers, benefits, and other issues consumers need to consider when making a buying decision.

Labels do more than communicate with consumers. They are also used by manufacturers and retailers as a tool for monitoring product performance and inventory. **Universal Product Codes (UPCs)**, those black stripes on packages, give companies a cost-effective method of tracking the movement of goods. Store checkout scanners read UPC codes and relay the identity, sales, and prices of all products to the retailer's computer system. Such data can help retailers and manufacturers measure the effectiveness of promotions such as coupons and in-store displays. They are also helpful for inventory control.

Product-Line and Product-Mix Strategies

In addition to developing branding, packaging, and labeling strategies, a company must decide how many products it will offer. To stay competitive, most companies continually add and drop products to ensure that declining items will be replaced by growth products. A **product line** is a group of products that are similar in terms of use or characteristics. The General Mills snack-food product line, for example, includes Bugles, Fruit Roll-Ups, Nature Valley Granola Bars, and Pop Secret popcorn. Within each product line, a company confronts decisions about the number of goods and services to offer.

An organization with several product lines has a **product mix**, a collection of goods or services offered for sale. For example, the General Mills product mix consists of cereals, baking products, desserts, snack foods, main meals, and so on (see Exhibit 11.9). Three important dimensions of a company's product mix are *width*, *length*, and *depth*. A company's product mix is *wide* if it has several different product lines. General Mills's product mix, for instance, is fairly wide with five or more product lines. A company's product mix is long if it carries several items in its product lines, as General Mills does. A product mix is deep if it has a number of versions of *each* product in a product line. General Mills, for example, produces several different versions of Cheerios—frosted, multigrain, and honey nut. The same is true for many other products in the company's other product lines.

When deciding on the dimensions of a product mix, a company must weigh the risks and rewards associated with various approaches. Some companies limit the number of product offerings and focus on selling a few selected items to be economical: Doing so keeps the production costs per unit down and limits selling expenses to a single salesforce. Other companies adopt a full-line strategy as a protection against shifts in technology, taste, and economic conditions.

As Exhibit 11.10 shows, companies can expand a product line in several ways. For instance, they can introduce additional items in a given product category under the same brand name—such as new flavors, forms, colors, ingredients, or package sizes.[49] Frito Lay, for example, extended the Doritos line with Salsa Verde and Flamin' Hot

Exhibit 11.9

The Product Mix at General Mills

Selected products from General Mills show a product mix that is fairly wide but that varies in length and depth within each product line.

Product Mix

	Ready-to-Eat Cereals	Snack Foods and Beverages	Baking Products and Desserts	Main Meals and Side Dishes	Dairy Products
Product Lines	Cheerios	Bugles Corn Snacks	Bisquick	Bacos Bits	Columbo Yogurt
	Cinnamon Toast Crunch	Chex Snack Mix	Gold Medal Flour	Chicken Helper	Yoplait Yogurt
	Cocoa Puffs	Fruit by the Foot	Sunkist Lemon Bars	Green Giant Vegetables	Yumsters Yogurt
	Kix	Fruit Roll-Ups	HomeStyle Frosting Mix	Hamburger Helper	Trix Yogurt
	Oatmeal Crisp	Nature Valley Granola Bars	Cinnamon Streusel Quick Bread Mix	Potato Buds	
	Raisin Nut Bran	Pop Secret Popcorn	Supermoist Cake Mix	Suddenly Salad	

METHOD OF EXPANSION	HOW IT WORKS	EXAMPLE
Line filling	Developing items to fill gaps in the market that have been overlooked by competitors or have emerged as consumers' tastes and needs shift	Alka-Seltzer Plus cold medicine
Line extension	Creating a new variation of a basic product	Tartar Control Crest toothpaste
Brand extension	Putting the brand for an existing product category into a new category	Virgin cola
Line stretching	Adding higher- or lower-priced items at either end of the product line to extend its appeal to new economic groups	Marriott Marquis hotel

Exhibit 11.10

Expanding the Product Line

Knowing that no product or category has an unlimited life cycle, companies use one or more of these product-line expansion methods to keep sales strong.

Sabrositos flavors aimed at the U.S. Hispanic market.[50] And Heinz squeezed more sales out of ketchup by adding green ketchup to its product line after young consumers identified color change as a desirable selling feature.[51]

Companies can also expand a product line by adding new but similar products bearing the same product name. Kraft, for example, has extended its Jell-O product line with new products such as gelatin in a cup, pudding in a cup, and cheesecake snacks in a cup. These products build on the convenience-with-quality image of the Jell-O family brand.[52] Building on the name recognition of an existing brand cuts the costs and risks of introducing new products. However, there are limits to how far a brand name can be stretched to accommodate new products and still fit the buyer's perception of what the brand stands for. Snickers ice cream bars and Dr. Scholl's socks and shoes worked as brand extensions, but Bic perfume and Rubbermaid computer accessories did not. When Kraft tried to extend the Chips Ahoy! brand with Ooey Gooey Warm 'N Chewy Chips Ahoy! (a microwavable version), the new cookies failed on a wide scale, forcing the company to spend $5.5 million to pull them off retail shelves.[53]

DEVELOPING PRICING STRATEGIES

A company's pricing decisions are determined by manufacturing and selling costs, competition, and the needs of wholesalers and retailers who distribute the product to the final customer. In addition, pricing is influenced by a firm's marketing objectives, government regulations, consumers' perceptions, and consumer demand.

- *Marketing objectives.* The first step in setting a price is to match it to the objectives you set in your strategic marketing plan. Is your goal to increase market share, increase sales, improve profits, project a particular image, or combat competition? In the wristwatch market, Swatch and Rolex have dramatically different approaches to pricing, with Rolex using premium pricing along with other marketing-mix elements to give its watches a luxury position. As you'll read at the end of the chapter, Adobe Systems ultimately decided to price its Acrobat Reader for free to stimulate sales for the full Acrobat product.

- *Government regulations.* Government plays a big role in pricing in many countries. To protect consumers and encourage fair competition, the U.S. government has enacted various price-related laws over the years. Three important classes of pricing are regulated: (1) *price fixing*—an agreement among two or more companies supplying the same type of products as to the prices they will charge; (2) *price discrimination*—the practice of unfairly offering attractive discounts to some customers but not to others; and (3) *deceptive pricing*—pricing schemes that are considered misleading.

■ *Consumer perceptions.* Another consideration is the perception of quality that your price will elicit from your customers. When people shop, they usually have a rough price range in mind. An unexpectedly low price triggers fear that the item is of low quality. South Korean carmaker Hyundai, for example, decided not to cut prices when the dollar gained strength against the Korean won because it had been making major strides in improving product quality and didn't want a low price to detract from its image.[54] On the other hand, an unexpectedly high price makes buyers question whether the product is worth the money.

■ *Consumer demand.* Whereas a company's costs establish a floor for prices, demand for a product establishes a ceiling. Theoretically, if the price for an item is too high, demand falls and the producers reduce their prices to stimulate demand. Conversely, if the price for an item is too low, demand increases and the producers are motivated to raise prices. As prices climb and profits improve, producers boost their output until supply and demand are in balance and prices stabilize. Nonetheless, the relationship between price and demand isn't always this perfect. Some goods and services are relatively insensitive to changes in price; others are highly responsive. Marketers refer to sensitivity as **price elasticity**—how responsive demand will be to a change in price. SanDisk, which makes electronic memory cards for digital cameras and other devices, largely attributes a recent 40 percent increase in revenue to lower prices, which spurred demand from consumers.[55]

price elasticity
A measure of the sensitivity of demand to changes in price

When companies set their prices they take these factors—among others—into account before choosing a general pricing approach. Common pricing approaches include cost-based, price-based, skimming, penetration pricing, and discounting.

Cost-Based and Price-Based Pricing

Many companies simplify the pricing task by using *cost-based pricing* (also known as *cost-plus pricing*). They price by starting with the cost of producing a good or a service and then add a markup to the cost of the product. This form of pricing, while simple, makes little sense. First, any pricing that ignores demand and competitor prices is not likely to lead to the best price. Second, although cost-based pricing may ensure a certain profit, companies using this strategy tend to sacrifice profit opportunity.

Recent thinking holds that cost should be the last item analyzed in the pricing formula, not the first. Companies that use *price-based pricing* can maximize their profit by first establishing an optimal price for a product or service. The product's price is based on an analysis of a product's competitive advantages, the users' perception of the item, and the market being targeted. Once the desired price has been established, the firm focuses its energies on keeping costs at a level that will allow a healthy profit. Although few businesses fail from overpricing their products, many more will fail from underpricing them.[56]

Price Skimming

A product's price seldom remains constant and will vary depending on the product's stage in its life cycle. During the introductory phase, for example, the objective might be to recover product-development costs as quickly as possible. To achieve this goal, the manufacturer might charge a high initial price—a practice known as **skimming**—and then drop the price later, when the product is no longer a novelty and competition heats up. Products such as HDTV and flat-screen monitors are perfect examples of this practice. Price skimming makes sense under two conditions: if the product's quality and image support a higher price, and if competitors cannot easily enter the market with competing products and undercut the price.

skimming
Charging a high price for a new product during the introductory stage and lowering the price later

Penetration Pricing

Rather than setting a high initial price to skim off a small but profitable market segment, a company might try to build sales volume by charging a low initial price, a practice known as **penetration pricing**. This approach has the added advantage of discouraging

penetration pricing
Introducing a new product at a low price in hopes of building sales volume quickly

competition, because the low price (which competitors would be pressured to match) limits the profit potential for everyone.

Penetration pricing can also help expand the entire product category by attracting customers who wouldn't have purchased at higher, skim-pricing levels. Furthermore, if a company is new to a category pioneered by another company, this strategy can help take customers away from the pioneer.[57] Still, the strategy makes most sense when the market is highly price sensitive so that a low price generates additional sales and the company can maintain its low-price position long enough to keep out competition.

Price Discounts

Once a company has set a product's price, it may choose to adjust that price from time to time to account for changing market situations or changing customer preferences. When you use **discount pricing**, you offer various types of temporary price reductions, depending on the type of customer being targeted and the type of item being offered. You may decide to offer a trade discount to wholesalers or retailers as a way of encouraging orders, or you may offer cash discounts to reward customers who pay cash or pay promptly. You may offer a quantity discount to buyers who buy large volumes, or you may offer a seasonal discount to buyers who buy merchandise or services out of season.

discount pricing
Offering a reduction in price

Another way to discount products is by *value pricing* them, charging a fairly affordable price for a high-quality offering. Many restaurants, including Friendly's, offer value menus for certain times of the day or certain customer segments, such as seniors. This strategy builds loyalty among price-conscious customers without damaging a product's quality image.

Although discounts are a popular way to boost sales of a product, the downside is that they can touch off price wars among competitors. Price wars encourage customers to focus only on a product's pricing and not on its value or benefits. Thus, they can hurt a business—even an entire industry—for years. The airline industry, for instance, has been struggling for years since it was deregulated, even before terrorism fears drove down business, thanks to a recurring pattern of price wars.

Summary of Learning Objectives

1 Explain what marketing is, and describe four utilities created by marketing.

Marketing is the process of planning and executing the conception, pricing, promotion, and distribution of ideas, goods, and services to create exchanges that satisfy individual and organizational objectives. Marketers enhance the appeal of their products and services by adding utility. Form utility is created when companies turn raw materials into finished goods desired by consumers. Time utility is created by making the product available when the consumer wants to buy it. Place utility is created when a product is made available at a location that is convenient for the consumer. Possession utility is created by facilitating the transfer of ownership from seller to buyer.

2 Explain why and how companies learn about their customers.

Companies learn about their customers so they can stay in touch with their current needs and wants, deliver quality products, and provide good customer service. Such attention tends to keep customers satisfied and helps retain their long-term loyalty. Moreover, studies show that sales to repeat customers are more profitable. Most companies learn about their customers by studying consumer behavior, conducting marketing research, and capturing and analyzing customer data.

3 Outline the three steps in the strategic marketing planning process.

The three steps in the strategic marketing planning process are (1) examining your current marketing situation, which includes reviewing your past performance, evaluating your competition, examining your internal strengths and weaknesses, and analyzing the external environment; (2) assessing your opportunities and setting your objectives; and (3) developing your marketing strategy, which covers segmenting your market, choosing your target markets, positioning your product, and creating a marketing mix to satisfy the target market.

4 **Define market segmentation, and cite six factors used to identify segments.**

Market segmentation is the process of subdividing a market into homogeneous groups to identify potential customers and to devise marketing approaches geared to their needs and interests. The six most common factors used to identify segments are demographics, geographics, psychographics, geodemographics, behavior, and usage.

5 **Highlight the four stages in the life cycle of a product and the marketing focus of each stage.**

Products start in the introductory stage where marketers focus on stimulating demand for the new product. As the product progresses through the growth stage, marketers focus on increasing the product's market share. During the maturity stage, marketers try to extend the life of the product by highlighting improvements or by repackaging the product in different sizes. Eventually, all products move to a decline stage, where the marketer must decide whether to keep the product and reduce its costs to compensate for declining sales or discontinue it.

6 **Discuss the functions of packaging and labeling.**

Packaging provides protection for the product, makes products easier to display, and attracts attention. In addition, packaging enhances the convenience of the product and communicates its attributes to the buyer. Labels help identify and distinguish the brand and product. They provide information about the product—including ingredients, risks, shelf life, and operating procedures. And they contain UPC codes, which are used for scanning sales information and monitoring inventory and pricing.

7 **Identify four ways of expanding a product line, and discuss two risks that product-line extensions pose.**

A product line can be expanded by filling gaps in the market, extending the line to include new varieties of existing products, extending the brand to new product categories, and stretching the line to include lower- or higher-priced items. Two of the biggest risks with product-line extensions include a loss of brand identity (weakening of the brand's meaning) and cannibalization of sales of other products in the product line.

8 **List seven factors that influence pricing decisions, and cite five common pricing methods.**

Pricing decisions are influenced by manufacturing and selling costs, competition, the needs of wholesalers and retailers who distribute the product to the final customer, a firm's marketing objectives, government regulations, consumer perceptions, and consumer demand. Five common pricing methods are cost-based, price-based, skimming, penetration pricing, and discounting.

Behind **the Scenes**

Turning a Profit by Giving Away the Product

Adobe Systems faced a formidable challenge. Its new Acrobat software turned somersaults over competition by removing critical formatting barriers so that documents shared electronically retained their original appearance. But only a few companies saw the software's benefits. Still, with the World Wide Web and graphical Internet browsers gaining popularity, Adobe knew that it had to move fast if Acrobat were to become the industrywide standard for viewing electronic documents across the web. It had to break through corporate barriers and convince consumers of the product's potential.

To create consumer awareness, Acrobat marketers designed a series of compelling advertisements that highlighted the many benefits of the software, including improved communication, reduced paperwork, and increased productivity. The ads further explained that the Acrobat Reader was only a small part of a much more dynamic software program

and that users could purchase the product's components separately: the complete Acrobat software program for about $250 or only the Reader for $50 a copy.

But few people were willing to pay $50 to view documents—especially documents that constituted a tiny minority of those available on the web. So Adobe shifted gears and decided to give away the Reader for free. Then, to expedite distribution, Adobe entered into an agreement with Netscape, the early leader in web browsers, to bundle a copy of the Reader with the browser software and made similar deals with IBM and Apple to include a copy of Reader software with all new computers. Moreover, it encouraged consumers to download copies of the Reader off the Internet at no charge.

Adobe's marketing strategy soon paid off. With more than 500 million copies of the Acrobat Reader distributed worldwide and 1,800 other software companies building

PDF compatibility into their products, PDF has indeed become the industry standard. Moreover, as the number of people using Adobe's Acrobat Reader skyrocketed, so did the demand for the full product required to create or edit PDF documents. Soon businesses and government agencies, including the Food and Drug Administration and the U.S. Postal Service, were using Acrobat to convert documents into PDF files to share with employees and customers over computer networks on the Internet. Organizations now use the Acrobat family to create online forms, assemble easily searchable electronic archives, automatically reformat web pages for handheld devices, and simplify the display of information for people with visual impairments.

Thanks to smart marketing, Adobe is now the second largest PC software company in the United States. The company employs over 2,900 people and generates over $1.2 billion in annual sales. Sales of Adobe's Photoshop, Illustrator, InDesign, and Premiere contribute the lion's share of that revenue, but some think Acrobat has the potential to eventually become Adobe's best-selling product. "To have a $300 million business that's potentially growing at 45 percent or greater is something that the company is very excited about," notes Adobe's CEO John Warnock. As he sees it, virtually everything you read via the Internet, whether on paper or on screen, could someday be processed through Adobe software.[58]

Critical Thinking Questions

1. Why was Adobe Acrobat a challenging product to market?
2. Why did Adobe decide to give away the Acrobat Reader software?
3. What pricing strategy does Adobe appear to be using by giving away the Reader?

LEARN MORE ONLINE

Go to Chapter 11 of this text's website at www.prenhall.com/ bovee, and click on the hotlink to the Adobe Systems website. After reviewing the site, analyze Adobe's product line: How many software products does Adobe produce? Is the company's product mix wide or narrow? Which of the following consumer product classifications best describes Adobe's Reader: convenience product, shopping product, specialty product, or unsought good? From a company's perspective, would you consider the entire Adobe Acrobat software package to be an organizational expense or a capital item? ■

Key Terms

behavioral segmentation (288)
brand (296)
brand mark (296)
brand names (296)
cause-related marketing (279)
co-branding (297)
cognitive dissonance (281)
customer relationship management (CRM) (284)
customer service (278)
database marketing (283)
demographics (288)
discount pricing (301)
distribution channels (292)
exchange process (279)
form utility (279)
generic products (297)
geodemographics (288)

geographic segmentation (288)
market (288)
market segmentation (288)
market share (287)
marketing (278)
marketing concept (280)
marketing mix (291)
marketing research (283)
marketing strategy (288)
national brands (297)
need (279)
penetration pricing (300)
place marketing (279)
place utility (279)
positioning (291)
possession utility (279)
price (292)
price elasticity (300)

private brands (297)
product (291)
product life cycle (295)
product line (298)
product mix (298)
promotion (292)
psychographics (288)
relationship marketing (283)
skimming (300)
target markets (289)
time utility (279)
trademark (297)
transaction (279)
utility (279)
Universal Product Codes (UPCs) (298)
wants (279)

Test Your Knowledge

Questions for Review

1. What are some of the characteristics of today's customers?
2. What is strategic marketing planning, and what is its purpose?
3. What external environmental factors affect strategic marketing decisions?
4. What are the four basic components of the marketing mix?
5. What are the functions of packaging and labeling?

Questions for Analysis

6. How can marketing research and database marketing help companies improve their marketing efforts?
7. Why do companies segment markets?
8. How could a marketer confuse a consumer when developing a product's positioning strategies?
9. Why is it important to review the objectives of a strategic marketing plan before setting a product's price?
10. **Ethical Considerations.** Why might an employee with high personal ethical standards act less ethically when developing packaging, labeling, or pricing strategies?

Questions for Application

11. How do airlines deal with the intangibility and perishability of the service they provide?

12. Think of a shopping product you recently purchased and review your decision process. Why did you need or want that product? How did the product's marketing influence your purchase decision? How did you investigate the product before making your purchase decision? Did you experience cognitive dissonance after your decision?
13. **Integrated.** Why is it important to analyze a firm's marketing plan before designing the production process for a service or a good? What kinds of information are generally included in a marketing plan that might affect the design of the production process as discussed in Chapter 8?
14. **Integrated.** How might these economic indicators discussed in Chapter 1 affect a company's marketing decisions: consumer price index, inflation, unemployment?

Practice Your Knowledge

Sharpening Your Communication Skills

Collect some examples of mail communications you have received from companies trying to sell you something. How do these communications try to get your attention? Highlight all the instances in which these communications use the word *you* or even your personal name. How is using the word *you* an effective way to communicate with customers? Does the communication appeal to your emotion or to your logic? How does the company highlight the benefits of its product or services? How does the company talk about price? Finally, how does the company motivate you to act? Bring your samples to class and be prepared to present your analysis of these factors to your classmates.

Building Your Team Skills

In the course of planning a marketing strategy, marketers need to analyze the external environment to consider how forces outside the firm may create new opportunities and challenges. One important environmental factor for merchandise buyers at Sears is weather conditions. For example, when merchandise buyers for lawn and garden products think about the assortment and number of products to purchase for the chain's stores, they don't place any orders without first poring over long-range weather forecasts for each market.

In particular, temperature and precipitation predictions for the coming 12 months are critical to the company's marketing plan, because they offer clues to consumer demand for barbecues, lawn furniture, gardening tools, and other merchandise. What other products would benefit from examining weather forecasts? With your team, brainstorm to identify at least three types of products (in addition to lawn and garden items) for which Sears should examine the weather as part of its analysis of the external environment. Share your recommendations with the entire class. How many teams identified the same products your team did?

Expand Your Knowledge

Discovering Career Opportunities

Jobs in the four Ps of marketing cover a wide range of activities, including a variety of jobs such as personal selling, advertising, marketing research, product management, and public relations. You can get more information about various marketing positions by consulting the *Career Information Center* guide to jobs and careers, the U.S. Employment Service's *Dictionary of Occupational Titles*, and online job-search websites such as Career Builder, www.careerbuilder.com, and Monster, www.monster.com.

1. Select a specific marketing job that interests you. Using one or more of the preceding resources, find out more about this chosen job. What specific duties and responsibilities do people in this position typically handle?
2. Search through help-wanted ads in newspapers, specialized magazines, or websites to find two openings in the field you are researching. What educational background and work experience are employers seeking in candidates for this position? What kind of work assignments are mentioned in these ads?

3. Now think about your talents, interests, and goals. How do your strengths fit with the requirements, duties, and responsibilities of this job? Do you think you would find this field enjoyable and rewarding? Why?

Developing Your Research Skills

From recent issues of business journals and newspapers (print or online editions), select an article that describes in some detail a particular company's attempt to build relationships with its customers (either in general or for a particular product or product line).

1. Describe the company's market. What geographic, demographic, behavioral, or psychographic segments of the market is the company targeting?

2. How does the company hold a dialogue with its customers? Does the company maintain a customer database? If so, what kinds of information does it gather?

3. According to the article, how successful has the company been in understanding its customers?

SEE IT ON THE WEB

For live links to the websites that follow, go to this text's website at www.prenhall.com/bovee. When you log on, select Chapter 11, then select "Featured Websites," click on the URL of the website you wish to visit, review the website, and answer the following questions:

1. What is the purpose of this website?

2. What kinds of information does this website contain? Please be specific.

3. How is the information provided at this website useful for businesspeople? Consumers?

4. How did you expand your knowledge of marketing, customers, products, or pricing by reviewing the material at this website? What new things did you learn about these topics?

Sign Up for Electronic Commerce 101

Think you may be interested in moving your business onto the Internet but you don't know where to start? Study the basics at Electronic Commerce 101 before you plan your marketing strategies. Find out how to succeed in electronic commerce. Read the beginners' guide and the step-by-step process of becoming e-commerce enabled. Learn how to process payments, credit cards, and e-cash. Find out the top 10 ways websites lose customers. Still have a question? This site has free advice from over 7,000 experts. www.ecommerce.about.com/smallbusiness/ecommerce/library/bl101

Fill Your Marketing Toolkit at MarketingPower.com

MarketingPower.com, a comprehensive site created by the American Marketing Association, offers an incredible array of articles, data, webcasts, and planning tools. Wondering about a marketing term? The online dictionary defines over 4,000 terms that marketing professionals use. Need demographic data to analyze a market? Get free summary, comparison, and ranking reports for the entire country. Looking for a marketing job? Check out the job board and career services. And while you're there, check out the benefits of joining the AMA. www.marketingpower.com

Protect Your Trademark

Do you have a winning idea for a new product? Don't forget to protect your trademark by registering it with the U.S. Patent and Trademark Office. Visit this government agency's website and learn the basic facts about registering a trademark, such as who is allowed to use the TM symbol and how a trademark differs from a service mark. Find out how the process works and how much it costs. In fact, why not search its database now to see whether anyone has already registered your trademark? www.uspto.gov

Companion Website

Learning Interactively

Go to the Companion Website at www.prenhall.com/bovee. For Chapter 11, take advantage of the interactive "Study Guide" to test your knowledge of the chapter. Get instant feedback on whether you need additional studying.

Also, visit this site's "Study Hall," where you'll find an abundance of valuable resources that will help you succeed in this course.

Video **Case**

Sending Products into Space: MCCI

LEARNING OBJECTIVES

The purpose of this video is to help you:

1. Recognize how and why a company develops specialized products for organizational customers.

2. Describe some of the decisions a company faces in pricing specialized products under long-term contracts for organizational customers.

3. Understand how a company can use quality to differentiate its products.

SYNOPSIS

MCCI, a 55-person company based in California, designs and produces highly specialized products that are customized to the detailed specifications of its organizational customers. When a telecommunications company or government agency needs a radio frequency filter for a new satellite, it calls on MCCI to design one for that situation. Custom-made from tiny components and precious materials, this filter must be top-quality to withstand powerful vibration and temperature extremes in space—and continue to perform exactly as promised for 20 years. Because some contracts cover products purchased over a decade or more, MCCI must carefully assess the risks of designing a product and pricing it for long-term profit. Yet speed is also a factor: MCCI once created a new product during a single weekend to win a contract from an important customer.

Discussion Questions

1. *For analysis:* Are MCCI's products capital or expense items? How do you know?

2. *For analysis:* Given its in-depth knowledge of the market, why does MCCI develop new products for individual customers rather than creating new products to meet general industry needs?

3. *For application:* The price of gold can fluctuate widely, depending on market conditions. How might this affect MCCI's pricing decisions for products that incorporate components made from gold?

4. *For application:* What factors must MCCI analyze as it prices a custom-designed product?

5. *For debate:* At the start of a long-term contract, should MCCI price a product to return little or no profit in the hope that it will be able to generate more profit from other products sold to this customer later in the contract period? Support your chosen position.

ONLINE EXPLORATION

One of MCCI's products went to Mars on the Sojourner Rover sent by NASA. What other kinds of goods and services does NASA buy? Visit its procurement website http://acquisition.jpl.nasa.gov and follow the link to see some of the requests for proposals on this site. Do any contain a document with questions and answers? Why would MCCI need to read such a document before preparing a proposal to develop a product for NASA? Now examine the listing of other links. How could MCCI use information from the sites on this listing in planning a product for NASA?

Chapter 12

Developing Distribution and Promotional Strategies

LEARNING OBJECTIVES

1 Explain what marketing intermediaries do and list their seven primary functions

2 Explain how wholesalers and retailers function as intermediaries

3 Discuss the key factors that influence channel design and selection

4 Differentiate between intensive, selective, and exclusive distribution strategies

5 Discuss the Internet's effect on the distribution function

6 Identify the five basic categories of promotion

7 Distinguish between the two main types of sales promotions and give examples of each

8 Discuss the use of integrated marketing communications

Behind **the Scenes**

Scaling New Heights at REI

www.rei.com

For more than six decades, Recreational Equipment, Inc. (REI) has been scaling new heights. Established in 1938 by two Seattle mountain climbers as a consumer cooperative, REI developed a reputation for providing outdoor enthusiasts with high-quality sports equipment at reasonable prices. By the mid-1990s, REI had grown into the nation's largest supplier of specialty outdoor gear, serving customers nationwide through some 50 retail stores and a thriving catalog business.

Offering everything from canoes to hiking gear, each REI store was a true interactive experience. Spanning from 10,000 to 95,000 square feet, the stores offered shoppers an avalanche of opportunities to test, touch, and play with products most stores kept in boxes or behind glass. Footwear test trails, water-filter testing stations, binocular demo stations, and rock-climbing walls were just a few of the reasons that shoppers flocked to REI stores.

REI has grown into a renowned supplier of specialty outdoor gear, selling through 60 retail stores in the United States and by direct sales via the Internet, telephone, and mail.

In spite of its success, REI was largely unknown outside the western U.S. region. Moreover, the company needed to find a way to keep customers and employees informed of the ever-changing array of products in the outdoor-gear industry. The Internet seemed like a perfect channel for accomplishing both objectives, but in the mid-1990s it was still a wild frontier—largely populated by techno-enthusiasts. Furthermore, experts warned retailers that opening an online presence would likely steal business from a company's existing retail channels.

REI was at a crossroads. The Internet was an exciting new channel but it was untraversed terrain. If you were a member of REI's management team, would you open an online store even if it might cannibalize the sales of your catalog and physical stores? If you chose the Internet route, would you keep your online business a separate entity, or would you integrate it with your existing operation?[1] ■

DEVELOPING DISTRIBUTION STRATEGIES

REI is just one example of how producers use intermediaries to get their products to market. Getting products to customers is the role of distribution, the third element of a firm's marketing mix—also known as *place*. As Chapter 11 points out, distribution channels or *marketing channels* are an organized network of firms that work together to get goods and services from producer to customer. A company's **distribution strategy**, which is its overall plan for moving products to buyers, plays a major role in the firm's success.

Think of all the products you buy: food, toiletries, clothing, sports equipment, train tickets, haircuts, gasoline, stationery, appliances, CDs, videotapes, books, and all the rest. How many of these products do you buy directly from the producer? For most people, the answer is not many. Instead, producers in many industries work with **marketing intermediaries** (previously known as *middlemen*) to bring their products to market.

distribution strategy
Firm's overall plan for moving products to intermediaries and final customers

marketing intermediaries
Businesspeople and organizations that channel goods and services from producers to customers

Understanding the Role of Marketing Intermediaries

The two main types of marketing intermediaries are wholesalers and retailers. **Wholesalers** sell primarily to retailers, to other wholesalers, and to organizational users such as government agencies, institutions, and commercial operations. In turn, the customers of wholesalers either resell the products or use them to make products of their own. Ingram Book Group, for example, the world's largest wholesaler of books and related products, supplies thousands of retail outlets from an inventory of more than 1 million items.[2] By contrast, **retailers** sell products to the final consumer for personal use. Retailers can operate out of a physical facility (supermarket, gas station, kiosk), through vending equipment (soft-drink machine, newspaper box, or automated teller), or from a virtual store (via telephone, catalog, or website). Most retailers today reach shoppers through a carefully balanced blend of store and nonstore retail outlets, as this part's special feature "E-Business in Action" highlights (see pages 333–334). The major types of retailers are described in Exhibit 12.1.

wholesalers
Firms that sell products to other firms for resale or for organizational use

retailers
Firms that sell goods and services to individuals for their own use rather than for resale

Exhibit 12.1   **Types of Retail Stores**

The definition of retailer covers many types of outlets. This table shows some of the most common types.

TYPE OF RETAILER	DESCRIPTION	EXAMPLES
Online retailer	Web-based store offering anything from a single product line to comprehensive selections in multiple product areas; can be web-only (e.g., Amazon.com) or integrated with physical stores (e.g., REI.com)	REI.com Amazon.com
Category killer	Type of specialty store focusing on specific products on giant scale and dominating retail sales in respective products categories	Office Depot Comp USA
Convenience store	Offers staple convenience goods, long service hours, quick checkouts	7-Eleven
Department store	Offers a wide variety of merchandise under one roof in departmentalized sections and many customer services	Sears J.C. Penney Nordstrom
Discount store	Offers a wide variety of merchandise at low prices and few services	Wal-Mart
Factory/retail outlet	Large outlet store selling discontinued items, overruns, and factory seconds	Nordstrom Rack Nike outlet store
Hypermarket	Giant store offering food and general merchandise at discount prices	Wal-Mart Super Centers Carrefour
Off-price store	Offers designer and brand-name merchandise at low prices and few services	T.J. Maxx Marshall's
Specialty store	Offers a complete selection in a narrow range of merchandise	Payless Shoes
Supermarket	Large, self-service store offering a wide selection of food and nonfood merchandise	Kroger Safeway
Warehouse club	Large, warehouse-style store that sells food and general merchandise at discount prices; some require club membership	Sam's Club Costco

Wholesalers and retailers are instrumental in creating three of the four forms of utility mentioned in Chapter 11: place utility, time utility, and possession utility. They provide an efficient process for transferring products from the producer to the customer, they reduce the number of transactions, and they ensure that goods and services are available at a convenient time and place for customers. To accomplish these goals, wholesalers and retailers perform a number of specific distribution functions that make life easier for both producers and customers:

- *Match buyers and sellers.* By making sellers' products available to multiple buyers, intermediaries such as REI reduce the number of transactions between producers and customers.

- *Provide market information.* Intermediaries such as REI collect valuable data about customer purchases: who buys, how often, and how much. Collecting such data allows them to spot buying patterns and to share marketplace information with producers.

- *Provide promotional and sales support.* Many intermediaries, such as Pepsi distributors, create advertising, produce eye-catching displays, and use other promotional devices for some or all of the products they sell. Some employ a salesforce, which can perform a number of selling functions.

- *Gather an assortment of goods.* REI, Amazon.com, Office Max, and other intermediaries receive bulk shipments from producers and break them into more convenient units by sorting, standardizing, and dividing bulk quantities into smaller packages.

- *Transport and store the product.* Intermediaries frequently maintain an inventory of merchandise that they acquire from producers so they can quickly fill customers' orders. In many cases, retailers purchase this merchandise from wholesalers who, in addition to breaking bulk, may also transport the goods from the producer to the retail outlets.

- *Assume risks.* When intermediaries accept goods from manufacturers, they often take on the risks associated with damage, theft, product perishability, and obsolescence. For example, if products stocked or displayed at REI are stolen, REI assumes responsibility for the loss.

- *Provide financing.* Large intermediaries sometimes provide loans to smaller producers.

As Exhibit 12.2 shows, without marketing intermediaries, the buying and selling process would be expensive and time-consuming.

How Intermediaries Simplify Commerce

Intermediaries actually reduce the price customers pay for many goods and services, because they reduce the number of contacts between producers and customers that would otherwise be necessary. They also create place, time, and possession utility.

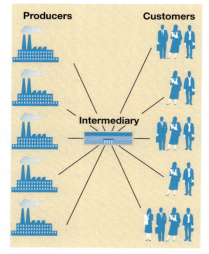

Number of transactions required when customers buy directly from manufacturers

Number of transactions required when buying is conducted via intermediary

Selecting Your Marketing Channels

Distribution channels come in all shapes and sizes. Some channels are short and simple; others are complex and involve many people and organizations. A company's decision about the number and type of intermediaries to use—its **distribution mix**—depends on the kind of product being sold and the marketing practices of the industry. An arrangement that works well for a power-tool and appliance manufacturer such as Black & Decker or a book publisher such as Prentice Hall would not necessarily work for an insurance company, a restaurant, a steel manufacturer, or a movie studio. In general, consumer products and business products tend to move through different channels (see Exhibit 12.3).

distribution mix
Combination of intermediaries and channels a producer uses to get a product to final customers

Length of Distribution Channels

Most businesses purchase goods they use in their operations directly from producers, so the distribution channel is short. Boeing, for example, purchases the parts and supplies it needs to build airplanes directly from over 15,800 companies, such as C&D Aerospace (builders of stowage bins, lavatories, and baggage compartment liners), and Crissair (manufacturer of fuel-system components).[3] In contrast, the channels for consumer goods are usually longer and more complex. Most consumer goods move through one of four primary channels:

- *Producer to consumer.* Producers who sell directly to consumers through catalogs, telemarketing, infomercials, and the Internet are using the shortest, simplest distribution channel. Dell Computer and other companies that sell directly to consumers are seeking closer relationships with customers and more control over pricing, promotion, service, and delivery.[4] Although this approach eliminates payments to channel members, it also forces producers to handle distribution functions such as storing inventory and delivering products.

- *Producer to retailer to consumer.* Some producers create longer channels by selling their products to retailers such as Ace Hardware, who then resell them to consumers. Weber grills, Benjamin Moore paint, and GE lightbulbs are typical of the many products distributed in this way.

Exhibit 12.3 Channels of Distribution

Producers of consumer and business goods and services must analyze the available channels of distribution available for their products so they can select the channels that best meet their marketing objectives and their customers' needs.

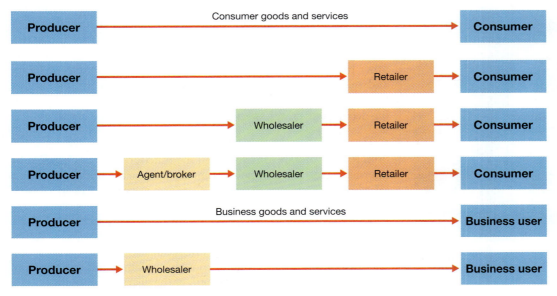

- *Producer to wholesaler to retailer to consumer.* Most manufacturers of supermarket and drugstore items rely on even longer channels. They sell their products to wholesalers, who in turn sell to the retailers. This approach works particularly well for small producers who lack the resources to sell or deliver merchandise to individual retail sites.

- *Producer to agent/broker to wholesaler to retailer to consumer.* Additional channel levels are common in certain industries, such as agriculture, where specialists are required to negotiate transactions or to perform interim functions such as sorting, grading, or subdividing the goods.

Factors That Influence Channel Selection

Should you sell directly to end users or rely on intermediaries? Which intermediaries should you choose? Should you try to sell your product in every available outlet or limit its distribution to a few exclusive outlets? Should you use more than one channel? These are some of the critical decisions that managers face when designing and selecting marketing channels for any product.

Building an effective channel system takes years and, like all marketing relationships, requires commitment. Thus, companies take extra care when establishing their initial marketing channels because changing distribution arrangements at a later date may prove difficult. As Chris DeNove, a channel expert, puts it, "It's much more difficult to modify an existing system than to start with a clean slate." Citing the automobile industry, for example, DeNove points out that "if an auto maker could start over now, none of them would create a franchise distribution system that looks like the existing one."[5]

When establishing marketing channels, companies must consider four key factors: market coverage, cost, control, and channel conflict.

Market Coverage The appropriate *market coverage*—the number of wholesalers or retailers that will carry a product—varies by type of product. Inexpensive convenience goods or organizational supplies such as computer paper and pens sell best if they are available in as many outlets as possible. Such **intensive distribution** requires wholesalers and retailers of many types. In contrast, shopping goods (goods that require some thought before being purchased) such as Sub-Zero refrigerators require different market coverage, because customers shop for such products by comparing features and prices. For these items, the best strategy is usually **selective distribution**, selling through a limited number of outlets that can give the product adequate sales and service support.

If producers of expensive specialty or technical products do not sell directly to customers, they may choose **exclusive distribution**, offering products in only one outlet in each market area. Vehicle manufacturers have traditionally relied on exclusive distribution agreements to sell through one dealership in each local area. By contrast, other firms use multiple channels to increase their market coverage and reach several target markets. Apparel manufacturers such as Champion frequently sell through a combination of channels, including department stores, specialty stores, the Internet, and catalogs.

Cost Costs play a major role in determining a firm's channel selection. It takes money to perform all the functions that are handled by intermediaries. Small or new companies often cannot afford to hire a salesforce large enough to sell directly to end users or to call on a host of retail outlets. Neither can they afford to build large warehouses and distribution centers or to buy trucks to transport their goods. These firms need the help of intermediaries who can spread the cost of such activities across a number of noncompeting products. With time and a larger sales base, a producer may build enough strength to take over some of these functions and reduce the length of the distribution channel.

intensive distribution
Market coverage strategy that tries to place a product in as many outlets as possible

selective distribution
Market coverage strategy that uses a limited number of outlets to distribute products

exclusive distribution
Market coverage strategy that gives intermediaries exclusive rights to sell a product in a specific geographical area

Marketers of luxury products often use exclusive distribution through carefully selected stores to ensure an optimum shopping experience for their customers.

Control   A third issue to consider when selecting distribution channels is control of how, where, when, and for how much your product is sold. Longer distribution channels mean less control for producers, who become increasingly distant from sellers and buyers as the number of intermediaries multiplies. On the other hand, companies may not want to concentrate too many distribution functions in the hands of too few intermediaries.

Control becomes critical when a firm's reputation is at stake. For instance, a designer of high-priced purses, such as Kate Spade or Louis Vuitton, generally limits distribution to exclusive boutiques or high-end retail stores such as Neiman Marcus. Otherwise, the brand could lose some of its appeal if the purses were sold by midpriced retailers such as J.C. Penney. Similarly, producers of complex technical products such as X-ray machines don't want their products handled by unqualified intermediaries that can't provide adequate customer service. A brand's reputation is also linked to, and at times dependent on, the success of the retailers it selects.

Channel Conflict   Because the success of individual channel members depends on the overall channel success, ideally all channel members should work together smoothly. However, individual channel members must also run their own businesses profitably, which means that they often disagree on the roles each member should play. Such disagreements create *channel conflict*.[6]

Channel conflict may arise when suppliers provide inadequate product support, when markets are oversaturated with intermediaries, or when companies sell products via multiple channels, each of which is competing for the same customers. For instance, Hallmark's decision to sell cards to mass-market outlets such as discount stores, supermarkets, and drugstores angered its 8,200 independent dealers, who were now forced to compete with large chains.[7] Similarly, when producers choose to sell direct to consumers via the Internet, they run the risk of damaging their existing relationships with other channel members. Some manufacturers who had hoped the Internet might let them get rid of their traditional distribution channels have found that a cooperative effort that uses the web to everyone's benefit makes more sense.[8] Such was the case when Levi Strauss decided to sell its jeans on the company website. Worried that they might lose jeans sales, retail channel members protested. Some even fought back by giving Levi's jeans less prominent display space in their stores. Eventually Levi Strauss caved in to retailer pressure and ceased selling merchandise directly to consumers via its website. The Levi's site now points shoppers to a selection of online retailers or local outlets.[9]

Managing Physical Distribution

Developing a distribution strategy involves more than selecting the most effective channels for selling a product. Companies must also decide on the best way to move their products and services through the channels so that they are available to the customers at the right place, at the right time, and in the right amount. **Physical distribution** encompasses all the activities required to move finished products from the producer to the customer, including order processing, inventory control, warehousing, materials handling, and outbound transportation (see Exhibit 12.4).

physical distribution
All the activities required to move finished products from the producer to the customer

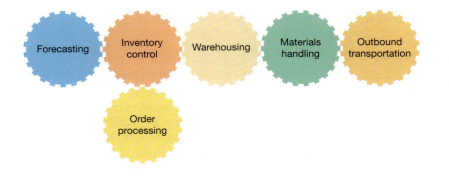

Exhibit 12.4

Steps in the Physical Distribution Process

The phases of a distribution system should mesh as smoothly as the cogs in a machine. Because the steps are interrelated, a change in one phase can affect the other phases. The objective of the process is to provide a target level of customer service at the lowest overall cost.

logistics
The planning, movement, and flow of goods and related information throughout the supply chain

The physical movement of goods may not appear glamorous or exciting, but it is vital to a company's success. To illustrate the importance of physical distribution, consider this: A typical box of breakfast cereal can spend as long as 104 days getting from factory to supermarket, moving haltingly through a series of wholesalers and distributors, each of which has a warehouse. In fact, so many physical distribution systems are burdened with duplication and inefficiency that in industry after industry executives have been placing one item near the top of the corporate agenda: **logistics**—the planning and movement of goods and information throughout the supply chain.

Hard pressed to knock out competitors on quality or price, companies are trying to gain an edge by streamlining processes that traverse companies and continents—no easy task, although the payback can be enormous. Over a two-year period, National Semiconductor was able to cut its standard delivery time 47 percent, reduce distribution costs 2.5 percent, and increase sales 34 percent. How? By shutting down six warehouses around the globe and airfreighting its microchips to customers worldwide from a new distribution center in Singapore.[10]

As National Semiconductor found, the key to success in managing physical distribution is to achieve a competitive level of customer service at the lowest total cost. Doing so requires trade-offs, because as the level of service improves, the cost of distribution increases. For instance, if you reduce the level of inventory to cut your storage costs, you run the risk of being unable to fill orders in a timely fashion. Or, if you use slower forms of transportation, you reduce your shipping costs, but you probably increase your storage costs. The trick is to optimize the *total* cost of achieving the desired level of service. This optimization requires a careful analysis of each step in the distribution process in relation to every other step. Let's take a closer look at each of these steps.

Order Processing

Order processing involves preparing orders for shipment and receiving orders when shipments arrive. It includes a number of activities, such as checking the customer's credit, recording the sale, making the appropriate accounting entries, arranging for the item to be shipped, adjusting the inventory records, and billing the customer. Because order processing involves direct interaction with the customer, it affects a company's reputation for customer service. Most companies establish standards for filling orders within a specific time period.

Inventory Control

As Chapter 8 discusses, in an ideal world, a company would always have just the right amount of goods on hand to fill the orders it receives. In reality, however, inventory and sales are seldom in perfect balance. Most firms like to build a supply of finished goods so that they can fill orders in a timely fashion. But how much inventory is enough? If your inventory is too large, you incur extra expenses for storage space, handling, insurance, and taxes; you also run the risk of product obsolescence. On the other hand, if your inventory is too low, you may lose sales when the product is not in stock. The objective of *inventory control* is to resolve these issues. Inventory managers decide how much product to keep on hand and when to replenish the supply of goods in inventory. They also decide how to allocate products to customers if orders exceed supply.

Warehousing

warehouse
Facility for storing inventory

distribution centers
Warehouse facilities that specialize in collecting and shipping merchandise

Products held in inventory are physically stored in a **warehouse**, which may be owned by the manufacturer, by an intermediary, or by a private company that leases space to others. Some warehouses are almost purely holding facilities in which goods are stored for relatively long periods. Other warehouses, known as **distribution centers**, serve as command posts for moving products to customers. In a typical distribution center, goods produced at a company's various locations are collected, sorted, coded, and redistributed to fill customer orders.

Some of today's most advanced physical distribution centers use satellite navigation and communication, voice-input computers, machine vision, robots, onboard computer logbooks, and planning software that relies on artificial intelligence. FedEx, for instance, runs a fully automated distribution center. The company's $180 million small-package sorting system processes hundreds of thousands of packages an hour. Each parcel is scanned four times, weighed, and measured; then its digital image is recorded on computer. In addition, the company's world shipping software streamlines customer billing, reduces shipping paperwork, and allows customers to track their shipments over the Internet.[11]

This $25 million sorting machine at Amazon.com's warehouse in Fernley, Nevada, reads bar codes on items, routes them into one of 2,100 chutes, and signals when an order is ready to be packed in a box. Source: Marilyn Newston/The New York Times.

Materials Handling

An important part of warehousing activities is **materials handling**, the movement of goods within and between physical distribution facilities. One main area of concern is storage method—whether to keep supplies and finished goods in individual packages, in large boxes, or in sealed shipping containers. The choice of storage method depends on how the product is shipped, in what quantities, and to which locations. For example, a firm that typically sends small quantities of goods to widely scattered customers would not want to use large containers. Materials handling also involves keeping track of inventory so that the company knows where in the distribution process its goods are located and when they need to be moved.

materials handling
Movement of goods within a firm's warehouse terminal, factory, or store

Outbound Transportation

For any business, the cost of transportation is normally the largest single item in the overall cost of physical distribution. Five common types of outbound transportation are rail, truck, water (ships), air (planes), and pipeline. When choosing among these five modes of transportation, managers weigh the advantages and disadvantages of each. In particular, they consider such factors as storage, financing, sales, inventory size, speed, product perishability, dependability, flexibility, and convenience—to name a few. The goal is to maximize the efficiency of the entire distribution process while minimizing overall cost.

Incorporating the Internet into Your Distribution Strategies

The Internet's efficient and effective global reach is revolutionizing the way goods and services are sold and distributed. Amazon.com's Jeff Bezos was a pioneer in recognizing the Internet's potential for making goods and services available to buyers. He reasoned that given a choice, many people would prefer the ease and convenience of online shopping to visiting a store every time they wanted to buy a book. He also believed that publishers would welcome Amazon.com as yet another way to get their books into the hands of readers. After investing millions in leading-edge distribution technology, the company continues to take advantage of this vital capability by expanding its product portfolio far beyond books.

Today, a growing number of businesses sell a huge selection of goods and services online. For some, such as Amazon.com, the Internet is their only marketing channel. But for others, such as REI, the Internet offers an additional way to sell to customers. An increasing number of businesses are using the Internet to improve the efficiency of their distribution systems and to expand their market reach. Others are using the Internet to eliminate the middleman entirely. After more than 100 years of offering medical insurance through 20,000 insurance agents, Provident American Life & Health Insurance Company dropped its agent network, changed its name to HealthAxis.com, and launched a website to sell a full line of insurance products directly to consumers. CEO Michael Ashker says that eliminating "costly middlemen in an industry where distribution is inefficient" allowed the company to cut its prices by 15 percent.[12]

In short, the Internet is a powerful force that is changing the role of traditional intermediaries. The livelihoods of travel agents, retailers, real estate agents, and independent sales representatives are threatened as never before, as the Internet increasingly allows sellers and buyers to find each other and do business directly or differently. For instance, between legitimate online music services such as RealNetworks Rhapsody and Apple's iTunes, illegal file downloads and other piracy, online CD stores such as Amazon.com, and ferocious low-price competitors such as Wal-Mart, some experts suggest that conventional music stores such as Tower Records will have to change dramatically if they hope to survive much longer.[13]

DEVELOPING PROMOTIONAL STRATEGIES

Although distribution is a critical element in the marketing mix, promotion is perhaps the one element you associate most with the marketing function. That's because promotion is highly visible to consumers. Chapter 11 defined promotion as a form of persuasive communication that motivates people to buy whatever an organization is selling—whether it's goods and services or places, people, and ideas. Promotion may take the form of direct, face-to-face communication or indirect communication through such media as television, radio, magazines, newspapers, direct mail, billboards, the Internet, floor ads, and other channels. How do you decide on which forms of promotion to use? Many firms develop a **promotional strategy**; that is, they define the direction and scope of the promotional activities their company will take to meet its marketing objectives.

Developing a promotional strategy encompasses several steps. You begin by setting your promotional goals. Next you take several product variables into consideration and decide on the optimal market approach before selecting your promotional mix. Finally, you fine-tune your product mix to make sure that all your promotional elements communicate the same message.

Setting Your Promotional Goals

You can use promotion to achieve three basic goals: to inform, to persuade, and to remind. *Informing* is the first promotional priority, because people cannot buy something until they are aware of it and know what it can do for them. Potential customers need to know where the item can be purchased, how much it costs, and how to use it. *Persuading* is also an important priority, because most people need to be encouraged to purchase something new or to switch brands. Advertising that meets this goal is classified as **persuasive advertising**. *Reminding* the customer of the product's availability and benefits is also important, because such reminders stimulate additional purchases. The term for such promotional efforts is **reminder advertising**.

Beyond these general objectives, your promotional strategy should accomplish specific objectives: It should attract new customers, increase usage among existing customers, aid distributors, stabilize sales, boost brand-name recognition, create sales leads, differentiate the product, and influence decision makers.

Analyzing Product Variables

A number of product and market factors also influence promotional choices. To begin with, you must consider the nature of your product. Various types of products lend themselves to differing forms of promotion. Simple, familiar items such as laundry detergent can be explained adequately through advertising, but personal selling is generally required to communicate the features of unfamiliar and sophisticated goods and services such as office-automation equipment or municipal waste-treatment facilities. Direct, personal contact is particularly important in promoting customized

promotional strategy
Statement or document that defines the direction and scope of the promotional activities that a company will use to meet its marketing objectives

persuasive advertising
Advertising designed to encourage customers to try new products or to switch brands

reminder advertising
Advertising intended to remind existing customers of a product's availability and benefits

services such as interior design, financial advice, or legal counsel. In general, consumer and organizational goods usually require different promotional mixes.

　　The product's price is also a factor in the selection of the promotional mix. Inexpensive items such as shaving cream or breakfast cereal sold to a mass market are well suited to advertising and sales promotion, which have a relatively low per-unit cost. At the other extreme, products with a high unit price, such as in-ground swimming pools, lend themselves to personal selling because the high cost of a sales call is justified by the price of the product. Furthermore, the nature of the selling process often demands face-to-face interaction between the buyer and seller.

　　Another factor that influences both the level and mix of promotional activity is the product's position in its life cycle. Early on, when the seller is trying to inform the customer about the product and build the distribution network, promotional efforts are in high gear. Selective advertising, sales promotion, and public relations are used to build awareness and to encourage early adopters to try the product; personal selling is used to gain the cooperation of intermediaries. Gillette, for example, spent $300 million to promote the launch of the Mach3 razor during its first year—on top of $750 million-plus in development costs—to accelerate the Mach3's transition from the costly introduction stage to the profitable growth stage faster than any previous Gillette razors. Just 18 months after the Mach3 was launched, sales for the product hit $1 billion, making it the company's most successful new product ever. The success of the Mach3 brand laid the foundation for successful follow-ons as well.[14]

　　As the market expands during the growth phase, the company broadens its advertising and sales-promotion activities to reach a wider audience and continues to use personal selling to expand the distribution network. When the product reaches maturity and competition is at its peak, the company's primary goal is to differentiate the product from rival brands. Advertising generally dominates the promotional mix during this phase, but sales promotion is an important supplemental tool, particularly for low-priced consumer products. As the product begins to decline, the level of promotion generally tapers off. Advertising and selling efforts are carefully targeted toward loyal, steady customers.

push strategy
Promotional approach designed to motivate wholesalers and retailers to push a producer's products to end users

pull strategy
Promotional strategy that stimulates customer demand, which then exerts pressure on wholesalers and retailers to carry a product

Deciding on Your Market Approach

The selection of your promotional mix also depends on whether you plan to focus your marketing effort on intermediaries or on final customers. If the focus is on intermediaries, the producer uses a **push strategy** to persuade wholesalers and retailers to carry the item. Producers may, for instance, offer wholesalers or retailers special discounts or incentives for purchasing larger quantities of the item. You would expect to see personal selling and sales promotions to dominate the promotional mix aimed at intermediaries. If the marketing focus is on end users, the producer uses a **pull strategy** to appeal directly to the ultimate customer, using advertising, direct mail, contests, discount coupons, and so on. With this approach,

A mature product such as blue jeans requires a different promotional strategy than a product in the introductory or growth stages in the product life cycle.

Where Did the Audience Go?

Looking around at today's media-saturated world, it's hard to imagine a time when "mass media" consisted of three nationwide television networks, radio, local newspapers, and a handful of popular magazines. If you wanted to launch a new product nationwide, you simply bought commercial time on ABC, CBS, or NBC, and you would've had a pretty good chance of reaching your target market. Advertisers didn't have to look very far to find consumers because consumers didn't have anywhere else to turn (and they didn't even have remote controls to mute commercials or change the channel).

Fast-forward to the 21st century, when advertisers wonder where everybody went. Consumers are still around, of course, but now they're scattered in smaller, isolated pockets all over the media landscape, from blogs to Internet radio to online e-zines to digital cable systems with hundreds of channels. With digital video recorders (DVRs) such as TiVo, they can zoom right past commercials they once had to sit through; 30 million households are expected to have DVRs by 2007. And many people, particularly younger consumers, are spending less time watching regular TV and more time playing video games or enjoying DVDs that NetFlix drops off in the mail. According to one study, in 1995, a national advertiser could reach 80 percent of U.S. women aged 18 to 49 by running a commercial just three times. To reach that same group in 2000 required 97 ads.

How can advertisers reach audiences that won't sit still and won't pay attention when they are sitting still? Nobody has the answer for every situation, but advertisers are trying plenty of possibilities. *Product placement*, in which advertisers put their products right into a TV show or movie, is more common than ever. Did you notice those Coke-logo beverage cups the judges drink from on *American Idol*? Coca-Cola paid $20 million to put them there. Another common move is taking the ads to wherever the customers are, from posters in rest rooms to TV screens positioned near checkout lines, gas pumps, and other places people are forced to wait. Highway billboards have gone high tech, too, with flashy electronic displays that can be altered by remote control to catch the eye of drivers stuck in traffic. One company pays college students to wear company logos on their foreheads. Tremor, a promotions company started by consumer giant Procter & Gamble, has recruited several hundred thousand teenagers to help promote its products—without pay. These boys and girls are treated to sneak previews and inside information about various products, and they're only too happy to share the news with their friends.

Television commercials aren't going away, of course, but advertisers are working harder to make them more entertaining and more memorable, if sometimes more risqué or even disgusting in some eyes. If you don't like these new ads, don't think you can get away by switching off the TV to play a video game instead; a number of games now have ads built right into them (and if you play networked games over the Internet, somebody's probably measuring your response to these ads, too).

Of course, every new solution seems to create another round of problems. With ads everywhere, consumers are now complaining that there's nowhere to hide. Until somebody dreams up a better way to reach consumers, though, chances are that wherever you go, you'll find an ad waiting for you—and it might be delivered by your best friend.

Questions for Critical Thinking

1. Do fragmented media make it easier or harder for marketers to engage in segmented or concentrated marketing? Explain your answer.
2. Is it ethical to engage consumers to help promote your products without explicitly telling them you're doing so? Explain your answer.

consumers learn of the product through promotion and request it from retailers, who respond by asking their wholesalers for it or by going directly to the producer (see Exhibit 12.5).

Many companies use both push and pull tactics to increase the impact of their promotional efforts. For example, when Schering-Plough introduced Claritin antihistamine, it used push tactics to educate physicians about the prescription drug's use and effectiveness, while it used pull tactics such as television and print advertising to increase market awareness and encourage consumers to ask for the new medication. This diverse, high-powered promotional mix helped Claritin capture a whopping 54 percent of the antihistamine drug market within a short time. Unfortunately, for Schering-Plough, competitors also caught on to the power of push-pull marketing and the patent on Claritin ran out in 2003 (meaning that competitors could make lower-cost generic versions), adding up to a short-lived advantage in the marketplace.[15]

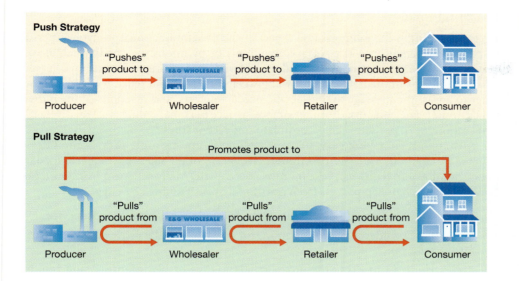

Exhibit 12.5

Push and Pull Strategies

In a push strategy, the manufacturer "pushes" products through the distribution channel, first promoting and distributing them to wholesalers, who then push them to retailers, who then push them to consumers. In a pull strategy, the manufacturer promotes its products directly to consumers who then "pull" the products through the distribution channel by requesting them from retailers, who then request them from wholesalers, who then request them from the manufacturer. Many companies use a combination of push and pull strategies.

The promotional strategy is also influenced by the size and concentration of the market. In markets with many widely dispersed buyers, advertising is generally the most economical way of communicating the product's features. In markets with relatively few customers, particularly when they are clustered in a limited area, personal selling is a practical promotional alternative. Many marketers use a combination of methods, often relying on advertising and public relations to build awareness and interest, following up with personal selling to complete the sale.

Selecting Your Promotional Mix

Within the framework of a company's promotional goods, product variables, and market approach, marketers use a mix of five activities to achieve their promotional objectives: personal selling, advertising, direct marketing, sales promotion, and public relations. These elements can be combined in various ways to create a **promotional mix** for a particular product or idea (see Exhibit 12.6).

promotional mix
Particular blend of personal selling, advertising, direct marketing, sales promotion, and public relations that a company uses to reach potential customers

Exhibit 12.6   **The Five Elements of Promotion**

The promotional mix typically includes a blend of various elements. The most effective mix depends on the nature of the market and the characteristics of the good or service being marketed. Over time, the mix for a particular product may change.

ACTIVITY	REACH	TIMING	FLEXIBILITY	COST/EXPOSURE
Personal selling	Direct personal interaction with limited reach	Regular, recurrent contact	Message tailored to customer and adjusted to reflect feedback	Relatively high
Advertising	Indirect interaction with large reach	Regular, recurrent contact	Standard, unvarying message	Low to moderate
Direct marketing	Direct personal interaction with large reach	Intermittent, based on short-term sales objectives	Customized, varying message	Relatively high
Sales promotion	Indirect interaction with large reach	Intermittent, based on short-term sales objectives	Standard, unvarying message	Varies
Public relations	Indirect interaction with large reach	Intermittent, as newsworthy events occur	Standard, unvarying message	No direct cost

Owens-Corning's FAST salesforce automation system makes working directly with customers easier than ever.

personal selling
In-person communication between a seller and one or more potential buyers

advertising
Paid, nonpersonal communication to a target market from an identified sponsor using mass communications channels

Personal Selling

Personal selling is the interpersonal aspect of the promotional mix. It involves person-to-person presentation—face-to-face, by phone, or by interactive media such as web-casting—for the purpose of making sales and building customer relationships. Personal selling allows for immediate interaction between the buyer and seller. It also enables the seller to adjust the message to the specific needs, interests, and reactions of the individual customer. The chief disadvantage of face-to-face personal selling is its relatively high cost—about $170 per sales call according to one recent study.[16]

Although it may look easy, personal selling is not a simple task. Some sales, of course, are made in a matter of minutes. However, other sales, particularly for large organizational purchases, can take months to complete. Many salespeople follow a carefully planned seven-step process from start to finish, as Exhibit 12.7 suggests:

- *Prospecting.* Finding and qualifying potential buyers of the product or service.
- *Preparing.* Considering various options for approaching the prospect and preparing for the sales call.
- *Approaching.* Contacting the prospect, getting his or her attention, and building interest in the product or service.
- *Presenting.* Communicating a message that persuades a prospect to buy.
- *Handling objections.* Countering the buyer's objections to purchasing a product or service with convincing claims.
- *Closing.* Asking the prospect to buy the product.
- *Following up.* Checking customer satisfaction following the sale and building good-will.

Technological advances are facilitating these steps and the entire selling process. Some companies are using custom software to provide online proposal-generation and order-management systems. The software relieves salespeople of nonproductive tasks and allows the sales reps to spend more time attending to customers' specific needs. Sales reps at Owens-Corning use laptops, the Internet, and a custom software package called Field Automation Sales Team (FAST) system to inquire about customers' backgrounds and sales histories, resolve customer service issues on the spot, modify pricing information as needed, print customized sales material, and more. Such technology empowers Owens-Corning reps: "They become the real managers of their own business and their own territories," says Owens-Corning's regional general manager.[17] For all its power, sales-force automation involves more engineering and maintenance work than some companies want to take on, but these firms can turn to web-based solutions such as Salesforce.com. Some 10,000 companies in dozens of industries now use the company's sales and customer service solutions.[18]

Advertising and Direct Marketing

Advertising and direct marketing are the two elements of a firm's promotional mix with which consumers are most familiar. **Advertising** consists of messages paid for by an identified sponsor and transmitted through a mass communication medium such as

---

Exhibit 12.7 **The Personal Selling Process**

The personal selling process can involve up to seven steps, starting with prospecting for sales leads and ending with following up after the sale has been closed.

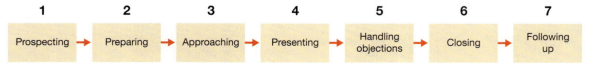

1	2	3	4	5	6	7
Prospecting	Preparing	Approaching	Presenting	Handling objections	Closing	Following up

television, radio, or newspapers. **Direct marketing** is defined by the Direct Marketing Association as distributing promotional materials directly to a consumer or business recipient for the purpose of generating (1) a response in the form of an order, (2) a request for further information, or (3) a visit to a store or other place of business for purchase of a specific product or service.[19]

All forms of advertising and direct marketing have three objectives: to create product awareness, to create and maintain the image of a product, and to stimulate consumer demand. Advertising and direct marketing are also the promotional approaches that best reach mass audiences quickly at a relatively low per-person cost. But, to be effective, your messages must be persuasive, stand out from the competition's, and motivate your target audience—a lofty goal considering that the average U.S. resident is exposed to roughly 250 ads every day.[20]

Of course, you're not allowed to stand out from the competition in ways that are deceptive. To limit promotional abuses, the Federal Trade Commission (FTC) and other government agencies have passed strict rules and regulations. One such rule is that *all statements of fact must be supported by evidence.* For example, the Food and Drug Administration ordered Glaxo Wellcome PLC, makers of the flu drug Relenza, to stop showing a widely aired commercial because it suggested that Relenza was more effective than had actually been demonstrated.[21] Another rule is that *sellers must not create an overall impression that is incorrect.* When the FTC concluded that an organization calling itself the National Consumer Council was actually a group of for-profit companies and was misrepresenting its ability to provide debt relief for consumers, the agency requested and received a temporary restraining order for the group to stop conducting business.[22] Most states also regulate promotional practices by certain businesses, such as liquor stores, stock brokerages, employment agencies, and loan companies.

Many individual companies and industries also practice self-regulation to restrain false and misleading promotion. The National Advertising Review Board, whose members include advertisers, agencies, and the general public, has a full-time professional staff that investigates complaints of deceptive advertising. If the complaint appears justified, the board tries to get the offending company to stop—even if it means referring the offender to proper government enforcement agencies.

Direct-Marketing Vehicles

Direct marketing is an effective promotional tool for many companies because it enables them to more precisely target and personalize messages to specific consumer and business segments and build long-term customer relationships.[23] The most popular direct-marketing vehicles are direct mail, targeted e-mail, telemarketing, and the Internet:

- *Direct mail.* The principal vehicle for direct marketing is **direct mail**, which includes catalogs, brochures, videotapes, CDs, and other promotional materials delivered through the postal service or private carriers such as Federal Express.

- *Target e-mail.* As millions of consumers and business employees got connected to e-mail in recent years, e-mail looked to be a promising medium for advertising. The ability to reach millions of people inexpensively and direct them to an e-commerce website was a compelling combination. As anyone with an e-mail account knows, however, legitimate e-mail campaigns are now getting buried in a deluge of spam campaigns that vary from the suspicious to the down-and-out illegal. Mike Gilbert, of Three A.M. Advertising, a Seattle ad agency with such clients as Microsoft and T-Mobile, has abandoned mass e-mailing for his clients because it risks tainting a valuable brand by associating it with spammers.[24] To avoid that problem and to help potential customers get the information they really do want, many mainstream companies now emphasize **permission marketing**, in which they first ask for permission before sending e-mail messages (usually through "opt-in" choices that are displayed on their websites).

Celebrity endorsers frequently license their names and images for use in advertising and direct marketing. Some endorsers also allow their names to be used as part of product names, as boxer George Foreman did with the George Foreman Grill.

direct marketing
Direct communication other than personal sales contacts designed to effect a measurable response

Business BUZZ

Phishing: The criminal practice of sending fraudulent e-mails designed to trick recipients into providing credit card numbers and other sensitive information; the messages typically link through to websites that look like legitimate e-commerce sites

direct mail
Advertising sent directly to potential customers, usually through the mail

permission marketing
Promotional campaigns that send information only to those people who've specifically asked to receive it

Technologies That Are Revolutionizing Business

Individualized advertising

Don't be surprised if you look out the window one morning to see clouds in the sky arranged in letters that spell out your name and invite you to try a refreshing bottle of Coke or remind you to get your oil changed at Jiffy Lube.

How it's changing business

Maybe it won't get quite that far, but advertisers are perfecting a variety of technologies that allow them to pinpoint individual audience members with customized messages. Given the continuing fragmentation of mainstream media and advertisers' growing disappointment in mass advertising that no longer brings in the results it used to, individualized advertising promises to be the next big thing in promotional strategies. A few examples: personalized magazine covers (including one that showed an aerial photograph of each subscriber's neighborhood with his or her home or office circled in red), commercials on digital cable systems that can be targeted to viewers in an individual neighborhood or even an individual household (with messages shaped by the demographics of the residents of the house), narrowly focused audio messages that can be aimed at a single shopper in a retail store, and Google's new Gmail e-mail service, which serves up ads based on specific words in your e-mail messages (if you invite a colleague out for sushi, for instance, ads for local sushi restaurants could appear next to your message).

Where you can learn more

Individualized advertising is still a young technology, so the key players and information sources are likely to change frequently in coming months and years. In the meantime, database and search engine queries for "personalized advertising," "customized advertising," and "individualized advertising," as well as variations on those terms, should yield interesting results.

Permission-based efforts also let recipients select the specific information they want, which benefits both recipients and marketers by making the communication more efficient. At Agilent Technologies' website, for instance, engineers and scientists who want e-mail updates on the company's test and measurement products can select from dozens of specific topics that match their professional interests.[25]

- *Telemarketing.* **Telemarketing**, or selling over the telephone, has long been popular with direct marketers, generating sales anywhere from 2 to 20 percent of the time. However, consumer complaints about interruptions led to the creation of the National Do Not Call Registry in 2003, partially blocking telemarketing access to millions of U.S. homes. The registry does not affect nonprofit organizations or several specific industries, including, ironically enough, the telephone companies themselves. Also, telemarketers are still allowed to call their existing customers, homes not registered on the do not call list, and other businesses—which is leading some telemarketers to target consumers at work.[26]

telemarketing
Selling or supporting the sales process over the telephone

product advertising
Advertising that tries to sell specific goods or services, generally by describing features, benefits, and, occasionally, price

institutional advertising
Advertising that seeks to create goodwill and to build a desired image for a company rather than to sell specific products

national advertising
Advertising sponsored by companies that sell products on a nationwide basis; refers to the geographic reach of the advertiser, not the geographic coverage of the ad

local advertising
Advertising sponsored by a local merchant

Advertising Categories

Advertising is commonly classified by type. **Product advertising** is the most common type, designed to sell specific goods or services, such as Kellogg's cereals, Sega video games, or Estée Lauder cosmetics. Product advertising generally describes the product's features and may mention its price. **Institutional advertising** is designed to create goodwill and build a desired image for a company rather than to sell specific products. As discussed in Chapter 2, many companies are now spending large sums for institutional advertising that focuses on *green marketing*, creating an image of companies as corporate conservationists. Institutional advertisers tout their actions, contributions, and philosophies not only as supporting the environmental movement but as leading the way. When utilized as *corporate advertising*, institutional advertising often promotes an entire line of a company's products. Institutional ads can also be used to remind investors that the company is doing well.

Advertising can also be classified according to the sponsor. **National advertising** is sponsored by companies that sell products on a nationwide basis. The term *national* refers to the level of the advertiser, not the geographic coverage of the ad. If a national manufacturer places an ad in only one city, the ad is still classified as a national ad. By contrast, **local advertising** is sponsored by a local merchant. Grocery store ads in the local newspaper are a good example. **Cooperative advertising** is a financial arrangement whereby companies with products sold nationally share the costs of local advertising with local merchants and wholesalers. As a result, it is a cross between local and national advertising.

Regardless of which type of advertising you use, you must get your message to your target audience by using suitable **media**, or channels of communication. Advertising media fall into six major categories, each with its own strengths and weaknesses, as highlighted in Exhibit 12.8. Your goal as a marketer is to select a **media mix**—the combination of print, broadcast, online, and other media that maximizes the return of your advertising investment.

As you can see in "The Rise, Fall—and Rise—of Online Advertising," the online possibilities continue to intrigue advertisers who want to use the web's interactive options to reach target audiences. The principal advantages of online marketing are timeliness, global reach, relatively low cost, and two-way communication using features such as chat and instant messaging. Not only can websites customize the words you see on screen based on your preferences and visitor profile, but with products such as Adobe Graphics Server, they can customize graphics on the fly for every site visitor.[27] For instance, if a clothing retailer knows that you prefer casual clothes rather than formal business attire, it can present those images when you visit.

cooperative advertising
Joint efforts between local and national advertisers, in which producers of nationally sold products share the costs of local advertising with local merchants and wholesalers

media
Communications channels, such as newspapers, radio, and television

media mix
Combination of various media options that a company uses in an advertising campaign

Exhibit 12.8 Advantages and Disadvantages of Major Advertising Media

When selecting the media mix, companies attempt to match the characteristics of the media audiences with the characteristics of the customer segments being targeted. A typical advertising campaign involves the use of several media.

MEDIUM	ADVANTAGES	DISADVANTAGES
Newspapers	Extensive market coverage; low cost; short lead time for placing ads; good local market coverage; geographic selectivity	Poor graphic quality; short life span; cluttered pages; visual competition from other ads
Television	Great impact; broad reach; appealing to senses of sight, sound, and motion; creative opportunities for demonstration; high attention; entertainment carryover	High cost for production and air time; less audience selectivity; long preparation time; commercial clutter; short life for message; vulnerability to remote controls; losing ground to new media options
Direct mail	Can deliver large amounts of information to narrowly selected audiences; excellent control over quality of message; personalization	High cost per contact; delivery delays; difficulty of obtaining desired mailing lists; customer resistance; generally poor image (junk mail)
E-mail	Extremely low cost; fast preparation and delivery; ability to customize and to provide links back to websites	Deluge of spam, much of it illegal or offensive, has tainted this medium for general advertising use, possibly beyond repair; many legitimate marketers use only permission-based (opt-in) e-mail now
Radio	Low cost; high frequency; immediacy; highly portable; high geographic and demographic selectivity	No visual possibilities; short life for message; commercial clutter; lower attention than television; lower level of engagement makes it easier to switch stations
Magazines	Good production quality; long life; local and regional market selectivity; authority and credibility; multiple readers	Limited demonstration possibilities; long lead time between placing and publishing ads; high cost; less compelling than other major media
Internet	Rich media options and creative flexibility can make ads more compelling and more effective; changes and additions can be made quickly and easily in most cases; webpages can provide an almost unlimited amount of information; can be personalized more than any other medium	Difficulty in measuring audiences and ad effectiveness, although improvements are being made; customer resistance; increasing clutter (such as pop-up ads); extreme fragmentation (millions of websites)

The Rise, Fall—and Rise—of Online Advertising

As the World Wide Web began to evolve from an online meeting place for scientists into a global playground and shopping mall, the question of advertising was inevitable. Hundreds of dot-com businesses were founded and funded on the idea that the web would turn into a major advertising medium. Many gave away free content (and a few even gave away free PCs), in the hope of attracting enough "eyeballs" to attract big-budget advertisers. Millions of websites popped up, and millions of consumers and businesses logged on. Everything was ready to go.

Except somebody forgot to tell the advertisers. A number of major players, such as McDonald's, with its $1 billion annual advertising budget, shunned web advertising. And advertisers who did plunge in often came away disappointed with low response rates. When the advertising revenue didn't materialize, most of the dot-coms struggled and many disappeared entirely.

With so many millions of people flocking to the web, why didn't it turn into the advertising dreamland that so many investors anticipated? After all, serious web surfers practically live online, their eyes glued to the screen. Sounds like a perfect advertising medium, but a combination of issues plagued early web advertising. One of the biggest was hyper-fragmentation; with millions of new websites popping up all around, advertisers weren't sure where to place their bets. This only added to the general uncertainty surrounding the web. National advertisers had decades of experience with television and radio advertising, and many weren't about to jeopardize sales on an unproven medium.

Other issues included measurement questions (businesses weren't quite sure how to gauge the effectiveness of online ads), buyer behavior (you'd never believe it now, but the early web was a fairly noncommercial place, where many people shunned the whole idea of advertising and e-commerce), seller behavior (such as failing to respond when sales leads came in from their websites), and too many websites that didn't take advantage of the medium (the biggest culprit: stale, static "brochure-ware" sites that merely duplicated printed brochures). For many people, advertising started to look like one more empty promise of the dot-com boom.

Through it all, though, some of the online pioneers persevered, learning from those early experiments, fine-tuning business models and creative approaches, and improving the technology. By 2003, online ad spending started to grow again. As broadband Internet access reached more consumers and businesses, advertisers could increase the use of *rich media* ads that combine audio, video, and animation. The result is a new generation of ads that are more entertaining and more informative—and often more effective. These new ads entice web visitors to play games, download helpful information, customize product choices, or sit back and enjoy "minimovies" that are 5 or 10 times longer than typical TV commercials.

While these improvements were coming along, a whole new category of advertising appeared: paid keyword searches on Google, Yahoo! and other search engines—those "sponsored links" that you see alongside your search results. In addition to targeted search advertising, technology has also improved advertisers' ability to track online behavior and customize ads based on users' web habits. (You know those times you hop online to plan your spring break, then suddenly start seeing ads for air travel, condo rentals on the beach, and other related products? That's not a coincidence.)

Moreover, the price for online ad space has dropped considerably from the dot-com fever days, giving advertisers one more reason to give the web another try. For instance, McDonald's is now spending an estimated 5 percent of its budget for ads on such youth-oriented sites as www.nick.com, www.disney.com, and www.foxkids.com. Five percent might not sound like a big commitment so far, but 5 percent of a billion dollars is a big number.

Online advertising will continue to evolve in the coming years as advertisers keep improving their tools and techniques—and continue to explore new options, such as advertising on blogs and Internet radio stations. It's been a bumpy ride, but this time online advertising looks like it's here to stay.

Questions for Critical Thinking

1. Why wouldn't a major advertiser such as McDonald's just spread its massive ad budget all over the web, buying ad space on hundreds or thousands of sites?
2. Do you think the creative flexibility of web advertising makes it a more compelling advertising medium than television or radio? Why or why not?

---

sales promotion
Wide range of events and activities (including coupons, rebates, contests, in-store demonstrations, free samples, trade shows, and point-of-purchase displays) designed to stimulate interest in a product

Sales Promotion

Sales promotion, which includes a wide range of events and activities designed to stimulate immediate interest in and encourage the purchase of your product or service, is the fourth element of the promotional mix. The impact of sales promotion activities is often short-term; thus, sales promotions are not as effective as advertising or personal selling in building long-term brand preference.[28] Sales promotion consists of two basic categories: consumer promotion and trade promotion.

Consumer Promotion   **Consumer promotion** is aimed directly at final users of the product. Companies use a variety of promotional tools and incentives to stimulate repeat purchases and to entice new users:

- *Coupons.* The biggest category of consumer promotion—and the most popular with consumers—is **coupons**, certificates that spur sales by giving buyers a discount when they purchase specified products. Customers redeem their coupons at the time of purchase.[29] Companies offer coupons on packages, in print ads, in direct mail, at the checkout, and on the Internet to encourage trial of new products, reach out to nonusers of mature products, encourage repeat buying, and temporarily lower a product's price.[30]

- *Rebates.* Similar to coupons, rebates are another popular promotional tool. Instead of receiving the discount at the time of purchase, buyers generally get reimbursement checks from the manufacturer by submitting proofs of purchase along with a prepared manufacturer's rebate form. Because many buyers neglect to redeem the rebates, the costs of running such programs remain relatively low. Moreover, rebates allow the manufacturer to promote the reduced price even though customers pay the full price at checkout.[31]

- *Point-of-purchase.* Another widely used consumer promotion technique is the **point-of-purchase (POP) display**, a device for showing a product in a way that stimulates immediate sales. It may be simple, such as the end-of-aisle stacks of soda pop in a supermarket or the racks of gum and mints at checkout counters, or it may be more elaborate, such as ad decals strategically placed on floor aisles. Simple or elaborate, point-of-purchase displays really work: Studies show that in almost every instance, such displays significantly increase sales.[32]

- *Special-event sponsorship.* Sponsoring special events has become one of the most popular sales-promotion tactics. Thousands of companies spend billions of dollars to sponsor events ranging from golf to opera. For instance, the Summer and Winter Olympic Games and the NFL Super Bowl are among the most watched television programs and always attract millions of dollars of event sponsorship.

- *Cross-promotion.* Another popular sales-promotion vehicle is **cross-promotion**, which involves using one brand to advertise another, noncompeting brand. Movies have become a regular vehicle for cross-promotion, for instance, with ties-ins to automobiles, soft drinks, fast food, toys, and other product categories.

- *Samples.* Samples are an effective way to introduce a new product, encourage nonusers to try an existing product, encourage current buyers to use the product in a new way, or expand distribution into new areas. Sampling has been around for decades, but it's alive and well in the computer age, too; many software companies let potential customers try their products for a limited period of time before making a purchase decision.

Other popular consumer sales-promotion techniques include in-store demonstrations, loyalty and frequency programs such as frequent-flyer miles, and **premiums**, which are free or bargain-priced items offered to encourage the consumer to buy a product. Contests, sweepstakes, and games are also quite popular in some industries and can generate a great deal of public attention, particularly when valuable or unusual prizes are offered. **Specialty advertising** (on pens, calendars, T-shirts, mouse pads, and so on) helps keep a company's name in front of customers for a long period of time.

consumer promotion
Sales promotion aimed at final consumers

coupons
Certificates that offer discounts on particular items and are redeemed at the time of purchase

point-of-purchase (POP) display
Advertising or other display materials set up at retail locations to promote products to potential customers as they are making their purchase decisions

cross-promotion
Jointly advertising two or more noncompeting brands

premiums
Free or bargain-priced items offered to encourage customers to buy a product

Once a mundane afterthought to costlier, more glamorous forms of advertising, product sampling is now seen by many marketers as a more cost-effective way to promote some products. Here Ben & Jerry's representatives serve up samples of Concession Obsession ice cream.

specialty advertising
Advertising that appears on various items such as coffee mugs, pens, and calendars, designed to help keep a company's name in front of customers

trade promotions
Sales-promotion efforts aimed at inducing distributors or retailers to push a producer's products

trade allowance
Discount offered by producers to wholesalers and retailers

public relations
Nonsales communication that businesses have with their various audiences (includes both communication with the general public and press relations)

news release
Brief statement or video program released to the press announcing new products, management changes, sales performance, and other potential news items

news conference
Gathering of media representatives at which companies announce new information; also called a press conference or press briefing

integrated marketing communications (IMC)
Strategy of coordinating and integrating all communications and promotional efforts with customers to ensure greater efficiency and effectiveness

Trade Promotion Although shoppers are more aware of consumer promotion, trade promotions actually account for the largest share of promotional spending. **Trade promotions** are aimed at inducing distributors or retailers to sell a company's products by offering them a discount on the product's price, or a **trade allowance**. The distributor or retailer can pocket the savings and increase company profits or can pass the savings on to the consumer to generate additional sales. Besides discounts, other popular trade-allowance forms are display premiums, dealer contests or sweepstakes, and travel bonus programs. All are designed to motivate distributors or retailers to push particular merchandise.

Public Relations

Public relations encompasses all the nonsales communications that businesses have with their many stakeholders—communities, investors, industry analysts, government agencies and officials, and the news media. Companies rely on public relations to build a favorable corporate image and foster positive relations with these groups.

In fact, successful companies recognize that a good reputation is one of a business's most important assets. A recent study shows that companies with a good public image have a big edge over less-respected companies. Customers are more than twice as likely to buy new products from companies they admire, which is why smart companies work hard to build and protect their reputations. Smart executives not only work to build a positive public image but also prepare a *crisis communication plan* to make sure they're ready to communicate in the event of accidents, financial stumbles, product tampering, or any disaster.

Two standard public relations tools are the news release and the news conference. A **news release** is a short memo sent to the media covering topics that are of potential news interest; a *video news release* is a brief videoclip sent to television stations. Companies use news releases in the hopes of getting favorable news coverage about themselves and their products. When a business has significant news to announce, it will often arrange a **news conference**. Both tools are used when the company's news is of widespread interest, when products need to be demonstrated, or when company officials want to be available to answer questions from the media.

Integrating Your Marketing Communications

With five major promotional methods available—personal selling, advertising, direct marketing, sales promotion, and public relations—how do you decide on the right mix for your product? There are no easy answers, because you must take many factors into account. In fact, when you consider all the ways that audiences can receive marketing messages today, the potential for confusion is not all that surprising. Besides the traditional media—radio, television, billboards, print ads, and direct-mail promotions—marketers are using websites, e-mail, kiosks in malls and airports, sponsorships, and a number of other vehicles to deliver messages to targeted audiences. Coordinating promotional and communication efforts is becoming vital if a company is to send a consistent message and boost that message's effectiveness.

Integrated marketing communications (IMC) is a strategy of coordinating and integrating all one's communications and promotional efforts to provide customers with clarity, consistency, and maximum communications impact. "It's everything from running ads to developing new media, to creating custom media, licensing, promotion, sweepstakes—every aspect of communicating to consumers," says one media expert.[33] The basics of IMC are quite simple: communicating with one voice and one message to the marketplace, as Exhibit 12.9 suggests.

The need for communicating with one voice is even greater today. Customers are exposed to a greater variety of marketing communications and don't necessarily distinguish among message sources the way marketers do. In the customer's mind, messages from different sources blur into one single message about the company. Thus, conflicting messages from different sources can result in confused company images and brand positions.[34]

Properly implemented, IMC increases marketing and promotional effectiveness. For instance, Southwest Airlines coordinates all marketing to establish and maintain a consistent image of low-fare, high-frequency service in new and existing markets. When

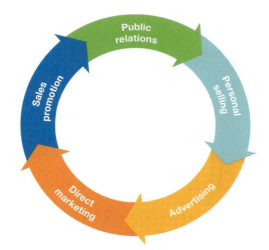

Exhibit 12.9

Integrated Marketing Communications

Coordinating the five elements of promotion delivers a consistent message to the marketplace.

the Texas-based airline beefed up service on the East Coast, it used public relations, special events, and advertising to whip up excitement by promoting a special Thanksgiving Day cross-country flight from Baltimore, Maryland, to Oakland, California, at the bargain rate of $99. The resulting media coverage effectively communicated the airline's low-price, flyer-friendly position. "We always start out with the public relations side in announcing inaugural services. Then we integrate government relations, community affairs, service announcements, special events, advertising, and promotion," says the head of Southwest's ad agency. The company's strategy is based on timing the promotional activities in advance of their entry into a given market, so that "by the time Southwest comes into the market, the airline already is part of the community."[35]

While integrating your communications and promotional efforts may seem logical and relatively simple, many organizations find IMC difficult to implement. They discover that over time their promotional mixes develop into collections of disconnected efforts. Organizational resistance is the primary cause for IMC failure. Many marketing departments are accustomed to autonomy and see IMC as a threat to their resources and decision-making power. Besides, moving to an IMC approach requires new ways of organizing, planning, and managing all marketing functions, and some marketing departments are not up to the task.[36]

Summary of Learning Objectives

1 **Explain what marketing intermediaries do, and list their seven primary functions.**

Marketing intermediaries, or middlemen, bring producers' products to market and help ensure that the goods and services are available in the right time, place, and amount. More specifically, intermediaries match buyers and sellers; provide market information; provide promotional and sales support; sort, standardize, and divide merchandise; transport and store the product; assume risks; and provide financing.

2 **Explain how wholesalers and retailers function as intermediaries.**

Wholesalers buy from producers and sell to retailers, to other wholesalers, and to organizational customers such as businesses, government agencies, and institutions. Retailers

buy from producers or wholesalers and sell the products to the final consumers.

3 **Discuss the key factors that influence channel design and selection.**

Channel design and selection are influenced by the type of product and industry practices. They are also influenced by a firm's desired market coverage (intense, selective, or exclusive), financial ability, desire for control, and potential for channel conflict.

4 **Differentiate between intensive, selective, and exclusive distribution strategies.**

With an intensive distribution strategy, a company attempts to saturate the market with its products by offering them in every available outlet. Companies that use a more selective approach to distribution choose a limited number of retailers that can adequately support the product. Firms that use exclusive distribution grant a single wholesaler or retailer the exclusive right to sell the product within a given geographic area.

5 Discuss the Internet's effect on the distribution function.

Companies are using the Internet to enhance their existing channel structures, expand their market reach, and add efficiencies to their channel structures. Some are eliminating layers of intermediaries from a marketing channel and transferring the eliminated intermediary functions to the Internet. In many cases, these changes—especially the bypassing of a channel—are causing channel conflict.

6 Identify the five basic categories of promotion.

The five basic categories of promotion are (1) personal selling, which involves contacting customers by phone, interactive media, or in person to make a sale; (2) advertising, which is a paid sponsored message transmitted by mass communication media; (3) direct marketing, which is the distribution of promotional material to customers via direct mail, e-mail, telemarketing, or the Internet to generate an order or other customer response; (4) sales promotion, which includes a number of tools designed to stimulate customer interest in a product and encourage a purchase; and

(5) public relations, which includes nonsales communications between businesses and their stakeholders to foster positive relationships.

7 Distinguish between the two main types of sales promotion, and give examples of each.

The two main types of sales promotion are consumer promotion and trade promotion. Consumer promotions are intended to motivate the final consumer to try new products or to experiment with the company's brands. Examples include coupons, cross-promotion, specialty advertising, premiums, point-of-purchase displays, and special events. Trade promotions are designed to induce wholesalers and retailers to stimulate sales of a producer's products. Examples include trade allowances, display premiums, dealer contests, and travel bonus programs.

8 Discuss the use of integrated marketing communications.

When companies use a greater variety of marketing communications, the likelihood of sending conflicting marketing messages to consumers increases. Integrated marketing communications (IMC) is a process of coordinating all of a company's communications and promotional efforts so that they present only one consistent message to the marketplace. Properly implemented, IMC increases marketing and promotional effectiveness.

Behind the Scenes

REI's Perfect Blend of Retail and E-Tail Channels

After weighing the advantages and disadvantages of establishing an online presence, REI banked on its six decades of experience, its powerful name, and its loyal customer base and ventured onto the web. In true trailblazer style, the company pressed ahead with its web store in 1996, when few traditional retailers were even considering online sales. "We knew it was going to cannibalize our catalog and retail sales," CEO Dennis Madsen predicted at the time, "but our philosophy was we better cannibalize ourselves or somebody will do it to us." Fortunately, his prediction turned out to be wrong.

Unlike many retailers at the time, who either shied away from the web or chose to operate their offline and online stores as independent channels, REI worked hard to develop a winning multichannel approach—one that successfully blended its online store with its offline business. Madsen and his team knew that by seamlessly operating the physical and online stores as one, the company could provide better customer service: Customers could return items purchased online or

through the catalog at any REI store and receive an instant credit or refund. Clerks could look up product information at store cash registers that were linked to the company's website and even sell items that were out of stock at one store but available at another. And members could use the website to check their patronage refunds and obtain members-only updates.

The company continued to mail millions of catalogs each year but encouraged shoppers to order via the web. It even placed Internet kiosks in stores. Poised among the backpacks, the kayaks, and freeze-dried meals, the kiosks let shoppers place online orders, get tips and techniques from outdoor experts, or download such customized items as topographic hiking maps, checklists for snow camping, and more. The kiosks not only enabled REI to offer broader product information but were ideal for smaller stores where carrying a complete assortment of goods was not possible.

Named by *Fortune* magazine as one of the top corporate websites, REI.com offered some 78,000 products—more than any physical REI store—and soon spanned 45,000 webpages. REI.com's e-tail shoppers placed nearly one-third of online orders after regular retail hours. "Our value proposition for REI.com was to deliver any product, at any time, to any place, and to answer any questions," says one REI executive. With the success of its online store, the company launched a second site to attract bargain hunters. The new website, www.REI-outlet.com, carried limited quantities of manufacturers' overstocks, seconds, and product closeouts at rock-bottom prices. It featured items that were not available at REI's physical stores, in its catalog, or on the main website, and it was linked to the company's main website. This strategy allowed REI to tailor messages to each consumer segment.

So what about REI's worry that the online stores would cannibalize their physical stores, that clicks would damage the bricks? According to Joan Broughton, REI's vice president in charge of multichannel programs, "Far from the concern of the web cannibalizing stores, we are using the Internet to measurably increase store sales while also lifting Internet sales." For instance, with nearly a quarter of the orders placed online, customers opt to have the merchandise delivered to their local REI store. And when they visit the stores to pick up their orders, more than a third of these cus-

tomers buy additional merchandise in person. Broughton also says that the coordinated channel effort also helps build a sense of community between the company and its customers. "Some of the e-commerce world does not seem to consider the physical location of its customers. It's almost as if they think of their customers as floating out there in cyberspace." As REI continues to grow across the country, those customers have a home no matter where they are.[37]

Critical Thinking Questions

1. Why would REI encourage online shoppers to have their orders delivered to store locations, since that isn't as convenient as home delivery?
2. Why would REI put website kiosks inside its retail stores?
3. How do REI's websites provide time utility?

LEARN MORE ONLINE

Go to Chapter 12 of this text's website at www.prenhall.com/bovee, and click on the REI hotlink. Review this website so you can answer these questions: How does REI promote its physical stores? What are REI's return policies for online customers? How do REI's online clinics, checklist, quick tips, and community forums help promote the store? ■

Key Terms

advertising (320)
consumer promotion (325)
cooperative advertising (323)
coupons (325)
cross-promotion (325)
direct mail (321)
direct marketing (321)
distribution centers (314)
distribution mix (311)
distribution strategy (308)
exclusive distribution (312)
institutional advertising (322)
integrated marketing communications (IMC) (326)
intensive distribution (312)
local advertising (322)

logistics (314)
marketing intermediaries (308)
materials handling (315)
media (323)
media mix (323)
national advertising (322)
news conference (326)
news release (326)
permission marketing (321)
personal selling (320)
persuasive advertising (316)
physical distribution (313)
point-of-purchase (POP) display (325)
premiums (325)
product advertising (322)

promotional mix (319)
promotional strategy (316)
public relations (326)
pull strategy (317)
push strategy 317)
reminder advertising (316)
retailers (309)
sales promotion (324)
selective distribution (312)
specialty advertising (326)
telemarketing (322)
trade allowance (326)
trade promotions (326)
warehouse (314)
wholesalers (309)

Test Your Knowledge

Questions for Review

1. What is a distribution channel?
2. What forms of utility do intermediaries create?
3. What are the two main types of intermediaries and how do they differ?
4. What are the three basic goals of promotion?
5. What are some common types of consumer promotion?

Questions for Analysis

6. How does the presence of intermediaries in the distribution channel affect the price of products?
7. What trade-offs must you consider when adopting a physical distribution system?
8. If a manufacturer starts to sell its goods on its company website, why might this arouse channel conflict?

9. Why is public relations an important element of a firm's promotional mix?

10. **Ethical Considerations.** Direct-mail marketers often publish different prices in different catalogs targeted at different market segments. When you call to order, the sales representative first asks for your customer or catalog number or ZIP code so that the rep knows which price to charge you.[38] Is this practice ethical?

Questions for Application

11. Local Better Business Bureaus monitor thousands of small-business ads each year. If the agency determines an advertiser is using false or misleading ads and refuses to change the ads, the case is referred to the FTC. Scan your local papers and highlight or clip ads that could

possibly mislead the public. What do you find misleading about the ad? How would you improve the ad?

12. Find three newspaper or magazine ads that you think are particularly effective and three more that you think are ineffective. What do you like about the effective ads? How might you improve the ineffective ads?

13. **Integrated.** Chapter 8 discussed the fact that supply-chain management integrates all the activities involved in the production of goods and services from suppliers to customers. What are the benefits of involving distributors in the design, manufacturing, or sale of a company's product or service?

14. **Integrated.** Which of the four basic functions of management discussed in Chapter 6 would be involved in decisions that establish or change a company's channels of distribution? Explain your answer.

Practice Your Knowledge

Sharpening Your Communication Skills

Select a product you're familiar with, and examine the strategies used to advertise and promote that product. Identify the media (website, print, television, radio, billboards, and so on) used to advertise the product. Consider the following:

- Where do the ads appear?
- Who is the target audience? Does the company attempt to appeal to a wide variety of people with differing ads?
- What creative theme or appeal is being used?
- Is the company taking advantage of any Internet technologies for promotion?

    Prepare a brief summary of your findings as directed by your instructor. Compare your findings with those of other

students, and note any differences or similarities in the promotion of your selected products.

Building Your Team Skills

In small groups discuss three or four recent ads or consumer promotions that you think were particularly effective. Using the knowledge you've gained from this chapter, try to come to consensus on what attributes contributed to the success of each ad or promotion. For instance, was it persuasive? Informative? Competitive? Creative? Did it stimulate you to buy the product? Why? Compare your results with those of other teams. Did you mention the same ads? Did you list the same attributes?

Expand Your Knowledge

Discovering Career Opportunities

Retailing is a dynamic, fast-paced field with many career opportunities in both store and nonstore settings. In addition to hiring full-time employees when needed, retailers of all types often hire extra employees on a temporary basis for peak selling periods, such as the year-end holidays. You can find out about seasonal and year-round job openings by checking newspaper classified ads, looking for signs in store windows, and browsing the websites of online retailers.

1. Select a major retailer, such as a chain store in your area or a retailer on the Internet. Is this a specialty store, discount store, department store, or another type of retailer?

2. Visit the website of the retailer you selected. Does the site discuss the company's hiring procedures? If so, what

are they? What qualifications are required for a position with the company?

3. Research your chosen retailer using library sources or online resources. Is this retailer expanding? Is it profitable? Has it recently acquired or been acquired by another firm? What are the implications of this acquisition for job opportunities?

Developing Your Research Skills

Find an article in a business journal or newspaper (online or print editions) discussing changes a company is making to its distribution strategy or channels. For example, is a manufacturer selling products direct to consumers? Is a physical retailer offering goods via a company website? Is a company eliminating the middleman? Has a nonstore retailer decided to open a physical store? Is a category killer opening smaller stores? Has a major retail tenant closed its stores in a mall?

1. What changes in the company's distribution structure or strategy have taken place? What additional changes, if any, are planned?

2. What were the reasons for the changes? What role, if any, did electronic commerce play in the changes?

3. If you were a stockholder in this company, would you view these changes as positive or negative? What, if anything, might you do differently?

SEE IT ON THE WEB

For live links to the websites that follow, go to this text's website at www.prenhall.com/bovee. When you log on, select Chapter 12, then select "Featured Websites," click on the URL of the website you wish to visit, review the website, and answer the following questions:

1. What is the purpose of this website?

2. What kinds of information does this website contain? Please be specific.

3. How is the information provided at this website useful for businesspeople? Consumers?

4. How did you expand your knowledge of distribution and promotion by reviewing the material at this website? What new things did you learn about these topics?

Explore the World of Wholesaling

Thinking about a career as a wholesale sales representative? The *Occupational Outlook Handbook* is a terrific source for learning about careers in business. Read the online material discussing the functions wholesale sales reps perform, the skills and experience manufacturers look for in candidates, and how to acquire any necessary training. Find out what a typical day on the job involves. How will you be compensated? Will travel be required? Will you be required to work long hours? What types of reports will you be expected to submit? Log on and learn now. A career in wholesale sales may be just the thing for you. http://stats.bls.gov/oco/ocos119.htm

Learn the Consumer Marketing Laws

Thinking about advertising or marketing your product? There are some laws you'll need to obey. Visit the Federal Trade Commission (FTC) website to learn how this agency protects consumers against unfair and deceptive marketing practices. Do you know what the FTC's policies are on deceptive pricing, use of the word *free*, or use of endorsements and testimonials? Find out what it means to substantiate product claims such as "tests prove," or "studies show." Learn what the rules are for unsolicited telephone calls and telephone slamming before you telemarket your product. Tune in to the FTC now and avoid making some serious mistakes later. www.ftc.gov

See How the Pros Put Marketing to Work

MarketingSherpa offers a compelling mix of articles, advice, and on-the-job interviews with marketing experts. The site's valuable content archives require nominal fees, but you can view the material for no charge for 10 days after it's first published, so visit frequently to get free insights into real-world marketing challenges. Plus, sign up for free e-newsletters in B2B and B2C marketing, e-mail marketing, marketing careers, and media relations. Check out Career Climber to see what's on the mind of top marketing people and to find job listings, salary benching, and career advice. www.marketingsherpa.com

Companion Website

Learning Interactively

Go to the Companion Website at www.prenhall.com/bovee. For Chapter 12, take advantage of the interactive "Study Guide" to test your knowledge of the chapter. Get instant feedback on whether you need additional studying.

Also, visit this site's "Study Hall," where you'll find an abundance of valuable resources that will help you succeed in this course.

Video **Case**

Revving Up Promotion: BMW Motorcycles

LEARNING OBJECTIVES

The purpose of this video is to help you:

1. Describe the purpose of product promotion.
2. Understand how and why a company must coordinate all the elements in its promotional mix.
3. Discuss how the message and the media work together in an effective advertising campaign.

SYNOPSIS

Although U.S. car buyers are extremely familiar with the BMW brand, the brand has a lower awareness among motorcycle buyers. This is a major challenge for BMW Motorcycles, which has been producing high-end motorcycles for more than 80 years. The company's promotional goal is to attract serious riders who are looking for an exceptional riding experience. To do so, its marketers carefully coordinate every promotional detail to convey a unified brand message positioning the BMW motorcycle as "the ultimate riding machine," as its advertising slogan states. Using print and television advertising, personal selling in dealerships, sales promotion, and a virtual showroom on the web, BMW is driving its brand message home to motorcycle enthusiasts across the United States.

Discussion Questions

1. *For analysis:* What are the advantages of using personal advertising copy and encouraging customers to become missionaries for BMW motorcycles?
2. *For analysis:* Why would BMW use its website as a virtual showroom rather than also selling online directly to consumers?
3. *For application:* What are some ways that BMW might use public relations to build brand awareness?
4. *For application:* How might BMW use direct mail to bring potential buyers into its motorcycle dealerships?
5. *For debate:* Should BMW develop and promote a new brand to differentiate its motorcycles from competing motorcycle brands as well as from BMW cars? Support your chosen position.

ONLINE EXPLORATION

Visit the BMW Motorcycle site, www.bmwmotorcycles.com, and notice the links on the homepage. Which elements of the promotional mix are in evidence on this site? How does this site support the company's "ultimate riding machine" brand message? How does the site make it easy for customers to obtain more information and ask questions about BMW motorcycles and dealer services? Do you find the site easy to navigate?

E-Business in Action

CLICKS AND BRICKS: BRIDGING THE PHYSICAL AND VIRTUAL WORLDS

When established retailers started to ponder a move to the web a few years ago, many experts advised them to keep their fledgling e-businesses separate. The thinking was that the creation of separate e-businesses would allow the web entity to speed up decision making, be more flexible, be more entrepreneurial, act independently, and thus compete more effectively with pure-play e-businesses (those that exist only on the Internet, such as Amazon.com). While some retailers embraced this approach, others debated whether to sell online at all. They worried about spreading their human and financial resources too thin. They worried about competing with their existing distributors, their competitors, and themselves (because their e-sales could cannibalize their physical-store sales).

Mixing Clicks with Bricks

In hindsight, the experts were wrong. Although financially the separate e-businesses promised considerable shareholder potential, running separate online and offline operations did not work.

Consider Barnes & Noble. To compete with Amazon.com, the company established a completely separate division—Barnes & Noble.com (www.bn.com)—and later spun the division off as a stand-alone company. But unlike pure-plays, barnesandnoble.com lacked a sense of urgency about the web and let Amazon capture the lion's share of initial e-business and publicity. Moreover, customers did not care that the two were separate entities. Web customers became confused and angry when they tried to return books purchased online to the physical Barnes & Noble bookstores, only to be turned away. Furthermore, the strategy forced the physical stores to compete with their online sibling and prevented them from sharing management teams, combining marketing programs, or achieving economies of scale.

It didn't take long for Barnes & Noble to realize its decision to separate its online and physical stores was flawed. So in 2000, Barnes & Noble integrated the two operations—making it possible for web customers to return purchases at a company's physical stores. In 2004, it took the final step and purchased Barnes & Noble.com, folding it back into the main company. Other companies have since followed Barnes & Noble's lead by reeling in their separate e-businesses.

Creating the Perfect Blend

After much debate, experts now agree that integrating a retailer's physical store operation with its web operation is the most effective approach to e-commerce. Mixing clicks with bricks (also known as *clicks-and-bricks* or *clicks-and-mortar*) makes a store's physical and web operations transparent to the customer. A Sears customer, for instance, can gather product information from Sears.com before heading to the outlet at the local mall. Salespeople can then add value by doing things the website can't—such as answering specific product questions and demonstrating products. Similarly, Circuit City's and Office Depot's customers can purchase what they want online and then pick up the products at the stores to avoid delivery fees. "It's a tremendous convenience for the customer," says one e-tailing expert. "They've done their research, compared prices, and paid. They can walk up to the pickup counter with a receipt, and they don't have to stand in line with everyone else."

A clicks-and-bricks strategy is also a boon for retailers. Multichannel customers who shop both online and in stores tend to be more loyal and spend more. Eddie Bauer (which sells products through catalogs, retail stores, and its website) reports that shoppers who use all three methods to purchase from the company spend five times more than those who shop only by catalog. Moreover, clicks-and-bricks retailers can use their websites to advertise, test merchandise, suggest gifts, increase product awareness, cross-promote online and offline products, and drive traffic to their physical stores or vice versa. Some are even using their websites to provide specialty items not available in stores. "We don't have the same real estate issues," says one spokesperson for the Gap, which offers plus sizes for men and women exclusively online. "It's an easy, lower-cost way to get merchandise out there quickly."

But, there are limitations to mixing clicks with bricks. Not all retailers, especially those that don't have a catalog business, are able to offer their entire inventory online, because of the expense of photographing and describing every item. This confuses customers. And delivery fees continue to be a barrier to online purchases, which is why so many companies offer free delivery when you spend, say, $100. Still, if you don't mix clicks with bricks, "you literally won't exist as a retailer," declares one e-commerce expert. The web is where most consumers do their initial phases of shopping—whether it's as basic as price comparison or searching for store locations.[39]

Questions for Critical Thinking

1. Why did retailers initially separate their physical and web stores?

2. Why did the strategy to separate online and offline stores fail?

3. What are the benefits of a clicks-and-bricks strategy?

BUSINESS PlanPro Exercises

Developing Marketing Strategies to Satisfy Customers

Review Appendix D, "Your Business Plan" (on pages 416–417), to learn how to use Business PlanPro Software so you can complete these exercises.

THINK LIKE A PRO

Objective: By completing these exercises you will become acquainted with the sections of a business plan that address a firm's product, pricing, promotion, and distribution strategies. You will use the sample business plan for Boulder Stop (listed as Sports Equipment-Cafe in the Sample Plan Browser) in this exercise.

1. Define the target market for Boulder Stop. How will the company differentiate its products and services from those of its competitors'?

2. Describe the company's pricing, promotion, sales, and distribution strategies. Which distribution channels will the company use to deliver its products?

3. Rank the company's three market segmentation categories according to their importance.

4. According to the Keys to Success section, what must Boulder Stop do to be successful?

CREATE YOUR OWN BUSINESS PLAN

Consider your own target market and customers as you continue working on the business plan you are creating. How will you segment your target market? Which customers are likely to buy your product or service? Describe your product, pricing, promotion, and distribution strategies. Now make some preliminary sales forecasts. Under which section headings will you present this information?

Part 6

Managing Financial Information and Resources

Chapter 13

Analyzing and Using Financial Information

LEARNING OBJECTIVES

After studying this chapter, you will be able to

1 Discuss how managers and outsiders use financial information

2 Describe what accountants do

3 Summarize the impact of the Sarbanes-Oxley Act

4 State the basic accounting equation and explain the purpose of double-entry bookkeeping and the matching principle

5 Differentiate between cash basis and accrual basis accounting

6 Explain the purpose of the balance sheet and identify its three main sections

7 Explain the purpose of the income statement and the statement of cash flows

8 Explain the purpose of ratio analysis and list the four main categories of financial ratios

9 Identify the responsibilities of a financial manager

Behind the Scenes

When Giants Fall: The Collapse of MCI

www.mci.com
Telecommunications giant MCI is a company of big numbers: 20 million customers, a 98,000-mile fiber optic network that connects 102,000 buildings in 2,800 cities across 140 countries, business offices in 65 countries on every continent except Antarctica—and the biggest bankruptcy in U.S. history. The company had assets of more than $100 billion when it asked the courts in 2002 for debt relief and temporary protection from creditors

Massive accounting fraud at WorldCom, as MCI was known at the time, led to the largest bankruptcy in U.S. history.

Until their scheme fell apart when a WorldCom employee blew the whistle on these executives, they had fooled the stock market, the company's board of directors, and most of WorldCom's workforce. The accounting frauds, which eventually totaled an estimated $11 billion, quickly caused the company's stock to tank as investors dumped their shares for any price they could get. Ebbers resigned under pressure in April 2002, trading in WorldCom

because it was no longer able to pay its bills. (The company was known as WorldCom at the time; it has since changed its name to MCI.)

Founder Bernie Ebbers built WorldCom through numerous acquisitions of other telecom companies. Because WorldCom used its own stock to help pay for these acquisitions, it counted on continuous increases in the price of that stock; and to keep the stock price moving upward, it had to keep demonstrating profitable growth to keep investors interested. However, with ferocious competition and the enormous cost of providing telecommunication services, WorldCom eventually found it couldn't meet the investor expectations it worked so hard to create.

When the real financial numbers wouldn't cooperate, a handful of high-ranking executives began to make up numbers that would. By understating expenses and overstating revenue, they created the illusion that WorldCom was doing much better than it really was.

stock was halted two months later, and WorldCom filed for bankruptcy a month after that.

Now what? What happens when a giant falls flat on its face? The company still served millions of customers and employed tens of thousands of people, but it was broke. As you might expect, quite a few people had strong interests in the situation, including criminal prosecutors who filed charges against the executives involved, creditors who wanted to know if and when they would get paid, and investors who wanted to know if they'd get anything for their WorldCom stock.

Sound like a business challenge you'd like to take on? If you were Michael Capellas, who stepped in as CEO after Ebbers was forced out, how would you get this giant back on its feet? What would you do to restore public confidence and protect the remaining jobs? Could you save WorldCom?[1] ■

UNDERSTANDING ACCOUNTING

accounting
Measuring, interpreting, and communicating financial information to support internal and external decision making

As Michael Capellas knows, it's difficult to manage a business today without accurate and up-to-date financial information. **Accounting** is the system a business uses to identify, measure, and communicate financial information to others, inside and outside the organization. Financial information is important to businesses such as MCI for two reasons: First, it helps managers and owners plan and control a company's operation and make informed business decisions. Second, it helps outsiders evaluate a business.

Suppliers, banks, and other lenders want to know whether a business is creditworthy; investors and shareholders are concerned with a company's profit potential; government agencies are interested in a business's tax accounting.

Because outsiders and insiders use accounting information for different purposes, accounting has two distinct facets. **Financial accounting** is concerned with preparing financial statements and other information for outsiders such as *stockholders* and *creditors* (people or organizations that have lent a company money or have extended them credit); **management accounting** is concerned with preparing cost analyses, profitability reports, budgets, and other information for insiders such as management and other company decision makers. To be useful, all accounting information must be accurate, objective, consistent over time, and comparable to information supplied by other companies.

What Accountants Do

Some people confuse the work accountants do with **bookkeeping**, which is the clerical function of recording the economic activities of a business. Although some accountants do perform bookkeeping functions, their work generally goes well beyond the scope of this activity. Accountants design accounting systems, prepare financial statements, analyze and interpret financial information, prepare financial forecasts and budgets, and prepare tax returns. Some accountants specialize in certain areas of accounting, such as **cost accounting** (computing and analyzing production costs), **tax accounting** (preparing tax returns and interpreting tax law), or **financial analysis** (evaluating a company's performance and the financial implications of strategic decisions such as product pricing, employee benefits, and business acquisitions).

In addition to traditional accounting work, accountants may also help clients improve business processes, plan for the future, evaluate product performance, analyze profitability by customer and product groups, design and install new computer systems, assist companies with decision making, and provide a variety of other management consulting services. Performing these functions requires a strong business background and a variety of business skills beyond accounting (see Exhibit 13.1).

Most accountants (about 65 percent) are **private accountants** (sometimes called *corporate accountants*). Private accountants work for a business, a government agency (such as the Internal Revenue Service, a school, or a local police department), or a nonprofit corporation (such as a church, charity, or hospital).[2] Private accountants generally work together as a team under the supervision of the organization's **controller**, who reports to

---

financial accounting
Area of accounting concerned with preparing financial information for users outside the organization

management accounting
Area of accounting concerned with preparing data for use by managers within the organization

bookkeeping
Recordkeeping, clerical aspect of accounting

cost accounting
Area of accounting focusing on the calculation of manufacturing and storage costs of products for use or sale in a business

tax accounting
Area of accounting focusing on tax preparation and tax planning

financial analysis
Process of evaluating a company's performance and analyzing the costs and benefits of a strategic action

private accountants
In-house accountants employed by organizations and businesses other than a public accounting firm; also called *corporate accountants*

controller
Highest-ranking accountant in a company, responsible for overseeing all accounting functions

---

Exhibit 13.1

Ten Most Important Skills for Accountants

Besides having a thorough knowledge of accounting, today's accountants need the right mix of personal and business skills to increase their chances for a successful career.

SKILLS
- Analytical
- Problem solving
- Interpersonal
- Listening
- Communication
- Leadership
- Decision making
- Time management
- Teamwork
- Computer

Accountants perform a variety of services for their clients beyond tax preparation and auditing. Many serve on strategic planning teams and help companies plan for the future.

certified public accountants (CPAs)
Professionally licensed accountants who meet certain requirements for education and experience and who pass a comprehensive examination

certified management accountants (CMAs)
Accountants who have fulfilled the requirements for certification as specialists in management accounting

public accountants
Professionals who provide accounting services to other businesses and individuals for a fee

audit
Formal evaluation of the fairness and reliability of a client's financial statements

the vice president of finance or the chief financial officer (CFO). Exhibit 13.2 shows the typical finance department of a large company. In smaller organizations, the controller may be in charge of the company's entire finance operation and report directly to the president.

Although certification is not required of private accountants, many are licensed **certified public accountants (CPAs)**, which means they have passed a rigorous state-certified licensing exam. To become eligible to sit for the exam, candidates must complete the equivalent of 120 to 150 semester hours of college-level course work and other requirements specified by the licensing state.[3] A growing number of private accountants are becoming **certified management accountants (CMAs)**; to do so they must pass a two-day exam (given by the Institute of Management Accountants) that is comparable in difficulty to the CPA exam.[4]

In contrast to private accountants, **public accountants** are independent of the businesses, organizations, and individuals they serve. Most public accountants are employed by public accounting firms that provide a variety of accounting and consulting services to their clients. Members of the firm generally are CPAs and must obtain CPA and state licensing certifications before they are eligible to conduct an **audit**—a formal evaluation of a company's accounting records and processes to ensure the integrity and reliability of a company's financial statements.

The Rules of Accounting

In order to make informed decisions, investors, bankers, suppliers, and other parties need some means to verify the quality of the financial information that companies release to the public. They also need some way to compare information from one company to the next. To accommodate these needs, financial accountants are expected to follow a number of rules, some of which are voluntary and some of which are required by law. The two most significant sets of rules are known as *GAAP*, which has evolved over decades, and *Sarbanes-Oxley*, new legislation that was passed in the wake of Enron and other recent accounting scandals.

GAAP

Companies whose stock is publicly traded in the United States are required to file audited financial statements with the Securities and Exchange Commission (SEC). During an audit, CPAs who work for an independent accounting firm, also known as

Exhibit 13.2

Typical Finance Department

Here is a typical finance department of a large company. In smaller companies, the controller may be the highest-ranking accountant and report directly to the president. The vice president in charge of finance is often called the chief financial officer (CFO).

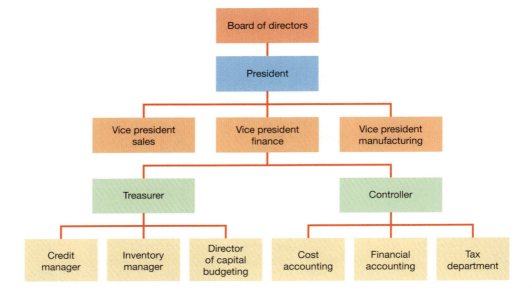

external auditors, review a client's financial records to determine whether the statements that summarize these records have been prepared in accordance with **generally accepted accounting principles (GAAP)**, basic accounting standards and procedures that have been agreed on by regulators, auditors, and companies over decades. GAAP aims to give a fair and true picture of a company's financial position.

Once the auditors have completed an audit, they attach a report summarizing their findings to the client's published financial statements. Sometimes these reports disclose information that might materially affect the client's financial position, such as the bankruptcy of a major supplier, a large obsolete inventory, costly environmental problems, or questionable accounting practices. Most companies, however, receive a clean audit report, which means that to the best of the auditors' knowledge the company's financial statements are accurate.

To assist with the auditing process, many large organizations use **internal auditors**—employees who investigate and evaluate the organization's internal operations and data to determine whether they are accurate and whether they comply with GAAP, federal laws, and industry regulations. Although this self-checking process is vital to an organization's financial health, an internal audit is not a substitute for having an independent auditor look things over and render an unbiased opinion.

All U.S. public companies such as MCI must publish their financial statements in accordance with GAAP. This requirement makes it possible for external users to compare the financial results of one company with those of another and to gain a general idea of a firm's relative effectiveness and its standing within a particular industry. From time to time, companies experience special situations, such as incurring a significant onetime loss, which managers believe may distort the overall financial picture. In the recent past, it was common for companies in these situations to publish *pro forma* or *non-GAAP* numbers that removed the effect of these deviations from the financial results. Some companies claimed their investors wanted to see these numbers, but critics say that too often the technique was used to hide losses that would depress stock prices. The SEC now requires companies that publish pro forma results to also publish GAAP-equivalent results so that investors can compare the difference.[5]

In the United States, the Financial Accounting Standards Board (FASB) is responsible for overseeing GAAP. Other countries have similar governing boards with accounting rules that don't always match GAAP conventions, which means that foreign companies such as Nissan or Toyota may report accounting data using rules that are different from those used by U.S. companies such as Ford or General Motors.

Foreign companies that list their securities on a U.S. stock exchange must, however, convert financial statements prepared under foreign accounting rules to GAAP. This requirement ensures that all companies listed on U.S. stock exchanges are on even ground. But it can also create problems for foreign companies. For instance, when the German firm Daimler-Benz first listed its stock on the New York Stock Exchange, the company's $102 million profit changed to a $579 million loss for the same period because of a difference between German accounting rules and U.S. GAAP.[6]

The International Accounting Standards Board (IASB) has been working for years to develop a uniform set of global accounting rules known to help eliminate such differences but has not yet been able to iron out all the differences from country to country. The IASB's proposed guidelines would simplify accounting for multinational companies, give foreign companies easier access to U.S. stock markets, and help investors select stocks from companies around the world.[7]

Sarbanes-Oxley

GAAP sets forth the principles and guidelines for companies and accountants to follow when preparing financial reports or recording accounting transactions, but high-profile scandals involving Enron, WorldCom, and other big corporations in recent years prove that it is still possible to get around the rules and deceive investors. To repair investor confidence, Congress passed the Public Company Accounting Reform and Investor

---

external auditors
Independent accounting firms that provide auditing servicing for public companies

generally accepted accounting principles (GAAP)
Professionally approved U.S. standards and practices used by accountants in the preparation of financial statements

internal auditors
Employees who analyze and evaluate a company's operations and data to determine their accuracy

Business BUZZ

Sox or Sarbox: Accounting slang for the Sarbanes-Oxley Act

Technologies That Are Revolutionizing Business

Compliance management software

The Sarbanes-Oxley Act requires publicly traded companies to regularly verify their internal accounting controls. To assist in this recurring task, a number of software companies now offer *compliance management software*.

How it's revolutionizing business

Verifying accounting controls can be a considerable task for large or decentralized companies with multiple accounting systems. For instance, one recent study found that the average billion-dollar public company has 48 separate financial systems. Rather than creating their own software solutions to the problem or adapting existing accounting software, many companies now turn to ready-made compliance management software. The costs can be considerable (up to $100,000 or more just to purchase the software and possibly many times more than that to have it customized and installed); the companies buying these solutions say it's cheaper and faster than building their own, plus they can take advantage of the compliance knowledge programmed into the software. Whether they build or buy, a number of firms are also using the new reporting requirements as an opportunity to streamline and improve their business operations.

Where you can learn more

Several professional publications are keeping an eye on the compliance software market, including *Computerworld* (www.computerworld.com), *CIO* (www.cio.com), *InformationWeek* (www.informationweek.com), *eWeek* (www.eweek.com), and *CFO* and *CFO IT* (www.cfo.com). Search their respective websites for "compliance software" to get the latest news.

Protection Act, usually referred to as **Sarbanes-Oxley**. The legislation aims to stop abuses and errors in several important areas. The act[8]

- Outlaws most loans by corporations to their own directors and executives
- Creates the Public Company Accounting Oversight Board (PCAOB) to oversee external auditors
- Requires corporate lawyers to report evidence of financial wrongdoing
- Prohibits external auditors from providing some nonaudit services
- Requires that audit committees on the board of directors have at least one financial expert and that the majority of board members be independent (not employed by the company in an executive position)
- Prohibits investment bankers from influencing stock analysts
- Requires CEOs and CFOs to sign statements attesting to the accuracy of their financial statements
- Requires companies to document and test their internal financial controls and processes

Sarbanes-Oxley
Comprehensive legislation, passed in the wake of Enron and other scandals, designed to improve integrity and accountability of financial information

The last two items in particular have generated lots of interest and some controversy among businesses. In a few of the recent scandals, top executives claimed not to know what was going on in their own companies, although "the idea that a CEO doesn't know what's going on in his company is ridiculous," according to United Technologies CEO George David. In any event, signing their financial statements under oath should have the intended effect of ensuring close attention to the details. However, the requirement to document and test financial controls has generated perhaps the most widespread discussion. Estimates of the cost of compliance vary widely, from a few hundred thousand dollars to several million, depending on the size of the company and initial state of its financial systems. According to one study, U.S. companies will need to spend a total of $7 billion to get into compliance initially.[9]

Is Sarbanes-Oxley the right idea—or even necessary? As you might expect with anything this complex and far-reaching, opinions vary widely. Most investors will surely welcome the changes. In contrast, in a recent survey, 54 percent of top executives felt it was unnecessary, and only 10 percent thought it was "very necessary." As the SEC continues to finalize rules (including determining how strict to make reporting requirements) and businesses respond, the true costs and benefits of Sarbanes-Oxley should become more visible.[10]

FUNDAMENTAL ACCOUNTING CONCEPTS

As pressure mounts for companies to produce cleaner financial statements and to disclose material information promptly, the need increases for all businesspeople—not just accountants—to understand basic accounting concepts. In the next sections we discuss the fundamental accounting concepts, explore the key elements of financial statements,

Putting Accountability Back into Public Accounting

For a profession that is supposed to be all about trust and financial responsibility, public accounting seems to be lurching from one scandal to another: billions of dollars in accounting fraud that slipped past auditors, multi-million-dollar fines for selling shady tax shelters, accountants arrested for destroying documents, accusations of over-billing, an endless parade of lawsuits from investors and clients—and the biggest black eye of them all, the collapse of the once-mighty accounting firm Arthur Andersen. How did all this happen, and how can the profession restore public confidence?

No situation this complex will surrender to a simple explanation, but observers point out several issues that have contributed to many of the recent problems:

- **Deliberate deception by corporate clients.** Auditors maintain that in many cases it's impossible to detect deliberately misleading bookkeeping, and it's unfair to hold them accountable when they don't. An auditor "cannot provide 100 percent guarantee against fraud," says Chuck Landes, director of auditing for the American Institute of Certified Public Accountants (AICPA).

- **Changes in accounting practices.** Some claim that auditors aren't looking in the right places. In the past, auditors used a labor-intensive process of sifting through thousands of transactions to determine if bookkeeping entries were correct. Now they focus on analyzing the computerized bookkeeping programs and internal controls. While this approach prevents low-level employees from swiping petty cash, it can't always catch executives who shift millions or billions around using creative accounting schemes.

- **Conflict of interest.** Others blame the conflict of interest that exists when an accounting firm earns millions performing consulting work for an audit client. "If you are auditing your own creations, it is very difficult to criticize them," says one accounting expert. Critics say these cozy relationships and lucrative consulting contracts discouraged some auditors from examining corporate books closely enough or challenging CEOs when potential irregularities did surface.

- **Overly aggressive business practices.** In 1991, the AICPA changed its code of conduct to allow tax accountants to charge performance-based fees, meaning that firms could charge a percentage of the money they saved clients by lowering their taxes. The IRS and industry insiders say this spawned a rash of overly aggressive tax shelters throughout the 1990s. When the IRS finally got its arms around the problem, it started banning these shelters, fining accountants who sold them, and recovering back taxes from clients who used them. Some of these clients are suing their accountants, claiming they were misled.

Between IRS crackdowns, new SEC requirements, and the numerous provisions of the Sarbanes-Oxley Act, the profession is certainly getting attention—some of it welcome, some of it not. For instance, auditors say Sarbanes-Oxley finally gives them the authority to stand up to executives who might be playing tricks with the numbers. The ban on selling certain kinds of consulting to auditing clients should help with the conflict of interest as well. At the same time, though, regulators and the AICPA are locking horns over the guidelines to implement Sarbanes-Oxley and other regulatory changes. The accountants say they have the expertise needed to write effective auditing rules; the regulators say the AICPA is more interested in protecting its members from lawsuits than in conducting proper audits.

With billions of dollars and the financial health of millions of people on the line, this battle is likely to go on for years. And the past few years have given everyone a clear and important reminder: Auditing is a vital function upon which free enterprise and the health of the global economy depend.

Questions for Critical Thinking
1. Should accounting firms be allowed to perform management consulting functions for their audit clients? Why or why not?
2. Why is the auditing function of such vital importance to the global economy?

and explain how managers and investors analyze a company's financial statements to make decisions.

In their work with financial data, accountants are guided by three basic concepts: the *fundamental accounting equation*, *double-entry bookkeeping*, and the *matching principle*. Let's take a closer look at each of these concepts.

assets
Any things of value owned or leased by a business

liabilities
Claims against a firm's assets by creditors

owners' equity
Portion of a company's assets that belongs to the owners after obligations to all creditors have been met

accounting equation
Basic accounting equation that assets equal liabilities plus owners' equity

double-entry bookkeeping
Way of recording financial transactions that requires two entries for every transaction so that the accounting equation is always kept in balance

matching principle
Fundamental principle requiring that expenses incurred in producing revenue be deducted from the revenues they generate during an accounting period

accrual basis
Accounting method in which revenue is recorded when a sale is made and expense is recorded when it is incurred

The Accounting Equation

For thousands of years, businesses and governments have kept records of their **assets**— valuable items they own or lease, such as equipment, cash, land, buildings, inventory, and investments. Claims against those assets are **liabilities**, or what the business owes to its creditors—such as banks and suppliers. For example, when a company borrows money to purchase a building, the lender or creditor has a claim against the company's assets. What remains after liabilities have been deducted from assets is **owners' equity**:

$$\text{Assets} - \text{Liabilities} = \text{Owners' equity}$$

Using the principles of algebra, this equation can be restated in a variety of formats. The most common is the simple **accounting equation**, which serves as the framework for the entire accounting process:

$$\text{Assets} = \text{Liabilities} + \text{Owners' equity}$$

This equation suggests that either creditors or owners provide all the assets in a corporation. Think of it this way: If you were starting a new business, you could contribute cash to the company to buy the assets you needed to run your business or you could borrow money from a bank (the creditor) or you could do both. The company's liabilities are placed before owners' equity in the accounting equation because creditors get paid first. After liabilities have been paid, anything left over belongs to the owners or, in the case of a corporation, to the shareholders. As a business engages in economic activity, the dollar amounts and composition of its assets, liabilities, and owners' equity change. However, the equation must always be in balance; in other words, one side of the equation must always equal the other side.

Double-Entry Bookkeeping and the Matching Principle

To keep the accounting equation in balance, most companies use a **double-entry bookkeeping** system that records every transaction affecting assets, liabilities, or owners' equity. For example, if MCI purchased a $6,000 computer system on credit, assets would increase by $6,000 (the cost of the system) and liabilities would also increase by $6,000 (the amount the company owes the vendor), keeping the accounting equation in balance. But if MCI paid cash outright for the equipment (instead of arranging for credit), the company's total assets and total liabilities would not change, because the $6,000 increase in equipment would be offset by an equal $6,000 reduction in cash. In fact, the company would just be switching assets—cash for equipment.

The **matching principle** requires that expenses incurred in producing revenues be deducted from the revenue they generated during the same accounting period. This matching of expenses and revenue is necessary for the company's financial statements to present an accurate picture of the profitability of a business. Accountants match revenue to expenses by adopting the **accrual basis** of accounting, which states that revenue is recognized when you make a sale or provide a service, not when you get paid. Similarly, your expenses are recorded when you receive the benefit of a service or when you use an asset to produce revenue—not when you pay for it. Accrual accounting focuses on the economic substance of the event instead of on the movement of cash. It's a way of recognizing that revenue can be earned either before or after cash is received and that expenses can be incurred when you receive a benefit (such as a shipment of supplies) whether before or after you pay for it.

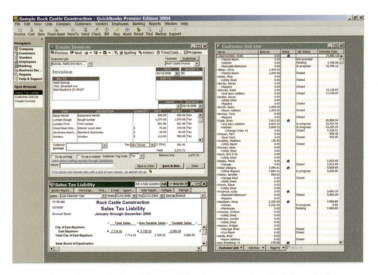

Accounting software designed for small businesses, such as QuickBooks from Intuit, simplifies bookkeeping and financial planning for small-business owners.

If a business runs on a **cash basis**, the company records revenue only when money from the sale is actually received. Your checkbook is an easy-to-understand cash-based accounting system: You record checks at the time of purchase and deposits at the time of receipt. Revenue thus equals cash received, and expenses equal cash paid. The trouble with cash-based accounting, however, is that it can be misleading. You can misrepresent expenses and income by the way you time payments. It's easy to inflate income, for example, by delaying the payment of bills. For that reason, public companies are required to keep their books on an accrual basis.

Depreciation, or the allocation of the cost of a tangible long-term asset over a period of time, is another way that companies match expenses with revenue. During the normal course of business, a company enters into many transactions that benefit more than one accounting period—such as the purchase of buildings, inventory, and equipment. When you buy a piece of real estate or equipment, instead of deducting the entire cost of the item at the time of purchase, you depreciate it, or spread its cost over the asset's useful life (because the asset will likely generate income for years to come). If the company were to expense long-term assets at the time of purchase, the financial performance of the company would be distorted in the year of purchase as well as in all future years when these assets generate revenue.

cash basis
Accounting method in which revenue is recorded when payment is received and expense is recorded when cash is paid

depreciation
Accounting procedure for systematically spreading the cost of a tangible asset over its estimated useful life

USING FINANCIAL STATEMENTS

A typical corporate accounting system handles thousands or even millions of individual transactions—debits and credits to be exact. During the accounting process, sales, purchases, and other transactions are recorded and classified into individual accounts. Once these individual transactions are recorded and then summarized, accountants must review the resulting transaction summaries and adjust or correct all errors or discrepancies before they can **close the books**, or transfer net revenue and expense items to *retained earnings*. Exhibit 13.3 presents the process for putting all of a company's financial data into standardized formats that can be used for decision making, analysis, and planning. To make sense of these individual transactions, accountants summarize them by preparing financial statements.

close the books
The act of transferring net revenue and expense account balances to retained earnings for the period

---

Exhibit 13.3   **The Accounting Process**

The accounting process involves numerous steps between recording the sales and other transactions to the internal and external reporting of summarized financial results.

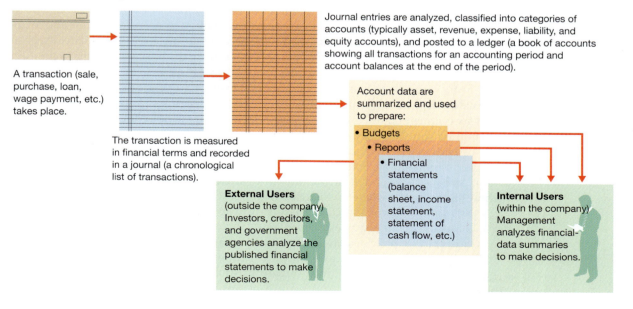

A transaction (sale, purchase, loan, wage payment, etc.) takes place.

The transaction is measured in financial terms and recorded in a journal (a chronological list of transactions).

Journal entries are analyzed, classified into categories of accounts (typically asset, revenue, expense, liability, and equity accounts), and posted to a ledger (a book of accounts showing all transactions for an accounting period and account balances at the end of the period).

Account data are summarized and used to prepare:
- Budgets
- Reports
- Financial statements (balance sheet, income statement, statement of cash flow, etc.)

External Users (outside the company) Investors, creditors, and government agencies analyze the published financial statements to make decisions.

Internal Users (within the company) Management analyzes financial-data summaries to make decisions.

Understanding Financial Statements

Financial statements consist of three separate yet interrelated reports: the *balance sheet*, the *income statement*, and the *statement of cash flows*. Together these statements provide information about an organization's financial strength and ability to meet current obligations, the effectiveness of its sales and collection efforts, and its effectiveness in managing its assets. Organizations and individuals use financial statements to spot opportunities and problems, to make business decisions, and to evaluate a company's past performance, present condition, and future prospects. Whether the company is a one-person consulting firm or a multinational with a hundred thousand employees, financial statements are a vital tool.

The following sections examine the financial statements of Computer Central, a company engaged in direct sales and distribution of brand-name personal computers (such as HP, Toshiba, and Apple) and related computer products (such as software, printer cartridges, and scanners). The company conducts its primary business from a combined telemarketing, corporate office, warehouse, and showroom facility in Denver, Colorado. There, Computer Central's 600-plus account executives service over 634,000 customers annually. In 2005 the company shipped over 2.3 million orders, amounting to more than $1.7 billion in sales—a 35 percent increase in sales from the prior year. The company's daily sales volume has grown considerably over the last decade—from $232,000 to $6.8 million. Because of this tremendous growth and the increasing demand for new computer products, the company recently purchased a 276,000-square-foot building. Keep these points in mind as you explore Computer Central's financial statements in the next sections.

Balance Sheet

balance sheet
Statement of a firm's financial position on a particular date; also known as a *statement of financial position*

The **balance sheet**, also known as the *statement of financial position*, is a snapshot of a company's financial position on a particular date, such as December 31, 2005. In effect, it freezes all business actions and provides a baseline from which a company can measure change. This statement is called a balance sheet because it includes all elements in the accounting equation and shows the balance between assets on one side of the equation and liabilities and owners' equity on the other side. In other words, as in the accounting equation, a change on one side of the balance sheet means changes elsewhere. Exhibit 13.4 is the balance sheet for Computer Central as of December 31, 2005.

In reality, however, no business can stand still while its financial condition is being examined. A business may make hundreds of transactions of various kinds every working day. Even during a holiday, office fixtures grow older and decrease in value and interest on savings accounts accumulates. Yet the accountant must set up a balance sheet so that managers and other interested parties can evaluate the business's financial position as if it were static, rather than ever changing.

calendar year
Twelve-month accounting period that begins on January 1 and ends on December 31

Every company prepares a balance sheet at least once a year, most often at the end of the **calendar year**, covering from January 1 to December 31. However, many business and government bodies use a **fiscal year**, which may be any 12 consecutive months. For example, a company may use a fiscal year of June 1 to May 31 because its peak selling season ends in May. Its fiscal year would then correspond to its full annual cycle of manufacturing and selling. Some companies prepare a balance sheet more often than once a year, perhaps at the end of each month or quarter. Thus, every balance sheet is dated to show the exact date when the financial snapshot was taken.

fiscal year
Any 12 consecutive months used as an accounting period

By reading a company's balance sheet you should be able to determine the size of the company, the major assets owned, any asset changes that occurred in recent periods, how the company's assets are financed, and any major changes that have occurred in the company's debt and equity in recent periods. Most companies classify assets, liabilities, and owners' equity into categories such as those shown in the Computer Central balance sheet.

Exhibit 13.4 **Balance Sheet for Computer Central**

The categories used on Computer Central's year-end balance sheet are typical.

Computer Central
Balance Sheet
As of December 31, 2005
(in thousands)

ASSETS

Current Assets
Cash	$ 4,230	
Marketable Securities	36,458	
Accounts Receivable	158,204	
Inventory	64,392	
Miscellaneous Prepaid and Deferred Items	6,504	
Total Current Assets		$269,788

Fixed Assets
Property and Equipment	53,188	
Less: Accumulated Depreciation	−16,132	
Total Fixed Assets		37,056

Other Assets		4,977
Total Assets		**$311,821**

Current Assets
Cash and other items that will or can be converted to cash within one year.

Fixed Assets
Long-term investments in buildings, equipment, furniture, and any other tangible property expected to be used in running the business for a period longer than one year.

LIABILITIES AND SHAREHOLDERS' EQUITY

Current Liabilities
Accounts Payable	$ 41,358	
Accrued Expenses	29,700	
Total Current Liabilities		$ 71,058

Long-Term Liabilities
Loans Payable	$ 15,000	
Total Long-Term Liabilities		15,000
Total Liabilities		86,058

Shareholders' Equity
Common Stock		
(21,571 shares @ $.01 par value)	$ 216	
Less: Treasury Stock (50,000 shares)	−2,089	
Paid-in Capital	81,352	
Retained Earnings	146,284	
Total Shareholders' Equity		225,763
Total Liabilities and Shareholders' Equity		**$311,821**

Current Liabilities
Amounts owed by the company that are to be repaid within one year.

Long-Term Liabilities
Debts that are due a year or more after the date of the balance sheet.

Shareholders' Equity
Money contributed to the company for ownership interests, as well as the accumulation of profits that have not been paid out as dividends (retained earnings).

Assets As discussed earlier in this chapter, an asset is something owned by a company that will be used to generate income. Assets can consist of cash, things that can be converted into cash (such as investments), and equipment needed to make products or to provide services. For example, Computer Central needs a warehouse and a sizable inventory to sell computer products to its customers. Most often, the asset section of the balance sheet is divided into current assets and *fixed assets*. **Current assets** include cash and other items that will or can become cash within the following year. **Fixed assets** (sometimes referred to as *property, plant*, and *equipment*) are long-term investments in build-

current assets
Cash and items that can be turned into cash within one year

fixed assets
Assets retained for long-term use, such as land, buildings, machinery, and equipment; also referred to as *property, plant, and equipment*

ings, equipment, furniture and fixtures, transportation equipment, land, and other tangible property used in running the business. Fixed assets have a useful life of more than one year. Computer Central's principal fixed asset is the company's warehouse facility.

Assets are listed in descending order by *liquidity*, or the ease with which they can be converted into cash. Thus, current assets are listed before fixed assets. The balance sheet gives a subtotal for each type of asset and then a grand total for all assets. Computer Central's current assets consist primarily of cash, investments in short-term marketable securities such as money-market funds, accounts receivable (or amounts due from customers), and inventory (such as computers, software, and other items the company sells to customers).

current liabilities
Obligations that must be met within a year

long-term liabilities
Obligations that fall due more than a year from the date of the balance sheet

Liabilities   Liabilities come after assets because they represent claims against the company's assets, as shown in the basic accounting equation: Assets = Liabilities + Owners' equity. Liabilities may be current or long-term, and they are listed in the order in which they will come due. The balance sheet gives subtotals for **current liabilities** (obligations that will have to be met within one year of the date of the balance sheet) and **long-term liabilities** (obligations that are due one year or more after the date of the balance sheet), and then it gives a grand total for all liabilities.

Current liabilities include accounts payable, short-term financing, and accrued expenses. *Accounts payable* includes the money the company owes its suppliers (such as Compaq and Toshiba) as well as money it owes vendors for miscellaneous services (such as electricity and telephone charges). *Short-term financing* consists of trade credit—the amount owed to suppliers for products purchased but not yet paid for—and commercial paper—short-term promissory notes of major corporations sold in denominations of $100,000 or more, with maturities of up to 270 days (the maximum allowed by the SEC without registration). *Accrued expenses* are expenses that have been incurred but for which bills have not yet been received. For example, because Computer Central's account executives earn commissions on computer sales to customers, the company has a liability to its account executives once the sale is made—regardless of when a check is issued to the employee. Thus, the company must record this liability because it represents a claim against company assets. If such expenses and their associated liabilities were not recorded, the company's financial statements would be misleading and would violate the matching principle (because the commission expenses that were earned at the time of sale would not be matched to the revenue generated from the sale).

lease
Legal agreement that obligates the user of an asset to make payments to the owner of the asset in exchange for using it

Long-term liabilities include loans, leases, and bonds. As Chapter 5 points out, bank loans may be secured or unsecured. The borrowing company makes principal and interest payments to the bank over the term of the loan, and its obligation is limited to these payments (see "Debt Versus Equity Financing" on pages 129–130). Leases are an alternative to loans. Rather than borrowing money to buy a piece of equipment, a firm may enter into a long-term **lease**, under which the owner of an item allows another party to use it in exchange for regular payments. Bonds are certificates that obligate the company to repay a certain sum, plus interest, to the bondholder on a specific date. Bonds are traded on organized securities exchanges and are discussed in detail in Chapter 14.

Computer Central's long-term liabilities are relatively small for a company its size. In 2005, the company purchased a new $30 million warehouse facility with $15 million in cash it had saved over many years and a five-year, $15 million bank loan. The company invests its excess cash in short-term marketable securities so it can earn interest on these funds until they are needed for future projects.

Businesses rely on bank loans as a chief source of long-term financing. Here bankers review a company's financial statements to determine if the firm is creditworthy.

Owners' Equity   The owners' investment in a business is listed on the balance sheet under owners' equity (or shareholders' equity for a corporation such as Computer Central). Sole proprietorships list owner's equity under the owner's name with the amount (assets minus liabilities). Small partnerships list each partner's share of the business separately, and large partnerships list the total of all partners' shares. Shareholders' equity for a corporation is presented in terms of the amount of common stock that is outstanding, meaning the amount that is in the hands of the shareholders. The combined amount of the assigned or par value of the common stock plus the amount paid over the par value (paid-in capital) represents the shareholders' total investment. Roughly $81 million was paid into the corporation by Computer Central shareholders at the time the company's shares were issued. In 2005, the company repurchased 50,000 shares of the company's own stock in the open market for $948,000. The company will use this *treasury stock* for its employee stock option plan and other general corporate purposes.

Shareholders' equity also includes a corporation's **retained earnings**—the portion of shareholders' equity that is not distributed to its owners in the form of dividends. Computer Central's retained earnings amount to $146 million. The company did not pay dividends. Instead, it is building its cash reserves for future asset purchases and to finance future growth.

Income Statement

If the balance sheet is a snapshot, the income statement is a movie. The **income statement** shows an organization's profit performance over a specific period of time, typically one year. It summarizes all **revenues** (or sales), the amounts that have been or are to be received from customers for goods or services delivered to them, and all **expenses**, the costs that have arisen in generating revenues. Expenses and income taxes are then subtracted from revenues to show the actual profit or loss of a company, a figure known as **net income**—profit, or the *bottom line*. By briefly reviewing a company's income statements you should have a general sense of the company's size, its trend in sales, its major expenses, and the resulting net income or loss. Owners, creditors, and investors can evaluate the company's past performance and future prospects by comparing net income for one year with net income for previous years. Exhibit 13.5 is the 2005 income statement for Computer Central, showing net income of almost $66 million. This is a 32 percent increase over the company's net income of $50 million for the previous year. Of course, as the WorldCom debacle illustrated, outsiders will get a distorted picture of profits if a company doesn't provide accurate and honest reports of revenues and expenses.

Expenses, the costs of doing business, include both the direct costs associated with creating or purchasing products for sale and the indirect costs associated with operating the business. Whether a company manufactures or purchases its inventory, the cost of storing the product for sale (such as heating the warehouse, paying the rent, and buying insurance on the storage facility) is added to the difference between the cost of the beginning inventory and the cost of the ending inventory in order to compute the actual cost of items that were sold during a period—or the **cost of goods sold**. The computation can be summarized as follows:

Cost of goods sold = Beginning inventory + Net purchases − Ending inventory

As shown in Exhibit 13.5, cost of goods sold is deducted from sales to obtain a company's **gross profit**—a key figure used in financial statement analysis. In addition to the costs directly associated with producing goods, companies deduct **operating expenses**, which include both *selling expenses* and *general expenses*, to compute a firm's *net operating income*, or the income that is generated from business operations. **Selling expenses** are operating expenses incurred through marketing and distributing the product (such as wages or salaries of salespeople, advertising, supplies, insurance for the sales operation, depreciation for the store and sales equipment, and other sales department expenses such as telephone charges). **General expenses** are operating expenses incurred in the overall administration of a business. They include professional services (accounting and legal fees), office salaries, depreciation of office equipment, insurance for office operations, supplies, and so on.

A firm's net operating income is then adjusted by the amount of any nonoperating income or expense items such as the gain or loss on the sale of a building. The result is the firm's net income or loss before income taxes (losses are shown in parentheses), a key figure used in budgeting, cash-flow analysis, and a variety of other financial computations. Finally, income taxes are deducted to compute the company's net income or loss for the period.

---

retained earnings
The portion of shareholders' equity earned by the company but not distributed to its owners in the form of dividends

income statement
Financial record of a company's revenues, expenses, and profits over a given period of time

revenues
Amount earned from sales of goods or services and inflow from miscellaneous sources such as interest, rent, and royalties

expenses
Costs created in the process of generating revenues

net income
Profit earned or loss incurred by a firm, determined by subtracting expenses from revenues; also called the *bottom line*

cost of goods sold
Cost of producing or acquiring a company's products for sale during a given period

gross profit
Amount remaining when the cost of goods sold is deducted from net sales; also known as *gross margin*

operating expenses
All costs of operation that are not included under cost of goods sold

selling expenses
All the operating expenses associated with marketing goods or services

general expenses
Operating expenses, such as office and administrative expenses, not directly associated with creating or marketing a good or a service

Exhibit 13.5 Income Statement for Computer Central

An income statement summarizes the company's financial operations over a particular accounting period, usually a year.

Revenues
Funds received from sales of goods and services to customers as well as other items such as rent, interest, and dividends. Net sales are gross sales less returns and allowances.

Cost of Goods Sold
Cost of merchandise or services that generate a company's income by adding purchases to beginning inventory and then subtracting ending inventory.

Operating Expenses
Generally classified as selling and general expenses. Selling expenses are those incurred through the marketing and distributing of the company's products. General expenses are operating expenses incurred in the overall administration of a business.

Net Income After Taxes
Profit or loss over a specific period determined by subtracting all expenses and taxes from revenues.

Computer Central
Income Statement
Year ended December 31, 2005
(in thousands)

Revenues		
Gross Sales	$1,991,489	
Less Sales Returns and Allowances	−258,000	
Net Sales		$1,733,489
Cost of Goods Sold		
Beginning Inventory	$ 61,941	
Add: Purchases During the Year	1,515,765	
Cost of Goods Available for Sale	−1,577,706	
Less: Ending Inventory	64,392	
Total Cost of Goods Sold		−1,513,314
Gross Profit		$ 220,175
Operating Expenses		
Selling Expenses	$ 75,523	
General Expenses	40,014	
Total Operating Expenses		115,537
Net Operating Income (Gross Profit Less Operating Expenses)		104,638
Other Income		4,373
Net Income Before Income Taxes		109,011
Less: Income Taxes		−43,170
Net Income After Taxes		$ 65,841

Statement of Cash Flows

statement of cash flows
Statement of a firm's cash receipts and cash payments that presents information on its sources and uses of cash

In addition to preparing a balance sheet and an income statement, all public companies and many privately owned companies prepare a **statement of cash flows** to show how much cash the company generated over time and where it went (see Exhibit 13.6). The statement of cash flows tracks the cash coming into and flowing out of a company's bank accounts. It reveals the increase or decrease in the company's cash for the period and summarizes (by category) the sources of that change. From a brief review of this statement you should have a general sense of the amount of cash created or consumed by daily operations, the amount of cash invested in fixed or other assets, the amount of debt borrowed or repaid, and the proceeds from the sale of stock or payments for dividends. In addition, an analysis of cash flows provides a good idea of a company's ability to pay its short-term obligations when they become due.

As Exhibit 13.6 shows, the cash-flow statement is organized into three parts. Computer Central's statement of cash flows shows that the company used $15 million of its cash reserves and the proceeds of a $15 million bank loan in 2005 to pay for its new facility.

Analyzing Financial Statements

Once financial statements have been prepared, managers and outsiders use these statements to evaluate the financial health of the organization, make business decisions, and spot opportunities for improvements by looking at the company's performance in relation to its past performance, the economy as a whole, and the performance of its competitors.

Exhibit 13.6 **Statement of Cash Flows for Computer Central**

A statement of cash flows shows a firm's cash receipts and cash payments as a result of three main activities—operating, investing, and financing—for a period.

Computer Central Statement of Cash Flows Year ended December 31, 2005 (in thousands)		
Cash Flows from Operating Activities*		
Net Income	$ 65,841	
Adjustments to Reconcile Net Income to		
Net Cash Provided by Operating Activities	–61,317	
Net Cash Provided by or Used in Operating Activities		$ 4,524
Cash Flows from Investing Activities		
Purchase of Property and Equipment	–30,110	
Purchase of Securities	–114,932	
Redemptions of Securities	112,463	
Net Cash Provided by or Used in Operating Activities		–32,579
Cash Flows from Financing Activities		
Loan Proceeds	15,000	
Purchase of Treasury Stock	–2,089	
Proceeds from Exercise of Stock Options	1,141	
Net Cash Provided by or Used in Financing Activities		14,052
Net (Decrease) Increase in Cash		–14,003
Cash and Cash Equivalents at Beginning of Year		$18,233
Cash and Cash Equivalents at End of Year		$ 4,230

Cash flows from operations
How much cash a company's business generates or uses contains clues to how healthy earnings are. Most companies start with net income from the income statement and detail items that cause income to differ from cash.

Cash flows from investments
Cash used to buy or received from selling stock, assets, and businesses, plus capital expenditures.

Cash flows from financing
Cash from or paid to outsiders—such as banks or stockholders. If positive, the company relied on outsiders for funds. If negative, the company may have paid down debt or bought back stock.

* Note: Numbers preceded by minus sign indicate cash outflows

Trend Analysis

The process of comparing financial data from year to year in order to see how they have changed is known as *trend analysis*. You can use trend analysis to uncover shifts in the nature of the business over time. Most large companies provide data for trend analysis in their annual reports. Their balance sheets and income statements typically show three to five years or more of data (making comparative statement analysis possible). Changes in other key items—such as revenues, income, earnings per share, and dividends per share—are usually presented in tables and graphs.

Of course, when you are comparing one period with another, it's important to take into account the effects of extraordinary or unusual items such as the sale of major assets, the purchase of a new line of products from another company, weather, or economic conditions that may have affected the company in one period but not the next. These extraordinary items are usually disclosed in the text portion of a company's annual report or in the notes to the financial statements.

Ratio Analysis

Managers and others compute financial ratios to facilitate the comparison of one company's financial results with those of competing firms and with industry averages. **Ratio analysis** compares two elements from the same year's financial figures. They are called *ratios* because they are computed by dividing one element of a financial statement by another. The advantage of using ratios is that it puts companies on the same footing; that is, it makes it possible to compare different-size companies and changing dollar

ratio analysis
Use of quantitative measures to evaluate a firm's financial performance

How to Read an Annual Report

Whether you're thinking of investing, becoming a supplier, or applying for a job, knowing how to read a company's annual report will be an important skill throughout your career. Thus, it's worth your while to consider the advice of *Newsweek* columnist Jane Bryant Quinn, who provided these pointers.

READ THE LETTERS

First, turn to the report of the certified public accountant. This third-party auditor will tell you right off the bat if the report conforms with generally accepted accounting principles. Now turn to the letter from the chairman. This letter should tell you how the company fared this year, but more important, the letter should tell you why. Keep an eye out for sentences that start with "Except for . . . " and "Despite the . . . " They're clues to problems. The chairman's letter should also give you insights into the company's future. For example, look for what's new in each line of business. Is management getting the company in good shape to weather the tough and competitive years ahead?

DIG INTO THE NUMBERS

Check out the trend in the company's working capital (the difference between current assets and current liabilities). If working capital is shrinking, it could mean trouble. One possibility: The company may not be able to keep dividends growing rapidly.

Another important number to analyze is earnings per share. Management can boost earnings by selling off a plant or by cutting the budget for research or advertising. See the footnotes; they often tell the whole story. If earnings are down only because of a change in accounting, maybe that's good! The company owes less tax and has more money in its pocket. If earnings are up, maybe that's bad. They may be up because of a special windfall that won't happen again next year. One good indicator is the trend in net sales. If sales increases are starting to slow, the company may be in trouble.

GET OUT YOUR CALCULATOR AND COMPARE

High and rising debt, relative to equity, may be no problem for a growing business. But it shows weakness in a company that's leveling out. So get out your calculator and divide long-term liabilities by shareholders' equity. That's the debt-to-equity ratio. A high ratio means the company borrows a lot of money to fund its growth. That's okay—if sales grow too, and if there's enough cash on hand to meet the payments. But if sales fall, watch out. The whole enterprise may slowly sink.

Remember, one ratio, one annual report, one chairman's letter won't tell you much. You have to compare. Is the company's debt-to-equity ratio better or worse than it used to be? Better or worse than the industry norms? In company watching, comparisons are all. They tell you if management is staying on top of things.

Questions for Critical Thinking

1. Why might a job seeker want to read a company's annual report before applying for a job with that company?
2. What types of valuable nonfinancial information might an annual report disclose to a potential supplier?

amounts. For example, by using ratios, you can easily compare a large supermarket's ability to generate profit out of sales with a similar statistic for a small grocery store.

The benefit of converting numbers into ratios can be explained by the following example: Suppose you wanted to know how well your favorite baseball player was performing this year. To find out, you would check the player's statistics—batting average, runs batted in (RBIs), hits, and home runs. In other words, you would look at data that have been arranged into meaningful statistics that allow you to compare present performance with past performance and with the performance of other players in the league. Financial ratios do the same thing. They convert the raw numbers from the current and prior years' financial statements into ratios that highlight important relationships or measures of performance.[11]

Just as baseball statistics focus on various aspects of performance (such as hitting or pitching), financial ratios help companies understand their current operations and answer key questions: Is inventory too large? Are credit customers paying too slowly? Can the company pay its bills? Ratios also set standards and benchmarks for gauging future business by comparing a company's scores with industry averages that show the performance of competition. Every industry tends to have its own "normal" ratios, which act as yardsticks for individual companies. Dun and Bradstreet, a credit rating firm, and Robert Morris Associates publish both average financial figures and ratios for a variety of industries and company sizes.

Before reviewing specific ratios, consider two rules of thumb: First, avoid drawing too strong a conclusion from any one ratio. For instance, even with a low batting average, a baseball player's RBIs may prove valuable in the team's lineup. Second, once ratios have presented a general indication, refer back to the specific data involved to see whether the numbers confirm what the ratios suggest. In other words, do a little investigating, because statistics can be misleading.

Types of Financial Ratios

Financial ratios can be organized into the following groups, as Exhibit 13.7 shows: profitability, liquidity, activity, and leverage (or debt).

Profitability Ratios   You can analyze how well a company is conducting its ongoing operations by computing **profitability ratios**, which show the state of the company's financial performance or how well it's generating profits. Three of the most common profitability ratios are **return on sales**, or profit margin (the net income a business makes per unit of sales); **return on investment (ROI)**, or return on equity (the income earned on the owner's investment); and **earnings per share** (the profit earned for each share of stock outstanding). Exhibit 13.7 shows how to compute these profitability ratios by using the financial information from Computer Central.

Liquidity Ratios   **Liquidity ratios** measure the ability of the firm to pay its short-term obligations. As you might expect, lenders and creditors are keenly interested in liquidity measures. Liquidity can be judged on the basis of *working capital*, the *current ratio*, and the *quick ratio*. A company's **working capital** (current assets minus current liabilities) is an indicator of liquidity because it represents current assets remaining after the payment of all current liabilities. The dollar amount of working capital can be misleading, however. For example, it may include the value of slow-moving inventory items that cannot be used to help pay a company's short-term debts.

A different picture of the company's liquidity is provided by the **current ratio**—current assets divided by current liabilities. This figure compares the current debt owed with the current assets available to pay that debt. The **quick ratio**, also called the *acid-test ratio*, is computed by subtracting inventory from current assets and then dividing the result by current liabilities. This ratio is often a better indicator of a firm's ability to pay creditors than the current ratio because the quick ratio leaves out inventories—which at times can be difficult to sell. Analysts generally consider a quick ratio of 1.0 to be reasonable, whereas a current ratio of 2.0 is considered a safe risk for short-term credit. Exhibit 13.7 shows that both the current and quick ratios of Computer Central are well above these benchmarks and industry averages.

Activity Ratios   A number of **activity ratios** may be used to analyze how well a company is managing its assets. The most common is the **inventory turnover ratio**, which measures how fast a company's inventory is turned into sales; in general, the quicker the better, because holding excess inventory can be expensive. When inventory sits on the shelf, money is tied up without earning interest; furthermore, the company incurs expenses for its storage, handling, insurance, and taxes. In addition, there is always a risk that the inventory will become obsolete before it can be converted into finished goods and sold. The firm's goal is to maintain enough inventory to fill orders in a timely fashion at the lowest cost.

Keep in mind that it's difficult to judge a company by its inventory level. For example, lower inventories might mean one of many things: You're running an efficient operation, the right inventory is not being stocked, or sales are booming and you need to increase your orders. Likewise, higher inventories could signal a decline in sales, careless

profitability ratios
Ratios that measure the overall financial performance of a firm

return on sales
Ratio between net income after taxes and net sales; also known as *profit margin*

return on investment (ROI)
Ratio between net income after taxes and total owners' equity; also known as *return on equity*

earnings per share
Measure of a firm's profitability for each share of outstanding stock, calculated by dividing net income after taxes by the average number of shares of common stock outstanding

liquidity ratios
Ratios that measure a firm's ability to meet its short-term obligations when they are due

working capital
Current assets minus current liabilities

current ratio
Measure of a firm's short-term liquidity, calculated by dividing current assets by current liabilities

quick ratio
Measure of a firm's short-term liquidity, calculated by adding cash, marketable securities, and receivables, then dividing that sum by current liabilities; also known as the *acid-test ratio*

activity ratios
Ratios that measure the effectiveness of the firm's use of its resources

inventory turnover ratio
Measure of the time a company takes to turn its inventory into sales, calculated by dividing cost of goods sold by the average value of inventory for a period

Exhibit 13.7   **How Well Does This Company Stack Up?**

Nearly all companies use ratios to evaluate how well the company is performing in relation to prior performance, the economy as a whole, and the company's competitors.

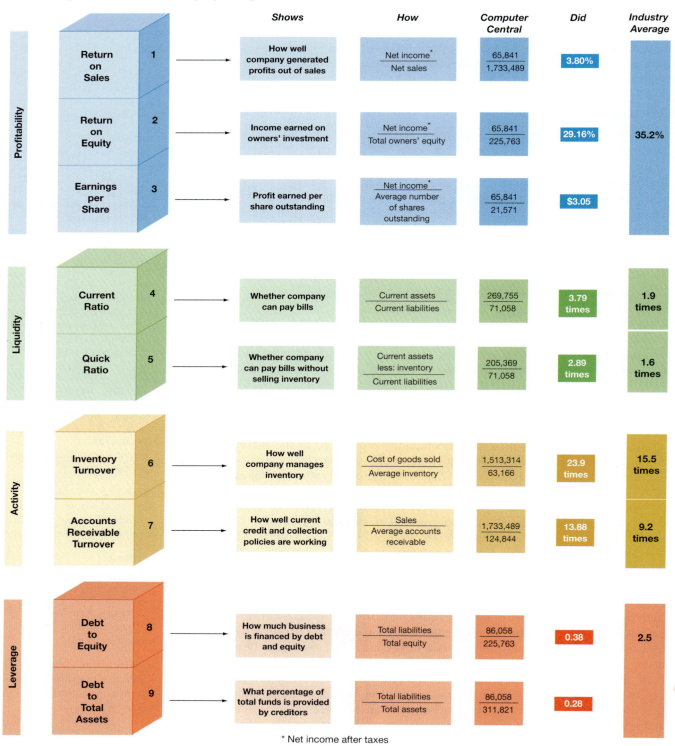

			Shows	How	Computer Central	Did	Industry Average
Profitability	Return on Sales	1	How well company generated profits out of sales	$\dfrac{\text{Net income}^*}{\text{Net sales}}$	$\dfrac{65,841}{1,733,489}$	3.80%	
	Return on Equity	2	Income earned on owners' investment	$\dfrac{\text{Net income}^*}{\text{Total owners' equity}}$	$\dfrac{65,841}{225,763}$	29.16%	35.2%
	Earnings per Share	3	Profit earned per share outstanding	$\dfrac{\text{Net income}^*}{\text{Average number of shares outstanding}}$	$\dfrac{65,841}{21,571}$	$3.05	
Liquidity	Current Ratio	4	Whether company can pay bills	$\dfrac{\text{Current assets}}{\text{Current liabilities}}$	$\dfrac{269,755}{71,058}$	3.79 times	1.9 times
	Quick Ratio	5	Whether company can pay bills without selling inventory	$\dfrac{\text{Current assets less: inventory}}{\text{Current liabilities}}$	$\dfrac{205,369}{71,058}$	2.89 times	1.6 times
Activity	Inventory Turnover	6	How well company manages inventory	$\dfrac{\text{Cost of goods sold}}{\text{Average inventory}}$	$\dfrac{1,513,314}{63,166}$	23.9 times	15.5 times
	Accounts Receivable Turnover	7	How well current credit and collection policies are working	$\dfrac{\text{Sales}}{\text{Average accounts receivable}}$	$\dfrac{1,733,489}{124,844}$	13.88 times	9.2 times
Leverage	Debt to Equity	8	How much business is financed by debt and equity	$\dfrac{\text{Total liabilities}}{\text{Total equity}}$	$\dfrac{86,058}{225,763}$	0.38	2.5
	Debt to Total Assets	9	What percentage of total funds is provided by creditors	$\dfrac{\text{Total liabilities}}{\text{Total assets}}$	$\dfrac{86,058}{311,821}$	0.28	

* Net income after taxes

ordering, or stocking up because of favorable pricing. The "ideal" turnover ratio varies with the type of operation. In 2005, Computer Central turned its inventory 23.9 times (see Exhibit 13.7). This rate is unusually high when compared with industry averages, and it suggests that the company stocks only enough inventory to fill current orders and cover a product's reorder time, as discussed in Chapter 8.

Another popular activity ratio is the **accounts receivable turnover ratio**, which measures how well a company's credit and collection policies are working by indicating how frequently accounts receivable are converted to cash. The volume of receivables outstanding depends on the financial manager's decisions regarding several issues, such as who qualifies for credit and who does not, how long customers are given to pay their bills, and how aggressive the firm is in collecting its debts. Be careful here as well. If the ratio is going up, you need to determine whether the company is doing a better job of collecting or sales are rising. If the ratio is going down, it may be because sales are decreasing or because collection efforts are lagging. In 2005, Computer Central turned its accounts receivable 13.88 times—considerably higher than the industry average (see Exhibit 13.7).

Leverage, or Debt, Ratios   You can measure a company's ability to pay its long-term debts by calculating its **debt ratios**, or leverage ratios. Lenders look at these ratios to determine whether the potential borrower has put enough money into the business to serve as a protective cushion for the loan. The **debt-to-equity ratio** (total liabilities divided by total equity) indicates the extent to which a business is financed by debt as opposed to invested capital (equity). From the lender's standpoint, the lower this ratio, the safer the company, because the company has less existing debt and may be able to repay additional money it wants to borrow. However, a company that is conservative in its long-term borrowing is not necessarily well managed; often a low level of debt is associated with a low growth rate. Computer Central's low debt-to-equity ratio of 38 percent (as shown in Exhibit 13.7) reflects the company's practice of financing its growth by using excess cash flow from operations and by selling shares of common stock to the public.

The **debt-to-total-assets ratio** (total liabilities divided by total assets) also serves as a simple measure of a company's ability to carry long-term debt. As a rule of thumb, the amount of debt should not exceed 50 percent of the value of total assets. For Computer Central, this ratio is a very low 28 percent and again reflects the company's policy of using retained earnings to finance its growth (see Exhibit 13.7). However, this ratio, too, is not a magic formula. Like grades on a report card, ratios are clues to performance. Managers, creditors, lenders, and investors can use them to get a fairly accurate idea of how a company is doing. But remember, one ratio by itself doesn't tell the whole story.

UNDERSTANDING FINANCIAL MANAGEMENT

Planning for a firm's current and future money needs is the foundation of **financial management**, or finance. This area of concern involves making decisions about alternative sources and uses of funds with the goal of maximizing a company's value (see Exhibit 13.8). To achieve this goal, financial managers develop and implement a firm's financial plan, monitor a firm's cash flow and decide how to create or use excess funds, budget for current and future expenditures, recommend specific investments, develop a plan to finance the enterprise for future growth, and interact with banks and capital markets.

Developing and Implementing a Financial Plan

One way companies make sure they have enough money is by developing a *financial plan*. Normally in the form of a budget, a **financial plan** is a document that shows the funds a firm will need for a period of time as well as the sources and uses of those funds. When you prepare a financial plan for a company, you have two objectives: achieving a positive cash

---

accounts receivable turnover ratio
Measure of time a company takes to turn its accounts receivable into cash, calculated by dividing sales by the average value of accounts receivable for a period

debt ratios
Ratios that measure a firm's reliance on debt financing of its operations (sometimes called *leverage ratios*)

debt-to-equity ratio
Measure of the extent to which a business is financed by debt as opposed to invested capital, calculated by dividing the company's total liabilities by owners' equity

debt-to-total-assets ratio
Measure of a firm's ability to carry long-term debt, calculated by dividing total liabilities by total assets

financial management
Effective acquisition and use of money

financial plan
A forecast of financial requirements and the financing sources to be used

Sources and Uses of a Company's Funds

Financial management involves finding suitable sources of funds and deciding on the most appropriate uses for those funds.

Sources of Funds		Uses of Funds
Sales from operations		Rent
Sales from assets		Utilities
Retained earnings		Plant and equipment
Trade credit	Management decides how to use funds	Materials
Commercial loans		Advertising and promotion
Bonds		Distribution
Stocks		Wages and salaries
		Personnel training
		Interest and dividends
		Taxes

flow and efficiently investing excess cash flow to make your company grow. Financial planning requires looking beyond the four walls of the company to answer questions such as: Is the company introducing a new product in the near future or expanding its market? Is the industry growing? Is the national economy declining? Is inflation heating up? Would an investment in new technology improve productivity?[12]

Monitoring Cash Flow

An underlying concept of any financial plan is that all money should be used productively. This concept is important because without cash a company cannot purchase the assets and supplies it needs to operate. In accounting, you prepare income statements to determine the net income of a firm. In finance, however, you focus on cash flows. Although the firm's income is important, cash flows are even more important because cash is necessary to purchase the assets required to continue operations and pay dividends to shareholders. Cash flows are generally related to net income; that is, companies with relatively high accounting profits generally have relatively high cash flows, but the relationship is not precise.

One way financial managers improve a company's cash flow is by monitoring its *working capital accounts*: cash, inventory, accounts receivable, and accounts payable. They use commonsense procedures such as shrinking accounts receivable collection periods, dispatching bills on a timely basis without paying bills earlier than necessary, controlling the level of inventory, and investing excess cash so the company can earn as much interest as possible. Aggressive financial managers use electronic cash management (the ability to access bank account information online) to move cash between accounts and pay bills on a daily basis; they also invest excess cash on hand in short-term investments called **marketable securities**. These interest-bearing or dividend-paying investments include money-market funds or publicly traded stocks such as IBM or Sears. They are said to be "marketable" because they can be easily converted back to cash. Because marketable securities are generally used as contingency funds, however, most financial managers invest these funds in government securities or securities of solid companies—ones perceived to have the least amount of risk. (Securities are discussed in detail in Chapter 14.)

Developing a Budget

In addition to developing a financial plan and monitoring cash flow, financial managers are responsible for developing a **budget**, a financial blueprint for a given period (often one year). Master (or operating) budgets help financial managers estimate the flow of

marketable securities
Stocks, bonds, and other investments that can be turned into cash quickly

budget
Planning and control tool that reflects expected revenues, operating expenses, and cash receipts and outlays

Companies plan for construction projects such as this one years in advance and reflect the costs of such long-term projects in their capital budgets.

money into and out of the business by structuring financial plans in a framework of a firm's total estimated revenues, expenses, and cash flows. Accountants provide much of the data required for budgets and are important members of the budget development team because they have a complete understanding of the company's operating costs.

The master operating budget sets a standard for expenditures, provides guidelines for controlling costs, and offers an integrated and detailed plan for the future. For example, by reviewing the budget of any airline you can determine whether the company plans on increasing its fleet of aircraft, adding more routes, hiring more employees,

Learning from Business Blunders

Oops: With a nationwide advertising campaign and free financing, Mitsubishi Motors went all out to entice young drivers to buy an Eclipse. The strategy worked—worked so well in fact that it cost the company nearly a billion dollars. Those young drivers took Mitsubishi up on the offer, then thousands of them defaulted on their loans when they couldn't make the payments. The bad debts cost the company $469 million. After fixing the credit problem, Mitsubishi then watched sales drop in half and had to spend $432 million more to buy back unsold inventory.

What You Can Learn: Two lessons: Credit can be as dangerous for buyers as it for sellers, and there is such a thing as a bad customer. Companies that go overboard in efforts to attract customers can find themselves in Mitsubishi's shoes, losing money on customers who couldn't afford their products in the first place.

increasing employees' pay, or continuing or abandoning any discounts for travelers. No wonder companies like to keep their budgets confidential. Once a budget has been developed, the finance manager compares actual results with projections to discover variances and recommends corrective action—a process known as **financial control**.

In addition to developing operating budgets, financial managers develop capital budgets to forecast and plan for a firm's **capital investments** such as major expenditures in buildings or equipment. Capital investments generally cover a period of several years and help the company grow. Before investments can be made, however, a firm must decide on which of the many possible capital investments to make, how to finance those that are undertaken, and even whether to make any capital investments at all. This process is called **capital budgeting**.

The process generally begins by having all divisions within a company submit their capital requests—essentially, "wish lists" of investments that would make the company more profitable and thus more valuable to its owners over time. Next, the financial manager decides which investments need evaluating and which don't. For example, the routine replacement of old equipment probably wouldn't need evaluating; however, the construction of a new manufacturing facility would. Finally, a financial evaluation is performed to determine whether the amount of money required for a particular investment will be greater than, equal to, or less than the amount of revenue it will generate. On the basis of this analysis, the financial manager can determine which projects to recommend to senior management for purchase approval.

financial control
The process of analyzing and adjusting the basic financial plan to correct for forecasted events that do not materialize

capital investments
Money paid to acquire something of permanent value in a business

capital budgeting
Process for evaluating proposed investments in select projects that provide the best long-term financial return

Summary of Learning Objectives

1 Discuss how managers and outsiders use financial information.

Managers use financial information to control a company's operation and to make informed business decisions. Outsiders use financial information to evaluate whether a business is creditworthy or a good investment. Specifically, banks want to know if a business is able to pay back a loan, investors want to know if the company is earning a profit, and governments want to be assured the company is paying the proper amount of taxes.

2 Describe what accountants do.

Accountants design and install accounting systems, prepare financial statements, analyze and interpret financial information, prepare financial forecasts and budgets, prepare tax returns, interpret tax law, compute and analyze production costs, evaluate a company's performance, and analyze the financial implications of business decisions. In addition to these functions, accountants help managers improve business procedures, plan for the future, evaluate product performance, analyze the firm's profitability, and design and install computer systems. Auditors are licensed certified public accountants who review accounting records and processes to assess whether they conform to GAAP and whether the company's financial statements fairly present the company's financial position and operating results.

3 Summarize the impact of the Sarbanes-Oxley Act.

Sarbanes-Oxley introduced a number of rules covering the way publicly traded companies manage and report their finances, including restricting loans to directors and executives, creating a new board to oversee public auditors, requiring cororate lawyers to report financial wrongdoing, requiring CEOs and CFOs to sign financial statements under oath, and requiring companies to document their financial systems.

4 State the basic accounting equation, and explain the purpose of double-entry bookkeeping and the matching principle.

The basic accounting equation is Assets = Liabilities + Owners' equity. Double-entry bookkeeping is a system of recording financial transactions to keep the accounting equation in balance. The matching principle makes sure that expenses incurred in producing revenues are deducted from the revenue they generated during the same accounting period.

5 Differentiate between cash basis and accrual basis accounting.

Cash basis accounting recognizes revenue at the time payment is received, whereas accrual basis accounting recognizes revenue at the time of sale, even if payment is not made.

6 Explain the purpose of the balance sheet, and identify its three main sections.

The balance sheet provides a snapshot of the business at a particular point in time. It shows the size of the company, the major assets owned, how the assets are financed, and the amount of owners' investment in the business. Its three main sections are assets, liabilities, and owners' equity.

7 Explain the purpose of the income statement.

The income statement reflects the results of operations over a period of time. It gives a general sense of a company's size and performance. The statement of cash flows shows how a company's cash was received and spent in three areas: operations, investments, and financing. It gives a general sense of the amount of cash created or consumed by daily operations, fixed assets, investments, and debt over a period of time.

8 Explain the purpose of ratio analysis, and list the four main categories of financial ratios.

Financial ratios provide information for analyzing the health and future prospects of a business. Ratios facilitate financial comparisons among different-size companies and between a company and industry averages. Most of the important ratios fall into one of four categories: profitability ratios, which show how well the company generates profits; liquidity ratios, which measure the company's ability to pay its short-term obligations; activity ratios, which analyze how well a company is managing its assets; and debt ratios, which measure a company's ability to pay its long-term debt.

9 Identify the responsibilities of a financial manager.

The responsibilities of a financial manager include developing and implementing a firm's financial plan, monitoring a firm's cash flow and deciding how to create or use excess funds, budgeting for current and future expenditures, recommending specific investments, raising capital to finance the enterprise for future growth, and interacting with banks and capital markets.

Behind the Scenes

Getting MCI Back on Its Feet

When Michael Capellas took over as WorldCom CEO in November 2002, he took the reins of a company on the brink of collapse. WorldCom was more than $30 billion in debt, investors and employees were angry and disillusioned, customers were worried about service disruptions, and prosecutors were banging on the door demanding justice.

The fiasco got the government's attention at the highest levels. The Justice Department and the U.S. Bankruptcy Court assigned former U.S. Attorney General Richard Thornburgh to investigate how a handful of high-ranking executives were able to perpetrate fraud on such a massive scale. Richard Breeden, a former chairman of the Securities and Exchange Commission (SEC), was given the role of guiding and monitoring the company's reform efforts. In a report that outlined 78 proposed changes, Breeden pointedly summarized the cause of the problem: "One cannot say that the checks and balances against excessive [executive] power within the old WorldCom didn't work adequately. Rather, the sad fact is that there were no checks and balances."

Implementing Breeden's reforms became Capellas's top priority. He changed the organizational structure, tightened finance and accounting policies (and started work toward replacing the company's 27 separate accounting systems with a single, integrated system), and overhauled corporate governance—including replacing the entire board of directors.

Capellas also had to face the problem of WorldCom's huge debt. As part of the settlement reached with the bankruptcy court, the government allowed the company to keep all of its assets, rather than selling them to pay creditors. It also forgave most of the $30 billion debt by giving those creditors ownership portions in a highly controversial agreement that gave some creditors more than others and gave shareholders nothing, although shareholders will receive a penalty payment assessed by the SEC. The rationale behind the agreement was that freeing the company from its huge debt would allow it to rebuild value for those creditor-owners and protect the jobs of its 55,000 employees.

The effort to restore public confidence also included changing the name from WorldCom to MCI (a company known as MCI had existed before; it was one of the firms Ebbers scooped up in his acquisition binge). Even this decision provoked a negative reaction from some observers, who said the company was simply trying to hide behind a new name.

What does the future hold for Capellas and MCI? Even though MCI emerged from bankruptcy in 2004 with realistic accounting measures and a stronger balance sheet, controversy and uncertainty are sure to be constant companions. For instance, the U.S. government recently prohibited the company from taking on new federal contracts, saying MCI still lacked sufficient ethical controls. (Noting that MCI still had progress to make in this respect, Capellas didn't appeal the decision.) Investigations continue into charges leveled by competitors that MCI has been improperly labeling or routing long-distance phone calls to avoid paying fees owed to these other companies. And in what could signal the final chapter in this complicated story, Capellas engaged an investment bank in late 2004 to explore the possibility of selling the company. Even if it does eventually disappear as a corporate entity, the legacy of MCI will live on through the financial damage it wreaked on thousands of the people and the changes it helped spur in the way U.S. corporations are managed and regulated.[13]

Critical Thinking Questions

1. Should the old WorldCom's outside auditors have been able to detect the $11 billion accounting fraud? Why or why not?
2. Why would the decision to relieve most of the MCI's debt help it return to profitability and growth quicker?
3. Why would the old WorldCom's 27 separate accounting systems likely have contributed to its financial problems?

LEARN MORE ONLINE

Visit the MCI website by going to Chapter 13 of this text's website at www.prenhall.com/bovee. Click on the company's hotlink, and review the company's latest financial statements. (Access the statements by clicking on About MCI, Investor Relations, and Annual Reports or Quarterly and Other Reports.) Then calculate the company's accounts receivable turnover, quick ratio, current ratio, and return on sales for the current and preceding year or quarter. What does each of these ratios show? How are the ratios trending from one period to the next? What might the trends indicate? (Note that you'll probably see results for 2003 and earlier identified as "Predecessor Company" to indicate these apply to the old WorldCom and results for 2004 and later as "Successor Company" to indicate MCI.) ■

Key Terms

accounting (336)
accounting equation (342)
accounts receivable turnover ratio (353)
accrual basis (342)
activity ratios (351)
assets (342)
audit (338)
balance sheet (344)
bookkeeping (337)
budget (354)
calendar year (344)
capital budgeting (355)
capital investments (355)
cash basis (343)
certified management accountants (CMAs) (338)

certified public accountants (CPAs) (338)
close the books (343)
controller (337)
cost accounting (337)
cost of goods sold (347)
current assets (345)
current liabilities (346)
current ratio (351)
debt ratios (353)
debt-to-equity ratio (353)
debt-to-total-assets ratio (353)
depreciation (343)
double-entry bookkeeping (342)
earnings per share (351)
expenses (347)
external auditors (339)

financial accounting (337)
financial analysis (337)
financial control (355)
financial management (353)
financial plan (353)
fiscal year (344)
fixed assets (345)
general expenses (347)
generally accepted accounting principles (GAAP) (339)
gross profit (347)
income statement (347)
internal auditors (339)
inventory turnover ratio (351)
lease (346)
liabilities (342)
liquidity ratios (351)

long-term liabilities (346)

management accounting (337)

marketable securities (354)

matching principle (342)

net income (347)

operating expenses (347)

owners' equity (342)

private accountants (337)

profitability ratios (351)

public accountants (338)

quick ratio (351)

ratio analysis (349)

retained earnings (347)

return on investment (ROI) (351)

return on sales (351)

revenues (347)

Sarbanes-Oxley (340)

selling expenses (347)

statement of cash flows (348)

tax accounting (337)

working capital (351)

Test Your Knowledge

Questions for Review

1. What is GAAP?
2. What is an audit and why is it performed?
3. What is the matching principle?
4. What are the three main profitability ratios, and how is each calculated?
5. What is the primary goal of financial management?

Questions for Analysis

6. Why is accounting important to business?
7. Why do some companies resort to accounting tricks, and what steps are being taken to clamp down on such wrongdoings?
8. Why are the costs of fixed assets depreciated?
9. Why do companies prepare budgets?
10. **Ethical Considerations.** In the process of closing the company books, you encounter a problematic transaction. One of the company's customers was charged twice for the same project materials, resulting in a $1,000 overcharge. You immediately notify the controller, whose response is, "Let it go, it happens often." What should you do now?

Questions for Application

11. The senior partner of an accounting firm is looking for ways to increase the firm's business. What other services besides traditional accounting can the firm offer to its clients? What new challenges might this additional work create?
12. Visit the websites of Ford Motor Company and General Motors Corporation and retrieve their annual reports. Using these financials, compute the working capital, current ratio, and quick ratio for each company. Does one company appear to be more liquid than the other? Why?
13. **Integrated.** Review the discussion of corporate governance in Chapter 6. How will Sarbanes-Oxley affect corporate boards and their relationship with CEOs?
14. **Integrated.** Your appliance manufacturing company recently implemented a just-in-time inventory system (see Chapter 8) for all parts used in the manufacturing process. How might you expect this move to affect the company's inventory turnover rate, current ratio, and quick ratio?

Practice Your Knowledge

Sharpening Your Communication Skills

Obtain a copy of the annual report of a business and examine what the report shows about finances and current operations. In addition to other chapter material, use the information in "How to Read an Annual Report" on page 350 as a guideline for understanding the annual report's content.

- Consider the statements made by the CEO regarding the past year: Did the company do well, or are changes in operations necessary to its future well-being? What are the projections for future growth in sales and profits?
- Examine the financial summaries for information about the fiscal condition of the company: Did the company show a profit?
- If possible, obtain a copy of the company's annual report from the previous year, and compare it with the current report to determine whether past projections were accurate.
- Prepare a brief written summary of your conclusions.

Building Your Team Skills

Divide into small groups and compute the following financial ratios for Alpine Manufacturing using the company's balance sheet and income statement. Compare your answers to those of your classmates:

- Profitability ratios: return on sales; return on equity; earnings per share
- Liquidity ratios: current ratio; quick ratio
- Activity ratios: inventory turnover; accounts receivable turnover
- Leverage ratios: debt to equity; debt to total assets

Alpine Manufacturing
Income Statement
Year Ended December 31, 2005

Sales	$1,800
Less: Cost of Goods Sold	1,000
Gross Profit	$ 800
Less: Total Operating Expenses	450
Net Operating Income Before Income Taxes	350
Less: Income Taxes	50
NET INCOME AFTER INCOME TAXES	$ 300

Alpine Manufacturing
Balance Sheet
December 31, 2005

ASSETS	
Cash	$ 100
Accounts Receivable (beginning balance $350)	300
Inventory (beginning balance $250)	300
Current Assets $	700
Fixed Assets	2,300
Total Assets	$3,000

LIABILITIES AND SHAREHOLDERS' EQUITY	
Current Liabilities (beginning balance $300)	$ 400
Long-Term Debts	1,600
Shareholders' Equity (100 common shares outstanding valued at $12 each)	1,000
Total Liabilities and Shareholders' Equity	$3,000

Expand Your Knowledge

Discovering Career Opportunities

People interested in entering the field of accounting can choose among a wide variety of careers with diverse responsibilities and challenges. Select one of the occupations mentioned in this chapter or in Appendix E, under the section "Careers in Finance and Accounting." Using Appendix E, library sources, or Internet websites from one of the major accounting firms or the AICPA, dig deeper to learn more about your chosen occupation.

1. What are the day-to-day duties of this occupation? How would these duties contribute to the financial success of a company?

2. What skills and educational qualifications would you need to enter this occupation? How do these qualifications fit with your current plans, skills, and interests?

3. What kinds of employers hire people for this position? According to your research, does the number of employers seem to be increasing or decreasing? How do you think this trend will affect your employment possibilities if you choose this career?

Developing Your Research Skills

Select an article from a business journal or newspaper (print or online editions) that discusses the quarterly or year-end performance of a company that industry analysts consider notable for either positive or negative reasons.

1. Did the company report a profit or a loss for this accounting period? What other performance indicators were reported? Is the company's performance improving or declining?

2. Did the company's performance match industry analysts' expectations, or was it a surprise? How did analysts or other experts respond to the firm's actual quarterly or year-end results?

3. What reasons were given for the company's improvement or decline in performance?

SEE IT ON THE WEB

For live links to the websites that follow, go to this text's website at www.prenhall.com/bovee. When you log on, select Chapter 13, then select "Featured Websites," click on the URL of the website you wish to visit, review the website, and answer the following questions:

1. What is the purpose of this website?
2. What kinds of information does this website contain? Please be specific.
3. How is the information provided at this website useful for businesspeople? Consumers?
4. How did you expand your knowledge of accounting by reviewing the material at this website? What new things did you learn about accounting?

Link Your Way to the World of Accounting

Looking for one accounting supersite packed with information and links to financial resources? Check out the WebCPA, an online launching point for accountants. This is the place to find answers to all kinds of questions about accounting, financial analysis, taxes, and more. Participate in one of the many focused discussion groups. Visit the niche sites for information on financial planning, practice management, technology consulting, or CPA requirements. Read the latest issues of *Accounting Today*, *Accounting Technology*, and the *Practical Accountant*. Don't leave without checking out the Career Center

where you'll find information on the latest accounting hot jobs and opportunities. www.webcpa.com

Sharpen Your Pencil

Take a virtual field trip to the Report Gallery, where you can click to view the annual reports of Allstate, Boeing, and many other U.S. and international firms. Select an annual report for any company and examine the financial statements, chairman's letter, and auditor's report. Was it a good or bad year for the company? Who are the company's auditors? Did they issue a clean audit report? www.reportgallery.com

Think Like an Accountant

Find out how the world of accounting is changing by exploring the valuable links at CPAnet. Learn about the many facets of accounting such as taxes, finance, auditing, and more. Follow the link to your state CPA society, and discover what it takes to become a CPA or how to prepare for the CPA exam. Learn how to read a financial report, and discover what financial statements say about your business. Check out the financial calculators. Increase your knowledge of accounting terms and accounting basics before participating in one of the site's discussion forums. CPAnet claims to be a complete resource for the accounting profession. www.cpanet.com

Companion Website

Learning Interactively

Go to the Companion Website at www.prenhall.com/bovee. For Chapter 13, take advantage of the interactive "Study Guide" to test your knowledge of the chapter. Get instant feedback on whether you need additional studying.

Also, visit this site's "Study Hall," where you'll find an abundance of valuable resources that will help you succeed in this course.

Video **Case**

Accounting for Billions of Burgers: McDonald's

LEARNING OBJECTIVES

The purpose of this video is to help you:

1. Understand the challenges a company may face in managing financial information from operations in multiple countries.

2. Consider how management and investors use the financial information reported by a public company.

3. Recognize how different laws and monetary systems can affect the accounting activities of a global corporation.

SYNOPSIS

Collecting, analyzing, and reporting financial data from 27,000 restaurants in more than 100 countries is no easy task, as the accounting experts at McDonald's know all too well. Every month, the individual restaurants send their sales figures to be consolidated with data from other restaurants at the local or country level. From there, the figures are sent to country-group offices and then to one of three major regional offices before going to their final destination at the McDonald's headquarters in Oak Brook, Illinois. In the past, financial information arrived in Illinois in bits and pieces, sent by courier, mail, or fax. Today, local and regional offices log on to a special secure website and enter their month-end figures, enabling the corporate controller to quickly produce financial statements and projections for internal and external use.

Discussion Questions

1. *For analysis:* Why does McDonald's use "constant currency" comparisons when reporting its financial results?

2. *For analysis:* What types of assets might McDonald's list for depreciation in its financial statements?

3. *For application:* What effect do the corporate income tax rates in the countries where McDonald's operates have on the income statements prepared in local offices?

4. *For application:* What problems might arise if individual McDonald's restaurants were required to enter sales data directly on the company's centralized accounting website, instead of following the current procedure of sending it through country and regional channels?

5. *For debate:* To help investors and analysts better assess the company's worldwide financial health, should McDonald's be required to disclose detailed financial results for every country and region? Support your chosen position.

ONLINE EXPLORATION

Visit the McDonald's corporate website at www.mcdonalds.com/corporate, locate the most recent financial report (quarterly or annual), and examine both overall and regional results. What aspects of its results does McDonald's highlight in this report? What does McDonald's say about its use of constant currency reporting? Which regions are doing particularly well? Which are lagging? How does management explain any differences in performance? What does McDonald's say about its use of constant currency reporting?

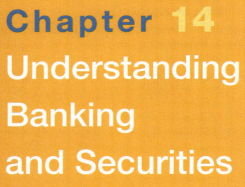

Chapter 14

Understanding Banking and Securities

LEARNING OBJECTIVES

After studying this chapter, you will be able to

1 Highlight the functions, characteristics, and common forms of money

2 Discuss the responsibilities and insurance methods of the FDIC

3 Discuss how industry deregulation and the repeal of the Glass-Steagall Act are affecting the banking industry

4 Differentiate among a stock's par value, its market value, and its book value

5 Highlight the distinguishing features of common stock, preferred stock, bonds, and mutual funds

6 Differentiate among an auction exchange, a dealer exchange, and an electronic communication network (ECN)

7 Explain how government regulation of securities trading tries to protect investors

Behind **the Scenes**

Schwab Puts It All Online

www.schwab.com

Charles Schwab is a trend-setter. When the SEC ended fixed-stock commissions in the 1970s, Schwab forged new ground by opening the discount brokerage house that now bears his name. Schwab's strategy: slash brokers' commissions, offer no-frills trading at a discount, and drive old-line firms out of business. When mutual funds became popular in the 1980s, the trendsetter revolutionized the mutual-fund industry by creating a mutual-fund supermarket. That is, investors could buy and sell hundreds of mutual funds in one account without incurring heavy fees.

First Charles Schwab grabbed huge chunks of market share from traditional brokers. Then it cleaned up in the discount and online markets. Now it's going after the full-service brokers—again.

In fact, Schwab has a history of making bet-the-company moves, but one move stands out in particular. When e-commerce took off in the mid-1990s, Schwab's co-CEO, David Pottruck, took a giant leap of faith. His strategy: leverage the power of the Internet and the company's nationwide network of customer centers to provide a convenient and economical way for investors to trade stocks.

Other brokerage houses were reluctant to follow in Schwab's e-commerce footsteps. They worried that moving securities trading to the Internet would cannibalize—even destroy—their traditional and lucrative businesses. But not Pottruck. Although the move would cut $150 million from expected revenue, he knew that offering both traditional trades and online trades (a strategy that came be to known as clicks-and-bricks) would eventually pay off. And it did.

Soon the company was bringing in client assets faster than any other discount or full-service U.S. brokerage: $51 billion in new-client assets poured into Schwab within a six-month period in 1998, and total customer accounts soon climbed from 3 million to over 6 million. That success jolted rival Merrill Lynch, the nation's largest full-service brokerage firm. In the past, Schwab had been little more than an annoyance to Merrill, the Wall Street titan. But once Schwab's total stock valuation passed that of Merrill's, the titan flexed its muscles and went after the trendsetter. Merrill Lynch matched Schwab's online trading fee, launched a website to rival Schwab's, and rolled out fee-based brokerage accounts.

At the turn of the 21st century, Schwab and Merrill's slugfest moved to a different arena when the dot-com bust sent the entire securities industry into a tailspin. With online trading falling off a cliff, Pottruck knew that it would take more than a slick website and discount trades to return the discount brokerage to its glory days. In fact, he announced that it was "time for Schwab to become pioneers again." But how? If you were David Pottruck, what would you do to gain more ground? What new services would you offer? What challenges would you expect to encounter en route?[1] ∎

MONEY AND FINANCIAL INSTITUTIONS

As David Pottruck knows, businesses and individuals have an abundance of options when it comes to investing money. They can deposit it in a bank account, purchase company stocks or bonds, or acquire real estate, artwork, or other assets that they hope will appreciate over time. This chapter discusses two investment options, banking and securities markets, starting with an explanation of the characteristics and types of money.

Following that is a look at common types of financial institutions, the services they provide, and the changing nature of the U.S. banking environment. The second half of the chapter explores three principal types of securities investments—stocks, bonds, and mutual funds—and discusses the types of securities markets where such investments are traded. The chapter concludes by looking at securities-trading procedures, performance barometers, and regulations.

Characteristics and Types of Money

money
Anything generally accepted as a means of paying for goods and services

Money is anything generally accepted as a means of paying for goods and services. To be an effective medium of exchange, money must have these important characteristics: It must be divisible, portable (easy to carry), durable, and difficult to counterfeit, and it should have a stable value. In addition, money must perform three basic functions: First, it must serve as a medium of exchange—a tool for simplifying transactions between buyers and sellers. Second, it must serve as a measure of value so that you don't have to negotiate the relative worth of dissimilar items every time you buy something. Finally, money must serve as a temporary store of value—a way of accumulating your wealth until you need it.

Paper money and coins are the most visible types of money, but money exists in a variety of forms, including

currency
Bills and coins that make up a country's cash money

demand deposit
Money that can be used by the customer at any time, such as checking accounts

time deposits
Bank accounts that pay interest and require advance notice before money can be withdrawn

- **Currency**: Coins, bills, traveler's checks, cashier's checks, and money orders
- **Demand deposit**: Money available immediately on demand, such as from checking accounts
- **Time deposits**: Accounts that pay interest and restrict the owner's right to withdraw funds on short notice, such as savings accounts, certificates of deposit, and money-market deposit accounts

Checking and Savings Accounts

checks
Written orders that tell the user's bank to pay a specific amount to a particular individual or business

Money you put into your checking account is a *demand deposit*, available immediately (on demand) through the use of **checks**, written orders that direct your bank to pay the stated amount of money to you or to someone else. Several types of checking accounts exist, each offering benefits in exchange for monthly fees, minimum account balances, or other requirements. For example, NOW (Negotiable Order of Withdrawal) checking accounts pay interest but limit the number of checks customers can write and impose a fee if the account balance falls below a minimum level.

You can also earn interest on the money you put in savings accounts. Originally, these accounts were known as *passbook savings accounts* because customers received a small passbook in which the bank recorded all deposits, withdrawals, and interest. Today, banks send out statements instead of passbooks, so these accounts have become known as *statement savings accounts*. In general, money in savings accounts can be withdrawn at any time, but certain types of savings accounts may require advance notice or impose withdrawal limits. For example, money in a *money-market deposit account* earns more interest, but you are allowed only a limited number of monthly withdrawals. Money held in a *certificate of deposit (CD)* earns an even higher interest rate, but you cannot withdraw the funds for a stated period, such as six months or more. If you want to make an early withdrawal from a CD, you will lose some or all of the interest you've earned.

Credit, Debit, and Smart Cards

credit cards
Plastic cards that allow the user to buy now and repay the loaned amount at a future date

For everyday access to short-term credit, banks and other institutions issue **credit cards**, plastic cards that entitle customers to make purchases now and repay the amount later. Credit cards are a popular substitute for currency and checks. Many credit card issuers charge an annual fee for Visa and MasterCard credit cards, and all charge interest on any unpaid credit card balance.

Surprise! You've Been Swiped

Thanks to some clever technology, thieves don't need to steal your credit card to steal your credit card information anymore. Using a technique called skimming, a thief steals card data by swiping the credit card through a small, hand-held magnetic card reader. The reader copies the card-holder's name, account number, and even the card valida-tion code—stored on the magnetic stripe—giving the counterfeiter all the data needed to create a perfect clone of the credit card. Readers can be purchased for as little as $100 over the Internet and are intended for legitimate use by banks, restaurants, retailers, and hotels. Unfortunately, some end up in the wrong hands.

Thieves and, increasingly, organized crime groups pay waiters and store clerks to steal information from credit cards using the concealed devices. By skimming 14 to 20 accounts, crooks can generate $50,000 to $60,000 worth of fraud that will probably go undiscovered until the victims get their bills—30 to 60 days after the crime. Moreover, skimmed data from, say, a customer in New York City or Washington can be e-mailed to Taiwan, Japan, or Europe and used for mail-order, telephone-order, or e-commerce overseas transactions within 24 to 48 hours of the theft. Professionals can even encode the stolen codes into a strip and use equipment to produce an electronically indistin-guishable counterfeit card.

While credit card issuers decline to say how much they are losing to skimmers—in part because they don't want to scare consumers out of using their plastic—industry ana-lysts estimate skimmers reap over $125 million annually. To curb the fraud, major credit card issuers are cooperating with the U.S. Secret Service to pool information about fraudulent transactions. For example, issuers can generate computer analyses that flag locations where numerous cards may have been skimmed. Or if someone in Hong Kong tries to buy something with a credit card that was used two hours earlier in Chicago, the computer will reject the transaction.

In the latest twist on skimming, thieves have begun attaching tiny memory devices to the card readers in gas pumps and privately owned ATMs (the type you often see in convenience stores). They sneak the recorder into the machine, temporarily wire it to the existing card reader, wait until it fills up with credit card data, then break into the machine again and retrieve the recorder.

What can you do to prevent your credit cards from get-ting skimmed? Not much, say experts, besides reading your bills closely, checking your accounts on the web or by phone during the month to make sure there are no surprises, and reporting improper charges promptly. Although you're not liable for fraudulent charges made to your accounts by skimmers or other scam artists, you do have to face the has-sle of getting the unauthorized transactions removed from your bills. Of course, you can always pay with old-fashioned cash. But if you carry lots of that around, you may have to worry about the old-fashioned robber.

Questions for Critical Thinking

1. To curb the abuse, why don't credit card issuers require customers to present additional personal validation data at the time of sale?
2. Why don't thieves skim debit cards too?

Credit cards have become immensely popular with consumers because they are convenient and allow people to postpone payment on purchases they make. They also help people manage their finances by either choosing to repay the full amount when they are billed or making small payments month by month until the debt has been repaid. Credit card companies make money by charging customers interest on their unpaid account balances and by charging businesses a processing fee, which can range from 2 to 5 percent of the value of each sales transaction paid by credit card. Nearly every store accepts credit cards, and mail-order merchants and Internet retailers are especially dependent on credit cards to facilitate purchases.

In addition to credit cards, many banks offer **debit cards**, plastic cards that function like checks in that the amount of a purchase is electronically deducted from the user's checking account and transferred to the retailer's account at the time of the sale. Debit cards are ideal for customers who must control their spending or stick to a budget. **Smart cards** are similar to debit cards; however, these plastic cards contain tiny com-puter chips that can store amounts of money (from the user's bank account) and selected data (such as shipping address, credit card information, frequent-flyer account numbers, health and insurance details, or other personal information). When a pur-chase is made, the store's equipment electronically deducts the amount from the value

debit cards
Plastic cards that allow the bank to take money from the user's demand-deposit account and transfer it to a retailer's account

smart cards
Plastic cards with embedded computer chips that store money drawn from the user's demand-deposit account as well as information that can be used for purchases

Technologies That Are Revolutionizing Business

Credit scoring software

Credit scoring software is a type of business intelligence software (see Chapter 6) that measures the credit worthiness of applications for credit cards, mortgages, and other forms of credit. It has the dual objective of filtering out applications that don't meet a lender's criteria while speeding up the process for applications that do meet the criteria. Most of these packages use variations on a scoring system originally developed by Fair Isaac Corporation.

How it's changing business

Using sophisticated mathematical models based on historical records, credit scoring software helps lenders decide which applicants to accept and how much credit to extend to each one. In addition, software with *predictive modeling* or *predictive analytics* helps predict which applicants will make the best customers (lowest risk and highest profit potential) for a given lender. For instance, customers who receive credit cards but never use them or who pay off their balance every month are less profitable than customers who tend to carry a balance and therefore pay interest charges every month. The software can also help detect fraudulent credit card applications, which cost card issuers $1 billion a year—a cost that gets passed on to consumers and businesses in the form of higher interest rates, higher fees, and tighter credit availability. Variations on credit scoring software are also used in the insurance industry to predict the likelihood that an applicant will file a claim in the future.

Where you can learn more

The details of the FICO model are confidential, but you can read more about the products offered by Fair Isaac at www.fairisaac.com. If you'd like to see what your own credit score is, you can buy a report at www.myfico.com.

stored on the smart card and reads and verifies requisite customer information. Users reload money from their bank accounts to their smart cards as needed.

Although popular in Europe, smart cards have been slow to catch on in the United States for two reasons: Low U.S. telephone rates (compared to those of European countries) make it affordable to verify credit card transactions over the phone, and it is not cost-effective for most U.S. businesses to replace current credit card infrastructures with smart-card readers and computer chip technology. Nevertheless, American Express has made inroads with its combination smart card and credit card, Blue. Designed to appeal to online shoppers, Blue comes with software and a small smart-card reader that plugs into the user's serial port. Customers who purchase online simply insert Blue into the reader and type in a password, and the digital information stored on the smart card tells the vendor the customer's credit card number, expiration date, and shipping address.[2]

Financial Institutions and Services

As a businessperson, you may or may not be responsible for writing company checks or investing a firm's money, but you will be receiving a paycheck and you will need to deposit that check into a financial institution or cash it so that you can pay your bills. In fact, no matter where in the world you live, work, or travel, today's businesses and individuals require a wide range of financial services.

Deposit and Nondeposit Financial Institutions

The types of services provided by a financial institution are generally governed by whether it is a *deposit institution* or *nondeposit institution*. Deposit institutions accept deposits from customers or members and offer checking and savings accounts, loans, and other banking services. Among the many deposit institutions are the following:

- *Commercial banks:* profit-oriented financial institutions that operate under state or national charters. Commercial banks make money by charging customers fees and higher interest rates on loans than the interest rates they pay on customers' deposits.

- *Thrifts, savings and loan associations* (which use most of their deposits to make home-mortgage loans), and *mutual savings banks* (which are owned by their depositors).

- *Credit unions:* nonprofit member-owned organizations that take deposits only from members, such as one company's employees or one union's members or another designated group. Credit unions generally pay favorable interest rates because they are tax-exempt institutions.

Nondeposit institutions offer specific financial services but do not accept deposits. Among the many nondeposit financial institutions are the following:

- *Insurance companies*, which provide insurance coverage for life, property, and other potential losses; they invest the payments they receive in real estate, in construction projects, and in other ways.
- *Pension funds*, which are set up by companies to provide retirement benefits for employees; money contributed by the company and its employees is put into securities and other investments.
- *Finance companies*, which lend money to consumers and businesses for home improvements, expansion, purchases, and other purposes.
- *Brokerage firms*, which allow investors to buy and sell stocks, bonds, and other investments; many also offer checking accounts, high-paying savings accounts, and loans to buy securities.

In the past, each financial institution focused on offering a particular set of financial services for specific customer groups. However, the competitive situation changed dramatically after the passage of the Depository Institutions Deregulation and Monetary Control Act of 1980. This law deregulated banking and made it possible for all financial institutions to offer a wider range of services—thereby blurring the line between banks and other financial institutions and encouraging more competition between different types of institutions.

Loans

Loans are one of the most important services financial institutions provide. Individuals usually apply for mortgage loans when they want to buy a home. They also look to banks and financial services firms for auto loans, home-improvement loans, student loans, and many other types of loans. Businesses rely on banks to provide loans for expansion, purchases of new equipment, construction or renovation of plants and facilities, or other large-scale projects. Some businesses obtain a working capital **line of credit**, which is an agreed-on maximum amount of money a bank is willing to lend to a business during a specific period of time, usually one year. Once a line of credit has been established, the business may obtain unsecured loans for any amount up to that limit, provided the bank has funds. The line of credit can be canceled at any time, so companies that want to be sure of obtaining credit when needed should arrange a revolving line of credit, which guarantees that the bank will honor the line of credit up to the stated amount.

line of credit
Arrangement in which the financial institution makes money available for use at any time after the loan has been approved

Electronic Banking

Most deposit institutions offer electronic banking services that may be conducted from sites other than the bank's physical location. For instance, all over the world, customers rely on **automated teller machines (ATMs)** to withdraw money from their demand-deposit accounts at any hour. Look around: ATMs are everywhere, from banks, malls, and supermarkets to airports, resorts, and tourist attractions. By linking with regional, national, and international ATM networks, banks let customers withdraw cash far from home, make deposits, and handle other transactions. To compete, more banks are jazzing up their ATMs. The latest ATMs are wired to the web and allow customers to pay insurance premiums and utility bills, print cashier's checks, and purchase stamps, movie tickets, ski lift tickets, DVDs, and even foreign currency.

automated teller machines (ATMs)
Electronic terminals that permit people to perform basic banking transactions 24 hours a day without a human teller

Electronic funds transfer systems (EFTS) are another form of electronic banking. These computerized systems allow users to conduct financial transactions efficiently from remote locations. More than one-third of all U.S. workers take advantage of EFTS when their employers use *direct deposit* to transfer wages directly into employees' bank accounts. This procedure saves employers and employees the worry and headache of handling large amounts of cash. Even the U.S. government uses EFTS for regular payments such as Social Security benefits.[3]

electronic funds transfer systems (EFTS)
Computerized systems for completing financial transactions

Electronic banking options such as ATMs offer speed and convenience, but many banks find that customers still want the personal communication offered by branches.

In addition to ATMs and EFTS, most major banks and many thrifts and community banks now offer Internet or online banking to accommodate the growing number of individuals and businesses that want to transfer money between accounts, check account balances, pay bills, apply for loans, and handle other transactions at any hour. Online banking is not only fast and easy for customers but also extremely cost-efficient for banks.[4] See "E-Business in Action" (pages 389–390) for more on the progress of online banking.

Bank Safety and Regulation

Banks are among the nation's most heavily regulated businesses. As many as 9,000 U.S. banks failed during the Depression years from 1929 to 1934. To restore public confidence in the banking system, the Banking Act of 1933 established the Federal Deposit Insurance Corporation (FDIC). The FDIC insures money on deposit in U.S. banks up to a maximum of $100,000 per account by collecting insurance premiums from member banks and depositing the premiums into the U.S. Treasury's Savings Association Insurance Fund (for thrifts) and Bank Insurance Fund (for commercial banks). Similar to the FDIC, the National Credit Union Association protects deposits in credit unions by collecting premiums from members and depositing them into funds.

In addition to FDIC protection against bank failure, a number of government agencies supervise and regulate banks and conduct periodic examinations to ensure that the bank is complying with regulations. State-chartered banks come under the watchful eyes of each state's banking commission; nationally chartered banks are under the federal Office of the Comptroller of the Currency; and thrifts are under the federal Office of Thrift Supervision. The overall health of the country's banking system is, ultimately, the responsibility of the Federal Reserve System, as Chapter 1 discusses.

The Evolving U.S. Banking Environment

Since the deregulation of the banking industry in 1980, the number of U.S. financial institutions has declined significantly. Today, the number of U.S. banks totals about 8,357 (a significant decline from the 14,146 main bank offices in 1934).[5] The decline is due in part to an increase in bank combinations, competitive pressure, and financial problems.

During the 1980s and 1990s, some U.S. banks, especially savings and loans, searched for higher profits by investing heavily in real estate and oil-drilling activities, by lending money to foreign governments, and by financing company buyouts. But when real estate markets collapsed, oil prices plummeted, and real estate developers went bankrupt, borrowers could not make payments on their bank loans. As a result, lending institutions were forced to close up shop or were taken over by stronger banks.

Also during that era, some U.S. banks sought strength, efficiency, and access to more customers by undergoing a series of mergers, acquisitions, and takeovers. Then, in 1999, Congress opened the floodgates for consolidation among banks, brokerage firms, and insurance companies by passing the 1999 Financial Services Modernization Act. This law repealed the Glass-Steagall Act (also known as the Banking Act of 1933) and portions of the 1956 Bank Holding Act, which for decades had kept banks out of the securities and insurance businesses. Originally enacted after the stock market crash of 1929 and the Great Depression, the Glass-Steagall Act was designed to restore confidence in U.S. financial houses by restricting investment banks and commercial banks from crossing into each others' businesses and potentially abusing their fiduciary duties at the expense of customers. Moreover, it ensured that a catastrophic failure in one part of the finance industry did not invade every other part, as it did in 1929. The 1956 Bank Holding Company Act restricted what banks could do in the insurance business.[6]

The repeal of the Glass-Steagall Act and the lifting of other bank restrictions have made it possible for banks to combine with other banks and insurance companies to create financial supermarkets. These mega-institutions offer customers a full range of services—from traditional loans to investment banking services to public stock offerings to insurance—blurring the line between bankers, brokers, and insurers. For example, Merrill Lynch and other major brokerage firms now offer federally insured interest-bearing savings and checking accounts among other bank products—in addition to securities trading.[7] E*Trade, which began as an online brokerage firm, has expanded its services to include banking. American Express has expanded beyond credit cards and now lends money to small businesses, and Charles Schwab has opened a mortgage bank.[8]

While some banks are focusing on becoming mega-institutions, others choose to remain comparatively smaller players. *Community banks* are smaller banks that concentrate on serving the needs of local consumers and businesses. Some community banks have multiple locations within a small, well-defined area. Others have expanded into new markets by opening branch operations or merging with banks across state lines. Such interstate operations were made possible by the Riegle-Neal Interstate Banking and Branching

Community bankers excel at personal service. They will meet with small-business owners and work with them on their business plan, and they will lend them money to help them grow their business to the next level.

Efficiency Act of 1994, a landmark law that reversed legislation dating back to 1927.[9] As a result, customers can now make deposits, cash checks, or handle any banking transaction in any branch of their bank, regardless of location.

TYPES OF SECURITIES INVESTMENTS

With the line between banks and brokerage houses such as Schwab blurring, consumers now have more options as to where they can purchase **securities**—stocks, bonds, and other investments—to meet their investment goals. Securities are traded in organized markets. Corporations sell stocks or bonds to finance their operations or expansion, while governments and municipalities issue bonds to raise money for building or public expenses—from national defense to road improvements. Here's a closer look at these three principal types of securities investments.

Stocks

As discussed in Chapter 4, a share of stock represents ownership in a corporation and is evidenced by a stock certificate. The number of stock shares a company sells depends on the amount of equity capital the company will require and on the price of each share it sells. A corporation's board of directors sets a maximum number of shares into which the business can be divided. In theory, all these shares—called **authorized stock**—may be sold at once. In practice, however, the company sells only a part of its authorized stock. The part sold and held by shareholders is called **issued stock**; the unsold portion is called **unissued stock**. From time to time a company may announce a **stock split**, in which it increases the number of shares that each stock certificate represents while proportionately lowering the value of each share. Companies generally use a stock split to make the share price more affordable. For instance, if a company with 1 million shares outstanding and a stock price of $50 per share announces a two-for-one split, it is doubling the number of shares. After the split, the company will have 2 million shares outstanding, and each original share will become two shares worth $25 each.

When stock is first issued, the company assigns a **par value**, or dollar value, to the stock primarily for bookkeeping purposes. Par value is also used to calculate dividends (for certain kinds of stock). Keep in mind that par value is not the same as the stock's *market value*, the price at which a share currently sells, or its *book value*, the amount of net assets of a corporation represented by one share of common stock.

securities
Investments such as stocks, bonds, options, futures, and commodities

authorized stock
Maximum number of ownership shares into which a corporation's board of directors decides the business can be divided

issued stock
Portion of authorized stock sold to and held by shareholders

unissued stock
Portion of authorized stock not yet sold to shareholders

stock split
Increase in the number of shares of ownership that each stock certificate represents, at a proportionate drop in each share's value

par value
As shown on the stock certificate, a value assigned to a stock for use in bookkeeping and in calculating dividends

Stock certificates represent a share of ownership of a company.

Common Stock

Most investors buy common stock, which represents an ownership interest in a publicly traded corporation. As Chapter 4 points out, shareholders of this class of stock vote to elect the company's board of directors, vote on other important corporate issues, and receive dividend payments from the company's profits. But they have no say in the day-to-day business activities. Still, common shareholders have the advantage of limited liability if the corporation gets into trouble, and as part owners, they share in the fortunes of the business and are eligible to receive dividends as long as they hold the stock. In addition, common shareholders stand to make a profit if the stock price goes up and they sell their shares for more than the purchase price. The reverse is also true: Shareholders of common stock can lose money if the market price drops and they sell the stock for less than they paid for it.

Preferred Stock

Investors who own preferred stock, the second major class of stock, enjoy higher dividends and a better claim (after creditors) on assets if the corporation fails. The amount of the dividend on preferred stock is printed on the stock certificate and set when the stock is first issued. If interest rates fluctuate, the market price of preferred stock will go up or down to adjust for the difference between the market interest rate and the stock's dividend. Preferred stock often comes with special privileges. *Convertible preferred stock* can be exchanged, if the shareholder chooses, for a certain number of shares of common stock issued by the company. *Cumulative preferred stock* has an additional advantage: If the issuing company stops paying dividends for any reason, the dividends on these shares will be held (accumulate) until preferred shareholders have been paid in full—before common stockholders are paid.

Bonds

Unlike stock, which gives the investor an ownership stake in the corporation, bonds are debt financing. A **bond** is a method of raising money in which the issuing organization borrows from an investor and issues a written pledge to make regular interest payments and then repay the borrowed amount later. When you invest in this type of security, you are lending money to the company, municipality, or government agency that issued the bond. Bonds are usually issued in multiples of $1,000, such as $5,000, $10,000, and $50,000. Also like stocks, bonds are evidenced by a certificate, which shows the issuer's name, the amount borrowed (the **principal**), the date this principal amount will be repaid, and the annual interest rate investors receive.

The interest is stated in terms of an annual percentage rate but is usually paid at six-month intervals. For example, the holder of a $1,000 bond that pays 8 percent interest due January 15 and July 15 could expect to receive $40 on each of those dates. A look at the financial section of any newspaper will show that some corporations sell new bonds at an interest rate two or three percentage points higher than that offered by other companies. Yet the terms of the bonds seem similar. Why? Because bonds are not guaranteed investments. The variations in interest rates reflect the degree of risk associated with the bond, which is closely tied to the financial stability of the issuing company. Agencies such as Standard & Poor's (S&P) and Moody's rate bonds on the basis of the issuers' financial strength. Exhibit 14.1 shows that the safest corporate bonds are rated AAA (S&P) and Aaa (Moody's). Low-rated bonds, known as *junk bonds*, pay higher interest rates to compensate investors for the higher risk.

bond
Method of funding in which the issuer borrows from an investor and provides a written promise to make regular interest payments and repay the borrowed amount in the future

principal
Amount of money a corporation borrows from an investor through the sale of a bond

BellSouth Telecommunications Bond Certificate
1. *Name of corporation issuing bond*
2. *Type of bond (debenture)*
3. *Face value of the bond*
4. *Annual interest rate (8.25%)*
5. *Maturity date (due 2032)*

Exhibit 14.1 Corporate Bond Ratings

Standard & Poor's (S&P) and Moody's Investors Service are two companies that rate the safety of corporate bonds. When its bonds receive a low rating, a company must pay a higher interest rate to compensate investors for the higher risk.

S&P	INTERPRETATION	MOODY'S	INTERPRETATION
AAA	Highest rating	Aaa	Prime quality
AA	Very strong capacity to pay	Aa	High grade
A	Strong capacity to pay; somewhat susceptible to changing business conditions	A	Upper-medium grade
BBB	More susceptible than A-rated bonds	Baa	Medium grade
BB	Somewhat speculative	Ba	Somewhat speculative
B	Speculative	B	Speculative
CCC	Vulnerable to nonpayment in default	Caa	Poor standing; may be in default
CC	Highly vulnerable to nonpayment	Ca	Highly speculative; often in default
C	Bankruptcy petition filed or similar action taken	C	Lowest rated; extremely poor chance of ever attaining real investment standing
D	In default		

Corporate Bonds

Companies issue a variety of corporate bonds. **Secured bonds** are backed by company-owned property (such as airplanes or plant equipment) that will pass to the bondholders if the issuer does not repay the amount borrowed. *Mortgage bonds*, one type of secured bond, are backed by real property owned by the issuing corporation. **Debentures** are unsecured bonds, backed only by the corporation's promise to pay. Because debentures are riskier than other types of bonds, investors who buy these bonds receive higher interest rates. **Convertible bonds** can be exchanged at the investor's option for a certain number of shares of the corporation's common stock. Because of this feature, convertible bonds generally pay lower interest rates.

U.S. Government Securities and Municipal Bonds

Just as corporations raise money by issuing bonds, so too do federal, state, city, and local governments and agencies. As an investor, you can buy a variety of U.S. government securities, including three types of bonds issued by the U.S. Treasury, U.S. savings bonds, and bonds issued by various U.S. municipalities.

Treasury bills (also referred to as *T-bills*) are short-term U.S. government bonds that are repaid in less than one year. Treasury bills are sold at a discount and redeemed at face value. The difference between the purchase price and the redemption price is, in effect, the interest earned for the time periods. **Treasury notes** are intermediate-term U.S. government bonds that are repaid from 1 to 10 years after they were initially issued. **Treasury bonds** are long-term U.S. government bonds that are repaid more than 10 years after they were initially issued. Both treasury notes and treasury bonds pay a fixed amount of interest twice a year. But in general, U.S. government securities pay lower interest than corporate bonds because they are considered safer: There is very little risk that the government will fail to repay bondholders as promised. Another benefit is that investors pay no state or local income tax on interest earned on these bonds. Also, these bonds can easily be bought or sold through the Treasury or in organized securities markets.

A traditional choice for many individual investors, **U.S. savings bonds** are issued by the U.S. government in amounts ranging from $50 to $10,000. Investors who buy

secured bonds
Bonds backed by specific assets that will be given to bondholders if the borrowed amount is not repaid

debentures
Corporate bonds backed only by the reputation of the issuer

convertible bonds
Corporate bonds that can be exchanged at the owner's discretion into common stock of the issuing company

Treasury bills
Short-term debt securities issued by the federal government; also referred to as *T-bills*

Treasury notes
Debt securities issued by the federal government that are repaid within 1 to 10 years after issuance

Treasury bonds
Debt securities issued by the federal government that are repaid more than 10 years after issuance

U.S. savings bonds
Debt instruments sold by the federal government in a variety of amounts

Series EE savings bonds pay just 50 percent of the stated value and receive the full face amount in as little as 17 years (the difference being earned interest). Once the bond's face value equals its redemption value, the bond continues to earn interest but only until 30 years after the bonds were issued (the bond's final maturity date). Other savings bonds are Series HH, which can be bought only by exchanging Series EE bonds, and Series I, which pay interest indexed to the inflation rate.

municipal bonds
Bonds issued by city, state, and government agencies to fund public services

general obligation bond
Municipal bond that is backed by the government's authority to collect taxes

revenue bond
Municipal bond backed by revenue generated from the projects it is financing

capital gains
Return that investors receive when they sell a security for a higher price than the purchase price

mutual funds
Financial organization pooling money to invest in diversified blends of stocks, bonds, or other securities

Municipal bonds (often called *munis*) are issued by states, cities, and special government agencies to raise money for public services such as building schools, highways, and airports. Investors can buy two types of municipal bonds: general obligation bonds and revenue bonds. A **general obligation bond** is a municipal bond backed by the taxing power of the issuing government. When interest payments come due, the issuer makes payments out of its tax receipts. In contrast, a **revenue bond** is a municipal bond backed by the money to be generated by the project being financed. As an example, revenue bonds issued by a city airport are paid from revenues raised by the airport's operation. To encourage investment, the federal government doesn't tax the interest that investors receive from municipal bonds. Also exempt from state income tax is the interest earned on municipal bonds that are issued by the governments within the taxpayer's home state. However, **capital gains**—the return investors get from selling a security for more than its purchase price—are taxed at both the federal and state levels.

Mutual Funds

Mutual funds are financial organizations that pool money from many investors to buy a diversified mix of stocks, bonds, or other securities. Charles Schwab helped make this type of investment popular when the company launched its OneSource no-fee mutual-fund supermarket in 1992. Mutual funds are particularly well suited for investors who wish to spread a fixed amount of money over a variety of investments and do not have the time or experience to search out and manage investment opportunities. *No-load funds* charge no fee to buy or sell shares, whereas *load funds* charge investors a commission to buy or sell shares. The most common types of loads are front end (assessed when you purchase the fund) and back end (assessed when you sell the fund).

Investment companies offer two types of mutual funds. An *open-end fund* issues additional shares as new investors ask to buy them. In essence, the fund's books never close. The number of shares outstanding changes daily as investors buy new shares or redeem old ones. These shares aren't traded in a separate market. *Closed-end funds*, on the other hand, raise all their money at once by distributing a fixed number of shares that trade much like stocks on major security exchanges. As soon as a certain number of shares are sold, the fund closes its books.

money-market funds
Mutual funds that invest in short-term securities and other liquid investments

Various mutual funds have different investment priorities. Among the most popular mutual funds are **money-market funds**, which invest in short-term securities and other liquid investments. *Growth funds* invest in stocks of rapidly growing companies. *Income funds* invest in securities that pay high dividends and interest. *Balanced funds* invest in a carefully chosen mix of stocks and bonds. *Sector funds* (also known as *specialty* or *industry funds*) invest in companies within a particular industry. *Global funds* invest in foreign and U.S. securities, whereas *international funds* invest strictly in foreign securities. And *index funds* buy stocks in companies included in specific market averages, such as the Standard & Poor's 500. You can buy shares in mutual funds through your broker or directly from the mutual-fund company.

For years, individual investors viewed mutual funds as a relatively safe and easy way to invest in the stock market, but that perception took a significant hit in 2003 when two types of widespread trading abuses came to light. The first is called *market timing*, in which a large shareholder in a mutual fund jumps in and out of the fund, trying to profit from short-term movements in the price. While this practice isn't illegal, it's unfair to smaller investors because fund managers can't manage their assets as effectively when huge sums of money are moving in and out of the fund on short notice. Moreover, although many mutual fund companies officially forbid it, the SEC discovered that half of the 88 largest fund companies were allowing it for selected customers.[10]

The second abuse, known as either *late trading* or *stale pricing*, occurs when fund managers let favored clients (usually wealthy individuals or institutions) essentially buy or sell shares in a fund after 4:00 P.M., when trading officially stops and the fund's price is fixed until the following day. The reason such moves are illegal and unfair to other investors in the fund is that these late traders can act on financial news that breaks after the 4:00 P.M. deadline, while still getting that day's price. In other words, these late traders can act on events that happen in the evening, while everyday investors are locked out until markets open the next day.

For example, on October 16, 2002, the stock market dropped a considerable amount, and the price of stock mutual funds, reflecting those price declines, declined as well. However, after closing time, IBM announced surprisingly good earnings news. Knowing that mutual funds would shoot up the next morning, Canary Capital Partners (one of the firms at the center of the scandal) loaded up on shares of a Bank of America mutual fund to which it had special access. Just like clockwork, Canary made a bundle as soon as the market opened the following day.[11]

After a whistle-blower at Canary tipped off the New York state attorney general's office, an investigation revealed that 25 percent of large fund companies had been allowing late trading. The investigation continues, but a number of people have been arrested already and regulators have assessed nearly $2 billion in fines.[12] The mutual-fund industry as a whole, which has enjoyed six decades of fairly lax oversight from Congress and the SEC, is likely to find itself under much closer scrutiny in the future.[13] How long will it take for investors to regain confidence in the markets after yet another scandal? That's anybody's guess.

SECURITIES MARKETS

Stocks and bonds are bought and sold in two kinds of marketplaces: primary markets and secondary markets. Newly issued shares or initial public offerings (IPOs) are sold in the **primary market**. Once these shares have been issued, subsequent investors can buy and sell them in the organized **secondary market** known as **stock exchanges** (or *securities exchanges*).

Securities Exchanges

The New York Stock Exchange (NYSE), also known as the "Big Board," is the world's largest securities exchange. The stocks and bonds of about 3,000 companies, with a combined market value topping $16 trillion, are traded on the exchange's floor.[14] After the NYSE, some of the largest stock exchanges are located in Tokyo, London, Frankfurt, Paris, Toronto, and Montreal. Many companies list their securities on more than one securities exchange. Thus, NYSE-listed stocks can also be bought and sold at one or more of the U.S. regional exchanges, such as the Pacific or Philadelphia exchanges, or in the *over-the-counter market*.

The **over-the-counter (OTC) market** consists of a network of registered stock and bond representatives who are spread out across the United States—and in some cases around the world. Most use a nationwide computer network owned by the National Association of Securities Dealers (NASD). This network is called **NASDAQ (National Association of Securities Dealers Automated Quotations)**, and it is the second-largest stock market in the United States. In 1998 NASD (owners of NASDAQ) acquired the American Stock Exchange (the world's third-largest auction exchange), making NASDAQ an even stronger competitor to the New York Stock Exchange.[15]

primary market
Market where firms sell new securities issued publicly for the first time

secondary market
Market where subsequent owners trade previously issued shares of stocks and bonds

stock exchanges
Location where traders buy and sell stocks and bonds

over-the-counter (OTC) market
Network of dealers who trade securities on computerized linkups rather than a trading floor

NASDAQ (National Association of Securities Dealers Automated Quotations)
National over-the-counter securities trading network

More than 3,000 companies trade their stock on the NASDAQ exchange, including such well-known firms as Merrill Lynch, 1-800-Flowers.com, Microsoft, and Apple Computer.

auction exchange
Centralized marketplace where securities are traded by specialists on behalf of investors

stock specialist
Intermediary who trades in a particular security on the floor of an auction exchange; "buyer of last resort"

dealer exchanges
Decentralized marketplaces where securities are bought and sold by dealers out of their own inventories

Exhibit 14.2

Old and New Ways to Buy Stocks

Some think that floor trading will become a thing of the past as electronic communication networks become increasingly popular.

How to Buy and Sell Securities

The process for buying and selling securities varies according to the type of exchange. As Exhibit 14.2 depicts, in an **auction exchange**, such as the New York Stock Exchange, all buy and sell orders (and all information concerning companies traded on that exchange) are funneled onto an auction floor. There, buyers and sellers are matched by a **stock specialist**, a broker who occupies a post on the trading floor and conducts all the trades in specific stocks via a central clearinghouse. If buying or selling imbalances occur in that stock, a specialist can halt trading to prevent the price from plunging without adequate cause. Specialists can also sell stock to customers out of their own inventory.[16] In contrast, a **dealer exchange**, such as NASDAQ, has no central marketplace for making transactions. Instead, all buy and sell orders are executed through

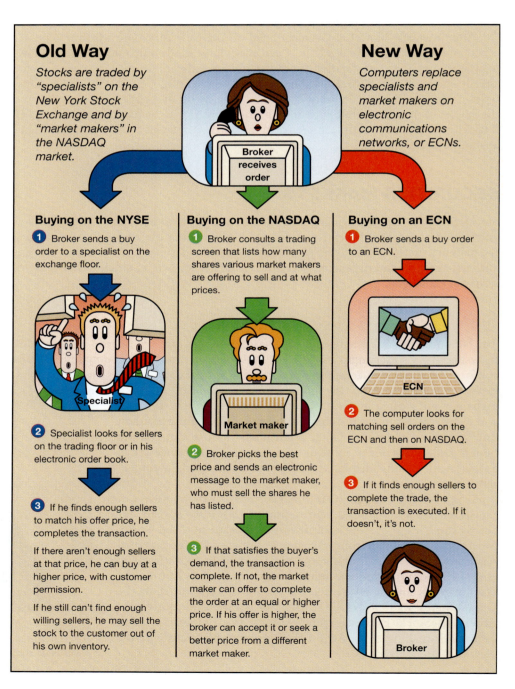

Old Way

Stocks are traded by "specialists" on the New York Stock Exchange and by "market makers" in the NASDAQ market.

New Way

Computers replace specialists and market makers on electronic communications networks, or ECNs.

Broker receives order

Buying on the NYSE

1 Broker sends a buy order to a specialist on the exchange floor.

Specialist

2 Specialist looks for sellers on the trading floor or in his electronic order book.

3 If he finds enough sellers to match his offer price, he completes the transaction.

If there aren't enough sellers at that price, he can buy at a higher price, with customer permission.

If he still can't find enough willing sellers, he may sell the stock to the customer out of his own inventory.

Buying on the NASDAQ

1 Broker consults a trading screen that lists how many shares various market makers are offering to sell and at what prices.

Market maker

2 Broker picks the best price and sends an electronic message to the market maker, who must sell the shares he has listed.

3 If that satisfies the buyer's demand, the transaction is complete. If not, the market maker can offer to complete the order at an equal or higher price. If his offer is higher, the broker can accept it or seek a better price from a different market maker.

Buying on an ECN

1 Broker sends a buy order to an ECN.

ECN

2 The computer looks for matching sell orders on the ECN and then on NASDAQ.

3 If it finds enough sellers to complete the trade, the transaction is executed. If it doesn't, it's not.

Broker

computers by **market makers**, registered stock and bond representatives who sell securities out of their own inventories.

Electronic communication networks (**ECNs**) use the Internet to link buyers and sellers. Frequently referred to as a virtual stock market, or cybermarket, ECNs have no exchange floors, specialists, or market makers. In fact, they are nothing more than computer networks with software programs that match buy and sell orders directly, cutting out the once-dominant market makers and specialists. Keep in mind that even though a company's stock is listed on an auction or dealer exchange, its shares may also be traded on an ECN. For instance, many brokerage firms use a combination of auction exchanges, dealer exchanges, and ECNs to execute their trades. In fact, more than a third of NASDAQ shares are traded on ECNs.[17]

Securities Brokers

Regardless of when, where, or how you trade securities, you must execute all trades by using a securities broker. Currently, individuals cannot interact with securities marketplaces or ECNs directly; purchases must be made through traditional stockbrokers—although some hope this will change soon.[18]

A **broker** is an expert who has passed a series of formal examinations and is legally registered to buy and sell securities on behalf of individual and institutional investors. As an investor, you pay *transaction costs* for every buy or sell order, to cover the broker's commission, which varies with the type of broker and the size of your trade: A *full-service broker* provides financial management services such as investment counseling and planning; a *discount broker* provides fewer or limited services and generally charges lower commissions than a full-service broker. Still, some discount brokers offer a range of services and resources that include free or low-cost research, customized tracking of securities, e-mails confirming trades, and electronic newsletters packed with investment advice.

Orders to Buy and Sell Securities

Before you start to trade, take time to think about your objectives, both long-term and short-term. Next, look at how various securities match your objectives and your attitude toward risk, because investing in stocks and bonds can involve potential losses, as many investors in recent years have been painfully reminded. Finally, consider the many ways you can have your broker buy or sell securities:

A **market order** tells the broker to buy or sell at the best price that can be negotiated at the moment. A **limit order** specifies the highest price you are willing to pay when buying or the lowest price at which you are willing to sell. A **stop order** tells the broker to sell if the price of your security drops to or below the price you set, protecting you from losing more money if prices are dropping. You can also place a time limit on your orders. An **open order** instructs the broker to leave the order open until you cancel it. A **day order** is valid only on the day you place it and should not be confused with a *day trader*, a stock trader who holds positions for a very short time (minutes to hours) and closes out these positions within the same day.

If you have special confidence in your broker's ability, you may place a **discretionary order**, which gives the broker the right to buy or sell your securities at the broker's discretion. In some cases, discretionary orders can save you from taking a loss, because the broker may have a better sense of when to sell a stock. If the broker's judgment proves wrong, however, you cannot hold the broker legally responsible for the consequences, so investigate your broker's background and think carefully before you give anyone the right to trade your securities.

Investors sometimes borrow cash to buy stocks, a practice known as **margin trading**. Instead of paying for the stock in full, you borrow some of the money from your stockbroker, paying interest on the borrowed money and leaving the stock with the broker as collateral. As we mentioned in Chapter 1, the Federal Reserve Board establishes margin requirements. Be aware, however, that margin trading increases risk. If the price of a stock you bought on margin goes down, you will have to give your broker more

market makers
Registered representatives who trade securities from their own inventories on dealer exchanges, making a ready market for buyers and sellers

electronic communication networks (ECNs)
Internet-based networks that match up buy and sell orders without using an intermediary

broker
An expert who has passed specific tests and is registered to trade securities for investors

market order
Authorization for a broker to buy or sell securities at the best price that can be negotiated at the moment

limit order
Market order that stipulates the highest or lowest price at which the customer is willing to trade securities

stop order
An order to sell a stock when its price falls to a particular point to limit an investor's losses

open order
Limit order that does not expire at the end of a trading day

day order
Any order to buy or sell a security that automatically expires if not executed on the day the order is placed

discretionary order
Market order that allows the broker to decide when to trade a security

margin trading
Borrowing money from brokers to buy stock, paying interest on the borrowed money, and leaving the stock with the broker as collateral

Put Your Money Where Your Mouse Is

The Internet has been hailed as the great equalizer between individual investors and Wall Street. Today's investors have access to a staggering amount of valuable information and investment tools—many of which are used by Wall Street professionals. But having access to information is one thing; using it wisely is another. So before you put money into any investment, learn as much as possible about the market, the security, its issuer, and its potential. Here are some tips to point you in the right direction.

For "how-to" advice, try the Motley Fool (www. fool.com), Quicken's financial site (www.quicken.com/investments), or *CNN/Money*'s website (http://money.cnn.com). For the latest online news and commentary about stocks, check out The Street (www.thestreet.com), CBS Market Watch (www. marketwatch.com), and Jag Notes (www.jagnotes.com). Be sure to research individual companies using your favorite search engine; stop by each company's website to read its press releases and financial statements. You can burrow even further into potential investments using these websites:

- Corporate financial data filed with the SEC (www. freeedgar.com)
- Morningstar mutual fund reports (www.morningstar. com)
- Bond prices and market performance (www.investing inbonds.com)

Before you invest real money, construct a hypothetical portfolio on Quicken, Yahoo!, or another financial website and watch how your investments fare. Track your favorite market index on MSN MoneyCentral (http://moneycentral. msn.com), and compare it to your personal investment portfolio. Are your proposed investments meeting, missing, or beating the market index?

Now you're in a better position to buy securities, but your research shouldn't end here. Even after you start trading, you need to stay on top of the latest news and industry developments that can affect the securities in which you have invested. And if a potential investment seems too good to be true, point your web browser to the North American Securities Administrators Association (www.nasaa.org) and get some tips on investment fraud. Remember, when it comes to investments, your web surfing can really pay off.

Questions for Critical Thinking

1. Why is it important to learn about a company's financial results and background before buying its stock or bonds?
2. What are the disadvantages of searching for investment information on the Internet?

---

money or the broker will sell your stock. Such forced sales can cause prices to fall even further, triggering a vicious cycle of sales and margin calls.[19]

If you believe that a stock's price is about to drop, you may choose a trading procedure known as **short selling**. With this procedure, you sell stock you borrow from a broker in the hope of buying it back later at a lower price. After you return the borrowed stock to the broker, you keep the price difference. For example, you might decide to borrow 25 shares that are selling for $30 per share and sell short because you think the share price is going to plummet. When the stock's price declines to $15, you buy 25 shares on the open market and make $15 profit on every share (minus transaction costs). Selling short is risky. If the stock had climbed to $32, you would have had to buy shares at that higher price, even though you would be losing money.

short selling
Selling stock borrowed from a broker with the intention of buying it back later at a lower price, repaying the broker, and keeping the profit

How to Analyze Financial News

Regardless of which trading procedures you use, you will want to monitor financial news sources to see how your investments are doing. Start with daily newspaper reports on securities markets. Other sources include newspapers aimed specifically at investors (such as *Investor's Business Daily* and *Barron's*) and general-interest business publications that follow the corporate world and give hints about investing (such as the *Wall Street Journal, Forbes, Fortune,* and *Business Week*). Standard & Poor's, Moody's Investor Service, and Value Line also publish newsletters and special reports on securities. Online sources include your brokerage firm's website plus a growing number of excellent financial websites listed in "Put Your Money Where Your Mouse Is."

What types of financial information should you be looking for? First, you want to determine the general direction of stock prices. If stock prices have been rising over a long period, the industry and the media will often describe this situation as a **bull market**. The reverse is a **bear market**, one characterized by a long-term trend of falling prices. You can see these broad market movements in Exhibit 14.3. Once you have the general picture, look at the timing. Has a bull market lasted for too long, suggesting that stocks are over-valued and a *correction* (tumbling prices) might be imminent? Also watch the volume of shares traded each day. If the stock market is down on heavy volume (that is, if prices are moving downward and a lot of trading is going on), investors may be trying to sell before prices go down further—a bearish sign.

bull market
Rising stock market

bear market
Falling stock market

Watching Market Indexes and Averages

One way to determine whether the market is bullish or bearish is to watch **market indexes** and averages, which use the performance of a representative sampling of stocks, bonds, or commodities as a gauge of broader market activity. The most famous U.S. stock average is the Dow Jones Industrial Average (DJIA), which tracks the prices of 30 *blue-chip* or well-established stocks, each representing a particular sector of the U.S. economy. Critics say the Dow is too narrow and too susceptible to short-term swings, lacks the right stocks, and gives too much weight to higher-priced shares. But advocates say the Dow's 30 stocks serve as a general barometer of market conditions, and the composition of the index is shuffled from time to time to reflect changes in the overall economy (for instance, such rising stars as Microsoft, Intel, and Home Depot were added in recent years).[20]

market indexes
Measures of market activity calculated from the prices of a selection of securities

Exhibit 14.3 **The Stock Market's Ups and Downs**

The peaks and valleys on this chart represent swings in the Dow Jones Industrial Average, the most widely used indicator of U.S. stock prices.

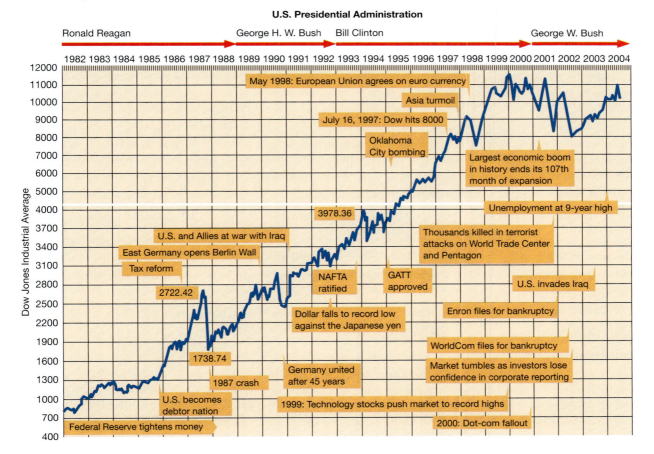

Another widely watched index is the Standard & Poor's 500 Stock Average (S&P 500), which tracks the performances of 500 corporate stocks, many more than the DJIA. This index is weighted by market value, not by stock price, so large companies carry far more weight than small companies.[21] The Wilshire 5000 Index, which actually covers some 7,000 stocks, is the broadest index measuring U.S. market performance. To get a sense of how technology stocks are doing, check the NASDAQ Composite Index, covering more than 3,000 over-the-counter stocks, including many high-tech firms. You can also look at indexes to learn about the performance of foreign markets, such as Japan's Nikkei 225 Index and the United Kingdom's FT-SE 100 Index.

Interpreting the Financial News

In addition to watching market trends, you will want to follow the securities you own and others that look like promising investments. For stocks, you can turn to the stock exchange report in major daily newspapers. Exhibit 14.4 shows how to read this report, which includes high and low prices for the past 52 weeks, the number of shares traded (volume), and the change from the previous day's closing price. U.S. securities markets began quoting security prices in decimals (dollars and cents) in 2000. Prior to that year,

---

Exhibit 14.4 **How to Read a Newspaper Stock Quotation**

Even before you invest, you will want to follow the latest quotations for your stock. This table shows you how to read the newspaper stock quotation tables.

(1)		(2)	(3)	(4)	(5)	(6)	(7)	(8)		(9)	(10)
52-WEEK HIGH	52-WEEK LOW	STOCK	SYM	DIV	YLD %	PE	VOL 100S	HI	LOW	LAST	NET CHG
43.84	34.45	JPMorgan Chase	JPM	1.37	3.6	20	9282	38.18	37.03	38.10	+0.61
47.94	22.25	Maytag	MYG	.72	2.3	33	9027	31.48	29.40	31.36	+1.16
39.50	23.53	Neiman Marc	NMGA	...	...	18	4217	27.03	23.75	27.03	+2.15
21.96	10.06	Office Depot	ODP	...	...	15	33898	12.80	11.05	12.77	+0.98

1. **52-week high/low:** Indicates the highest and lowest trading price of the stock in the past 52 weeks plus the most recent week but not the most recent trading day (adjusted for splits). Stocks are quoted in dollars and cents. In most newspapers, boldfaced entries indicate stocks whose price changed by at least 4% but only if the change was at least 75 cents a share.

2. **Stock:** The company's name may be abbreviated. A capital letter usually means a new word. In this example, Neiman Marc is Neiman Marcus.

3. **Symbol:** Symbol under which this stock is traded on stock exchanges.

4. **Dividend:** Dividends are usually annual payments based on the last quarterly or semiannual declaration, although not all stocks pay dividends. Special or extra dividends or payments are identified in footnotes.

5. **Yield:** The percentage yield shows dividends as a percentage of the share price.

6. **PE:** Price-to-earnings ratio, calculated by dividing the stock's closing price by the earnings per share for the latest four quarters.

7. **Volume:** Daily total of shares traded, in hundreds. A listing of 888 indicates 88,800 shares were traded during that day.

8. **High/Low:** The stock's highest and lowest price for that day.

9. **Last:** Closing price of the stock that day.

10. **Net change:** Change in share price from the close of the previous trading day.

Common Stock Footnotes: d—new 52-week low; n—new; pf—preferred; s—stock split or stock dividend of 25 percent or more in previous 52 weeks; u—new 52-week high; v—trading halted on primary market; vi—in bankruptcy; x—ex dividend (the buyer won't receive a recently declared dividend, but the seller will)

(1) COMPANY	(2) CUR YLD	(3) VOL	(4) CLOSE	(5) NET CHG
NYTel 6 1/8 10	6.6	11	93.40	−.25
PacBell 6 1/4 05	6.4	10	98.40	+.25
Safwy 9 7/8 07	8.4	20	117.50	+3.60
StoneC 11 1/4 06	11.1	24	103.50	−1.10
TimeWar 9 1/8 13	8.3	30	109.75	−.50

1. **Company:** Name of company issuing the bond, such as New York Telephone, and bond description, such as 6 1/8 percent bond maturing in 2010.

2. **Current Yield:** Annual interest of $1,000 bond divided by the closing price shown. The yield for New York Telephone is $61.25 + $933.75 = 0.06559, or approximately 6.6 percent.

3. **Volume:** Number of bonds traded (in thousands) that day.

4. **Close:** Price of the bond at the close of the last day's business.

5. **Net change:** Change in bond price from the close of the previous trading day.

Exhibit 14.5

How to Read a Newspaper Bond Quotation

When newspapers carry bond quotations, they show prices as a percentage of the bond's value, which is typically $1,000.

prices were quoted in fractions as small as 1/16. Using decimals in trading makes stock prices easier for many investors to understand. Moreover, quoting shares down to the penny permits stocks to be priced in smaller increments.[22]

Included in the stock exchange report is the **price-earnings ratio**, or *p/e ratio* (also known as the *price-earnings multiple*), which is computed by dividing a stock's market price by its *prior* year's earnings per share. Some investors also calculate a forward p/e ratio using *expected* year earnings in the ratio's denominator. Bear in mind that if a stock's p/e ratio is well below the industry norm, either the company is in trouble or it's an undiscovered gem with a relatively low stock price. For more detailed data on a stock, consult the company's annual reports or documents filed with the Securities and Exchange Commission (SEC).

To follow specific bonds, check the bond quotation tables in major newspapers (see Exhibit 14.5). When reading these tables, remember that the price is quoted as a percentage of the bond's value. For example, a $1,000 bond shown closing at 65 actually sold at $650.

Newspapers and business publications also include tables of price quotations for investments such as mutual funds, commodities, options, and government securities (see Exhibit 14.6). These same publications also carry news about current challenges the securities industry is facing, securities regulations, reported frauds, and proposals to improve investor protection.

price-earnings ratio
Ratio calculated by dividing a stock's market price by its prior year's earnings per share

Industry Challenges

Securities marketplaces are facing a number of challenges today. Until recently, big Wall Street firms have lived with costly stock exchange floors, specialists, and market makers because the system worked well enough. But now these systems are under attack. As the chairman of the NASD puts it, "the old methods of exchanging stocks no longer meet the needs of the investing consumer."[23] Discount brokers, ECNs, large securities institutions such as Merrill Lynch and Goldman Sachs (which are investing in ECNs), and consumers are pushing traditional securities exchanges to offer electronic trading options within their exchanges.[24] As a result, the NYSE recently rolled out Direct Plus, which automatically executes trading orders for up to 2,099 shares—80 percent of all transactions—in five seconds.[25] Moreover, some of Wall Street's largest brokers are lobbying the SEC to adopt a sweeping new market system that includes a central display of all stock quotes.[26]

Exhibit 14.6 How to Read a Newspaper Mutual Fund Quotation

A mutual fund listing shows the new asset value of one share (the price at which one share is trading) and the change in trading price from one day to the next.

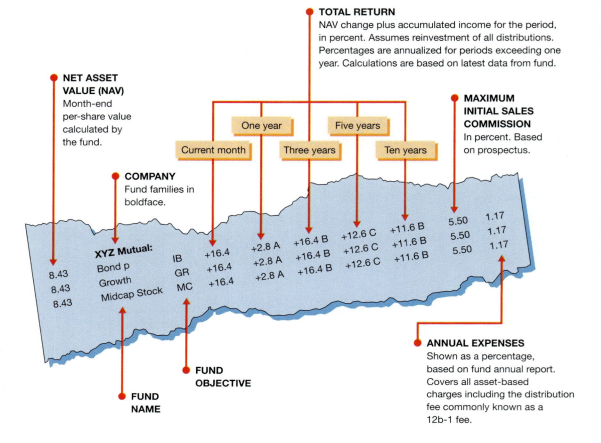

TOTAL RETURN
NAV change plus accumulated income for the period, in percent. Assumes reinvestment of all distributions. Percentages are annualized for periods exceeding one year. Calculations are based on latest data from fund.

NET ASSET VALUE (NAV)
Month-end per-share value calculated by the fund.

MAXIMUM INITIAL SALES COMMISSION
In percent. Based on prospectus.

One year   Five years

Current month   Three years   Ten years

COMPANY
Fund families in boldface.

XYZ Mutual:
Bond p   IB   +16.4   +2.8 A   +16.4 B   +12.6 C   +11.6 B   5.50   1.17
Growth   GR   +16.4   +2.8 A   +16.4 B   +12.6 C   +11.6 B   5.50   1.17
Midcap Stock   MC   +16.4   +2.8 A   +16.4 B   +12.6 C   +11.6 B   5.50   1.17

8.43
8.43
8.43

FUND NAME

FUND OBJECTIVE

ANNUAL EXPENSES
Shown as a percentage, based on fund annual report. Covers all asset-based charges including the distribution fee commonly known as a 12b-1 fee.

The push toward round-the-clock trading is another challenge securities markets are facing. Extending traditional trading hours of 9:30 A.M. to 4:00 P.M. (Eastern U.S. time zone) by adding early morning and late-night trading sessions is the next revolution sweeping Wall Street. *After-hours trading* or *extended-hours trading* refers to the purchase and sale of publicly traded stocks after the major stock markets, such as the NYSE and NASDAQ, close. Many securities exchanges now offer after-hours trading via ECNs that typically operate from 8:00 A.M. to 9:15 A.M. and 4:15 P.M. to 7:00 or 8:00 P.M., although some operate 24 hours a day. The biggest advantage to extended-hours trading is that it accommodates traders who live in regions outside the Eastern U.S. time zone. The biggest disadvantage, however, is lack of volume. Most institutional investors close up shop after the NYSE closing bell. Nonetheless, to remain competitive, many traditional securities exchanges have already extended their traditional trading hours.[27]

Online trading is another phenomenon that has revolutionized the securities industry, as the Charles Schwab chapter-opening vignette shows. When online trading first became popular in the 1990s, many full-service brokerages such as Merrill Lynch resisted offering such services because they worried about losing their lucrative commissions. But now, most full-service firms offer some form of online trading to remain competitive in the marketplace.

Investors who choose online trading execute their trades via a brokerage firm's website instead of phoning a firm's brokers. Convenience, control, and lower commissions are the main advantages of online trading. Still, online trading is not for everyone. When you trade online, you trade alone, with no one to check for mistakes or offer advice. Moreover, online trading websites have had their share of problems. The top five consumer complaints filed with the SEC against online brokers include (1) failure to process orders or delays in executing orders, (2) difficulty in accessing one's account or contacting a broker, (3) errors in processing orders, (4) execution of orders at higher prices than posted on the website, and (5) errors and omissions in account records and documents.[28]

Regulation of Securities Markets

Whether you buy and sell securities online or use a traditional full-service house, your trades are governed by a network of state and federal laws. Combined with industry self-regulation, these laws are designed to ensure that you and all investors receive accurate information and that no one artificially manipulates the market price of a given security. Trading in stocks and bonds is monitored by the Securities and Exchange Commission. In addition, the SEC works closely with the stock exchanges and NASD to police securities transactions and maintain the system's integrity. As recent scandals have shown, however, even all these watchdog efforts can't always catch people who are determined to manipulate the market in some way.

SEC Filing Requirements

Companies must meet certain requirements (which include filing a blizzard of registration papers and reports) to be listed on any stock exchange (see Exhibit 14.7). Similarly, brokers must operate according to the rules of the exchanges, rules that are largely

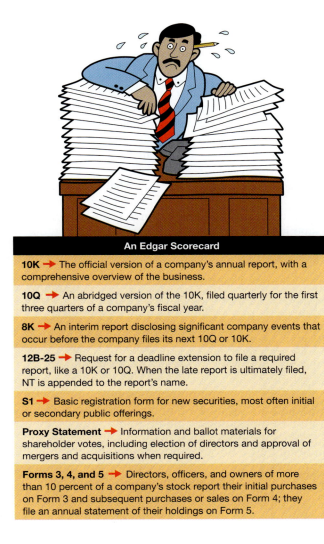

An Edgar Scorecard

10K ➡ The official version of a company's annual report, with a comprehensive overview of the business.

10Q ➡ An abridged version of the 10K, filed quarterly for the first three quarters of a company's fiscal year.

8K ➡ An interim report disclosing significant company events that occur before the company files its next 10Q or 10K.

12B-25 ➡ Request for a deadline extension to file a required report, like a 10K or 10Q. When the late report is ultimately filed, NT is appended to the report's name.

S1 ➡ Basic registration form for new securities, most often initial or secondary public offerings.

Proxy Statement ➡ Information and ballot materials for shareholder votes, including election of directors and approval of mergers and acquisitions when required.

Forms 3, 4, and 5 ➡ Directors, officers, and owners of more than 10 percent of a company's stock report their initial purchases on Form 3 and subsequent purchases or sales on Form 4; they file an annual statement of their holdings on Form 5.

Exhibit 14.7

An Edgar Scorecard

To successfully navigate the Securities and Exchange Commission's Edgar database of corporate filings, it helps to know the most common filings required of publicly traded companies and their content.

designed to protect investors. Overseeing all these details keeps the SEC very busy indeed. Every year the SEC screens over 15,200 annual reports, 40,000 investor complaints, 14,000 prospectuses (a legal statement that describes the objectives of a specific investment), and 6,500 proxy statements (a shareholder's written authorization giving someone else the authority to cast his or her vote). The agency's website contains a mountain of public documents that investors can browse, download, or print to learn more about publicly traded companies.[29]

Regulation Fair Disclosure

Regulation Fair Disclosure (FD) was adopted by the SEC in 2000 to create a level playing field for all investors. Specifically, the regulation mandates that any news with the potential to affect the price of a stock must be released to everyone simultaneously. In other words, the regulation prohibits companies from "selectively disclosing" important information (such as earnings estimates) to big institutional shareholders and Wall Street analysts ahead of regular investors. Otherwise, early news recipients would be able to "make a profit or avoid a loss at the expense of those kept in the dark."[30]

In spite of its good intentions, the regulation could have unintended consequences, say critics. Some worry that instead of giving small and large investors equal access to market-sensitive information, the regulation could cut down on the amount of information received by everyone. Part of the problem stems from the fact that the SEC has not clearly defined what it means by *market-sensitive* information, so companies are opting to err on the side of silence. Moreover, some companies claim it's too difficult to give small investors the same level of information that they have selectively provided to investment analysts.[31]

Business BUZZ

Pump and Dump: An illegal stock manipulation maneuver in which a small group of people buy a stock, "pump" the price up by talking it up enthusiastically in chat rooms and other web forums, wait until enough receptive listeners jump on the bandwagon to push the price up, then "dump" it by selling out before the price inevitably falls again

Securities Fraud

The combination of a "get-rich" mindset and the huge number of people now investing online has resulted in a rise in the number of Internet stock scams. Today, with just an e-mail address list and a message-board alias or two, penny-stock promoters can dupe tens of thousands (if not millions) of investors by making false claims about a company, watching investors eager to make a fast profit pump up the company's stock price, then selling or dumping their penny shares at inflated prices and pocketing a handsome profit.

In fact, the problem has become so pervasive that the Department of Justice, the FTC, the U.S. Attorney's offices, and even the FBI have stepped up efforts to police such fraud. Even NASD has developed an Internet search engine to find phrases such as "too good to be true," and it monitors securities chat forums for fraudulent or misleading

---

Exhibit 14.8

10 Questions to Ask Before You Invest

You can avoid getting taken in an online stock scam by asking yourself these 10 questions before you invest.

1. Is the investment registered with the SEC and your state's securities agency?
2. Have you read the company's audited financial statements?
3. Is the person recommending this investment a registered broker?
4. What does the person promoting the investment have to gain?
5. If the tip came from an online bulletin board or e-mail, is the author identifiable or using an alias? Is there any reason to trust that person?
6. Are you being pressured to act before you can evaluate the investment?
7. Does the investment promise you'll get rich quick, using words like "guaranteed," "high return," or "risk free"?
8. Does the investment match your objectives? Could you afford to lose all of the money you invest?
9. How easy would it be to sell the investment later? Remember, stocks with fewer shares are easy for promoters to manipulate and hard for investors to sell if the price starts falling.
10. Does the investment originate overseas? If yes, beware: It is tougher to track money sent abroad and harder for burned investors to have recourse to justice.

information.[32] As an investor, your best defense against fraud is to carefully research securities before you buy and to steer clear of any investment that seems too good to be true (see Exhibit 14.8).

Two particular forms of securities fraud making the headlines today are insider trading and accounting fraud. **Insider trading** occurs when people buy or sell a stock based on information that is not available to the general public, such as a company merger or new discovery. Insider trading can produce big profits for the unscrupulous, but it can also claim many victims. Acquisition companies, for example, are forced to pay higher-than-expected premiums to buy a target company when leaks trigger a run-up in the target's stock price. And shareholders who rely on the integrity of corporate executives can lose billions while company insiders and their associates profit from the information.

Accounting trickery is another form of securities fraud, as Chapter 13 points out. In fact, the unusually high number of companies engaging in accounting tricks and fraud at the turn of this century has not only kept regulators busy but taken its toll on U.S. securities markets and the global economy.

Learning from Business Blunders

Oops: You know that e-commerce has truly spanned the globe when you can get scammed out of money from halfway around the world. Anyone with an e-mail account has probably seen the Nigerian investment scam. Someone claiming to be connected to somebody connected to the Nigerian government or the national oil company claims to have a way to shuttle millions of dollars out of the country if only you'll provide some up-front money to shake the whole thing loose. Sounds crazy, but the scheme has already defrauded hopeful e-mail recipients out of more than $100 million in the United States alone. One retired man from Florida shelled out more than $300,000 before he realized he'd been had.

What You Can Learn: If it sounds too good to be true, it is. This rule applies in the stock market, in the grocery market—pretty much anywhere on planet Earth. If you're ever tempted by this or any other investment pitch, stop and ask yourself a couple of questions: (1) Why are they offering this to *me*, out of the 5 or 6 billion people in the world? (2) What would have to happen for me to make any money from this deal? If you can't make the connection between your investment and the promised payoff, that's a good sign there won't be one.

---

insider trading
Use of nonpublic information to make an investment profit

Summary of Learning Objectives

1 Highlight the functions, characteristics, and common forms of money.

Money functions as a medium of exchange, a measure of value, and a store of value. It must be divisible, portable, durable, stable, and difficult to counterfeit. Common forms of money include currency, such as coins, bills, traveler's checks, cashier's checks, and money orders; demand deposits, such as checking accounts; and time deposits, such as savings accounts, certificates of deposit, and money-market deposit accounts.

2 Discuss the responsibilities and insurance methods of the FDIC.

The Federal Deposit Insurance Corporation is a federal insurance program that protects deposits in member banks. Banks pay premiums to the FDIC, which insures funds on deposit with a particular bank for up to $100,000 in case of bank failure. The FDIC supervises the Bank Insurance Fund, which covers deposits in commercial banks and savings banks, and the Savings Association Insurance Fund, which covers deposits in savings and loan associations.

3 Discuss how deregulation and the repeal of the Glass-Steagall Act are affecting the banking industry.

Deregulation and the repeal of the Glass-Steagall Act are fueling a raft of megamergers among banks, insurance companies, and brokerage firms and increasing the competition among these institutions. As a result, the line between the types of financial services offered by banks, securities brokers, and insurance companies is blurring. Meanwhile, community banks are stepping in to fill a void created by bank consolidations by focusing on the needs of local customers (generally, small businesses).

4 Differentiate among a stock's par value, its market value, and its book value.

Par value is the dollar value assigned to a stock for book-keeping and for dividend calculations. Market value is the price at which a share of stock is currently selling. Book value is the portion of a corporation's net assets represented by a single share of common stock.

5 Highlight the distinguishing features of common stock, preferred stock, bonds, and mutual funds.

Common stock gives shareholders an ownership interest in the company, the right to elect directors and vote on important issues, and the chance to earn dividends and share in the fortunes of the company—while limiting the shareholder's liability to the price paid for the shares. Preferred stock gives shareholders a higher dividend than common stock and a preferred claim over creditors if the corporation fails. Special types of preferred stock have certain privileges. Bonds are long-term loans investors make to the issuing entity in return for a stated interest amount. The loan or principal is paid back to the bondholder over the life of the bond. Bonds may be secured, unsecured, or convertible. They may be issued by corporations or federal, state, city, and local agencies. Mutual funds are pools of money drawn from many investors to buy a variety of stocks, bonds, and other marketable securities. The primary benefit of this investment is diversification.

6 Differentiate among an auction exchange, a dealer exchange, and an electronic communication network (ECN).

Auction exchanges such as the New York Stock Exchange funnel all buy and sell orders into one centralized location. Dealer exchanges such as NASDAQ are decentralized marketplaces in which dealers, known as market makers, are connected electronically to handle buy and sell orders without a single, centralized trading floor. Electronic computerized networks (ECNs) match buy and sell orders directly (cutting out the market makers and specialists); ECNs operate globally, and they operate economically.

7 Explain how government regulation of securities trading tries to protect investors.

The government tries to prevent fraud in the securities markets by requiring companies to file registration papers, fulfill certain requirements, and file periodic information reports so that investors receive accurate information. Government regulations also control the listing of companies on stock exchanges and prohibit such fraudulent acts as improper release of information, insider trading, stock scams, and other acts designed to deceive investors.

Behind **the Scenes**

Transforming the Trendsetter

Facing increased competition from rival Merrill Lynch, a stock market tailspin at the turn of the century, and defection of wealthier customers to firms that offered a full range of services and advice, Schwab set out to once again rewrite the rules on Wall Street. From now on it would target more profitable customers—those with $500,000 to $5 million to invest. Schwab would advise on trades, not just execute them, and the company would provide other investment services for a fee.

In May 2000, the company purchased U.S. Trust Co., an old-line money-management firm, for $3.2 billion. The acquisition gave Schwab a toehold in providing advice to the wealthy. Then David Pottruck set out to turn Schwab into a full-service brokerage by adding such services as wireless trading, account management, strategic investment advice, financial planning, portfolio evaluations, and new online research tools that let customers take investment courses and hear live audio feeds of lectures. For a flat fee (based on a percentage of assets), Schwab's Private Client customers could meet face-to-face (or by phone) with an adviser to work out a personal investment plan. In keeping with Schwab's tradition, however, the advisers did not actually manage the client's money or decide what customers should buy and sell. They simply provided investment advice.

Schwab's new advice-based services were taking off when the firm was thrown off course. The financial aftershocks of the September 11, 2001, terrorist attacks and a wave of corporate scandals sent consumer confidence and securities markets into a nosedive. It was time for Pottruck to rewrite the rules on Wall Street—again.

Turning Wall Street's woes into a competitive advantage, he launched an aggressive marketing campaign with hard-hitting print and TV ads that emphasized rivals' shortcomings. The ads explained that unlike competitors, Schwab's brokers weren't paid based on how much they encouraged customers to trade. Nor was Schwab tied to big corporate clients via investment banking relationships. The ads also promoted Schwab's new stock-rating system—one that used a sophisticated, unbiased, in-house computer model to generate stock picks and that rated an equal number of stocks as buys as it did sells. Pottruck believed that this computerized approach would appeal to customers who had lost faith in the advice of brokers driven by commissions or investment-banking relationships.

Whether Schwab can successfully evolve into a "different kind" of full-service firm remains to be seen. "The changes we're making are profound," admits Pottruck. We are "retesting what the company stands for." Still, he knows that changing the company's image as a discount broker to one that provides investment advice worth listening to will require much more than an expensive marketing campaign and a new stock-rating system. For one thing, competition in the field of investment advice is fierce. For another, the company must train employees who were hired mainly as order takers to become qualified financial advisers. Moreover, by offering investment advice, Schwab is putting its relationship with thousands of independent advisers at risk. These independent advisers use Schwab to process their trades and provide custody for their clients' funds.

Unfortunately for David Pottruck, he will have to view Schwab's progress from the outside. After several disagreements with the company's board of directors, he was replaced as CEO in 2004 when Charles Schwab came out of semi-retirement to retake the reins.

Whether the challenges are internal or external, however, Schwab is willing to face them head on to gain ground. After all, Schwab has a history of zigging when everyone else zags. Time and again, Charles Schwab's rivals have dismissed the firm's ideas as impractical or unnecessary. And time and again, the firm has wrought major changes in the way Wall Street operates.[33]

Critical Thinking Questions

1. How and why has Charles Schwab continually reinvented itself?
2. Why did Pottruck decide to morph Schwab into a full-service firm?
3. What risks is Schwab taking by adding new services and targeting wealthier clients?

LEARN MORE ONLINE

Visit the corporate website of Charles Schwab by going to Chapter 14 of this text's website at www.prenhall.com/bovee, and clicking on the Charles Schwab hotlink. Review the website. What is Schwab's point of view on evaluating stocks? What makes Schwab different from other brokerage houses? ∎

Key Terms

auction exchange (374)
authorized stock (369)
automated teller machines (ATMs) (367)
bear market (377)
bond (370)
broker (375)
bull market (377)
capital gains (372)
checks (364)
convertible bonds (371)
credit cards (364)
currency (364)
day order (375)
dealer exchange (374)
debentures (371)
debit cards (365)
demand deposit (364)
discretionary order (375)
electronic communication networks (ECNs) (375)

electronic funds transfer systems (EFTS) (367)
general obligation bond (372)
insider trading (383)
issued stock (369)
limit order (375)
line of credit (367)
margin trading (375)
market indexes (377)
market makers (375)
market order (375)
money (364)
money-market funds (372)
municipal bonds (372)
mutual funds (372)
NASDAQ (National Association of Securities Dealers Automated Quotations) (373)
open order (375)
over-the-counter (OTC) market (373)

par value (369)
price-earnings ratio (379)
primary market (373)
principal (370)
revenue bond (372)
secondary market (373)
secured bonds (371)
securities (369)
short selling (376)
smart cards (365)
stock exchanges (373)
stock specialist (374)
stock split (369)
stop order (375)
time deposits (364)
Treasury bills (371)
Treasury bonds (371)
Treasury notes (371)
unissued stock (369)
U.S. savings bonds (371)

Test Your Knowledge

Questions for Review

1. How do credit cards, debit cards, and smart cards work?
2. What are examples of deposit and nondeposit financial institutions?

3. What are the differences between a Treasury bill, a Treasury note, a U.S. savings bond, a general bond, and a revenue bond?
4. What happens during a 2-for-1 stock split?

5. What is the function of the Securities and Exchange Commission?

Questions for Analysis

6. How can smaller community banks compete with large commercial banks?
7. What are some of the advantages of mutual funds?
8. When might an investor sell a stock short? What risks are involved in selling short?
9. How are the Internet and e-commerce redefining the banking and investment industry?
10. **Ethical Considerations.** You work in the research-and-development department of a large corporation and have been involved in a discovery that could lead to a new, profitable product. News of the discovery has not been made public. Is it legal for you to buy stock in the company? Now assume the same scenario but you talk to your friend about your discovery while dining at a restaurant. The person at the next table overhears the conversation. Is it legal for the eavesdropper to buy the company's stock before the public announcement of the news?

Questions for Application

11. What are the advantages and disadvantages of using cash, checks, credit cards, and debit cards to pay for goods and services?
12. If you were thinking about buying shares of AT&T, under what circumstances would you place a market order, a limit order, an open order, and a discretionary order?
13. **Integrated.** Besides watching market indexes, which economic statistics discussed in Chapter 1 might investors want to monitor? Why?
14. **Integrated.** Look back at Chapter 6 and review the discussion of mission statements. Suppose you were thinking about purchasing 100 shares of common stock in General Electric. Why might you want to first review the company's mission statement? What would you be looking for in the company's mission statement that could help you decide whether or not to invest?

Practice Your Knowledge

Sharpening Your Communication Skills

Interviewing a broker is one of the most important steps you can take before hiring that broker to execute your trades or manage your funds and investment portfolio. Practice your communication skills by developing two sets of questions:

1. Questions you might ask a stockbroker to help you decide whether you would use his or her services.
2. Questions you might pose to that broker to help you evaluate the merits of purchasing a specific security.

Building Your Team Skills

You and your team are going to pool your money and invest $5,000. Before you plunge into any investments, how can you prepare yourselves to be good investors? First, consider your group's goals. What will you and your teammates do with any profits generated by your investments? Once you have agreed on a goal for your team's profits, think about how much money you will need to achieve this goal and how soon you want to achieve it.

Next, think about how much risk you personally are willing to take to achieve the goal. Bear in mind that safer investments generally offer lower returns than riskier investments—and certain investments, such as stocks, can lose money. Now hold a group discussion to find a level of risk that feels comfortable for everyone on your team.

Once your team has decided how much risk to take, consider which investments are best suited to your group's goals and chosen risk level. Will you choose stocks, bonds, a combination of both, or other securities? What are the advantages and disadvantages of each type of investment for your team's situation? Then come to a decision about specific investment opportunities—particular stocks, for example—that your group would like to investigate further.

Compare your group's goal, risk level, and investment possibilities with those of the other teams in your class and discuss the differences and similarities you see.

Expand Your Knowledge

Discovering Career Opportunities

Think you might be interested in a job in the securities and commodities industry? This industry has one of the most highly educated and skilled workforces of any industry. And the requirements for entry are high—most brokerage clerks have a college degree. Log on to the Bureau of Labor Statistics, Career Guide to Industries, at www.bls.gov/oco.cg, and click on Financial and Insurance, then click on

Securities and Commodities. Read the article, then answer these questions:

1. What are the licensing and continuing education requirements for securities brokers?
2. What is the typical starting position for many people in the securities industry?
3. What factors are expected to contribute to the projected long-term growth of this industry?

Developing Your Research Skills

Since the turn of the century, the stocks of several high-profile companies, such as Tyco, Enron, and WorldCom, tumbled following their disclosures of negative company information. Use computer resources or business journals to find a company whose disclosure of negative information dramatically affected its securities. Then perform some research on that company so you can answer the following questions:

1. On what exchanges do the company's shares trade and under what ticker symbol?

2. What negative information did the company disclose? When? Did the company commit a fraudulent act? How did the information affect the company as a whole?

3. How did the negative information impact the company's securities? What was the company's stock price prior to the release of the negative information? Following the release of the information? What was the stock's 52-week high and low during the year the disclosure was made?

4. How did the DJIA and NASDAQ perform on the day the negative information was made public?

SEE IT ON THE WEB

For live links to the websites that follow, go to this text's website at www.prenhall.com/bovee. When you log on, select Chapter 14, then select "Featured Websites," click on the URL of the website you wish to visit, review the website, and answer the following questions:

1. What is the purpose of this website?

2. What kinds of information does this website contain? Please be specific.

3. How is the information provided at this website useful for businesspeople? Consumers?

4. How did you expand your knowledge of banking and securities markets by reviewing the material at this website? What new things did you learn about these topics?

Tour the U.S. Treasury

Take a virtual tour of the U.S. Treasury at www.ustreas.gov and click on Education to visit the Learning Vault. Once you're inside the vault, read about the duties and functions of the U.S. Treasury, explore the fact sheets, and discover how money gets into circulation. Then explore this department from the inside out by clicking on the Site Index and following the links. Do you know how many notes a day the Bureau of Engraving and Printing (BEP) produces? Do you know how long $10 billion would last if you spent one dollar every second of every day? To find out, fol-low the link to BEP and brush up on your money facts. www.ustreas.gov

Stock Up at the NYSE

Tour the New York Stock Exchange at www.nyse.com. Visit the trading floor and learn about the hectic pace of trading. Find out why having a seat doesn't necessarily mean you'll have a chance to sit down. Listen in on a stock transaction and discover how a stock is bought and sold. Learn how investors are protected and how unusual stock transactions are spotted. Get the latest market information as well as a historical perspective of the exchange. www.nyse.com

Invest Wisely—Like a Fool

Here's a fun securities website you can fool around at for a while. Visit the Motley Fool and don't be afraid to ask a foolish investment question or two. (The idea of an investing Fool is somebody who's not afraid to ask tough questions of the rich and powerful.) Roll up your sleeves and do a little work on your own. Discover the strategies, ideas, and information needed to make investment decisions at Fool's School. Learn the steps to investing foolishly. Read the investing basics and learn how to value stocks, analyze stocks, or pick a stockbroker. Expand your knowledge of stocks, bonds, and mutual funds. Finally, discover the keys to successful investing. www.fool.com

Companion Website

Learning Interactively

Go to the Companion Website at www.prenhall.com/bovee. For Chapter 14, take advantage of the interactive "Study Guide" to test your knowledge of the chapter. Get instant feedback on whether you need additional studying.

Also, visit this site's "Study Hall," where you'll find an abundance of valuable resources that will help you succeed in this course.

Video **Case**

Learn More to Earn More with Motley Fool

LEARNING OBJECTIVES

The purpose of this video is to help you:

1. Identify the wide variety of investments available to individuals.
2. Describe the process by which securities are bought and sold.
3. Recognize the risks involved in commodities and other investments.

SYNOPSIS

Despite new reports about lottery winners and others who have become millionaires overnight, individuals have a better chance of getting rich if they learn to select investments that are appropriate for their long-term financial goals. Experts advise looking for investments that will beat inflation and keep up with or—ideally—beat general market returns. Individuals can invest in preferred or common stock, newly issued stock from initial public offerings (IPOs), managed or index mutual funds, bonds, or commodities. These investments are far from risk-free, however; commodities and IPOs can be particularly risky. Therefore, individuals should become educated about securities and investment strategies by surfing Web sites such as the Motley Fool (www.fool.com).

Discussion Questions

1. *For analysis:* Why is the Securities and Exchange Commission concerned about stock rumors that circulate on the Internet?

2. *For analysis:* Why do Motley Fool's experts advise individuals to invest in index funds rather than in actively managed mutual funds?
3. *For application:* What should you consider when deciding whether to buy and sell stock through a broker, through a web-based brokerage, or directly through the company issuing the stock?
4. *For application:* If you were about to retire, why might you invest in preferred stock rather than common stock?
5. *For debate:* Should stock rumors that circulate on the Internet be covered by the individual's constitutional right to freedom of speech rather than being regulated by the SEC? Support your chosen position.

ONLINE EXPLORATION

Mutual funds that seek out environmentally and socially conscious firms in which to invest are becoming more popular because they offer investors a way to earn returns that don't offend their principles. Investigate the following websites: www.socialfunds.com, www.ethicalfunds.com, and www.domini.com. What types of firms does each fund avoid? What type does each prefer to invest in? Would you choose one of these funds if you wanted to invest in a mutual fund? Explain your answer.

E-Business in Action

INTERNET BANKS HIT A BRICK WALL

When online-only banks began popping up in the late 1990s, many believed they would revolutionize retail banking. Lower transaction costs, no physical building costs, and smaller staffs than physical banks meant that online banks could afford to offer customers higher interest rates on deposits, little or no transaction fees, and lower interest rates on loans. Furthermore, customers could bank at home 24 hours a day, seven days a week. They could move money from a savings account to a checking account—or even into the stock market—whenever they pleased. But the promise that banking customers would flock to online banks and abandon traditional banks never quite materialized. Online *banking* has taken off like a wildfire in the past few years, but most of the business has been won by traditional banks such as Bank of America and Wells Fargo, not by online-only start-ups.

Tough Sell

Why didn't online banks take off as some expected? As with a number of new Internet-only businesses, online banks faced these roadblocks:

- *Lack of name recognition.* To attract new customers, online banks launched their e-businesses with expensive marketing campaigns, eliminating much of the Internet cost advantage.

- *No in-person service.* Customers appreciated the cost advantages online banks offered, but without branches, many online banks lacked a concrete place for customers to resolve problems. Customers wanted the assurance that someone was there (in person) if they needed help.

- *Limited services.* Customers still needed to venture into the physical world to get services online banks did not offer: ATMs, safe deposit boxes, or business loans. Moreover, without access to a network of ATMs, customers faced hefty ATM fees and were required to deposit money into their accounts by mail.

To overcome these challenges, some online banks got physical by opening service centers, setting up kiosks, and establishing ATM networks. Others offered rebates on ATM surcharges their customers paid to other banks. Still others, such as Juniper Financial, formed alliances with stores such as Mail Boxes Etc. (now known as The UPS Store) so customers could deposit checks nationwide. But these actions were not enough to fend off the awakening giants.

Bricks-and-Mortar Banks Wake Up

Rather than give traditional (bricks-and-mortar) banks a run for their money, online banks gave them ideas. Some traditional banks established partnerships with key online players or swallowed them up altogether. Others, such as Bank One, established their own virtual banks—keeping them separate entities. But in spite of their efforts, few traditional banks generated profits from their online banking ventures. Online-only banking did not reach the mass appeal needed to justify the huge investment and operating costs involved. So most traditional banks eventually folded their online ventures into the parent organization. For instance, in 2001 WingspanBank.com, Bank One's highly publicized online venture, was folded into the parent organization. And customers of Security First Network Bank became a part of RBC Centura, a North Carolina-based physical bank.

From Competitive Edge to Commodity

The playing field has changed considerably since virtual banking first emerged. Online banking has moved from becoming a competitive edge to a commodity. Today, roughly 40 million U.S. households do at least some of their banking online, and online banking continues to grow rapidly. More than half of all banks offer some form of online banking services, such as money transfer, bill payment, loan applications, and account management. Some, such as Citibank, allow customers to set up a personal account and aggregate all the services they use into one webpage interface at the My Citi site.

Online-only banks didn't disappear entirely, of course, and several still compete with better rates on savings deposits than their bricks-and-mortar competitors frequently offer. However, in a slightly surprising twist, even as online banking becomes ever more popular, so do physical bank branches. The top six U.S. banks built more than 500 new branches in 2004 alone. It seems U.S. consumers like to have their cake and eat it too, which could be the ultimate reason that Internet banks never quite revolutionized the banking business the way many people predicted.[34]

Questions for Critical Thinking

1. What challenges did online-only banking face in the competitive banking environment, and what steps did they take to overcome these challenges?

2. Why did most pure Internet banks close up or fold into their parent organizations?

3. What banking services, if any, do you perform online? What do you like and dislike about banking online?

BUSINESS PlanPro Exercises

Developing Marketing Strategies to Satisfy Customers

Review Appendix D, Your Business Plan (on pages 416–417), to learn how to use Business PlanPro Software so you can complete these exercises.

THINK LIKE A PRO

Objective: By completing these exercises you will become acquainted with the sections of a business plan that address a company's financial and operational projections. You will use the sample business plan for Fantastic Florals (listed as Import—Artificial Flowers in the Sample Plan Browser) in this exercise.

1. Identify the source(s) Fantastic Florals will use to fund its start-up costs. Why is it important to indicate how much start-up money will be used to fund assets versus expenses?

2. Review the financial assumptions, sales tables and graphs, and other financial information included in the Fantastic Florals plan. Assuming the financial projections are on target, would an investment of $75,000 for a 20 percent ownership stake in the company be prudent? Explain your answer. Which financial statement(s) did you use to make your decision?

3. Examine the company's projected gross margin for the years covered by the plan. How does Fantastic Florals' gross margin compare with the industry profile? How might a potential investor view this comparison?

CREATE YOUR OWN BUSINESS PLAN

Return to the plan you are developing for your own business. How will you categorize your revenue and expense items? Will you break down your sales by product type, by service, or by location? What general operating and product-related expenses will you incur? Set up your basic revenue and expense categories and build the framework for your profit and loss statement. How do the categories in your plan compare to those used by Fantastic Florals?

Appendix B
The U.S. Legal System

The U.S. Legal System

Throughout this textbook, you encountered a number of regulatory agencies, such as the FDA, FTC, EPA, and SEC, whose function is to protect society from the potential abuses of business. Federal, state, and local governments work in numerous ways to protect both individuals and other businesses from corporate wrongdoing. Laws also spell out accepted ways of performing many essential business functions—along with the penalties for failing to comply. In other words, like the average person, companies must obey the law or face the consequences.

As you read this material, keep in mind that many companies conduct business overseas. Thus, in addition to knowing U.S. laws, these companies must also be familiar with **international law**, the principles, customs, and rules that govern the relationships between sovereign states and international organizations and persons.[1] Successful global business requires an understanding of the domestic laws of trading partners as well as of established international trading standards and legal guidelines.

Global companies, such as Coca-Cola, must have a firm grasp of international law.

Sources of Law

A *law* is a rule developed by a society to govern the conduct of, and relationships among, its members. The U.S. Constitution, including the Bill of Rights, is the foundation for U.S. laws. Because the Constitution is a general document, laws offering specific answers to specific problems are constantly embellishing its basic principles. However, law is not static; it develops in response to changing conditions and social standards. Individual laws originate in various ways: through legislative action (*statutory law*), through administrative rulings (*administrative law*), and through customs and judicial precedents (*common law*). To one degree or another, all three forms of law affect businesses. Moreover, at times the three forms of law may overlap so that the differences between them become indistinguishable. Nonetheless, in cases where the three forms of law appear to conflict, statutory law generally prevails.

Statutory Law

Statutory law is law written by the U.S. Congress, state legislatures, and local governments. One of the most important elements of statutory law that affects businesses is the **Uniform Commercial Code (UCC)**. Designed to mitigate differences between state statutory laws and to simplify interstate commerce, this code is a comprehensive, systematic collection of statutes in a particular legal area.[2] For example, the UCC provides a nationwide standard in many issues of commercial law, such as sales contracts, bank deposits, and warranties. The UCC has been adopted in its entirety in 49 states and the District of Columbia, and about half of it has been adopted in Louisiana.

Administrative Law

Once laws have been passed by a state legislature or Congress, an administrative agency or commission typically takes responsibility for enforcing them. That agency may be called on to clarify a regulation's intent, often by consulting representatives of the affected industry. The administrative agency may then write more specific regulations, which are considered **administrative law**.

Government agencies cannot, however, create regulations out of thin air; the agency's regulations must be linked to specific statutes to be legal. For example, one of the responsibilities of the Food and Drug Administration (FDA) is ensuring the accuracy of pharmaceutical marketing efforts. When the FDA determined that Pfizer's Warner-Lambert division had falsely promoted the epilepsy drug Neurontin as effective for other ailments, including bipolar disorder, it fined the company $430 million.[3]

Administrative agencies also have the power to investigate corporations suspected of breaking administrative laws. A corporation found to be misbehaving may agree to a **consent order**, which allows the company to promise to stop doing something without actually admitting to any illegal behavior. As an alternative to entering into a consent order, the administrative agency may start legal proceedings against the company in a hearing presided over by an administrative law judge. During such a hearing, witnesses are called and evidence is presented to determine the facts of the situation. The judge then issues a decision, which may impose corrective actions on the company. If either party objects to the decision, the party may file an appeal to the appropriate federal court.[4]

Common Law

Common law, which originates in courtrooms and judges' decisions, began in England many centuries ago and was transported to the United States by the colonists. It is applied in all states except Louisiana (which follows a French model). Common law is sometimes called the "unwritten law" to distinguish it from legislative acts and administrative-agency regulations, which are written documents. Instead, common law is established through custom and the precedents set in courtroom proceedings.

Despite its unwritten nature, common law has great continuity, which derives from the doctrine of *stare decisis* (Latin for "to stand by decisions"). What the *stare decisis*

doctrine means is that judges' decisions establish a precedent for deciding future cases of a similar nature. Because common law is based on what has gone before, the legal framework develops gradually.

In the United States, common law is applied and interpreted in the system of courts (see Exhibit B.1). Common law thus develops through the decisions in trial courts, special courts, and appellate courts. The U.S. Supreme Court (or the highest court of a state when state laws are involved) sets precedents for entire legal systems. Lower courts must then abide by those precedents as they pertain to similar cases.

In all but six states, business cases are heard in standard trial courts. However, many corporations and states are pushing for the establishment of a network of special business courts. Advocates say that the special nature of business legal disputes requires experienced judges who understand business issues. They also feel that a system of business courts would go a long way toward reducing the expense and unpredictability of business litigation. However, opponents say that business courts are likely to favor local companies in disputes involving out-of-state litigants. Moreover, they say that the courts are likely to come under the influence of powerful business special-interest groups. Regardless, the national trend appears to be moving in the direction of special business courts; more than a dozen states now have business courts or business-only court sessions.[5]

Business Law

Although businesses must comply with the full body of laws that apply to individuals, a subset of laws can be defined more precisely as **business law**. This includes those elements of law that directly affect business activities. For example, laws pertaining to business licensing, employee safety, and corporate income taxes can all be considered business law. The most

The U.S. Court System

A legal proceeding may begin in a trial court or an administrative agency (examples of each are given here). An unfavorable decision may be appealed to a higher court at the federal or state level. (The court of appeals is the highest court in states that have no state supreme court; some other states have no intermediate appellate court.) The U.S. Supreme Court, the country's highest court, is the court of final appeal.

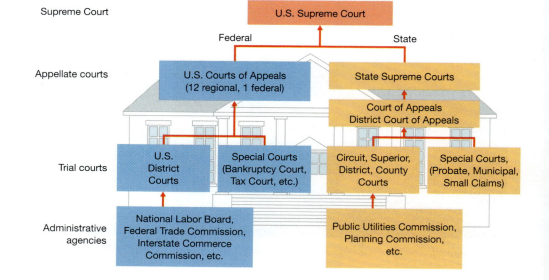

important categories of laws affecting business include torts, contracts, agency, property transactions, patents, trademarks, copyrights, negotiable instruments, and bankruptcy.

Torts

A **tort** is a noncriminal act (other than breach of contract) that results in injury to a person or to property.[6] A tort can be either intentional or the result of negligence. The victim of a tort is legally entitled to some form of financial compensation, or **damages**, for his or her loss and suffering. This compensation is also known as a *compensatory damage award*. In some cases, the victim may also receive a *punitive damage award* to punish the wrongdoer if the misdeed was deemed particularly bad. Extremely large punitive damages occasionally grab headlines and generate criticism and calls for reform of the tort process. However, a Cornell University study found that punitive damages are awarded in only about 6 percent of cases nationwide and that the majority of such awards are in line with compensatory damage awards.[7]

Intentional Torts

An **intentional tort** is a willful act that results in injury. For example, accidentally hitting a softball through someone's window is a tort, but purposely cutting down someone's tree because it obscures your view is an intentional tort. Note that *intent* in this case does not mean the intent to cause harm; it is the intent to commit a specific act. Some intentional torts involve communication of false statements that harm another's reputation. If the communication is in writing or on television, it is called *libel*; if it is spoken, it is *slander*.[8] For example, Jose Santos, the winning jockey in the 2003 Kentucky Derby, recently sued the *Miami Herald* for printing an article that accused him of using an electrical prod during the race. Although race officials subsequently cleared Santos of any improper behavior, the outcome of his case will depend on whether he can prove that the paper knowingly published false information.[9]

Negligence and Product Liability

In contrast to intentional torts, torts of **negligence** involve a failure to use a reasonable amount of care necessary to protect others from unreasonable risk of injury.[10] Cases of alleged negligence often involve **product liability**, which is a product's capacity to cause damages or injury for which the producer or seller is held responsible. Product liability is one of the most hotly contested aspects of business law today, with consumer advocates pointing to the number of product-related injuries and deaths every year—some 28 million injuries and 22,000 deaths—and business advocates pointing to the high cost of product-liability lawsuits—as much as $150 billion every year.[11]

A company may also be held liable for injury caused by a defective product even if the company used all reasonable care in the manufacture, distribution, or sale of its product.

Such **strict product liability** makes it possible to assign liability without assigning fault. It must only be established that (1) the company is in the business of selling the product, (2) the product reached the customer or user without substantial change in its condition, (3) the product was defective, (4) the defective condition rendered the product unreasonably dangerous, and (5) the defective product caused the injury.[12]

With so much at stake, including the magnitude of legal fees in many cases, it's no surprise that product-liability lawsuits generate so much controversy. Although few people would argue that individual victims of harmful goods and services shouldn't be entitled to some sort of compensation, many people now ask whether the system needs reforms. For instance, a recent survey suggested a majority of U.S. consumers favor such reforms as limiting the fees that lawyers can earn in product-liability lawsuits, placing limits on the amount of money awarded for pain and suffering, and enacting sanctions against attorneys who file frivolous lawsuits.[13] In addition, business leaders point out that the billions of dollars consumed by legal fees and damage awards raise prices for all consumers and, in some cases, limit the product choices available in the marketplace. As is often the case in complex situations such as this, both sides have valid points to make.

Contracts

Broadly defined, a **contract** is an exchange of promises between two or more parties that is enforceable by law. Many business transactions—including buying and selling products, hiring employees, purchasing group insurance, and licensing technology—involve contracts. Contracts may be either express or implied. An **express contract** is derived from the words (either oral or written) of the parties; an **implied contract** stems from the actions or conduct of the parties.[14]

Elements of a Contract

The law of contracts deals largely with identifying the exchanges that can be classified as contracts. The following factors must usually be present for a contract to be valid and enforceable:

- *An offer must be made.* One party must propose that an agreement be entered into. The offer may be oral or written, but it must be firm, definite, and specific enough to make it clear that someone intends to be legally bound by the offer. Finally, the offer must be communicated to the intended party or parties.

- *An offer must be accepted.* For an offer to be accepted, there must be clear intent (spoken, written, or by action) to enter into the contract. An implied contract arises when a person requests or accepts something and the other party has indicated that payment is expected. If, for example, your car breaks down on the road and you call a mobile mechanic and ask him or her to repair it, you are obligated to pay the reasonable value for the services, even if you didn't agree to specific charges beforehand. However, when a specific offer is made, the acceptance must satisfy the terms of the offer. For example, if someone offers you a car for $18,000, and you say you would take it for $15,000, you have not accepted the offer. Your response is a *counteroffer*, which may or may not be accepted by the salesperson.

■ *Both parties must give consideration.* A contract is legally binding only when the parties have bargained with each other and have exchanged something of value, which is called the **consideration**. The relative value of each party's consideration does not generally matter to the courts. In other words, if you make a deal with someone and later decide you didn't get enough in the deal, that result is not the court's concern. You entered into the deal with the original consideration in mind, and that fact is legally sufficient.[15]

■ *Both parties must give genuine assent.* To have a legally enforceable contract, both parties must agree to it voluntarily. The contract must be free of fraud, duress, undue influence, and mutual mistake.[16] If only one party makes a mistake, it ordinarily does not affect the contract. On the other hand, if both parties make a mistake, the agreement would be void. For example, if both the buyer and the seller of a business believed the business was profitable, when in reality it was operating at a loss, their agreement would be void.

■ *Both parties must be competent.* The law gives certain classes of people only a limited capacity to enter into contracts. Minors, people who are senile or insane, and in some cases those who are intoxicated cannot usually be bound by a contract for anything but the bare necessities: food, clothing, shelter, and medical care.

■ *The contract must not involve an illegal act.* Courts will not enforce a promise that involves an illegal act. For example, a drug dealer cannot get help from the courts to enforce a contract to deliver illegal drugs at a prearranged price.

■ *The contract must be in proper form.* Most contracts can be made orally, by an act, or by a casually written document; however, certain contracts are required by law to be in writing. For example, the transfer of goods worth $500 or more must be accompanied by a written document. The written form is also required for all real estate contracts.

A contract need not be long; all these elements of a contract may be contained in a simple document (see Exhibit B.2). In fact, a personal check is one type of simple contract.

Contract Performance

Contracts normally expire when the agreed-to conditions have been met, called *performance* in legal terms. However, not all contracts run their expected course. Both parties involved can agree to back out of the contract, for instance. In other cases, one party fails to live up to the terms of the

Exhibit B.2 **Elements of a Contract**

This simple document contains all the essential elements of a valid contract.

> The band titled XYZ agrees to provide entertainment at the Club de Hohenzollern on April 30, 2005, between 8:30 p.m. and midnight.
>
> The band will be paid $500.00 for its performance.
>
> Signed on the date of
> *February 19, 2005*
>
> *Violetta Harvey*
>
> Violetta Harvey,
> Manager,
> Club de Hohenzollern
> and
>
> *Ralph Perkins*
>
> Ralph Perkins,
> Manager, XYZ

contract, a situation called **breach of contract**. The other party has several options at that point:

■ *Discharge.* When one party violates the terms of the agreement, generally the other party is under no obligation to continue with his or her end of the contract. In other words, the second party is discharged from the contract.

■ *Damages.* A party has the right to sue in court for damages that were foreseeable at the time the contract was entered into and that result from the other party's failure to fulfill the contract. The amount of damages awarded usually reflects the amount of profit lost and often includes court costs as well, although figuring out fair amounts is not always easy. When talk-show host Rosie O'Donnell and publisher Gruner + Jahr USA sued each other for more than $100 million each over the collapse of the magazine *Rosie*, a judge determined that neither side deserved anything.[17]

■ *Specific performance.* A party can be compelled to live up to the terms of the contract if money damages would not be adequate.

To control the increasing costs of litigation, more and more companies are now experimenting with alternatives to the courtroom. These include independent mediators, who sit down with the two parties and try to hammer out a satisfactory solution to contract problems, and mandatory arbitration, in which an impartial arbitrator or arbitration panel hears evidence from both sides and makes a legally binding

Step 1: All current legal proceedings against the firm are halted. A decision is made to either liquidate or reorganize the firm, based on the value of the firm's assets. If liquidation is chosen, the firm's assets are transferred to a trustee, who sells them to pay the firm's debts. If reorganization is chosen, go to step 2.

Step 2: The courts may appoint a trustee to operate the firm, or current management may continue to operate it. A reorganization plan is developed either by current management, by the trustee, or by a committee of creditors. When plan is developed, go to step 3.

Step 3: Creditors and shareholders vote on the reorganization plan. Plan is ratified if (1) at least one-half of creditors vote in favor and if their claims against the company represent at least two-thirds of total claims; (2) at least two-thirds of shareholders approve the plan; and (3) the plan is confirmed by the court. When plan is ratified, go to step 4.

Step 4: The plan guarantees creditors new securities, and sometimes cash, in exchange for dismissal of their claims. With the firm discharged from its debts, it is free to start anew without the weight of past failures.

Exhibit B.3

Steps in Chapter 11 Bankruptcy Proceedings

Chapter 11 bankruptcy may buy a debtor time to reorganize finances and continue operating. However, using this device to evade financial obligations is extremely risky from a legal standpoint, and declaring bankruptcy may severely damage the reputation and credit rating of a firm or an individual.

sanctity of the copyright extends to online publishing. This law makes it a crime to possess or distribute multiple copies of online copyrighted material for profit or not. Specifically, it closes the loophole that had allowed the distribution of copyrighted material as long as the offender didn't seek profit. Penalties include fines up to $250,000 and five years in prison.[25] To avoid potential copyright infringements, experts suggest that authors include copyright and trademark notices on webpages that contain protected material, include a link on each page to a detailed copyright notice that explains what users can and cannot do, and place disclaimers on all pages that contain links to other sites.[26]

Negotiable Instruments

Whenever you write a personal check, you are creating a **negotiable instrument**, a transferable document that represents a promise to pay a specified amount. (*Negotiable* in this sense means that it can be sold or used as payment of a debt; an *instrument* is simply a written document that expresses a legal agreement.) In addition to checks, negotiable instruments include certificates of deposit, promissory notes, and commercial paper. To be negotiable, an instrument must meet several criteria:[27]

- It must be in writing and signed by the person who created it.

- It must have an unconditional promise to pay a specified sum of money.

- It must be payable either on demand or at a specified date in the future.

- It must be payable either to some specified person or organization or to the person holding it (the bearer).

You can see how a personal check meets those criteria; when you write one, you are agreeing to pay the amount of the check to the person or organization to whom you're writing it.

Bankruptcy

Even though the U.S. legal system establishes the rules of fair play and offers protection from the unscrupulous, it can't prevent most businesses from taking on too much debt. The legal system does, however, provide help for businesses that find themselves in deep financial trouble. **Bankruptcy** is the legal means of relief for debtors (either individuals or businesses) who are unable to meet their financial obligations.[28]

Voluntary bankruptcy is initiated by the debtor; *involuntary bankruptcy* is initiated by creditors. The law provides for several types of bankruptcy, which are commonly referred to by chapter number of the Bankruptcy Reform Act. In a Chapter 7 bankruptcy, the debtor's assets will be sold and the proceeds divided equitably among the creditors. Under Chapter 11 (which is usually aimed at businesses but does not exclude individuals other than stockbrokers), a business is allowed to get back on its feet and continue functioning while it arranges to pay its debts.[29] For the steps involved in a Chapter 11 bankruptcy, see Exhibit B.3. If a company emerges from Chapter 11 as a leaner, healthier organization, creditors generally benefit. That's because once a company is back on its financial feet it can resume payments to creditors. Polaroid, for example, emerged from Chapter 11 bankruptcy in 2002, less than nine months after it filed for protection. The outcome resulted in a court-approved sale of substantially all of Polaroid's business to One Equity Partners. Both the secured and unsecured creditors supported the sale in anticipation of receiving payments on their outstanding debt balances.[30]

As Exhibit B.4 shows, a number of Chapter 11 bankruptcies of epic proportions have been filed in the past few years. Banking failures dominated the early 1990s, whereas technology and energy failures dominated in the early years of the new millennium.

Largest U.S. Bankruptcies Since 1990

Companies in banking, energy, and technology dominate the list of the largest U.S. corporate bankruptcies in recent years.

COMPANY	YEAR OF BANKRUPTCY	ASSETS PRIOR TO BANKRUPTCY ($ BILLIONS)
WorldCom, Inc.	2002	$103.9
Enron Corp.	2001	$63.4
Conseco, Inc.	2002	$61.4
Global Crossing Ltd.	2002	$30.2
Pacific Gas and Electric Co.	2001	$29.8
Adelphia Communications	2002	$21.5
Mirant Corporation	2003	$19.4
First Executive Corp.	1991	$15.2
Gibraltar Financial Corp.	1990	$15.0
Kmart Corp.	2002	$14.6
FINOVA Group, Inc.	2001	$14.1
HomeFed Corp.	1992	$13.9
Southeast Banking Corporation	1991	$13.4
NTL, Inc.	2002	$13.0
Reliance Group Holdings, Inc.	2001	$12.6
Imperial Corp. of America	1990	$12.3
UAL Corp.	2002	$12.2
Federal-Mogul Corp.	2001	$10.2
First City Bancorp of Texas	1992	$9.9
First Capital Holdings	1991	$9.7

Appendix Glossary

administrative law   Rules, regulations, and interpretations of statutory law set forth by administrative agencies and commissions

agency   Business relationship that exists when one party (the principal) authorizes another party (the agent) to enter into contracts on the principal's behalf

bankruptcy   Legal procedure by which a person or a business that is unable to meet financial obligations is relieved of debt

breach of contract   Failure to live up to the terms of a contract, with no legal excuse

business law   Those elements of law that directly influence or control business activities

common law   Law based on the precedents established by judges' decisions

consent order   Settlement in which an individual or organization promises to discontinue some illegal activity without admitting guilt

consideration   Negotiated exchange necessary to make a contract legally binding

contract   Legally enforceable exchange of promises between two or more parties

damages   Financial compensation to an injured party for loss and suffering

deed   Legal document by which an owner transfers the title, or ownership rights, to real property to a new owner

express contract   Contract derived from words, either oral or written

implied contract   Contract derived from actions or conduct

intellectual property   Intangible personal property, such as ideas, songs, trade secrets, and computer programs, that are protected by patents, trademarks, and copyrights

intentional tort   Willful act that results in injury

international law Principles, customs, and rules that govern the international relationships between states, organizations, and persons

negligence Tort in which a reasonable amount of care to protect others from risk of injury is not used

negotiable instrument Transferable document that represents a promise to pay a specified amount

personal property All property that is not real property

power of attorney Written authorization for one party to legally act for another

product liability The capacity of a product to cause harm or damage for which the producer or seller is held accountable

property Rights held regarding any tangible or intangible object

real property Land and everything permanently attached to it

stare decisis Concept of using previous judicial decisions as the basis for deciding similar court cases

statutory law Statute, or law, created by a legislature

strict product liability Liability for injury caused by a defective product when all reasonable care is used in its manufacture, distribution, or sale; no fault is assigned

tort Noncriminal act (other than breach of contract) that results in injury to a person or to property

Uniform Commercial Code (UCC) Set of standardized laws, adopted by most states, that govern business transactions

warranty Statement specifying what the producer of a product will do to compensate the buyer if the product is defective or if it malfunctions

Appendix C
Personal Finance: Getting Set for Life

Will You Control Your Money, or Will Your Money Control You?

In your years as a consumer and a wage earner, even if it's only been from part-time jobs so far, you've already established a relationship with money. How would you characterize that relationship? Positive or negative? Are you in control of your money, or does money—and a frequent lack of it—control you? Unfortunately, too many people in the United States find themselves in the second situation, with heavy debt loads, a constant cycle of struggle from one paycheck to the next, and worries about the future. In a recent survey, 64 percent of U.S. adults said they were living paycheck to paycheck, and 71 percent said that getting out of debt is their

By establishing positive financial habits now, you can avoid the money worries that plague millions of U.S. consumers

primary financial goal.[1] When people get stuck in this mode, money often controls their lives because it's a constant source of worry.

The good news is that with some basic information in hand, you can almost always improve your financial well-being and take control of your money. The timing might seem ironic, but the best time to establish a positive relationship with money is right now, when you're still a student. If you build good habits now, when money is often scarce, you'll be taking a major step toward getting set for life. Conversely, if you fall into bad habits now, you could find yourself struggling and worrying for years to come. You'd be amazed at how many graduates think that their financial lives will improve dramatically when they start earning a "real" paycheck, only to discover that their bills and their debts increase even faster than their earnings.

This appendix will help you understand the basic principles of personal finances and give you a solid foundation for managing your money. Before exploring some helpful strategies for each stage of your life, the following sections emphasize three lessons that every consumer and wage earner needs to know and offer a brief look at the financial planning process.

Three Simple—but Vital—Financial Lessons

If you've ever read a copy of the *Wall Street Journal*, *Barron's*, or another financial publication, you might have gotten the sense that money management is complex and jargon infested. However, unless you become a financial professional, you don't need to worry about the intricacies of "high finance." A few simple lessons will serve you well, starting with three ideas that will have enormous impact on your financial future: (1) the value of your money is constantly changing, so you need to understand how time affects your financial health, (2) small sacrifices early in life can have huge payback later in life, and (3) every financial decision you make involves trade-offs. Taking these three ideas to heart will improve every aspect of your money management efforts, no matter how basic or sophisticated your finances.

The Value of Your Money Is Constantly Changing

If you remember only one thing from this discussion of personal finance, make sure this thought stays with you: A dollar today does not equal a dollar tomorrow. If you've successfully invested a dollar, it will be worth a little more tomorrow. However, if you charged a dollar's worth of purchases on a credit card, you're going to owe a little more than a dollar tomorrow. And even if you hold it tightly in your hand, that dollar will be worth a little less tomorrow, thanks to **inflation**—the tendency of prices to increase over time. When prices go up, your **buying power** goes down, so that dollar will buy less and less with each passing day.

These effects are so gradual that they are usually impossible to notice from one day to the next, but they can have a staggering impact on your finances over time. Put time to work for you, and you'll join that happy segment of the population whose finances are stable and under control. Let time work against you, and you could get trapped in an endless cycle of stress and debt.

A simple example will demonstrate the power of time. Let's say you inherit $10,000 today and have two choices: hide it under your mattress or invest it in the stock market. Now fast-forward 10 years. If you hid the $10,000 under your mattress, it'll now be worth only $7,000 or so (assuming today's inflation rates stay about the same). It will still *look* like $10,000, but because of inflation, it'll *spend* like $7,000. On the other hand, if you invested it in the stock market, you could have $18,000 or more, assuming stock market returns track historical patterns. That's a difference of $11,000 between the two choices, more than your inheritance to begin with.

Now let's say you didn't get that inheritance but you did get the urge to treat your best friends to a relaxing, luxury vacation. You don't have the cash, but you do have a shiny new credit card with a $10,000 limit, so away you go. The bill arrives a few days after you return home, and you start paying a modest amount, say $150 a month. At 13 percent interest, which is not unusual for a credit card, it'll take you just about 10 years to pay off the $10,000 you borrowed—and you'll end up paying $18,000, nearly twice what you thought that vacation was costing you. Doesn't seem so relaxing now, does it?

Depending on the financial decisions you make, then, time can be your best friend or your worst enemy. The **time value of money** refers to increases in money as a result of accumulating interest.[2] Time is even more powerful when your investment or debt is subject to **compounding**, which occurs when new interest is applied to interest that has already accumulated. Financial planners often talk about the "magic of compounding," and it really can feel like magic— good magic if it's compounded interest on savings, bad magic if it's compounded interest on debt. For example, Exhibit C.1 shows how $10,000 grows in a savings account that pays 3 percent annually, compounded monthly.

Granted, you're not going to get wealthy with 3 percent interest, but if you leave your money in this account for 10 years, you'd accumulate more than $1,600 in compounded interest. (Unfortunately, inflation would probably erode all your gains in this case, which is why you don't want to keep much of your savings in a savings account, as you'll see later.)

Small Sacrifices Early in Life Can Produce Big Payoffs

If you're currently living the life of a typical college student, you probably can't wait to move on and move up in life. You'll land that first "real" job, then get a nicer apartment, buy a new car, replace those ratty clothes you've been wearing for four years, and stop eating ramen seven nights a

Month	Balance	Interest
0	$10,000.00	$0.00
1	10,025.00	25.00
2	10,050.06	25.06
3	10,075.19	25.13
4	10,100.38	25.19
5	10,125.63	25.25
6	10,150.94	25.31
7	10,176.32	25.38
8	10,201.76	25.44
9	10,227.26	25.50
10	10,252.83	25.57
11	10,278.46	25.63
12	10,304.16	25.70

(1) Opening balance

(3) Balance at beginning of 2nd month: $10,000.00 + 25.00

(5) Balance at beginning of 3rd month: $10,025.00 + 25.06

(2) Interest after 1st month: $10,000 × 0.25%

(4) Interest after 2nd month: $10,250 × 0.25%

Exhibit C.1

Compounding and the Time Value of Money

The "magic of compounding" accelerates savings (or debt) by calculating new interest on both the existing balance and previously accumulated interest.

Exhibit C.2 Building a Million

To amass $1 million by age 65 (assuming 10 percent return on your investments and 4 percent inflation), you can save $330,000 by starting 20 years earlier.

STARTING AGE	MONTHLY INVESTMENT	TOTAL INVESTMENT
25	$904	$434,880
35	$1,643	$591,480
45	$3,188	$765,120

week. This might be the last thing you want to hear, but if you can convince yourself to continue your frugal ways for a few more years, you'll benefit tremendously in the long run.

Let's say that by age 65 you'd like to have a retirement fund of $1 million in *today's dollars*, which means it's adjusted for inflation. Compare the scenarios in Exhibit C.2 (which assume 10 percent annual return on your investments, which is in line with historical stock market investments, and 4 percent annual inflation). If you start investing at age 25, you'll need to invest $904 a month. If you wait until age 35 to start, you'll need to invest $1,643 a month to reach $1 million. Wait until age 45, and you'll need to invest $3,188 a month. In other words, the longer you wait, the more painful it gets. But that's not all. The longer you wait, the more you need to invest in total dollars, too—$330,000 more if you start at age 45 instead of age 25.

Of course, saving $904 a month during the early years of your career is no easy task, and it may be impossible, depending on your starting salary. In addition to the endless temptations to spend, you may also face the costs of starting a family, for instance. However, you'd be amazed at how much you can save every month by forgoing that new car, renting a cheaper apartment, buying modestly priced clothes, and watching your entertainment expenses closely. A few simple choices can often free up hundreds of dollars every month. And if you join the growing number of college graduates who plan to move back in with their parents during the initial years of their careers, you can really pile up the savings.[3] Even if you can save only a few hundred dollars every month early in your career, the earlier you start, the better off you'll be. Just keep increasing your monthly investment every time your salary increases and do everything you can to take advantage of the time value of money.

Every Decision Involves Trade-Offs

By now, you've probably noticed that the time value of money and frugal living involve lots of choices. In fact, virtually every financial decision you make, from buying a cup of coffee to buying a house, involves a **trade-off**, in which you have to give up one thing to gain something else. If your

family and friends give you $2,000 for graduation, should you run right out and buy alloy wheels and a custom exhaust system for your car? Or should you invest that $2,000 in the stock market and invest another $200 every month, so that in five or six years you could have enough to buy a new car—in cash, with no monthly payments? Then, while your friends are shelling out $300 or $400 in payments for their new cars, you can be investing that amount every month and build up enough money to start your own business or perhaps retire a few years early.

Even the smallest habits and choices have consequences. Addicted to potato chips? Let's say you spend $3.19 for a big bag two or three times a week. Kick that habit now and invest the money instead. Over the course of 40 years, you could earn enough to treat yourself to a new luxury car when you retire. Sounds crazy, but over the course of many years, even tiny amounts of money can add up to large sums.

Not all your choices will be so simple, of course. Most of the examples presented so far have involved trading current pleasures and luxuries for future financial gain—a dilemma you'll be facing most of your life, by the way. Other choices involve risks versus rewards. Should you buy life insurance to provide for your family or invest the money and hope it'll grow fast enough to provide your loved ones with enough to get by on in the event of your death? Should you invest your money in a safe but slow-growing investment or an investment that offers the potential for high growth—but the risk that you could lose everything? As you gain experience with financial choices, you'll recognize your own level of *risk tolerance*. For instance, if you're lying awake at night worrying about a high-risk stock you just purchased, you may have a lower level of risk tolerance and you'll probably want to stick with safer, saner investments.

Figuring out the best choice is difficult in many cases, but simply recognizing that every decision involves a trade-off will improve your decision making. Too often, people get into trouble by looking at *only* the risk (which can stop them from making choices that might in fact be better for them in the long run) or *only* the potential rewards (which can lure them into making choices that are too risky). Consider all the consequences of every choice you make, and you'll start making better financial decisions.

You'll pick up many other financial tips as you start investing, buying houses, selecting insurance, and making other financial choices, but these three concepts will always apply. With those thoughts in mind, it's time to take a look at the financial planning process.

Creating Your Personal Financial Plan

Creating and following a sensible financial plan is the only sure way to stay in control of your finances. A good plan can help you get the most from whatever amount of money you have, identify the funds you'll need to get

Exhibit C.3 **The Financial Planning Process**

The financial planning process starts with an honest assessment of where you are now, followed by setting goals, defining and implementing plans, measuring your progress, then adjusting if needed.

through life's major expenses, increase your financial independence and confidence, minimize the time and energy you need to manage your finances, and answer a question that vexes millions of people every year: Where did all my money go?

Many people discover they'd rather turn the planning task over to a professional financial planner. And even if you do most of your planning yourself, you may encounter special situations or major transactions in which you'd like the advice of an expert. The right advice at the right time can mean all the difference. Unfortunately, finding the right adviser is not a simple task: Some 250,000 people in the United States offer their services as financial advisers.[4] Before you sign on with anyone, make sure you understand what advice you need and who can provide it. Ask for references, professional credentials, investing strategies, and most important of all, how the adviser is paid.[5]

Fee-only planners charge you for their services, either an hourly rate or a percentage of the assets they're managing for you. In theory, the major advantage of fee-only planners is complete objectivity, as they don't make money on the specific decisions they recommend for you. In contrast, **commission-based planners** are paid commissions on the financial products they sell you, such as insurance policies and mutual funds. While you can certainly receive good advice from a commission-based planner, make sure he or she has a wide range of offerings for you. Otherwise, you're likely to be hampered by limited choices.[6] Of course, since these types of planners are selling you something, make sure their recommendations are really the best choices for your financial needs. If you can't get a good recommendation from family members or colleagues, consider a matchmaker such as www.wiseradvisor.com, an impartial service that helps investors find advisers.

Even if you decide to rely on a full-service financial adviser to guide your decisions, stay informed and actively involved. Lawsuits against financial advisers have risen dramatically in recent years, as clients seek compensation for losses in the stock market, for tax shelters (investments designed primarily to reduce tax obligations) that the Internal Revenue Service (IRS) later ruled were "abusive," or for other financial missteps. Some observers attribute this trend to clients who are simply angry and frustrated that many stocks crumbled after the dot-com boom. In other cases, however, clients have sued advisers who led them into overly complex or even illegal investment and tax schemes.[7] Keep in mind that even if you get advice, you are ultimately responsible for—and in control of—the choices involving your money. Don't count on anyone else to secure your financial future for you.

Planning can be as simple or as complex as you're inclined to make it, as long as you follow the basic steps shown in Exhibit C.3.[8] The following sections discuss each step in more detail.

Figure Out Where You Are Now

Successful financial planning starts with a careful examination of where you stand right now, financially speaking. Before you can move ahead, you need to add up what you own and what you owe, where your money is going, and how you're using credit. You might not like what you see, but if your finances are heading downhill, the sooner you learn that, the sooner you can fix it.

Start by listing your **assets**—the things you own—and your **liabilities**—the amounts of money you owe. Assets include both *financial assets,* such as bank accounts, mutual funds, retirement accounts, and money that people owe you, and *physical assets,* such as cars, houses, and artwork. Liabilities include credit card debts, car loans, home mortgages, and student loans. After you've itemized everything you own and everything you owe, calculate your **net worth** by subtracting your liabilities from your assets. The **balance sheet** in Exhibit C.4 shows Devon Anderson's net worth. Her net worth is currently negative, but that's certainly not uncommon for college students. The important thing for Devon at this point is that she knows how much she's worth, so she has a baseline to build on.

Your balance sheet gives you a snapshot of where you stand at a particular point in time. The second major planning tool is your **income and expense statement**, or simply *income statement.* This statement answers that all-important question of where your money is going month by month. Start by adding up all your sources of income from jobs, parents, investments, and so on. If you have

Exhibit C.4

Devon Anderson's Net Worth

Devon Anderson's net worth is currently negative, driven in large part by her school loans. However, she now knows exactly where she stands and can start working to improve her balance.

ASSETS		
Cash accounts	Checking account	$450.67
	Savings account	927.89
Investments	50 shares Microsoft	1,302.50
Retirement accounts	(none)	
Automobiles	2001 Escort	5,500.00
Personal property	Jewelry	1,800.00
	Furniture	2,000.00
	Computer	450.00
Total assets		**$12,431.06**

LIABILITIES		
Current bills (due within 30 days)	Rent	$650.00
	Visa	120.00
	MasterCard	195.00
	Car payment	327.25
Credit card debt	Visa	1,185.34
	MasterCard	2,431.60
Housing debt	(none)	
Automobile loans	2001 Escort	3,880.10
Other debt	Student loans	22,560.00
Total liabilities		**$31,349.29**
Net worth (total assets − total liabilities)		**($18,918.23)**

irregular income, such as a onetime cash infusion from your parents at the beginning of each semester, divide it by the number of months it needs to cover to give you an average monthly value. Next, list all your expenses. If you're in the habit of using debit cards, credit cards, or a checkbook for most of your expenses, this task is fairly easy, since your statements will show where the money is going. However, if you tend to use cash for a lot of purchases, you'll need to get in the habit of recording those purchases. (Using cash has the major advantage of limiting your spending to money that you actually have, but it doesn't leave a "paper trail," so you have to keep track of the spending yourself.) Exhibit C.5 shows Devon's income and expense statement.

Assembling your balance sheet and your income and expense statement can be a chore the first time around, but updating it as you make progress is much easier. By the way, software such as Intuit Quicken or Microsoft Money can simplify these tasks, but it's not absolutely necessary. You can do all your record keeping in a spreadsheet (the software is probably already on your computer), or simply keep records in a notebook. How you record your data is less important than making sure you do it.

Set Realistic Financial Goals

Now that you've gotten through the chore of assessing your current financial situation, the next step is setting goals. Take some time with this step. Your goals will drive all your financial decisions from here on out, so make sure they're the right ones for you. For instance, saving up for an early retirement requires a different financial strategy than saving up to take a year off in the middle of your career. Think carefully about what you really value in life. Discuss your dreams and plans with family and friends. Is making a million dollars by the time you're 30 or 40 your most important goal, and are you willing to work around the clock to get there? Or would you rather accumulate wealth more slowly and live at a more relaxed pace? Do you want to start a family when you're 25? 35? Perhaps being able to take care of an aging relative is important. In spite of what you might hear in TV commercials, you can't have it all, but you can make trade-offs that are compatible with your personal goals and values.

No matter what they might be, effective financial goals have two aspects in common: They are *specific* and they are *realistic.* "I want to be rich" and "I just don't want to have to

INCOME	
Wages (take home, average per month)	$1,230.00
Help from the parents	450.00
Total income	**$1680.00**

EXPENSES (AVERAGE MONTHLY)	
Rent	$650.00
Gas bill	34.00
Electric bill	76.00
Cell phone	98.00
Food	315.00
Misc. household supplies	45.00
School materials & supplies	22.00
Car payment	327.25
Gasoline	38.00
Sailing club	78.25
Clothes	188.00
Entertainment & fast food	325.00
Visa payment	120.00
MasterCard payment	195.00
Total expenses	**$2,511.50**
Monthly difference	**($831.50)**

Exhibit C.5

Devon Anderson's Income and Expense Statement

Devon was surprised to learn that she has been spending over $800 more every month than she takes in. Since she can't work any more hours without compromising her studies and she is reluctant to ask her parents for more, the only solution is to cut expenses. After some careful thought, she realizes that by cutting her cell phone usage in half (or finding a better deal), dropping the sailing club, economizing on groceries, and cutting way back on entertainment, fast food, and new clothes, she can almost break even every month.

worry about money" are not good goal statements because both are too general to give you any guidance. For one person, "not worrying about money" could require $100,000 a year, but another person might get by on only $50,000 a year. You can certainly start with a general desire, such as wealth or freedom from worry, but you need to translate that into real numbers so you can craft a meaningful plan.

In addition to making them specific, make sure your goals are realistic. Lots of young people start out life saying they'd like to make a million by age 30 or retire by age 40. These are wonderful desires, but for most people, they simply aren't realistic. The problem with having unrealistic goals is that you'll be repeatedly frustrated by your inability to meet them, and you're more likely to give up on your financial plan as a result.[9] While amassing a million dollars in the first 10 years of your career is highly unlikely, amassing a million dollars in 40, 30, or sometimes even 20 years is quite attainable for many professional wage earners. A few minutes with a financial calculator will help you assess the various possibilities and determine what is reasonable for you. (If you don't have a calculator with financial functions or software such as Quicken or Money, visit www.choosetosave.org/tools, which

offers a wide variety of online calculators. In fact, just playing around with the many calculators on this site will teach you a fair amount about financial planning.)

Many people find it helpful to divide financial goals into short, medium, and long term. Your personal time frame for each might vary, but in general, short-term goals will get you through your current financial situation, medium-term goals will get you into the next stage in your life, and long-term goals will get you completely set for life. For some people, this planning might split up into 1 year or less, 2 to 5 years, and 6 years and beyond. For others, short term might be the next 5 years, medium could be 6 to 10, and long term beyond 10 years.[10] The important thing is to consider the phases in your life and establish goals for each phase. Also, think carefully about the type of goals you wish to achieve. For instance, acquiring a ranch might be a significant goal for you, whereas someone who loves to travel may have little interest in real estate. Similarly, if you find that you have a low tolerance for risk or a number of loved ones depend on you, comprehensive insurance coverage might be a significant goal. So go ahead and earn that million if you want to, but make sure you know *why* you're earning it.

You can find a wide range of free financial-planning tools online, such as these calculators offered by the "Choose to Save" program at www.choosetosave.org.

Create and Implement a Practical Plan to Meet Your Goals

You've thought about your goals and defined some that are specific and realistic. You're inspired and ready to start. What's next? For all the thousands of books, television shows, magazines, software products, and websites devoted to money, financial success really boils down to one beautifully—and brutally—simple formula: Earn more, spend less, and make better choices with what you have left over. On the plus side, this is an easy concept to understand. On the minus side, it's completely unforgiving. If you're spending more than you're earning or making bad choices with your savings and investments, you're never going to reach your goals until you can turn things around. The sections on life stages later in this appendix explore some of the details of these three components, but here's a brief overview to put it all in context.

- **Earn more.** Particularly in the early stages of your career, income from your job will probably provide most or all of your income, so be sure to maximize your earning potential. As you get more established and have the opportunity to invest, you can start earning income from real estate, stocks and other investments, and perhaps businesses that you either own yourself or own a share of. As you move into retirement, your sources of income will shift to returns from your own investments, along

with both employer- and government-funded retirement plans. For most people, earning power continues to build to a peak between the ages of 45 and 55, then declines into and through retirement.[11]

- **Spend less.** Regardless of how much control you have over your income (and there are times and circumstances in life when you probably can't expect to change your earning power), you always have some control over how you spend your money. The first and most important step to spending less is maintaining a personal budget. For most people, budgeting sounds like about as much fun as having root canal surgery, but it shouldn't be that way. Don't think of budgeting as a straightjacket that crimps your style; think of it as a way to free up more cash so that you can accomplish those wonderful goals you've set for yourself. When you skip a night out at the clubs or squeeze another year out of your car, think of that ranch in Montana or that business you want to start. As with dieting, exercise, and other personal improvement regimes, sticking to a budget is difficult at first, but as you start to see some positive results, you'll be motivated to continue. Another important aspect of budgeting is understanding *why* you spend money, particularly on things you don't need and can't afford.[12] Don't try to spend your way out of depression, for instance; "retail therapy" never really solves anything and only makes financial matters worse. If you're prone to budget meltdowns, try to make everything as automatic as possible. For example, have your employer invest part of your salary in a company-sponsored investment program or have a mutual fund company pull money from your checking account every month.

- **Make better choices.** Now that you've maximized your income and minimized your expenses, success comes down to making better choices with the money you have to save and invest (and the occasional bit of good luck, but you can't control that part, obviously). Investing can be a complex subject, with literally thousands of places to put your money. As with everything else in personal finance, the more you know, the better you're likely to perform. You can learn a tremendous amount at websites such as Motley Fool (www.fool.com), Kiplinger.com (www.kiplinger.com), and Investopedia (www.investopedia.com). Don't make investments that you don't understand, whether it's some exotic financial scheme or simply the stock of a company that doesn't make sense to you. Proceed at your own pace, such as starting with an *index mutual fund* (which tracks the overall performance of the stock market) instead of trying to pick individual stocks.

In addition to your other healthy financial habits, get in the habit of keeping good records of income, expenses, investments, and other financial matters. Doing so will not only help you track your progress, but the IRS also requires you to keep a variety of tax-related records. For a good overview of both suggested and required records, refer to Publication 552

Investopedia.com is one of many websites that offer free, self-paced learning materials for people who want to take control of their finances.

(for personal records) and Publication 583 (for business records), both of which are available online at www.irs.gov.

Finally, make sure that anyone who plays a role in the plan, whether roommates sharing grocery costs or family members sharing all aspects of finances, buys into the plan. One of the most critical aspects of successful financial planning is discipline, and a plan will fall apart if some people follow it and some don't. Money is one of the most common issues in relationship problems and divorces, so talk things over calmly and honestly with your partner or spouse. Getting everyone to agree to—and commit to—the plan will reduce stress and increase the chances of success.[13]

Periodically Measure Your Progress

To make sure you're on track to meet your goals, get in the habit of periodically checking your progress. Is your net worth increasing? (It might still be moving up toward zero, but that's progress!) Are your expenses under control? However, don't obsess over your finances. Life's too short, and there are too many other pleasurable ways to spend your time. You don't need to check your stock portfolio a dozen times a day or lie in bed every night dreaming up new ways to snip nickels and dimes out of your budget. After a while, you'll get a sense of how often you need to measure your progress to make sure you stay on track toward your goals. In general, check your income and expenses at least once a month to make sure you're staying within budget. For larger assets such as your house, you might want to verify approximate values once or twice a year.

However, don't put off checking your financial health so long that you don't notice problems such as poorly performing investments or small expenses that somehow ballooned into big expenses. If you're using a financial planner, don't wait for an annual statement. Find out where you stand at least once a quarter.

Adjust Your Goals and Plans as Needed

At various points in your life, you'll find that your goals or your financial status have changed enough to require adjustments to your plan. Whenever you pass through one of life's major transitions, such as getting married, having children, changing jobs, or buying a house, chances are you'll need to make some revisions. For instance, many first-time home buyers are surprised by the amount of money it takes to maintain a house, particularly a "fixer-upper" that needs a lot of work. To keep your income and expenses in balance, you may find you need to make sacrifices elsewhere in your budget.

In fact, if you're like most college students, you'll go through at least four major stages in your financial life: getting through college, establishing a financial foundation, building your net worth and preparing for life's major expenses, and planning for retirement. (If you're back in college after having been in the workforce for a while, your situation might vary.) The following sections give you an overview of the decisions to consider at each major stage in your life.

Life Stage 1: Getting Through College

The most important financial advice for college students can be summed up in a single phrase: Make sure you graduate. With tuition and expenses rising so rapidly these days, completing your education can be a mammoth struggle, to be sure, but if you leave school early, you will dramatically reduce your earning power throughout your entire career. In today's job market, the average difference between having a bachelor's degree and not having one is at least $15,000 a year. Advanced degrees add even more to your earning power.[14] Multiply those numbers by 40 or 45 years in the workforce, and a college diploma can be worth a half million dollars or more. No matter how desperate things might be, do everything possible to stay in school. Ask for advice—and help—if you need it. Many people find doing so uncomfortable or embarrassing, but you're almost guaranteed to regret it later if you don't ask when you really do need help. Talk to a counselor in your school's financial aid office. Ask friends and family for advice. If you have a job, see whether your employer is willing to assist with school expenses. Make sure you're getting all the financial aid you're eligible for, too. A number of websites can help you explore all the options, including www.fastweb.com, www.fafsa.gov, and www.loans4students.org.

Is it a good idea to borrow money to get through college? Absolutely, as long as the money goes toward the essential elements of your education and not toward the weekend's entertainment possibilities. This point leads to the second most important piece of advice for college students: Don't dig yourself into a giant hole with credit card debt. The average U.S. college student today has over $3,000 in credit card debt, and one in 10 has nearly $8,000.[15] If you're already in a hole, don't panic, but do stop digging.

Your first step to recovery is to recognize that you're at a make-or-break point in both your college career and your life as a whole. No amount of extracurricular fun is worth the damage that a credit card mess can inflict on your life. Excessive credit card debt from college can follow you for decades, limiting your ability to pay off student loans and purchase a car or a house, warns Sophia Jackson, a North Carolina financial adviser who counsels many students from schools in the area. She describes debt problems with college-age consumers as "absolutely epidemic."[16] Too many students drop out of college because of credit card debt, and many more spend years after graduation paying off debt they probably shouldn't have accumulated in the first place. Don't assume you can ring up a big balance during college and easily pay it off when you start working, either. Many graduates entering the workforce are disappointed to find themselves bringing home less and paying out more than they expected. You'll be facing student loan repayments and a host of new expenses, from housing to transportation to a business-quality wardrobe; you can't afford to devote a big chunk of your new salary to paying off your beer and pizza bills from the previous four years.

Your second step is to compile your income and expense statement as described earlier so you know where all that borrowed money is going. Do a thorough and honest evaluation of your expenses: How much of your spending is going toward junk food, clubbing, concert tickets, video games, and other nonessentials? At first, it won't seem possible that these small-ticket items can add up to big trouble, but it happens to thousands of college students every year. Most colleges and college towns offer a wide spectrum of free and low-cost entertainment options. With a little effort and creativity, anyone can find ways to reduce nonessential expenses, often by hundreds of dollars a month. As noted earlier, a few sacrifices now can make all the difference.

Do you really need it? Every purchase you make now means you have less money to save and invest for the future.

Life Stage 2: Building Your Financial Foundation

Whew, you made it. You scraped by to graduation, found a decent job, and now are ready to get really serious about financial planning. First, give yourself a pat on the back; it's a major accomplishment in life. Second, dust off that financial plan you put together in college. It's time to update it to reflect your new status in life. Third, don't lose those frugal habits you learned in college. Keep your *fixed expenses*, those bills you have to pay every month no matter what, as low as possible. Some of these expenses are mandatory, such as transportation and housing, but others may not be. Such things as gym and club memberships, additional phone lines, and subscriptions have a tendency to creep into your budget and gradually raise your expenses. Before you know it, you could be shelling out hundreds of dollars a month on these recurring but often nonessential expenses.

Among the important decisions you may need to make at this stage involve paying for transportation and housing, taking steps to maximize your earning power, and managing your cash and credit wisely.

Paying for Transportation

Transportation is likely to be one of your biggest ongoing expenses, if transportation for you means owning or leasing a vehicle. The *true cost* of owning a vehicle is significantly higher than the price tag. You'll probably have to finance it, you'll definitely need to insure it, and you'll face recurring costs for fuel and maintenance. And unfortunately, unlike houses, which often *appreciate* in value, cars always *depreciate* in value (with extremely rare exceptions, such as classic cars). In fact, that lovely new ride can lose as much as 20 percent of its value the instant you drive away from the dealership. If you pay $25,000 for a car, for example, your net worth could drop $5,000 before you've driven your first mile. And if you took out a five-, six-, or seven-year loan, you'll probably owe more than the car is worth for the first several years, a situation known as having an "upside-down" loan. In fact, 40 percent of new-car buyers now owe more on their trade-ins than those cars are worth.[17]

There is good news, however. Most cars tend not to depreciate much during their second, third, and fourth years, then plummet again after five years. You can take advantage of this effect by looking for a used car that is one year old, driving it for three years, then selling it.[18] Automotive websites such as www.edmunds.com offer a wealth of information about depreciation and other costs, including the true cost of owning any given model. Also check with your insurance company before buying any car, as some models cost considerably more to insure.

Negotiating the purchase of a car ranks high on most consumers' list of dreaded experiences. You can level the playing field, at least somewhat, by remembering two important issues. First, most buyers worry only about the monthly payment, which can be a costly mistake. Salespeople usually negotiate with four or even five variables at once, including the monthly payment, purchase price, down payment, value of your trade-in, and terms of your loan. If you don't pay attention to these other variables, you can get a low monthly payment and still get a bad deal. Experts suggest arranging your financing ahead of time, then negotiating only the purchase price when you're at the dealership.[19] If you're not comfortable negotiating, consider using a car-buying service such as CarsDirect.com (www.carsdirect.com).

Leasing, rather than buying, is a popular option with many consumers. In general, the biggest advantage of leasing is lower monthly payments than with a purchase (or a nicer car for the same monthly payment, depending on how you look at it). However, leases are even more complicated than purchases, so it's even more important to know what you're getting into. Also, leases usually aren't the best choice for consumers who want to minimize their long-term costs. To learn more about leasing, visit www.leaseguide.com.

Paying for Housing

Housing also presents you with a lease-versus-buy decision, although purchasing a house has two huge advantages that purchasing a car doesn't have: Most houses appreciate in value, and the interest on the **mortgage** reduces taxable income. And compared to renting, buying your own place also lets you build **equity**, the portion of the house's value that you own. These three factors mean that real estate is nearly always a recommended investment for anyone who can afford it. However, there are times when renting makes better financial sense. The **closing costs** for real estate—all the fees and commissions associated with buying or selling a house—can be considerable. Closing costs can represent from 3 to 6 percent of the price of a home. Depending on how fast your house's value rises, you may need to stay there two or three years just to recoup your closing costs before selling.

If you think that a job change, an upcoming marriage, or any other event in your life might require you to move in the near future, plug your numbers into a "rent versus own" calculator to see which option makes more sense. You can find several of these calculators online; two handy examples are at HomeLoanCenter.com (www.homeloancenter.com/loancalculator/maincalculator.aspx, then select "Rent vs. Own") and Choose to Save (www.choosetosave.org/tools/fincalcs.htm#bud, then select "Am I Better Off Renting?" from the list of home mortgage calculators).

When you are ready to buy, take your time. Choosing a house to buy is the most complicated financial decision many people will ever make, involving everything from property values in the neighborhood to the condition of the house to the details of the financial transaction.

Buying a house could be the most important financial decision you ever make.

Fortunately, you can learn more about home ownership from a number of sources. Check local lenders and real estate agencies for free seminars. Online sources include the U.S. Department of Housing and Urban Development (www.hud.gov) and MSN House and Home (http://houseandhome.msn.com). Buying your own house can and should be a wonderful experience, but don't let emotional factors lead you to a decision that doesn't make financial sense. Keep in mind that a house is both a home and an investment.

Maximizing Your Earning Power

Why do some people peak at earning $40,000 or $50,000 a year while others go on to earn 2 or 3 or 10 times that much? Because your salary is likely to be the primary "engine" of your financial success, this question warrants careful consideration. The profession you choose is one of the biggest factors, of course, but even within a given profession, you'll often find a wide range of income levels. A number of factors influence these variations, including education, individual talents, ambition, location, contacts, and good old-fashioned luck. You can change some of these factors throughout your career, but some you can't. However, compensation experts stress that virtually everyone can improve his or her earning power by following these tips:[20]

- *Know what you're worth.* The more informed you are about your competitive value in the marketplace, the better chance you have of negotiating a salary that reflects your worth. Several websites offer salary-level information that will help you decide your personal value, including www.bls.gov, www.salary.com, www.vault.com, and www.salaryexpert.com. (Some of these sites charge a modest fee for customized reports, but the information could be worth many times what you pay for it.)

■ *Be ready to articulate your value.* In addition to knowing what other people in your profession make, you need to be able to explain to your current employer or a potential new employer why you're worth the money you think you deserve. Collect concrete examples of how you've helped companies earn more or spend less in the past—and be ready to explain how you can do so in the future. Moreover, seek out opportunities that let you increase and demonstrate your worth.

■ *Don't overlook the value of employee benefits, performance incentives, and perks.* For instance, even if you can't negotiate the salary you'd really like, maybe you can negotiate extra time off or a flexible schedule that would allow you to run a home-based business on the side. Or perhaps you can negotiate a bonus arrangement that rewards you for higher-than-average performance.

■ *Understand the salary structure in your company.* If you hope to rise through the ranks and make $200,000 as a vice president, for instance, but the CEO is making only $150,000, your goal is obviously unrealistic. Some companies pay top performers well above market average, whereas others stick closely to industry norms.

■ *Study top performers.* Some employees have the misperception that top executives must have "clawed their way" to the top or stepped on everyone else on their way up. In most cases, the opposite is true. Employees and managers who continue to rise through the organization do so because they make people around them successful. Being successful on your own is one thing; helping an entire department or an entire company be successful is the kind of behavior that catches the attention of the people who write the really big paychecks.

Managing Cash

When those paychecks start rolling in, you'll need to set up a system of **cash management**, your personal system for handling cash and other **liquid assets**, which are those that can be quickly and easily converted to cash. You have many alternatives nowadays for storing cash, from a basic savings account to a variety of investment funds, but most offer interest rates that are below the average level of inflation. In other words, if you were to keep all your money in such places, your buying power would slowly but surely erode over time. Consequently, the basic challenge of cash management is keeping enough cash or other liquid assets available to cover your near-term needs without keeping so much cash that you lose out on investment growth opportunities or fall prey to inflation. Once again, your budget planning will come to the rescue by showing you how much money you need month to month. Financial experts also recommend keeping anywhere from three to six months' worth of basic living expenses in an *emergency fund* that you can access if you find yourself between jobs or have other unexpected needs.

Chapter 14 introduced the wide variety of financial institutions that offer ways to store and protect your cash.

Just as there are a number of alternatives to the traditional bank these days, you can also choose from several different options for holding cash (see Exhibit C.6 for a summary of their advantages and disadvantages):[21]

■ *Checking accounts.* Whether it's a traditional checking account from your neighborhood bank, an online account at an Internet bank, or a brokerage account with check-writing privileges, your checking account will serve as your primary cash management tool. A checking account can be either a demand deposit, which doesn't pay interest, or an interest-bearing or negotiable order of withdrawal (NOW) account.

■ *Savings accounts.* Savings accounts are convenient places to store small amounts of money. Many savings accounts can be linked to a checking account for quick access to your cash. Although they're convenient and safe, savings accounts nearly always offer interest rates below average inflation rates, so the buying power of your account steadily diminishes.

■ *Money market accounts.* Money market accounts, sometimes called money market deposit accounts, are an alternative to savings accounts; the primary difference is that they have variable interest rates that are usually higher than savings account rates.

■ *Money market mutual funds.* Money market mutual funds, sometimes called money funds, are similar to stock mutual funds, although they invest in *debt instruments* such as bonds, rather than stocks.

■ *Asset management accounts.* Brokerage firms and mutual fund companies frequently offer **asset management accounts** as a way to manage cash that isn't currently invested in stocks or stock mutual funds.

■ *Certificate of deposits.* With a certificate of deposit (CD), you are essentially lending a specific amount of money to a bank or other institution for a specific length of time and a specific interest rate. The length of time can range from a week to several years; the longer the time span and the larger the amount, the higher the interest rate.

No matter which types of accounts you choose, make sure you understand all the associated fees—which might not be clearly labeled as fees, either. Some accounts charge a fee every month, some charge fees when your balance drops below a certain amount or you write too many checks, and so on. For accounts with checking capability, **overdraft fees** can chew up hundreds of dollars if you bounce checks frequently. Also, be sure to verify your account statement every month and **reconcile** your checking account to make sure you and the bank agree on the balance.

Managing Credit

Even if you never want to use a credit card or borrow money, it's increasingly difficult to get by without credit in today's consumer environment. For instance, car rental companies usually require a credit card before you can rent a car, and

Exhibit C.6   **Places to Stash Your Cash**

You can find quite a few places to park your cash, but they're not all created equal.

TYPE OF ACCOUNT	ADVANTAGES	DISADVANTAGES
Checking account (demand deposit)	Convenient, usually no minimum balance needed to open, often provides online banking and access via ATMs, insured against losses due to bank failure	Does not earn any interest
Checking account (NOW account)	Convenience of a regular checking account, plus you earn interest on your balance; insured	Some institutions require a minimum balance to open an account; modest interest rates
Savings account	Slightly higher interest rate than on typical checking account, often linked to a checking account for simple transfers; insured	Low interest rates; not as liquid as checking accounts (except for linked accounts, in which you can easily transfer funds to checking)
Money market deposit account	Higher interest rates than checking or savings accounts; insured	High minimum balances; limited check writing; fees can limit real returns
Money market mutual fund	Higher interest rates than many other cash management options	Not insured (but limited exposure to risk); minimum balance requirements; limited check writing
Asset management account	Convenience of having cash readily available for investment purposes; higher interest rates than regular checking or savings accounts; consolidated statements show most of your cash management and investing activity	Expensive (high monthly fees); large minimum balances; restrictions on check writing privileges (such as high minimum amounts) can limit usefulness as regular checking account; not insured against losses
Certificate of deposit	Higher interest rates that are fixed and therefore predictable; insured	Minimum balance requirements; limited liquidity (your money is tied up for weeks, months, or years)

landlords want to verify your **credit history**, a record of your mortgages, consumer loans (such as financing provided by a home appliance store), credit card accounts, and bill-paying performance. Banks and other companies voluntarily provide this information to **credit bureaus**, businesses that compile **credit reports**. As you read in Chapter 10, an increasing number of employers are looking into the credit history of job applicants as well. Moreover, you may find yourself in need of a loan you didn't anticipate, and getting a loan without a credit history is not easy. Consequently, building and maintaining a solid credit history needs to be a part of your lifetime financial plan.

To build a good credit history, apply for a modest amount of sensible credit (a credit card, auto loan, or a line of credit at a bank, for instance), use that credit periodically, and make sure that at least some credit is being established in your name. If an account is in someone else's name, such as a parent, spouse, or domestic partner, you won't "get credit" for a good payment history, even if you provide some or all of the money.[22] This situation can be a troublesome one for married women in households where most of the accounts are in the husband's name. Applying for credit after a divorce or death of the husband can be difficult for women who haven't built up credit in their own names. Most important of all is to pay all your bills on time. If you find that you can't pay a particular bill on time, call the company and explain your situation. You may get some leniency by showing that you're making a good faith effort to pay your bill.

Experts also recommend that you verify the accuracy of your credit report once a year. Mistakes do creep into credit reports from time to time, and you also need to make sure you haven't been a victim of **identity theft**, in which someone illegally applies for credit using your name. Actually, you don't have just one credit report. The three major credit reporting agencies in the United States each keep a file on you and provide their own credit reports to lenders, landlords, and others with a valid need to see them. For more information, visit Experian (www.experian.com), TransUnion (www.transunion.com), or Equifax (www.equifax.com).

Managing your credit wisely will help you avoid one of the most traumatic events that can befall a consumer: **personal bankruptcy**. You have several options for declaring bankruptcy, but none of them is desirable and all should be avoided by every means possible. Declaring bankruptcy, even if for an unavoidable reason such as medical costs or loss of a spouse, is sometimes called "the 10-year mistake" because it stays on your credit record for 10 years.[23] Bankruptcy is not a simple cure-all, as it is sometimes presented. If you are considering bankruptcy, talk to a counselor first. Start with the National Foundation for Credit Counseling (www.nfcc.org). Wherever you turn for advice, make sure you understand it thoroughly and understand why the organization would be motivated to give you that particular advice. You've probably seen ads (and a torrent of spam e-mail) offering ways to get out from under your debt. Many of these schemes involve declaring bankruptcy, which may not be the right choice for you.[24]

Stage 3: Increasing Your Net Worth and Preparing for Life's Major Expenses

With your basic needs taken care of and a solid foundation under your feet, the next stage of your financial life is increasing your net worth and preparing for both expected and unexpected expenses. Some of the major decisions at this stage include investments, taxes, insurance, your children's education, and emergency planning.

Investing: Building Your Nest Egg

The various cash management options described earlier can be an effective way to store and protect money you already have, but they aren't terribly good at generating more money. That's the goal of *investing*, in which you buy something of value with the idea that it will increase in value before you sell it to someone else. You read about the most common financial investment vehicles in Chapter 14: stocks, mutual funds, and bonds. Real estate is the other major category of investment for most people, not only their own homes but also rental properties and commercial real estate. The final category of investments includes precious metals (primarily gold), gems, and collectibles such as sports or movie memorabilia.

The details of successful investing in these various areas differ widely, but six general rules apply to all of them:

- *Don't invest cash that you may need in the short term.* You may not be able to *liquidate* the investment (selling it to retrieve your cash) in time, or the value may be temporarily down, in which case you'll permanently lose money.

- *Don't invest in anything you don't understand or haven't thoroughly evaluated.* If you can't point to specific reasons that the investment should increase in value, you're simply guessing or gambling.

- *Don't invest on emotion.* You might love eating at a certain restaurant chain, shopping at a particular online retailer, or collecting baseball cards, but that doesn't mean any of these is automatically a good investment.

- *Understand the risks.* Aside from Treasury bills and U.S. savings bonds, virtually no investment can guarantee that you'll make money or even protect the money you originally invested. You could lose most or all of your money, thanks to the risk/reward trade-off discussed earlier. To give yourself the opportunity to realize higher gains, you nearly always need to accept higher levels of risk.

- *Beware of anybody who promises guaranteed results or instant wealth.* Chances are that person will profit more by snaring you into the investment than you'll earn from the investment yourself.

- *Given the risks involved, don't put all your eggs in one basket.* Diversify your investments to make sure you don't leave yourself vulnerable to downturns in a single stock or piece of real estate, for instance.

If you plan to invest in a specific area, you would be wise to take a course in that area or commit to learning on your own. Most of the websites mentioned throughout this appendix offer information, and some offer formal courses you can take online. Investment clubs are an increasingly popular way to learn and pool your resources with other individual investors, too. In the beginning, don't worry about the details of particular stocks or the intricacies of real estate investment trusts and other more advanced concepts. Focus on the fundamentals: Why do stock prices increase or decrease? What effect do interest rates have on bonds? How can a particular house increase in value dramatically while another in the same neighborhood stays flat?

Create a mock portfolio to test your stock-market skills before you invest real money in the market.

You can also practice investing without risking any money. This is a smart move early in your career, when you're still getting on your feet and may not have much money to invest yet. After you've learned the basics of stock investing, for instance, set up a "mock portfolio" on one of the many online sites that provide free portfolio tracking. Month by month, monitor the performance of your choices. Whenever you see a big increase or decrease, dig deeper to understand why. By practicing first, you can learn from your mistakes before those mistakes cost you any money.

Taxes: Minimizing the Bite

Taxes will be a constant factor in your personal financial planning. You pay *sales tax* on many of the products you buy (in all but five states at present); you pay federal *excise taxes* on certain purchases such as gasoline and phone service; you pay *property tax* on real estate; and you pay *income tax* on both earned income (wages, salaries, tips, bonuses, commissions, and business profits) and investment income. The total taxes paid by individuals vary widely, but you can safely assume that taxes will consume 30 to 40 cents of every dollar you make.

Your personal tax strategy should focus on minimizing the taxes you are required to pay, without running afoul of the law or harming your financial progress (for instance, you usually don't want to skip an investment opportunity just because you'll have to pay tax on your gains). Put another way, you are expected to pay your fair share of taxes, but no one expects you to pay more than your share.

You can reduce taxes in three basic ways: (1) by reducing your consumption of goods and services that are subject to either sales tax or excise taxes, (2) by reducing your *taxable income*, or (3) by reducing your tax through the use of *tax credits*. Reducing consumption is a straightforward concept, although there are obviously limits to how far you can reduce consumption and therefore this portion of your tax obligation.

Reducing your taxable income is more complicated but can have a great impact on your finances (by the way, reducing your taxable income means reducing the part of your income that is subject to local, state, or federal income tax, not reducing your overall income level). Authorities such as the IRS allow a variety of **deductions**, such as interest paid on home mortgages and the costs associated with using part of your home for office space. Qualifying deductions can be subtracted from your *gross income* to lower your taxable income. A portion of your income is also *exempt* from federal income tax, based on the number of dependents in your household. The more **exemptions** you can legally claim, the lower your taxable income. You can also lower your taxable income by investing a portion of your income in *tax-exempt* or *tax-deferred* investments. With **tax-exempt investments** (which are primarily bonds issued by local governments), you don't have to pay federal income tax on any income you earn from the investment. With **tax-deferred investments**, such as 401(k) plans and individual retirement accounts (IRAs), you can deduct the amount of money you invest

every year from your gross income, and you don't have to pay tax on income from the investment until you withdraw money during retirement.

Unlike deductions, which only reduce your taxable income and therefore reduce your tax burden by your tax rate, **tax credits** reduce your tax obligation directly. In other words, a $100 *deduction* reduces your tax bill by $28 (if you're in the 28 percent tax bracket, for instance), whereas a $100 *credit* reduces your tax bill by $100.

Personal tax software such as TurboTax (www.turbotax.com) or TaxCut (www.taxcut.com) can guide you through the process of finding deductions and credits. For more complex scenarios, though, it's always a good idea to get the advice of a professional tax adviser.

Insurance: Protecting Yourself, Your Family, and Your Assets

Unfortunately, things go wrong in life, from accidents to health problems to the death of an income provider. Insurance is designed to protect you, your family, and your assets if and when these unpleasant events occur. In a sense, insurance is the ultimate risk/reward trade-off decision. If you had an ironclad guarantee that you would never get sick or injured, you would have no need for health insurance. However, there's a reasonable chance that you will need medical attention at some point, and major injuries and illness can generate many thousands of dollars of unplanned expenses. Consequently, most people consider it a reasonable trade-off to pay for health insurance to protect themselves from catastrophic financial blows. Exhibit C.7 provides a brief overview of your most significant insurance options.

Another vital step to protecting your family, and one that is often overlooked by younger people, is preparing a **will**, a legal document that specifies what happens to your assets (as well as who will be legal guardian of your children, if you have any) in the event of your death.

Stage 4: Plan for a Secure, Independent Retirement

Retirement? You're only 25 years old (or 35 or 45). Yes, but as you saw earlier in the discussion of compound interest, it's never too early to start planning for retirement. It's tempting to picture retirement as a carefree time when you can finally ditch your job and focus on hobbies, travel, volunteer work, and the hundred other activities you haven't had time for all your life. Sadly, the reality for millions of retired people today is much different. Between skyrocketing medical costs, the dot-com devastation in the stock market, and lower than expected company pensions in some cases, retirement for many people is a never-ending financial struggle with little hope for improvement.

Understanding Your Insurance Options

You can buy insurance for every eventuality from earthquake damage to vacation interruptions, but the most common and most important types include medical, disability, auto, home owners', and life insurance.

CATEGORY	HIGHLIGHTS
Medical insurance	Usually purchased as part of group coverage, such as through an employer or a union; individual or single family is available but often more expensive; most plans offer a variety of cost and coverage options—for instance, to lower your monthly costs you can select a higher deductible, which is the amount you have to pay before insurance coverage kicks in; selecting the right plan requires a careful analysis of your needs and financial circumstances
Disability insurance	Temporarily replaces a portion of your salary if you are unable to work; various policies have different definitions of "disability" and restrictions on coverage and payments
Auto insurance	Most states now have *compulsory liability insurance laws*, meaning that you have to prove that you are covered for any damage you might cause as a driver; coverage for your vehicle can be both *collision* (damages resulting from collisions) and *comprehensive* (other damages or theft); you can also buy coverage to protect yourself from illegally uninsured motorists
Home owners' insurance	Most policies include both *property loss coverage* (to replace or repair the home and its contents) and *liability coverage* (to protect you in case someone sues you); often required by the lender when you have a mortgage
Life insurance	Primary purpose is to provide for others in the event that your death would create a financial hardship for them; common forms are *term life* (limited duration, less expensive, no investment value), *whole-life* (permanent coverage, builds cash value over time, more expensive than term life), and *universal life* (similar to whole-life but more flexible)

Perhaps the most important step you can take toward a more positive retirement is to shed all of the misconceptions that people often have about retirement planning:[25]

- *My living expenses will drop so I'll need less money.* Some of your expenses may well drop, but rising health-care costs will probably swamp reductions in housing, clothing, and other personal costs.

- *I'll live for roughly 15 years after I retire.* The big advantage of that expensive health care is that people are living longer and longer. You could live for 20 or 30 years after you retire.

- *Social Security will cover my basic living expenses.* Social Security probably won't cover even your basic requirements, and the entire system is in serious financial trouble. While it's unlikely that political leaders would ever let Social Security collapse, the safest bet is to not count on it at all.

- *Your employer will keep funding your pension and health insurance.* Thousands of retirees in recent years have been devastated by former employers who either curtailed or eliminated pension and health coverage.

- *I can't save much right now, so there's no point in saving anything at all.* If you find yourself thinking this, remind yourself of the magic of compounding. Over time, small amounts grow into large amounts of money. Do whatever it takes to get started now.

- *You have plenty of time to worry about retirement later.* Unfortunately, you don't. The longer you wait, the harder it will become to ensure a comfortable retirement. If you're not prepared, your only option will be to continue working well into your 70s or 80s.

In other words, the situation is serious. However, that doesn't mean it's hopeless—not by any means. You control your destiny, and you don't need to abandon all pleasures and comforts now to make it happen. However, you do need to put a plan together and start saving now. Make retirement planning a positive part of your personal financial planning, part of your dream of living the life you want to live.

Appendix Glossary

asset management accounts   Cash management accounts offered by brokerage firms and mutual fund companies, frequently as a way to manage cash that isn't currently invested elsewhere

assets   The physical things, such as real estate and artwork, and financial elements, such as cash and stocks, that you own

balance sheet   A summary of your assets and liabilities; the difference between the two subtotals is your net worth

buying power   The real value of money, adjusted for inflation; inflation raises prices, which in turn reduces buying power

cash management   All of the planning and activities associated with managing your cash and other liquid assets

closing costs   Fees associated with buying and selling a house

commission-based planners   Financial advisers who are paid commissions on the financial products they sell you, such as insurance policies and mutual funds

compounding   The acceleration of balances caused by applying new interest to interest that has already accumulated

credit bureaus   Businesses that compile credit information on businesses and individual consumers

credit history   A record of your mortgages, consumer loans, credit card accounts (including credit limits and current balances), and bill-paying performance

credit reports   Reports generated by credit bureaus, showing an individual's credit usage and payment history

deductions   Opportunities to reduce taxable income by subtracting the cost of a specific item, such as business expenses or interest paid on home mortgages

equity   The portion of a house's current value that you own

exemptions   Reductions to taxable income based on the number of dependents in the household

fee-only planners   Financial advisers who charge a fee for their services, rather than earning a commission on financial services they sell you

identity theft   A crime in which someone illegally applies for credit in someone else's name

income and expense statement   A listing of your monthly inflows (income) and outflows (expenses); also called an *income statement*

inflation   The tendency of prices to increase over time

liabilities   Amounts of money you owe

liquid assets   Assets that can be quickly and easily converted to cash

mortgage   A loan used to purchase real estate

net worth   The difference between your assets and your liabilities

overdraft fees   Penalties charged against your checking account when you write checks that total more than your available balance

personal bankruptcy   A condition in which a consumer is unable to repay his or her debts; depending on the type of bankruptcy, a court will either forgive many of the person's debts or establish a compatible repayment plan

reconcile   The process of comparing the balance you believe is in your account with the balance the bank believes is in your account

tax credits   Direct reductions in your tax obligation

tax-deferred investments   Investments such as 401(k) plans and IRAs that let you deduct the amount of your investments from your gross income (thereby lowering your taxable income); you don't have to pay tax on any of the income from these investments until you start to withdraw money during retirement

tax-exempt investments   Investments (usually municipal bonds) whose income is not subject to federal income tax

time value of money   The increasing value of money as a result of accumulating interest

trade-off   A decision-making condition in which you have to give up one or more benefits to gain other benefits

will   A legal document that specifies what happens to your assets, who will execute your estate (carry out the terms of your will), and who will be the legal guardian of your children, if you have any, in the event of your death

Appendix D
Your Business Plan

Getting Started with Business PlanPro Software

Business PlanPro (BPP) software is a template for crafting a winning business plan. The software is designed to stimulate your thinking about the many tasks and decisions that go into planning and running a business. The software can't do your thinking for you, of course, but it does lead you through a thought process by asking you to respond to questions about your business and to provide data for the preformatted tables and charts. Accompanying instructions, examples, and sample business plans provide you with a full range of assistance you can use to draft your own comprehensive business plan. By working through the exercises at the end of each text part, you will gain a practical skill for your business career.

When installing the software, be sure to install Adobe Acrobat Reader software if you don't already have it on your computer; you'll need it to view the sample business plans included with the disk and downloadable from the web. You can get an overview of the BPP software by clicking on the Help menu from the main screen, then selecting About Business PlanPro. Under the Help menu, you can click on contents and then Getting Help for operational instructions or to look up business terms in the software's Glossary. For quick answers to questions about using the software, look under the How Do I menu at the top right of the screen. An overview of the software's features is also on the web at www.paloalto.com/prenticehall.

Navigating the Software

One of the best ways to become familiar with the BPP software is by navigating one of the BPP sample business plans. Launch the BPP software, then click on Create a New Business Plan to reach the main screen. Now choose File from the menu and click Open Sample. This brings you to the Sample Plan Browser. An alternate way to get to this screen is by clicking on the Research It menu along the left of the screen, then selecting Sample Plan Browser.

The names of the sample plans are listed on the left, and the first page of plans bundled with the software can be seen on the right. To view a sample plan, double-click on the plan name. To page through a plan, simply click on the arrows on the bottom of the frame in which the plan pages appear. If you have an Internet connection, the software will download the latest version of the sample plan. You can also check the web at www.bplans.com/sp to search through dozens of sample plans created using BPP software.

To see how a sample plan in the BPP software is organized or to move between sections in your order, click the Show/Hide Navigation icon to the right of the printer icon on the menu above the sample plan page. When you click on a section name, the plan displays that page.

As you will see when exploring the sample plans, the Executive Summary section provides a brief overview of the business plan. The Company Summary discusses company specifics such as the mission and ownership. The Products and Services section describes exactly what the company is selling. The Market Analysis examines the company's market, including competitors and customers. The Strategy and Implementation section indicates the company's broad course of action in the market, its sales goals, and how it will implement the plan. The Management Summary introduces the organizational structure and management personnel. Finally, the Financial Plan section presents profit-and-loss projections and other financial plans.

You may find it helpful to print out a full copy of the sample plan you have selected and review it as you navigate its contents on your screen. This way you can see how the software uses the information to construct a formal business plan. To print out the sample plan, click on the Printer icon and select Plan. You may also choose to print selected sections or the instructions or examples for a business plan. Once you've finished viewing or printing sample plans, click to close the frame and return to the main screen.

You have multiple options for accessing the same information, as shown under the View menu. The Plan Manager option guides you through the process of researching a plan, building it, distributing and delivering it, and making it happen. The Plan Outline option allows you to develop the plan section by section in outline form. To access the text mode option, where you write your business plan's text, select Text Mode from the View menu. You can move between sections by selecting from topics in the Topic drop-down menu above the text screen or using the forward and backward arrows at the right of the Topic menu. To view related tables and charts, click the Table mode or the Chart mode under the View menu.

Creating a Winning Business Plan

The exercises included at the end of each text part use the knowledge you've gained from reading that text part. Each exercise has two tasks: Think Like a Pro tasks require you to navigate the software, find and review information in the sample business plans, and evaluate and critique some of the thinking that went behind these plans. By reviewing these sample plans with a critical eye, you will begin to sharpen your own business planning skills. Create Your Own Business Plan tasks are an opportunity for you to apply your business-planning skills to create your own winning business plan. So begin thinking now about the type of business you'd like to own or manage some day. Then develop and refine your business strategies as you work through the exercises.

Appendix E
Careers in Business and the Employment Search

Looking Ahead to Your Career

Finding the right job at every stage of your career is a lifelong process of seeking the best fit between what you want to do and what employers are willing to pay you to do. For instance, if money is more important to you than anything else, you can certainly pursue jobs that promise high pay; just be aware that most of these jobs require years of experience and many produce a lot of stress, require frequent travel, or have other drawbacks you'll want to consider. In contrast, if location, lifestyle, intriguing work, or other factors are more important to you, you may well have to sacrifice some level of pay to achieve them. The important thing is to know what you want to do, what you have to offer, and how to make yourself more attractive to employers.

What Do You Want to Do?

Economic necessities and the vagaries of the marketplace will influence much of what happens in your career, of course; nevertheless, it's wise to start your employment search by examining your own values and interests. Identify what you want to do first, then see whether you can find a position that satisfies you at a personal level while also meeting your financial needs.

- *What would you like to do every day?* Conduct research into occupations that interest you. Find out what people really do every day. Ask friends, relatives, or alumni from your school. On the web, visit Career One Stop, www.careeronestop.com, which offers a vast array of career resources, including short online videos of real people doing real work in hundreds of different professions.

- *How would you like to work?* Consider how much independence you want on the job, how much variety you like, and whether you prefer to work with products, machines, people, ideas, figures, or some combination thereof. Do you like physical work, mental work, or a mix? Constant change or a predictable role?

- *What specific compensation do you expect?* What do you hope to earn in your first year? What kind of pay increase do you expect each year? What's your ultimate earnings goal? Would you be comfortable getting paid on com-

mission, or do you prefer a steady paycheck? Are you willing to settle for less money in order to do something you really love?

- *Can you establish some general career goals?* Consider where you'd like to start, where you'd like to go from there, and the ultimate position you'd like to attain. Do you want to be a corporate executive or a technical specialist? How important are power and influence to you?

- *What size company would you prefer?* Do you like the idea of working for a small, entrepreneurial operation? Would you prefer a large corporation? Do you want to work on your own?

- *What type of operation is appealing to you?* Would you prefer to work for a profit-making company or a non-profit organization? Are you interested in service or manufacturing? Do you require regular, predictable hours or can you handle a flexible or unpredictable schedule? Do you prefer consistent work throughout the year or seasonal cycles (as in education, accounting, or retailing)?

- *What facilities do you envision?* Would you prefer a downtown high-rise building, an office park in the suburbs, a shop on Main Street in a small town—or perhaps no office at all?

- *What sort of corporate culture are you most comfortable with?* Would you be happy in a formal hierarchy with clear reporting relationships? Or do you prefer less structure? Teamwork or individualism? Do you like a competitive environment? What qualities do you want in a boss?

- *What location would you like?* Would you like to work in a city, a suburb, a small town, an industrial area, or an uptown setting? Do you favor a particular part of the country? Do you like working indoors or outdoors? In another country?

What Do You Have to Offer?

Knowing what you *want* to do is one thing. Knowing what you *can* do is another. You may already have a good idea of what you can offer employers. If not, some brainstorming can help you identify your skills, interests, and characteristics.

Start by jotting down 10 achievements you're proud of, such as learning to ski, taking a prize-winning photo, tutoring a child, or editing your school paper. Think carefully about what specific skills these achievements demanded of you. For example, leadership skills, speaking ability, and artistic talent may have helped you coordinate a winning presentation to your school's administration. As you analyze your achievements, you'll begin to recognize a pattern of skills. Which of them might be valuable to potential employers?

Next, look at your educational preparation, work experience, and extracurricular activities. What do your knowledge and experience qualify you to do? What have you learned from volunteer work or class projects that could benefit you on the job? Have you held any offices, won any awards or scholarships, mastered a second language?

Take stock of your personal characteristics. Are you aggressive, a born leader? Or would you rather follow? Are you outgoing, articulate, great with people? Or do you prefer working alone? Make a list of what you believe are your four or five most important qualities. Ask a relative or friend to rate your traits as well.

If you're having difficulty figuring out your interests, characteristics, or capabilities, consult your college placement office. Many campuses administer a variety of tests to help you identify interests, aptitudes, and personality traits. These tests won't reveal your "perfect" job, but they'll help you focus on the types of work best suited to your personality.

How Can You Make Yourself More Valuable?

While you're figuring out what you want from a job and what you can offer an employer, you can take positive steps toward actually building your career. You can do a lot before you graduate from college and even while you are seeking employment:

- *Keep an employment portfolio.* Collect anything that shows your ability to perform, whether it's in school, on the job, or in other venues. Your portfolio is a great resource for writing your résumé, and it gives employers tangible evidence of your professionalism. Many colleges now offer students the chance to create an *e-portfolio*, a multimedia presentation of your skills and experiences. It's an extensive résumé that links to an electronic collection of your student papers, solutions to tough problems, internship and work projects, and anything else that demonstrates your accomplishments and activities.[1] To distribute the portfolio to potential employers, you can burn a CD-ROM or store your portfolio on a website—whether it's a personal site, your college's site (if student pages are available), or a site such as www.collegegrad.com. (However, you *must* check with an employer before including any items that belong to the company or contain sensitive information.)

- *Take interim assignments.* As you search for a permanent job, consider temporary jobs, freelance work, or internships. These temporary assignments not only help you gain valuable experience and relevant contacts but also provide you with important references and with items for your portfolio.[2]

- *Continue to polish and update your skills.* Join networks of professional colleagues and friends who can help you keep up with your occupation and industry. Many professional societies have student chapters or offer students discounted memberships. Take courses and pursue other educational or life experiences that would be hard to get while working full-time.

Seeking Employment Opportunities and Information

Whether your major is business, biology, or political science, once you know what you want and what you have to offer, you can start finding an employer to match. If you haven't already committed yourself to any particular career field, review the career tables in the *Occupational Outlook Handbook*, a nationally recognized source of career information published by the U.S. Bureau of Labor Statistics. Revised every two years, the handbook (available in print and online at www.bls.gov/oco) describes what workers do on the job, working conditions, the training and education needed, earnings, and expected job prospects in a wide range of occupations.[3]

Here is a brief overview of the future outlook for a number of careers in business:

- *Careers in management.* Today's business environment requires the skills of effective managers to reduce costs, streamline operations, develop marketing strategies, and supervise workers. As discussed in Chapter 6, managers perform four basic functions: planning, organizing, leading, and controlling. Facing increased competition, many businesses are becoming more dependent on the expertise of outside management consultants—one of the fastest-growing occupations of all jobs. Outside management consultants perform many important tasks, but chief among them is evaluating operating conditions and making recommendations to improve effectiveness. To find out more about what you can do with a degree in management and the typical courses management majors take, log on to the Prentice Hall Student Success SuperSite at www.prenhall.com/success/MajorExp/mgmt.html.

- *Careers in human resources.* As discussed in Chapters 9 and 10, human resources managers plan and direct human resource activities that include recruiting, training and development, compensation and benefits, employee and labor relations, and health and safety. Additionally, human resources managers develop and implement human resources systems and practices to accommodate a firm's strategy and to motivate and manage diverse workforces. Large numbers of job openings are expected in the human resources field in the near future. Efforts to recruit quality employees and to provide more employee training programs should create new human resources positions. With a vast supply of qualified workers and new college graduates, however, the job market for human resources is likely to remain competitive.

- *Careers in computers and information systems.* Job opportunities abound for trained information technology workers. As competition and advanced technologies force companies to upgrade and improve their computer systems, the number of computer-related positions continues to escalate. Within the computer field, only two categories of jobs are expected to decrease: computer operators and data-entry clerks. More user-friendly computer software has greatly reduced the need for operators and data-entry processors, but displaced workers who keep up with changing technology should have few problems moving into other areas of computer support. To find out more about careers in computer science and information systems, log on to the Prentice Hall Student Success SuperSite at www.prenhall.com/success/MajorExp/CSImajors.html, then explore the various specialties listed.

- *Careers in sales and marketing.* Increasing competition in products and services should create greater needs for effective sales and marketing personnel in the future. Employment opportunities for retail salespersons look good because of the need to replace the large number of workers who transfer to other occupations or leave the workforce each year. Opportunities for part-time work should be abundant. Employment for insurance and real estate agents, however, is expected to grow more slowly than average. Computer technology will allow established agents to increase their sales volume and eliminate the need for additional marketing personnel in these fields. For additional information on the types of courses marketing majors take and what you can do with a degree in marketing see Chapters 11 through 12 and log on to the Prentice Hall Student Success SuperSite at www.prenhall.com/success/MajorExp/mktg.html.

- *Careers in finance and accounting.* As Chapter 13 points out, accountants and financial managers are needed in almost every industry. Most positions in finance and accounting are expected to grow as fast as the average for all occupations in the near future, as continued growth in the economy and population is expected to create more demand for trained financial personnel. To find out more about careers in finance and accounting, log on to the Prentice Hall Student Success SuperSite at www.prenhall.com/success/MajorExp/acct.html, and select finance or accounting.

- *Careers in economics.* As Chapter 1 discusses, economists study how society distributes scarce resources such as land, labor, raw materials, and machinery to produce goods and services. They conduct research, collect and analyze data, monitor economic trends, and develop forecasts. Economists are needed in many industries and spend time applying economic theory to analyze issues that are important to their firms. For example, they might analyze the effects of global economic activity on the demand for the company's product, conduct a cost-benefit analysis of the projects the company is considering, or determine the effects of government regulations or taxes on the company. Employment of economists is expected to grow about as fast as the average for all occupations, with the best opportunities in private industry—especially research, testing, and consulting firms—as more companies contract out for economic research services. To find out more about what you can do with a degree in economics and the typical courses economics majors take, log on to the Prentice Hall Student Success SuperSite at www.prenhall.com/success/MajorExp/econ.html.

- *Careers in communications.* As businesses recognize the need for effective communications with their customers and the public, employment of communications personnel is expected to grow as fast or faster than the average for all occupations in the near future. Recent college graduates may face keen competition for entry positions in communications as the number of applicants is expected to exceed the number of job openings. Newly created jobs in the ever-expanding computer world—such as graphic designers for websites or technical writers for instruction manuals—are expected to improve the career outlook for new communications graduates.

Exhibit E.1 lists the 30 business occupations (including management positions) that are projected to grow the fastest between now and 2012. Keep in mind that most of the high-growth jobs require college degrees, and many of the hottest jobs in today's business world demand technological and computer skills. Even if you're interested in finance, human resources, or marketing positions, you'll need basic computer skills to snare the best jobs in your desired field of work.

Sources of Employment Information

One effective approach to the employment process is to gather as much information as you can, narrowing it as you go until you know precisely the companies you want to contact. Begin by finding out where the job opportunities are, which industries are strong, which parts of the country are booming, and which specific job categories offer the best prospects for the future.

From there you can investigate individual organizations, doing your best to learn as much about them as possible. Here are some good information sources:

- *Business and financial news.* If you don't already do so, subscribe to a major newspaper (print or online editions) and scan the business pages every day. Watch

Exhibit E.1	The 25 Fastest-Growing Business Occupations

According to government estimates, these 25 business occupations are expected to grow the fastest between 2002 and 2012. (The list does not include technical specialties such as engineering or computer programming.)

OCCUPATION	2002 EMPLOYMENT (THOUSANDS)	PROJECTED INCREASES BY 2012	
		NUMBER OF NEW JOBS (THOUSANDS)	% INCREASE
Computer and information systems managers	284	103	36.1
Personal financial advisers	126	44	34.6
Sales managers	343	105	30.5
Management analysts	577	176	30.4
Medical and health services managers	244	71	29.3
Agents and business managers of artists, performers, and athletes	15	4	27.8
Human resources, training, and labor relations specialists	474	131	27.7
All other business operations specialists	1,056	290	27.5
Advertising and promotions managers	85	21	25.0
Public relations managers	69	16	23.4
Marketing managers	203	43	21.3
Meeting and convention planners	37	8	21.3
Administrative services managers	321	63	19.8
Transportation, storage, and distribution managers	111	22	19.7
Accountants and auditors	1,055	205	19.5
Human resources managers	202	39	19.4
Credit analysts	66	12	18.7
Financial analysts	172	32	18.7
Cost estimators	188	35	18.6
General and operations managers	2,049	376	18.4
Financial managers	599	109	18.3
Appraisers and assessors of real estate	88	16	17.6
Chief executives	553	93	16.7
Claims adjusters, appraisers, examiners, and investigators	241	34	14.0
Budget analysts	62	9	14.0

some of the television programs that focus on business, such as *Wall Street Week*. You can find information about the future of specific jobs in the *Dictionary of Occupational Titles* (U.S. Employment Service), the employment publications of Science Research Associates, and the *Occupational Outlook Handbook* (U.S. Bureau of Labor Statistics). This last reference is available both in print and online at www.bls.gov. Of course, with all the business information available today, it's easy to get lost in the details. Try not to get too caught up in the daily particulars of business. Start by examining "big picture" topics, such as trends, issues, industry-wide challenges, and careers, before delving into specific companies that look attractive.

Job fairs can be a great source of information about new career opportunities.

- *Networking.* Networking is the process of making informal connections with a broad sphere of mutually beneficial business contacts. According to one recent survey, networking is the most common way that employees find jobs.[4] Networking takes place wherever and whenever people talk: at industry functions, social gatherings, sports events and recreational activities, online chat rooms (including sponsored online networking sites such as http://network.monster.com), alumni reunions, and so on. You may be able to network with executives in your field by joining or participating in student business organizations, especially those with ties to professional organizations such as the American Marketing Association or the American Management Association. Keep in mind that novice job seekers sometimes misunderstand networking and unknowingly commit breaches of etiquette. Networking isn't a matter of walking up to strangers at social events, handing over your résumé, and asking them to find you a job. Rather, it involves the sharing of information between people who might be able to offer mutual help at some point in the future. Think of it as an organic process, in which you cultivate the possibility of finding that perfect opportunity. Networking can take time, and it can operate in unpredictable ways. You may not get results for months, so it's important to start early and make it part of your lifelong program of career management.

- *College placement offices.* Also known as career centers, college placement offices offer individual counseling, credential services, job fairs, on-campus interviews, and job listings. Staff members give advice on résumé writing and provide workshops in job-search techniques, interview techniques, and more.[5]

Employment Information on the Web

The web offers an amazing amount of company and employment information, both general and specific:

- *Discussion groups.* Using the web, you can locate and communicate with potential employers through numerous types of discussion groups dedicated to your field. Search for Usenet newsgroups in the fields you're interested in (visit www.google.com, click on Groups, then enter keywords such as "marketing" or "research"). Commercial systems such as AOL have numerous discussion groups as well.

- *Career counseling websites.* You can also find job counseling online. You might begin your self-assessment, for example, with the Keirsey Temperament Sorter, an online personality test at www.advisorteam.com. For excellent job-seeking pointers and counseling, visit college- and university-run online career centers. Major online job boards such as Monster.com also offer a variety of career planning resources.

- *Company websites.* Most companies, even small firms, offer at least basic information about themselves on their websites. Look for the "About Us" or "Company" part of the site to find a company profile, executive biographies, press releases, financial information, and information on employment opportunities. You'll often find information about an organization's mission, products, annual reports, and employee benefits. You can also e-mail organizations and ask for annual reports, descriptive brochures, or newsletters. Look for outside sources as well, including the business sections of local newspapers and trade publications that cover the company's industries and markets.

- *Job boards.* As Chapter 10 pointed out, online job boards have become an integral part of most companies' recruiting procedures, so be sure to check them out. In addition to the major sites such as Monster, Yahoo! Hotjobs, and CareerBuilder, look for niche boards that address special-interest and specific career fields (see Exhibit E.2). Your placement office probably has an up-to-date list as well.

Preparing Your Résumé

A **résumé** is a structured, written summary of a person's education, employment background, and job qualifications. Although many people have misconceptions about résumés (see Exhibit E.3 on page 424), the fact is that a résumé is a form of advertising. It is intended to stimulate an employer's interest in you—in meeting you and learning more about you. A successful résumé inspires a prospective employer to invite you to interview with the company. Thus, your purpose in writing your résumé is to create interest—*not* to tell readers everything about you. In fact, it may be best to only hint at some things and leave the reader wanting more. The

Exhibit E.2　**Netting a Job on the Web**

Begin your job search with these helpful online career resources.

WEBSITE*	URL	HIGHLIGHTS
Riley Guide	www.rileyguide.com	Vast collection of links to both general and specialized job sites for every career imaginable; don't miss this one—it'll save you hours or days of searching
America's CareerOneStop	www.careeronestop.org	Comprehensive, government-funded site that includes America's Career InfoNet and America's Job Bank; learn more about the workplace in general as well as specific careers; offers information on typical wages and employment trends and identifies education, knowledge, and skills requirements for most occupations
Monster	www.monster.com	World's largest job site with hundreds of thousands of openings, many from hard-to-find smaller companies; extensive collection of advice on the job-search process
MonsterTrak	www.monstertrak.com	Focused on job searches for new college grads; your school's career center site probably links here
Yahoo! Hotjobs	hotjobs.yahoo.com	Another leading job board, formed by recent merger of Hotjobs and Yahoo! careers
CareerBuilder	www.careerbuilder.com	Fast-growing site affiliated with more than 100 local newspapers around the country
USA Jobs	www.usajobs.opm.gov	The official job search site for the U.S. government, featuring everything from economists to astronauts to border patrol agents
IMDiversity	www.imdiversity.com	Good resource on diversity in the workplace, with job postings from companies that have made a special commitment to promoting diversity in their workforces
Dice.com	www.dice.com	One of the best sites for high-technology jobs
Net-Temps	www.nettemps.com	Popular site for contractors and freelancers looking for short-term assignments
InternshipPrograms.com	www.internships.wetfeet.com	Posts listings from companies looking for interns in a wide variety of professions

* Note: This list represents only a small fraction of the job-posting sites and other resources available online; be sure to check with your college's career center for the latest information.

potential employer will then have even more reason to contact you.[6]

Your résumé is one of the most important documents you'll ever write. You can help ensure success by remembering four things: First, treat your résumé with the respect it deserves. Until you're able to meet with employers in person, your résumé is all they have of you. Until that first personal contact occurs, you *are* your résumé, and a single mistake or oversight can cost you interview opportunities. Second, give yourself plenty of time. Don't put off preparing your résumé until the last second and then try to write it in one sitting. Let this special document stew and try out different ideas and phrases until you hit on the right combination. Also, give yourself plenty of time to proofread the résumé when you're

finished—and ask several other people to proofread it as well. Third, learn from good models. You can find thousands of sample résumés online at college websites and job sites such as Monster.com. Fourth, don't get frustrated by the conflicting advice you'll read about résumés; they are more art than science. Consider the alternatives and choose the approach that makes the most sense in your specific situation.

By the way, if anyone asks to see your "CV," they're referring to your *curriculum vitae*, the term used instead of *résumé* in some professions and in many countries outside the United States. Résumés and CVs are essentially the same, although CVs can be more detailed. If you need to adapt a U.S.-style résumé to CV format, or vice versa, Monster.com has helpful guidelines on the subject.

FALLACY	FACT
✗ The purpose of a résumé is to list all your skills and abilities.	✓ The purpose of a résumé is to kindle employer interest and generate an interview.
✗ A good résumé will get you the job you want.	✓ All a résumé can do is get you in the door.
✗ Your résumé will be read carefully and thoroughly by an interested employer.	✓ Your résumé probably has less than 45 seconds to make an impression.
✗ The more good information you present about yourself in your résumé, the better.	✓ Too much information on a résumé may actually kill the reader's appetite to know more.
✗ If you want a really good résumé, have it prepared by a résumé service.	✓ Prepare your own résumé—unless the position is especially high-level or specialized. Even then, you should check carefully before using a service.

Controlling the Format and Style

To give your printed résumé the best appearance possible, use a clean typeface on high-grade, letter-size bond paper in white or a very light earth tone. Avoid gimmicky preprinted papers (which can make you look unprofessional) or papers with speckled or other nonplain backgrounds (which can cause problems with scanning or photocopying). Your stationery and envelope should match. Leave ample margins all around, and make sure that any corrections are unnoticeable. Avoid italic typefaces, which are difficult to read, and use a quality printer.

Try to keep your résumé to one page. If you have a great deal of experience and are applying for a higher-level position, you may need to prepare a somewhat longer résumé. The important thing is to have enough space to present a persuasive, but accurate, portrait of your skills and accomplishments.

Lay out your résumé so that the information is easy to grasp.[7] Break up the text with headings that call attention to various aspects of your background, such as work experience and education. Underline or boldface key points, or set them off in the left margin. Use indented lists to itemize your most important qualifications. Leave plenty of white space, even if you're forced to use two pages. Pay attention to mechanics and details. Make sure that headings and itemized lists are grammatically parallel and that grammar, spelling, and punctuation are correct.

Write in a simple and direct style to save your reader time. Use short, crisp phrases instead of whole sentences, and focus on what your reader needs to know. Avoid using the word *I*. Instead, you might say, "Led a team of volunteers that raised $45,000 for a community center" or "Managed a fast-food restaurant and four employees."

Think about your résumé from the employer's perspective. Ask yourself: What key qualifications will an employer be looking for? Which of these are my greatest strengths? What will set me apart from other candidates? What are my greatest accomplishments, and what was produced as a result? Then tailor your résumé to appeal to the employer's needs.

Keeping Your Résumé Honest

At some point in the writing process, you're sure to run into the question of honesty. A claim may be clearly wrong ("So what if I didn't get those last two credits—I got the same education as people who did graduate, so it's OK to say that I graduated too"). Or a rationalization may be more subtle ("Even though the task was to organize the company picnic, I did a good job, so it should qualify as 'project management'"). Either way, the information is dishonest.

Somehow, the idea that "everybody lies on their résumés" has crept into popular consciousness, and dishonesty in the job search process has reached epidemic proportions. As many as half of the résumés now sent to employers contain false information. And it's not just the simple fudging of a fact here and there. Dishonest applicants are getting creative—and bold. Don't have the college degree you want? You can buy a degree from one of the websites that now offer fake diplomas. Better yet, pay a computer hacker to insert your name into a prestigious university's graduation records, in case somebody checks. Aren't really working in that impressive job at a well-known company? You can always list it on your résumé and sign up for a service that provides phony employment verification.[8]

Applicants with integrity know they don't need to stoop to lying to compete in the job market. If you are tempted to stretch the truth, bear in mind that professional recruiters have seen every trick in the book, and employers who are fed up with the dishonesty are getting more aggressive at uncovering the truth. Roughly 80 percent now contact references and conduct criminal background checks, and many do credit checks when the job involves financial responsibility.[9] And even if you get past these filters with fraudulent information, you'll probably be exposed on the job when you can't live up to your own résumé. Such fabrications have been known to catch up to people many years into their careers, with embarrassing consequences.

To maintain a high standard of honesty in your résumé, subject any questionable entries to two simple tests: First, if something is not true, don't include it—don't try to rationalize it, excuse it, or make it sound better than it is; simply leave it out. A second and more subtle test, helpful for those borderline issues, is asking whether you'd be comfortable sharing a particular piece of information face-to-face. If you wouldn't be comfortable saying it in person, don't say it in your résumé. These tests will help ensure a factual résumé that represents who you are and lead you toward jobs that are truly right for you.

Organizing Your Résumé Around Your Strengths

As you compose your résumé, try to emphasize the information that has a bearing on your career objective, and minimize or exclude any that is irrelevant or counterproductive. To interest potential employers in your résumé, call attention to your best features and downplay your weaknesses—but be sure you do so without distorting or misrepresenting the facts.[10] Do you have something in your history that might trigger an employer's red flag? Following are some common problems and some quick suggestions for overcoming them:[11]

- *Frequent job changes.* Group all contract and temporary jobs under one heading if they're similar.

- *Gaps in work history.* Mention relevant experience and education gained during time gaps, such as volunteer or community work. If gaps are due to personal problems such as drug, alcohol abuse, or mental illness, offer honest but general explanations about your absences ("I had serious health concerns and had to take time off to fully recover").

- *Inexperience.* Do related volunteer work. List relevant course work and internships. Offer hiring incentives such as "willing to work nights and weekends."

- *Overqualification.* Tone down your résumé, focusing exclusively on pertinent experience and skills.

- *Long-term employment with one company.* Itemize each position held at the firm to show "interior mobility" and increased responsibilities. Don't include obsolete skills and job titles.

- *Job termination for cause.* Be honest with interviewers. Show you're a hard-working employee and counter their concerns with proof such as recommendations and examples of completed projects.

- *Criminal record.* Consider sending out a "broadcast letter" about your skills and experience, rather than a résumé and cover letter. Prepare answers to questions that interviewers will probably pose ("You may wonder whether I will be a trustworthy employee. I'd like to offer you a list of references from previous bosses and co-workers who will attest to my integrity. I learned some hard lessons during that difficult time in my life, and now I'm fully rehabilitated").

To focus attention on your strongest points, adopt the appropriate organizational approach—make your résumé chronological, functional, or a combination of the two. The "right" choice depends on your background and your goals.

The Chronological Résumé

In a **chronological résumé**, the work-experience section dominates and is placed in the most prominent slot, immediately after the name and address and optional objective. You develop this section by listing your jobs sequentially in reverse order, beginning with the most recent position and working backward toward earlier jobs. Under each listing, describe your responsibilities and accomplishments, giving the most space to the most recent positions. If you're just graduating from college with limited professional experience, you can vary this chronological approach by putting your educational qualifications before your experience, thereby focusing attention on your academic credentials.

The chronological approach is the most common way to organize a résumé, and many employers prefer it. This approach has three key advantages: (1) Employers are familiar with it and can easily find information, (2) it highlights growth and career progression, and (3) it highlights employment continuity and stability.[12] As vice president with Korn/Ferry International, Robert Nesbit speaks for many recruiters: "Unless you have a really compelling reason, don't use any but the standard chronological format. Your résumé should not read like a treasure map, full of minute clues to the whereabouts of your jobs and experience. I want to be able to grasp quickly where a candidate has worked, how long, and in what capacities."[13]

The chronological approach is especially appropriate if you have a strong employment history and are aiming for a job that builds on your current career path (see Exhibit E.4).

The Functional Résumé

A **functional résumé**, sometimes called a *skills résumé*, emphasizes your skills and capabilities, identifying employers and academic experience in subordinate sections. This pattern stresses individual areas of competence, so it's useful for people who are just entering the job market, want to redirect their careers, or have little continuous career-

Exhibit E.4   **Chronological Résumé**

Roberto Cortez calls attention to his most recent achievements by setting them off in list form with bullets. The section titled "Intercultural and Technical Skills" emphasizes his international background, fluency in Spanish, and extensive computer skills—all of which are important qualifications for his target position.

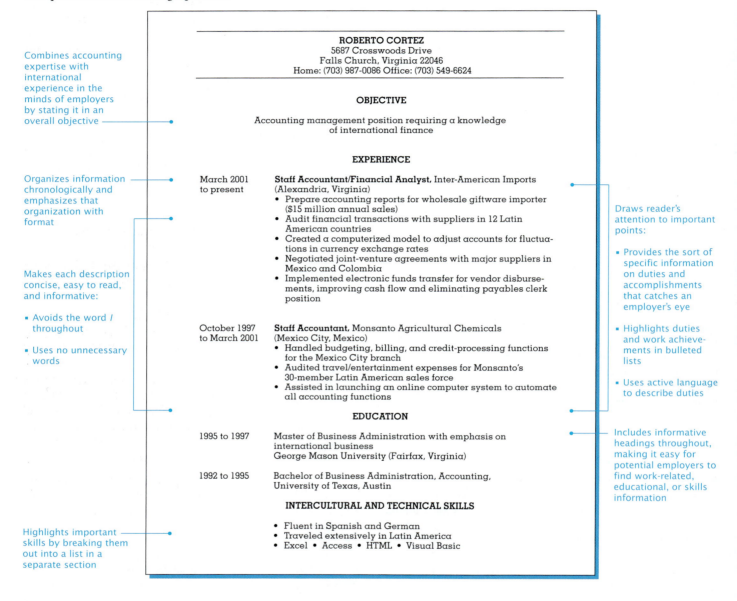

Combines accounting expertise with international experience in the minds of employers by stating it in an overall objective

Organizes information chronologically and emphasizes that organization with format

Makes each description concise, easy to read, and informative:
- Avoids the word *I* throughout
- Uses no unnecessary words

Highlights important skills by breaking them out into a list in a separate section

Draws reader's attention to important points:
- Provides the sort of specific information on duties and accomplishments that catches an employer's eye
- Highlights duties and work achievements in bulleted lists
- Uses active language to describe duties

Includes informative headings throughout, making it easy for potential employers to find work-related, educational, or skills information

ROBERTO CORTEZ
5687 Crosswoods Drive
Falls Church, Virginia 22046
Home: (703) 987-0086 Office: (703) 549-6624

OBJECTIVE

Accounting management position requiring a knowledge of international finance

EXPERIENCE

March 2001 to present — **Staff Accountant/Financial Analyst,** Inter-American Imports (Alexandria, Virginia)
- Prepare accounting reports for wholesale giftware importer ($15 million annual sales)
- Audit financial transactions with suppliers in 12 Latin American countries
- Created a computerized model to adjust accounts for fluctuations in currency exchange rates
- Negotiated joint-venture agreements with major suppliers in Mexico and Colombia
- Implemented electronic funds transfer for vendor disbursements, improving cash flow and eliminating payables clerk position

October 1997 to March 2001 — **Staff Accountant,** Monsanto Agricultural Chemicals (Mexico City, Mexico)
- Handled budgeting, billing, and credit-processing functions for the Mexico City branch
- Audited travel/entertainment expenses for Monsanto's 30-member Latin American sales force
- Assisted in launching an online computer system to automate all accounting functions

EDUCATION

1995 to 1997 — Master of Business Administration with emphasis on international business
George Mason University (Fairfax, Virginia)

1992 to 1995 — Bachelor of Business Administration, Accounting, University of Texas, Austin

INTERCULTURAL AND TECHNICAL SKILLS

- Fluent in Spanish and German
- Traveled extensively in Latin America
- Excel • Access • HTML • Visual Basic

related experience. The functional approach also has three advantages: (1) Without having to read through job descriptions, employers can see what you can do for them, (2) you can emphasize earlier job experience, and (3) you can de-emphasize any lack of career progress or lengthy unemployment. However, you should be aware that not all employers like the functional résumé, perhaps partly because it can obscure your work history and partly because it's less common. In any event, many seasoned employment professionals are suspicious of this résumé style, and some assume that candidates who use it are trying to hide something. In fact, Monster.com lists the functional résumé as one of employers' "Top 10 Pet Peeves."[14] If you don't have a strong, uninterrupted history of relevant work, the combination résumé might be a better choice.

The Combination Résumé

A **combination résumé** includes the best features of the chronological and functional approaches. Nevertheless, it is not commonly used, and it has two major disadvantages: (1) It tends to be longer, and (2) it can be repetitious if you

Under Jeff Taylor's guidance, Monster.com now lists close to 40 million résumés on its recruitment website.

have to list your accomplishments and skills in both the functional section and the chronological job descriptions.[15]

As you look at a number of sample résumés, you'll probably notice variations on the three basic formats presented here. Study these other options in light of effective communication principles; if you find one that seems like the best fit for your unique situation, by all means use it.

Producing Your Résumé

With less than a minute to make a good impression, your résumé needs to look sharp and grab a recruiter's interest in the first few lines. A typical recruiter devotes 45 seconds to each résumé before tossing it into either the "maybe" or the "reject" pile. Few recruiters read every résumé from top to bottom; most give them a quick glance to look for keywords and accomplishments. If yours doesn't stand out—or stands out in a negative way—chances are a recruiter won't look at it long enough to judge your qualifications.[16]

Good design is a must, and it's not hard to achieve. Good designs feature simplicity, order, plenty of white space, and straightforward typefaces such as Times Roman or Arial (most of the fonts on your computer are not appropriate for a résumé). Make your subheadings easy to find and easy to read, placing them either above each section or in the left margin. Use lists to itemize your most important qualifications, and leave plenty of white space, even if doing so forces you to use two pages rather than one. Color is not necessary by any means, but if you add color, make it subtle and sophisticated, such as a thin horizontal line under your name and address. The most common way to get into trou-

ble with résumé design is going overboard. If any part of the design "jumps out at you," get rid of it. You want people to be impressed with the information on your résumé, not the number of colors in your printer.

Until just a few years ago, producing résumés was a simple matter: You printed or photocopied as many as you needed and mailed them out. Not anymore. Depending on the companies you apply to, you might want to produce your résumé in as many as six forms:

- *Printed traditional résumé.* Format your traditional résumé simply but elegantly to make the best impression on your employer. Naturally, printed versions must be delivered by hand or by mail.

- *Printed scannable résumé.* Prepare a printed version of your résumé that is unformatted and thus electronically scannable so that employers can store your information in their database.

- *Electronic plain-text file.* Create an electronic plain-text file to use when uploading your résumé information into web forms or inserting it into e-mail messages.

- *Microsoft Word file.* Keep a Microsoft Word file of your traditional résumé so that you can upload it on certain websites.

- *HTML format.* By creating an HTML version, you can post your résumé on your own website, on a page provided by your college, or some of the many job board sites now available.

- *Electronic PDF file.* This is an optional step, but a portable document format (PDF) file of your traditional résumé provides a simple, safe format to attach to e-mail messages. Creating PDFs requires special software, but a PDF can be a helpful item to have on hand in case an employer asks you to e-mail your résumé.

Producing most of these formats is a straightforward task, but printing a scannable résumé and creating a plain-text file require careful attention to some important details.

Printing a Scannable Résumé

To cope with the flood of unsolicited paper résumés in recent years, many companies now optically scan incoming résumés into a database. When hiring managers want to interview candidates for job openings, they search the database for the most attractive candidates, using keywords appropriate to a specific position. The system then displays a list of possible candidates, each with a percentage score indicating how closely the résumé reflects the employer's requirements.[17] Nearly all large companies now use these systems, as do many midsized companies and even some smaller firms.[18]

The emergence of such scanning systems has important implications for your résumé. First, computers are interested only in matching information to search parameters, not in artistic attempts at résumé design. A human being may never actually see the résumé as you submitted it, so don't worry about it looking depressingly dull; computers prefer it that way. Second, *optical character recognition (OCR) software* doesn't technically "read" anything; it merely looks for shapes that match stored profiles of characters. Although printing your name in some gothic font might look grand to you, it will look like nonsense to the OCR software. If the OCR software can't make sense of your fancy fonts or creative page layout, it will enter gibberish into the database (for instance, your name might go in as "W[$..3r ?00!#" instead of "Walter Jones"). Third, even the most sophisticated databases cannot conduct a search with the nuance and intuition of an experienced human recruiter. Therefore, choosing the keywords for your résumé is a critical step. A human might know that "data-driven webpage design" means that you know XML, but the database probably won't make that connection.

The solution to these issues is twofold: (1) use a plain font and simplified design, and (2) compile your list of keywords carefully.

A scannable résumé contains the same information as your traditional résumé but is formatted to be OCR-friendly (see Exhibit E.5):[19]

- Use a clean, common sans serif font such as Optima or Arial, and size it between 10 and 14 points.

- Make sure that characters do not touch one another (whether numbers, letters, or symbols—including the slash [/]).

- Don't use side-by-side columns (the OCR software reads one line all the way across the page).

- Don't use ampersands (&), percent signs (%), foreign-language characters (such as é and ö), or bullet symbols (use a dash—not a lowercase 'o'—in place of a bullet symbol).

- Put each phone number and e-mail address on its own line.

- Print on white, plain paper (speckles and other background coloration can confuse the OCR software).

Your scannable résumé will probably be longer than your traditional résumé because you can't compress text into columns and because you need plenty of white space between headings and sections. If your scannable résumé runs more than one page, make sure your name appears on every subsequent page (in case the pages become separated). Before sending a scannable résumé, check the company's website or call the human resources department to see whether it has any specific requirements other than those discussed here.

When adding a keyword summary to your résumé, keep your audience in mind. Employers generally search for nouns (since verbs tend to be generic rather than specific to a particular position or skill), so make your keywords nouns as well. Use abbreviations sparingly and only when they are well known and unambiguous, such as *MBA*. Include in your list between 20 and 30 words and phrases that define your skills, experience, education, professional affiliations, and so on. Place this list right after your name and address.

One good way to identify which keywords to include in your summary is to underline all the skills listed in ads for the types of jobs you're interested in. (Another advantage of staying current by reading periodicals, networking, and so on is that you'll develop a good ear for current terminology.) Be sure to include only those keywords that correspond with your skills and experience. Trying to get ahead of the competition by listing skills you don't have is unethical; moreover, your efforts will be quickly exposed when your keywords don't match your job experience or educational background.

Creating a Plain-Text File of Your Résumé

An increasingly common way to get your information into an employer's database is by entering a *plain-text* version (sometimes referred to as an *ASCII text version*) of your résumé into an online form. This approach has the same goal as a scannable résumé, but it's faster, easier, and less prone to errors than the scanning process. If you have the option of mailing a scannable résumé or submitting plain text online, go with plain text.

In addition, when employers or networking contacts ask you to e-mail your résumé, they'll often want to receive it in plain-text format in the body of your e-mail message. Thanks to the prevalence of computer viruses these days, many employers will refuse to open an e-mail attachment.

Plain text is just what it sounds like: no font selections, no bullet symbols, no colors, no lines or boxes, and so on. A plain-text version is easy to create with your word processor. Start with the file you used to create your traditional printed résumé, use the *save as* choice to save it as "plain text" or whichever similarly labeled option your software has, then verify the result.

The verification step is crucial because you can never be quite sure what happens to your layout. Open the text file to view the layout, but don't use your word processor; instead, open the file with a basic text editor (such as Notepad on Windows PCs). If necessary, reformat the page manually, moving text and inserting spaces as needed. For simplicity's sake, left justify all your headings, rather than trying to center them manually. You can put headings in all caps or underline them with a row of dashes to separate them from blocks of text.

Preparing Your Application Letter

Whenever you submit your résumé, accompany it with a cover, or application, letter to let readers know what you're sending, why you're sending it, and how they can benefit from reading it. Because your application letter is in your own style (rather than the choppy, shorthand style of your résumé), it gives you a chance to show your communication skills and some personality.

Always send your résumé(s) and application letter together, because each has a unique job to perform. The purpose of your résumé is to get employers interested enough to contact you for an interview. The purpose of your application letter is to get employers interested enough to read your résumé.

Exhibit E.5 Electronic Résumé

Because some of his target employers will be scanning his résumé into a database, and because he wants to submit his résumé via e-mail or post it on the Internet, Roberto Cortez created an electronic résumé by changing his formatting and adding a list of keywords. However, the information remains essentially the same.

Removes all boldfacing, rules, bullets, and two-column formatting

Includes carefully selected keywords that describe Cortez's skills and accomplishments

Uses a dash in bulleted lists

Singles Cortez out from the crowd by including in the key-word section specific attributes such as "team player" and "willing to travel"

Uses ample white space to make his plain-text résumé easier to scan

Roberto Cortez
5687 Crosswoods Drive
Falls Church, Virginia 22046
Home: (703) 987-0086   Office: (703) 549-6624
RCortez@silvernet.com

KEY WORDS

Financial executive, accounting management, international finance, financial analyst, accounting reports, financial audit, computerized accounting model, exchange rates, joint-venture agreements, budgets, billing, credit processing, online systems, MBA, fluent Spanish, fluent German, Excel, Access, Visual Basic, team player, willing to travel

OBJECTIVE

Accounting management position requiring a knowledge of international finance

EXPERIENCE

Staff Accountant/Financial Analyst, Inter-American Imports (Alexandria, Virginia), March 2001 to present
— Prepare accounting reports for wholesale giftware importer, annual sales of $15 million
— Audit financial transactions with suppliers in 12 Latin American countries
— Created a computerized model to adjust for fluctuations in currency exchange rates
— Negotiated joint-venture agreements with suppliers in Mexico and Colombia
— Implemented electronic funds transfer for vendor disbursements, improving cash flow and eliminating payables clerk position

Staff Accountant, Monsanto Agricultural Chemicals (Mexico City, Mexico), October 1997 to March 2001
— Handled budgeting, billing, and credit-processing functions for the Mexico City branch
— Audited travel/entertainment expenses for Monsanto's 30-member Latin American sales force
— Assisted in launching an online computer system to automate accounting

EDUCATION

Master of Business Administration with emphasis in international business, George Mason University (Fairfax, Virginia), 1995 to 1997

Bachelor of Business Administration, Accounting, University of Texas (Austin, Texas), 1992 to 1995

INTERCULTURAL AND TECHNICAL SKILLS

Fluent in Spanish and German
Traveled extensively in Latin America
Excel, Access, HTML, Visual Basic

Before drafting a letter, learn something about the organization you're applying to; then focus on your audience so that you can show you've done your homework. Imagine yourself in the recruiter's situation, and show how your background and talents will solve a particular problem or fill a specific need the company has. The more you can learn about the organization, the better you'll be able to capture the reader's attention and convey your interest in the company. During your research, find out the name, title, and department of the person you're writing to. Reaching and

addressing the right person is the most effective way to gain attention. Avoid phrases such as "To Whom It May Concern" and "Dear Sir."

When putting yourself in your reader's shoes, remember that this person's in-box is probably overflowing with résumés and cover letters. So respect your reader's time. Steer clear of gimmicks, which almost never work, and include nothing in your cover letter that already appears in your résumé. Keep your letter straightforward, fact-based, short, upbeat, and professional (see Exhibit E.6).

Exhibit E.6 **Application Letter**

In her unsolicited application letter, Glenda Johns manages to give a snapshot of her qualifications and skills without repeating what is said in her résumé.

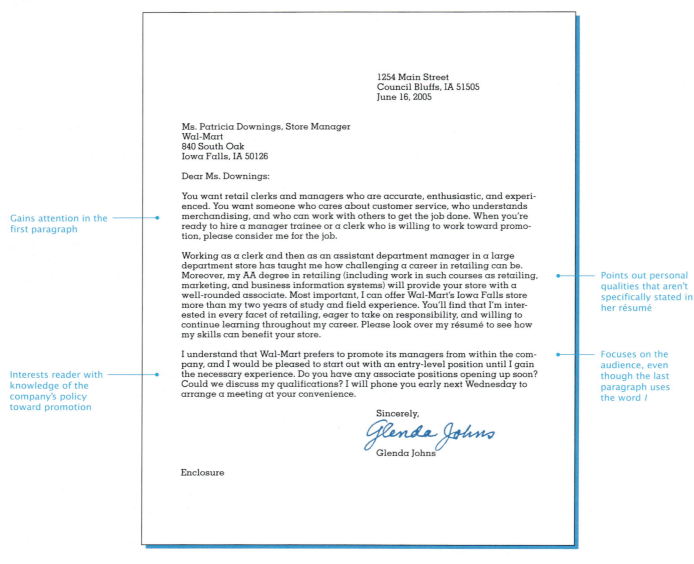

Gains attention in the first paragraph

Interests reader with knowledge of the company's policy toward promotion

Points out personal qualities that aren't specifically stated in her résumé

Focuses on the audience, even though the last paragraph uses the word *I*

1254 Main Street
Council Bluffs, IA 51505
June 16, 2005

Ms. Patricia Downings, Store Manager
Wal-Mart
840 South Oak
Iowa Falls, IA 50126

Dear Ms. Downings:

You want retail clerks and managers who are accurate, enthusiastic, and experienced. You want someone who cares about customer service, who understands merchandising, and who can work with others to get the job done. When you're ready to hire a manager trainee or a clerk who is willing to work toward promotion, please consider me for the job.

Working as a clerk and then as an assistant department manager in a large department store has taught me how challenging a career in retailing can be. Moreover, my AA degree in retailing (including work in such courses as retailing, marketing, and business information systems) will provide your store with a well-rounded associate. Most important, I can offer Wal-Mart's Iowa Falls store more than my two years of study and field experience. You'll find that I'm interested in every facet of retailing, eager to take on responsibility, and willing to continue learning throughout my career. Please look over my résumé to see how my skills can benefit your store.

I understand that Wal-Mart prefers to promote its managers from within the company, and I would be pleased to start out with an entry-level position until I gain the necessary experience. Do you have any associate positions opening up soon? Could we discuss my qualifications? I will phone you early next Wednesday to arrange a meeting at your convenience.

Sincerely,

Glenda Johns

Glenda Johns

Enclosure

Following Up on Your Application

If your application letter and résumé fail to bring a response within a month or so, follow up with a second letter to keep your file active. This follow-up letter also gives you a chance to update your original application with any recent job-related information. Even if you've received a letter acknowledging your application and saying that it will be kept on file, don't hesitate to send a follow-up letter three months later to show that you are still interested. Such a letter can demonstrate that you're sincerely interested in working for the organization, that you're persistent in pursuing your goals, and that you're upgrading your skills to make yourself a better employee. And it might just get you an interview.

Interviewing with Potential Employers

Approach job interviews with a sound appreciation of their dual purpose: The organization's main objective is to find the best person available for the job; the applicant's main objective is to find the job best suited to his or her goals and capabilities.

In general, the easiest way to connect with a big company is through your campus placement office; the most efficient way to approach a smaller business is by contacting the company directly. In either case, you move to the next stage and prepare to meet with a recruiter during an **employment interview**, a formal meeting during which an employer and an applicant ask questions and exchange information to see whether the applicant and the organization are a good match.

Most employers conduct two or three interviews before deciding whether to offer a person a job. The first interview, generally held on campus, is the **preliminary screening interview**, which helps employers eliminate unqualified applicants from the hiring process. Those candidates who best meet the organization's requirements are invited to visit company offices for further evaluation. Some organizations make a decision at that point, but many schedule a third interview to complete the evaluation process before extending a job offer.

Because the interview takes time, start seeking interviews well in advance of the date you want to start work. It takes an average of 10 interviews to get one job offer. If you hope to have several offers to choose from, you can expect to go through 20 or 30 interviews during your job search.[20] Some students start their job search as early as nine months before graduation. Early planning is even more crucial during downturns in the economy because many employers become more selective when times are tough.

What Employers Look For

Today's employers want candidates who are experienced, intelligent, good communicators, enthusiastic, creative, and motivated. In addition to these qualities, candidates must also fit in with the organization and meet the basic qualifications for the job.

To determine whether a candidate will be compatible with the other people in the organization, some interviewers may ask you questions about your interests, hobbies, awareness of world events, and so forth. Others may consider your personal style. You're likely to impress an employer by being open, enthusiastic, and interested. Still others may look for courtesy, sincerity, willingness to learn, and a style that is positive and self-confident. All of these qualities help a new employee adapt to a new workplace and new responsibilities.

When you're invited to interview for a position, the interviewer may already have some idea of whether you have the right qualifications, based on a review of your résumé. But during the interview, you'll be asked to describe your education and previous jobs in more depth so that the interviewer can determine how well your skills match the requirements. When describing your skills, be honest. If you don't know how to do something, say so. In many cases, the interviewer will be seeking someone with the flexibility to apply diverse skills in several areas.

What Applicants Need to Find Out

What things should you find out about the prospective job and employer? By doing a little advance research and asking the right questions during the interview (see Exhibit E.7), you can probably find answers to these questions and more:

- Are these my kind of people?
- Can I do this work?
- Will I enjoy the work?
- Is this job what I want?
- Does the job pay what I'm worth?
- What kind of person would I be working for?
- What sort of future can I look forward to with this organization?

QUESTIONS ABOUT THE JOB	QUESTIONS ABOUT THE ORGANIZATION
What are the job's major responsibilities?	Who are your organization's major competitors, and what are their strengths and weaknesses?
What qualities do you want in the person who fills this position?	What makes your organization different from others in the industry?
Do you want to know more about my related training?	What are your organization's major markets?
What is the first problem that needs the attention of the person you hire?	Does the organization have any plans for new products? Acquisitions?
Would relocation be required now or in the future?	How would you define your organization's managerial philosophy?
Why is this job now vacant?	What additional training does your organization provide?
What can you tell me about the person I would report to?	Do employees have an opportunity to continue their education with help from the organization?
How do you measure success for someone in this position?	

Exhibit E.7

Fifteen Questions to Ask the Interviewer

Learn as much as you can about potential employers by asking these questions.

How to Prepare for a Job Interview

It's perfectly normal to feel a little anxious before an interview. Don't worry too much, however; preparation will help you perform well. Learning about the organization and the job is important because it enables you to consider the employer's point of view. Here are some pointers to guide that preparation:

■ *Think ahead about questions.* Most job interviews are essentially question-and-answer sessions: You answer the interviewer's questions about your background, and you ask questions of your own to determine whether the job and the organization are right for you. By planning for your interviews, you can handle these exchanges intelligently (see Exhibit E.8). Of course, you don't want to memorize responses or sound overrehearsed.

■ *Bolster your confidence.* By overcoming your tendencies to feel self-conscious or nervous during an interview, you can build your confidence and make a better impression. If some aspect of your background or appearance makes you uneasy, correct it or exercise positive traits to offset it, such as warmth, wit, intelligence, or charm. Instead of dwelling on your weaknesses, focus on your strengths so that you can emphasize them to an interviewer.

■ *Polish your interview style.* Confidence helps you walk into an interview and give the interviewer an impression of poise, good manners, and good judgment. In the United States, you're more likely to be invited back for a second interview or offered a job if you maintain eye contact, smile frequently, sit in an attentive position, and use frequent hand gestures. These nonverbal signals convince the interviewer that you're alert, assertive, dependable, confident, responsible, and energetic.[21] Work on eliminating speech mannerisms such as "you know," "like," and "um." Speak in your natural tone, and try to vary the pitch, rate, and volume of your voice to express enthusiasm and energy.

■ *Plan to look good.* The best policy is to dress conservatively. Wear the best-quality businesslike clothing you can, preferably in a dark, solid color. Avoid flamboyant styles, colors, and prints. Clean, unwrinkled clothes, well-shined shoes, neatly styled and combed hair, clean fingernails, and fresh breath help make a good first impression. Don't spoil the effect by smoking cigarettes before or during the interview. Finally, remember that one of the best ways to look good is to smile at appropriate moments.

■ *Be ready when you arrive.* Be sure you know when and where the interview will be held. Take a small notebook, a pen, a list of your questions, a folder with two copies of your résumé, an outline of your research findings about the organization, and any correspondence about the position. You may also want to take a small calendar, a transcript of your college grades, a list of references, and, if

appropriate, samples of your work. After you arrive, relax. You may have to wait, so bring something to read or to occupy your time (the less frivolous or controversial, the better).

How to Follow Up After the Interview

Touching base with the prospective employer after the interview, either by phone or in writing, shows that you really want the job and are determined to get it. It also brings your name to the interviewer's attention again and reminds him or her that you're waiting to know the decision.

The two most common forms of follow-up, the thank-you note and the inquiry, are generally handled by letter or e-mail. But a phone call can be just as effective, particularly if the employer favors a casual, personal style. Express your thanks within two days after the interview, even if you feel you have little chance for the job. In a brief message, acknowledge the interviewer's time and courtesy, convey your continued interest, and ask politely for a decision. If you're not advised of the interviewer's decision by the promised date or within two weeks, you might make an inquiry, particularly if you don't want to accept a job offer from a second firm before you have an answer from the first. Assume that a simple oversight is the reason for the delay, not outright rejection.

Building Your Career

Having the right skills is one way to build toward a career. Employers seek people who are able and willing to adapt to diverse situations, who thrive in an ever-changing workplace, and who continue to learn throughout their careers. In addition, companies want team players with strong work records and leaders who are versatile. Many companies encourage managers to get varied job experience.[22] In some cases, your chances of being hired are better if you've studied abroad or learned another language. Many employers expect college graduates to have a sound understanding of international affairs, and they're looking for employees with intercultural sensitivity and an ability to adapt in other cultures.[23]

Compile an employment portfolio. Get a three-ring notebook and a package of plastic sleeves that open at the top. Collect anything that shows your ability to perform, such as classroom or work evaluations, certificates, awards, and papers you've written. An employment portfolio serves as an excellent resource when writing your résumé and provides employers with tangible evidence of your professionalism.

As you search for a permanent job that fulfills your career goals, take interim job assignments, participate in an internship program, and consider temporary work or freelance jobs. Not only will these temporary assignments help you gain valuable experience and relevant contacts, but they will also provide you with important

QUESTIONS ABOUT COLLEGE

1. What courses in college did you like most? Least? Why?

2. Do you think your extracurricular activities in college were worth the time spent on them? Why or why not?

3. When did you choose your college major? Did you ever change your major? If so, why?

4. Do you feel you did the best scholastic work you are capable of?

5. Which of your college years was the toughest? Why?

QUESTIONS ABOUT EMPLOYERS AND JOBS

6. What jobs have you held? Why did you leave?

7. What percentage of your college expenses did you earn? How?

8. Why did you choose your particular field of work?

9. What are the disadvantages of your chosen field?

10. Have you served in the military? What rank did you achieve? What jobs did you perform?

11. What do you think about how this industry operates today?

12. Why do you think you would like this particular type of job?

QUESTIONS ABOUT PERSONAL ATTITUDES AND PREFERENCES

13. Do you prefer to work in any specific geographic location? If so, why?

14. How much money do you hope to be earning in 5 years? In 10 years?

15. What do you think determines a person's progress in a good organization?

16. What personal characteristics do you feel are necessary for success in your chosen field?

17. Tell me a story.

18. Do you like to travel?

19. Do you think grades should be considered by employers? Why or why not?

QUESTIONS ABOUT WORK HABITS

20. Do you prefer working with others or by yourself?

21. What type of boss do you prefer?

22. Have you ever had any difficulty getting along with colleagues or supervisors? With instructors? With other students?

23. Would you prefer to work in a large or a small organization? Why?

24. How do you feel about overtime work?

25. What have you done that shows initiative and willingness to work?

Exhibit E.8

Twenty-five Common Interview Questions

Prepare for an interview in advance by thinking about your answers to these questions.

references and with items for your portfolio.[24] Employers will be more willing to find (or even to create) a position for someone they've learned to respect, and your temporary or freelance work gives them a chance to see what you can do.

If you're unable to find actual job experience, work on polishing and updating your skills. Network with professional colleagues and friends who can help you stay abreast of your occupation and industry. While you're waiting for responses to your résumé or your last interview, take a computer course or gain some other educational or life experience that would be difficult while working full-time. Become familiar with the services offered by your campus career center (or placement office). These centers offer individual placement counseling, credential services, job fairs, on-campus interviews, job listings, advice on computerized résumé-writing software, workshops in job-search techniques, résumé preparation, interview techniques, and more.[25]

Even after an employer hires you, continue improving your skills to distinguish yourself from your peers and to make yourself more valuable to current and potential employers:[26]

- Acquire as much technical knowledge as you can, build broad-based life experience, and develop your social skills.

- Learn to respond to change in positive, constructive ways; this will help you adapt if your "perfect" career path eludes your grasp.

- Keep up with developments in your industry and the economy at large; read widely and subscribe to free e-mail newsletters.

- Learn to see each job, even so-called entry-level jobs, as an opportunity to learn more and to expand your knowledge, experience, and social skills.

- Take on as much responsibility as you can outside your job description.

- Share what you know with others instead of hoarding knowledge in the hope of becoming indispensable; helping others excel is a skill, too.

- Understand the big picture; knowing your own job inside and out isn't enough any more.

- Understand that what counts isn't only who you know but also what you know and who knows you.

Appendix Glossary

chronological résumé Most traditional type of résumé, listing employment history sequentially in reverse order so that the most recent experience is listed first

combination résumé A hybrid of a chronological and functional résumé that contains elements of both

employment interview Formal meeting during which an employer and an applicant ask questions and exchange information to see whether the applicant and the organization are a good match

functional résumé Résumé organized around a list of skills and accomplishments, subordinating employers and academic experience in order to stress individual areas of competence; frowned on by many recruiters

preliminary screening interview Meeting between an employer's representative and a candidate for the purpose of eliminating unqualified applicants from the hiring process

résumé Form of advertising that lists a person's education, employment background, and job qualifications in order to obtain an interview

REFERENCES

Notes

Chapter 1

1. Jeff Leeds, "Online Song Sales, Though Rising Fast, Are at Most a Hopeful Blip," *Los Angeles Times*, 1 February 2004, C1; Apple iTunes website [accessed 30 March 2004] www.apple.com/itunes; Pui-Wing Tam and Nick Wingfield, "Apple's iTunes to Fall Short on Song Sales," *Wall Street Journal*, 16 March 2004, B3; Bob Tedeschi, "Music at Your Fingertips, but a Battle Among Those Selling It to You," *New York Times,* 1 December 2003, C21; Gloria Goodale, "'Don't Call Me a Pirate, I'm an Online Fan;' One Girl's Downloading Habits Reveal the Gulf Between the Music Industry and Teens," *Christian Science Monitor*, 18 July 2003, 13; John Schwartz and John Markoff, "Power Players: Big Names Are Jumping into the Crowded Online Music Field," *New York Times*, 12 January 2004 [accessed 30 March 2004] www.nytimes.com; Peter Lewis, "Gadgets: Drop a Quarter in the Internet," *Fortune,* 14 March 2004 [accessed 30 March 2004] www.fortune.com.

2. Ken Stammen, "Where Big Planes Are Born," *Cincinnati Post*, 12 September 2000, 7C.

3. IBM 2002 Annual Report [accessed 29 March 2004] www.ibm.com.

4. David Cay Johnson, "In the New Economics: Fast-Food Factories?" *Wall Street Journal*, 20 February 2004, C2.

5. U.S. Bureau of Labor Statistics website [accessed 29 March 2004] www.bls.gov.

6. U.S. Department of Commerce, Bureau of Economic Analysis website [accessed 24 September 1999] beadata.bea.doc.gov/bea/dn2/gpoc.htm; "Fortune 1000 Ranked Within Industry," *Fortune*, 26 April 1999, F51–F73.

7. *Statistical Abstract of the United States*, 1996 (Washington, D.C.: GPO, 1996), 56–59, 394, 396.

8. Robert L. Heilbroner and Lester C. Thurow, *Economics Explained* (New York: Simon & Schuster, 1994), 29–30.

9. Ronald M. Ayers and Robert A. Collinge, *Economics: Explore and Apply* (Upper Saddle River, N.J.: Pearson Prentice Hall, 2005), 97–103.

10. Heilbroner and Thurow, *Economics Explained*, 250.

11. Heilbroner and Thurow, *Economics Explained*, 250.

12. Greg Steinmetz, "Her Majesty May Sell Part of London's Tube, Angering Some in U.K.," *Wall Street Journal*, 14 October 1999, A1, A12; Erik Eckholm, "Chinese Restate Goals to Reorganize State Companies," *New York Times*, 23 September 1999, A10; Dexter Roberts, "China's New Revolution," *BusinessWeek*, 27 September 1999, 72–78.

13. Martin Peers, "Show of Strength: How Media Giants Are Reassembling the Old Oligopoly," *Wall Street Journal*, 15 September 2003, A1, A11.

14. Brier Dudley and Kim Peterson, "Microsoft Legal Maneuvers Could Offset EU Sanctions," *Seattle Times*, 25 March 2004 [accessed 27 March 2004] www.seattle-times.com.

15. Kenneth N. Gilpin, "Antitrust Challenge Stops United Merger with U.S. Airways," *New York Times*, 26 July 2001, B1, B2; Patrick M. Reilly, "Barnes & Noble Closes Book on Attempt to Buy Ingram Amid FTC Objections," *Wall Street Journal*, 3 June 1999, B16.

16. Elizabeth Hurt, "AOL/Time Warner Merger Approved," *Business 2.0* [accessed 29 March 2004] www.business2.com.

17. Jim Rossi, "The Electric Deregulation Fiasco: Looking to Regulatory Federalism to Promote a Balance Between Markets and the Provision of Public Goods," *Michigan Law Review*, May 2002, 1768–1790; Ferdinand E. Banks, "A Simple Economic Analysis of Deregulation Failure," *OPEC Review*, June 2002, 169–181.

18. Jeannine Aversa, "Fed Ends String of Rate Cuts," *Journal-Gazette*, 31 January 2001, 7B.

19. Anna Bernasek, "The $44 Trillion Abyss," *Fortune*, 24 November 2003, 113–116; Mike Allen, "Bush Pledges Effort to Balance Budget by 2004," *Washington Post*, 17 April 2002, A6; Richard W. Stevenson, "2 Parties Predict a Sharp Increase in Spending by U.S.," *New York Times*, 12 May 2002, sec. 1, 1; Martin Kasindorf and Ken Fireman, "The Clinton Budget/2002 Solution," *Newsday*, 7 February 1997, A4; Gilbert C. Alston, "Balancing the Federal Budget," *Los Angeles Times*, 14 February 1997, B8.

20. Kathleen Madigan, "Keep Your Nest Egg Safe—Watch Housing Data," *BusinessWeek*, 17 April 2000, 208–210.

21. Kevin Maney, "The Economy According to eBay," *USA Today*, 29 December 2003, B1.

22. Sue Kirchhoff, "Delicate Balance Helps USA Battle Deflation, Inflation," *USA Today*, 5 March 2003, B–B2.

23. U.S. Bureau of Labor Statistics website [accessed 29 March 2004] www.bls.gov; Jyoti Thottam, "Why Aren't Your Prices Falling?" *Time*, 26 May 2003, 53.

24. Stephen Baker, "Where Danger Lurks," *BusinessWeek*, 25 August 2003, 114–118.

25. See note 1.

Appendix A

1. Open Directory [accessed 13 December 2003] www.dmoz.com.

2. LookSmart.com [accessed 13 December 2003] www.looksmart.com.

3. AllTheWeb.com advanced search page [accessed 13 December 2003] www.alltheweb.com; Google advanced search page [accessed 13 December 2003] www.google.com; Yahoo! advanced search page [accessed 13 December 2003] www.yahoo.com.

4. NewsGator website [accessed 13 December 2003] www.newsgator.com; NewzCrawler website [accessed 13 December 2003] www.newzcrawler.com.

5. Robert D. Hof, Gary McWilliams, and Gabrielle Saveri, "The Click Here Economy," *BusinessWeek*, 22 June 1998, 122–128; Tim McCollum, "End Your Internet Anxieties Now," *Nation's Business*, April 1999, 19–26.

6. Mary Kathleen Flynn, "Courting Calls," *U.S. News & World Report*, 2 February 2004, 40–42; Donny Jackson, "VoIP Recognition," *Telephony*, 26 January 2004 [accessed 19 May 2004] www.highbeam.com.

7. David Morse, ed., *CyberDictionary: Your Guide to the Wired World* (Santa Monica, Calif.: Knowledge Exchange, 1996), 113.

8. Morse, *CyberDictionary*, 233.

9. Michael Taylor, "Intranets—A New Technology Changes All the Rules," *Telecommunication*, January 1997, 39–40.

10. Stephanie Armour, "Workers Just Click to Enroll for Benefits," *USA Today*, 8

November 2000, B1; Charlene Marmer Solomon, "Sharing Information Across Borders and Time Zones," *Global Workforce*, March 1998, 13–18; Eryn Brown, "9 Ways to Win on the Web," *Fortune*, 24 May 1999, 112.

11. Material for this section was taken from Courtland L. Bovée and John V. Thill, *Business Communication Today*, 6th ed. (Upper Saddle River, N.J.: Prentice Hall, 1999), 348–352.

12. John R. L. Rizza, "Extranets: The Internet Gets Down to Business," *Entrepreneurial Edge*, 3, 1998, 76–78; Samuel Greengard, "Extranets Linking Employees with Your Vendors," *Workforce*, November 1997, 28–34.

13. Andy Reinhardt, "The Paperless Manual," *BusinessWeek e.Biz*, 18 September 2000, EB92.

14. Heather Green, "The Underground Internet," *BusinessWeek*, 15 September 2003, 80–82.

15. Efraim Turban, Jae Lee, David King, and H. Michael Chung, *Electronic Commerce, A Managerial Perspective* (Upper Saddle River, N.J.: Prentice Hall, 2000), 15–16.

16. Laurie Windham, *Dead Ahead* (New York: Allworth Press, 1999), 31–32.

17. Walid Mougayar, *Opening Digital Markets* (New York: McGraw-Hill, 1998), 29–35.

18. Turban et al., *Electronic Commerce, A Managerial Perspective*, 15–16.

19. Korper and Ellis, *The E-Commerce Book: Building the E-Empire* (San Diego, Calif.: Academic Press, 2000), 4.

20. Jeff Howe, "Big Boss Is Watching," *Yahoo! Internet Life*, October 2000, 105–107.

21. Elisa Deardorff, "With Voice Mail, You Never Know Who's Listening," *Chicago Tribune*, 1 June 1998, B1, B8; "40 Fired for Sex-Site Abuse," *CNN America*, 6 October 1999, www.cnnfn.com/1999/10/06/companies/Xerox.

22. Sushil K. Sharma and Jatinder N. D. Gupta, "Improving Workers' Productivity and Reducing Internet Abuse," *Journal of Computer Information Systems*, Winter 2003–2004, 74+.

23. Samuel Greengard, "How Secure Is Your Data?" *Workforce*, May 1998, 52–60; Nikhil Hutheesing and Philip E. Ross, "Hackerphobia," *Forbes*, 23 March 1998, 150–154.

24. Dan Luzadder, "Corporate Security Gets Urgent," *Interactive Week*, 23 October 2001, www.techupdate.zdnet.com/techupdate/stories/main/0,14179,2819412,00.html.

25. Luzadder, "Corporate Security Gets Urgent."

26. Richard Behar, "Fear Along the Firewall," *Fortune*, 15 October 2001, 145–148; Brian Fonseca, "Study: Viruses Cost $12B in '99," *InfoWorld.com*, 17 January 2000 [accessed 5 November 2001]

www.computerworld.com; David S. Bernstein, "We've Been Hacked," *Inc. Tech 2000*, no. 3, 106+.

27. Behar, "Fear Along the Firewall," 145–148.

28. Steve Patterson, "Congress to Weigh Privacy Right vs. Security Need; Legislation May Mean Intrusiveness," *Florida Times Union*, 24 September 2001, A-1.

29. Del Jones, "Businesses Battle over Intellectual Property," *USA Today*, 2 August 2000, 1B, 2B; Greengard, "How Secure Is Your Data?" 52–60.

Chapter 2

1. Patagonia website [accessed 1 April 2004] www.patagonia.com; Monte Burke, "The World According to Yvon," *Forbes*, 26 November 2001, 236; Dianna Edwards, "A Mountain of Trust," *Step-By-Step Graphics*, September–October 2001, 30–39; Jennifer Laabs, "Mixing Business with Passion," *Workforce*, March 2000, 80–87; Roger Rosenblatt, "The Root of All Good: Reaching the Top by Doing the Right Thing," *Time*, 18 October 1999, 88–91; Michael Lear-Olimpi, "Management Mountaineer," *Warehousing Management*, January–February 1999, 23–30; Larry Armstrong, "Patagonia Sticks to Its Knitting," *BusinessWeek*, 7 December 1998, 68; Nancy Rivera Brooks, "Companies Give Green Power the Green Light," *Los Angeles Times*, 27 September 1998, D8; Charlene Marmer Solomon, "A Day in the Life of Terri Wolfe: Maintaining Corporate Culture," *Workforce*, June 1998, 94–95; Jacqueline Ottman, "Proven Environmental Commitment Helps Create Committed Customers," *Marketing News*, 2 February 1998, 5–6; Dawn Hobbs, "Patagonia Ranked 24th by Magazine," *Los Angeles Times*, 23 December 1997, B1; Jim Collins, "The Foundation for Doing Good," *Inc.*, December 1997, 41–42; "It's Not Easy Being Green," *BusinessWeek*, 24 November 1997, 180; Paul C. Judge and Melissa Downing, "A Lean, Green Fulfillment Machine," *Catalog Age*, June 1997, 63; "Patagonia, A Green Endeavor," *Apparel Industry Magazine*, February 1997, 46–48; Polly LaBarre, "Patagonia Comes of Age," *IndustryWeek*, 3 April 1995, 42; John Steinbreder, "Yvon Chouinard, Founder and Owner of the Patagonia Outdoor," *Sports Illustrated*, 2 November 1991, 200.

2. "Timeline of Enron's Collapse," *Washington Post*, 27 January 2004 [accessed 2 April 2004] www.washingtonpost.com; Ellen Florian, "Scandal Cheat Sheet," *Fortune*, 7 July 2003, 48–49.

3. Carrie Johnson and Peter Behr, "Andersen Guilty of Obstruction: Accounting Firm Will End Audit Work," *Washington Post*, 16 June 2002, A1+.

4. Carrie Johnson, "Mistrial in Tyco Case; Judge Blames Outside Pressure on Jury,"

Seattle Times [accessed 3 April 2004] www.seattletimes.com.

5. Carrie Johnson and Christopher Stern, "Adelphia Founder, Sons Charged," *Washington Post*, 25 July 2002, A1+.

6. Christopher Stern, "WorldCom Plans New Job Cuts," *Washington Post*, 16 January 2004, E1.

7. Keith Naughton and Mark Hosenball, "Ford Vs. Firestone," *Newsweek*, 18 September 2000, 26–33; Keith Naughton, "Spinning out of Control," *Newsweek*, 11 September 2000, 58; Stephen Power and Bob Simison, "Firestone Knew of Tire Safety Problems," *Wall Street Journal*, 7 September 2000, A3; Timothy Aeppel, Clare Ansberry, Milo Geyelin, and Robert L. Simison, "Road Signs: How Ford, Firestone Let the Warnings Slide By as Debacle Developed," *Wall Street Journal*, 6 September 2000, A1; Robert L. Simison, Norihiko Shirouzu, and Timothy Aeppel, "Ford Says It Knew of Venezuelan Tire Failures in 1998," *Wall Street Journal*, 30 August 2000, A3; Robert L. Simison, Norihiko Shirouzu, Timothy Aeppel, and Todd Zaun, "Pressure Points: Tension Between Ford and Firestone Mounts Amid Recall Efforts," *Wall Street Journal*, 28 August 2000, A1; Alejandro Bodipo-Memba, "Lawsuits Outlive Recalls; Liability, Safety Worries Hound Ford, Firestone," *Detroit Free Press*, 30 March 2002 [accessed 3 April 2004] www.ebsco.com.

8. "Staying Current: Sarbanes-Oxley Compliance Cost," The Controller's Report, November 2003, 2–3; Jorge E. Guerra, "The Sarbanes-Oxley Act and Evolution of Corporate Governance," *CPA Journal*, March 2004, 14+; Justin Schack, "The Anti-IPO," *Institutional Investor*, June 2003, 24.

9. Peter Asmus, "100 Best Corporate Citizens: 2003," *Business Ethics*, Spring 2003, 6–10.

10. Elaine Appleton Grant, "Let the Good Works Roll," *Inc.*, February 2003, 51–54.

11. Alicia Zappier, "P & G, Unilever Talk Settlement in Hair Care Spy Case," *Drug Store News*, 24 September 2001, 45.

12. Michael McCarthy, "Recent Crop of Sneaky Ads Backfires," *USA Today*, 17 July 2001, 3B; "Publishers Clearing House Strikes Deceptive-Practices Accord," *New York Times*, 23 August 2000, A16.

13. Aaron Bernstein, Brian Grow, Darnell Little, Stanley Holmes, and Diane Brady, "Bracing for a Backlash," *BusinessWeek*, 4 February 2002, 32–36.

14. Suzanne Wooley, "The Hustlers Queue Up on the Net," *BusinessWeek*, 20 November 1995, 146–148.

15. Amy Zipkin, "Getting Religion on Corporate Ethics," *New York Times*, 18 October 2000, C1, C10.

16. John S. McClenahen, "Your Employees Know Better," *IndustryWeek*, 1 March 1999, 12–14.

17. Betsy Stevens, "Communicating Ethical Values: A Study of Employee Perceptions," *Journal of Business Ethics*, June 1999, 113–120.

18. Steven Greenhouse, "Time Records Often Altered, Job Experts Say," *New York Times*, 4 April 2004 [accessed 4 April 2004] www.nytimes.com.

19. Milton Bordwin, "The Three R's of Ethics," *Management Review*, June 1998, 59–61.

20. Mark Seivar, personal communication, 2 April 1998; "1-800-Jus-tice or 1-800-Rat-fink," *Reputation Management*, March–April 1995, 31–34; Margaret Kaeter, "The 5th Annual Business Ethics Awards for Excellence in Ethics," *Business Ethics*, December 1993, 26–29.

21. Richard Lacayo and Amanda Ripley, "Persons of the Year," *Time*, 20 December 2002–6 January 2003, 60.

22. Mahzarin R. Banaji, Max H. Bazerman, and Dolly Chugh, "How (Un)Ethical Are You?" *Harvard Business Review*, December 2003, 56–64.

23. See letters in *New York Times*, 25 August 1918, and *New York Herald*, 1 October 1918.

24. "Business of Social Responsibility," *Businessline*, 3 August 1999, 1.

25. "Does It Pay to Be Ethical?" *Business Ethics*, March–April 1997, 14–16; Don L. Boroughs, "The Bottom Line on Ethics," *U.S. News & World Report*, 20 March 1995, 61–66.

26. Ann Graham, "Lynn Sharp Paine: The Thought Leader Interview," *Strategy + Business*, Summer 2003, 97–105.

27. Joseph Weber, "3M's Big Cleanup," *BusinessWeek*, 5 June 2000, 96–98.

28. Stephanie Strom, "Gates Aims Billions to Attack Illnesses of World's Neediest," *New York Times*, 13 July 2003, 1, 15.

29. Thomas A. Fogarty, "Corporations Use Causes for Effect," *USA Today*, 10 November 1997, 7B; PeaceWorks website [accessed 22 June 1999] www.peaceworks.net; Florence Fabricant, "A Young Entrepreneur Makes Food, Not War," *New York Times*, 30 November 1996, sec. International Business, 21.

30. Jim Hopkins, "Ben & Jerry's Co-Founder to Try 'Venture Philanthropy,'" *USA Today*, 7 August 2001, B1.

31. Anna Muoio, ed., "Ways to Give Back," *Fast Company*, December–January 1998, 113+.

32. William H. Miller, "Cracks in the Green Wall," *IndustryWeek*, 19 January 1998, 58–65.

33. U.S. Department of Energy website [accessed 3 April 2004] www.energy.gov.

34. Bruce Barcott, "Changing All the Rules," *New York Times Magazine*, 4 April 2004 [accessed 4 April 2004] www.nytimes.com.

35. "Hummer Mania," CBSNews.com [accessed 3 April 2004] www.cbsnews.com;

Danny Hakim, "To Avoid Fuel Limits, Subaru Is Turning a Sedan into a Truck," *New York Times*, 13 January 2004 [accessed 13 January 2004] www.nytimes.com.

36. Traci Watson, "Smoggy Skies Persist Despite Decade of Work," *USA Today*, 16 October 2003, 6A.

37. "Tap Water at Risk: Bush Administration Actions Endanger America's Drinking Water Supplies," Natural Resources Defense Council website [accessed 4 April 2004] www.ndrc.org.

38. "What's on Tap? Grading Drinking Water in U.S. Cities," Natural Resources Defense Council website [accessed 4 April 2004] www.ndrc.org.

39. Paul Rauber, "Saving the Environment," *The Nation*, 8 March 2004 [accessed 3 April 2004] www.highbeam.com.

40. Marc Gunther, "Tree Huggers, Soy Lovers, and Profits," *Fortune*, 23 June 2003, 98–103.

41. "The IW Survey: Encouraging Findings," *IndustryWeek*, 19 January 1998, 62.

42. John Markoff, "Technology's Toxic Trash Is Sent to Poor Nations," *New York Times*, 25 February 2002, C1, C4.

43. Kirk Spitzer, "Companies Divert Enough Waste to Fill Five Astrodomes," *Gannett News Service*, 2 November 1995.

44. Laura Shapiro, "The War of the Labels," *Newsweek*, 5 October 1992, 63, 66.

45. Chris Burritt, "Fallout from the Tobacco Settlement," *Atlanta Journal and Constitution*, 22 June 1997, A14; Jolie Solomon, "Smoke Signals," *Newsweek*, 28 April 1997, 50–51; Marilyn Elias, "Mortality Rate Rose Through '80s," *USA Today*, 17 April 1997, B3; Mike France, Monica Larner, and Dave Lindorff, "The World War on Tobacco," *Business Week*, 11 November 1996; Richard Lacayo, "Put Out the Butt, Junior," *Time*, 2 September 1996, 51; Elizabeth Gleick, "Smoking Guns," *Time*, 1 April 1996, 50.

46. John A. Byrne, Leslie Brown, and Joyce Barnathan, "Directors in the Hot Seat," *BusinessWeek*, 8 December 1997, 100, 102, 104.

47. "Injuries, Illnesses, and Fatalities," Bureau of Labor Statistics [accessed 26 February 2002] www.bls.gov/iif.

48. Yochi J. Dreazen, "New OSHA Proposal Enrages Businesses," *Wall Street Journal*, 8 November 2000, A2, A6; Robert Manor, "OSHA's Ergonomic Rules Rile Business," *Chicago Tribune*, 14 November 2000, sec. 1, 1.

49. Wendy Bounds and Hilary Stout, "Sweatshop Pact: Good Fit or Threadbare?" *Wall Street Journal*, 10 April 1997, A2; Ellen Neuborne, "Nike to Take a Hit in Labor Report," *USA Today*, 27 March 1997, B1; William J. Holstein et al., "Santa's

Sweatshop," *U.S. News & World Report*, 16 December 1996, 50–60; Stephanie Strom, "From Sweetheart to Scapegoat," *New York Times*, 27 June 1996, C1, 16; Nancy Gibbs, "Cause Celeb: Two High-Profile Endorsers Are Props in a Worldwide Debate Over Sweatshops and the Use of Child Labor," *Time*, 17 June 1996; Ellen Neuborne, "Labor's Shopping List: No Sweatshops," *USA Today*, 5 December 1995, B1; Bob Herbert, "A Sweatshop Victory," *New York Times*, 22 December 1995, A15.

50. Asmus, "100 Best Corporate Citizens: 2003," 6–10.

51. See Note 1.

52. Geanne Rosenberg, "Truth and Consequences," *Working Woman*, June/August 1998, 79–80.

Chapter 3

1. Adapted from "About Whirlpool Corp.," Whirlpool website [accessed 5 April 2004] www.whirlpool.com; Regina Fazio Maruca, "The Right Way to Go Global," *Harvard Business Review*, March–April 1994, 135–145; Deborah Duarte and Nancy Snyder, "From Experience: Facilitating Global Organizational Learning in Product Development at Whirlpool Corporation," *Journal of Product Innovation Management* 14, no. 1 (January 1997): 48–55; Joe Jancsurak, "Whirlpool: U.S. Leader Pursues Global Blueprint," *Appliance Manufacturer* 45, no. 2 (February 1997): G21; Carl Quintanilla, "Despite Setbacks, Whirlpool Pursues Overseas Markets," *Wall Street Journal*, 9 December 1997, B4; Ian Katz, "Whirlpool: In the Wringer," *BusinessWeek*, 14 December 1998, 83+; Gale Cutler, "Asia Challenges Whirlpool Technology," *Research Technology Management*, September–October 1998, 4–6; "Whirlpool Europe and Tupperware Europe Announce Strategic Alliance," Investor Relations, 28 April 1999, Whirlpool website [accessed 5 May 1999] www.whirlpoolcorp.com.

2. Holley H. Ulbrich and Mellie L. Warner, *Managerial Economics* (New York: Barron's Educational Series, 1990), 190.

3. Patrick Lane, "World Trade Survey: Why Trade Is Good for You," *The Economist*, 3 (October 1998): S4–S6.

4. "U.S. International Transactions," U.S. Bureau of Economic Analysis website [accessed 5 April 2004] www.bea.doc.gov.

5. Robert J. Samuelson, "Trading with the Enemy," *Newsweek*, 1 April 1996, 41; Amy Borrus, Pete Engardio, and Dexter Roberts, "The New Trade Superpower," *BusinessWeek*, 16 October 1995, 56–57; David A. Andelman, "Marco Polo Revisited," *American Management Journal*, August 1995, 10–12; John Greenwald, "Get Asia Now, Pay Later," *Time*, 10 October 1994, 61; Simons, "High-Tech Jobs for Sale," 59.

6. James Cox, "Tariffs Shield Some U.S. Products," *USA Today*, 6 May 1999, 1B.

7. Eric Schmitt, "U.S. Backs off Sanctions, Seeing Poor Effect Abroad," *New York Times*, 31 July 1998, A1, A6; Robert T. Gray, "Book Review," *Nation's Business*, January 1999, 47.

8. "Saudi Arabia Hopes to Join WTO by 2002," *Reuters Business Report*, 3 August 1997.

9. "Airbus to Resume Talks on Status," *New York Times*, 5 May 1999, C4; Daniel Michaels, "Airbus Industrie's Partners Are Close to Establishing a Single Corporation," *Wall Street Journal*, 8 June 2000, A20; Daniel Michaels, "Country by Country—Flying High," *Wall Street Journal*, 25 September 2000, R18.

10. "Japanese Steelmakers Face U.S. Penalties in Antidumping Case," *Wall Street Journal*, 3 August 2000, C19.

11. Cox, "Tariffs Shield Some U.S. Products," 1B, 2B.

12. "APEC Ministers Commit to Sustainable Development," *Xinhau News Agency*, 11 June 1997; Fred C. Bergsten, "An Asian Push for World-Wide Free Trade: The Case for APEC," *The Economist*, 6 January 1996, 62; "U.S. Must Press to Reduce Trade Barriers in Asia, Pacific, Congress Told," *Gannett News Service*, 1995.

13. Michael M. Phillips, "One by One," *Wall Street Journal*, 26 April 1999, R4, R7.

14. Christopher Koch, "It's a Wired, Wired World," *Webmaster*, March 1997, 50–55.

15. Masaaki Kotabe and Maria Cecilia Coutinho de Arruda, "South America's Free Trade Gambit," *Marketing Management*, Spring 1998, 38+.

16. "Grand Illusions," *The Economist*, 4 March 1995, 87; Bob Davis, "Global Paradox: Growth of Trade Binds Nations, But It Also Can Spur Separatism," *Wall Street Journal*, 20 June 1994, A1, A6; Barbara Rudolph, "Megamarket," *Time*, 10 August 1992, 43–44; Peter Truell, "Free Trade May Suffer from Regional Blocs," *Wall Street Journal*, 1 July 1991, A1.

17. Patrice M. Jones, "Leaving Trade Pact's Woes Behind," *Chicago Tribune*, 10 May 2000, sec. 3, 42.

18. Rafael A. Lecuona, "Economic Integration: NAFTA and MERCOSUR, A Comparative Analysis," *International Journal on World Peace*, December 1999, 27–49.

19. Emeric Lepourte, "Europe's Challenge to the U.S. in South America's Biggest Market," *Christian Science Monitor*, 8 April 1997, 19; Mario Osava, "Mercosur: Free Trade with Europe More Advantageous Than FTAA," *Inter Press English News Wire*, 6 May 1997; Robert Maynard, "At a Crossroads in Latin America," *Nation's Business*, April 1996, 38–39; Gregory L. Miles and Loubna Freih, "Join the Caribbean Revolution," *International Business*, September 1994, 42–54; Matt Moffett, "Spreading the Gospel,"

Wall Street Journal, 28 October 1994, R12.

20. Lecuona, "Economic Integration: NAFTA and MERCOSUR, A Comparative Analysis."

21. Geri Smith and Cristina Lindblad, "Mexico: Was NAFTA Worth It?" *BusinessWeek*, 22 December 2003, 66–72; Charles J. Walen, "NAFTA's Scorecard: So Far, So Good," *BusinessWeek*, 9 July 2001, 54–56.

22. Smith and Lindblad, "Mexico: Was NAFTA Worth It?" 68; Geri Smith, "Betting on Free Trade," *BusinessWeek*, 23 April 2001, 60–62.

23. Europa (EU gateway site) [accessed 5 April 2004] www.europa.eu.int.

24. Brandon Mitchener, "Increasingly Rules of Global Economy Are Set in Brussels," *Wall Street Journal*, 23 April 2002, A1, A10.

25. Mitchener, "Increasingly Rules of Global Economy Are Set in Brussels," A1, A10.

26. Thomas Kamm, "EU Certifies Participants for Euro," *Wall Street Journal*, 26 March 1998, A14; Mitchener, "Increasingly Rules of Global Economy Are Set in Brussels," A1, A10.

27. Thane Peterson, "The Euro," *BusinessWeek*, 27 April 1998, 90–94; Joan Warner, "The Great Money Bazaar," *BusinessWeek*, 27 April 1998, 96–98; Gail Edmondson, "Industrial Evolution," *BusinessWeek*, 27 April 1998, 100–101.

28. Michael H. Mescon, Courtland L. Bovée, and John V. Thill, *Business Today*, 10th ed. (Upper Saddle River, N.J.: Prentice Hall, 2002), 69.

29. John Alden, "What in the World Drives UPS?" *International Business*, March/April 1998, 6–7; UPS website [accessed 4 March 2002] www.ups.com.

30. "Getting It Right in Japan," *International Business*, May–June 1997, 19.

31. Gary M. Wederspahn, "Exporting Corporate Ethics," *Global Workforce*, January 1997, 29–30; Dana Milbank and Marcus W. Brauchli, "Greasing Wheels," *Wall Street Journal*, 29 September 1995, A1, A7.

32. James Wilfong and Toni Seger, *Taking Your Business Global* (Franklin Lakes, N.J.: Career Press, 1997), 289.

33. Jules Abend, "Jockey Colors Its World," *Bobbin*, February 1999, 50–54.

34. Ricky W. Griffin and Michael W. Pustay, *International Business* (Reading, Mass.: Addison-Wesley, 1999), 415.

35. "Padgett Surveys Franchise/Small Business Sectors," *Franchising World*, March–April 1995, 46; John Stansworth, "Penetrating the Myths Surrounding Franchise Failure Rates—Some Old Lessons for New Business," *International Small Business Journal*, January–March 1995, 59–63; Laura Koss-Feder, "Building Better Franchise Relations," *Hotel & Motel Management*, 6 March 1995, 18; Carol Steinberg, "Franchise Fever," *World Trade*, July 1992, 86, 88, 90–91; John O'Dell,

"Franchising America," *Los Angeles Times*, 25 June 1989, sec. IV, 1.

36. Dori Jones Yang, "An American (Coffee) in Paris—and Rome," *U.S. News and World Report*, 19 February 2001, 47.

37. One World website [accessed 16 May 2000] oneworldalliance.com.

38. Lewis M. Simons, "High-Tech Jobs for Sale," *Time*, 22 July 1996, 59.

39. Alden, "What in the World Drives UPS?" 6–7.

40. Ernest Beck and Emily Nelson, "As Wal-Mart Invades Europe, Rivals Rush to Match Its Formula," *Wall Street Journal*, 6 October 1999, A1, A6.

41. "Foreign Investment in U.S. Reaches 54.4 Billion Dollars in 1995," *Xinhua News Agency*, 1996.

42. *Big Emerging Markets: 1996 Outlook* (Washington, D.C.: GPO, 1996); Nicholas D. Kristof and Sheryl WuDunn, "The World's Ills May Be Obvious, But Their Cure Is Not," *New York Times*, 18 February 1999 [accessed 19 February 1999] www.nytimes.com/library/world/global/021699global-econ.html.

43. Paulo Prado and Bruce Orwall, "A Certain 'Je Ne Sais Quoi' at Disney's New Park," *Wall Street Journal*, 12 March 2002, B1, B4.

44. Tim O'Brien, "Disneyland Paris Caters to European Tastes, Lowers Costs and Refines Service," *Amusement Business*, 5 May 1997, 18; "Disneyland Paris: How Beauty Became a Beast," *Reputation Management*, March–April 1995, 35–37.

45. Erin White and Jeffrey A. Trachtenberg, "'One Size Doesn't Fit All': At WPP, Sir Martin Sorrell Sees Limits to Globalization," *Wall Street Journal*, 1 October 2003, B1, B2.

46. Joel Millman and Ann Zimmerman, "'Repats' Help Payless Shoes Branch Out in Latin America," *Wall Street Journal*, 24 December 2003, B1, B2.

47. Michael J. Mandel, "Rethinking the Economy," *BusinessWeek*, 1 October 2001, 28–33.

48. James Cox, "U.S. Slowdown Would Ripple Around Globe," *USA Today*, 22 January 2001, 1B–2B.

49. Cox, "U.S. Slowdown Would Ripple Around Globe," 1B–2B.

50. Jeffrey E. Garten, "The Wrong Time for Companies to Beat a Global Retreat," *BusinessWeek*, 17 December 2001, 22.

51. "Is It At Risk?—Globalization," *The Economist*, 2 February 2002, 65–68.

52. Brian O'Keefe, "Global Brands," *Fortune*, 26 November 2001, 102–110.

53. Ben Van Houten, "Where Are They Now?" *Restaurant Business*, 15 November 2001, 22–30.

54. Peter Engardio and Rich Miller, "What's At Stake?" *BusinessWeek*, 22 October 2001, 34–37; Chris Woodyard, "Stepped-up Security Siphons Companies' Cash," *USA*

Today, 22 October 2001, 1B, 2B.

55. Toni Locy, "Anti-Terror Law Puts New Demands on Business," *USA Today,* 26 February 2004, 5A.

56. Paul Magnusson, "Your Jitters Are Their Lifeblood," *BusinessWeek,* 14 April 2003, 41; Del Jones, "Executives Pessimistic About Disaster Readiness, Survey Finds," *USA Today,* 5 August 2003, 12B; Gary Fields, "FedEx Takes Direct Approach to Terrorism," *Wall Street Journal,* 9 October 2003, A4.

57. Mandel, "Rethinking the Economy," 28–33.

58. See Note 1.

59. Adam Zagorin, "The Great Banana War," *Time,* 8 February 1999 [accessed 11 May 1999] www.pathfinder.com.

60. "USAJobs: International Trade Specialist," USA Jobs website [accessed 17 June 1999] www.usajobs.opm.gov/wfjic/jobs/BL2896.htm.

Chapter 4

1. Adapted from *Business Wire,* "FedEx Completes Acquisition of Kinko's; Strategic Move Allows FedEx to Capitalize on Key Business Trends," 12 February 2004 [accessed 7 April 2004] www.highbeam.com; Woody Baird, "FedEx Buying Kinko's for $2.4 Billion," *AP Online,* 31 December 2003 [accessed 7 April 2004] www.highbeam.com; "Kinko Deal Yields Payoff for Buyout Firm," *AP Online,* 30 December 2003 [accessed 7 April 2004] www.highbeam.com; Kinko's website [accessed 7 April 2004] www.kinkos.com; Shawn Tully, "A Better Taskmaster than the Market," *Fortune,* 26 October 1998, 277–286; Laurie J. Flynn, "For the Officeless, A Place to Call Home," *New York Times,* 6 July 1998, 1, 4; Michele Marchetti, "Getting the Kinks Out," *Sales and Marketing Management,* March 1997, 56–64; "Man of Few Words," *Sales and Marketing Management,* March 1997, 63; "Kinko's Improves Image of Businesses with Top-Notch Proposals and Presentations Capabilities; Presentations a Growing Percentage of Customer Work at Kinko's," *Business Wire,* 28 September 1997; "Kinko's Strengthens Office Product Assortment," *Discount Store News,* 17 November 1997, 6, 70; Ann Marsh, "Kinko's Grows Up—Almost," *Forbes,* 1 December 1997, 270–272; "Kinko's Strikes Deal for Mideast Growth," *Graphic Arts Monthly,* January 1998, 22; Lori Ioannou and Paul Orfalea, "Interview: The Brains Behind Kinko's," *Your Company,* 1 May 1999, 621.

2. Mitchell Pacelle and Ianthe Jeanne Dugan, "Partners Forever? Within Andersen, Personal Liability May Bring Ruin," *Wall Street Journal,* 2 April 2002, C1, C16.

3. Norman M. Scarborough and Thomas W. Zimmerer, *Effective Small Business Management* (Upper Saddle River, N.J.:

Prentice Hall, 2000), 84.

4. James W. Cortada, "Do You Take This Partner," *Total Quality Review,* November–December 1995, 11.

5. Laurence Zuckerman, "UPS Hears Market's Song, and Plans to Sell Some Stock," *New York Times,* 22 July 1999, A1, C23.

6. Vivien Kellerman, "A Growing Business Takes the Corporate Plunge," *New York Times,* 23 July 1994, sec. Your Money, 31.

7. "Fortune 5 Hundred Largest U.S. Corporations," *Fortune,* 15 April 2002, F1–F20.

8. Wal-Mart website [accessed 5 April 2002] www.walmart.com; U.S. Census Bureau website [accessed 5 April 2002] www.census.gov.

9. Scarborough and Zimmerer, *Effective Small Business Management,* 90.

10. Robert G. Goldstein, Russell Shapiro, and Edward A. Hauder, "So Many Choices of Business Entities—Which One Is Best for Your Needs?" *Insight (CPA Society),* February/March 1999, 10–16.

11. John M. Cunningham, "What's Behind New Hampshire's LLC 'Revolution'?" *New Hampshire Business Review,* 19 September–2 October 2003, 27A.

12. Rana Dogar, "Crony Baloney," *Working Woman,* January 1997; Richard H. Koppes, "Institutional Investors, Now in Control of More Than Half the Shares of U.S. Corporations, Demand More Accountability," *National Law Journal,* 14 April 1997, B5; John A. Byrne, "The Best & Worst Boards," *BusinessWeek,* 25 November 1996, 82–84; Anthony Bianco, John Byrne, Richard Melcher, and Mark Maremont, "The Rush to Quality on Corporate Boards," *BusinessWeek,* 3 March 1997, 34–35.

13. *Business Wire,* "CalPERS to Vote Proxy Against Safeway Directors," 7 April 2004, [accessed 8 April 2004] www.highbeam.com.

14. Gary Strauss, "From Public Service to Private Payday," *USA Today,* 17 April 2000, 1B, 2B.

15. "Cleaning up the Boardroom," *New York Times,* 8 March 2002, A20.

16. Floyd Norris, "Ebbers and Passive Directors Blamed for WorldCom Woes: Board That Made Decisions in Haste with No Questioning," *Wall Street Journal,* 10 June 2003, C1, C2.

17. Marc Gunther, "Boards Beware!" *Fortune,* 10 November 2003, 171–178.

18. Pamela Yip, "Reforms Empower Corporate Boards, Shareholders," *Dallas Morning News,* 7 March 2004 [accessed 7 April 2004] www.highbeam.com.

19. "Mergers & Acquisitions Explained," Thomson Investors Network [accessed 8 April 2004] www.thomsoninvest.net.

20. "Mergers & Acquisitions Explained."

21. The PSI Opportunity (online newsletter), PSI website [accessed 8 April 2004] www.psiusa.com.

22. Nancy K. Kubasek, Bartley A. Brennan, and M. Neil Browne, *The Legal Environment of Business* 3d ed. (Upper Saddle River, N.J.: Pearson Education, 2003), 691.

23. Irene Macauley, "Corporate Governance: Crown Charters to Dotcoms," Museum of American Financial History website [accessed 8 April 2004] www.financialhistory.org.

24. *PR Newswire,* "Bank of America Completes FleetBoston Merger; Starting Today, Customers Have Access to Full ATM Network" [accessed 8 April 2004] www.highbeam.com.

25. Brian Caulfield, "Saving $3 Billion the HP Way," *Business 2.0,* May 2003, 52–54.

26. Caulfield, "Saving $3 Billion the HP Way"; Quentin Hardy, "We Did It," *Forbes,* 11 August 2003.

27. Caulfield, "Saving $3 Billion the HP Way"; Hardy, "We Did It."

28. David A. Nadler, "10 Steps to a Happy Merger," *New York Times,* 15 March 1998, BU14.

29. Peter Passell, "Do Mergers Really Yield Big Benefits?" *New York Times,* 14 May 1998, C1, C2.

30. Alex Taylor III, "More Mergers. Dumb Idea," *Fortune,* 15 February 1999, 26–27.

31. Stephen Labaton, "800-Pound Gorillas," *New York Times,* 11 June 2000, sec. 4, 1; Martin Peers, Nick Wingfield, and Laura Landro, "AOL, Time Warner Set Plan to Link in Mammoth Merger," *Wall Street Journal,* 11 January 2000, A1, A6; Thomas E. Weber, Martin Peers, and Nick Wingfield, "Two Titans in a Strategic Bind Bet on a Futuristic Megadeal," *Wall Street Journal,* 11 January 2000, B1, B12; "AOL and Time Warner Will Merge to Create World's First Internet-Age Media and Communications Company," America Online website [accessed 11 January 2000] media.web.aol.com/media/press.cfm.

32. Merrill Goozner and John Schmeltzer, "Mass Exodus Hits Corporate Names," *Chicago Tribune,* 12 May 1998, sec. 3, 1, 3; Bill Vlasic, "The First Global Car Colossus," *BusinessWeek,* 18 May 1998, 40–43; Abid Aslam, "Exxon-Mobil Merger Could Poison the Well," *Inter Press Service English News Wire,* 2 December 1998, Electric Library [accessed 2 June 1999]; Agis Salpukas, "Do Oil and Bigger Oil Mix?" *New York Times,* 2 December 1998, C1, C4.

33. Pui-Wing Tam, "H-P's Board Says It Won't Nominate Dissident Walter Hewlett for Re-Election," *Wall Street Journal,* 2 April 2002, A3, A6; Brian Hale, "Dissident Hewlett Director Sues over Merger Vote," *The Times,* 29 March 2002, 31.

34. Joann S. Lublin, "'Poison Pills' Are Giving Shareholders a Big Headache, Union Proposals Assert," *Wall Street Journal,* 23 May 1997, C1.

35. Thomas Mulligan, "ITT Takes Starwood Offer," *Los Angeles Times,* 13 November 1997,

D2; Kathleen Morris, "Behind the New Deal Mania," *BusinessWeek*, 3 November 1997, 36.
36. Martha Groves and Stuart Silverstein, "Levi Strauss Offers Year's Pay as Incentive Bonus," *Los Angeles Times*, 13 June 1996, A1.
37. "RadioShack Recognized for Contributions to Wireless Industry," *PR Newswire*, 21 March 2002, 1; "Verizon Wireless and RadioShack to Unveil Nationwide Store-Within-A-Store," *PR Newswire*, 7 May 2001.
38. Michael Hickins, "Searching for Allies," *Management Review*, January 2000, 54–58.
39. Gary Dessler, *Management*, 2d ed. (Upper Saddle River, N.J.: Prentice Hall, 2001), 45.
40. See Note 1.

Chapter 5
1. Adapted from Susan Gosselin, "Pizza Wars," *The Lane Report*, 1 September 2001, 46; Kirsten Haukebo, "Papa John's Dad Finds His Calling," *USA Today*, 22 February 2000, 3B; Ron Ruggles, "John Schnatter: Mom Never Thought There'd Be Days Like This, But Papa John's CEO Is Rolling in Dough," *Nation's Restaurant News*, January 2000, 158–160; Amy Zuber, "Papa John's European Expansion to Mushroom via Perfect Pizza Buy," *Nation's Restaurant News*, 13 December 1999, 8; Alynda Wheat, "Striking It Rich the Low-Tech Way," *Fortune*, 27 September 1999, 86; Amy Zuber, "Papa John's Acquires Minnesota Pizza Co.," *Nation's Restaurant News*, 12 April 1999, 4, 91; Anne Field, "Piping-Hot Performance," *Success*, March 1999, 76–80; John Greenwald, "Slice, Dice, and Devour," *Time*, 26 October 1998, 64–66; Papa John's website [accessed 10 April 2004] www.papajohns.com.
2. U.S. Small Business Administration website [accessed 11 April 2004] www.sba.gov; Jim Hopkins, "Entrepreneur 101: Supervising Employees," *USA Today*, 12 September 2001, 9B; Claudia H. Deutsch, "When a Big Company Hatches a Lot of Little Ideas," *New York Times*, 23 September 1998, D4.
3. Small Business Administration Office of Advocacy website [accessed 17 March 2002] www.sba.gov/advo.
4. Small Business Administration website [accessed 11 April 2004].
5. Janice Castro, "Big vs. Small," *Time*, 5 September 1988, 49; Steve Solomon, *Small Business USA* (New York: Crown, 1986), 124.
6. Lloyd Gite and Dawn M. Baskerville, "Black Women Entrepreneurs on the Rise," *Black Enterprise*, August 1996, 73–74.
7. Bill Meyers, "It's a Small-Business World," *USA Today*, 30 July 1999, B1, B2.
8. LeapFrog website [accessed 11 April 2004] www.leapfrog.com.
9. "Matters of Fact," *Inc.*, April 1985, 32.
10. Donna Fenn, "The Buyers," *Inc.*, June 1996, 46–52.

11. Brian O'Reilly, "The New Face of Small Business," *Fortune*, 2 May 1994, 82–88.
12. Michael Moeller, Steve Hamm, and Timothy J. Mullaney, "Remaking Microsoft," *BusinessWeek*, 17 May 1999, 106–116.
13. Timothy D. Schelhardt, "David in Goliath," *Wall Street Journal*, 23 May 1996, R14; Deutsch, "When a Big Company Hatches a Lot of Little Ideas."
14. Adam Cohen, "Her Own Bubble Economy," *Time Bonus Section—Your Business*, April 2001, Y14.
15. Tim McCollum, "A High-Tech Edge for Home Offices," *Nation's Business*, December 1998, 52–54.
16. *Inc. Special Edition—The State of Small Business 1997*, 20 May 1997, 112; James Wilfong and Toni Seger, *Taking Your Business Global* (Franklin Lakes, N.J.: Career Press, 1997), 84.
17. Jim Hopkins, "Female-Owned Companies Flourish," *USA Today*, 6 May 2003, B1.
18. Stephanie Armour, "Many Turn to Start-Ups for Freedom," *USA Today*, 8 June 1998, 1B, 2B; "The Top 500 Women-Owned Businesses," *Working Woman*, May 1998, 50.
19. Small Business Association website [accessed 17 March 2002] www.sba.gov.
20. Small Business Administration Office of Advocacy website [accessed 11 April 2004] www.sba.gov/advo.
21. Jim Hopkins, "Hispanic-Owned Companies See Strong Growth Spurt," *USA Today*, 2 July 2003, B1.
22. Jim Hopkins, "Bad Times Spawn Great Start-Ups," *USA Today*, 18 December 2001, 1B; Alan Cohen, "Your Next Business," *FSB*, February 2002, 33–40.
23. Jim Hopkins, "Entrepreneur 101: Supervising Employees," *USA Today*, 12 September 2001, 9B.
24. Wilfong and Seger, *Taking Your Business Global*, 78–80; Kelly J. Andrews, "Born or Bred?" *Entrepreneurial Edge* 3 (1998), 24–28.
25. Jane Applegate, *Succeeding in Small Business* (New York: Plume/Penguin, 1992), 1.
26. Michelle Conlin, "It's in the Bag," *Forbes*, 28 December 1998, 86, 90; Edie Cohen, "Ace of Spades," *Interior Design*, April 2001, 198–205.
27. Lisa J. Moore and Sharon F. Golden, "You Can Plan to Expand or Just Let It Happen," *U.S. News & World Report*, 23 October 1989, 78; John Case, "The Origins of Entrepreneurship," *Inc.*, June 1989, 56.
28. Norm Brodsky, "Caveat Emptor," *Inc.*, August 1998, 31–32; "Why Buy a Business?" CCH Toolkit website [accessed 20 May 1999] aol.toolkit.cch.com/text/PO1_0820.asp.
29. "McBusiness," *Inc. State of Small Business 2001*, 34.
30. Richard Gibson, "Franchise Fever," *Wall Street Journal*, 15 December 2003, R1.

31. Roberta Maynard, "Choosing a Franchise," *Nation's Business*, October 1996, 56–63.
32. Latonya West, "Success Is Convenient," *Minorities in Business*, [undated], 22–26.
33. Jeffrey A. Tannenbaum, "Taking a Bath," *Wall Street Journal*, 22 June 1998, 27.
34. Papa John's website [accessed 20 March 2002] www.papajohns.com.
35. Michael Hopkins, "Zen and the Art of the Self-Managed Company," *Inc.*, November 2000, 54–63.
36. Roberta Maynard, "The Changing Landscape," *Nation's Business*, January 1997, 54–55.
37. "McBusiness," *Inc. State of Small Business 2001*, 58.
38. Joseph W. Duncan, "The True Failure Rate of Start-Ups," *D&B Reports*, January–February 1994; Maggie Jones, "Smart Cookies," *Working Woman*, April 1995, 50–52; Janice Maloney, "Failure May Not Be So Bad After All," *New York Times*, 23 September 1998, 12.
39. Juan Hovey, "Risky Business," *IndustryWeek*, 15 May 2000, 75–76.
40. Sharon Nelton, "Coming to Grips with Growth," *Nation's Business*, February 1998, 26–32.
41. Michael Selz, "Here's the Problem," *Wall Street Journal—Breakaway Special Report Winter 1999*, 22 February 1999, 12.
42. Jerry Useem, "The Secret of My Success," *Inc.*, May 1998, 67–80.
43. Maloney, "Failure May Not Be So Bad After All."
44. SCORE website [accessed 11 April 2004] www.score.org.
45. J. Tol Broome, Jr., "SCORE's Impact on Small Firms," *Nation's Business*, January 1999, 41–43; Robert McGarvey, "Peak Performance," *American Way*, July 1996, 56–60.
46. Loren Fox, "Hatching New Companies," *Upside*, February 2000, 144–152.
47. Dale Buss, "Bringing New Firms out of Their Shell," *Nation's Business*, March 1997, 48–50; Fox, "Hatching New Companies."
48. Jonathan Katz, "Hatching Ideas," *IndustryWeek*, 18 September 2000, 63–65.
49. Buss, "Bringing New Firms out of Their Shell."
50. McGarvey, "Peak Performance."
51. Papa John's website [accessed 20 March 2002] www.papajohns.com.
52. Jim Hopkins, "Corporate Giants Bankroll Start-Ups," *USA Today*, 29 March 2001, B1.
53. Bob Zider, "How Venture Capital Works," *Harvard Business Review*, November/December 1998, 131–139.
54. "Cash Flow," *Inc. State of Small Business 2001*, 76.
55. Brian Caulfield, Michael V. Copeland, Bridget Finn, David Howard, Kevin Kelleher,

Matthew Maier, Om Malik, Jordan Robertson, and Owen Thomas, "12 Hot Startups," *Business 2.0*, January/February 2004, 93–98.
56. Dori Jones Yang, "Venture Capitalists Seek Less Adventure," *U.S. News & World Report*, 4 June 2001, 39.
57. Barbara Darrow, "Touched By an Angel," *Computer Reseller News*, 17 April 2000, 152, 156.
58. Jane Easter Bahls, "Cyber Cash"; "Startup Financing: Finding an Angel to Get Going," CCH Business Owners Toolkit website [accessed 20 May 1999] aol.toolkit.cch.com/columns/Starting/225-99AngelR.asp.
59. Darrow, "Touched By an Angel," 152, 156.
60. Rodney Ho, "Banking on Plastic," *Wall Street Journal*, 9 March 1998, A1, A8.
61. Joel Russell, "Credit Card Capitalism," *Hispanic Business*, March 1998, 40.
62. Henry Wichmann, Jr., Charles Harter, and H. Charles Sparks, "Big Cash for Small Business," *Journal of Accountancy*, July 1999, 64–72.
63. Wilfong and Seger, *Taking Your Business Global*, 20.
64. Ronaleen R. Roha, "Big Loans for Small Businesses," *Changing Times*, April 1989, 105–109; "Small Loans, Big Problems," *Economist*, 28 January 1995, 73; Elizabeth Kadetsky, "Small Loans, Big Dreams," *Working Woman*, February 1995, 46–49; Reid Rutherford, "Securitizing Small Business Loans: A Banker's Action Plan," *Commercial Lending Review*, Winter 1994–1995, 62–74.
65. Roha, "Big Loans for Small Businesses," 105.
66. Susan Hodges, "Microloans Fuel Big Ideas," *Nation's Business*, February 1997, 34–35.
67. Karen Gutloff, "Five Alternative Ways to Finance Your Business," *Black Enterprise*, March 1998, 81–85.
68. See Note 1.

Chapter 6
1. Adapted from Nokia website [accessed 13 April 2004] www.nokia.com; "Nokia Defends Itself Against Securities Fraud Complaint," Business CustomWire, 7 April 2004 [accessed 13 April 2004] www.ebsco.com; Janet Guyon, "Nokia Rocks Its Rivals," *Fortune*, 4 March 2002, 115–118; Dan Steinbock, *The Nokia Revolution* (New York: American Management Association, 2001); Kerry Capell, William Echikson, and Peter Elstrom, "Surprise! Nokia Doesn't Walk on Water," *BusinessWeek*, 25 June 2001, 49; John S. McClenahen, "CEO of the Year: Nokia's Jorma Ollila Wants to Unwire the World," *IndustryWeek*, 20 November 2000, 38–44; "Nokia: A Finnish Fable," *The Economist*, 14 October 2000, 83–85; Stephen Baker with Inka Resch and Roger O.

Crockett, "Nokia's Costly Stumble," *BusinessWeek*, 14 August 2000, 42; "Business: Star Turn," *The Economist*, 5 August 2000, 60; Maryanne Murry Buechner, "Making the Call," *Time*, 29 May 2000, 64–65; Justin Fox, "Nokia's Secret Code," *Fortune*, 1 May 2000; 160–174; Adrian Wooldridge, "Survey: Telecommunications: To the Finland Base Station," *The Economist*, 9 October 1999, S23–S27; Stephen Baker and Robert McNatt, "Now Nokia Is Net Crazy," *BusinessWeek*, 5 April 1999, 6; "Jorma Ollila: Finn Fatale," *BusinessWeek*, 11 January 1999, 78; Stephen Baker with Roger O. Crockett and Neil Gross, "Nokia," *BusinessWeek*, 10 August 1998, 54.
2. Richard L. Daft, *Management*, 4th ed. (Fort Worth, Tex.: Dryden Press, 1997), 8.
3. Courtland L. Bovée, John V. Thill, Marian Burk Wood, and George P. Dovel, *Management* (New York: McGraw-Hill, 1993), 220; David H. Holt, *Management: Principles and Practices*, 2d ed. (Upper Saddle River, N.J.: Prentice Hall, 1990), 10–12; James A. F. Stoner, *Management*, 4th ed. (Upper Saddle River, N.J.: Prentice Hall, 1989), 15–18.
4. Gillian Flynn, "A Flight Plan for Success," *Workforce*, July 1997, 72–128.
5. Stephen P. Robbins, *Managing Today* (Upper Saddle River, N.J.: Prentice Hall, 1997), 452.
6. Leonard Goodstein, Timothy Nolan, and J. William Pfeiffer, *Applied Strategic Planning* (New York: McGraw-Hill, 1993), 169–192.
7. Aimee L. Stern, "Management: You Can Keep Your Staff on the Competitive Track If You . . . Inspire Your Team with a Mission Statement," *Your Company*, 1 August 1997, 36.
8. Cornelis A. de Kluyver and John A Pearce II, *Strategy: A View from the Top* (Upper Saddle River, N.J.: Prentice-Hall, 2003), 62.
9. Daft, *Management*, 4th ed., 221–223, 260–262.
10. de Kluyver and Pearce, *Strategy: A View from the Top*, 55–56.
11. Judy A. Smith, "Crisis Communications: The War on Two Fronts," *Industry Week*, 20 May 1996, 136; John F. Reukus, "Hazard Communication," *Occupational Hazards*, February 1998, 39; Kim M. Gibson and Steven H. Smith, "Do We Understand Each Other?" *Journal of Accountancy*, January 1998, 53.
12. Timothy Aeppel, Clare Ansberry, Milo Geyelin, and Robert L. Simison, "Road Signs: How Ford, Firestone Let the Warnings Slide By as Debacle Developed," *Wall Street Journal*, 6 September 2000, A1; Joann Muller, David Welch, Jeff Green, Lorraine Woellert, and Nicole St. Pierre, "A Crisis of Confidence," *BusinessWeek*, 18 September 2000, 40–42.
13. Michael Moeller, Steve Hamm, and

Timothy J. Mullaney, "Remaking Microsoft," *BusinessWeek*, 17 May 1999, 106–116.
14. Stephanie Armour, "Once Plagued by Pink Slips, Now They're in Driver's Seat," *USA Today*, 14 May 1998, 1B–2B.
15. Daft, *Management*, 4th ed., 219–221.
16. Gary A. Yukl, *Leadership in Organizations*, 2d ed. (Upper Saddle River, N.J.: Prentice Hall, 1989), 9, 175–176.
17. Daniel Goleman, "What Makes a Leader?" *Harvard Business Review*, November–December 1998, 92–102; Shari Caudron, "The Hard Case for Soft Skills," *Workforce*, July 1999, 60–66.
18. Daft, *Management*, 4th ed., 498–499.
19. Jenny Anderson, "Al Gets the Chainsaw," *Institutional Investor*, October 1999, 224.
20. Michael A. Verespej, "Lead, Don't Manage," *IndustryWeek*, 4 March 1996, 58.
21. Stratford Sherman, "Secrets of HP's 'Muddled' Team," *Fortune*, 18 March 1996, 116–120.
22. Daniel Goleman, "Leadership That Gets Results," *Harvard Business Review*, March–April 2000, 78–90.
23. Richard L. Daft, *Management*, 6th ed. (Mason, Ohio: South-Western, 2003), 526.
24. Stephen P. Robbins and David A. De Cenzo, *Fundamentals of Management*, 4th ed. (Upper Saddle River, N.J.: Prentice Hall, 2004), 325.
25. John A. Byrne, "How to Lead Now," *Fast Company*, August 2003, 62–70.
26. Stephen P. Robbins and David A. De Cenzo, *Fundamentals of Management*, 2d ed. (Upper Saddle River, N.J.: Prentice Hall, 1998), 55–56; James Waldroop and Timothy Butler, "The Executive as Coach," *Harvard Business Review*, November–December 1996, 113.
27. Kathryn Tyler, "Scoring Big in the Workplace," *HR Magazine*, June 2000, 96–106.
28. "The Advantage of Female Mentoring," *Working Woman*, October 1991, 104.
29. David Welch and Kathleen Kerwin, "Rick Wagoner's Game Plan," *BusinessWeek*, 10 February 2003, 52–60.
30. Richard L. Daft, *Management*, 6th ed. (Mason, Ohio: South-Western, 2003), 382; Robbins and De Cenzo, *Fundamentals of Management*, 4th ed., 209.
31. Michael Been and Nitin Nohria, "Cracking the Code of Change," *Harvard Business Review*, May–June 2000, 133–141.
32. Robbins and De Cenzo, *Fundamentals of Management*, 4th ed., 211; Daft, *Management*, 6th ed., 384, 396.
33. Robbins and De Cenzo, *Fundamentals of Management*, 4th ed., 210–211.
34. Patrick J. Sauer, "Open-Door Management," *Inc.*, June 2003, 44.
35. Melanie Trottman, "Inside Southwest Airlines, Stories Culture Feels Strains," *Wall Street Journal*, 11 July 2003, A1, A6.
36. Kostas N. Dervitsiotis, "The Challenge of Managing Organizational Change," *Total*

Quality Management, February 1998, 109–122.

37. George Taninecz, "Borg-Warner Automotive," *IndustryWeek*, 19 October 1998, 44–46.

38. Bovée et al., *Management*, 680.

39. Michael A. Verespej, "Stability Before Growth," *IndustryWeek*, 15 April 1996, 12–16.

40. James R. Lackritz, "TQM Within Fortune 500 Corporations," *Quality Progress*, February 1997, 69–72.

41. David Sirota, Brian Usilaner, and Michelle S. Weber, "Sustaining Quality Improvement," *Total Quality Review*, March–April 1994, 23; Joe Batten, "A Total Quality Culture," *Management Review*, May 1994, 61; Rahul Jacon, "More Than a Dying Fad?" *Fortune*, 18 October 1993, 66–72.

42. Lackritz, "TQM Within Fortune 500 Corporations."

43. Robert L. Katz, "Skills of an Effective Administrator," *Harvard Business Review*, September–October 1974. Reprinted in *Paths Toward Personal Progress: Leaders Are Made, Not Born* (Boston: Harvard Business Review, 1983), 23–35; Mike Dawson, "Leaders Versus Managers," *Systems Management*, March 1995, 32; R. S. Dreyer, "Do Good Bosses Make Lousy Leaders?" *Supervision*, March 1995, 19–20; Michael Maccoby, "Teams Need Open Leaders," *Research-Technology Management*, January–February 1995, 57–59.

44. Robert E. Kaplan and Robert B. Kaiser, "Developing Versatile Leadership," *MIT Sloan Management Review*, Summer 2003, 19–26.

45. Courtland L. Bovée and John V. Thill, *Business Communication Today*, 6th ed. (Upper Saddle River, N.J.: Prentice Hall, 2000), 4.

46. Daft, *Management*, 4th ed., 128; Kathryn M. Bartol and David C. Martin, *Management* (New York: McGraw-Hill, 1991), 268–272.

47. Bartol and Martin, *Management*, 268–272; Ricky W. Griffin, *Management*, 3d ed. (Boston: Houghton Mifflin, 1990), 131–137.

48. Robbins, *Managing Today*, 72.

49. See note 1.

Chapter 7

1. Mike Duff, "Top-Shelf Employees Keep Container Store on Track," *DSN Retailing Today*, 8 March 2004, 7, 49; Bob Nelson, "The Buzz at The Container Store," *Corporate Meetings & Incentives*, June 2003, 32; Jennifer Saba, "Balancing Act," *Potentials*, 1 October 2003 [accessed 15 April 2004] www.highbeam.com; Peter S. Cohan, "Corporate Heroes," *Financial Executive*, 1 March 2003 [accessed 15 April 2004] www.highbeam.com; Margaret Steen, "Container Store's Focus on Training a

Strong Appeal to Employees," *Mercury News* (San Jose, CA), 6 November 2003 [accessed 15 April 2004] www.highbeam.com; Holly Hayes, "Container Store Brings Clutter Control to San Jose, Calif.," 17 October 2003, *Mercury News* (San Jose, CA), 1F; "Performance Through People Award," press release, 10 September 2003; David Lipke, "Container Store's CEO: People Are Most Valued Asset," 13 January 2003, *HFN* [accessed 9 March 2003] www.highbeam.com; Lorrie Grant, "Container Store's Workers Huddle Up to Help You Out," 30 April 2002, *USA Today*, B1; Container Store website [accessed 14 April 2004] www.containerstore.com.

2. Richard L. Daft, *Management*, 4th ed. (Fort Worth, Tex.: Dryden Press, 1997), 358.

3. Rob Goffee and Gareth Jones, "What Holds the Modern Company Together?" *Harvard Business Review*, November–December 1996, 134–145.

4. Peter F. Drucker, "Management's New Paradigms," *Forbes*, 5 October 1998, 152–176.

5. Stephen P. Robbins, *Managing Today!* (Upper Saddle River, N.J.: Prentice Hall, 1997), 193; Daft, *Management*, 320.

6. Stephen P. Robbins and David A. De Cenzo, *Fundamentals of Management*, 2d ed. (Upper Saddle River, N.J.: Prentice Hall, 1998), 201; Daft, *Management*, 321.

7. "Sharing Knowledge Through BP's Virtual Team Network," *Harvard Business Review*, September–October 1997, 152–153; British Petroleum website [accessed 20 April 2002] www.bp.com.

8. Alan Webber, "The Best Organization Is No Organization," *USA Today*, 13A; Eve Tahmincioglu, "How GM's Team Approach Works," *Gannett News Service*, 24 April 1996, S11.

9. Fred R. David, *Strategic Management*, 6th ed. (Upper Saddle River, N.J.: Prentice Hall, 1997), 225; Kathryn M. Bartol and David C. Martin, *Management* (New York: McGraw-Hill, 1991), 352.

10. Kevin Kelleher, "The Drug Pipeline Flows Again," *Business 2.0*, April 2004 [accessed 15 April 2004] www.business2.com.

11. Daft, *Management*, 325.

12. Courtland L. Bovée, John V. Thill, Marian Wood, and George Dovel, *Management* (New York: McGraw-Hill, 1993), 285.

13. Bartol and Martin, *Management*, 370–371.

14. Gary Izumo, "Teamwork Holds Key to Organization Success," *Los Angeles Times*, 20 August 1996, D9; Daft, *Management*, 328–329; David, *Strategic Management*, 223.

15. Gareth R. Jones, *Organizational Theory, Design, and Change*, 4th ed. (Upper Saddle River, N.J.: Prentice Hall, 2004), 167.

16. John A. Byrne, "The Horizontal Corporation," *BusinessWeek*, 20 December 1993, 76–81; "Is a Horizontal Organization for You?" *Fortune*, 3 April 1995, 96; Rahul Jacob, "The Struggle to Create an Organization for the 21st Century," *Fortune*, 3 April 1995, 90–96.

17. Steven Burke, "Acer Restructures into Six Divisions," *Computer Reseller News*, 13 July 1998, 10; Acer America website [accessed 20 July 2000] www.acer.com/aac/about/pro-file.htm.

18. Daft, *Management*, 328–329; David, *Strategic Management*, 223; Bartol and Martin, *Management*, 376.

19. Dan Dimancescu and Kemp Dwenger, "Smoothing the Product Development Path," *Management Review*, 1 January 1996, 36.

20. Dimancescu and Dwenger, "Smoothing the Product Development Path."

21. Robbins, *Managing Today!* 209; Daft, *Management*, 333–336.

22. Daft, *Management*, 340–343; Robbins, *Managing Today!*, 213–214.

23. Daft, *Management*, 340–343; Robbins, *Managing Today!*, 213–214.

24. "The Horizontal Corporation."

25. Daft, *Management*, 352–353; Richards, *Strategic Management*, 217; Bartol and Martin, *Management*, 357–358.

26. Arthur D. Wainwright, "People-First Strategies Get Implemented," *Strategy and Leadership*, January–February 1997, 12–17.

27. Stephen P. Robbins, *Essentials of Organizational Behavior*, 6th ed. (Upper Saddle River, N.J.: Prentice Hall, 2000), 105.

28. Daft, *Management*, 591; Robbins, *Managing Today!*, 295.

29. "Microsoft Teamwork," *Executive Excellence*, 6 July 1996, 6–7.

30. Jeffrey Pfeffer, "When It Comes to 'Best Practices'—Why Do Smart Organizations Occasionally Do Dumb Things?" *Organizational Dynamics*, 1 June 1996, 33; LaMar A. Trego, "Reengineering Starts with a 'Clean Sheet of Paper,'" *Manage*, 1 July 1996, 17.

31. Daft, *Management*, 594–595; Robbins and De Cenzo, *Fundamentals of Management*, 336; Robbins, *Managing Today!*, 309.

32. Pfeffer, "When It Comes to 'Best Practices.'"

33. Scott Kirsner, "Every Day, It's a New Place," *Fast Company*, April–May 1998, 132–134.

34. Daft, *Management*, 594; Robbins and De Cenzo, *Fundamentals of Management*, 336.

35. Jenny C. McCune, "On the Train Gang: In the New Flat Organizations, Employees Who Want to Be Competitive Must Be Versatile Enough to Perform a Variety of Tasks," *Management Review*, 1 October 1994, 57.

36. Daft, *Management*, 594; Robbins and De Cenzo, *Fundamentals of Management*, 338; Robbins, *Managing Today!*, 310–311.

37. Seth Lubove, "Destroying the Old Hierarchies," *Forbes*, 3 June 1996, 62–64.
38. Clyde Fessler, "Rotating Leadership at Harley-Davidson: From Hierarchy to Interdependence," *Strategy & Leadership*, July–August 1997, 42–43; Mark A. Brunelli, "How Harley-Davidson Uses Cross-Functional Teams," *Purchasing*, 4 November 1999, 148.
39. Ellen Neuborne, "Companies Save, But Workers Pay," *USA Today*, 25 February 1997, B1; Daft, *Management*, 594; Robbins and De Cenzo, *Fundamentals of Management*, 338; Robbins, *Managing Today!*, 310.
40. Richard Moderow, "Teamwork Is the Key to Cutting Costs," *Modern Healthcare*, 29 April 1996, 138.
41. Daft, *Management*, 594.
42. Robbins, *Essentials of Organizational Behavior*, 109.
43. Deborah L. Duarte and Nancy Tennant Snyder, *Mastering Virtual Teams* (San Francisco: Jossey-Bass Publishers, 1999), 23.
44. "Sharing Knowledge Through BP's Virtual Team Network," *Harvard Business Review*, September–October 1997, 152–153.
45. Barbara De Lollis, "Virtual Meeting Companies Get Boost as Travel Wanes," *USA Today*, 18 March 2003, 10B.
46. Daft, *Management*, 612–615.
47. Robbins, *Essentials of Organizational Behavior*, 98.
48. Ross Sherwood, "The Boss's Open Door Means More Time for Employees," *Reuters Business Report*, 30 September 1996.
49. Neuborne, "Companies Save, But Workers Pay," B2; Charles L. Parnell, "Teamwork: Not a New Idea, But It's Transforming the Workplace," *Vital Speeches of the Day*, 1 November 1996, 46.
50. Robbins and De Cenzo, *Fundamentals of Management*, 151.
51. Larry Cole and Michael Cole, "Why Is the Teamwork Buzz Word Not Working?" *Communication World*, February/March 1999, 29; Patricia Buhler, "Managing in the 90s: Creating Flexibility in Today's Workplace," *Supervision*, January 1997, 24+; Allison W. Amason, Allen C. Hochwarter, Wayne A. Thompson, and Kenneth R. Harrison, "Conflict: An Important Dimension in Successful Management Teams," *Organizational Dynamics*, Autumn 1995, 20+.
52. "Team Players," *Executive Excellence*, May 1999, 18.
53. Robbins and De Cenzo, *Fundamentals of Management*, 334–335; Daft, *Management*, 602–603.
54. Robbins, *Managing Today!*, 297–298; Daft, *Management*, 604–607.
55. Thomas K. Capozzoli, "Conflict Resolution—A Key Ingredient in Successful Teams," *Supervision*, November 1999, 14–16.
56. Daft, *Management*, 609–612.

57. Steven Crom and Herbert France, "Teamwork Brings Breakthrough Improvements in Quality and Climate," *Quality Progress*, March 1996, 39–41.
58. David, *Strategic Management*, 221.
59. "Better Meetings Benefit Everyone: How to Make Yours More Productive," *Working Communicator Bonus Report*, July 1998, 1.
60. Ken Blanchard, "Meetings Can Be Effective," *Supervisory Management*, October 1992, 5.
61. "Better Meetings Benefit Everyone."
62. See Note 1.

Chapter 8
1. Adapted from Jonathan Fahey, "Love into Money," *Forbes*, 7 January 2002, 60–65; Vincent J. Orange and David E. Robinson, "The Role of Certification in the Buyer/Planner Position: A Case Study at Harley-Davidson Motor Company," *Hospital/Materiel Management Quarterly*, February 1999, 28–36; Leslie P. Norton, "Potholes Ahead?" *Barron's*, 1 February 1999, 16–17; Bruce Caldwell, "Harley-Davidson Revs Up IT Horsepower," *Internetweek*, 7 December 1998, 63; Peter Bradley, "Harley-Davidson Keeps Its Eyes on the Road," *Logistics Management and Distribution Report*, August 1998, 68–73; Harley-Davidson website [accessed 17 April 2004] www.harley-davidson.com.
2. Roberta A. Russell and Bernard W. Taylor III, *Operations Management: Focusing on Quality and Competitiveness*, 2d ed. (Upper Saddle River, N.J.: Prentice Hall, 1998), 21.
3. Robert Kreitner, *Management*, 9th ed. (Boston: Houghton-Mifflin, 2004), 576–578.
4. T. J. Becker, "Have It Your Way," *The Edward Lowe Report*, February 2002, 1–3, 12.
5. Philip Siekman, "The Smart Car Is Looking More So," *Fortune*, 15 April 2002, 310(I)–310(P).
6. Gene Bylinsky, "For Sale: Japanese Plants in the U.S.," *Fortune*, 21 February 2000, 240B–240D.
7. Hansell, "Is This the Factory of the Future?"; Pete Engardio, "Souping Up the Supply Chain," *BusinessWeek*, 31 August 1998, 110–112.
8. Faye Bowers, "Building a 747: 43 Days and 3 Million Fasteners," *Christian Science Monitor*, 29 October 1997 [accessed 16 April 2004] www.csmonitor.com.
9. Ronald Henkoff, "Boeing's Big Problem," *Fortune*, 12 January 1998, 96–103; James Wallace, "How Boeing Blew It," *Sales and Marketing Management*, February 1998, 52–57; John Greenwald, "Is Boeing out of Its Spin?" *Time*, 13 July 1998, 67–69; John T. Landry, "Supply Chain Management: The Case for Alliances," *Harvard Business Review*, November–December 1998, 24–25.
10. Robert J. Trent, "What Everyone Needs to Know About SCM," *Supply Chain*

Management Review, 1 March 2004 [accessed 16 April 2004] www.manufacturing.net.
11. Mark M. Davis, Nicholas J. Aquilano, and Richard B. Chase, *Fundamentals of Operations Management* (Boston: Irwin McGraw-Hill, 1999), 382.
12. Jane C. Linder, "Transformational Outsourcing," *MIT Sloan Management Review*, Winter 2004, 52–58.
13. John Greenwald, "Cruise Lines Go Overboard," *Time*, 11 May 1998, 42–45.
14. Joseph G. Monks, *Operations Management, Theory and Problems* (New York: McGraw-Hill, 1987), 77–78.
15. Davis, Aquilano, and Chase, *Fundamentals of Operations Management*, 241–242.
16. Mark Landler, "Slovakia No Longer a Laggard in Automaking," *New York Times*, 13 April 2004 [accessed 15 April 2004] www.nytimes.com.
17. Jae K. Shim and Joel G. Siegel, *Operations Management* (Hauppauge, N.Y.: Barron's Educational Series, 1999), 206.
18. Monks, *Operations Management, Theory and Problems*, 2–3.
19. Shim and Siegel, *Operations Management*, 206.
20. Monks, *Operations Management, Theory and Problems*, 125.
21. Davis, Aquilano, and Chase, *Fundamentals of Operations Management*, 254; Richard L. Daft, *Management*, 4th ed. (Fort Worth, Tex.: Dryden Press, 1997), 718.
22. Kathryn M. Bartol and David C. Martin, *Management* (New York: McGraw-Hill, 1991), 307–308.
23. Larry E. Long and Nancy Long, *Introduction to Computers and Information Systems*, 5th ed. (Upper Saddle River, N.J.: Prentice Hall, 1997), 84.
24. Stuart F. Brown, "Giving More Jobs to Electronic Eyes," *Fortune*, 16 February 1998, 104B–104D.
25. "IBM and Dassault Awarded Boeing CATIA Contract," *CAD/CAM Update*, 1 January 1997, 1–8.
26. Russell and Taylor, *Operations Management*, 211.
27. "CAD/CAM Industry Embracing Intranet-Based Technologies," *Computer Dealer News* 12 (28 November 1996): 21.
28. Drew Winter, "C3P: New Acronym Signals Big Change at Ford," *Ward's Auto World* 32 (1 August 1996): 34; Thomas Hoffman, "Ford to Cut Its Prototype Costs," *Computerworld*, 30 September 1996, 65; Drew Winter, "Massive Changes Coming in Computer Engineering," *Ward's Auto World* 32 (1 April 1996): 34.
29. Davis, Aquilano, and Chase, *Fundamentals of Operations Management*, 64; Russell and Taylor, *Operations Management*, 257–258.
30. Brian S. Moskal, "Born to Be Real," *Industry Week*, 2 August 1993, 14–18.

31. Russell and Taylor, *Operations Management*, 255–256.

32. John H. Sheridan, "Agile Manufacturing: Stepping Beyond Lean Production," *Industry Week*, 19 April 1993, 30–46.

33. Robyn Meredith, "Porsche Goes Soccer Mom," *Forbes*, 4 February 2000, 54.

34. Brian McWilliams, "Re-engineering the Small Factory," *Inc. Technology* 1 (1996): 44–45.

35. James A. Senn, *Information Technology: Principles, Practices, Opportunities*, 3d ed. (Upper Saddle River, N.J.: Prentice-Hall, 2004), 328.

36. Helen Gurevich, "Surviving the Enterprise Integration War," *Health Management Technology*, February 2004, 66+; Mark Jones, "Ingram Micro: The Trouble with XML and Web Services," *InfoWorld*, 9 November 2001 [accessed 17 April] www.infoworld.com; "Companies Continue to Find Benefit in EDI Investments," *Electronic Commerce News*, 1 March 2004, 1.

37. Greg Ip, "Risky Business," *Wall Street Journal*, 24 October 2001, A1, A4.

38. Jon E. Hilsenrath, "Parts Shortages Hamper Electronics Makers: Surging Demand Shows Flaw in Just-in-Time Chains," *Wall Street Journal*, 7 July 2000, B5.

39. Shim and Siegel, *Operations Management*, 326.

40. Russell and Taylor, *Operations Management*, 712–733.

41. Patricia W. Hamilton, "Getting a Grip on Inventory," *D&B Reports*, March–April 1994, 32.

42. Russell and Taylor, *Operations Management*, 652–653.

43. Trent, "What Everyone Needs to Know About SCM."

44. David Hughes, "Life-Cycle Software," *Aviation Week & Space Technology*, 18 August 2003 [accessed 17 April 2004] www.ebsco.com.

45. Tim Laseter and Keith Oliver, "When Will Supply Chain Management Grow Up?" *strategy+business*, Fall 2003, 32–36; Trent, "What Everyone Needs to Know About SCM."

46. Laura Rock Kopczak and M. Eric Johnson, "The Supply-Chain Management Effect," *MIT Sloan Management Review*, Spring 2003, 27–34.

47. George Taninecz, "Forging the Chain," *Industry Week*, 15 May 2000, 40–46.

48. Laseter and Oliver, "When Will Supply Chain Management Grow Up?"

49. Alan Young, "Healing Corrupted by Practices of Big Pharma," *Toronto Star*, 11 April 2004 [accessed 17 April 2004] www.highbeam.com; Kathleen Longcore, "Group Aims to Fix Medical Mistakes, Shorten Recovery with Technology," *Grand Rapids Press* (Grand Rapids, MI), 3 April 2004 [accessed 17 April 2004] www.highbeam.com.

50. Karl Ritzler, "A Mercedes Made from Scratch," *Atlanta Journal and Constitution*, 30 May 1997, S1.

51. Del Jones, "Training and Service at Top of Winners' List," *USA Today*, 17 October 1996, 5B.

52. John A. Byrne, "Never Mind the Buzzwords. Roll Up Your Sleeves," *BusinessWeek*, 22 January 1996, 84.

53. Davis, Aquilano, and Chase, *Fundamentals of Operations Management*, 177–179; Russell and Taylor, *Operations Management*, 131.

54. William M. Carley, "Charging Ahead: To Keep GE's Profits Rising, Welch Pushes Quality-Control Plan," *Wall Street Journal*, 13 January 1997, A1, A6.

55. Russell and Taylor, *Operations Management*, 131.

56. Gillian Babicz, "ISO 9004: The Other Half of the Consistent Pair," *Quality*, June 2001, 50–53; David Drickhemer, "Standards Shake-Up," *IndustryWeek*, 5 March 2001, 37–40.

57. Hugh D. Menzies, "Global Guide: Quality Counts When Wooing Overseas Clients," *Your Company*, 1 June 1997, 64; Michael E. Raynor, "Worldwide Winners," *Total Quality Management*, July–August 1993, 43–48; Greg Bounds, Lyle Yorks, Mel Adams, and Gipsie Ranney, *Beyond Total Quality Management: Toward the Emerging Paradigm* (New York: McGraw-Hill, 1994), 212; Russell and Taylor, *Operations Management*, 115–116.

58. See Note 1.

Chapter 9

1. Adapted from Atlas Container website [accessed 30 April 2004] www.atlascontainer.com; John Case, "The Power of Listening," *Inc.*, March 2003, 76–84; Esther Durkalski, "Workplace Perks Spark Happy Employees," *Paperboard Packaging*, May 2001, 28+; Steven Averett, "Provocative Politics," *Industrial Engineer*, May 2003, 28+; Esther Durkalski, "Mapping Its Future," *Paperboard Packaging*, October 2001 [accessed 30 April 2004] www.highbeam.com.

2. Dennis C. Kinlaw, "What Employees See Is What Organizations Get," *Management Solutions*, March 1988, 38–41.

3. Michael A. Verespej, "Balancing Act," *IndustryWeek*, 15 May 2000, 81–85.

4. Stephen P. Robbins and David A. DeCenzo, *Fundamentals of Management*, 4th ed. (Upper Saddle River, N.J.: Prentice Hall, 2004), 284.

5. John McMorrow, "Future Trends in Human Resources," *HR Focus*, September 1999, 8–9.

6. Robert B. Reich, "The Company of the Future," *Fast Company*, November 1998, 124–150.

7. Richard L. Daft, *Management*, 6th ed. (Mason, Ohio: Thomson South-Western, 2003), 552–553.

8. Douglas McGregor, *The Human Side of Enterprise* (New York: McGraw-Hill, 1960).

9. Rudy M. Yandrick, "Help Employees Reach for the Stars," *HRMagazine*, 1 January 1997 [accessed 26 April 2004] www.highbeam.com.

10. Daft, *Management*, 6th ed., 554–555.

11. Eryn Brown, "How to Get Paid What You're Worth," *Business 2.0*, May 2004, 102–110.

12. Robbins and DeCenzo, *Fundamentals of Management*, 289.

13. Bob Parks, "Where the Customer Service Rep Is King," *Business 2.0*, June 2003, 70–72.

14. Reich, "The Company of the Future."

15. Aaron Bernstein, "We Want You to Stay. Really," *BusinessWeek*, 22 June 1998, 67–72; Carol Kleiman, "The New Loyalty: A Work in Progress," *Chicago Tribune*, 15 August 1999, sec. 6, 1.

16. Kelly Barron and Ann Marsch, "The Skills Gap," *Forbes*, 23 February 1998, 44–45.

17. Greg Jaffe and Douglas A. Blackmon, "Just in Time. When UPS Demanded Workers, Louisville Did the Delivering," *Wall Street Journal*, 24 April 1998, A1, A10; James Ott, "UPS Hub 2000 at Louisville Marks New Airport Era," 20 July 1998, 47+.

18. Stephanie Armour, "Companies Hire Even as They Lay Off," *USA Today*, 15 May 2001, A1.

19. Carlos Tejeda and Gary McWilliams, "New Recipe for Cost Savings: Replace Expensive Workers," *Wall Street Journal*, 11 June 2003, A1, A6.

20. Michelle Kessler, "Days of BMW Signing Bonuses Long Gone," *USA Today*, 14 April 2002, 3B.

21. Jennifer Laabs, "The New Loyalty: Grasp It. Earn It. Keep It," *Workforce*, November 1998, 35–39.

22. Emily Thornton, "No Room at the Top," *BusinessWeek*, 9 August 1999, 50; Michael A. Lev, "Lifetime Jobs May Be at Death's Door as Japan Tradition," *Chicago Tribune*, 11 October 1998, sec. 5, 1, 18.

23. John Greenwald, "Spinning Away," *Time*, 26 August 1996, 30–31.

24. Stephanie Armour, "Blame It on Downsizing, E-Mail, Laptops, and Dual-Career Families," *USA Today*, 13 March 1998, B1; Jennifer Laabs, "Workforce Overload," *Workforce*, January 1999, 30–37.

25. Michelle Conlin, Peter Coy, Ann Therese, and Gabrielle Saveri, "The Wild New Workforce," *BusinessWeek*, 6 December 1999, 39–44.

26. Richard L. Daft, *Management*, 4th ed. (Fort Worth, Tex.: Dryden Press, 1997), 771.

27. Stephanie Armour, "Workplace Demands Taking Up More Weekends," *USA Today*, 24 April 1998, B1; Laabs, "Workforce Overload."

28. Armour, "Workplace Demands Taking Up More Weekends."

29. Laabs, "Workforce Overload."

30. Michael A. Verespej, "Stressed Out," *IndustryWeek*, 21 February 2000, 30–34.

31. Verespej, "Balancing Act."

32. John W. Newstrom and Keith Davis, *Organizational Behavior: Human Behavior at Work*, 9th ed. (New York: McGraw-Hill, 1993), 345.

33. Joanne Cole, "De-Stressing the Workplace," *HR Focus*, October 1999, 1, 10.

34. Jennifer Bresnehan, "The Elusive Muse," *CIO Enterprise*, 15 October 1997, 52; Kerry A. Dolan, "When Money Isn't Enough," *Forbes*, 18 November 1996, 164–170.

35. Rona Gindin, "Dealing with a Multicultural Workforce," *Nation's Restaurant News*, September–October 1998, 31, 83; Howard Gleckman, "A Rich Stew in the Melting Pot," *BusinessWeek*, 31 August 1998, 76+; Toby B. Gooley, "A World of Difference," *Logistics Management and Distribution Report*, June 2000, 51–55; William H. Miller, "Beneath the Surface," *Industry Week*, 20 September 1999, 13–16.

36. Linda Beamer and Iris Varner, *Intercultural Communication in the Workplace*, 2d ed. (New York: McGraw-Hill Irwin, 2001), xiii.

37. Kelly Greene, "Many Older Workers to Delay Retirement Until After Age 70," *Wall Street Journal*, 23 September 2003, D2.

38. Kim Clark, "A Fondness for Gray Hair," *U.S. News & World Report*, 8 March 2004, 56–58; Donna Fenn, "Respect Your Elders," *Inc.*, September 2003, 29–30; "Work Force Facts," *Chicago Tribune*, 10 September 2000, sec. 6, 1.

39. Clark, "A Fondness for Gray Hair," 56; Stephanie Armour, "Maturing Boomers Smack 'Silver Ceiling,'" *USA Today*, 16 August 2001, 1A, 2A.

40. Nina Munk, "Finished at Forty," *Fortune*, 1 February 1999, 56–60.

41. Lisa Carricaburu, "Utah Ranks Among Nation's Worst in Gender Wage Disparities," *Salt Lake Tribune*, 22 April 2004 [accessed 29 April 2004] www.highbeam.com.

42. United Press International, "Women Increase Employment, Not Salaries," 8 March 2004 [accessed 29 April 2004] www.highbeam.com; Gary Strauss and Del Jones, "Too Bright Spotlight Burns Female CEOs," *USA Today*, 18 December 2000, 3B.

43. "Gender Diversity Linked to Bottom-Line Performance," *MSI*, 1 April 2004 [accessed 29 April 2004] www.highbeam.com.

44. M. June Allard, "Theoretical Underpinnings of Diversity," in Carol Harvey and M. June Allard, *Understanding and Managing Diversity*, 2d ed. (Upper Saddle River, N.J.: Prentice Hall, 2002), 7.

45. "One-Fifth of Women Are Harassed Sexually," *HR Focus*, April 2002, 2.

46. Michael Barrier, "Sexual Harassment," *Nation's Business*, December 1998, 15–19.

47. Marianne Lavelle, "The New Rules of Sexual Harassment," *U.S. News & World Report*, 6 July 1998, 30–31.

48. Joseph White and Carol Hymowitz, "Broken Glass: Watershed Generation of Women Executives Is Rising to the Top," *Wall Street Journal*, 10 February 1997, A1, 6; Andrea Adelson, "Casual, Worker-Friendly, and a Moneymaker, Too: At Patagonia, Glass Ceiling Is Sky-High," *New York Times*, 30 June 1996, sec. Earning It, 8; Reed Abelson, "A Push from the Top Shatters a Glass Ceiling," *New York Times*, 22 August 1999, Y21, Y23.

49. Crockett, "Winning Competitive Advantage Through a Diverse Workforce."

50. Mahlon Apgar IV, "The Alternative Workplace: Changing Where and How People Work," *Harvard Business Review*, May–June 1998, 121–136.

51. Charlene Marmer Solomon, "Flexibility Comes out of Flux," *Personnel Journal*, June 1996, 38–40.

52. ITAC press release, "Home-Based Telework by U.S. Employees Grows Nearly 40% Since 2001," International Telework Association and Council website, 4 September 2003 [accessed 24 April 2004] www.telecommute.org.

53. Susan Campbell, "More Hartford, Conn.-Area Workers Telecommute to Beat Winter Blues," *Hartford Courant*, 5 February 2004 [accessed 24 April 2004] www.highbeam.com.

54. Doreen Carvajal, "It's All About the Coffepot," *International Herald Tribune*, 4 February 2004 [accessed 24 April 2004] www.highbeam.com.

55. Apgar, "The Alternative Workplace."

56. Carol Leonetti Dannhauser, "Who's in the Home Office?" *American Demographics*, June 1999, 50–56.

57. Apgar, "The Alternative Workplace."

58. Melanie Warner, "Working at Home—The Right Way to Be a Star in Your Bunny Slippers," *Fortune*, 3 March 1997, 166; Lin Grensing-Pophal, "Employing the Best People—From Afar," *Workforce*, March 1997, 30–32.

59. Kemba J. Dunham, "Telecommuters' Lament," *Wall Street Journal*, 31 October 2000, B1, B8.

60. Carvajal, "It's All About the Coffepot."

61. Lisa Chadderdon, "Merrill Lynch Works—At Home," *Fast Company*, April–May 1998, 70–72.

62. Shari Caudron, "Workers' Ideas for Improving Alternative Work Situations," Workforce, December 1998, 42–46.

63. Thomas A. Kochan and Harry C. Katz, *Collective Bargaining and Industrial Relations* (Homewood, Ill.: Irwin, 1988), 165.

64. Catherine Yang et al., "Low-Wage Lessons," *BusinessWeek*, 11 November 1996, 108–110.

65. Martha Irvine, "Organizing Twentysomethings," *Los Angeles Times*, 7 September 1997, D5.

66. Michael A. Verespej, "What's Behind the Strife?" *IndustryWeek*, 1 February 1999, 58–62; Keith Bradsher, "General Motors and the U.A.W. Agree on End to Strike," *New York Times*, 29 July 1998, A1, C6.

67. *World Almanac and Book of Facts* (New York: Scripps Howard, 1989), 161.

68. Eugene H. Methvin, "The Union Label: With the Level of Union Violence on the Rise, Congress Must, Again, Deal with the Courts," *National Review*, 29 September 1997, 47; Anya Sacharow, "Walking the Line in Detroit," *Newspapers*, 22 July 1996, 8–13.

69. Paul D. Staudohar, "Labor Relations in Basketball: The Lockout of 1998–99," *Monthly Labor Review*, April 1999, 3–9; E. Edward Herman, *Collective Bargaining and Labor Relations*, 4th ed. (Upper Saddle River, N.J.: Prentice Hall, 1998), 61; "NLRB Permits Replacements During Legal Lockout," *Personnel Journal*, January 1987, 14–15.

70. Nancy Cleeland, "Union Membership Steady in 2001 at 13.5% of Nation's Workforce," *Los Angeles Times*, 18 January 2002, C3; Steven Greenhouse, "Unions Hit Lowest Point in 6 Decades," *New York Times*, 21 January 2001, 1, 20.

71. International Labour Organization, *World Labour Report*, 4 November 1997 [accessed 7 November 1997] www.ilo.org.

72. Steven Greenhouse, "Unions to Push to Make Organizing Easier," *New York Times*, 31 August 2003, 16.

73. Lloyd G. Reynolds, Stanley H. Masters, and Colletta H. Moser, *Labor Economics and Labor Relations*, 11th ed. (Upper Saddle River, N.J.: Prentice Hall, 1998), 497; Indiana University News Bureau, "Trends in U.S. Labor Movement," *Futurist*, January–February 1996, 44; Barbara Presley Noble, "Reinventing Labor: An Interview with Union President Lynn Williams," *Harvard Business Review*, July–August 1993, 115–125.

74. Steven Greenhouse, "Wal-Mart, Driving Workers and Supermarkets Crazy," *New York Times*, 19 October 2003, 3; Janet Adamy, "Supermarkets Get Concessions; Wal-Mart Wage Gap Remains," *Wall Street Journal*, 1 March 2004, B2; Martin Kasindork, "Strikes Strain Southern California," *USA Today*, 20 October 2003, 3A.

75. Michael Arndt, "Salvation from the Shop Floor," *BusinessWeek*, 3 February 2003, 100–101; Stanley Holmes, "Boeing: Putting Out Labor Fires," *BusinessWeek*, 29 December 2003, 43; Jill Jusko, "Nature Versus Nurture," *IndustryWeek*, July 2003, 40–42; David Kiley, "Foreign Companies Cast Long Shadow on UAW Negotiations," *USA Today*, 6 August 2003, B1.

76. See Note 1.

Chapter 10

1. Adapted from Starbucks website [accessed 1 May 2004] www.starbucks.com; "Mr. Coffee," *Context*, August–September 2001, 20–25; Jennifer Ordonez, "Starbucks' Schultz to Leave Top Post, Lead Global Effort," *Wall Street Journal*, 7 April 2000, B3; Karyn Strauss, "Howard Schultz: Starbucks' CEO Serves a Blend of Community, Employee Commitment," *Nation's Restaurant News*, January 2000, 162–163; Carla Joinson, "The Cost of Doing Business?" *HR Magazine*, December 1999, 86–92; "Interview with Howard Schultz: Sharing Success," *Executive Excellence*, November 1999, 16–17; Kelly Barron, "The Cappuccino Conundrum," *Forbes*, 22 February 1999, 54–55; Naomi Weiss, "How Starbucks Impassions Workers to Drive Growth," *Workforce*, August 1998, 60–64; Scott S. Smith, "Grounds for Success," *Entrepreneur*, May 1998, 120–126; "Face Value: Perky People," *The Economist*, 30 May 1998, 66; Howard Schultz and Dori Jones Yang, "Starbucks: Making Values Pay," *Fortune*, 29 September 1997, 261–272.
2. Kris Maher, "Human-Resources Directors Are Assuming Strategic Roles," *Wall Street Journal*, 17 June 2003, B8.
3. Gary Dessler, *A Framework for Human Resource Management* (Upper Saddle River, N.J.: Pearson Prentice Hall, 2004), 74–75.
4. Shari Randall, "Succession Planning Is More Than a Game of Chance," *Workforce Management* [accessed 1 May 2004], www.workforce.com.
5. David Koeppel, "The New Cost of Keeping Workers Happy," *New York Times*, 7 March 2004, 11.
6. Joanne Cole, "Permatemps Pose New Challenges for HR," *HR Focus*, December 1999, 7–8; Sharon R. Cohany, "Workers in Alternative Employment Arrangements: A Second Look," *Monthly Labor Review*, November 1998, 3–21.
7. Steven Greenhouse, "Equal Work, Less-Equal Perks," *New York Times*, 30 March 1998, C1, C6; Aaron Bernstein, "When Is a Temp Not a Temp?" *BusinessWeek*, 7 December 1998, 90–92.
8. "Employee or Independent Contractor? How to Tell," *HR Focus*, January 2004, 7, 10.
9. United States Immigration Support website [accessed 1 May 2004] www.immigrationconsultant.org; Barry Newman, "Safe Crossing: One Solution to Illegal Workers Takes Form: H-2B," *Wall Street Journal*, 14 April 2004, A1, A12.
10. Spencer E. Ante and Paul Magnusson, "Too Many Visas for Techies?" *BusinessWeek*, 25 August 2003, 39.
11. Joellen Perry, "Help Wanted," *U.S. News & World Report*, 8 March 2004, 48–54.
12. William J. Stevenson, *Production Operations Management*, 6th ed. (Boston: Irwin McGraw-Hill, 1999), 698; Laurie Edwards, "When Outsourcing Is Appropriate," *Wall Street and Technology*, July 1998, 96–98.
13. Dessler, *A Framework for Human Resource Management*, 72.
14. Stephanie Armour, "Some Companies Choose No-Layoff Policy," *USA Today*, 17 December 2001, 1B.
15. "How to Make Your Recruitment & Applicant Tracking System Pay Off," *HR Focus*, December 2003, 3–4.
16. Samuel Greengard, "Gimme Attitude," *Workforce Management*, July 2003, 56–60.
17. George Donnelly, "Recruiting, Retention, and Returns," *CFO Magazine*, March 2000 [accessed 10 April 2000] www.cfonet.com/html/Articles/CFO/2000/00MArecr.html.
18. Audrey Arthur, "How Much Should Employers Know?" *Black Enterprise*, October 1997, 56; Anthony Ramirez, "Name, Résumé, References. And How's Your Credit?" *New York Times*, 31 August 1997, F8.
19. Jonathan Segal, "When Norman Bates and Baby Jane Act Out at Work," *HR Magazine*, 1 February 1996, 31; Jenny C. McCune, "Companies Grapple with Workplace Violence," *Management Review*, March 1994, 52–57.
20. Kris Maher, "The Jungle: Focus on Recruitment, Pay and Getting Ahead," *Wall Street Journal*, 20 January 2004, B8.
21. Andy Meisler, "Negative Results," *Workforce Management*, October 2003, 35–40.
22. Tyler D. Hartwell, Paul D. Steele, and Nathaniel F. Rodman, "Workplace Alcohol-Testing Programs: Prevalence and Trends," *Monthly Labor Review*, June 1998, 27–34; "Substance Abuse in the Workplace," *HR Focus*, February 1997, 1, 4+.
23. Meisler, "Negative Results," 35–40.
24. Tammy Galvin, "2003 Industry Report," *Training*, October 2003, 21+.
25. Randall S. Schuler, *Managing Human Resources* (Cincinnati, Ohio: South-Western College Publishing, 1998), 386.
26. Katharine Mieszkowski, "Report from the Future," *Fast Company*, February–March 1998, 28–30.
27. Galvin, "2003 Industry Report."
28. Kevin Dobbs, "Tires Plus Takes the Training High Road," *Training*, April 2000, 56–63.
29. Adolph Haasen and Gordon F. Shea, *A Better Place to Work* (New York: American Management Association, 1997), 19–20.
30. Galvin, "2003 Industry Report."
31. Dessler, *A Framework for Human Resource Management*, 198.
32. PerformanceNow.com website [accessed 2 May 2004] www.performancenow.com; Dessler, *A Framework for Human Resource Management*, 199.
33. Kate Ludeman, "How to Conduct Self-Directed 360," *Training and Development*, July 2000, 44–47; Cassandra Hayes, "To Tell the Truth," *Black Enterprise*, December 1998, 55.
34. Gina Imperato, "How to Give Good Feedback," *Fast Company*, September 1998, 144–156.
35. Jeff St. John, "Kennewick, Wash., 'Snoop' Software Maker Also Protects Privacy," *Tri-City Herald* (Kennewick, Wash.), 17 April 2004 [accessed 2 May 2004] www.highbeam.com; Dessler, *A Framework for Human Resource Management*, 204–205.
36. Dessler, *A Framework for Human Resource Management*, 223–225.
37. Matthew Grim, "Wal-Mart Uber Alles," *American Demographics*, October 2003, 38–39; Jeffrey E. Garten, "Wal-Mart Gives Globalism a Bad Name," *BusinessWeek*, 8 March 2004, 24; Jerry Useem, "Should We Admire Wal-Mart?" *Fortune*, 8 March 2004, 118–120.
38. Elayne Robertson Demby, "Two Stores Refuse to Join the Race to the Bottom for Benefits and Wages," *Workforce Management*, February 2004, 57–59; Stanley Holmes and Wendy Zellner, "The Costco Way," *BusinessWeek*, 12 April 2004, 76–77.
39. Jennifer Reingold, "CEOs Who Should Lose Their Jobs," *Fast Company*, October 2003, 68–80; Louis Lavelle, "Executive Pay," *BusinessWeek*, 21 April 2003, 86–90; Jerry Useem, "Have They No Shame?" *Fortune*, 28 April 2003, 57–64.
40. Starbucks website [accessed 2 May 2004] www.starbucks.com.
41. Fiona Jebb, "Flex Appeal," *Management Today* (London), July 1998, 66–69; Milton Zall, "Implementing a Flexible Benefits Plan," *Fleet Equipment*, May 1999, B4–B8.
42. Joseph Pereira, "Parting Shot: To Save on Health-Care Costs, Firms Fire Disabled Workers," *Wall Street Journal*, 14 July 2003, A1, A7; Timothy Aeppel, "Ill Will: Skyrocketing Health Costs Start to Pit Worker vs. Worker," *Wall Street Journal*, 17 July 2003, A1, A6; Vanessa Furhmans, "To Stem Abuses, Employers Audit Workers' Health Claims," *Wall Street Journal*, 31 March 2004, B1, B7; Milt Freudenheim, "Employees Paying Ever-Bigger Share for Health Care," *New York Times*, A1, C2; Julie Appleby, "Employers Get Nosy About Workers' Health," *USA Today*, 6 March 2003, B1–B2; Ellen E. Schultz and Theo Francis, "Employers' Caps Raise Retirees' Health-Care Costs," *Wall Street Journal*, 25 November 2003, B1, B11; Vanessa Fuhrmans, "Company Health Plans Try to Drop Spouses," *Wall Street Journal*, 9 September 2003, D1, D2.
43. Don L. Boroughs, "The Bottom Line on Ethics," *U.S. News & World Report*, 20 March 1995, 63–54.

44. Richard D. Pearce, "The Small Employer Retirement Plan Void," *Compensation and Benefits Management*, Winter 1999, 51–55.

45. James H. Dulebohn, Brian Murray, and Minghe Sun, "Selection Among Employer-Sponsored Pension Plans: The Role of Individual Differences," *Personal Psychology*, Summer 2000, 405–432.

46. Keith Naughton, "Business's Killer I.O.U.," *Newsweek*, 6 October 2003, 42–44; Christine Dugas, "Companies Consider Pension Freezes," *USA Today*, 7 January 2004, B1.

47. George Van Dyke, "Examining Your 401k," *Business Credit*, January 2000, 59.

48. Paul J. Lim, "Losing Altitude," *U.S. News & World Report*, 21 April 2003, 58–60; Paul J. Lim and Matthew Benjamin, "The 401(k) Stumbles," *U.S. News & World Report*, 24 December 2001, 30–32.

49. Dessler, *A Framework for Human Resource Management*, 282.

50. Robert A Guth and Joann S. Lublin, "Tarnished Gold: Microsoft Ushers Out Era of Options," *Wall Street Journal*, 9 July 2003, A1, A9; John Markoff and David Leonhardt, "Microsoft Will Award Stock, Not Options, to Employees," *New York Times*, 9 July 2003, A1, C4.

51. Gillian Flynn, "Employees Need an FMLA Brush-up," *Workforce 76*, no. 4 (April 1997): 101–104; Barbara Presley Noble, "At Work: We're Doing Just Fine, Thank You," *New York Times*, 20 March 1994, 25.

52. Stephanie Armour, "Ford Plans Ambitious Child-Care Program for Workers," *USA Today*, 22 November 2000, B1.

53. "Workplace Briefs," Gannett News Service, 24 April 1997; Julia Lawlor, "The Bottom Line," *Working Woman*, July–August 1996, 54–58, 74–76.

54. Stephanie Armour, "Employers Stepping Up in Elder Care," *USA Today*, 3 August 2000, 3B.

55. Del Jones, "Firms Take New Look at Sick Days," *USA Today*, 8 October 1996, 8B.

56. William Atkinson, "Wellness, Employee Assistance Programs: Investments, Not Costs," *Bobbin*, May 2000, 42–48.

57. Atkinson, "Wellness, Employee Assistance Programs."

58. Atkinson, "Wellness, Employee Assistance Programs"; Kevin Dobbs, Jack Gordon, and David Stamps, "EAPs Cheap But Popular Perk," *Training*, February 2000, 26.

59. "50 Benefits and Perks That Make Employees Want to Stay Forever," *HR Focus*, July 2000, S2–S3.

60. Edward Iwata, "Staff-Hungry Tech Firms Cast Exotic Lures," *USA Today*, 1 February 2000, B1.

61. Adam Cohen and Cathy Booth Thomas, "Inside a Layoff," *Time*, 16 April 2001, 38–40.

62. Rodney Ho, "AT&T's Offer of $10,000 May Test Entrepreneurship of Laid-Off Workers," *Wall Street Journal*, 12 March 1997; David Fischer and Kevin Whitelaw, "A New Way to Shine Up Corporate Profits," *U.S. News & World Report*, 15 April 1996, 55.

63. John Jude Moran, *Employment Law: New Challenges in the Business Environment*, 2d ed. (Upper Saddle River, N.J.: Prentice Hall, 2002), 127; Dan Seligman, "The Right to Fire," *Forbes*, 10 November 2003, 126–128.

64. See Note 1.

65. Donald P. Shuit, "Board Games," *Workforce Management*, November 2003, 37–44; "The Pros and Cons of Online Recruiting," *HR Focus*, April 2004, S2; Efraim Turban, Jae Lee, David King, and H. Michael Chung, *Electronic Commerce: A Managerial Perspective* (Upper Saddle River, N.J.: Prentice Hall, 2000), 164–168; Marlene Piturro, "The Power of E-Cruiting," *Management Review*, January 2000, 33–38; "Online Recruiting: What Works, What Doesn't," *HR Focus*, March 2000, 11–15; "More Pros and Cons to Internet Recruiting," *HR Focus*, May 2000, 8; Christopher Caggiano, "The Truth About Internet Recruiting," *Inc.*, December 1999, 156; Peter Buxbaum, "Where's Dilbert?" *Chief Executive* [accessed 2 March 2000] www.chiefexecutive.net/mag/150tech/part1c.htm; James R. Borck, "Recruiting Systems Control Résumé Chaos," *InfoWorld*, 24 July 2000, 47–48; Bill Leonard, "Online and Overwhelmed," *HR Magazine*, August 2000, 36–42; Milton Zall, "Internet Recruiting," *Strategic Finance*, June 2000, 66–72; "Why Your Web Site Is More Important Than Ever to New Hires," *HR Focus*, June 2000, 9; Rachel Emma Silverman, "Recruiters' Hunt for Résumés Is Nocturnal Game," *Wall Street Journal*, 20 September 2000, B1–B4.

Chapter 11

1. Adapted from Adobe website [accessed 4 May 2004] www.adobe.com; "Adobe Named by Fortune as One of the 100 Best Companies to Work for in America," *Business Wire*, 24 January 2002, 1; Mylene Mangalindan, "Adobe Cuts Revenue and Profit Targets, Reduces Staff 5%, Blaming Economy," *Wall Street Journal*, 31 October 2001, B6; Melinda Patterson Grenier, "Turning Popularity into Profitability: Adobe Had a Popular Product; Making It Profitable Took Some Work," *Wall Street Journal*, 15 October 2001, R18; Karen Southwick, "How Far Can Serendipity Carry Adobe?" *Upside*, September 1995, 46; Kennedy Grey, "Rekindling an Old Spirit," *MC Technology Marketing Intelligence*, August 2000, 64–70; Paul Andrews, "Microsoft Can't Topple Adobe Acrobat," *Seattle Times*, 1 April 2002, C1.

2. "AMA Board Approves New Marketing Definition," *Marketing News*, 1 March 1985, 1.

3. Al Ries and Jack Trout, *The 22 Immutable Laws of Marketing* (New York: Harper Collins, 1994), 19–25.

4. Stan Choe, "Businesses Still Barter, in Simple or Complex Exchanges," *Charlotte Observer*, 30 March 2004 [accessed 5 May 2004] www.highbeam.com.

5. June Lee Risser, "Customers Come First," *MM*, November/December 2003, 22–26.

6. Peter Fingar, Harsha Kumar, and Tarun Sharma, *Enterprise E-Commerce* (Tampa, Fla.: Meghan-Kiffer Press, 2000), 24, 109.

7. Barbara Whitaker, "House Hunting with Cursor and Click," *New York Times*, 24 September 1998, D1, D5.

8. Pierre M. Loewe and Mark S. Bonchek, "The Retail Revolution," *Management Review*, April 1999, 38–44.

9. Dan Hill, "Why They Buy," *Across the Board*, November–December 2003, 27–32; Eric Roston, "The Why of Buy," *Time*, April 2004.

10. James C. Anderson and James A. Narus, *Business Market Management: Understanding, Creating, and Delivering Value*, 2d ed. (Upper Saddle River, N.J.: Pearson Prentice Hall, 2004), 114–116; Philip Kotler and Gary Armstrong, *Principles of Marketing*, 10th ed. (Upper Saddle River, N.J.: Pearson Prentice Hall, 2004), 215, 224–226.

11. Nancy Beth Jackson, "Opinions to Spare? Click Here," *New York Times*, E1, E7.

12. Janet Novack, "The Data Miners," *Forbes*, 12 February 1996, 96–97; Don Peppers and Martha Rogers, *Enterprise One to One* (New York: Doubleday, 1997), 120–121.

13. Louisa Wah, "The Almighty Customer," *Management Review*, February 1999, 16–22; James Lardner, "Your Every Command," *U.S. News & World Report*, 5 July 1999, 44–46.

14. Hal Lancaster, "Managing Your Career: Giving Good Service, Never an Easy Task, Is Getting a Lot Harder," *Wall Street Journal*, 9 June 1998, B1.

15. Janet Willen, "The Customer Is Wrong," *Business97*, October–November 1997, 40–42; William H. Davidow and Bro Uttal, *Total Customer Service: The Ultimate Weapon* (New York: Harper & Row, 1989), 8; Valarie A. Zeithaml, A. Parasuraman, and Leonard L. Berry, *Delivering Quality Service* (New York: Free Press, 1990), 9; George J. Castellese, "Customer Service . . . Building a Winning Team," *Supervision*, January 1995, 9–13; Erica G. Sorohan and Catherine M. Petrini, "Dumpsters, Ducks, and Customer Service," *Training and Development*, January 1995, 9.

16. Bruce Horovitz, "You Want It Your Way," *USA Today*, 5–7 March 2004, 1A–2A.

17. Lisa Takeuchi Cullen, "Have It Your Way," *Time*, 23 December 2002, 42–43.

18. Don Peppers, Martha Rogers, and Bob Dorf, "Is Your Company Ready for One-to-

One Marketing?" *Harvard Business Review*, January–February 1999.

19. Malcolm H. B. McDonald, "Ten Barriers to Marketing Planning," *Journal of Product and Brand Management*, Fall 1992, 51–64.

20. Brian Grow and Gerry Khermouch, "The Low-Carb Fight Ahead," *BusinessWeek*, 22 December 2003, 48.

21. May Wong, "Encyclopedias Gather Dust in Internet Age," *AP Online* [accessed 5 May 2004] www.highbeam.com; Encyclopaedia Britannica website [accessed 5 May 2004] www.britannica.com; Leslie Kaufman, "Playing Catch-Up at the Online Mall," *New York Times*, 21 February 1999, sec. 3, 1, 6; Gary Samuels, "CD-ROMs First Big Victim," *Forbes*, 28 February 1994, 42–44; Richard A. Melcher, "Dusting Off the Britannica," *BusinessWeek*, 20 October 1997, 143–146.

22. Malcolm McDonald and John W. Leppard, *Marketing by Matrix* (Lincolnwood, Ill.: NTC, 1993), 10; H. Igor Ansoff, "Strategies for Diversification," *Harvard Business Review*, November–December 1957, 113–124; H. Igor Ansoff, *Corporate Strategy* (New York: McGraw-Hill, 1965).

23. Alex Taylor III, "How to Murder the Competition," *Fortune*, 22 February 1993, 87, 90.

24. Scott Hays, "Exceptional Customer Service Takes the 'Ritz' Touch," *Workforce*, January 1999, 99–102.

25. Jennifer Barron and Jill Hollingshead, "Making Segmentation Work," *MM*, January–February 2002, 24–28.

26. Haya El Nassar and Paul Overberg, "Old Labels Just Don't Stick in 21st Century," *USA Today*, 17 December 2003; Michael J. Weiss, *The Clustering of America* (New York: Harper & Row, 1988), 41.

27. Horacio D. Rozanski, Gerry Bollman, and Martin Lipman, "Seize the Occasion," *Strategy and Business*, Third Quarter 2001, 42–51.

28. David Shani and Sujana Chalasani, "Exploring Niches Using Relationship Marketing," *Journal of Business and Industrial Marketing*, no. 4 (1993): 58–66.

29. Courtland L. Bovée, Michael J. Houston, and John V. Thill, *Marketing*, 2d ed. (New York: McGraw-Hill, 1994), 224.

30. Daniel Roth, "First: From Poster Boy to Whipping Boy," *Fortune*, 6 July 1998, 28–29.

31. Gary Armstrong and Philip Kotler, *Marketing: An Introduction*, 5th ed. (Upper Saddle River, N.J.: Prentice Hall, 2000), 201–204.

32. Armstrong and Kotler, *Marketing: An Introduction*, 206.

33. Steve Hamm, "Why High Tech Has to Stay Humble," *BusinessWeek*, 19 January 2004, 76–77.

34. Armstrong and Kotler, *Marketing: An Introduction*, 329.

35. Michael R. Solomon and Elnora W. Stuart, *Marketing: Real People, Real Choices*, 3d ed. (Upper Saddle River, N.J.: Prentice Hall, 2003), 263.

36. Lev Grossman, "The Quest for Cool," *Time*, 8 September 2003, 48–54.

37. Poul Funder Larsen, "Better Is . . . Better," *Wall Street Journal*, 22 September 2003, R6, R11.

38. Philip Kotler and Gary Armstrong, *Principles of Marketing*, 9th ed. (Upper Saddle River, N.J.: Prentice Hall, 2001), 296.

39. Gary Hamel, *Lessons in Leadership Lecture*, Northern Illinois University, 23 October 1997.

40. "Preparing for a Point to Point World," *Marketing Management* 3, no. 4 (Spring 1995): 30–40.

41. Claudia H. Deutsch, "Deep in Debt Since 1988, Polaroid Files for Bankruptcy," *New York Times*, 13 October 2001, C1, C14.

42. Bruce Horovitz, "Cookie Makers Bake Up New Twists," *USA Today*, 27 March 2001, 3B.

43. Marcia Mogelonsky, "Product Overload?" *American Demographics*, August 1998, 65–69.

44. Michael McCarthy, "Brands That Lose Their Punch Get Yanked," *USA Today*, 13 December 2000, 3B.

45. James Bandler, "Ending Era, Kodak Will Stop Selling Most Film Cameras," *Wall Street Journal*, 14 January 2004, B1, B4.

46. Thomas K. Grose, "Brand New Goods," *Time.com*, 1 November 1999 [accessed 17 February 2001] www.time.com/time/magazine/article/0,9171,33124-1,00.html.

47. Jagdish N. Sheth and Rajendra S. Sisodia, "Feeling the Heat," *Marketing Management* 4, no. 2 (Fall 1995): 9–23.

48. Claudia H. Deutsch, "Will That Be Paper or Pixel?" *New York Times*, 4 August 2000, C1, C4.

49. Armstrong and Kotler, *Marketing: An Introduction*, 234.

50. Roberta Bernstein, "Food for Thought," *American Demographics*, May 2000, 39–42.

51. Gary Strauss, "Squeezing New from Old," *USA Today*, 4 January 2001, 1B–2B.

52. Nina Munk, "Gap Gets It," *Fortune*, 3 August 1998, 68–82.

53. Sarah Ellison, "Kraft's Stale Strategy," *Wall Street Journal*, 18 December 2003, B1, B6.

54. Terril Yue Jones, "Fearing the Old Shoddy Image," *Forbes*, 12 January 1998 [accessed 16 June 1999] www.forbes.com/forbes/98/0112/6101064a.htm.

55. "Q2 2004 SanDisk Corp. Earnings Conference Call," *Fair Disclosure Wire*, 14 July 2004 [accessed 3 August 2004] www.highbeam.com.

56. Thomas T. Nagle, "Managing Price Competition," *Marketing Management* 2, no.

1 (1993): 38–45; Sheth and Sisodia, "Feeling the Heat," 21.

57. Gurumurthy Kalyanaram and Ragu Gurumurthy, "Market Entry Strategies: Pioneers Versus Late Arrivals," *Strategy & Business*, Third Quarter 1998 [accessed 16 June 1999] www.strategy-business.com.

58. See Note 1.

Chapter 12

1. REI website [accessed 7 May 2004] www.rei.com; "REI Store Pickup Lifts Store and Internet Sales," *Business Wire*, 22 September 2003 [accessed 7 May 2004] www.highbeam.com; Ken Yamada, "Web Trails," *Forbes Best of the Web*, 3 December 2001, 15; Mike Troy, "REI.com Scales Online Heights," *DSN Retailing Today*, 8 May 2000, 6; Kellee Harris, "Online Travel Revs Up Revenues," *Sporting Goods Business*, 1 February 2000, 16; Lawrence M. Fisher, "REI Climbs Online: A Clicks-and-Mortar Chronicle," *Strategy & Business*, First Quarter 2000 [accessed 13 October 2000] www.strategy-business.com/casestudy/00111; "REI Scales New Heights with Second-Generation Web Sites and IBM," IBM E-Business Case Studies [accessed 10 March 2000] www.ibm.com/e-business/case_studies/rei.phtml; Kristin Carpenter, "REI.com," *Sporting Goods Business*, 6 July 1999, 57; David Orenstein, "Retailers Find Uses for Web Inside Stores," *Computerworld*, 11 January 1999, 41; Sharon Machlis, "Outdoor Goods Seller Creates Online Outlet," *Computerworld*, 14 December 1998, 51–53; Kerry A. Dolan, "Backpackers Meet Bottom Line," *Forbes*, 16 November 1998, 161; Kristin Carpenter, "REI Venturing Out with Off-Price Web Site," *Sporting Goods Business*, 10 August 1998, 22.

2. Ingram Book Group website [accessed 7 May 2004] www.ingrambook.com.

3. Felix Sanchez, "Boeing Honors Its Top Suppliers," *Press-Telegram* (Long Beach, Calif.), 15 February 2002 [accessed 7 May 2004] www.highbeam.com.

4. Lisa Chadderdon, "How Dell Sells on the Web," *Fast Company*, September 1998, 58, 60.

5. Gregory L. White, "GM Is Forming Unit to Buy Dealerships," *Wall Street Journal*, 24 September 1999, A3; Joann Muller, "Meet Your Local GM Dealer: GM," *BusinessWeek*, 11 October 1999, 48.

6. Philip Kotler and Gary Armstrong, *Principles of Marketing*, 9th ed. (Upper Saddle River, N.J.: Prentice Hall, 2001), 435.

7. "Hallmark, a New Name in Mass Retailing," *Supermarket Business*, March 1997, 84; Daniel Roth, "Card Sharks," *Forbes*, 7 October 1996, 14; Julie Rygh, "Hallmark Cards Find Success with New Expressions Brand," *Knight-Ridder/Tribune Business News*, 31 August 1997, 831B0958.

8. Andrew J. Rohm and Fareena Sultan, "The Evolution of E-Business," *MM*, January/February 2004, 32–37.

9. Levi Strauss website [accessed 6 May 2004] www.levistrauss.com; Michael S. Katz and Jeffrey Rothfeder, "Crossing the Digital Divide," *Strategy & Business*, First Quarter 2000, 26–41; Anne Stuart, "Clicks & Bricks," *CIO*, 15 March 2000, 76–84.

10. Ronald Henkoff, "Delivering the Goods," *Fortune*, 28 November 1994, 64–78.

11. Colleen Gourley, "Retail Logistics in Cyberspace," *Distribution*, December 1996, 29; Dave Hirschman, "FedEx Starts Up Package Sorting System at Memphis Tenn. Airport," *Knight-Ridder/Tribune Business News*, 28 September 1997, 928B0953; "FedEx and Technology—Maintaining a Competitive Edge," *PresWIRE*, 2 December 1996.

12. Marcia Stepanek, "Closed, Gone to the Net," *BusinessWeek*, 7 June 1999, 113–114.

13. Louise Lee and Kerry Capell, "Taps for Music Retailers?" *BusinessWeek*, 23 June 2003, 40; Paul Keegan, "Is the Music Store Over?" *Business 2.0*, March 2004, 115–119.

14. Gillette website [accessed 7 May 2004] www.gillette.com; Mark Maremont, "How Gillette Brought Its Mach3 to Market," *Wall Street Journal*, 15 April 1998, B1, B4; Jeremy Kahn, "Gillette Loses Face," *Fortune*, 8 November 1999, 147–148.

15. Amy Barrett, "Schering's Dr. Feelbetter?" *BusinessWeek*, 23 June 2003, 55+; "FDA Gives Final Approval to Loratadine, Generic Equivalent of Claritin," *Biotech Week*, 17 September 2003, 235–236; David J. Morrow, "From Lab to Patient, by Way of Your Den," *New York Times*, 7 June 1998, sec. 3, 1, 10.

16. Michele Marchetti, "What a Sales Call Costs," *Sales and Marketing Management*, September 2000, 80–82.

17. David Prater, "The Third Time's the Charm," *Sales and Marketing Management*, September 2000, 100–104; Gary Armstrong and Philip Kotler, *Marketing: An Introduction* (Upper Saddle River, N.J.: Prentice Hall, 2000), 454.

18. Salesforce.com website [accessed 7 May 2004] www.salesforce.com.

19. Direct Marketing Association website [accessed 23 November 1997] www.the-dma.org/servicec1/libres-home1b.shtml.

20. Dennis K. Berman, "From Cell Phones to Sell Phones," *BusinessWeek*, 11 September 2000, 88–90.

21. Chris Adams, "FDA Tells Glaxo to Halt Airing Flu Commercial," *Wall Street Journal*, 14 January 2000, B3.

22. "FTC: Bogus 'Nonprofit' Debt Negotiation Companies Misled Consumers in Financial Trouble and Violated Do Not Call Registry," FTC website, 5 May 2004 [accessed 7 May 2004] www.ftc.gov.

23. "Direct Hit," *The Economist*, 9 January 1999, 55–57.

24. Heidi Dietrich, "Direct Marketer Steers Away from E-Mail Ads," *Puget Sound Business Journal*, 23–29 April 2004, 28.

25. Agilent Technologies website [accessed 6 May 2004] www.agilent.com.

26. Ellen Neuborne, "Telemarketing After 'Do Not Call,'" *Inc.*, November 2003, 32–34.

27. Adobe website [accessed 7 May 2004] www.adobe.com.

28. Armstrong and Kotler, *Marketing: An Introduction*, 409.

29. "Coupons, Samples Drive Consumer Shopping Decisions," Cox Direct, 8 September 1998 [accessed 24 May 1999] www.justdelivered.com/itm/pressreleases/pr-090898-2.htm.

30. Paulette Thomas, "'e-Clicking' Coupons Online Has a Cost: Privacy," *Wall Street Journal*, 18 June 1998, B1, B8.

31. William M. Bulkeley, "Rebates' Secret Appeal to Manufacturers: Few Customers Actually Redeem Them," *Wall Street Journal*, 10 February 1998, B1, B8.

32. Lisa Z. Eccles, "Point of Purchase Advertising," *Advertising Age Supplement*, 26 September 1994, 1–6.

33. Verne Gay, "Milk, the Magazine," *American Demographics*, February 2000, 32–33.

34. Armstrong and Kotler, *Marketing: An Introduction*, 405.

35. Wendy Zellner, "Southwest's New Direction," *BusinessWeek*, 8 February 1999, 58–59; Jennifer Lawrence, "Integrated Mix Makes Expansion Fly," *Advertising Age—Special Integrated Marketing Report*, 4 November 1993, S10–S12.

36. Janet Smith, "Integrated Marketing," *American Demographics*, November 1995, 62.

37. See Note 1.

38. Bill Gates, *Business @ the Speed of Thought* (New York: Warner Books, 1999), 76; Elizabeth Weise, "Sizing Up Web Shoppers for the Perfect Fit," *USA Today*, 21 April 1999, 4D.

39. Jim Milliot, "B&N-B&N.com Closing Delayed," *Publishers Weekly*, 4 March 2004 [accessed 7 May 2004] www.publishersweekly.com; Allison Kaplan, "Retailers Taking New Approach to Internet," *Knight Ridder Tribune News Service*, 11 June 2002, 1; Gerry Khermouch and Nanette Byrnes, "Come Back to Papa," *BusinessWeek*, 19 February 2001, 42; Rebecca Quick, "Returns to Sender," *Wall Street Journal*, 17 July 2000, R8; Greg Farrell, "Clicks-and-Mortar World Values Brands," *USA Today*, 5 October 1999, B1, B2; Ranjay Gulati and Jason Garino, "Get the Right Mix of Bricks and Clicks," *Harvard Business Review*, May–June 2000, 107–114; Anne Stuart, "Clicks & Bricks," *CIO*, 15 March 2000, 76–84; Jason Anders, "Sibling Rivalry," *Wall Street Journal*, 17 July 2000, R16; William M. Bulkeley, "Clicks and Mortar," *Wall Street Journal*, 17 July 2000, R4; Allanna Sullivan, "From a Call to a Click," *Wall Street Journal*, 17 July 2000, R30; Suein L. Hwang, "Clicks and Bricks," *Wall Street Journal*, 17 April 2000, R8, R10; Jeffrey Rothfeder, "Toys 'R' Us Battles Back," *Strategy and Business*, Quarter 2, 2000; Dennis K. Berman and Heather Green, "Cliff Hanger Christmas," *Business Week E.Biz*, 23 October 2000, EB30–EB38; Jerry Useem, "Dot-Coms: What Have We Learned?" *Fortune*, 30 October 2000, 82–104.

Chapter 13

1. Adapted from Peter J. Howe, "MCI Chief Unveils Global Vision for Telecom Giant," *Boston Globe*, 24 September 2004 [accessed 15 October 2004] www.highbeam.com; Andrew Backover, "MCI Monitor Calls for Power Shift," *USA Today*, 23 August 2003 [accessed 15 October 2004] www.usatoday.com; Liesbeth Evers, "Capellas Faces Cuts to £24m WorldCom Pay Package," *Accountancy Age*, 12 November 2002 [accessed 15 October 2004] www.accountancyage.com; Craig Schneider, "MCI: Ringing in Reform," CFO, 21 October 2003 [accessed 15 October 2004] www.cfo.com; "Ebbers to Face WorldCom Fraud Charges," *Accountancy Age*, 3 March 2004 [accessed 13 October 2004] www.accountancyage.com; "Ex-WorldCom Execs Face Criminal Charges," *Accountancy Age*, 28 August 2003 [accessed 13 October 2004] www.accountancyage.com; Kevin Maney, Andrew Backover, and Elliot Blair Smith, "Straightening Out the Story on Telecom's Routing Game," *USA Today*, 26 August 2003 [accessed 15 October 2004] www.usatoday.com; Larry Schlesinger, "WorldCom report: Recovery Is on Track," *Accountancy Age*, 6 October 2003 [accessed 13 October 2004] www.accountancyage.com; James Hester, "US Draws Up Corporate Governance Blueprint," *Accountancy Age*, 26 August 2003 [accessed 13 October 2004] www.accountancyage.com; Robert Jaques, "Customers Set to Abandon WorldCom/MCI," *Accountancy Age*, 6 October 2003 [accessed 13 October 2004] www.accountancyage.com; Liz Loxton, "Judge Approves MCI Recovery Plans," *Accountancy Age*, 11 April 2003 [accessed 13 October 2004] www.accountancyage.com; "MCI Just Can't Escape Its Past," *Accountancy Age*, 8 July 2003 [accessed 13 October 2004] www.accountancyage.com; Paul Grant, "MCI Excluded from U.S. Government Work," *Accountancy Age*, 8 January 2003 [accessed 13 October 2004] www.accountancyage.com; "Emergence News," MCI website, [accessed 13 October 2004] www.mci.com; Om Malik, "One Scandal That Won't Die," Business 2.0, 29 July 2003 [accessed 13 October 2004] www.business2.com; Susie Gharib, television interview with Michael Capellas on *Nightly Business Report*, 20 April 2004 [access 15 October 2004] www.highbeam.com.

2. Robert Stuart, "Accountants in Management—A Globally Changing Role," *CMA Magazine*, 1 February 1997, 5.

3. Melody Petersen, "Shortage of Accounting Students Raises Concern on Audit Quality," *New York Times*, 19 February 1999, C1, C3.

4. Jack L. Smith, Robert M. Keith, and William L. Stephens, *Accounting Principles*, 4th ed. (New York: McGraw-Hill, 1993), 16–17.

5. Matt Krantz, "Some Major Companies Still Use Pro Forma Accounting," *USA Today*, 11 August 2003, B1; "'Pro Forma' Financial Information: Tips for Investors," SEC website [accessed 9 May 2004] www.sec.gov; David Henry and Robert Berner, "Ouch! Real Numbers," *BusinessWeek*, 24 March 2003, 72–73.

6. Steve Zwick, "The Price of Transparency," *Time*, 19 February 2001, B8–B11.

7. Kerry Capell and David Henry, "When Bankers Keep Saying *Non*," *BusinessWeek*, 1 March 2004, 54.

8. "Summary of SEC Actions and SEC Related Provisions Pursuant to the Sarbanes-Oxley Act of 2002," SEC website [accessed 9 May 2004] www.sec.gov; "Sarbanes-Oxley Act's Progress," *USA Today*, 26 December 2002 [accessed 9 May 2004] www.high-beam.com.

9. David Henry and Amy Borrus, "Honesty Is a Pricey Policy," *BusinessWeek*, 27 October 2003, 100–101.

10. Ben Worthen, "A Funny Thing Happened on the Way to Compliance (It Got Easier for CIOs)," *CIO*, 1 December 2003 [accessed 9 May 2004] www.cio.com; "SEC Approves Listing Exchange Rules," *Internal Auditor*, 1 December 2003 [accessed 9 May 2004] www.highbeam.com; Henry and Borrus, "Honesty Is a Pricey Policy."

11. Frank Evans, "A Road Map to Your Financial Report," *Management Review*, October 1993, 39–47.

12. David H. Bangs, Jr., "Financial Troubleshooting," *Soundview Executive Book Summaries* 15, no. 5 (May 1993).

13. See Note 1.

Chapter 14

1. Adapted from Patrick McGeehan, "Charles Schwab to Give Up Title at Brokerage Firm," *New York Times*, 1 February 2003, C1; "Company News; Charles Schwab Reports a $79 Million Loss in Quarter," *New York Times*, 22 January 2003, C1; Patrick McGeehan, "Seeing Long Trading Slump, Schwab Sets More Cutbacks," *New York Times*, 13 August 2002, C2; Louise Lee and Emily Thorton, "Schwab vs. Wall Street," *BusinessWeek*, 3 June 2002, 62–71; Louise

Lee, "Will Investors Pay for Schwab's Advice?" *BusinessWeek*, 21 January 2002, 36; Fred Vogelstein, "Can Schwab Get Its Mojo Back?" *Fortune*, 17 September 2001, 93–98; Susanne Craig, "Schwab Unveils a New Service, Chides Brokers," *Wall Street Journal*, 17 May 2002, C1, C13; Charles Gasparino and Ken Brown, "Discounted, Schwab's Own Stock Suffers from Move into Online Trading," *Wall Street Journal*, 19 June 2001, A1, A6; Rebecca Buckman, "Schwab, Once a Predator, Is Now Prey," *Wall Street Journal*, 8 December 1999, C1; Louise Lee, "When You're No. 1, You Try Harder," *BusinessWeek E.Biz*, 18 September 2000, EB88.

2. Mandy Andress, "Smart Is Not Enough: Cards Must Also Be Easy and Useful," *InfoWorld*, 16 October 2000, 94; Mary Shacklett, "American Express' Blue Is Setting the Pace in U.S. Smart Card Market," *Credit Union Magazine*, September 2000, 16A–17A.

3. Thomas McCarroll, "No Checks. No Cash. No Fuss?" *Time*, 9 May 1994, 60–61.

4. Scott Woolley, "Virtual Banker," *Forbes*, 15 June 1998 [accessed 28 July 1999] www.forbes.com/forbes/98/0615/6112127a.htm; Dean Foust, "Will Online Banking Replace the ATM?" *Yahoo! Internet Life*, November 1998, 114–118.

5. John C. Soper, "What's Next for Consolidation in Banking?" *Business Economics*, April 2001, 39.

6. Stephan Labaton, "Accord Reached on Lifting Depression-Era Barriers Among Financial Industries," *New York Times*, 23 October 1999, A1, B4.

7. Patrick McGeehan, "Merrill Lynch Is Set to Move into Banking," *New York Times*, 26 January 2000, C1, C6.

8. Rob Blackwell, "Wal-Mart, TD: Could They Make It Work?" *American Banker*, 13 January 2002, 1; Leah Nathans Spiro, "The Coca-Cola of Personal Finance," *BusinessWeek*, 20 April 1998, 37–38; Joseph Nocera, "E-Banking Is Necessary—Banks Are Not," *Fortune*, 11 May 1998, 84–85; Glenn Coleman, "The Battle for Your Money," *Money*, December 1999, 134–140; Lorrie Grant, "Retail King Gets Thrifty Idea," *USA Today*, 30 June 1999, B1; Niamh Ring, "Why Schwab Wants Another Charter to Add Bank Services," *American Banker*, 1 March 2002, 1.

9. "Important Banking Legislation," FDIC [accessed 28 July 1999] www.fdic.gov/pub-lish/banklaws.html; "Interstate Branching," The Federal Reserve Board [accessed 23 July 1999] www.bog.frb.fed.us/generalinfo/isb.

10. Peter Elkind, "The Secrets of Eddie Stern," *Fortune*, 19 April 2004, 106–127.

11. Elkind, "The Secrets of Eddie Stern."

12. Elkind, "The Secrets of Eddie Stern."

13. Paula Dwyer, "Breach of Trust," *BusinessWeek*, 15 December 2003, 98–108.

14. New York Stock Exchange website [accessed 23 July 2002] www.nyse.com.

15. James K. Glassman, "Manager's Journal: Who Needs Stock Exchanges? Not Investors," *Wall Street Journal*, 8 May 2000, A42.

16. Julie Bort, "Trading Places," *Computerworld*, 27 May 1996, 1051.

17. Neil Weinberg, "The Big Board Comes Back from the Brink," *Forbes*, 13 November 2000, 274–281.

18. Lee Copeland, "After-Hours Trading," *Computerworld*, 27 March 2000, 57.

19. John R. Dorfman, "Crash Courses," *Wall Street Journal*, 28 May 1996, R12–R13.

20. Katrina Brooker, "Could the Dow Become Extinct?" *Fortune*, 15 February 1999, 194–195; Anita Raghavan and Nancy Ann Jeffrey, "What, How, Why—So What Is the Dow Jones Industrial Average, Anyway?" *Wall Street Journal*, 28 May 1996, R30; E. S. Browning, "New Economy Stocks Join Industrials," *Wall Street Journal*, 27 October 1999, C1, C15.

21. Jeffrey M. Laderman, "Why It's So Tough to Beat the S&P," *BusinessWeek*, 24 March 1997, 82–83.

22. E. S. Browning, "Journal Goes 'Decimal' With Nasdaq Tables," *Wall Street Journal*, 2 August 2000, C1; "SEC Orders Decimal Stock Prices," *Chicago Tribune*, 29 January 2000, sec. 2, 2.

23. Diana B. Henriques, "Stock Markets, Facing Threats, Pursue Changes," *New York Times on the Web*, 6 March 1999 [accessed 7 March 1999] www.nytimes.com/library/financial/030799market-changes.htm.

24. Mike McNamee and Paula Dwyer, "A Revolt at NASD?" *BusinessWeek*, 2 August 1999, 70–71.

25. Weinberg, "The Big Board Comes Back from the Brink."

26. Michael Schroeder and Randall Smith, "Sweeping Change in Market Structure Sought," *Wall Street Journal*, 29 February 2000, C1.

27. Copeland, "After-Hours Trading."

28. SEC website [accessed 21 December 2000] www.sec.gov/consumer/jdatacom.htm.

29. David Diamond, "The Web's Most Wanted," *Business 2.0*, August 1999, 120–128.

30. Thor Valdmanis and Tom Lowry, "Wall Street's New Breed Revives Inside Trading," *USA Today*, 4 November 1999, 1B.

31. Joseph Nocera, "No Whispering Allowed," *Money*, December 2000, 71–74; Heather Timmons, "The Full Disclosure Rule Could Mean More Secrets," *BusinessWeek*, 9 October 2000, 198; Lee Clifford, "The SEC Wants to Open the Info Vault," *Fortune*, 13 November 2000, 434.

32. Rebecca Buckman, "NASD Maps War on Claims on Internet," *Wall Street Journal*, 24 March 1997, B98W.

33. See Note 1.

34. John Kimelman, "How Internet Banks Have Inched Ahead on Rates," *New York*

Times, 28 December 2003, 6; Rick Brooks and Charles Forelle, "Despite Online-Banking Boom, Branches Remain King," *Wall Street Journal*, 29 October 2003, B1–B2; Christine Dugas, "Banks Race to Add Branches," *USA Today*, 20–22 January 2003, 1A; Pallavi Gogoi, "The Hot News in Banking: Bricks and Mortar," *BusinessWeek*, 21 April 2003, 83–84; Mark Sievewright, "Traditional vs. Virtual Service," *Credit Union Magazine*, February 2002, 26; Eileen Colkin, "Citibank," *Information Week*, 27 August 2001, 30; Andrew Ross Sorkin, "Put Your Money Where Your Modem Is," *New York Times*, 30 May 2002, G1; Erica Garcia, "What's Left of the Online Banks," *Money*, October 2001, 167; Jathon Sapsford, "Consumers Take Notice of Online Banks," *Wall Street Journal*, 28 November 2000, C1, C19; Lauren Bielski, "Online Banking Yet to Deliver," American Bankers Association, *ABA Banking Journal*, September 2000, 6, 12+; Heather Timmons, "Online Banks Can't Go It Alone," *BusinessWeek*, 31 July 2000, 86–87; Mark Skousen, "Online Banking's Goodies," *Forbes*, 12 June 2000, P366+; Tony Stanco, "Internet Banking—Some Big Players, But Little Returns So Far," *Boardwatch*, March 2000, 86–90; Carrick Mollenkamp, "Old-Line Banks Advance in Bricks-vs.-Clicks Battle," *Wall Street Journal*, 21 January 2000, C1.

Appendix B

1. Bill Shaw and Art Wolfe, *The Structure of the Legal Environment: Law, Ethics, and Business*, 2d ed. (Boston: PWS-Kent, 1991), 635.
2. Shaw and Wolfe, *The Structure of the Legal Environment*, 146.
3. "Pfizer Fined for False Advertising; Company to Pay $430 Million U.S.," *Toronto Star*, 14 May 2004 [accessed 16 May 2004] www.highbeam.com.
4. George A. Steiner and John F. Steiner, *Business, Government, and Society* (New York: McGraw-Hill, 1991), 149.
5. Paula Burkes Erickson, "Oklahoma Bill Proposes Business Courts," *Daily Oklahoman*, 23 February 2004 [accessed 16 May 2004] www.highbeam.com.
6. Thomas W. Dunfee, Frank F. Gibson, John D. Blackburn, Douglas Whitman, F. William McCarty, and Bartley A. Brennan, *Modern Business Law* (New York: Random House, 1989), 164.
7. Jacqueline Bueno, "Home Depot to Fight Sex-Bias Charges," *Wall Street Journal*, 19 September 1997, B5; Edward Felsenthal, "Punitive Awards Are Called Modest, Rare," *Wall Street Journal*, 17 June 1996, B2.
8. Bartley A. Brennan and Nancy K. Kubasek, *The Legal Environment of Business* (New York: McGraw-Hill, 1990), 183.
9. "'03 Derby Controversy: Santos Seeks $48M in Damages for Libel," *Newsday*, 10 May 2004 [accessed 16 May 2004] www.highbeam.com.

10. Brennan and Kubasek, *The Legal Environment of Business*, 184.
11. Nancy K. Kubasek, Bartley A. Brennan, and M. Neil Browne, *The Legal Environment of Business*, 3d ed. (Upper Saddle River, N.J.: Prentice Hall, 2003), 325; "Reasonable Product-Liability Reform," *Nation's Business*, 1 September 1997, 88.
12. Dunfee et al., *Modern Business Law*, 569.
13. Michael Ha, "Public Banks Many Tort Reforms," *National Underwriter*, 19 April 2004, 10.
14. Dunfee et al., *Modern Business Law*, 236.
15. Dunfee et al., *Modern Business Law*, 284–297; Brennan and Kubasek, *The Legal Environment of Business*, 125–127; Douglas Whitman and John William Gergacz, *The Legal Environment of Business*, 2d ed. (New York: Random House, 1988), 196–197; *The Lawyer's Almanac* (Upper Saddle River, N.J.: Prentice Hall Law & Business, 1991), 888.
16. Brennan and Kubasek, *The Legal Environment of Business*, 128.
17. Samuel Maull, "Judge Rules No Damages to Rosie, Publisher," AP Online, 20 February 2004 [accessed 16 May 2004] www.highbeam.com.
18. Roy Furchgott, "Opposition Builds to Mandatory Arbitration at Work," *New York Times*, 20 July 1997, F11; Barry Meier, "In Fine Print, Customers Lose Ability to Sue," *New York Times*, 10 March 1997, A1, C7.
19. Richard M. Steuer, *A Guide to Marketing Law: What Every Seller Should Know* (New York: Harcourt Brace Jovanovich, 1986), 151–152.
20. Dunfee et al., *Modern Business Law*, 745, 749.
21. Brennan and Kubasek, *The Legal Environment of Business*, 160; Whitman and Gergacz, *The Legal Environment of Business*, 260.
22. Henry R. Cheeseman, *Business Law*, 4th ed. (Upper Saddle River, N.J.: Prentice Hall, 2001), 324.
23. James Connell, "Tech Brief: Apple Look-Alike Suit Settled," *International Herald Tribune*, 7 June 2001, 17; David P. Hamilton, "Apple Sues Future Power and Daewoo, Alleging They Copied Design of iMac," *Wall Street Journal*, 2 July 1999, B4; "Injunction Is Issued Against Makers of iMac Look Alikes," *Wall Street Journal*, 9 November 1999, B25.
24. Cheeseman, *Business Law*, 330.
25. Mike Snider, "Law Targets Copyright Theft Online," *USA Today*, 18 December 1998, A1.
26. Tariq K. Muhammad, "Real Law in a Virtual World," *Black Enterprise*, December 1996, 44.
27. Jerry M. Rosenberg, *Dictionary of Business and Management* (New York: Wiley, 1983), 340.
28. Ronald A. Anderson, Ivan Fox, and David P. Twomey, *Business Law* (Cincinnati:

South-Western Publishing, 1987), 635.
29. Brennan and Kubasek, *The Legal Environment of Business*, 516–517.
30. "Polaroid Finalizes Sale, Emerges from Chapter 11," *TWICE*, 8 July 2002, 37; Polaroid website [accessed 29 July 2002] www.polaroid.com.

Appendix C

1. Lawrence J. Gitman and Michael D. Joehnk, *Personal Financial Planning*, 10th ed. (Mason, Ohio: Thomson South-Western, 2005), 27.
2. Jack R. Kapoor, Les R. Dlabay, and Robert J. Hughes, *Personal Finance*, 7th ed. (New York: McGraw-Hill/Irwin, 2004), 18.
3. Anne Kim, "Moving In, Moving On," *Seattle Times*, 8 May 2004 [accessed 13 May 2004] www.seattletimes.com.
4. Kapoor et al., *Personal Finance*, 33.
5. "How to Choose a Financial Advisor," WiserAdvisor.com [accessed 21 May 2004] www.wiseradvisor.com.
6. Arthur J. Keown, *Personal Finance: Turning Money into Wealth*, 3d ed. (Upper Saddle River, N.J.: Prentice Hall, 2003) 52–53.
7. Albert B. Crenshaw and Brooke A. Masters, "Big Four Face Legal Trouble, Lost Business; IRS, Clients Challenge Tax-Shelter Advice," *Washington Post*, 12 February 2003 [accessed 21 May 2004] www.highbeam.com; Jerry L. Reiter, "The Blame Game," *Registered Rep*, 2 January 2003 [accessed 21 May 2004] www.highbeam.com.
8. Kapoor et al., *Personal Finance*, 11; Gitman and Joehnk, *Personal Financial Planning*, 5.
9. Gitman and Joehnk, *Personal Financial Planning*, 15.
10. Deborah Fowles, "Financial Advice for Your 20s," About.com [accessed 22 May 2004] www.about.com; Gitman and Joehnk, *Personal Financial Planning*, 15.
11. Ana M. Aizcorbe, Arthur B. Kennickell, and Keven B. Moore, "Recent Changes in U.S. Family Finances: Evidence from the 1998 and 2001 Survey of Consumer Finances," *Federal Reserve Bulletin*, January 2003, 4.
12. Deborah Fowles, "The Psychology of Spending Money," About.com [accessed 22 May 2004] www.about.com.
13. Gitman and Joehnk, *Personal Financial Planning*, 15.
14. "More College Grads, Fewer Home-Grown," *Seattle Times*, 17 May 2004 [accessed 17 May 2004] www.seattletimes.com.
15. Kimberly E. Mock, *Athens Banner-Herald*, "Good Credit Skills Are Essential for Georgia's College Students," 23 February 2004 [accessed 4 May 2004] www.highbeam.com.
16. Lucy Lazarony, "Credit Cards Teaching Students a Costly Lesson," Bankrate.com, 5

June 1998 [accessed 22 May 2004] www.bankrate.com.

17. David Kiley, "Car Buyers Pay More, Owe More Longer," *USA Today*, 17 February 2004, B1; Lucy Lazarony, "It's a Good Time to Be a New-Car Shopper," Bankrate.com, 5 March 2003 [accessed 22 May 2004] www.bankrate.com.

18. Philip Reed, "Drive a (Nearly) New Car for (Almost) Nothing," Edmunds.com [accessed 22 May 2004] www.edmunds.com.

19. Chandler Phillips, "Confessions of a Car Salesman," Edmunds.com [accessed 22 May 2004] www.edmunds.com.

20. Eryn Brown, "Hot to Get Paid What You're Worth," *Business 2.0*, May 2004, 102–110, 134.

21. Keown, *Personal Finance: Turning Money into Wealth*, 143–148; Gitman and Joehnk, *Personal Financial Planning*, 140–147.

22. "How to Establish Credit," CreditInfoWeb.com [accessed 23 May 2004] www.creditinfoweb.com.

23. Kapoor et al., *Personal Finance*, 222.

24. "Ads Promising Debt Relief May Be Offering Bankruptcy," FTC Consumer Alert [accessed 23 May 2004] www.ftc.gov.

25. Kapoor et al., *Personal Finance*, 582.

Appendix E

1. Jeffrey R. Young, "'E-Portfolios' Could Give Students a New Sense of Their Accomplishments," *The Chronicle of Higher Education*, 8 March 2002, A31.

2. Nancy M. Somerick, "Managing a Communication Internship Program," *Bulletin of the Association for Business Communication* 56, no. 3 (1993): 10–20.

3. Bureau of Labor Statistics, *1998–99 Occupational Outlook Handbook* [accessed 10 August 1999] www.bls.gov/oco; Webmaster career information from Excite Careers, Internet Industry Focus [accessed 10 August 1999] http://careers.excite.com/cgi-cls/display.exe?xc-xca+Career+WetFeet1 Industry+HiTech_InternetWebmaster.

4. Caroline A. Drakeley, "Viral Networking: Tactics in Today's Job Market," Intercom, September–October 2003, 4+.

5. Cheryl L. Noll, "Collaborating with the Career Planning and Placement Center in the Job-Search Project," *Business Communication Quarterly* 58, no. 3 (1995): 53–55.

6. Rockport Institute, "How to Write a Masterpiece of a Résumé" [accessed 16 October 1998] www.rockportinstitute.com/résumés.html.

7. Janice Tovey, "Using Visual Theory in the Creation of Résumés: A Bibliography," *The Bulletin of the Association for Business Communication* 54, no. 3 (September 1991): 97–99.

8. "Resume Fraud Gets Slicker and Easier," CNN.com [accessed 11 March 2004] www.cnn.com.

9. "Resume Fraud Gets Slicker and Easier"; Employment Screening Resources website [accessed 18 March 2004] www.erscheck.com.

10. Pam Stanley-Weigand, "Organizing the Writing of Your Résumé," *Bulletin of the Association for Business Communication* 54, no. 3 (September 1991): 11–12.

11. Susan Vaughn, "Answer the Hard Questions Before Asked," *Los Angeles Times*, 29 July 2001, W1–W2.

12. Richard H. Beatty and Nicholas C. Burkholder, *The Executive Career Guide for MBAs* (New York: Wiley, 1996), 133.

13. Adapted from Burdette E. Bostwick, *How to Find the Job You've Always Wanted* (New York: Wiley, 1982), 69–70.

14. Norma Mushkat Gaffin, "Recruiters' Top 10 Resume Pet Peeves," Monster.com [accessed 19 February 2004] www.monster.com; Beatty and Burkholder, *The Executive Career Guide for MBAs*, 151.

15. Rockport Institute, "How to Write a Masterpiece of a Résumé."

16. Beverly Culwell-Block and Jean Anna Sellers, "Résumé Content and Format—Do the Authorities Agree?" *Bulletin of the Association for Business Communication* 57, no. 4 (1994): 27–30.

17. Ellen Joe Pollock, "Sir: Your Application for a Job Is Rejected; Sincerely, Hal 9000," *Wall Street Journal*, 30 July 1998, A1, A12.

18. "Scannable Résumé Design," ResumeEdge.com [accessed 19 February 2004] www.resumeedge.com.

19. Kim Isaacs, "Tips for Creating a Scannable Résumé," Monster.com [accessed 19 February 2004] www.monster.com.

20. William J. Banis, "The Art of Writing Job-Search Letters," *CPC Annual*, 36th ed., 2 (1992): 42–50.

21. Robert Gifford, Cheuk Fan Ng, and Margaret Wilkinson, "Nonverbal Cues in the Employment Interview: Links Between Applicant Qualities and Interviewer Judgments," *Journal of Applied Psychology* 70, no. 4 (1985): 729.

22. Amanda Bennett, "GE Redesigns Rungs of Career Ladder," *Wall Street Journal*, 15 March 1993, B1, B3.

23. Robin White Goode, "International and Foreign Language Skills Have an Edge," *Black Enterprise*, May 1995, 53.

24. Nancy M. Somerick, "Managing a Communication Internship Program," *Bulletin of the Association for Business Communication* 56, no. 3 (1993): 10–20.

25. Noll, "Collaborating with the Career Planning and Placement Center in the Job-Search Project," 53–55.

26. Joan Lloyd, "Changing Workplace Requires You to Alter Your Career Outlook," *Milwaukee Journal Sentinel*, 4 July 1999, 1; Camille DeBell, "Ninety Years in the World of Work in America," *Career Development Quarterly* 50, no. 1 (September 2001): 77–88.

Illustration and Text Credits

Chapter 1

1. Exhibit 1.1, U.S. Department of Commerce, Bureau of Economic Analysis [accessed 27 March 2004] beadata.bea.doc.gov.

2. Exhibit 1.2, Adapted from Christopher Caggiano, "Will the Real Bootstrappers Please Stand Up?" *Inc.*, August 1995, 34; Mike Hofman, "Capitalism—A Bootstrappers' Hall of Fame," *Inc.*, August 1997, 54–57; Hoover's, [accessed 27 March 2004] www.hoovers.com.

3. Exhibit 1.3, Adapted from Monica Kearns, "Whatever Happened to the New Economy?" *State Legislatures*, February 2002, 24–27.

4. Exhibit 1.4, Adapted from Chris Woodyard, "Firms Stretch Travel Dollars," *USA Today*, 16 March 1999, B1–B2.

5. (Learning from Business Blunders) Adapted from Adam Horowitz, Mark Athitakis, Mark Lasswell, and Owen Thomas, "The 101 Dumbest Moments in Business," *Business 2.0* [accessed 27 March 2004] www.business2.com.

6. (Technologies That Are Revolutionizing Business) Adapted from Jefferson Graham, "Instant Messaging Programs Are No Longer Just for Messages," *USA Today*, 20 October 2003, 5D; Todd R. Weiss, "Microsoft Targets Corporate Instant Messaging Customers," *Computerworld*, 18 November 2002, 12; "Banks Adopt Instant Messaging to Create a Global Business Network," *Computer Weekly*, 25 April 2002, 40; Michael D. Osterman, "Instant Messaging in the Enterprise," *Business Communications Review*, January 2003, 59–62; John Pallato, "Instant Messaging Unites Work Groups and Inspires Collaboration," *Internet World*, December 2002, 14+; Mark Gibbs, "Racing to Instant Messaging," *NetworkWorld*, 17 February 2003, 74.

7. (LivePerson Puts a Pulse on the Web) Adapted from LivePerson website [accessed 27 March 2004], www.liveperson.com; Mary Wagner, "The Long Road to Online Checkout," *Internet World*, April 2001 [accessed 7 May 2001] www.internetretailer.com; Karen J. Bannan, "Burning Up the Wires," *PSINet eBusiness*, Winter 2001, 48–51; Bruce Horovitz, "Site Untangles E-Customer Service Mess," *USA Today*, 23 November 1999 [accessed 7 May 2001] www.usatoday.com; "LivePerson Reels in $19 Million," *Red Herring*, 10 August 1999

[accessed 7 May 2001] www.redherring.com; Connie Guglielmo, "LivePerson Puts a Pulse into Web Interaction," *ZDNet*, 21 June 1999 [accessed 7 May 2001] www.zdnet.com; Vanessa Geneva Melter, "Closing the Sale with Interactive Chat," *ShopGuide News*, 7 June 1999 [accessed 7 May 2001] www.shopguide.com; Jennifer Gilbert, "LivePerson Focuses on the Human Touch," *Advertising Age*, 1 June 1999 [accessed 7 May 2001] adage.com; Craig Bicknell, "Somebody Freakin' Talk to Me!" *Wired*, 1 June 1999 [accessed 7 May 2001] www.wired.com.
8. (The Electronic Economy: Redefining Reality) Adapted from Stephen Baker, "Where Danger Lurks," *BusinessWeek*, 25 August 2003, 114–118; W. Brian Arthur, "Why Tech Is Still the Future," *Fortune*, 24 November 2003, 119–125; Keven Anderson, "Delivery at Internet Speed," BBC News Online, 22 December 1999 [accessed 30 March 2004] news.bbc.co.uk.
9. (Business Buzz) Adapted from Wordspy.com [accessed 15 April 2004] www.wordspy.com.

Chapter 2
1. Exhibit 2.1, Adapted from *The Institute of Electrical and Electronics Engineers* [accessed 21 July 1999] ieeeusa.org/documents/career/career_library/ethics.html.
2. Exhibit 2.2, "American Workers Do the Right Thing," *HRFocus*, March 1999, 4.
3. Exhibit 2.3, Adapted from Manuel G. Velasquez, *Business Ethics: Concepts and Cases* (Upper Saddle River, N.J.: Prentice Hall, 1998), 87; Joseph L. Badaracco, Jr., "Business Ethics: Four Spheres of Executive Responsibility," *California Management Review*, Spring 1992, 64–79; Kenneth Blanchard and Norman Vincent Peale, *The Power of Ethical Management* (Reprint, 1989; New York: Fawcett Crest, 1991), 7–17; John R. Boatright, *Ethics and the Conduct of Business* (Upper Saddle River, N.J.: Prentice Hall, 1996), 35–39, 59–64, 79–86.
4. Exhibit 2.4, Weld Royal, "Real Expectations," *Industry Week*, 4 September 2000, 32.
5. Exhibit 2.6, 2002 Census of Fatal Occupational Injuries, U.S. Bureau of Labor Statistics [accessed 1 April 2004] www.bls.gov.
6. (Learning from Business Blunders) Adapted from Adam Horowitz, Mark Athitakis, Mark Lasswell, and Owen Thomas, "The 101 Dumbest Moments in Business," *Business 2.0* [accessed 27 March 2004] www.business2.com; Bob Garfield, "KFC Serves Big, Fat Bucket of Nonsense in 'Healthy' Spots," *Advertising Age*, 3 November 2003, 61; "KFC Blunders in Healthy Ads," *Advertising Age*, 3 November 2003, 22.

7. (Technologies That Are Revolutionizing Business) Adapted from "Benetton Explains RFID Privacy Flap," RFID Journal [accessed 1 April 2004] www.rfidjournal.com; David LaGress, "They Know Where You Are," *U.S. News & World Report*, 8 September 2003, 32–38; Christopher Elliott, "Some Rental Cars Are Keeping Tabs on Drivers," *New York Times*, 13 January 2004, C6.
8. (Ben & Jerry's: A Double Scoop of Irony?) Adapted from Ben & Jerry's website [accessed 1 April 2004] www.benjerry.com; George F. Will, "Being Green and Ben & Jerry's," *Newsweek*, 6 May 2002, 72; Edward O. Welles, "Ben's Big Flop," *Inc.*, September 1998, 40+; Constance L. Hays, "Getting Serious at Ben & Jerry's," *New York Times*, 22 May 1998, C1, C3; Constance L. Hays, "Ben & Jerry's to Unilever, with Attitude," *New York Times*, 13 April 2000, C1, C20; Fred Bayles, "Reviews in on Ben & Jerry's Sweet Deal," *USA Today*, 20 April 2000, 3A.
9. (Actions Speak Louder Than Codes) Adapted from Craig Dreilinger, "Get Real (and Ethics Will Follow)," *Workforce*, August 1998, 101–102; Louisa Wah, "Workplace Conscience Needs a Boost," *American Management Association International*, July–August 1998; "Ethics Are Questionable in the Workplace," *HRFocus*, June 1998, 7.
10. (Business Buzz) Adapted from Wordspy.com [accessed 15 April 2004] www.wordspy.com.

Chapter 3
1. Exhibit 3.1, U.S. Bureau of Economic Analysis website [accessed 5 April 2004] www.bea.doc.gov.
2. Exhibit 3.2, "U.S. International Transactions," U.S. Bureau of Economic Analysis website [accessed 5 April 2004] www.bea.doc.gov.
3. Exhibit 3.4, *USA Today Snapshot*, "Going Global Has Its Barriers," *USA Today*, 3 May 2000, B1.
4. Exhibit 3.5, John V. Thill and Courtland L. Bovée, *Excellence in Business Communication* (Upper Saddle River, N.J.: Prentice Hall, 2002), 33.
5. (Technologies That Are Revolutionizing Business) Adapted from Rick Whiting, "Innovation: Videoconferencing's Virtual Room," *InformationWeek*, 1 April 2002, 14; Mark Alpert, "Long-Distance Robots," *Scientific American*, December 2001, 94; Teliris website [accessed 8 August 2003] www.teliris.com.
6. (Learning from Business Blunders) Adapted from David A. Ricks, *Blunders in International Business*, 3d ed. (Oxford, England: Blackwell Business, 1997), 134.
7. (How to Avoid Business Mistakes Abroad) Adapted from David Ricks, "How to Avoid Business Blunders Abroad," *Business*, April–June 1984, 3–11.

8. (China's Counterfeit Economy) Adapted from Robyn Meredith, "Microsoft's Long March," *Forbes*, 17 February 2003, 78–86; Chris Buckley, "Helped by Technology, Piracy of DVD's Runs Rampant in China," *New York Times*, 18 August 2003, C9; Todd Zaun and Karen Leggert, "Road Warriors," *Wall Street Journal*, 25 July 2001, A1, A4; Steve Friess, "Product Piracy Poses Biggest Threat to China's Economic Status," *USA Today*, 28 June 2001, 6B; Richard Behar, "Beijing's Phony War on Fakes," *Fortune*, 30 October 2000, 188+; Susan V. Lawrence, "For Better or Worse," *Far Eastern Economic Review*, 5 October 2000, 60; Lorien Holland, "A Brave New World," *Far Eastern Economic Review*, 5 October 2000, 46–48; Trish Saywell, "Fakes Cost Real Cash," *Far Eastern Economic Review*, 5 October 2000, 57–58; Dexter Roberts, Frederik Balfour, Paul Magnusson, Pete Engardio, and Jennifer Lee, "China's Piracy Plague," *BusinessWeek*, 5 June 2000, 44–48.
9. (E-Business in Action) Adapted from "China Is World's No. 2 Spam Receiver," ChinaTechNews.com, 17 March 2004 [accessed 5 April 2004] www.chinatechnews.com; Bruce Einhorn, "The Net's Second Superpower," *BusinessWeek*, 15 March 2004, 54–56; David J. Lynch, "Surf's Up in China, Where Millions Are Going Online," *USA Today*, 8 October 2003, B1–2; "China Pulls Plug on Internet Blogs," ChinaTechNews.com, 17 March 2004 [accessed 5 April 2004] www.chinatechnews.com; "China Suspends Registration of New Net Cafés," 3 March 2004 [accessed 5 April 2004] www.chinatechnews.com.
10. (Business Buzz) Adapted from Wordspy.com [accessed 15 April 2004] www.wordspy.com.

Chapter 4
1. Exhibit 4.2, "Business Enterprise," *2003 Statistical Abstract of the United States*, 495.
2. Exhibit 4.4, Mergerstat, "M&A Activity: U.S. and U.S. Cross-Border Transactions" [accessed 11 April 2004] www.mergerstat.com.
3. (Technologies That Are Revolutionizing Business) Adapted from Tony Kontzer, "Learning to Share," *InformationWeek*, 5 May 2003, 28; Jon Udell, "Uniting Under Groove," *InfoWorld*, 17 February 2003 [accessed 9 September 2003] www.elibrary.com; Alison Overholt, "Virtually There?" *Fast Company*, 14 February 2002, 108.
4. (Learning from Business Blunders) Adapted from Andy Holloway, "Wasting Time," *Canadian Business*, 1 March 2004, 95+; John Motavalli, "More AOL Woes for Time Warner," *Television Week*, 5 January 2004, 1+; Andy Kessler, "Here's the Sinking Case of AOL Time Warner," *Wall Street Journal Online*, 8 October 2002; Frank Ahrens, "At AOL and Disney, Uneasy Chairs,"

Washington Post, 18 September 2002, E01; Martin Peers, "Will Steve Case Leave AOL?" *Wall Street Journal*, 12 September 2002, B1, B7; Jeremy Kahn and Bill Powell, "Can These Guys Fix AOL?" *Fortune*, 2 September 2002, 95–100; Tom Lowry, "The Sinkhole of 'Synergy,'" *BusinessWeek*, 26 August 2002, 22; Catherine Yang, "Can Miller Put the Oomph Back in AOL?" *BusinessWeek*, 26 August 2002, 42; Frank Ahrens, Merissa Marr, "Old-school media reassert control," *Toronto Star*, 30 July 2002; "Big Media Mergers Raise Big Doubts; Is Synergy Achievable—or Even Desirable?" *Washington Post*, 14 May 2002, A01.

5. (Hey, Wanna Lose a Few Billion? We've Got a Sure Deal for You) Adapted from Larry Selden and Geoffrey Colvin, "M&A Needn't Be a Loser's Game," *Harvard Business Review*, June 2003, 70–79; Amy Kover, "Big Banks Debunked," *Fortune*, 21 February 2000, 187–194; Erick Schonfeld, "Have the Urge to Merge? You'd Better Think Twice," *Fortune*, 31 March 1997, 114–116; Phillip L. Zweig et al., "The Case Against Mergers," *BusinessWeek*, 30 October 1995, 122–130; Kevin Kelly et al., "Mergers Today, Trouble Tomorrow?" *BusinessWeek*, 12 September 1994; "How to Merge," *The Economist*, 9 January 1999, 21–23; "Study Says Mergers Often Don't Aid Investors," *New York Times*, 1 December 1999, C9.

6. (DaimlerChrysler: Merger of Equals or Global Fender Bender?) Adapted from Christiaan Hetzner and Chang-Ran Kim, "Daimler Boss Set to Ride Out Storm," *Birmingham Post*, 6 April 2004 [accessed 7 April 2004] www.highbeam.com; Roberto A. Weber and Colin F. Camerer, "Cultural Conflict and Merger Failure: An Experimental Approach," *Management Science*, April 2003, 400–415; Bill Vlasic and Bradley A. Stertz, "How the DaimlerChrysler Marriage of Equals Got Taken for a Ride," *BusinessWeek*, 5 June 2000, 86–92; Jeffrey Ball and Scott Miller, "Full Speed Ahead: Stuttgart's Control Grows with Shakeup at DaimlerChrysler," *Wall Street Journal*, 24 September 1999, A1, A8; Robert L. Simison and Scott Miller, "Making Digital Decisions," *Wall Street Journal*, 24 September 1999, B1, B4; Keith Bradsher, "A Struggle over Culture and Turf at Auto Giant," *New York Times*, 25 September 1999, B1, B14; Message from DaimlerChrysler Chairman to Company Employees, *Wall Street Journal*, 24 September 1999, A15; Joann Muller, Kathleen Kerwin, and Jack Ewing, "Man with a Plan," *BusinessWeek*, 4 October 1999, 34–35; Frank Gibney, Jr., "Worldwide Fender Bender," *Time*, 24 May 1999, 58–62; Daniel McGinn and Stefan Theil, "Hands on the Wheel," *Newsweek*, 12 April 1999, 49–52; Alex Taylor III, "The Germans Take Charge," *Fortune*, 11 January 1999, 92–96; Barrett Seaman and Ron Stodghill II, "The Daimler-Chrysler Deal: Here Comes the Road Test," *Time*, 18 May 1999, 66–69; Bill Vlasic, Kathleen Kerwin, David Woodruff, Thane Peterson, and Leah Nathans Spiro, "The First Global Car Colossus," *BusinessWeek*, 18 May 1998, 40–43; Joann Muller, "Lessons from a Casualty of the Culture Wars," *BusinessWeek*, 29 November 1999, 198; Rovert McNatt, "Chrysler: Not Quite So Equal," *BusinessWeek*, 13 November 2000, 14.

7. (Business Buzz) Adapted from Wordspy.com [accessed 15 April 2004] www.wordspy.com.

Chapter 5

1. Exhibit 5.1, Adapted from Carrie Dolan, "Entrepreneurs Often Fail as Managers," *Wall Street Journal*, 15 May 1989, B1. Reprinted by permission of The Wall Street Journal, © 1989 Dow Jones & Company, Inc. All Rights Reserved Worldwide.

2. Exhibit 5.2, Anne R. Carey and Grant Jerding, *USA Snapshot, USA Today*, 26 March 1998, B1.

3. Exhibit 5.3, *Business Know How* [accessed 19 September 1997] www.business-knowhow.com.

4. Exhibit 5.4, Adapted from Norman M. Scarborough and Thomas W. Zimmerer, *Effective Small Business Management* (Upper Saddle River, N.J.: Prentice Hall, 2000), 8–13.

5. Exhibit 5.6, Adapted from Norman M. Scarborough and Thomas W. Zimmerer, *Effective Small Business Management* (Upper Saddle River, N.J.: Prentice Hall, 2000), 27–29.

6. (E-Business in Action) Adapted from Jennifer Reingold, Carleen Hawn, Keith H. Hammonds, Ryan Underwood, and Linda Tischler, "What We Learned in the New Economy," *Fast Company*, March 2003, 9+; AP Worldstream, "eBay Tops Wall Street Expectations, Improves Outlook for 2004," 21 January 2004 [accessed 10 April 2004] www.highbeam.com; David Moschella, "Revenge of the Dot-coms," *Computerworld*, 26 January 2004 [accessed 10 April 2004] www.highbeam.com; Paulette Thomas, "The Morning After," *Wall Street Journal*, 27 March 2002, R12; Michael Totty and Ann Grimes, "If at First You Don't Succeed," *Wall Street Journal*, 11 February 2002, R6–R7; J. William Gurley, "Startups, Beware: Obey the Law of Supply and Demand," *Fortune*, 29 May 2000, 278; William M. Bulkeley and Jim Carlton, "E-Tail Gets Derailed: How Web Upstarts Misjudged the Game," *Wall Street Journal*, 5 April 2000, A1, A6; Leslie Kaufman, "After Taking a Beating, Dot-Coms Now Seek Financial Saviors," *New York Times*, 18 April 2000, C1, C18; Kevin Maney, "Net Start-Ups Pull Out of the Garage," *USA Today*, 1 October 1999, 1B, 2B; Matt Krantz, "E-Retailers Run Low on Fuel," *USA Today*, 26 April 2000, 1B, 2B; "Survival of the Fastest," *Inc. Tech*, 16 November 1999, 44–58; Darnell Little, "Peapod Is in a Pickle," *BusinessWeek*, 3 April 2000, 41; Heather Green, Nanette Byrnes, Norm Alster, and Arlene Weintraub, "The Dot.Coms Are Falling to Earth," *BusinessWeek*, 17 April 2000, 48–49; John A. Byrne, "The Fall of a Dot-Com," *BusinessWeek*, 1 May 2000, 150–160; Stephanie N. Mehta, "As Investors Play VC, It's Dot-Com Doomsday," *Fortune*, 1 May 2000, 40–41; David P. Hamilton and Mylene Mangalindan, "Angels of Death," *Wall Street Journal*, 25 May 2000, A1, A8; Luisa Kroll, "When the Music Stops," *Forbes*, 15 May 2000, 182; Chris Farrell, "Death of the Dot-Coms?" *BusinessWeek*, 22 May 2000, 104E6; John Steele Gordon, "The Golden Spike," *Forbes ASAP*, 21 February 2000, 118–122; Eric W. Pfeiffer, "Where Are We in the Revolution?" *Forbes ASAP*, 21 February 2000, 68–70; James Lardner and Paul Sloan, "The Anatomy of Sickly IPOs," *U.S. News and World Report*, 29 May 2000, 42; Hillary Stout, "Crunch Time," *Wall Street Journal*, 7 June 2000, B1; Jerry Useem, "Dot-Coms—What Have We Learned?" *Fortune*, 30 October 2000, 82–104; Heather Green and Norm Alster, "Guess What—Venture Capitalists Aren't Geniuses," *BusinessWeek*, 10 July 2000, 98; Thomas E. Weber, "What Were We Thinking?" *Wall Street Journal*, 18 July 2000, B1, B4; Greg Ip, Susan Pulliam, Scott Thurm, and Ruth Simon, "The Color Green," *Wall Street Journal*, 14 July 2000, A1, A8; "Business Brief—Value America: Bankruptcy Code Filing Is Made by the Company," *Wall Street Journal*, 14 August 2000, B2.

7. (Learning from Business Blunders) Adapted from Eve Tahmincioglu, "Even the Best Ideas Don't Sell Themselves," *New York Times*, 9 October 2003, C9.

8. (Technologies That Are Revolutionizing Business) Adapted from David Pescovitz, "Technology of the Year: Social Network Applications," *Business 2.0*, November 2003, 113–114; Spoke website [accessed 11 April 2004] www.spoke.com; LinkedIn website [accessed 11 April 2004] www.linkedin.com; Ryze website [accessed 11 April 2004] www.ryze.com.

9. (Create a Winning Website) Adapted from Brian Hurley and Peter Birkwood, *A Small Business Guide to Doing Big Business on the Internet* (Bellingham, Washington: International Self-Counsel Press, 1996), 124–134; "Design a Better Web Site," *Journal of Accountancy*, August 1998, 18; Anita Dennis, "A Home on the Web," *Journal of Accountancy*, August 1998, 29–31.

10. (Blueprint for a Comprehensive Business Plan) Adapted from J. Tol Broome, Jr., "How to Write a Business Plan," *Nation's Business*, February 1993, 29–30; Albert Richards, "The Ernst & Young Business Plan Guide," *R & D Management*, April 1995, 253;

David Lanchner, "How Chitchat Became a Valuable Business Plan," *Global Finance*, February 1995, 54–56; Marguerita Ashby-Berger, "My Business Plan—And What Really Happened," *Small Business Forum*, Winter 1994–1995, 24–35; Stanley R. Rich and David E. Gumpert, *Business Plans That Win $$$* (New York: Harper Row, 1985).
11. (Business Buzz) Adapted from Wordspy.com [accessed 15 April 2004] www.wordspy.com.

Chapter 6

1. Exhibit 6.2, Adapted from Dell Computer website [accessed 15 June 1999] www.dell.com/corporate/vision/mission.htm.
2. Exhibit 6.4, Adapted from and reprinted by permission of *Harvard Business Review*, an exhibit from "How to Choose a Leadership Pattern" by Robert Tannenbaum and Warren H. Schmidt, May–June 1973. Copyright © 1973 by the President and Fellows of Harvard College, all rights reserved.
3. Exhibit 6.6, Adapted from Courtland Bovée et al., *Management* (New York: McGraw-Hill, 1993), 678.
4. Exhibit 6.7, Adapted from Fred Vogelstein, "Mighty Amazon," *Fortune*, 26 May 2003, 60–74; Stuart Crainer, "The 75 Greatest Management Decisions Ever Made," *Management Review*, November 1998, 17–23.
5. (Learning from Business Blunders) Adapted from Richard Pérez-Peña and Matthew L. Wald, "Basic Failures by Ohio Utility Set Off Blackout, Report Finds," *New York Times*, 20 November 2003, A1; "US Blackout: Interim Report," *Power Economics*, January 2004, 9; Edward Iwata, "Report: Major Blackout Could Have Been Prevented," *USA Today*, 6 April 2004, A1.
6. (Technologies That Are Revolutionizing Business) Adapted from TechEncyclopedia, [accessed 13 April 2004] www.techweb.com/encyclopedia; Business Objects websites [accessed 13 April 2004] www.businessobjects.com; Cognos website [accessed 13 April 2004] www.cognos.com.
7. (JetBlue: Tough Management Decisions in Tough Times) Adapted from Michael Arndt and Wendy Zellner, "American Draws a Bead on JetBlue," *BusinessWeek*, 24 June 2002, 48; Sally B. Donnelly, "Blue Skies," *Time*, 30 July 2001, 23–27; Paul C. Judge, "How Will Your Company Adapt?" *Fast Company*, December 2001, 128–132; Robert Whalen, "JetBlue Turning Profit as Industry Struggles," *The Record*, 27 December 2001, B1; Tom Fredrickson, "Plane Sailing," *Crain's New York Business*, 12 November 2001, 1.
8. (How Much Do You Know About the Company's Culture?) Adapted from Andrew Bird, "Do You Know What Your Corporate Culture Is?" *CPA Insight*, February, March 1999, 25–26; Gail H. Vergara, "Finding a Compatible Corporate Culture," *Healthcare Executive*, January/February 1999, 46–47; Hal Lancaster, "To Avoid a Job Failure, Learn the Culture of a Company First," *Wall Street Journal*, 14 July 1998, B1.
9. (Business Buzz) Adapted from Wordspy.com [accessed 15 April 2004] www.wordspy.com.

Chapter 7

1. Exhibit 7.4, Adapted from Steven Burke, "Acer Restructures into Six Divisions," *Computer Reseller News*, 13 July 1998, 10.
2. (Technologies That Are Revolutionizing Business) Adapted from Wavelink case study, "Tesco Picks Wavelink to Manage Over 5000 Wireless Access Points Across More Than 600 Stores," Wavelink website [accessed 14 April 2004] www.wavelink.com; Cisco case study, "University of Wyoming—Rocky Mountain Campus Builds Rock-Solid Wireless Network," Cisco website [accessed 14 April 2004] www.cisco.com; "Wireless Access Point (WLAN) Basics," Caltech Information Technology Services website [accessed 14 April 2004] www.its.caltech.edu.
3. (Learning from Business Blunders) Adapted from Clayton M. Christensen and Michael E. Raynor, "Why Hard-Nosed Executives Should Care About Management Theory," *Harvard Business Review*, September 2003, 67–74; Martha McKay, "Lucent Turns Its First Profit in 14 Quarters," *The Record* (Bergen County, NJ), 23 October 2003 [accessed 14 April 2004] www.highbeam.com.
4. (Mervyn's Calls SWAT Team to the Rescue) Adapted from Peter Carvonara, "Mervyn's Calls in the SWAT Team," *Fast Company*, April–May 1998, 54–56; Richard Halverson, "Ulrich Delivers Ultimatum to Mervyn's: Improve Sales Performance, or Else," *Discount Store News*, 26 October 1998, 3,126.
5. (Don't Leave Home to Go to Work: American Express Company's Virtual Environment) American Express Company website [accessed 20 April 2002] www.americanexpress.com; Sally Richards, "Make the Most of Your First Job," *Information Week*, 21 June 1999, 183–186; Tim Greene, "American Express: Don't Leave Home to Go to Work," *Network World*, 8 March 1999, 25; Mahlon Apgar IV, "The Alternative Workplace: Changing Where and How People Work," *Harvard Business Review*, May/June 1998, 121–130; "How Senior Executives at American Express View the Alternative Workplace," *Harvard Business Review*, May/June 1998, 132–133; Michelle Marchetti, "Master Motivators," *Sales and Marketing Management*, April 1998, 38–44; Carrie Shook, "Leader, Not Boss," *Forbes*, 1 December 1997, 52–54.
6. (Business Buzz) Adapted from Wordspy.com [accessed 15 April 2004] www.wordspy.com.

Chapter 8

1. Exhibit 8.2, Adapted from Mark M. Davis, Nicholas J. Aquilano, and Richard B. Chase, *Fundamentals of Operations Management* (Boston: Irwin McGraw-Hill, 1999), 7.
2. (Technologies That Are Revolutionizing Business) Adapted from Barnaby J. Feder, "Technology: Bashful vs. Brash in the New Field of Nanotech," *New York Times*, 15 March 2004 [accessed 16 April 2004] "Nanotechnology Basics," Nanotechnology Now website [accessed 16 April 2004] www.nanotech-now.com; Center for Responsible Nanotechnology website [accessed 16 April 2004] www.crnano.org; Gary Stix, "Little Big Science," *Scientific American*, 16 September 2001 [accessed 16 April 2004] www.sciam.com; Tim Harper, "Small Wonders," *Business 2.0*, July 2002 [accessed 16 April 2004] www.business2.com; Erick Schonfeld, "A Peek at IBM's Nanotech Research," *Business 2.0*, 5 December 2003 [accessed 16 April 2004] www.business2.com; David Pescovitz, "The Best New Technologies of 2003," *Business 2.0*, November 2003, 109–116.
3. (Learning From Business Blunders) Adapted from Adam Horowitz, Mark Athitakis, Mark Lasswell, and Owen Thomas, "The 101 Dumbest Moments in Business," *Business 2.0* [accessed 27 March 2004] www.business2.com; David Lazarus, "Pakistani Threatened UCSF to Get Paid, She Says," *San Francisco Chronicle*, 12 November 2003 [accessed 17 April 2004] www.sfgate.com.
4. (A Bike That Really Travels) Adapted from Lisa Marshall, "A Bike That Really Travels," *Boulder Daily Camera*, June 1999; Bike Friday website [accessed 11 August 2000] www.bikefriday.com; Tim Stevens, "Pedal Pushers," *Industry Week*, 17 July 2000, 46–52.
5. (Offshoring: Profits, Yes, But at What Cost?) Adapted from Stephanie Amour and Michelle Kessler, "USA's New Money-Saving Export: White-Collar Jobs," *USA Today*, 5 August 2003, B1–B2; Steve Lohr, "Offshore Jobs in Technology: Opportunity or Threat?" *New York Times*, 22 December 2003, C1, C6; Kris Maher, "Next on the Outsourcing List," *Wall Street Journal*, 28 March 2004, B1, B8; Jennifer Reingold, "Into Thin Air," *Fast Company*, April 2004, 76–82; Paul Craig Roberts, "The Harsh Truth About Outsourcing," 22 March 2004, 48; Craig Karmin, " 'Offshoring' Can Generate Jobs in the U.S.," *Wall Street Journal*, 16 March 2004, B1, B7; Bernard J. La Londe, "From Outsourcing to 'Offshoring'—Part 1," *Supply Chain Management Review*, 1 March 2004 [accessed 16 April 2004] www.manufacturing.net; Paul Kaihla, "Straws in the Wind," Business 2.0, 27 April 2004 [accessed 22 July 2004] www.business2.com.

6. (E-Commerce in Action) Adapted from Erik Heinrich, "What Can Work: One Buyer, Many Sellers," *Toronto Sun*, 23 October 2003 [accessed 17 April] www.highbeam.com; Peter Loftus, "E-Commerce: Business to Business—Exchanges Making It Work," *Wall Street Journal*, 11 February 2002, R16; Ralph Kisiel, "Automakers Saving by Using Covisint," *Crain's Detroit Business*, 21 January 2002, 12; Eric Young, "Web Marketplaces That Really Work," *Fortune Tech Review*, Winter 2002, 10; J. William Gurley, "Big Company.com: Should You Start a B2B Exchange?" *Fortune*, 3 April 2000, 260+; Peter D. Henig, "Revenge of the Bricks," *Red Herring*, August 2000, 121–134; Daniel Lyons, "B2Bluster," *Forbes*, 1 May 2000, 122–126; Steven Kaplan and Mohanbir Sawhney, "E-hubs: The New B2B Marketplaces," *Harvard Business Review*, May–June 2000, 97–100; Robert D. Hof, "Who Will Profit from the Internet Agora?" *BusinessWeek E.Biz*, 5 June 2000, EB56–EB62; Joseph B. White, "Getting Into Gear," *Wall Street Journal*, 17 April 2000, R65; Douglas A. Blackmon, "Where the Money Is," *Wall Street Journal*, 17 April 2000, R30–R32; Edward Iwata, "Despite the Hype, B2B Marketplaces Struggle," *USA Today*, 10 May 2000, 1B–2B; Jack Trout, "Stupid Net Tricks," *Business 2.0*, May 2000, 76–77; John W. Verity, "Invoice? What's an Invoice?" *BusinessWeek*, 10 June 1996, 110–112; Christina Binkley, "Hyatt Plans Internet Firm with Marriott," *Wall Street Journal*, 2 May 2000, A3, A6; Clint Willis, "B2B . . . to Be?" *Forbes ASAP*, 21 August 2000, 125–130; Jason Anders, "Yesterday's Darling," *Wall Street Journal*, 23 October 2000, R8.
7. (Business Buzz) Adapted from Wordspy.com [accessed 15 April 2004] www.wordspy.com.

Chapter 9
1 Exhibit 9.2, *Management, 4th ed.*, by Richard L. Daft copyright © 1997 by Harcourt Inc., reproduced by permission of the publisher.
2. Exhibit 9.3, Douglas McGregor, *The Human Side of Enterprise* (New York: McGraw-Hill, 1960).
3. Exhibit 9.4, Adapted from Stephen P. Robbins and David A. DeCenzo, *Fundamentals of Management*, 4th ed. (Upper Saddle River, N.J.: Prentice Hall, 2004), 289.
4. Exhibit 9.6, Adapted from Jennifer Laabs, "The New Loyalty: Grasp It. Earn It. Keep It." *Workforce*, November 1998, 35–39.
5. Exhibit 9.7, *USA Today Snapshot*, "9-to-5 Not for Everyone," *USA Today*, 13 October 1999, B1.
6. (Learning from Business Blunders) Adapted from Adam Horowitz, Mark Athitakis, Mark Lasswell, and Owen

Thomas, "The 101 Dumbest Moments in Business," *Business 2.0* [accessed 24 April 2004] www.business2.com; "The Best & Worst Managers of 2003," *BusinessWeek*, 12 January 2004, 55–85; Gretchen Morgenson, "It's Awards Time on Wall Street: From Epic to Comic Wall Street Watch," *International Herald Tribune*, 30 December 2003 [accessed 24 April 2004] www.highbeam.com; Rick Moriarty, "Low-Flying Airline; American Struggles to Recover from 9/11, Bankruptcy, Executive Pay Scandal," *The Post-Standard* (Syracuse, N.Y.), 15 December 2003 [accessed 24 April 2004] www.highbeam.com.
7. (Technologies That Are Revolutionizing Business) Adapted from Rich Karlgaard, "Outsource Yourself," *Forbes*, 19 April 2004 [accessed 24 April 2004] www.highbeam.com; David Kirkpatrick, "Big-League R&D Gets Its Own eBay," *Fortune*, 3 May 2004 [accessed 24 April 2004] www.highbeam.com; Joseph N. Pelton, "The Rise of Telecities: Decentralizing the Global Society," *The Futurist*, 1 January 2004 [accessed 24 April 2004] www.highbeam.com.
8. (Too Many Workers? Not for Long) Adapted from John S. McClenahen, "The Next Crisis: Two Few Workers," *IndustryWeek*, May 2003, 41–45; Ken Dychtwald, Tamara Erickson, and Bob Morison, "It's Time to Retire Retirement," *Harvard Business Review*, March 2004, 48–57; Paul Kaihla, "The Coming Job Boom," *Business 2.0*, September 2003, 97–105; Stephanie Armour, "More Moms Make Kids Their Career of Choice," *USA Today*, 12 March 2002, 1B; Aaron Bernstein, "Too Many Workers? Not for Long," *BusinessWeek*, 20 May 2002, 126–130; Steven A. Nyce and Sylvester J. Schieber, "The Decade of the Employee: The Workforce in the Coming Decade," *Benefits Quarterly*, First Quarter 2002, 60–79; Paul Gores, "Economist Calls Recession Mild, Predicts Labor Shortage Will Return," *Knight Ridder Tribune Business News*, 10 February 2002; Nancy Pounds, "Nation Expert Sees Skilled Worker Need Despite Recent Layoffs," *Alaska Journal of Commerce*, 28 October 2001, 19.
9. (Chuckle While You Work) Adapted from Tim Larimer, "Having Any Fun?" *Time*, November 2003; Harvey Meyer, "Fun for Everyone," *Journal of Business Strategy*, March–April 1999, 13–17; Erika Rasmusson, "A Funny Thing Happened on the Way to Work," *Sales and Marketing Management*, March 1999, 97–98; Peter Baker, "Work: Have Fun. And That's An Order," *The Observer*, 3 January 1999, 11+; Melanie Payne, "Chuckle While You Work," *San Diego Union-Tribune*, 19 October 1998, E1–E2; Maggie Jackson, "Corporate America Lightens Up: Laughing Workers Are Happy Workers," *The Salt Lake Tribune*, 4 May 1997,

E1; Diane E. Lewis, "Employers Find Humor Can Improve Morale, Profits," *Boston Globe*, 1 April 1997, C5; R. J. King, "Here's a Laugh: Speaker Shows How Office Humor Helps," *Detroit News*, 15 February 1996, B3; Katy Robinson, "Use Laughter to Brighten Your Office," *Idaho Statesman*, 18 October 1995, 1.
10. (Business Buzz) Adapted from Wordspy.com [accessed 25 April 2004] www.wordspy.com.

Chapter 10
1. Exhibit 10.1, Adapted from Henry R. Cheeseman, *Contemporary Business and E-Commerce Law*, 4th ed. (Upper Saddle River, N.J.: Prentice Hall, 2003), 628–631.
2. Exhibit 10.4, Monster.com [accessed 1 August 2004], www.monster.com.
3. Exhibit 10.6, "Checking Out New Hires," *USA Today Snapshot*, 18 May 2000, B1.
4. (Learning from Business Blunders) Adapted from Steven Greenhouse, "Workers Assail Night Lock-Ins by Wal-Mart," *New York Times*, 18 January 2004, 1, 23; Steven Greenhouse, "Wal-Mart Raids by U.S. Aimed at Illegal Aliens," *New York Times*, 24 October 2003, A1, A19; Jeffrey E. Garten, "Wal-Mart Gives Globalism a Bad Name," *BusinessWeek*, 8 March 2004, 24; "Wal-Mart Suit Gets Class-Action Status in Massachusetts," *Wall Street Journal*, 19 January 2004, A2.
5. (Technologies That Are Revolutionizing Business) Adapted from IBM Accessibility Center [accessed 30 April 2004] www-3.ibm.com/able; AssistiveTech.net [accessed 30 April 2004] www.assistivetech.net, Business Leadership Network website [accessed 30 April 2004] www.usblin.com; National Institute on Disability and Rehabilitation Research website [accessed 30 April 2004] www.ed.gov/about/offices/list/osers/nidrr; Rehabilitation Engineering and Assistive Technology Society of North America website [accessed 30 April 2004] www.resna.org.
6. (Click and Learn: E-Training Today's Employees) Adapted from Joe Mullich, "A Second Act for E-Learning," *Workforce Management*, February 2004, 51–55; Gail Johnson, "Brewing the Perfect Blend," *Training*, December 2003, 30+; Michael A. Verespej, "Click and Learn," *Industry Week*, 15 January 2001, 31–36; Elisabeth Goodridge, "Slowing Economy Sparks Boom in E-Learning," 12 November 2001, 100–104; Cynthia Pantazis, "Maximizing E-Learning to Train the 21st Century Workforce," *Public Personnel Management*, Spring 2002, 21–26; Mary Lord, "They're Online and on the Job," *U.S. News & World Report*, 15 October 2001, 72–78.
7. (Should Employees Pay to Keep Their Jobs?) Adapted from Dean Foust, Michelle Conlin, Peter Burrows, and Roger O. Crockett, "A Smarter Squeeze?"

BusinessWeek, 31 December 2001, 42–44; Daniel Eisenberg, "Paying to Keep Your Job," *Time*, 15 October 2001, 80–84; Stephanie Armour, "Workers Take Pay Cuts over Pink Slips," *USA Today*, 13 April 2001, 1B; Carole Bula, "Your Bagel or Your Job," *Time*, 12 February 2001, 68; Stephanie Armour, "Companies Get Creative to Avoid Layoffs," *USA Today*, 5 September 2001, 1B.
8. (Business Buzz) Adapted from Wordspy.com [accessed 30 April 2004] www.wordspy.com.

Chapter 11
1. Exhibit 11.1, Gary Armstrong and Philip Kotler, *Marketing: An Introduction*, 5th ed. (Upper Saddle River, N.J.: Prentice Hall, 2000), 5 (Figure 1.1—Core marketing concepts).
2. Exhibit 11.5, Gary Armstrong and Philip Kotler, *Marketing: An Introduction*, 5th ed. (Upper Saddle River, N.J.: Prentice Hall, 2000), 201.
3. (Learning from Business Blunders) Adapted from Pamela Paul, "It's Mind Vending," *Time*, 15 September 2003; Hallmark website [accessed 4 May 2004] www.hallmark.com; "Every Day, 10,000 Baby Boomers Turn 50; Nobody Said Getting Old Would Be Easy," *Seattle Post-Intelligencer*, 27 March 1997 [accessed 4 May 2004] www.highbeam.com.
4. (Technologies That Are Revolutionizing Business) Adapted from TechEncyclopedia, TechWeb.com [accessed 4 May 2004] www.techweb.com; Ganesh Variar, "Only the Best Survive: The Combination of Integration and BI Were the Standouts of the 2003 IT Landscape," *Intelligent Enterprise*, January 2004 [accessed 4 May 2004] www.highbeam.com; Angoss website [accessed 4 May 2004] www.angoss.com.
5. (Your Right to Privacy Versus the Marketing Databases) Adapted from Linda Stern, "Is Orwell Your Banker?" *Newsweek*, 8 April 2002, 59; Mike France and Heather Green, "Privacy in an Age of Terror," *BusinessWeek*, 5 November 2001, 83–87; Amy Harmon, "F.T.C. to Propose Laws to Protect Children Online," *New York Times*, 4 June 1998, C1, C6; Andrew L. Shapiro, "Privacy for Sale," *The Nation*, 23 June 1997, 11–16; Bruce Horovitz, "Marketers Tap Data We Once Called Our Own," *USA Today*, 19 December 1995, 1A–2A; Stephen Baker, "Europe's Privacy Cops," *BusinessWeek*, 2 November 1998, 49, 51.
6. (Questionable Marketing Tactics on Campus) Adapted from Kimberly E. Mock, "Good Credit Skills Are Essential for Georgia's College Students," *Athens Banner-Herald*, 23 February 2004 [accessed 4 May 2004] www.highbeam.com; Charles Haddad, "Congratulations, Grads—You're Bankrupt," *BusinessWeek*, 21 May 2001, 48; Christine Dugas, "Colleges Target Card Solicitors,"

USA Today, 12 March 1999, B1; Lisa Toloken, "Turning the Tables on Campus," *Credit Card Management*, May 1999, 76–79; "Credit Cards Given to College Students a Marketing Issue," *Marketing News*, 27 September 1999, 38.
7. (Business Buzz) Adapted from Wordspy.com [accessed 3 May 2004] www.wordspy.com.

Chapter 12
1. Exhibit 12.2, Adapted from Philip Kotler, *Marketing Management*, 10th ed. (Upper Saddle River, N.J.: Prentice Hall, 2000), 491.
2. (Technologies That Are Revolutionizing Business) Adapted from "Nick Gillespie Discusses the Personalized Cover of Reason Magazine and the Possibilities of Database Technology" (interview), Talk of the Nation, National Public Radio, 4 May 2003 [accessed 6 May 2004] www.highbeam.com; Kevin J. Delaney, "Will Users Care if Gmail Invades Privacy?" *Wall Street Journal*, 6 April 2004, B1, B3; Allison Fass, "Spot On," *Forbes*, 23 June 2003, 140; "Hey You! How About Lunch?" *Wall Street Journal*, 1 April 2004, B1, B5.
3. (Learning from Business Blunders) Adapted from Evite website [accessed 6 May 2004] www.evite.com; "Desktop," *Rocky Mountain News* (Denver), 1 September 2003 [accessed 6 May 2004] www.highbeam.com; Adam Horowitz, Mark Athitakis, Mark Lasswell, and Owen Thomas, "The 101 Dumbest Moments in Business," *Business 2.0* [accessed 6 May 2004] www.business2.com.
4. (Where Did the Audience Go?) Adapted from Mike Drexler, "Media Midlife Crisis: The Changes are Monumental," *Adweek,* 9 February 2004 [accessed 6 May 2004] www.highbeam.com; Kevin J. Delaney and Robert A. Guth, "Beep. Foosh. Buy Me. Pow." *Wall Street Journal*, 8 April 2004, B1, B7; Stuart Elliot, "Advertising," *New York Times*, 14 April 2004, C8; Melanie Wells, "Kid Nabbing," *Forbes,* 2 February 2004, 84–88; Kimberly Palmer, "Highway Ads Take High-Tech Turn," *Wall Street Journal,* 13 September 2003, B5; Brian Hindo, "Ad Space," *BusinessWeek*, 12 January 2004, 14; Ellen Neuborne, "Dude, Where My Ad?" *Inc.,* April 2004, 56–57; Erin White, "Look Up for New Products in Aisle 5," *Wall Street Journal,* 23 March 2004, B11; Ronald Grover, "Can Mad Ave. Make Zap-Proof Ads?" *BusinessWeek*, 2 February 2004, 36; Mathew Boyle, "Brand Killers," *Fortune*, 88–100.
5. (Business Buzz) Adapted from " 'Phishing' Scams Shooting Up," CNN.com, 6 May 2004 [accessed 6 May 2004] www.cnn.com.

Chapter 13
1. Exhibit 13.1, Adapted from Gary Siegel and Bud Kulesza, "The Practice of Management Accounting," *Management Accounting*, April 1996, 20; "Up the Ladder of

Success," *Journal of Accountancy*, November 2000, 24.
2. (Technologies That Are Revolutionizing Business) Adapted from Dennis Callaghan, "Sarbanes-Oxley: Road to Compliance," *eWeek*, 16 February 2004 [accessed 8 May 2004] www.eweek.com; Ellen Florian, "Can Tech Untangle Sarbanes-Oxley?" *Fortune*, 29 September 2003, 125–128; Thomas Hoffman, "Big Companies Turn to Packaged Sarb-Ox Apps," *Computerworld*, 1 March 2004 [accessed 8 May 2004] www.computerworld.com.
3. (Learning from Business Blunders) Adapted from Adam Horowitz, Mark Athitakis, Mark Lasswell, and Owen Thomas, "The 101 Dumbest Moments in Business," *Business 2.0* [accessed 3 August 2004] www.business2.com.
4. (Putting Accountability Back into Public Accounting) Adapted from Daren Fonda, "Revenge of the Bean Counters," *Time*, 29 March 2004, 38–39; Greg Farrell and Andrew Backover, "Stage Is Set for Auditors, Management to Clash," *USA Today*, 20 February 2003 [accessed 9 May 2004] www.highbeam.com; Thomas A. Fogarty, "Accounting Oversight Agency Targets Abusive Tax Shelters," *USA Today*, 21 November 2003, 3B; Janice Revell, "The Fires That Won't Go Out," *Fortune*, 13 October 2003, 139–142; Jeremy Kahn, "Do Accountants Have a Future?" *Fortune*, 3 March 2003, 115–116; David Henry and Mike McNamee, "Bloodied and Bowed," *BusinessWeek*, 20 January 2003, 56–57; Thaddeus Herrick and Alexei Barrionuevo, "Were Auditor and Client Too Close-Knit?" *Wall Street Journal*, 21 January 2002, C1, C5; Jeremy Kahn, "One Plus One Makes What?" *Fortune*, 7 January 2002, 88–90; Nanette Byrnes, "Auditing Here, Consulting over There," *BusinessWeek*, 8 April 2002, 34–36; Nanette Byrnes, "Accounting in Crisis," *BusinessWeek*, 28 January 2002; 42–48; Ken Brown, "Auditors' Methods Make It Hard to Catch Fraud by Executives," *Wall Street Journal*, 8 July 2002, C1, C16.
5. (How to Read an Annual Report) Adapted from Manual Schiffres, "All the Good News That Fits," *U.S. News and World Report*, 14 April 1998, 50–51; Janice Revell, "Annual Reports Decided," *Fortune*, 25 June 2001, 176; "The P&L: Your Score Card of Profitability," *The Edward Lowe Report*, August 2001, 1–3.

Chapter 14
1. Exhibit 14.2, Fred Vogelstein, "A Virtual Stock Market," *U.S. News and World Report*, 26 April 1999, 47–48; Exhibit is on page 48— Robert Kemp U.S. News & World Report
2. Exhibit 14.6, "How to Read the Monthly Performance Tables," *Wall Street Journal*, 5 June 2000, R2.

3. Exhibit 14.7, Richard Korman, "Mining for Nuggets of Financial Data," *New York Times*, 21 June 1998, BU5.

4. Exhibit 14.8, Amy Feldman, "The Seedy World of Online Stock Scams," *Money*, February 2000, 143–148.

5. (Technologies That Are Revolutionizing Business) Adapted from "Fair Isaac Launches Strategy Science Institute; First Educational Forum Spurs Client Empowerment in Applying Advanced Analytics to Improve Critical Business Decisions," *Business Wire* [accessed 10 May 2004] www.highbeam.com; Fair Isaac website [accessed 10 May 2004] www.fairisaac.com; "Idea Bank," *Orlando Sentinel*, 5 August 2002 [accessed 10 May 2004] www.highbeam.com.

6. (Learning from Business Blunders) Adapted from Peter Carbonara, "The Scam That Will Not Die," *Business Credit*, 1 July 2003 [accessed 10 May 2004] www.high-beam.com; "Profile: Recent Confidence Scams from Nigeria Have Their Roots in Depression-Era Scam That Targeted the Midwest," All Things Considered, National Public Radio, 29 July 2002 [accessed 10 May 2004] www.highbeam.com; Jim Stratton, "Notorious E-Mail Scam Snares Savings of Volusia, Fla., Retiree," *Orlando Sentinel*, 23 December 2003 [accessed 10 May 2004] www.highbeam.com.

7. (Surprise! You've Been Swiped) Adapted from Walt Bogdanich, "Criminals Focus on ATMs, Weak Link in Banking System," *New York Times*, 3 August 2003, 1, 22; Richard Burnett, "Florida Warns of Credit Card Fraud at Gasoline Pumps," *Orlando Sentinel*, 26 January 2004 [accessed 10 May 2004] www.highbeam.com; Tom Lowry, "Thieves Swipe Credit with Card Readers," *USA Today*, 28 June 1999, 1B; Elaine Shannon, "A New Credit-Card Scam," *Time*, 5 June 2000, 54–55; Linda Punch, "Card Fraud: Down but Not Out," *Credit Card Management*, June 1999, 30–42; Bill Orr, "Will E-Commerce Reverse Card Fraud Trend?" *American Bankers Association*, April 2000, 59–62.

8. (Business Buzz) Adapted from Investopedia.com [accessed 10 May 2004] www.investopedia.com.

Appendix B

1. Exhibit B.1, Adapted from Bartley A. Brennan and Nancy Kubasek, *The Legal Environment of Business* (New York: Macmillan, 1988), 24; Douglas Whitman and John Gergacz, *The Legal Environment of Business*, 2d ed. (New York: Random House, 1988), 22, 25.

2. Exhibit B.3, Adapted from Richard A. Brealely and Stewart C. Myers, *Principles of Corporate Finance*, 4th ed. (New York: McGraw-Hill, 1991), 761–765.

3. Exhibit B.4, Adapted from BankruptcyData.Com [accessed 16 May 2004] www.bankruptcydata.com.

Appendix C

1. Exhibit C.6, Adapted from Lawrence J. Gitman and Michael D. Joehnk, *Personal Financial Planning*, 10th ed. (Mason, Ohio: Thomson South-Western, 2005), 139–143; Jack R. Kapoor, Les R. Dlabay, and Robert J. Hughes, *Personal Finance*, 7th ed. (New York: McGraw-Hill/Irwin, 2004), 141; Arthur J. Keown, *Personal Finance: Turning Money into Wealth*, 3d ed. (Upper Saddle River, N.J.: Prentice Hall, 2003), 150.

Appendix E

1. Exhibit E.1, Adapted from Daniel E. Hecker, "Occupational Employment Projections to 2012," *Monthly Labor Review*, February 2004, 80–105.

2. Exhibit E.7, Adapted from Marilyn Sherman, "Questions R Us: What to Ask at a Job Interview," *Career World*, January 2004, 20; H. Lee Rust, *Job Search: The Complete Manual for Jobseekers* (New York: American Management Association, 1979), 56.

Photo Credits

Chapter 1

1	AP/Wide World Photos
2, 22	AP/Wide World Photos
3	AP/Wide World Photos
9	AP/Wide World Photos
13	Erik Freeland/Corbis/SABA Press Photos, Inc.
14	AP/Wide World Photos

Appendix A

29	Amazon
32	Chris Stewart/Black Star

Chapter 2

38	Steve Cole/Getty Images, Inc.—Photodisc
39, 58	Pictor/ImageState/International Stock Photography, Ltd.
42	AP Wide World Photos
50	Jeff Christensen/Reuters/Land Ladov LLC
52	Calvin Larsen/Photo Researchers, Inc.
52	Basel Action Network (BAN)
53	Mark Graham
54	Getty Images, Inc.—Liaison

Chapter 3

63	AP Wide World Photos
64, 83	Kraipit Phahvut/SIPA Press
68	Corbis NY
72	Michel Poro/Getty Images, Inc.—Liaison
73	Horacio Paone/New York Times Pictures
78	AP Wide World Photos

81	Mehdi Fedouach/AFP/Getty Images, Inc.—Liaison

Chapter 4

90	The Image Works
91, 108	Dan Lamont Photography
96	AP Wide World Photos
97	Jodi L. Jacobson
97	Giboux/Getty Images, Inc.—Liaison
100	Gary I. Rothstein/Corbis/Sygma
103	AP Wide World Photos

Chapter 5

113	Masterfile Corporation
114, 132	Jim Whitmer Photography
115	Philip Saltonstall
118	T. Michael Keza Photography
124	Subway Restaurants/DAI
126	Corbis/Bettmann
127	T. Michael Keza Photography
131	Richard Howard Photography

Chapter 6

140	Masterfile Corporation
141, 160	Suomen Kuvapalveluoy/Corbis/Sygma
142	Peter Endig/DPA/Landov LLC
146	AP Wide World Photos
149	AP Wide World Photos
156	William Mercer McLeod

Chapter 7

165	John Henley/Corbis/Bettmann
166, 186	AP Wide World Photos
175	Rob Crandall/Stock Boston
177	AP Wide World Photos
182	Andy Freeberg Photography
184	Masterfile Corporation

Chapter 8

191	Peter Arnold, Inc.
192, 213	Butler Photography
195	Jeff Morgan/Alamy Images
196	Martyn Goddard/Corbis/Bettmann
198	Jonathan Atkin
199	Corbis/Bettmann
206	Leslie Garland Picture Library/Alamy Images
207	Corbis/Bettmann
211	Jim West

Chapter 9

220	Alamy Images
221, 243	Atlas Container Corporation
223	Corbis NY
230	John Kringas/The Chicago Tribune
233	AP Wide World Photos
236	Nancy Pierce/New York Times Pictures
241	Corbis NY

Chapter 10

248	Corbis NY
249, 269	Michael Newman/PhotoEdit

Glossary

absolute advantage A nation's ability to produce a particular product with fewer resources per unit of output than any other nation

accountability Obligation to report results to supervisors or team members and to justify outcomes that fall below expectations

accounting Measuring, interpreting, and communicating financial information to support internal and external decision making

accounting equation Basic accounting equation that assets equals liabilities plus owners' equity

accounts receivable turnover ratio Measure of time a company takes to turn its accounts receivable into cash, calculated by dividing sales by the average value of accounts receivable for a period

accrual basis Accounting method in which revenue is recorded when a sale is made and expense is recorded when it is incurred

acquisition Form of business combination in which one company buys another company's voting stock

activity ratios Ratios that measure the effectiveness of the firm's use of its resources

administrative skills Technical skills in information gathering, data analysis, planning, organizing, and other aspects of managerial work

advertising Paid, nonpersonal communication to a target market from an identified sponsor using mass communications channels

affirmative action Activities undertaken by businesses to recruit and promote women and minorities, based on an analysis of the workforce and the available labor pool

analytic system Production process that breaks incoming materials into various component products and divisional patterns simultaneously

arbitration Process for resolving a labor-contract dispute in which an impartial third party studies the issues and makes a binding decision

assets Any things of value owned or leased by a business

attrition Loss of employees for reasons other than termination

auction exchange Centralized marketplace where securities are traded by specialists on behalf of investors

audit Formal evaluation of the fairness and reliability of a client's financial statements

authority Power granted by the organization to make decisions, take actions, and allocate resources to accomplish goals

authorized stock Maximum number of ownership shares into which a corporation's board of directors decides the business can be divided

autocratic leaders Leaders who do not involve others in decision making

automated teller machines (ATMs) Electronic terminals that permit people to perform basic banking transactions 24 hours a day without a human teller

balance of payments Sum of all payments one nation receives from other nations minus the sum of all payments it makes to other nations, over some specified period of time

balance of trade Total value of the products a nation exports minus the total value of the products it imports, over some period of time

balance sheet Statement of a firm's financial position on a particular date; also known as a statement of financial position

barriers to entry Factors that make it difficult to launch a business in a particular industry economics

bear market Falling stock market

behavior modification Systematic use of rewards and punishments to change human behavior

behavioral segmentation Categorization of customers according to their relationship with products or response to product characteristics

blogs Web-based journals, usually presented by a single writer and updated frequently

board of directors Group of people, elected by the shareholders, who have the ultimate authority in guiding the affairs of a corporation

bond Method of funding in which the issuer borrows from an investor and provides a written promise to make regular interest payments and repay the borrowed amount in the future

bonus Cash payment, in addition to the regular wage or salary, that serves as a reward for achievement

bookkeeping Record keeping, clerical aspect of accounting

bookmark A browser feature that places selected URLs in a file for quick access, allowing you to automatically return to the website by clicking on the site's name

Boolean operators The term Boolean refers to a system of logical thought developed by the English mathematician George Boole; it uses the operators AND, OR, and NOT

boycott Union activity in which members and sympathizers refuse to buy or handle the product of a target company

brand A name, term, sign, symbol, design, or combination of these used to identify the products of a firm and to differentiate them from competing products

brand mark Portion of a brand that cannot be expressed verbally

brand names Portion of a brand that can be expressed orally, including letters, words, or numbers

broadband Exact definitions vary, but generally, broadband refers to any method of Internet access that offers higher speeds than dial-up

broker An expert who has passed specific tests and is registered to trade securities for investors

browser Software, such as Microsoft's Internet Explorer or Netscape Navigator, that enables a computer to search for, display, and download the multimedia information that appears on the World Wide Web

budget Planning and control tool that reflects expected revenues, operating expenses, and cash receipts and outlays

bull market Rising stock market

business A profit-seeking activity that provides goods and services that a society wants or needs

business cycle Fluctuations in the rate of growth that an economy experiences over a period of several years

business plan A written document that provides an orderly statement of a company's goals and a plan for achieving those goals

business-to-business e-commerce Electronic commerce that involves transactions between companies and their suppliers, manufacturers, or other companies

business-to-consumer e-commerce Electronic commerce that involves transactions between businesses and the end user or consumer

calendar year Twelve-month accounting period that begins on January 1 and ends on December 31

capacity planning A long-term strategic decision that determines the level of resources available to an organization to meet customer demand

capital budgeting Process for evaluating proposed investments in select projects that provide the best long-term financial return

capital gains Return that investors receive when they sell a security for a higher price than the purchase price

capital investments Money paid to acquire something of permanent value in a business

capital The physical, human-made elements used to produce goods and services, such as factories and computers; can also refer to the funds that finance the operations of a business

capital-intensive businesses Businesses that require large investments in capital assets

capitalism Economic system based on economic freedom and competition

cash basis Accounting method in which revenue is recorded when payment is received and expense is recorded when cash is paid

cause-related marketing Identification and marketing of a social issue, cause, or idea to selected target markets

cellular layout Method of arranging a facility so that parts with similar shapes or processing requirements are processed together in work centers

centralization Concentration of decision-making authority at the top of the organization

certificate Document that proves stock ownership

certified management accountants (CMAs) Accountants who have fulfilled the requirements for certification as specialists in management accounting

certified public accountants (CPAs) Professionally licensed accountants who meet certain requirements for education and experience and who pass a comprehensive examination

chain of command Pathway for the flow of authority from one management level to the next

chat A form of interactive communication that enables computer users in separate locations to have real-time conversations. Usually takes place at websites called chat rooms

checks Written orders that tell the user's bank to pay a specific amount to a particular individual or business

chief executive officer (CEO) Person appointed by a corporation's board of directors to carry out the board's policies and supervise the activities of the corporation

close the books The act of transferring net revenue and expense account balances to retained earnings for the period

coaching Helping employees reach their highest potential by meeting with them, discussing problems that hinder their ability to work effectively, and offering suggestions and encouragement to overcome these problems

co-branding Partnership between two or more companies to closely link their brand names together for a single product

code of ethics Written statement setting forth the principles that guide an organization's decisions

cognitive dissonance Tension that exists when a person's beliefs don't match his or her behaviors; a common example is buyer's remorse, when someone regrets a purchase immediately after making it

cohesiveness A measure of how committed the team members are to their team's goals

collective bargaining Process used by unions and management to negotiate work contracts

commissions Payments to employees equal to a certain percentage of sales made

committee Team that may become a permanent part of the organization and is designed to deal with regularly recurring tasks

common stock Shares whose owners have voting rights and have the last claim on distributed profits and assets

communism Economic system in which the government owns and operates all productive resources and determines all significant economic choices

comparative advantage theory Theory that states that a country should produce and sell to other countries those items it produces most efficiently

compensation Money, benefits, and services paid to employees for their work

competition Rivalry among businesses for the same customer

competitive advantage Ability to perform in one or more ways that competitors cannot match

computer-aided design (CAD) Use of computer graphics and mathematical modeling in the development of products

computer-aided engineering (CAE) Use of computers to test products without building an actual model

computer-aided manufacturing (CAM) Use of computers to control production equipment

computer-integrated manufacturing (CIM) Computer-based systems, including CAD and CAM, that coordinate and control all the elements of design and production

conceptual skills Ability to understand the relationship of parts to the whole

conflict of interest Situation in which a business decision may be influenced by the potential for personal gain

consolidation Combination of two or more companies in which the old companies cease to exist and a new enterprise is created

consumer price index (CPI) Monthly statistic that measures changes in the prices of about 400 goods and services that consumers buy

consumer promotion Sales promotion aimed at final consumers

consumerism Movement that pressures businesses to consider consumer needs and interests

consumer-to-consumer e-commerce Electronic commerce that involves transactions between consumers

contingency leadership Adapting the leadership style to what is most appropriate, given current business conditions

controller Highest-ranking accountant in a company, responsible for overseeing all accounting functions

controlling Process of measuring progress against goals and objectives and correcting deviations if results are not as expected

convertible bonds Corporate bonds that can be exchanged at the owner's discretion into common stock of the issuing company

cooperative advertising Joint efforts between local and national advertisers, in which producers of nationally sold products share the costs of local advertising with local merchants and wholesalers

corporate culture A set of shared values and norms that support the management system and that guide management and employee behavior

corporation Legally chartered enterprise having most of the legal rights of a person, including the right to conduct business, to own and sell property, to borrow money, and to sue or be sued; owners of the corporation enjoy limited liability

cost accounting Area of accounting focusing on the calculation of manufacturing and storage costs of products for use or sale in a business

cost of goods sold Cost of producing or acquiring a company's products for sale during a given period

coupons Certificates that offer discounts on particular items and are redeemed at the time of purchase

cracking Entering a computer network for nondestructive reasons, such as to play a prank

credit cards Plastic cards that allow the user to buy now and repay the loaned amount at a future date

crisis management System for minimizing the harm that might result from some unusually threatening situations

critical path In a PERT network diagram, the sequence of operations that requires the longest time to complete

cross-functional teams Teams that draw together employees from different functional areas

cross-promotion Jointly advertising two or more noncompeting brands

currency Bills and coins that make up a country's cash money

current assets Cash and items that can be turned into cash within one year

current liabilities Obligations that must be met within a year

current ratio Measure of a firm's short-term liquidity, calculated by dividing current assets by current liabilities

customer divisions Divisional structure that focuses on customers or clients

customer relationship management (CRM) Computer systems designed to collect information and coordinate activities related to a company's interactions with each of its customers

customer service Efforts a company makes to satisfy its customers to help them realize the greatest possible value from the products they are purchasing

customized production Production of individual goods and services for individual customers

cyberterrorism Orchestrated attacks on a company's information systems for political or economic purposes

data Recorded facts and statistics; data need to be converted to information before they can help people solve business problems

database marketing Process of building, maintaining, and using customer databases for the purpose of contacting customers and transacting business

day order Any order to buy or sell a security that automatically expires if not executed on the day the order is placed

dealer exchanges Decentralized marketplaces where securities are bought and sold by dealers out of their own inventories

debentures Corporate bonds backed only by the reputation of the issuer

debit cards Plastic cards that allow the bank to take money from the user's demand-deposit account and transfer it to a retailer's account

debt ratios Ratios that measure a firm's reliance on debt financing of its operations (sometimes called leverage ratios)

debt-to-equity ratio Measure of the extent to which a business is financed by debt as opposed to invested capital, calculated by dividing the company's total liabilities by owners' equity

debt-to-total-assets ratio Measure of a firm's ability to carry long-term debt, calculated by dividing total liabilities by total assets

decentralization Delegation of decision-making authority to employees in lower-level positions

decision making Process of identifying a decision situation, analyzing the problem, weighing the alternatives, choosing an alternative and implementing it, and evaluating the results

deflation Economic condition in which prices fall steadily throughout the economy

delegation Assignment of work and the authority and responsibility required to complete it

demand Buyers' willingness and ability to purchase products

demand deposit Money that can be used by the customer at any time, such as checking accounts

democratic leaders Leaders who delegate authority and involve employees in decision making

demographics Study of statistical characteristics of a population

departmentalization Grouping people within an organization according to function, division, matrix, or network

depreciation Accounting procedure for systematically spreading the cost of a tangible asset over its estimated useful life

digital subscriber line (DSL) High-speed phone line that carries both voice and data

direct mail Advertising sent directly to potential customers, usually through the U.S. Postal Service

direct marketing Direct communication other than personal sales contacts designed to effect a measurable response

discount pricing Offering a reduction in price

discount rate Interest rate the Federal Reserve charges on loans to commercial banks

discretionary order Market order that allows the broker to decide when to trade a security

discrimination In a social and economic sense, denial of opportunities to individuals on the basis of some characteristic that has no bearing on their ability to perform in a job

discussion mailing lists E-mail lists that allow people to discuss a common interest by posting messages, which are received by everyone in the group

dispatching Issuing work orders and schedules to department heads and supervisors

distribution centers Warehouse facilities that specialize in collecting and shipping merchandise

distribution channels Systems for moving goods and services from producers to customers; also known as marketing channels

distribution mix Combination of intermediaries and channels a producer uses to get a product to end users

distribution strategy Firm's overall plan for moving products to intermediaries and final customers

diversity initiatives Company policies designed to enhance opportunities for minorities and to promote understanding of diverse cultures, customs, and talents

dividends Distributions of corporate assets to shareholders in the form of cash or other assets

divisional structure Grouping departments according to similarities in product, process, customer, or geography

domain name The portion of an Internet address that identifies the host and indicates the type of organization it is

double-entry bookkeeping Way of recording financial transactions that requires two entries for every transaction so that the accounting equation is always kept in balance

download Transmitting a file from one computer system to another; on the Internet, bringing data from the Internet into your computer

dumping Charging less than the actual cost or less than the home-country price for goods sold in other countries

earnings per share Measure of a firm's profitability for each share of outstanding stock, calculated by dividing net income after taxes by the average number of shares of common stock

ecology Study of the relationships among living things in the water, air, and soil, their environments, and the nutrients that support them

economic indicators Statistics that measure variables in the economy

economic system Means by which a society distributes its resources to satisfy its people's needs

economics The study of how society uses scarce resources to produce and distribute goods and services

economies of scale Savings from manufacturing, marketing, or buying in large quantities

electronic business (e-business) A company that has transformed its key business processes to incorporate Internet technology into every phase of the operation

electronic commerce (e-commerce) The general term for the buying and selling of goods and services on the Internet

electronic communication networks (ECNs) Internet-based networks that match up buy and sell orders without using a middleman

electronic data interchange (EDI) Use of information systems that transmit documents such as invoices and purchase orders between computers, thereby lowering ordering costs and paperwork

electronic funds transfer systems (EFTS) Computerized systems for completing financial transactions

electronic performance monitoring (EPM) Real-time, computer-based evaluation of employee performance

e-mail Communication system that enables computers to transmit and receive written messages over electronic networks

embargo Total ban on trade with a particular nation (a sanction) or of a particular product

employee assistance programs (EAPs) Company-sponsored counseling or referral plans for employees with personal problems

employee benefits Compensation other than wages, salaries, and incentive programs

employee retention Efforts to keep current employees

employee stock-ownership plan (ESOP) Program enabling employees to become partial owners of a company

enterprise resource planning (ERP) A comprehensive database system that expands beyond the production function to include other groups such as sales and accounting

entrepreneurs Businesspeople who create and run new businesses and accept the risks involved in the private enterprise system

equilibrium price Point at which quantity supplied equals quantity demanded

equity theory A theory that suggests employees base their level of satisfaction on the ratio of their inputs to the job and the outputs or rewards they receive from it

ethical dilemma Situation in which both sides of an issue can be supported with valid arguments

ethical lapse Situation in which an individual makes a decision that is morally wrong, illegal, or unethical

ethics The rules or standards governing the conduct of a person or group

euro A unified currency used by most nations in the European Union

exchange process Act of obtaining a desired object from another party by offering something of value in return

exchange rate Rate at which the money of one country is traded for the money of another

exclusive distribution Market coverage strategy that gives intermediaries exclusive rights to sell a product in a specific geographical area

expectancy theory Suggests that the effort employees put into their work depends on expectations about their own ability to perform, expectations about the rewards that the organization will give in response to that performance, and the attractiveness of those rewards relative to their individual goals

expenses Costs created in the process of generating revenues

exporting Selling and shipping goods or services to another country

external auditors Independent accounting firms that provide auditing servicing for public companies

extranet Similar to an intranet but extending the network to select people outside the organization

factors of production Basic inputs that a society uses to produce goods and services, including natural resources, labor, capital, entrepreneurship, and knowledge

file transfer protocol (FTP) A software protocol that lets you copy or move files from a remote computer—called an FTP site—to your computer over the Internet; it is the Internet facility for downloading and uploading files

financial accounting Area of accounting concerned with preparing financial information for users outside the organization

financial analysis Process of evaluating a company's performance and analyzing the costs and benefits of a strategic action

financial control The process of analyzing and adjusting the basic financial plan to correct for forecasted events that do not materialize

financial management Effective acquisition and use of money

financial plan A forecast of financial requirements and the financing sources to be used

firewall Computer hardware and software that protects part or all of a private computer network attached to the Internet by preventing public Internet users from accessing it

first-line managers Those at the lowest level of the management hierarchy; they supervise the operating employees and implement the plans set at the higher management levels; also called supervisory managers

fiscal policy Use of government revenue collection and spending to influence the business cycle

fiscal year Any 12 consecutive months used as an accounting period

fixed assets Assets retained for long-term use, such as land, buildings, machinery, and equipment; also referred to as property, plant, and equipment

fixed-position layout Method of arranging a facility so that the product is stationary and equipment and personnel come to it

flat organizations Organizations with a wide span of management and few hierarchical levels

flexible manufacturing system (FMS) Production system using computer-controlled machines that can adapt to various versions of the same operation

flextime Scheduling system in which employees are allowed certain options regarding time of arrival and departure

foreign direct investment (FDI) Investment of money by foreign companies in domestic business enterprises

form utility Consumer value created by converting raw materials and other inputs into finished goods and services

formal organization A framework officially established by managers for accomplishing tasks that lead to achieving the organization's goals

franchise Business arrangement in which a small business obtains rights to sell the goods or services of the supplier (franchisor)

franchisee Small-business owner who contracts for the right to sell goods or services of the supplier (franchisor) in exchange for some payment

franchisor Supplier that grants a franchise to an individual or group (franchisee) in exchange for payments

free riders Team members who do not contribute sufficiently to the group's activities because members are not being held individually accountable for their work

free trade International trade unencumbered by restrictive measures

free-market system Economic system in which decisions about what to produce and in what quantities are decided by the market's buyers and sellers

functional structure Grouping workers according to their similar skills, resource use, and expertise

functional teams Teams whose members come from a single functional department and that are based on the organization's vertical structure

Gantt chart Bar chart used to control schedules by showing how long each part of a production process should take and when it should take place

general expenses Operating expenses, such as office and administrative expenses, not directly associated with creating or marketing a good or a service

general obligation bond Municipal bond that is backed by the government's authority to collect taxes

general partnership Partnership in which all partners have the right to participate as co-owners and are individually liable for the business's debts

generally accepted accounting principles (GAAP) Professionally approved U.S. standards and practices used by accountants in the preparation of financial statements

generic products Products characterized by a plain label, with no advertising and no brand name

geodemographics Method of combining geographical data with demographic data to develop profiles of neighborhood segments

geographic divisions Divisional structure based on location of operations

geographic segmentation Categorization of customers according to their geographical location

glass ceiling Invisible barrier attributable to subtle discrimination that keeps women out of the top positions in business

globalization Tendency of the world's economies to act as a single interdependent economy

goal Broad, long-range target or aim

goal-setting theory Motivational theory suggesting that setting goals can be an effective way to motivate employees

goods-producing businesses Businesses that produce tangible products

gross domestic product (GDP) Value of all the final goods and services produced by businesses located within a nation's borders; excludes receipts from overseas operations of domestic companies

gross national product (GNP) Value of all the final goods and services produced by domestic businesses that includes receipts from overseas operations and excludes receipts from foreign-owned businesses within a nation's borders

gross profit Amount remaining when the cost of goods sold is deducted from net sales; also known as gross margin

hacking Breaking into a computer network to steal, delete, or change data

holding company Company that owns most, if not all, of another company's stock but does not actively participate in the management of that other company

homepage The primary website for an organization or individual; the first hypertext document displayed on a website

hostile takeovers Situations in which an outside party buys enough stock in a corporation to take control against the wishes of the board of directors and corporate officers

human relations Interaction among people within an organization for the purpose of achieving organizational and personal goals

human resources All the people who work for an organization

human resources management (HRM) Specialized function of planning how to obtain employees, oversee their training, evaluate them, and compensate them

hybrid structure Structure designs that combine elements of functional, divisional, matrix, and network organizations

hygiene factors Aspects of the work environment that are associated with dissatisfaction

hyperlink A highlighted word or image on a webpage or document that automatically allows people to move to another webpage or document when clicked on with a mouse

hypertext markup language (HTML) The software language used to create, present, and link pages on the World Wide Web

hypertext transfer protocol (HTTP) A communications protocol that allows people to navigate among documents or pages linked by hypertext and to download pages from the World Wide Web

importing Purchasing goods or services from another country and bringing them into one's own country

incentives Cash payments to employees who produce at a desired level or whose unit (often the company as a whole) produces at a desired level

income statement Financial record of a company's revenues, expenses, and profits over a given period of time

incubators Facilities that house small businesses during their early growth phase

inflation Economic condition in which prices rise steadily throughout the economy

informal organization Network of informal employee interactions that are not defined by the formal structure

information Insights, summaries, analyses, comparisons, and other meaningful elements of knowledge

initial public offering (IPO) Corporation's first offering of stock to the public

injunction Court order prohibiting certain actions by striking workers

insider trading The use of unpublicized information that an individual gains from the course of his or her job to benefit from fluctuations in the stock market

insider trading Use of material nonpublic information to make an investment profit

instant messaging (IM) Online conversations in which any number of computer users can type in messages to each other and receive responses in real time

institutional advertising Advertising that seeks to create goodwill and to build a desired image for a company rather than to sell specific products

integrated marketing communications (IMC) Strategy of coordinating and integrating communications and promotional efforts with customers to ensure greater efficiency and effectiveness

intensive distribution Market coverage strategy that tries to place a product in as many outlets as possible

internal auditors Employees who analyze and evaluate a company's operations and data to determine their accuracy

Internet A worldwide collection of interconnected networks that enables users to share information electronically and provides digital access to a wide variety of services

Internet service provider (ISP) A company that provides access to the Internet, usually for a monthly fee, via telephone lines, cable, or satellite; ISPs can be local companies or specialists such as America Online

Internet telephony Telephone service that uses the Internet instead of traditional phone lines; also called VoIP

interpersonal skills Skills required to understand other people and to interact effectively with them

intranet A private network, set up within a corporation or organization, that operates over the Internet and may be used to link geographically remote sites

inventory Goods kept in stock for the production process or for sales to final customers

inventory control System for determining the right quantity of various items to have on hand and keeping track of their location, use, and condition

inventory turnover ratio Measure of the time a company takes to turn its inventory into sales, calculated by dividing cost of goods sold by the average value of inventory for a period

ISO 9000 A collection of global standards set by the International Organization for Standardization establishing a minimum level of acceptable quality

issued stock Portion of authorized stock sold to and held by shareholders

job analysis Process by which jobs are studied to determine the tasks and dynamics involved in performing them

job description Statement of the tasks involved in a given job and the conditions under which the holder of the job will work

job enrichment Reducing work specialization and making work more meaningful by adding to the responsibilities of each job

job redesign Designing a better fit between employees' skills and their work to increase job satisfaction

job sharing Splitting a single full-time job between two employees for their convenience

job specification Statement describing the kind of person who would be best for a given job—including the skills, education, and previous experience that the job requires

joint venture Cooperative partnership in which organizations share investment costs, risks, management, and profits in the development, production, or selling of products

just-in-time (JIT) system Continuous system that pulls materials through the production process, making sure that all materials arrive just when they are needed with minimal inventory and waste

knowledge Expertise gained through experience or association

labor unions Organizations of employees formed to protect and advance their members' interests

labor-intensive businesses Businesses in which labor costs are more significant than capital costs

laissez-faire leaders Leaders who leave the actual decision making up to employees

layoffs Termination of employees for economic or business reasons

lead time Period that elapses between the ordering of materials and their arrival from the supplier

leading Process of guiding and motivating people to work toward organizational goals

lease Legal agreement that obligates the user of an asset to make payments to the owner of the asset in exchange for using it

leveraged buyouts (LBO) Situation in which individuals or groups of investors purchase companies primarily with debt secured by the company's assets

liabilities Claims against a firm's assets by creditors

licensing Agreement to produce and market another company's product in exchange for a royalty or fee

limit order Market order that stipulates the highest or lowest price at which the customer is willing to trade securities

limited liability companies (LLCs) Organizations that combine the benefits of S corporations and limited partnerships without the drawbacks of either

limited partnership Partnership composed of one or more general partners and one or more partners whose liability is usually limited to the amount of their capital investment

line of credit Arrangement in which the financial institution makes money available for use at any time after the loan has been approved

line organization Chain-of-command system that establishes a clear line of authority flowing from the top down

line-and-staff organization Organization system that has a clear chain of command but that also includes functional groups of people who provide advice and specialized services

liquidity The level of ease with which an asset can be converted to cash

local advertising Advertising sponsored by a local merchant

lockouts Management tactics in which union members are prevented from entering a business during a strike in order to force union acceptance of management's last contract proposal

logistics The planning, movement, and flow of goods and related information throughout the supply chain

long-term liabilities Obligations that fall due more than a year from the date of the balance sheet

management Process of coordinating resources to meet organizational goals

management accounting Area of accounting concerned with preparing data for use by managers within the organization

management by objectives (MBO) A motivational approach in which managers and employees work together to structure personal goals and objectives for every individ-

ual, department, and project to mesh with the organization's goals

management pyramid Organizational structure comprising top, middle, and lower management

mandatory retirement Required dismissal of an employee who reaches a certain age

manufacturing resource planning (MRP II) Computer-based system that integrates data from all departments to manage inventory and production planning and control

margin trading Borrowing money from brokers to buy stock, paying interest on the borrowed money, and leaving the stock with the broker as collateral

market Network of dealers who trade securities on computerized linkups rather than a trading floor

market People or businesses who need or want a product and have the money to buy it

market indexes Measures of market activity calculated from the prices of a selection of securities

market makers Registered representatives who trade securities from their own inventories on dealer exchanges, making a ready market for buyers and sellers

market order Authorization for a broker to buy or sell securities at the best price that can be negotiated at the moment

market segmentation Division of total market into smaller, relatively homogeneous groups

market share A firm's portion of the total sales in a market

marketable securities Stocks, bonds, and other investments that can be turned into cash quickly

marketing Process of planning and executing the conception, pricing, promotion, and distribution of ideas, goods, and services to create and maintain relationships that satisfy individual and organizational objectives

marketing concept Approach to business management that stresses customer needs and wants, seeks long-term profitability, and integrates marketing with other functional units within the organization

marketing intermediaries Businesspeople and organizations that channel goods and services from producers to consumers

marketing mix The four key elements of marketing strategy: product, price, distribution (place), and promotion

marketing research The collection and analysis of information for making marketing decisions

marketing strategy Overall plan for marketing a product

mass customization Producing partially customized goods and services by combining mass production techniques with individual customization

mass production Production of uniform products in large quantities

matching principle Fundamental principle requiring that expenses incurred in producing revenue be deducted from the revenues they generate during an accounting period

material requirements planning (MRP) Method of getting the correct materials where they are needed, on time, and without carrying unnecessary inventory

materials handling Movement of goods within a firm's warehouse terminal, factory, or store

matrix structure Assigning employees to both a functional group and a project team (thus using functional and divisional patterns simultaneously)

media Communications channels, such as newspapers, radio, and television

media mix Combination of various media options that a company uses in an advertising campaign

mediation Process for resolving a labor-contract dispute in which a neutral third party meets with both sides and attempts to steer them toward a solution

mentor Experienced manager or employee with a wide network of industry colleagues who can explain office politics, serve as a role model for appropriate business behavior, and help other employees negotiate the corporate structure

merger Combination of two companies in which one company purchases the other and assumes control of its property and liabilities

metacrawlers Special engines that search several search engines at once

middle managers Those in the middle of the management hierarchy; they develop plans to implement the goals of top managers and coordinate the work of first-line managers

mission statement A statement of the organization's purpose, basic goals, and philosophies

mobile commerce (m-commerce) Transaction of electronic commerce using wireless devices and wireless Internet access instead of PC-based technology

monetary policy Government policy and actions taken by the Federal Reserve Board to regulate the nation's money supply

money Anything generally accepted as a means of paying for goods and services

money-market funds Mutual funds that invest in short-term securities and other liquid investments

monopolistic competition Situation in which many sellers differentiate their products from those of competitors in at least some small way

monopoly Market in which there are no direct competitors so that one company dominates

morale Attitude an individual has toward his or her job and employer

motivation Force that moves someone to take action

motivators Factors of human relations in business that may increase motivation

multimedia Typically used to mean the combination of more than one presentation medium—such as text, sound, graphics, and video

multinational corporations (MNCs) Companies with operations in more than one country

municipal bonds Bonds issued by city, state, and government agencies to fund public services

mutual funds Financial organization pooling money to invest in diversified blends of stocks, bonds, or other securities

NASDAQ (National Association of Securities Dealers Automated Quotations) National over-the-counter securities trading network

national advertising Advertising sponsored by companies that sell products on a nationwide basis; refers to the geographic reach of the advertiser, not the geographic coverage of the ad

national brands Brands owned by the manufacturers and distributed nationally

natural resources Land, forests, minerals, water, and other tangible assets usable in their natural state

need Difference between a person's actual state and his or her ideal state; provides the basic motivation to make a purchase

net income Profit earned or loss incurred by a firm, determined by subtracting expenses from revenues; also called the bottom line

network structure Electronically connecting separate companies that perform selected tasks for a small headquarters organization

news conference Gathering of media representatives at which companies announce new information; also called a press briefing

news release Brief statement or video program released to the press announcing new products, management changes, sales performance, and other potential news items

nonprofit organizations Firms whose primary objective is something other than returning a profit to their owners

norms Informal standards of conduct that guide team behavior

objective Specific, short-range target or aim

oligopoly Market dominated by a few producers

online database A collection of data arranged for ease and speed in searching and retrieving online

open order Limit order that does not expire at the end of a trading day

operating expenses All costs of operation that are not included under cost of goods sold

operational plans Plans that lay out the actions and the resource allocation needed to achieve operational objectives and to support tactical plans; usually defined for less than one year and developed by first-line managers

organization chart Diagram showing how employees and tasks are grouped and where the lines of communication and authority flow

organization structure Framework enabling managers to divide responsibilities, ensure employee accountability, and distribute decision-making authority

organizing Process of arranging resources to carry out the organization's plans

orientation Session or procedure for acclimating a new employee to the organization

outsource Subcontracting work to outside companies

outstanding liquidity ratios Ratios that measure a firm's ability to meet its short-term obligations when they are due

owners' equity Portion of a company's assets that belongs to the owners after obligations to all creditors have been met

par value As shown on the stock certificate, a value assigned to a stock for use in bookkeeping and in calculating dividends

parent company Company that owns most, if not all, of another company's stock and that takes an active part in managing that other company

participative management Sharing information with employees and involving them in decision making

partnership Unincorporated business owned and operated by two or more persons under a voluntary legal association

penetration pricing Introducing a new product at a low price in hopes of building sales volume quickly

pension plans Generally refers to traditional, defined benefit retirement plans

performance appraisal Evaluation of an employee's work according to specific criteria

permission marketing Promotional campaigns that send information only to those people who've specifically asked to receive it

perpetual inventory System that uses computers to monitor inventory levels and automatically generate purchase orders when supplies are needed

personal selling In-person communication between a seller and one or more potential buyers

persuasive advertising Advertising designed to encourage product sampling and brand switching

philanthropic Descriptive term for altruistic actions such as donating money, time, goods, or services to charitable, humanitarian, or educational institutions

physical distribution All the activities required to move finished products from the producer to the consumer

picketing Strike activity in which union members march before company entrances to persuade nonstriking employees to walk off the job and to persuade customers and others to cease doing business with the company

place marketing Marketing efforts to attract people and organizations to a particular geographical area

place utility Consumer value added by making a product available in a convenient location

planned system Economic system in which the government controls most of the factors of production and regulates their allocation

planning Establishing objectives and goals for an organization and determining the best ways to accomplish them

point-of-purchase (POP) display Advertising or other display materials set up at retail locations to promote products to potential customers as they are making their purchase decisions

pollution Damage to or destruction of the natural environment caused by the discharge of harmful substances

positioning Using promotion, product, distribution, and price to differentiate a good or service from those of competitors in the mind of the prospective buyer

possession utility Consumer value created when someone takes ownership of a product

preferred stock Shares that give their owners first claim on a company's dividends and assets after paying all debts

premiums Free or bargain-priced items offered to encourage consumers to buy a product

price The amount of money charged for a product or service

price-earnings ratio Ratio calculated by dividing a stock's market price by its prior year's earnings per share

price elasticity A measure of the sensitivity of demand to changes in price

primary market Market where firms sell new securities issued publicly for the first time

prime interest rate (prime) Lowest interest rate banks offer on short-term loans to preferred borrowers

principal Amount of money a corporation borrows from an investor through the sale of a bond

private accountants In-house accountants employed by organizations and businesses other than a public accounting firm; also called corporate accountants

private brands Brands that carry the label of a retailer or a wholesaler rather than a manufacturer

private corporation Company owned by private individuals or companies

privatizing The conversion of public ownership to private ownership

problem-solving team Informal team of 5 to 12 employees from the same department who meet voluntarily to find ways of improving quality, efficiency, and the work environment

process divisions Divisional structure based on the major steps of a production process

process layout Method of arranging a facility so that production tasks are carried out in separate departments containing specialized equipment and personnel

product Good or service used as the basis of commerce

product advertising Advertising that tries to sell specific goods or services, generally by describing features, benefits, and, occasionally, price

product divisions Divisional structure based on products

production Transformation of resources into goods or services that people need or want

product layout Method of arranging a facility so that production proceeds along a line of workstations

product life cycle Four basic stages through which a product progresses: introduction, growth, maturity, and decline

product line A series of related products offered by a firm

product mix Complete list of all products that a company offers for sale

production and operations management (POM) Coordination of an organization's resources for the manufacture of goods or the delivery of services

production forecasts Estimates of how much of a company's goods and services must be produced in order to meet future demand

profit Money left over after expenses and taxes have been deducted from revenue generated by selling goods and services

profit sharing System for distributing a portion of the company's profits to employees

profitability ratios Ratios that measure the overall financial performance of a firm

program evaluation and review technique (PERT) A planning tool that managers of complex projects use to determine the optimal order of activities, the expected time for project completion, and the best use of resources

promotion Wide variety of persuasive techniques used by companies to communicate with their target markets and the general public

promotional mix Particular blend of personal selling, advertising, direct marketing, sales promotion, and public relations that a company uses to reach potential customers

promotional strategy Statement or document that defines the direction and scope of the promotional activities that a company will use to meet its marketing objectives

protectionism Government policies aimed at shielding a country's industries from foreign competition

proxy Document authorizing another person to vote on behalf of a shareholder in a corporation

psychographics Classification of customers on the basis of their psychological makeup

public accountants Professionals who provide accounting services to other businesses and individuals for a fee

public corporation Corporation that actively sells stock on the open market

public relations Nonsales communication that businesses have with their various audiences (includes both communication with the general public and press relations)

pull strategy Promotional strategy that stimulates consumer demand, which then exerts pressure on wholesalers and retailers to carry a product

purchasing Acquiring the raw materials, parts, components, supplies, and finished products needed to produce goods and services

pure competition Situation in which so many buyers and sellers exist that no single buyer or seller can individually influence market prices

push strategy Promotional approach designed to motivate wholesalers and retailers to push a producer's products to end users

quality A measure of how closely a product conforms to predetermined standards and customer expectations

quality assurance System of policies, practices, and procedures implemented throughout the company to create and produce quality goods and services

quality control Routine checking and testing of a finished product for quality against an established standard

quality of work life (QWL) Overall environment that results from job and work conditions

quick ratio Measure of a firm's short-term liquidity, calculated by adding cash, marketable securities, and receivables, then dividing that sum by current liabilities; also known as the acid-test ratio

quotas Fixed limits on the quantity of imports a nation will allow for a specific product

ratio analysis Use of quantitative measures to evaluate a firm's financial performance

recession Period during which national income, employment, and production all fall

recruiting Process of attracting appropriate applicants for an organization's jobs

reinforcement theory A motivational approach based on the idea that managers can motivate employees by influencing their behaviors with positive and negative rewards

relationship marketing A focus on developing and maintaining long-term relationships with customers, suppliers, and distributors for mutual benefit

reminder advertising Advertising intended to remind existing customers of a product's availability and benefits

replacement chart A planning tool that identifies the most vital employees in the organization and any available information related to their potential replacement

responsibility Obligation to perform the duties and achieve the goals and objectives associated with a particular position

retailers Firms that sell goods and services to individuals for their own use rather than for resale

retained earnings The portion of shareholders' equity earned by the company but not distributed to its owners in the form of dividends

retirement plans Company-sponsored programs for providing retirees with income

return on investment (ROI) Ratio between net income after taxes and total owners' equity; also known as return on equity

return on sales Ratio between net income after taxes and net sales; also known as profit margin

revenue bond Municipal bond backed by revenue generated from the projects it is financing

revenues Amount earned from sales of goods or services and inflow from miscellaneous sources such as interest, rent, and royalties

robots Programmable machines that can complete a variety of tasks by working with tools and materials

roles Behavioral patterns associated with or expected of certain positions

routing Specifying the sequence of operations and the path the work will take through the production facility

S corporation Corporation with no more than 75 shareholders that may be taxed as a partnership; also known as a subchapter S corporation

salary Fixed cash compensation for work, usually by yearly amount; independent of the number of hours worked

sales promotion Wide range of events and activities (including coupons, rebates, contests, in-store demonstrations, free samples, trade shows, and point-of-purchase displays) designed to stimulate interest in a product

Sarbanes-Oxley Comprehensive legislation, passed in the wake of Enron and other scandals, designed to improve integrity and accountability of financial information

scheduling Process of determining how long each production operation takes and then setting a starting and ending time for each

scientific management Management approach designed to improve employees' efficiency by scientifically studying their work

search engines Internet tools for finding websites on the topics of your choice

secondary market Market where subsequent owners trade previously issued shares of stocks and bonds

secured bonds Bonds backed by specific assets that will be given to bondholders if the borrowed amount is not repaid

secured loans Loans backed up with something of value that the lender can claim in case of default, such as a piece of property

securities Investments such as stocks, bonds, options, futures, and commodities

selective distribution Market coverage strategy that uses a limited number of outlets to distribute products

self-managed teams Teams in which members are responsible for an entire process or operation

selling expenses All the operating expenses associated with marketing goods or services

service businesses Businesses that provide intangible products or perform useful labor on behalf of another

setup costs Expenses incurred each time a producer organizes resources to begin producing goods or services

sexism Discrimination on the basis of gender

sexual harassment Unwelcome sexual advance, request for sexual favors, or other verbal or physical conduct of a sexual nature within the workplace

shareholders Owners of a corporation stock

short selling Selling stock borrowed from a broker with the intention of buying it back later at a lower price, repaying the broker, and keeping the profit

situational leadership A variation on contingency leadership in which the manager adapts his or her style based on the readiness of employees to accept changes or task responsibilities

skills inventory A list of the skills a company needs from its workforce, along with the specific skills that individual employees currently possess

skimming Charging a high price for a new product during the introductory stage and lowering the price later

small business Company that is independently owned and operated, is not dominant in its field, and meets certain criteria for the number of employees and annual sales revenue

smart cards Plastic cards with embedded computer chips that store money drawn from the user's demand-deposit account as well as information that can be used for purchases

social audit Assessment of a company's performance in the area of social responsibility

social responsibility The concern of businesses for the welfare of society as a whole

socialism Economic system characterized by public ownership and operation of key industries combined with private ownership and operation of less-vital industries

sole proprietorship Business owned by a single individual

span of management Number of people under one manager's control; also known as span of control

special-purpose teams Temporary teams that exist outside the formal organization hierarchy and are created to achieve a specific goal

specialty advertising Advertising that appears on various items such as coffee mugs, pens, and calendars, designed to help keep a company's name in front of customers

stakeholders Individuals or groups to whom business has a responsibility

standards Criteria against which performance is measured

start-up companies New ventures

statement of cash flows Statement of a firm's cash receipts and cash payments that presents information on its sources and uses of cash

statistical process control (SPC) Use of random sampling and control charts to monitor the production process

statistical quality control (SQC) Monitoring all aspects of the production process to see whether the process is operating as it should

stock Shares of ownership in a corporation

stock exchanges Location where traders buy and sell stocks and bonds over-the-counter (OTC)

stock options Contract allowing the holder to purchase or sell a certain number of shares of a particular stock at a given price by a certain date

stock specialist Intermediary who trades in a particular security on the floor of an auction exchange; "buyer of last resort"

stock split Increase in the number of shares of ownership that each stock certificate represents, at a proportionate drop in each share's value

stop order An order to sell a stock when its price falls to a particular point to limit an investor's losses

strategic alliance Long-term relationship in which two or more companies share ideas, resources, and technologies in order to establish competitive advantages

strategic plans Plans that establish the actions and the resource allocation required to accomplish strategic goals; usually defined for periods of two to five years and developed by top managers

strike Temporary work stoppage by employees who want management to accept their union's demands

strikebreakers Nonunion workers hired to replace striking workers

subsidiary corporations Corporations whose stock is owned entirely or almost entirely by another corporation

succession planning Workforce planning efforts that identify possible replacements for specific employees, usually senior executives

supply Specific quantity of a product that the seller is able and willing to provide

supply chain The collection of suppliers and systems that provide all of the materials and supplies required to create finished products and deliver them to final customers

supply-chain management (SCM) An approach to coordinating and optimizing the flow of goods, services, information, and capabilities throughout the entire supply chain, including outside business partners

synthetic system Production process that combines two or more materials or components to create finished products; the reverse of an analytic system

tactical plans Plans that define the actions and the resource allocation necessary to achieve tactical objectives and to support strategic plans; usually defined for a period of one to three years and developed by middle managers

tall organizations Organizations with a narrow span of management and many hierarchical levels

target markets Specific customer groups or segments to whom a company wants to sell a particular product

tariffs Taxes levied on imports

task force Team of people from several departments who are temporarily brought together to address a specific issue

tax accounting Area of accounting focusing on tax preparation and tax planning

team A unit of two or more people who share a mission and collective responsibility as they work together to achieve a goal

technical skills Ability and knowledge to perform the mechanics of a particular job

telecommute To work from home and communicate with the company's main office via computer and communication devices

telecommuting Working from home and communicating with the company's main office via computer and communication devices

telemarketing Selling or supporting the sales process over the telephone

telnet A way to access a remote computer via the Internet

termination Act of getting rid of an employee through layoff or firing

Theory X Managerial assumption that employees are irresponsible, are unambitious, and dislike work and that managers must use force, control, or threats to motivate them

Theory Y Managerial assumption that employees like work, are naturally committed to certain goals, are capable of creativity, and seek out responsibility under the right conditions

Theory Z Human relations approach that emphasizes involving employees at all levels and treating them like family

time deposits Bank accounts that pay interest and require advance notice before money can be withdrawn

time utility Consumer value added by making a product available at a convenient time

top managers Those at the highest level of the organization's management hierarchy; they are responsible for setting strategic goals, and they have the most power and responsibility in the organization

total quality management (TQM) Comprehensive, strategic management approach that builds quality into every organizational process as a way of improving customer satisfaction

trade allowance Discount offered by producers to wholesalers and retailers

trade deficit Unfavorable trade balance created when a country imports more than it exports

trade promotions Sales-promotion efforts aimed at inducing distributors or retailers to push a producer's products

trade surplus Favorable trade balance created when a country exports more than it imports

trademark Brand that has been given legal protection so that its owner has exclusive rights to its use

trading blocs Organizations of nations that remove barriers to trade among their members and that establish uniform barriers to trade with nonmember nations

transaction Exchange between parties

transactional leaders Managers who focus on meeting established goals, making sure current business operations run smoothly

transformational leaders Managers who can reshape the destinies of their organizations by inspiring employees to rise above self-interest and create new levels of success for the company as a whole

Treasury bills Short-term debt securities issued by the federal government; also referred to as T-bills

Treasury bonds Debt securities issued by the federal government that are repaid more than 10 years after issuance

Treasury notes Debt securities issued by the federal government that are repaid within 1 to 10 years after issuance

U.S. savings bonds Debt instruments sold by the federal government in a variety of amounts

uniform resource locator (URL) Web address that gives the exact location of an Internet resource

unissued stock Portion of authorized stock not yet sold to shareholders

Universal Product Codes (UPCs) A bar code on a product's package that provides information read by optical scanners

unlimited liability Legal condition under which any damages or debts attributable to the business can also be attached to the owner because the two have no separate legal existence

unsecured loans Loans requiring no collateral but a good credit rating

upload Sending a file from your computer to a server or host system

Usenet newsgroups One or more discussion groups on the Internet where people with similar interests can post articles and reply to messages

utility Power of a good or service to satisfy a human need

value chain All of the functions required to transform inputs into outputs (goods and services), along with the business functions that support the transformation process

venture capitalists Investment specialists who provide money to finance new businesses or turnarounds in exchange for a portion of the ownership, with the objective of making a considerable profit on the investment; also called VCs

virtual teams Team that uses communication technology to bring geographically distant employees together to achieve goals

viruses Form of computer sabotage embedded in software or passed from one computer to the next that changes or deletes computer files or programs

vision A viable view of the future that is rooted in but improves on the present

wages Cash payment based on the number of hours the employee has worked or the number of units the employee has produced

wants Things that are desirable in light of a person's experiences, culture, and personality

warehouse Facility for storing inventory

Web directory A search tool that searches for information by subject categories, created by real people rather than by automation

webpages Related files containing multimedia data that are made available on a website

website A related collection of files on the World Wide Web

wholesalers Firms that sell products to other firms for resale or for organizational use

work specialization Specialization in or responsibility for some portion of an organization's overall work tasks; also called division of labor

worker buyout Distribution of financial incentives to employees who voluntarily depart; usually undertaken in order to reduce the payroll

working capital Current assets minus current liabilities

World Wide Web (WWW) A hypertext-based system for finding and accessing Internet resources such as text, graphics, sound, and other multimedia resources

worms Form of computer sabotage sent by e-mail that reproduces—taking up network space and snarling connections

XML A standardized web language that goes beyond basic HTML, defining content or data, in addition to displaying formatting

Company/Brand/Organization Index

Subject Index